Trace fossils

Proceedings of an International Conference held at Liverpool
University, 6, 7, 8 January 1970 under the auspices of the
Liverpool Geological Society and sponsored by the
International Union of Geological Sciences.

Edited by
T. P. CRIMES
and
J. C. HARPER
Assisted by
Glenys W. Flinn

Department of Geology
University of Liverpool

Seel House Press, Liverpool

THE SEEL HOUSE PRESS
Seel Street, Liverpool L1 4AY

First Edition, 7 December 1970

Printed in Great Britain by
LIVERPOOL LETTERPRESS LIMITED
(Member of the Seel House Press)
Seel Street, Liverpool L1 4AY

Contents

Preface

The papers in this book were presented at an International Conference in Liverpool from 6–8 January 1970. The Conference was convened and organised by Dr. T. P. Crimes, held under the auspices of the Liverpool Geological Society and sponsored by the International Union of Geological Sciences.

We are grateful to Dr. A. Hallam, Professor Scott Simpson and Professor A. Seilacher who each acted as Chairman for one day of the proceedings. We wish to thank those students who assisted in the registration of delegates and particularly Miss Gillian Trent who also rendered considerable help during the Conference. We have also been assisted by Mrs. G. Flynn who edited the references and compiled the subject index; Mr. J. Lynch who redrew some of the diagrams and designed the cover; and Miss H. Longworth who undertook much of the typing associated with the Conference. We are particularly grateful to Mrs. Vivienne Crimes who provided invaluable help in the organisation both before and during the Conference and also compiled the trace fossil index.

The Conference, the first to be convened on the subject of trace fossils, attracted a large international audience including representatives of 18 countries. It is clear from this, and also from the ever increasing number of papers being published on trace fossils, that interest in the subject is increasing rapidly. It is attracting the attention not only of palaeontologists but also stratigraphers, sedimentologists, and biologists, as will be clear from the papers contained in this volume.

In the absence of international agreement on trace fossil nomenclature, we have attempted, as far as possible, to maintain a constant format for the taxonomic descriptions and wherever possible have followed the international code of zoological nomenclature. Nevertheless, we are aware that in a few instances the taxonomy is not fully in accord with accepted zoological procedure but we hope this will at least draw attention to the urgent need for rules to deal with trace fossils.

Finally, we would wish to thank the authors for their assistance in submitting papers on time and for reading the proofs promptly, both of which have helped in the rapid publication of this volume.

T. P. Crimes
J. C. Harper

Department of Geology,
The University,   15 August 1970
Liverpool L69 3BX,
United Kingdom.

The distribution and significance of trace fossils in the uppermost Jurassic rocks of the Boulonnais, Northern France

D. V. Ager and Peigi Wallace

Trace fossils cannot and should not be studied *in vacuo*. In the magnificent Jurassic cliff sections of Kimmeridgian to "Purbeckian" age between Boulogne and Wissant (Pas-de-Calais) in northern France, beautifully preserved trace fossils form part of a coherent story of shallow-water sedimentation and contemporaneous marine life. Three sequences of shallowing and emergence each carry a similar trace fossil succession, though with significant differences. Generally the succession is as follows: (i) horizontal *Rhizocorallium,* (ii) large *Thalassinoides* of the "*Spongia paradoxica*" type, (iii) obliquely oriented *Rhizocorallium* (or small *Thalassinoides* in protected environments), (iv) *Diplocraterion* in intertidal sediments. There are several other trace fossils present, but never in significant numbers.

1. Introduction

Sediments of Kimmeridgian and later Jurassic age are very well displayed in the cliffs between Boulogne and Wissant (Pas-de-Calais) on the north French coast. They consist predominantly of shallow marine sandstones and shales; trace fossils are abundantly distributed throughout. The classic accounts of these rocks by Pruvost (1925) and by Pruvost and Pringle (1924) contain no mention of trace fossils other than the "problematical" *Spongia paradoxica*, nor do the numerous minor papers published on the area since. Two papers by the present authors (1966 a, b) include a revision of the succession in terms of lithological formations and a brief summary of the trace fossils as part of the successive biofacies.

Within the succession generally, and especially in those parts of it that seem to represent deposition in the shallowest water, there is abundant bioturbation and various burrows and trails that are not specially considered here.

The forms that are both easily identifiable and significant are the more or less horizontal U-burrows *Rhizocorallium,* the branching burrows of *Thalassinoides* (with their tuberculate counterparts *Ophiomorpha*) and the vertical U-burrows such as *Diplocraterion.*

It is interesting to compare the faunas in general of the uppermost Jurassic of the Boulonnais with those of equivalent strata in England. The most striking resemblance is with the well-known fauna of the Portland Stone. The abundance of trigoniids and other large bivalves, gastropods, serpulids and giant ammonites is a positive resemblance, in spite of a complete difference in sediment type. Equally striking is the virtual absence in the Portlandian strata of both the Dorset and the Boulonnais facies of major groups such as corals, brachiopods, belemnites and all echinoderms apart from occasional *Hemicidaris*. One suspects some sort of salinity control as suggested for the northern European facies generally by Hallam (personal communication), but it is difficult to find concrete evidence.

In the cliffs of the Boulonnais (Fig. 1), the succession is repeated several times as a

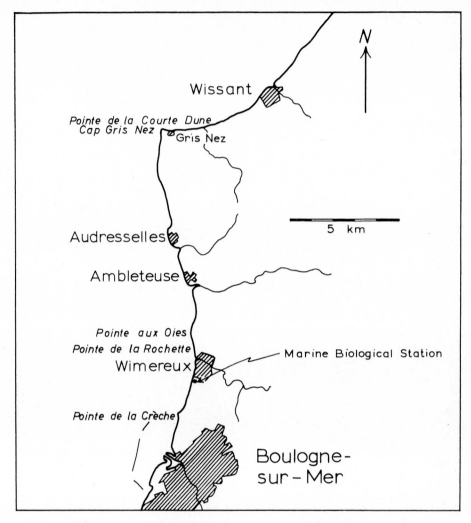

Fig. 1. Locality map of the Jurassic coast sections of the Boulonnais.

result of gentle folding and faulting. The following four sections are worthy of special consideration:

(i) that between the north end of Boulogne-sur-Mer and the Marine Biological Station at Wimereux.

(ii) that between Ambleteuse and Audresselles.

(iii) that between Cap Gris Nez and Pointe de la Courte Dune.

(iv) that between the north end of Wimereux and Pointe aux Oies.

The sections in and south of Boulogne are not considered here since they are too poorly exposed and those between Audresselles and Cap Gris Nez are omitted because the accessible parts of the cliff are almost all at the same stratigraphical level and do not add anything to the other sections.

The succession may be summarised as follows:

"Purbeckian"	Calcaire des Oies
Portlandian	Grès des Oies
	Assises de Croi
Kimmeridgian	Argiles de Wimereux
	Argiles de la Crèche
	Grès de la Crèche
	Schistes de Chatillon
	Grès de Chatillon
	Calcaires du Moulin Wibert
	Argiles du Moulin Wibert

The above sections exhibit this succession with considerable overlap and display marked lateral variations. Each will be considered in turn.

2. The Boulogne-Wimereux section

The oldest sediments exposed in the cliffs of the Boulonnais are seen in the core of the monocline between the entrance to Boulogne harbour and the headland to the north usually known as La Crèche. The youngest Jurassic beds exposed in the cliffs approaching Wimereux are the Grès des Oies, so this section is almost complete in itself. However, the upper part of the succession is not well displayed here and much of the Argiles de la Crèche and the Argiles de Wimereux are not accessible at beach level because of faulting; the lower part of the succession (Fig. 2) is therefore the most interesting. This was summarised briefly by Ziegler (1962 p. 15).

The lowest two formations—the Argiles du Moulin Wibert and the Calcaires du Moulin Wibert—are not clearly separable. Together they may be regarded as a thick shale sequence having layers of calcareous nodules and thin bands of argillaceous calcilutites that become increasingly closely spaced upwards. The division between the two formations is thus based upon dominance of clays below and of limestones above.

In the lower part, the shaly clays contain shell debris, drift-wood and some large bivalves. The thinner calcareous bands usually consist of *Exogyra* coquinoids whilst the thicker bands are calcilutites with large articulated bivalves, notably *Laevitrigonia* and *Gervillella*. One shale bed (**25**—numbers in heavy type refer to bed numbers in the relevant formation and section, Figs. 2, 4, 5 and 6) yields occasional specimens of one of the rare brachiopods of the coast sections, the terebratulid *Rouillieria? boloniensis*. The bivalves commonly lie on their sides in this formation but are not usually disarticulated. Identifiable trace fossils have not been observed in the Argiles du Moulin Wibert, but *Rhizocorallium* appears in what is here regarded as the bottom bed (**1**) of the succeeding Calcaires du Moulin Wibert.

Much of this formation consists of reworked shelly deposits lacking trace fossils but several horizons contain horizontal *Rhizocorallium* (**1, 3, 7, 13**). Disarticulated and broken shell material is abundant and consists of the genera mentioned above. In the best *Rhizocorallium* horizon (**13**) the trace fossils are perceptibly smaller than those lower down; they also have a slightly preferred orientation towards the southwest, though this is probably not statistically significant.

There is clear evidence of shallowing water as one passes into the succeeding Grès de Chatillon. Cross-bedded and ripple-marked sandstones and uncemented yellow sands dominate the succession. The shelly fossils are mostly similar to those lower down but there are important newcomers such as the echinoid *Pygurus,* which has been compared with modern "sand-dollars" (Ager and Wallace 1966a p.401) and which occurs here in life position. Many of the beds are intensely bioturbated; oblique U-burrows of *Rhizocorallium* type occur at several levels (especially **8**), mainly descending from ripple-marked surfaces which also exhibit abundant molluscan trails. *Thalassinoides* also occurs at one horizon (**9, 10**), locally showing the typical tuberculate appearance of *Ophiomorpha*. The difference between these two nominal genera seems to relate chiefly to the nature of the sediment in which they occur. *Ophiomorpha* is characteristic of the sandier horizons while *Thalassinoides* s.s. is found in the more argillaceous and calcareous deposits.

Above the Grès de Chatillon, dipping steeply in the north limb of the monocline, are the Schistes de Chatillon. These mark a return to the deeper water conditions of the Argiles du Moulin Wibert which they closely resemble in both lithology and fauna. The chief fossil is *Exogyra virgula,* preserved in coquinoid bands. No trace fossils have been seen in the La Crèche section, though they are known elsewhere from this formation (see below).

The succeeding Grès de la Crèche represents a return to shallower conditions similar to those of the Grès de Chatillon, though the environment probably reached an even higher energy level. The Grès de la Crèche caps the south side of the headland bearing that name, but dips down steeply to undulate at beach level on the north side of the headland. This is a convenient place to see its great lateral variability and to demonstrate the lateral equivalence of certain of the trace fossils (see Fig. 3).

The cross-bedded sands of the lower part of the formation on the south side of La Crèche are locally cemented into large sphaeroidal doggers or "boules" (Section L). There are several levels of irregular and indeterminate bioturbation, but towards the top distinct levels of *Rhizocorallium* occur in more evenly bedded sediment (base of Section K).

The middle part of the formation consists of unconsolidated cross-bedded sands in which trace fossils have not been observed.

The upper part of the formation contains *Thalassinoides* together with shells and bones that are very much reworked and broken (Sections A-H). There is a distinct erosion level near the middle of the upper part from which *Diplocraterion* and other vertical burrows extend downwards. Horizontal *Rhizocorallium* reappears in the thinner bedded strata at the top of the formation.

The succeeding Argiles de la Crèche (exposed on the north side of the headland, but generally difficult of access), mark a return to muddy deposition. The fauna consists mainly of small, drifted molluscs and wood; hardly anything occurs in life position and little or no burrowing is preserved, although a prominent limestone band high in the cliff carries some of the best horizontal *Rhizocorallium* in the area.

The junction between the Argiles de la Crèche and the succeeding Argiles de Wimereux is difficult to reach in the cliffs to the south of that town. It is noteworthy as being marked by two obvious calcareous bands instead of the three seen to the north. The upper band shows some burrowing.

Fig. 2. Columnar section of the succession at La Crèche. Legend: 1 Coarse sandstone; 2 Fine sandstone; 3 Shaly clay; 4 Limestone; 5 Sandy limestone; 6 Calcareous sand; 7 Argillaceous limestone; 8 Nodule bed; 9 Cross bedding; 10 Ripple marks; 11 Bioturbation; 12 Shell debris; 13 Horizontal *Rhizocorallium*; 14 Oblique *Rhizocorallium*; 15 *Thalassinoides*; 16 *Laevitrigonia*; 17 *Gervillella*; 18 *Exogyra*; 19 *Rouillieria? boloniensis*; 20 Wood fragments.

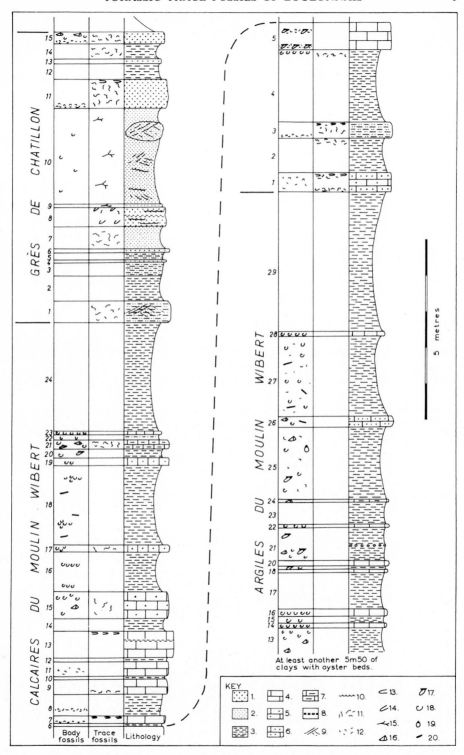

Fig. 2

The higher part of the Argiles de Wimereux is faulted down to beach level and contains small, obscure, swirl-like structures, evidently feeding burrows filled with glauconitic sand in the clay matrix. The burrows cannot be assigned with confidence to any named trace fossil, but may be attributable to *Zoophycos* s.l. They occur just below the prominent Tour de Croi Nodule Bed which marks the base of the Assises de Croi. They are associated with abundant drift-wood and occasional pavloviid ammonites.

The Tour de Croi Nodule Bed here has been discussed elsewhere (Ager and Wallace *opera cit.*). It is accompanied by a marked colour change in the sediment and clearly indicates an important break in deposition. The phosphatic nodules are associated with abundant small articulated bivalves, ammonites of *Pavlovia rotunda* type, drift-wood and many other fossils. There is little doubt that it corresponds with the important *rotunda* nodule horizon in England. Larger ammonites and oysters occur a metre or so higher up the succession. The bed, which is locally bioturbated, is thought to represent very slow deposition in relatively deep water.

The Assises de Croi at this locality are very similar to their outcrop in the cliffs north of Wimereux and are best considered there.

3. The Ambleteuse-Audresselles section

The low cliff between these two villages displays an almost continuous section between the Grès de Chatillon and the Grès de la Crèche, mainly in the Schistes de Chatillon (Fig. 4). The succession was summarised briefly by Ziegler (1962 p. 16).

The Grès de Chatillon is seen in a series of low, rocky platforms on the beach just north of Ambleteuse and contains what is probably the greatest variety and abundance of trace fossils in the area. The formation consists essentially of a series of fine to medium sandstones with shaly partings. Four such distinct sandstones are distinguishable in this section; all contain *Rhizocorallium*-type burrows, ranging from horizontal to angles of 45° to the bedding.

The lowest complete sandstone (**11a**) contains strongly oblique *Rhizocorallium* in its main part accompanied by concentrically striated burrows and horizontal *Rhizocorallium* and *Ophiomorpha* on the upper ripple-marked surface immediately subjacent to a shale parting. The lower part of the overlying cross-bedded sandstone (**11b**) is intensely bioturbated, with clusters of large, upward radiating burrows of *Phycodes* type. These are succeeded by steeply dipping *Rhizocorallium* in the middle of the sandstone and slightly oblique *Rhizocorallium* at the top.

The succeeding sandstone (**11c**) is finer grained and intensely bioturbated, especially in the upper part with many oblique *Rhizocorallium* and *Ophiomorpha* on the top bedding plane. The top sandstone of this main bed (**11d**) is thinner than the others but has a similarly ripple-marked upper surface with slightly oblique *Rhizocorallium,* trails, oysters and other bivalves. After a sandstone-shale interval, the formation is topped by an intensely bioturbated sandstone with horizontal

Fig. 3. Lateral variation in the Grès de la Crèche at La Crèche. Legend: 1 Coarse sandstone; 2 Fine sandstone; 3 Sandy clay; 4 Shaly clay; 5 Limestone; 6 Sandy limestone; 7 Cross bedding; 8 Concretions; 9 Shell fragments; 10 Bivalves; 11 Gastropods; 12 Wood fragments; 13 *Laevitrigonia*; 14 *Perna*; 15 *Exogyra*; 16 Bioturbation; 17 *Thalassinoides*; 18 Horizontal *Rhizocorallium*; 19 Oblique *Rhizocorallium*; 20 *Diplocraterion*.

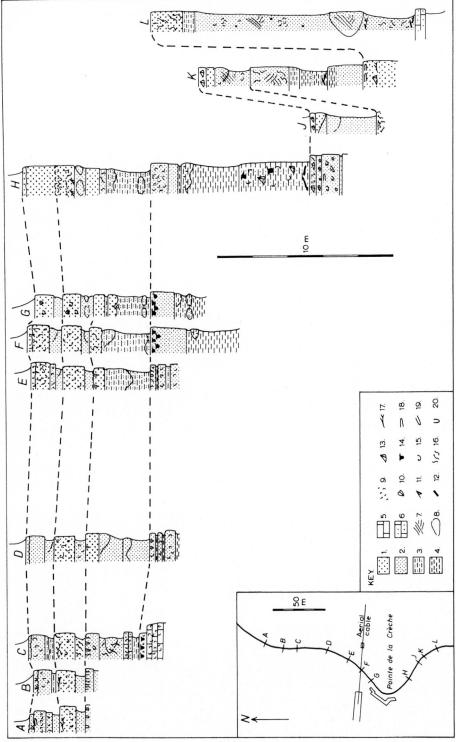

Fig. 3

Rhizocorallium on the upper surface, accompanied by large *Laevitrigonia* and serpulid clusters.

The succeeding Schistes de Chatillon have the same characters as elsewhere, but can be examined at this locality in greater detail. The sandy beds within the lower part of the shales show bioturbation and some trails, and then oyster-rich shales pass up into a prominent coquinoid limestone which heralds the characteristic *Exogyra virgula* bands of the upper part of the formation. The first such bed, which may be called the "Main Oyster Bed" (8), has large horizontal *Rhizocorallium* on its upper surface. Both this and a subsequent *Rhizocorallium* horizon show a slight tendency to parallel orientation on northeast-southwest lines, but this is probably not significant.

This bed and the subsequent *Exogyra* coquinoid bands, which relieve the monotony of the upper part of the Schistes de Chatillon, contain pebbles and phosphatic nodules which may indicate halts in deposition and the formation of a hard, shelly sea floor.

The top of this formation is not clearly discernible in the main section. The Grès de la Crèche appears as large rounded "boules" immediately below the houses of Audresselles, but is not in immediate contact with the shales. Just south of the village the Grès de Chatillon appears again in a faulted anticline.

However, in the highest part of the cliff between Audresselles and Ambleteuse, and especially in fallen blocks, a passage upwards into sandier lithologies is seen. This is presumably the base of the Grès de la Crèche. There is an immediate incoming of the trace fossil *Thalassinoides,* up to 2·5 cm in diameter, accompanied by general bioturbation, *Laevitrigonia,* large oysters and ammonites. In places the *Thalassinoides* are seen to pass into the *Ophiomorpha* form, and in the middle of the main sandstone there is a layer of oblique *Rhizocorallium* dipping at about 30°.

A further section on the north side of Audresselles is worth mentioning in passing. This is the section beyond the small fault just north of the village where the coast road comes close to the cliff edge. It shows the Grès de Chatillon with abundant trace fossils and ripple-marked surfaces, which serves to confirm the section described from near Ambleteuse.

4. The Cap Gris Nez section

The chief interest of this section lies in the Grès de la Crèche (Fig. 5). Older beds, especially the Schistes de Chatillon, are exposed on the south side of the headland, in the folds on the beach and in the cliff below Gris Nez village as well as in the cliff and beach between that village and Pointe de la Courte Dune. These contain carbonate bands, some composed almost entirely of the shells of *Exogyra virgula* while others lack shells but have abundant horizontal *Rhizocorallium*.

The change from the shales of the Schistes de Chatillon to the sandstones of the Grès de la Crèche is quite abrupt. As the sediments change to cross-bedded sands, sandstones and sandy limestones, the shelly fauna and the trace fossils also change. The small oysters are replaced by large bivalves, notably *Laevitrigonia* and *Perna,* with the latter especially abundant in an impersistent clay in the middle of the

Fig. 4. Columnar section of the succession between Ambleteuse and Audresselles. Legend: 1 Sandstone; 2 Sandy clay; 3 Shaly clay; 4 Limestone; 5 Sandy limestone; 6 Phosphatic nodules; 7 Cross bedding; 8 Ripple marks; 9 Shell debris; 10 Bioturbation; 11 *Exogyra*; 12 *Laevitrigonia*; 13 Ammonite; 14 Gastropod; 15 Serpulids; 16 Wood fragments; 17 Burrowing bivalve; 18 Horizontal *Rhizocorallium*; 19 Oblique *Rhizocorallium*; 20 *Thalassinoides*.

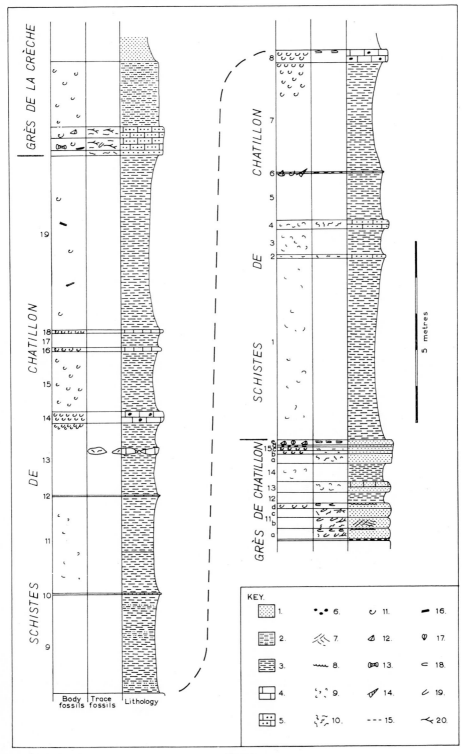

Fig. 4

B

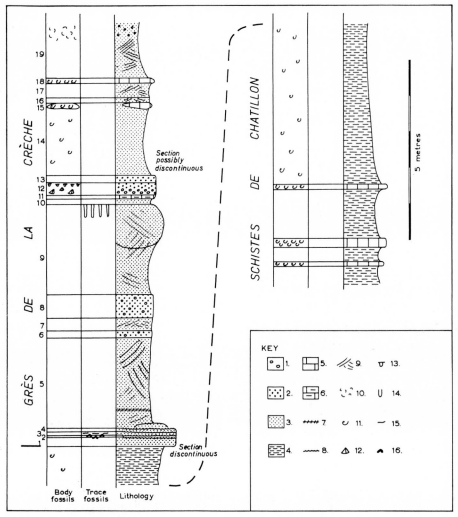

Fig. 5. Columnar section of the succession at Cap Gris Nez. Legend: 1 Pebbles; 2 Coarse sandstone; 3 Fine sandstone; 4 Shaly clay; 5 Limestone; 6 Argillaceous limestone; 7 Humus band; 8 Ripple marks; 9 Cross bedding; 10 Shell debris; 11 *Exogyra*; 12 *Laevitrigonia*; 13 *Perna bouchardi*; 14 *Diplocraterion*; 15 Horizontal burrows; 16 "*Asterosoma*"-like mounds.

formation. The horizontal *Rhizocorallium* is replaced by a more varied suite of trace fossils, most notably *Thalassinoides, Asterosoma?, Diplocraterion* and *Corophioides*.

This suite is not generally distributed and intermixed, however. Irregular faecal mounds of *Asterosoma* type occur only in ripple-marked sandstones at the bottom of the succession (**2**). Higher up, within the cross-bedded sands which are only locally cemented, the small diameter variety of *Thalassinoides* is found sparingly.

About half-way up the formation (its full thickness here is not clearly determinable) there are several erosion levels marked by thin conglomerates (**12**) and drifts of broken shell material. At one of the more obvious of these levels there is a concentration of vertical U-burrows (**19**). These burrows were previously figured (Ager and Wallace 1966b pl. 21A and 1966a fig. 6) and have been referred to *Corophioides*. There is considerable taxonomic confusion over trace fossils of this kind, but it now seems probable that they should be placed in the long-ranging ichnogenus *Diplocraterion* (which was formerly reserved for Palaeozoic forms or even just Lower Cambrian forms according to the *Treatise*). The traces are typical vertical, protrusive parallel-sided U-burrows with spreiten. They consistently reach 30 to 35 cm in depth. Associated with these, however, are smaller forms of a similar type, which more closely resemble burrows of the living *Corophium* and which may, therefore, be referrable to *Corophioides* or *Glossifungites*. More rare in occurrence are simple, wide U-burrows without spreiten, which may be called *Arenicolites*.

There is little doubt in the authors' minds that these trace fossils represent an episode of inter-tidal emergence, when the danger of such environmental extremes as desiccation and erosion necessitated deep burrowing. The contrast between the shallow burrowing seen elsewhere in the succession and the deep burrowing seen at this one horizon is reminiscent of the contrast emphasised by Rhoads (1966; 1967) between the present day subtidal and inter-tidal burrowing activity. Though it is fully realised that the modern situation may not be quite as simple as this, the coincidence of the burrowing maximum of 30 cm cited by Rhoads for inter-tidal conditions and the depths observed here is worthy of comment.

5. The Wimereux-Pointe aux Oies section

This is the best section in the area for studying the upper part of the succession. The Grès de la Crèche is exposed at low tide just north of Wimereux, and the general gentle northerly dip brings down the highest beds of the Jurassic in the headland of Pointe aux Oies about 1·5 km to the north (Fig. 6).

The Argiles de la Crèche are exposed in the low cliffs immediately north of the town of Wimereux. The shales and thin sandstones of this formation show very few trace fossils. Bedding planes covered with small, disarticulated bivalves are the rule.

The base of the Argiles de Wimereux is marked by the triple limestone band referred to earlier (**2, 4, 6**). Phosphatic nodule beds lie both immediately below the lowest limestone and immediately above the highest (**1, 7**) and are known as the La Rochette Nodule Bed; this marks an important change in fauna though not in lithology (Ager and Wallace 1966a p. 405).

Immediately above the Nodule Bed, the small bivalves of the lower formation are replaced by large articulated bivalves such as *Perna, Lima, Astarte, Laevitrigonia* and *Ostrea*. *Perna* valves are almost invariably bored by *Lithodomus,* but few other trace fossils could be distinguished, chiefly because of the extremely tumbled and glutinous nature of the section. Ammonites, bones, vertebrae and large pieces of wood are also fairly common.

The *Lima* Bed forms a prominent marker halfway up the formation (**8**) and has been discussed in a previous paper (Ager and Wallace 1966a p. 403 and 406). The fauna of this thin bed, notably *Lima bononiensis* and *Pleuromya,* is preserved almost entirely in life position; the upper surface shows vertical borings that indicate early lithification.

The upper part of the Argiles de Wimereux is similar to the lower part, though perhaps more nodular, but detailed work is needed on the whole formation. Gaping, but still articulated bivalves are common in the upper part of the formation, and imply sedimentation in quiet, comparatively deep water.

The Tour de Croi Nodule Bed marks the base of the succeeding formation. It is
exposed on the north side of the bay between Pointe de la Rochette and Pointe aux
Oies. It indicates an important break in deposition and marks the start of a long
shallowing sequence. The lower part of the Assises de Croi above seems to represent
relatively deep water sedimentation with little or no burrowing. The macrofauna
consists of pelagic elements, notably large oyster-encrusted ammonites and large
bivalves in life position. Even *Pinna,* which is very easily reworked, is characteristically vertical and undisturbed in this section (e.g. **17**), suggesting little wave or
current disturbance. Several levels show evidence of a contemporaneous hard
bottom encrusted with small oysters and serpulids.

A fallen block having a lithology characteristic of this facies has been seen from
here, packed with randomly oriented horizontal *Rhizocorallium.* Unfortunately,
these have not been found *in situ* but other evidence indicates that they belong in
this part of the sequence.

Higher up is a distinctive sequence of iron-stained alternating glauconitic silty
clays and sandy calcareous layers. The bedding is extremely irregular and is
entirely absent in the silts or silty clays, where it has been destroyed by the intense
bioturbation. The succession given in Figure 6 is true only of a series of linked
sections, for most of the beds change within a few metres laterally. Shell debris,
especially small oysters and serpulids, is common throughout.

Apart from the rare *Rhizocorallium* mentioned above, which are probably
restricted to a single horizon, the only identifiable trace fossil appears to be
Thalassinoides. This becomes much more obvious in the overlying formation,
largely because of a change in lithology.

The change from the Assises de Croi to the Grès des Oies is essentially one from
dark grey sandy limestones to buff or khaki calcareous sandstones, interbedded
with bioturbated sands rather than silts. Immediately after the change, there also
appears the first of a notable series of diapiric structures (**1**).

Less than a metre from the base and above the first diapirs is the most distinctive
of the *Thalassinoides* beds (**2**). This bed shows the well-known "*Spongia paradoxica*"
type burrow, with smooth-walled tubes about 5 cm in diameter that branch
dichotomously at regular intervals. It is the "true" *Thalassinoides* as here understood and a feature of this form is its frequent association with the large bivalve
Ceratomya. The latter is always seen as internal moulds of closed, articulated
valves, lying on its side. It does not seem likely that the mollusc was responsible for
the burrows.

This *Thalassinoides* Bed splits in two southwards in the cliffs and is always
associated with diapiric structures in its lower part. *Thalassinoides*-type structures
are locally cemented in the diapirs and show up for this reason.

Just over a metre higher up is a very distinctive bed, seen all round the headland
of Pointe aux Oies, with very abundant horizontal *Rhizocorallium* on its upper
surface (**4**). The bed is a sandy calcarenite and appears to be the "*Ampullina* Bed" of
earlier literature (Pruvost and Pringle 1924) since locally it contains very abundant
thick-shelled gastropods of this type.

Fig. 6. Columnar section of the succession between Pointe aux Oies and Wimereux. Legend:
1 Sandstone; 2 Silty clay; 3 Shaly clay; 4 Limestone; 5 Sandy limestone; 6 Argillaceous
limestone; 7 Calcareous marl; 8 Pebbles; 9 Phosphatic nodules; 10 Cross bedding; 11 Diapiric structure; 12 Shell debris; 13 Calcareous algae; 14 *Exogyra*; 15 *Laevitrigonia*; 16 *Lima*;
17 *Pinna*; 18 Pectinid; 19 *Astarte*; 20 Bivalve; 21 Ammonite; 22 Gastropod; 23 Arthropod
fragments; 24 Bone fragments; 25 Serpulids; 26 Wood fragments; 27 Bioturbation; 28
Thalassinoides; 29 Horizontal *Rhizocorallium*; 30 "*Zoophycos*"-like structures.

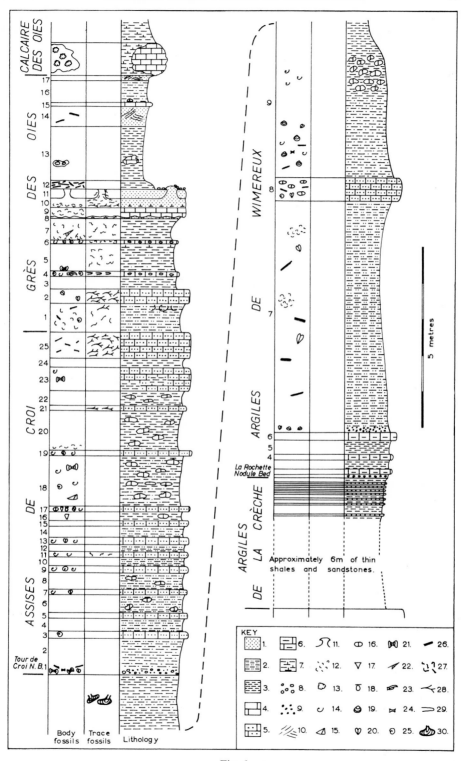

Fig. 6

The *Rhizocorallium* here is of a large size, up to nearly 11 cm in overall diameter. Indications of parallel orientation were noted locally but measurement of a very large number of specimens failed to reveal any significant orientation.

About halfway up the formation, immediately below a horizon of well-developed diapiric structures (**11**), there is intensive bioturbation of another type. Burrows here could again be referred to *Thalassinoides*, since they consist essentially of repeatedly Y-branched burrows, but this form is much smaller than the *Thalassinoides* described from lower down in the succession. The burrows are characteristically about 1 cm in diameter and were almost certainly the work of an animal different from that producing the usual *Thalassinoides*.

The diapirs at this level are large, exceptionally clear and well-developed (Ager and Wallace 1966a fig. 7). The fine-grained sand of which they are composed appears to have pushed up through the overlying sediment and "overflowed" at the surface. Associated with the diapirs are small diameter burrows which appear to post-date the sediment movement. Presumably the organisms responsible congregated at the sandstone pipes because of the rising water, which may have been saline in an otherwise desiccating or freshwater environment.

Immediately above the diapirs is a locally developed thin pebbly layer which seems to be the equivalent of the thick and famous conglomerate at the headland of La Rochette to the south. The latter cannot be accurately placed in the succession because it occurs high in the cliff and can only be studied in fallen blocks. It is noteworthy, however, that as the conglomerate thickens southwards to this point, the diapirs die out. It may be that they were developed in quiet intertidal conditions behind the protection of a pebble bank. The occasional presence of the coral *Isastraea* encrusting pebbles in the conglomerate may be significant in that it implies very shallow depths.

The beds above the diapirs are extremely variable, even within the small area of Pointe aux Oies. Locally a thick lignitic bed (**12**) is developed at the base of the clays with calcareous algal masses (**13**), which directly overlie the diapirs, but these pass into cross-bedded sands within a few metres (Ager and Wallace 1966a fig. 8).

These lithologies pass upwards into limestones with algal "burrs" which are very reminiscent of those in the English Purbeckian (Calcaire des Oies). It is tempting to postulate a connection between the rising waters of the diapirs and the development of the sphaeroidal algal masses. Certainly they occur together but the evidence is insufficient to draw any valid conclusions.

6. The significance of the trace fossils

Though trace fossils may be found in all the formations seen in the Boulonnais cliffs, it must be emphasised that they are confined to certain beds and there are often considerable thicknesses where trace fossils are completely absent. Also, as in most shallow marine sequences, much of the bioturbation cannot be assigned to particular ichnogenera.

Nevertheless, there are clear associations between trace fossil forms and particular lithologies. There are also clear and repeated successions of trace fossils, which always occur in the same order and which seem to relate to the depth of water and energy level of the contemporary environment (Table 1).

It must be emphasised that all the environments represented in these cliffs were probably comparatively shallow water and the trace fossils all belong within Seilacher's original "*Cruziana* facies".

Table 1

Formation	Trace Fossils	Postulated Environment
Calcaire des Oies	—	Fresh water
Grès des Oies	Small *Thalassinoides*	Low energy, intertidal
	Rhizocorallium	Low energy, infralittoral
	Large *Thalassinoides*	High energy, infralittoral
Assises de Croi	Large *Thalassinoides*	High energy, infralittoral
	Rhizocorallium	Low energy, fairly deep infralittoral
Assises de Wimereux	*Zoophycos?*	Low energy, deep infralittoral or ? circalittoral
Argiles de la Crèche	*Rhizocorallium*	Low energy, fairly deep infralittoral
Grès de la Crèche	*Diplocraterion*	High energy, intertidal
Schistes de Chatillon	Large *Thalassinoides* *Rhizocorallium*	High energy, infralittoral Low energy, fairly deep infralittoral
Grès de Chatillon	Oblique *Rhizocorallium*	High energy, just subtidal
	Large *Thalassinoides/ Ophiomorpha*	High energy, infralittoral
Calcaires du Moulin Wibert	*Rhizocorallium*	Low energy, fairly deep infralittoral
Argiles du Moulin Wibert	—	Low energy, deep infralittoral

We can, however, deduce the following environmental succession:

(i) Deeper-water, flat-bedded, muddy sediments—horizontal *Rhizocorallium*.

(ii) Shallower-water, high-energy, thick-bedded sediments—large *Thalassinoides* (locally *Ophiomorpha*) etc.

(iii) Subtidal, thin-bedded, ripple-marked, sandy sediments—oblique *Rhizocorallium* becoming steeper into shallower water; other arthropod burrows and trails.

(iv) Intertidal, high-energy, sandy sediments with erosion levels—vertical *Diplocraterion, Corophioides* and other deep arthropod and worm burrows.

(v) Alternatively to (iii) or (iv), in low-energy intertidal or just subtidal sediments, perhaps only in protected situations—small *Thalassinoides*.

It is interesting to compare this succession with that postulated in the pioneer work of Farrow (1967) on the Middle Jurassic trace fossils of Yorkshire. One noteworthy difference is the apparent absence of *Teichichnus* in the Boulonnais sections, which may mean that the deeper-water facies of the Yorkshire story are not represented, though this seems doubtful in view of the abundance of the supposedly even deeper-water Pernidae. Also, *Asterosoma* of the Yorkshire type is absent, though there is a form somewhat resembling it at one level in the Grès de la Crèche. The most interesting forms which are present in the Boulonnais and have not been described from Yorkshire are *Diplocraterion* and its associates in what is here interpreted as an intertidal environment.

Efforts were made to see if there was any pattern of orientation in the Boulonnais trace fossils comparable to that described by Farrow. At certain levels and localities a suggestion of parallelism in *Rhizocorallium* was noted, with the distal ends of the burrows directed to the southwest (i.e. normal to the postulated shoreline), but a large number of measurements failed to reveal any statistical significance. What is more, if any preferred orientation exists it is in the deeper facies rather than in the shallower (i.e. the reverse of Farrow's picture). No preferred orientation was observed in *Thalassinoides,* though such orientation would be very difficult to measure. The *Diplocraterion* burrows probably are parallel, but since most of the specimens observed were on fallen blocks, orientation could not be measured.

As a general conclusion, Table 1 might be simplified into three ichnofacies: (i) a deeper, low-energy, horizontal *Rhizocorallium* facies; (ii) a shallow, high-energy *Thalassinoides* and oblique *Rhizocorallium* facies and (iii) an intertidal *Diplocraterion* facies.

It must be emphasised, however, that the trace fossil distributions probably relate to energy level and sediment type as well as to bathymetry. Thus in the Pointe aux Oies section, *Rhizocorallium* appears above *Thalassinoides* in a shallowing sequence probably due to the onset at this locality of protected low-energy conditions in shallow water, prior to the development of diapiric structures and freshwater deposits.

The repeated facies belts suggested by Farrow (*op. cit.*) have not been seen in the Boulonnais and it is thought that they are more likely to relate to oscillatory conditions in Yorkshire rather than to a single shallowing sequence.

The best illustration of the relationship of the trace fossils to sedimentary type is provided by the *Thalassinoides/Ophiomorpha* transition seen in the Grès de Chatillon. This transition was first suggested to the authors by H. Doust as a result of his work on the Miocene trace fossils of the Sirte Basin in eastern Libya. He pointed out that *Ophiomorpha* there is found in coarse-grained deposits, whereas *Thalassinoides* is typical of fine-grained sediments, though it commonly roots from and is filled with sand or calcarenite. This is confirmed in the Boulonnais section.

The absence of vertical *Ophiomorpha* here is interesting, since it might be expected in the shallowest water facies (as it is commonly seen in British and French Tertiary deposits). This may be explained, however, by the very restricted nature of this particular facies in the Boulonnais and the absence of appropriate sediments.

A much closer parallel than that described by Farrow is seen in the survey by Seilacher (1967) based largely on Palaeozoic studies. This paper confirmed the present authors' earlier views that it was possible to subdivide the shallowest water facies, as seen in the Boulonnais, on the basis of trace fossils.

Seilacher recognised two marine ichnofacies in the shallower part of his previously all-embracing "*Cruziana* facies". These were the "*Glossifungites* facies" and the "*Skolithos* facies". He also suggested that these could be related to particular depths of water on the basis of modern comparisons, though he gave no actual figures.

A deeper facies is possibly represented in the Argiles de Wimereux, though the trace fossils in question are obscure and the present authors would not regard them as reliable depth indicators.

Seilacher's "*Cruziana* facies", as now restricted (1967), would include both the horizontal *Rhizocorallium* facies of the Boulonnais and the large *Thalassinoides* facies. His "*Glossifungites*" and "*Skolithos* facies" are referred to "omission surfaces" and littoral sands respectively, but in general correspond to the oblique *Rhizocorallium* and *Diplocraterion* facies of this study.

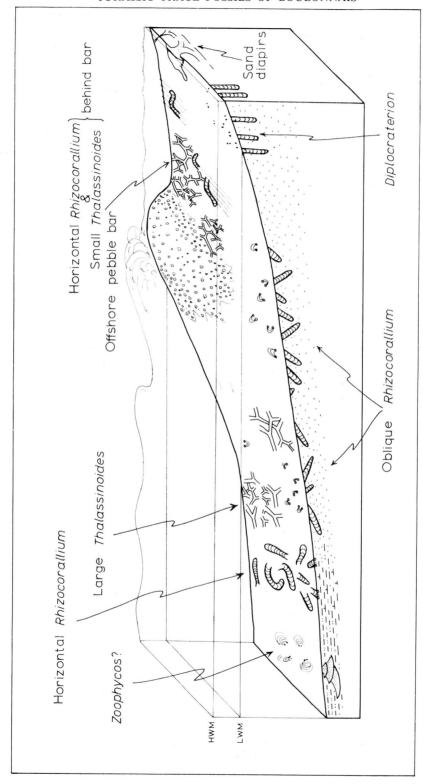

Fig. 7. Block diagram showing the postulated environments of the more important trace fossils.

Seilacher's conclusion that there is a general gradation from vertical burrows in the shallowest water to horizontal burrows in deeper water is certainly confirmed by this study, though the authors believe that this is related not simply to the trend from suspension to sediment feeding, but also and most dramatically to the dangers of desiccation and disinterment in the inter-tidal environment.

References

AGER, D. V. and WALLACE, P. 1966a. The environmental history of the Boulonnais, France. *Proc. Geol. Ass.* **77**, 385.

—— 1966b. Easter field meeting in the Boulonnais, France. *Proc. Geol. Ass.* **77**, 419.

FARROW, G. E. 1966. Bathymetric zonation of Jurassic trace fossils from the coast of Yorkshire, England. *Palaeogeogr. Palaeoclimatol. Palaeoecol.* **2**, 103.

PRUVOST, P. 1925. Observations sur la structure du Cap Gris Nez et sur les mouvements qui ont affecté le pays Boulonnais après le dépôt du Jurassique. *Bull. Servs Carte géol. Fr.* **28**, 1.

—— and PRINGLE, J. 1924. A synopsis of the geology of the Boulonnais, including a correlation of the Mesozoic rocks with those of England, with report of excursion. *Proc. Geol. Ass.* **35**, 29.

RHOADS, D. C. 1966. Depth of burrowing by benthonic marine organisms: a key to nearshore—offshore relationships. *Abstracts geol. Soc. Am.* p. 176.

—— 1967. Biogenic reworking of intertidal and subtidal sediments in Barnstable Harbour and Buzzards Bay, Massachusetts. *J. Geol.* **75**, 461.

SEILACHER, A. 1967. Bathymetry of trace fossils. *Mar. Geol.* **5**, 413.

ZIEGLER, B. 1962. Die Ammoniten-gattung *Aulacostephanus* im Oberjura (Taxionomie, Stratigraphie, Biologie). *Palaeontographica* **119 (A)**, 1.

D. V. Ager, Department of Geology, University College, Swansea, U.K.

P. Wallace, Department of Geology, Imperial College, London, S.W.7., U.K.

Trace fossils from the late Precambrian and Lower Cambrian of Finnmark, Norway.

N. L. Banks

A conformable succession of dominantly shallow marine sediments of late Precambrian and Lower Cambrian age is present in the Tanafjord area of Finnmark, northern Norway. In this succession trace fossils first occur a short distance above the late Precambrian (Varangian) tillites. Their abundance and diversity increases rapidly in latest Precambrian and early Cambrian sediments. The absence of biogenic activity in older sediments is not due to the lack of suitable sedimentary facies. The incoming and diversification of trace fossils reflects principally the development of the Phyla Annelida, Arthropoda and Mollusca. The rate of early metazoan evolution and the factors which controlled it are briefly discussed.

1. Introduction

What is the earliest evidence of undoubted metazoan life? How rapidly did the Metazoa evolve in late Precambrian and Cambrian times? In investigating these problems, trace fossils as well as body fossils may give some indications as to the state of development of certain phyla. Some trace fossils are sufficiently distinctive to allow reasonable inferences to be made as to the phylum of the animal concerned (Glaessner 1969). With the appearance of metamerically segmented worms (i.e. annelids), sustained burrowing became possible for the first time in metazoan history (Clark 1964). Thus the first occurrence of well-developed burrow systems may reflect the initial development of the Phylum Annelida. From studies of the ecology of modern animals and the functional morphology of fossils, it seems likely that most biogenic structures in Palaeozioc sediments were produced by members of the Phyla Annelida, Arthropoda and Mollusca. It is universally agreed by zoologists that these phyla are closely linked in their origins, and probably all evolved at about the same time. Thus the development of trace fossils in late Precambrian and early Cambrian times probably more accurately reflects the evolution of these phyla than of metazoans as a whole.

Trace fossils from late Precambrian and Cambrian strata have been described and discussed by many authors. Seilacher (1956) described material from Pakistan and the U.S.A. and concluded that trace fossils were very rare in Precambrian rocks and showed an explosive differentiation at the beginning of the Cambrian. Glaessner (1969) studied trace fossils from late Precambrian and Cambrian successions in southern and central Australia and supported Seilacher's thesis of a rapid differentiation of soft bodied benthonic life at the base of the Cambrian. However, he also showed that several distinctive forms occur in late Precambrian rocks.

The purpose of this paper is to describe the incoming and development of trace fossils in a conformable succession of late Precambrian and Lower Cambrian sediments in the Tanafjord area of Finnmark, northern Norway, and to attempt to distinguish between those changes in biogenic activity which are the result of variations in the sedimentary environment, and those which may be reflections of the evolution of animal life at that time.

2. Geological background

The geology of the Tanafjord area of Finnmark (Fig. 1) was first elucidated by Føyn (1937) following the observations of Holtedahl (1918; 1931). The most complete section of the latest Precambrian and younger rocks is found on the Digermul Peninsula where Reading (1965) established the presence of a conformable succession of sedimentary rocks, 3000 m thick, extending from late Precambrian (Varangian, Eocambrian) tillites through the Cambrian and into the Tremadoc (Fig. 2). The succession can be divided into two parts:

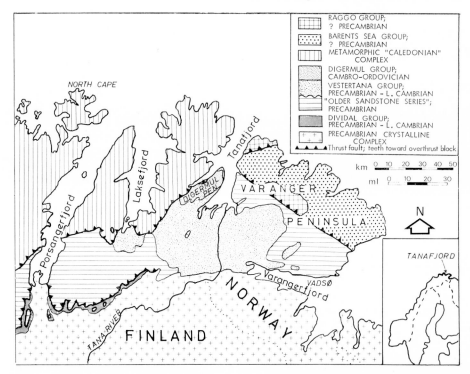

Fig. 1. Geological Map of East and Mid Finnmark. After Føyn (1937; 1967), Reading (1965) and Siedlecka and Siedlecki (1967).

   2. Digermul Group: 1500 m—Duolbasgaissa, Kistedal and Berlogaissa Formations. Lower Cambrian—Tremadoc.

   1. Vestertana Group: 1550 m—Lower Tillite, Nyborg, Upper Tillite, Stappogiedde and Breivik Formations. Precambrian-Lower Cambrian.

Reading considered that the majority of the sediments were deposited in a shallow marine basin, although occasional deepening allowed sedimentation by turbidity currents to occur in a non-agitated environment.

Together with the sediments of the unconformably underlying "Older Sandstone Series" this succession forms a northward thickening wedge of dominantly clastic miogeosynclinal sediments. This wedge is bounded to the south by the Fenno-scandian basement, to the northwest by an overthrust "Caledonian" metamorphic complex and to the northeast it is separated by a tectonic discontinuity from the sediments of the Barents Sea Group (Siedlecka and Siedlecki 1967). Part of the wedge can be correlated with the Dividal Group (Føyn 1967), a relatively condensed succession of late Precambrian and Cambrian sediments whose outcrop can be traced from Finnmark, through northern Sweden into southern Scandinavia.

Palaeontological studies on the Digermul Peninsula by Henningsmoen (in Reading 1965) revealed good Middle Cambrian and younger faunas although only fragments of *Holmia* sp. were found below the Middle Cambrian. I have now found several specimens of *Platysolenites antiquissimus* Eichwald at a horizon about 150 m above the base of the Breivik Formation (Fig. 2). This fossil, recently interpreted by Hamar (1967) as a serpulid worm tube, is well known from other localities in Finnmark (Føyn 1967), from southern Scandinavia and the Baltic regions. It is considered indicative of a very low horizon in the Lower Cambrian which is thus at least 950 m thick in this succession.

3. Depositional history

Only a brief description and discussion of the sedimentology need be given here but a more detailed account has been given by Banks *et al.* (in press). The main sedimentological features of the succession are summarised in Figure 2.

The sedimentation of the two tillites and the immediately adjacent sediments was described in detail by Reading and Walker (1966). The upper part of the Nyborg Formation is a well developed regressive sequence passing from distal turbidites through proximal turbidites into a wide variety of shallow marine sediments. The latter include herring-bone cross-stratified sandstones of probable tidal origin. The unconformity at the base of the Upper Tillite is considered to be due to glacial scouring and it is probable that no significant time break is represented. Above the Upper Tillite the transition from the Lillevatn Member to the Innerelv Member was interpreted by Reading and Walker (1966) as a transgressive sequence, passing from a fluviatile facies through a sub-tidal facies into a basinal facies with mudstone deposition.

Two periods of shallowing occurred within the Innerelv Member. They are indicated by transitions from mudstone through thin bedded fine sandstones and siltstones into medium to thick bedded lenticular sandstones; the latter often sit within large low-angle scours which also contain irregularly bedded, rippled, fine sandstones and siltstones resembling the sandy streak facies of de Raaf *et al.* (1965). The scours may have been produced by exceptional wave activity associated with storms.

Quiet basin mudstones occur again at the top of the Innerelv Member and pass gradually upward into red siltstones and sandstones which mark the base of the Manndraperelv Member. This member includes a lower unit consisting predominantly of fine red sandstones, deposited in a fairly active offshore environment, which is overlain by two regressive cycles 40–90 m thick. These cycles pass up from thin turbidites with interbedded mudstones into more proximal turbidites and

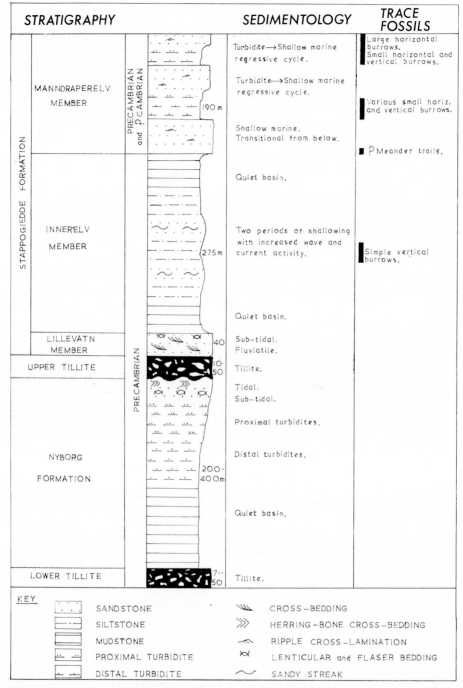

Figs.2a (above) and 2b (opposite). Sedimentological interpretation and trace fossils of the Vestertana Group and the lower part of the Digermul Group. Partly after Reading and Walker (1966).

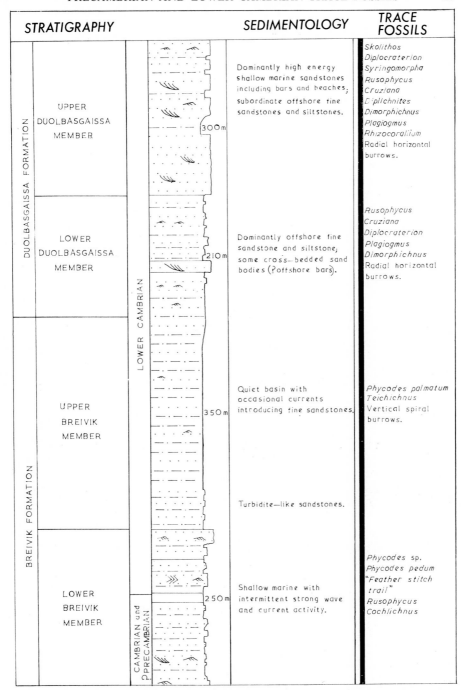

Fig. 2b.

then into shallow marine sandstones. The majority of the upper sandstones are similar to those of the lower unit, but in one section lagoonal and swash zone facies are also present. All the evidence from sedimentary structures, vertical and lateral facies relationships and petrography suggests that the sediments of the upper parts of the cycles represent true marine rather than deltaic conditions.

The transition upward from the Manndraperelv Member (Stappogiedde Formation) into the Breivik Formation is lithologically gradational. The Lower Breivik Member, a series of rapidly alternating sandstones, siltstones and mudstones, is sedimentologically complex, but in general appears to have been deposited in a shallow marine environment, mostly above wave base. Large fluctuations in current strength are indicated by the interbedding of cross-stratified clean sandstones with siltstones and mudstones. Lenticular and flaser bedding (Reineck 1967) occur and some horizons are extensively bioturbated.

The transition into the Upper Breivik Member is abrupt. The lower part of the Upper Breivik Member consists of siltstones with occasional sharp-based fine sandstones which often fill channels, and were probably deposited by turbidity currents. This facies passes upward into silts with many thin rippled sandstones which are interpreted as having been deposited in a gently agitated "shelf" environment.

The sediments of the Duolbasgaissa Formation were deposited in a nearer shore environment. Offshore thin bedded fine sandstones and siltstones interfinger with coarser sand bodies deposited under higher energy conditions. These sand bodies consist mainly of cross-bedded and flat-bedded orthoquartzites which were deposited as a series of bars and beach/barrier sands. The Lower Member consists almost entirely of the offshore facies whilst in the Upper Member thick sand bodies predominate.

4. Trace fossils

Trace fossils have been recorded from the Digermul Peninsula by Strand (1935), Føyn (1937) and Reading (1965). Reading considered that trace fossils first occurred in the upper part of the Nyborg Formation but the specimen on which this statement was based is now believed to be of inorganic origin (Reading personal communication). Further study of the Nyborg Formation has failed, as yet, to provide any evidence of animal life (M. B. Edwards personal communication and my own observations). Similarly, studies in the "Older Sandstone Series", a series of shallow marine and fluviatile sediments lying with slight regional unconformity

Plate 1

a Hypichnial casts; passively filled simple vertical burrows. 150 m above base of Innerelv Member ($\times 1$).

b Hypichnial and exichnial casts showing various burrowing patterns. Turbidite facies, 75 m above base of Manndraperelv Member ($\times 0.9$).

c Simple horizontal burrows; hypichnial and exichnial casts. Shallow marine facies, 180 m above base of Manndraperelv Member ($\times 1.2$).

d Hypichnial and exichnial casts showing horizontal burrows with occasional branching. Turbidite facies, 75 m above base of Manndraperelv Member ($\times 0.075$).

All specimens from Digermul Peninsula.

PLATE 1

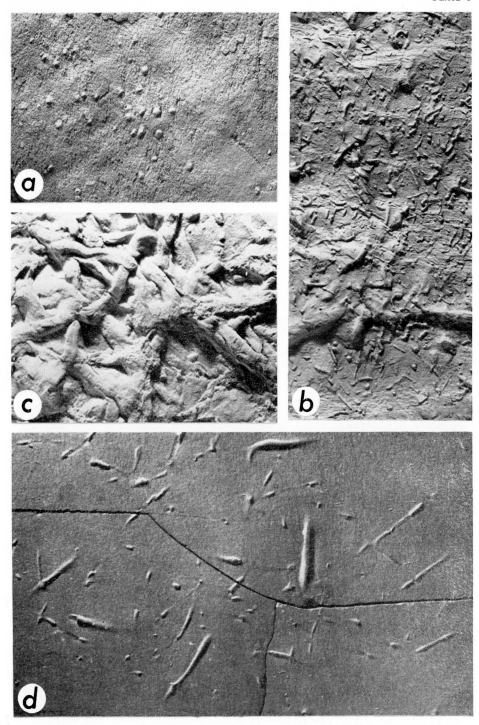

below the Lower Tillite, have also failed to reveal the presence of trace fossils (W. P. Geddes personal communication).

The general sequence of trace fossils is summarised in Figure 2. Brief descriptions are given below of some of the early forms and more general comments are made about some of the well known later types. The classification of Martinsson (1965) is used to describe the mode of preservation of the specimens.

Innerelv Member. The first undoubted trace fossils occur 140–150 m above the base of the member in a facies of interlaminated siltstone and mudstone. In the field they appear as circular protuberances (hypichnial casts) on the bases of siltstone laminae (Pl. 1a). The diameter of the protuberances is 1-2 m. Occasionally they occur in pairs but usually there is no pattern to their distribution. No sign of burrowing can be seen in the overlying siltstone and the structures are interpreted as being passive infillings of vertical burrows.

Manndraperelv Member. Trace fossils occur intermittently throughout this member. In general they are very rare in the shallow water sandstones but common in the turbidites, where several types are present. This distribution is probably a function of the higher preservation potential of trace fossils in the latter environment. However, it may also reflect the original distribution of the infaunal population.

In the turbidite facies trace fossils are found on the undersurfaces of sandstones and siltstones. They occur most frequently on the bases of thin beds ($<$5 cm) although they are occasionally seen associated with thicker beds. The most common forms are:

(i) Cylindroidal burrow tubes, approximately 1 mm in diameter, infilled with fine sand or silt and often densely covering undersurfaces of beds and developed as a number of different forms (Pl. 1b). These forms include regularly sinuous horizontal burrows, loosely coiled (spiral) horizontal burrows (cf. *Helicolithus*), short horizontal burrows with Y-shaped branching, and a variety of other patterns, including vertical non-septate U-tubes. The polychaete worm *Notomastus* is known to produce rather similar burrows with short branches and spiral structures in the present day sediments of the North Sea (Reineck *et al.* 1967).

(ii) Dominantly horizontal burrows, circular or elliptical in cross-section, 2–3 mm in diameter, straight or slightly curving, often branching every 2–4 cm. The branches usually diverge at angles of 60–90°. Other more irregularly branching forms also occur. They are found as exichnial sand-filled casts lying closely below a sandstone bed or as hypichnial casts (Pl. 1d). Most of the trace fossils in this facies were probably produced by worms.

The undersurfaces of many sandstone beds show delicate groove marks produced by tools carried by the current which deposited the sand. These marks often consist of sets of fine sub-parallel striations. These are usually straight and continuous, but occasionally are gently curved, discontinuous, and occur in sets

---

Plate 2

a *Phycodes pedum* Seilacher, Lower Breivik Member ($\times$ 1·3).

b "*Feather-stitch trail*", Lower Breivik Member ($\times$ 1).

c Vertical spiral burrow, Upper Breivik Member ($\times$ 0·55).

d Horizontal burrows with lateral grooves; hypichnial casts. Shallow marine facies, 180 m above base of Manndraperelv Member ($\times$ 1).

e cf. *Teichichnus*, Upper Breivik Member ($\times$ 0·6).

All specimens from Digermul Peninsula.

PLATE 2

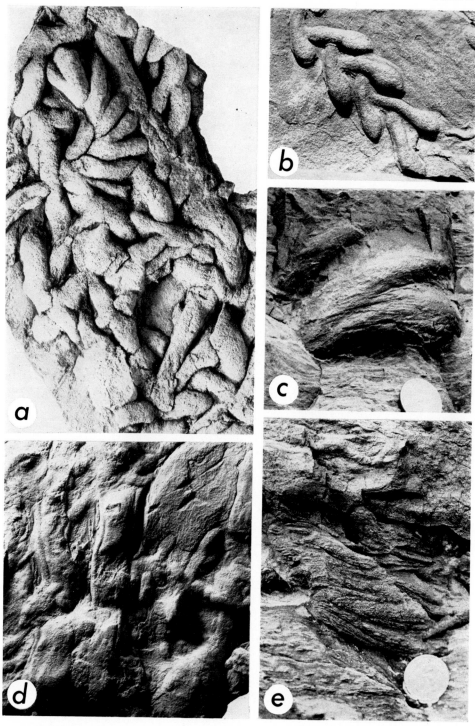

resembling in part the trace fossil *Dimorphichnus* Seilacher. Seilacher (1955) interpreted these marks as the tracks of a sideways-moving trilobite. It seems possible that many of these delicate markings could have been produced by the hard exoskeletons of arthropods during transport. The tool could either have been an animal dead or alive, or exoskeletons previously discarded by ecdysis. Similar structures have been described by Seilacher (1960) and Martinsson (1965). If this is so, it provides indirect evidence for the existence of arthropods at this time, although no hard parts were preserved.

In the shallow marine facies, some poorly preserved trace fossils occur a few metres above the base of the Member. They resemble structures described by Glaessner (1969 fig. 5c, d) from the Pound Quartzite of South Australia which he interpreted as meander trails.

Several types of trace fossil appear in the uppermost part of the Member. These include:

(i) Horizontal burrows 5–10 mm wide and up to 10 mm deep with well-developed lateral grooves. They are found as hypichnial or exichnial sand filled casts (Pl. 2d). The lateral grooves suggest that the animal which produced the structure may have been an arthropod.

(ii) Horizontal burrows 3–5 mm in width, without ornamentation, randomly curved and frequently crossing, found as exichnial or hypichnial sand filled casts (Pl. 1c).

(iii) Small vertical U-tubes with the width of the U *c.* 2 cm (*?Diplocraterion*) and several irregular types of horizontal and vertical burrows.

Lower Breivik Member. Here biogenic activity has reached an intensity at which marked modification of the sedimentary lamination is often visible. Many horizontal burrows are present, the majority being simple sand-filled tubes which lack any distinctive character. The trace fossil assemblage is dominated by *Phycodes*. Most specimens can be referred to *Phycodes pedum* Seilacher or are closely related to this species (Pl. 2a). *Phycodes pedum* first occurs in the lowest 3 m of the member and is persistent throughout it. The diameter of the burrow tubes varies from 2–20 mm. Seilacher (1955) considered that this species might serve as a Cambrian index fossil of world-wide extent. Its wide distribution is further confirmed by its presence in Finnmark and also in Australia (Glaessner). Its first occurrence in Finnmark, 140–150 m below the level of *Platysolenites*, suggests that the organisms responsible had developed in very earliest Cambrian, or perhaps even latest Precambrian times. *P. pedum* is now known to range up into the Lower Ordovician (Seilacher, personal communication). Probably closely related to *Phycodes pedum* is the so-called "*Feather-stitch trail*" (Pl. 2b); this, like *Phycodes,* is best interpreted as a feeding burrow.

Rusophycus is first seen about 70 m above the base of the member. *Rusophycus* is used here in general discussion to refer to paired sets of claw impressions which can be interpreted as resting marks (presumably of trilobites in most cases). *Cruziana* is used for more continuous markings, usually interpreted as the result of furrowing through the sediment.

Plate 3

a *Plagiogmus* sp., Lower Duolbasgaissa Member ($\times 1$).

b Radial horizontal burrow patterns; exichnial casts, Lower Duolbasgaissa Member ($\times 0.09$).

c *Rusophycus* sp., Lower Duolbasgaissa Member ($\times 1.25$).

d Large tracks cf. *Dimorphichnus* sp., Lower Duolbasgaissa Member ($\times 0.07$).

All specimens from Digermul Peninsula.

PLATE 3

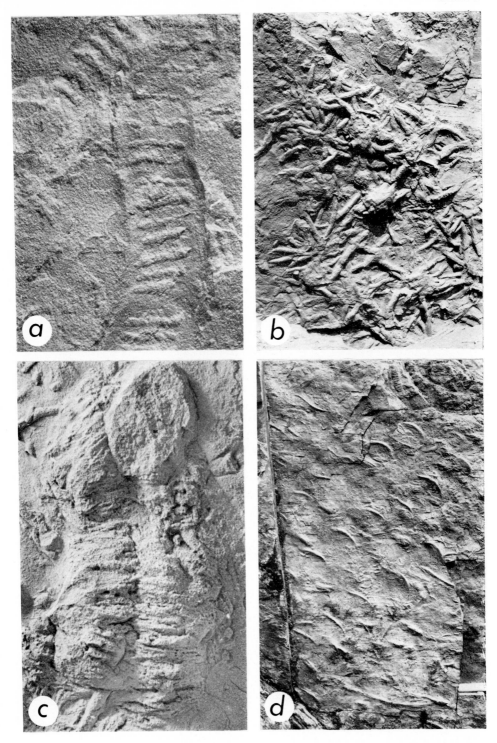

Some *Rusophycus* are only very shallowly dug paired sets of scratch marks (cf. Cloud and Nelson 1966 fig. 1g); others are much more deeply excavated bilobate pits. The top surfaces of sandstone beds show a number of epichnial grooves. These include regular sinuous trails (*Cochlichnus*) and bilobate trails with lateral lobe-like elevations similar to the trails produced by recent crustaceans (Nathorst 1881).

Upper Breivik Member. In the lower part vertically-stacked horizontal burrows which compare with *Teichichnus* are common (Pl. 2e) and are associated with various types of vertical spiral burrows. Some of these spiral burrows are irregular (Pl. 2c) whilst others maintain a constant whorl diameter and compare with the Mesozoic-Tertiary form *Gyrolithes* except that they are much smaller (tube diameter usually less than 5 mm). In the upper parts of the Member numerous small horizontal burrows occur associated with occasional specimens of *Phycodes palmatum* (Hall), a species described in detail by Seilacher (1955).

Duolbasgaissa Formation. Three intergradational trace fossil assemblages can be recognised in this Formation. The finest grained offshore siltstone and sandstone facies is dominated by large horizontal burrows (Pl. 3b). These are sometimes found in the form of radiating tunnels from a central chamber; scratch marks on the burrow walls suggest that they were probably produced by arthropods, although worms cannot be ruled out. The radiating burrow pattern has some similarity to that of *Volkichnium* figured by Pfeiffer (1965) but the Finnmark specimens are larger and laterally more extensive.

When the beds become sandier this form, though still present, becomes less common and *Rusophycus* (Pl. 3c), *Cruziana*, cf. *Dimorphichnus* (Pl. 3d), *Diplichnites*, *Plagiogmus* (Pl. 3a) and small *Diplocraterion* appear.

In the highest energy facies consisting of flat- and cross-bedded orthoquartzites, the assemblage consists of *Skolithos*, large *Diplocraterion* (width of U *c.* 12 cm), *Syringomorpha* and *Rusophycus*. Thus with increasing current activity there is a passage through the *Cruziana* facies of Seilacher (1967) into his *Skolithos* facies.

Several different forms of *Rusophycus* and *Cruziana* occur within this Formation and these are distinct from those found above and below this level. In the Upper Member some very large forms are present which resemble *C. dispar* Linnarsson. Cloud and Nelson (1966) suggested that the organisms responsible for these structures were more prone to a sedentary life in the Cambrian than in younger rocks. It is certainly true that *Rusophycus* is much more common than *Cruziana* in the Lower Cambrian of Finnmark, but in the overlying Kistedal Formation (Middle–Upper Cambrian) the reverse relationship is true.

5. Discussion

Seilacher (1964; 1967) has shown that trace fossils can be useful as environmental indicators. A clear relationship between sedimentary facies and the morphology of the trace fossils occurring in those facies is displayed in the upper part of the Finnmark succession. Such a relationship also demonstrates the wide ecological diversity already attained by animals in the Lower Cambrian.

It is thus important to consider whether changes in the environment can account, in whole or in part, for the increase in trace fossil activity which has been described. From the earlier discussion of the depositional history this seems to be unlikely. A turbidite facies in the inter-tillite Nyborg Formation has no trace fossils, whilst a similar facies in the younger Manndraperelv Member has abundant trails and burrows. Broadly similar, shallow marine facies occur in parts of the Nyborg

Formation, the Manndraperelv Member and the Lower Breivik Member. In the Nyborg Formation biogenic activity is absent, in the Manndraperelv Member it is present but rare, and in the Lower Breivik Member it is abundant. It is possible that further study may eventually lead to the discovery of trace fossils in the Nyborg Formation, but the overall pattern of their development in the Finnmark succession is abundantly clear.

From the evidence of this succession the following tentative suggestions are made:

(i) Before and during the time of the late Precambrian glaciation in Finnmark, animals capable of producing recognisable trace fossils did not exist, or were at a very early stage of development.

(ii) They first appeared soon after the cessation of glacial sedimentation and developed rapidly, so that by the end of the Lower Cambrian a level of biogenic activity had been reached which is comparable with that existing in many younger sediments of similar facies.

To see whether the suggestions made above are typical on a world-wide scale it is important to compare the evidence from as many areas as possible. Such a review is beyond the scope of this paper, but a few points can be mentioned. Firstly, at other localities in Finnmark, where the equivalent successions are often of somewhat different facies to that on the Digermul Peninsula, the same general trend in trace fossil evolution is seen. Secondly, in the Adelaide Series of South Australia the development of trace fossils is similar to that in Finnmark. The earliest occurs a short distance above the upper of two tillites; several forms are found in the Pound Quartzite associated with the Ediacara fauna while the Lower Cambrian contains a rich assemblage (Glaessner 1969)

It is not known whether the widespread late Precambrian glacial sediments are broadly time-equivalents. It would be of considerable interest to know the absolute ages of the tillites from the point of view of estimating the rate of early metazoan evolution. On the basis of isotopic dating presented by Dunn et al. (1966) the Australian tillites may be about 680–750 m.y. old. Banks et al. (1969) consider that the glaciation in Finnmark probably ended 15–43 m.y. before the beginning of the Cambrian (all dates recalculated where necessary using a Rb^{87} half-life of 5.0×10^{10} m.y. to enable comparison). The base of the Cambrian is poorly defined geochronologically but by recalculating Cowie's (1964) figure a date of 606 m.y. is obtained. Thus, in Australia the record of undoubted metazoan life apparently extends back about 100 m.y. before the Cambrian whilst in Finnmark this period is less than about 40 m.y. However such estimates must, at present, be regarded as tentative.

Many supposed trace fossils have been described from much older sediments. The great majority of these can, however, now be attributed to inorganic processes (Cloud 1968b; Glaessner 1969) but there remains a small number of specimens whose origins are problematical. Nevertheless, it is unlikely that any true trace fossils exist in rocks which are significantly older than about 700 m.y. The idea that Precambrian metazoan life is restricted to a relatively short period prior to the Cambrian appears to be coming increasingly accepted (Cloud 1968b; McAlester 1968).

If it is true that there was an extensive late Precambrian glaciation it seems possible that it may have had some effect on the development of life. Harland and Wilson (1956) and Rudwick (1964) considered that there was a causal relationship between the amelioration of climate at the end of the glaciation and the basal Cambrian transgression; the former provided a trigger for the rapid evolution of life at the beginning of the Cambrian. Whilst the effect of an ameliorating climate cannot be discounted there is little evidence to link a possible eustatic rise in sea level in early Cambrian times with the glacial episodes preserved in the stratigraphical record. On the other hand, the presence of distinct faunal provinces in the Cambrian may reflect the existence of high temperature gradients between the poles and the equator at that time. Such a situation, would tend to contribute towards a high rate of phyletic evolution because of the high provinciality and relatively small species populations within each province (Valentine 1968).

Whatever the effects of climatic factors on evolution I do not consider it likely that they were fundamental in controlling the development of life. A more plausible theory is that which relates major evolutionary advance to the gradual build up of atmospheric oxygen (Nursall 1959; Berkner and Marshall 1964; 1965; Cloud 1968a, b).

6. Conclusions

(i) Trace fossils first appear a short distance above the tillites and increase rapidly in abundance and diversity in latest Precambrian and Lower Cambrian times.

(ii) The sequence of trace fossil assemblages is partly controlled by changes of sedimentary facies but these are not responsible for the overall increase in trace fossils.

(iii) The incoming of trace fossils reflects the development of annelids, arthropods and molluscs rather than of metazoans as a whole.

(iv) Trace fossils are unlikely to occur in any rocks which are significantly older than 700 m.y.

(v) The build up of atmospheric oxygen is considered to be the fundamental factor controlling the development of life. Climatic factors were probably of only minor importance.

Acknowledgements. I am grateful to Dr. W. J. Kennedy and Dr. H. G. Reading for their help and encouragement at all stages of this work. I am indebted to Professors M. F. Glaessner, W. Häntzschel and A. Seilacher for helpful discussion and to Professor Glaessner for allowing me to see the manuscript of his paper on trace fossils from Australia. I would also like to thank those colleagues at Oxford who have commented on the manuscript, and the technical staff of the Department of Geology and Mineralogy who assisted in the preparation of the plates and figures. I am grateful to Dr. R. G. Walker for allowing me to use his photograph of the "*Feather-stitch trail*". The work was carried out during the tenure of a postgraduate studentship awarded by Shell International Petroleum Co. Ltd.

References

BANKS, N. L., EDWARDS, M. B., GEDDES, W. P., HOBDAY, D. K. and READING, H. G. Late Precambrian and Cambro-Ordovician sedimentation in East Finnmark. *Norg. geol. Unders.* In press.

——, —— and READING, H. G. 1969. Written contribution to the memoir *Late Pre-Cambrian glaciation in Scotland* by A. M. Spencer. *Proc. geol. Soc.* No. 1657, 191.

BERKNER, L. V. and MARSHALL, L. C. 1964. The history of oxygenic concentration in the Earth's atmosphere. *Discuss. Faraday Soc.* **37**, 122.

—— and —— 1965. History of major atmospheric components. *Proc. nat. Acad. Sci. U.S.A.* **53**, 1215.

CLARK, R. B. 1964. *Dynamics in metazoan evolution.* Clarendon Press, Oxford.

CLOUD, P. E. 1968a. Atmospheric and hydrospheric evolution on the primitive Earth. *Science, N.Y.* **148**, 729.

—— 1968b. Premetazoan evolution and the origins of the Metazoa. In *Evolution and environment* (Ed. E. T. Drake). Yale Univ. Press, New Haven and London.

—— and NELSON, C. A. 1966. Phanerozoic-Cryptozoic and related transitions: new evidence. *Science, N.Y.* **154**, 766.

COWIE, J. W. 1964. The Cambrian Period. In *The Phanerozoic time-scale* (Ed. W. B. Harland *et al.*) *Q.J. geol. Soc. Lond.* **120**S Supplement, 255.

DUNN, P. R., PLUMB, K. A. and ROBERTS, H. G. 1966. A proposal for the time-stratigraphic subdivision of the Australian Precambrian. *J. geol. Soc. Aust.* **13**, 593.

FØYN, S. 1937. The Eo-Cambrian series of the Tana district, Northern Norway. *Norsk. geol. Tidsskr.* **17**, 65,

—— 1967. Dividal-gruppen ("Hyolithus-sonen") i Finnmark og dens forhold til de eokambrisk-kambriske formasjoner. *Norg. geol. Unders.* No. 249, 1.

GLAESSNER, M. F. 1969. Trace fossils from the Precambrian and basal Cambrian. *Lethaia.* **2**, 369.

HAMAR, G. 1967. *Platysolenites antiquissimus* Eichw. (Vermes) from the Lower Cambrian of northern Norway. *Norg. geol. Unders.* No. 249, 87.

HARLAND, W. B. and WILSON, C. B. 1956. The Hecla Hoek Succession in Ny Friesland, Spitsbergen. *Geol. Mag.* **93**, 265.

HOLTEDAHL, O. 1918. Bidrag til Finmarkens geologi. *Norg. geol. Unders.* **84**, 1.

—— 1931. Additional observations on the rock formation of Finmarken, Northern Norway. *Norsk geol. Tidsskr.* **11**, 241.

MCALESTER, A. L. 1968. *The history of life.* Prentice-Hall, Englewood Cliffs (N.J.).

MARTINSSON, A. 1965. Aspects of a Middle Cambrian thanatotope on Öland. *Geol. För. Stockh. Förh.* **87**, 181.

NATHORST, A. G. 1881. Om spår af nagra evertebrerade djur m. m. och delas paleontologiska betydelse. *K. svenska Vetensk-Akad. Handl.* **18**, No. 7.

NURSALL, J. R. 1959. Oxygen as a prerequisite to the origin of the Metazoa. *Nature, Lond.* **183**, 1170.

PFEIFFER, H. 1965. *Volkichnium volki* n. gen.; n. sp. (Lebens-Spuren) aus den Phycoden Schichten Thüringens. *Geologie* **14**, 1266.

RAAF, J. F. M. DE, READING, H. G. and WALKER, R. G. 1965. Cyclic sedimentation in the Lower Westphalian of North Devon, England. *Sedimentology,* **4**, 1.

READING, H. G. 1965. Eocambrian and Lower Palaeozoic geology of the Digermul Peninsula Tanafjord, Finnmark. *Norg. geol. Unders.* No. 243, 167.

—— and WALKER, R. G. 1966. Sedimentation of Eocambrian tillites and associated sediments in Finnmark, northern Norway. *Palaeogeogr. Palaeoclimatol. Palaeoecol.* **2**, 177.

REINECK, H. E. 1967. Layered sediments of tidal flats, beaches, and shelf bottoms of the North Sea. In *Estuaries* (Ed. G. H. Lauff). *Publs Am. Ass. Advmt Sci.* **83**, 191.

——, GUTMANN, W. F. and HERTWECK, G. 1967. Das Schlickgebiet südlich Helgoland als Beispiel rezenter Schelfablagerungen. *Senckenberg. leth.* **48**, 219.

RUDWICK, M. J. S. 1964. The Infra-Cambrian glaciation and the origin of the Cambrian fauna. In *Problems in climatology* (Ed. A. E. N. Nairn). John Wiley, London, p. 150.

SEILACHER, A. 1955. Spuren und Lebenweise der Trilobiten, Spuren und Facies im Unterkambrium. In *Beiträge zur Kenntnis des Kambriums in der Salt Range (Pakistan)*, by O. H. Schindewolf and A. Seilacher. *Abh. mat. naturw. Kl. Akad. Wiss. Mainz. Jahrg.* 1955, p. 343.

—— 1956. Der Beginn des Kambriums als biologische Wende. *Neues Jb. Geol. Päläont. Abh.* **96**, 421.

—— 1960. Strömüngsanzeichen im Hunsruckschiefer. *Notizbl. hess. Landesamt. Bodenforsch. Wiesbaden.* **88**, 88.

—— 1964. Biogenic sedimentary structures. In *Approaches to Paleoecology* (Ed. J. Imbrie and N. Newell). Wiley, New York, p. 296.

—— 1967. Bathymetry of trace fossils. *Mar. Geol.* **5**, 413.

SIEDLECKA, A. and SIEDLECKI, ST. 1967. Some new aspects of the geology of Varanger Peninsula (Northern Norway). *Norg. geol. Unders.* No. 247, 288.

STRAND, T. 1935. A Cambrian fauna from Finnmark. *Norsk geol. Tidsskr.* **15,** 19.

VALENTINE, J. W. 1968. Climatic regulation of species diversification and extinction. *Bull. geol. Soc. Am.* **79,** 273.

N. L. Banks, Department of Geology, The University, Oxford, OX1 3PR, U.K.

Rusophycus as an indication of early Cambrian age

J. Bergström

An unexpected find of probable trilobite resting trails in the barren Hardeberga Sandstone *sensu stricto* draws attention to:— (i) the danger of using the absence of fossils as a means of correlation; (ii) the possibility put forward by Seilacher (1956) of using trace fossils for distinguishing between Cambrian and Eocambrian beds; (iii) the question of the age of the Hardeberga-Ringsaker Quartzite complex in Scandinavia. *Rusophycus parallelum* ichnosp. nov. is described.

1. Introduction

In the spring of 1969 Mr. Bo Arvidsson, works engineer at the Hardeberga quarry, east of Lund, South Sweden (Fig. 1) collected a rock specimen with ripple marks and two oval imprints. Dr. Lars Nilsson at the Institute of Geography of Lund kindly informed me about the new find. The three of us then managed to trace with reasonable certainty the stratigraphic origin, which proved to be within the supposedly unfossiliferous lower part of the arenitic sequence, which is commonly believed to be of early Cambrian age. The unfossiliferous part was distinguished by its supposed lack of fossils (Hadding 1929) as a separate formation, now known as the Hardeberga Sandstone *sensu stricto* (Regnéll 1960). The stratigraphic term "Hardeberga Sandstone" was originally introduced by Angelin in 1877 to cover the whole sequence of Lower Cambrian arenites in Scania, South Sweden.

The different meaning of the term Hardeberga Sandstone as understood by different authors, the lack of any specific name for the formation above the restricted Hardeberga Sandstone, and the confusion regarding the stratigraphic range of different fossils, makes a stratigraphic discussion necessary. A more detailed discussion will be published elsewhere (Bergström 1970).

2. Stratigraphic setting

Within the arenitic sequence, there is a more or less gradual change from poorly fossiliferous quartzitic sandstones upwards into calcareous glauconitic and phosphoritic sandstones, with a variety of trace fossils and some body fossils. At the type locality for the Hardeberga Sandstone *sensu stricto*, the Hardeberga quarry, the lowermost trace fossil horizon is known as the *Syringomorpha* Sandstone and lies within the poorly fossiliferous, white and quartzitic sequence. Unfortunately, this horizon cannot be traced with certainty outside the type locality.

With the restriction in the meaning of the term Hardeberga Sandstone, the upper part of the arenitic sequence (except possibly the topmost few metres) was

35

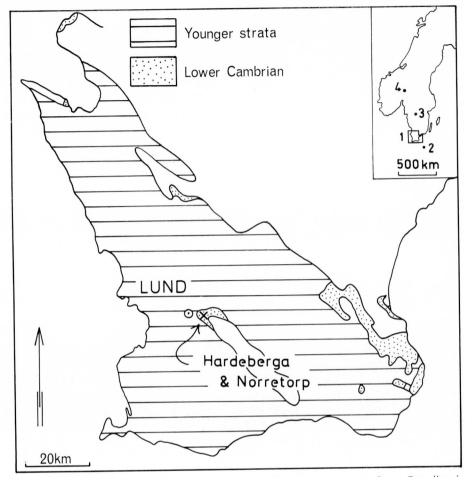

Fig. 1. Map of Scania with position of the Hardeberga Quarry at Norretorp. Inset: Scandinavia with 1 Scania; 2 Bornholm; 3 Västergötland; 4 the Mjøsa district.

left without a formation name. The main part of this sequence, the "sandstone with *Diplocraterion, Skolithos,* etc." of Regnéll (1960), is characterized by its trace fossils (Fig. 2). Within this sequence there is a fairly distinct lithological boundary between the pure white quartzitic beds below and the greyish impure sandstone above. The white quartzitic sequence appears to be barren except at a few levels.

The difficulties in treating this stratigraphic interval have forced me to introduce a few changes in the stratigraphic nomenclature (Bergström 1970). Firstly, the upper limit of the white quartzitic formation is set at the distinct lithologic boundary referred to above, notwithstanding the fact that a few trace fossils occur further down. In the Hardeberga quarry, this boundary is about 12 m above the boundary between the Hardeberga Sandstone *s.s.* and the "sandstone with *Diplocraterion, Skolithos,* etc." The name of this lower formation is here changed to "Hardeberga Quartzite". Secondly, the impure sandstone above the Hardeberga Quartzite and below the Rispebjerg Sandstone (Fig. 2), is called the "Norretorp Sandstone".

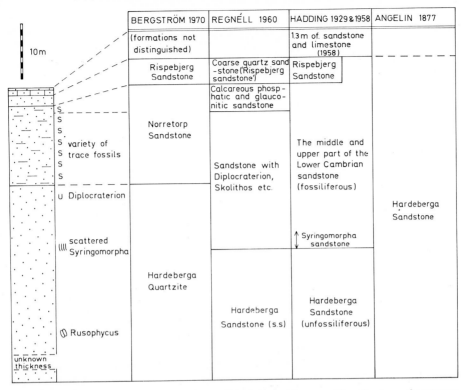

Fig. 2. The Lower Cambrian succession at Hardeberga Quarry. Classification of sequence according to different authors. Vertical scale only approximate.

The *Rusophycus* which is the subject of this report was found in the Hardeberga Sandstone as defined by Hadding, probably some 15 m below the upper boundary of this formation, and well inside the supposedly unfossiliferous sequence. This level is about 27 m below the top of the Hardeberga Quartzite.

3. Systematic description

Ichnogenus RUSOPHYCUS Hall 1852

Rusophycus parallelum ichnosp. nov.

Plate 1

Holotype. LM LO 4353T. Institute of Palaeontology, University of Lund, Lund, Sweden.

Locality and horizon. Hardeberga Quartzite, 25 to 30 m below the upper boundary, in the Hardeberga quarry, Scania, South Sweden. Grid reference: Topographical map of Sweden (Topografisk karta över Sverige), on 1:50 000, map sheet 2c Malmö NO, UB 927743.

Diagnosis. A *Rusophycus* with parallel sides, low relief, and traces of two distal claws.

Description. Two *Rusophycus* specimens were found, both on the same slab (Pl. 1). One of them is complete, whereas the other is cut off by the edge of the slab. The complete specimen is about 60 mm long and 40 mm wide. The other one, truncated at its posterior end, is about 50 mm wide, and the preserved length about 40 mm. The width is remarkably constant along the trail; 10 mm in front of the posterior end of the complete specimen it is still about 35 mm.

Both trails are quite shallow. The complete specimen is at its maximum only 3 mm deep in its posterior half and still shallower in the anterior half, where it crosses a ripple ridge at an oblique angle. In spite of a ripple amplitude of about 6 mm even the ripple ridge is only slightly affected by the trail, which thus neatly follows the ripple-mark topography. The other, truncated, specimen does not cross any ripple ridge as far as can be seen. Its depth is less than 5 mm.

In the complete trail, the individual appendage scars are transverse. They curve slightly backwards close to the sagittal line. There is possibly a faint indication of the imprint of two distal claws in a few places. In the truncated specimen the individual scars are directed more obliquely inwards-backwards, and in this case the imprints of two distal claws are readily discernible.

Discussion. The trails were undoubtedly made by an arthropod. Morphologically this arthropod must have been fairly short and broad. Its width must have been subequal along the body, and there appears to be appreciable tapering only very close to the posterior end. Apparently there was no posterior spine. Furthermore, the walking legs were serially arranged and present along the body to the posterior end. These features rule out a merostome as the trace maker. Certain and presumed trails of xiphosurans (Caster 1938), as well as of aglaspidids (Radwański and Roniewicz 1967; Bergström 1968), are distinctly different from the Hardeberga trails. Instead, these trails are of the general morphological type which have generally been assigned to trilobites.

The similarities between the two specimens are greater than the differences, and as both are found on the same surface it seems probable that they were made by the same kind of animal. As is evident from the size difference, however, they were made by two separate individuals.

There is little doubt that the trails are resting trails. This is neatly shown by the specimen crossing the ridge of a ripple without really affecting the ridge. As the crossing is oblique, the animal cannot have followed the curvature of the subsurface by simple bending of the body. Thus the animal must have been standing on its appendages rather than resting on the margins of the dorsal exoskeleton, except perhaps at the ripple ridge. The relation between length and width seems to show that the trail was made by the whole animal, unless it was vermiform.

Plate 1

a Slab of Hardeberga Quartzite with ripples and two *Rusophycus* specimens, preserved as epichnia.

b Holotype (LM LO 4353T) of *Rusophycus parallelum* ichnosp. nov. A *Kjerulfia* contour is added to show the probable general outline of the trail-maker (modified from *Treatise of Invertebrate Paleontology* Pt 0, fig. 137, 1a).

c Truncated specimen (LM LO 4354t) of *Rusophycus parallelum* ichnosp. nov. Note bifid nature of individual leg imprints. Photograph from artificial cast.

PLATE 1

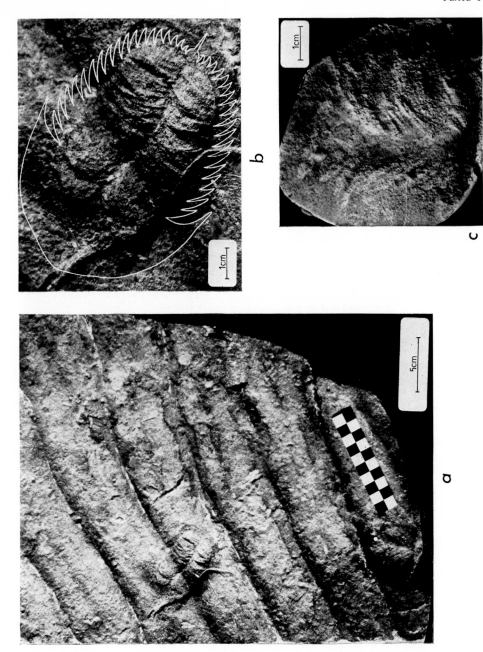

No trilobite is known from the Hardeberga Sandstone, nor from the overlying *Diplocraterion* Sandstone. The succeeding part of the sequence is characterized by the presence of what may be the oldest trilobites hitherto found in Sweden, *viz. Holmia torelli* Moberg and *Kjerulfia lundgreni* Moberg. These two forms, and especially the latter, possess exactly the broadly oval outline that would be expected from the trace-making animal. The size of the trails also corresponds to these two trilobites. Two strong distal claws were apparently present in some redlichiids, as shown by Seilacher (1955) on *Redlichia?* and Martinsson (1965) on *Paradoxides?*. According to Öpik (1958) *Redlichia* was probably much closer to olenellids than appears from the Treatise classification. Thus a close correspondance in appendage features would not be surprising.

It is concluded that the traces were produced by some early trilobite, either a species of *Kjerulfia* or a form similar to *Kjerulfia* in outline, and most probably an olenellid.

4. Correlation

In different areas of Baltoscandia, the Cambro-Silurian sedimentation began with the deposition of arenites, which are usually nearly barren in their lower parts. The apparent absence of fossils has made correlation difficult, and the arenitic formations have sometimes been referred to the Lower Cambrian and sometimes to the Eocambrian.

It is reasonable to suppose that the initial sedimentation was comparatively rapid, not least because an appreciable amount of weathered material must have been available. Thus the deposition of the comparatively thick sequences of arenitic beds may have occurred during a short time interval. The difference in time between the deposition of the lowermost beds and the first beds with reliable zone fossils may thus be comparatively small. The absence of fossils in the lowermost parts of the formations may merely be a result of the habitats; proximity to the shore and clean sand, devoid of detritus, made the environment unfriendly to life.

On the other hand, life probably flourished in adjoining areas, and now and then individuals would have visited the barren sand areas, as shown by the *Rusophycus* in the Hardeberga Quartzite. This demonstrates the danger of using the supposed absence of fossils as a means of correlation, in this case as a means of placing the Eocambrian-Cambrian boundary immediately beneath the fossiliferous beds. As with the Hardeberga Quartzite, there is no particular reason to believe that the similar and possibly contemporaneous Balka Sandstone of Bornholm, the Ringsaker Quartzite in the Mjøsa District, or the Vemdal or Ström Quartzites in the Caledonian area should be regarded as Eocambrian (Fig. 3).

The find of a *Rusophycus* in the Hardeberga Quartzite underlines the possibility, put forward by Seilacher in 1956, of using trace fossils to distinguish between Cambrian and Eocambrian beds. Trilobites are generally said to occur for the first time well up in Lower Cambrian strata, i.e. above a pre-*Holmia* horizon. However, all trilobites cannot have come into existence with a sudden and simultaneous explosion at the base of the Cambrian, and they may well have been present in Eocambrian times.

Thus, on balance I find it very probable that the Hardeberga Quartzite and contemporary arenites belong to the Lower Cambrian, and not necessarily even to the lowermost part of it.

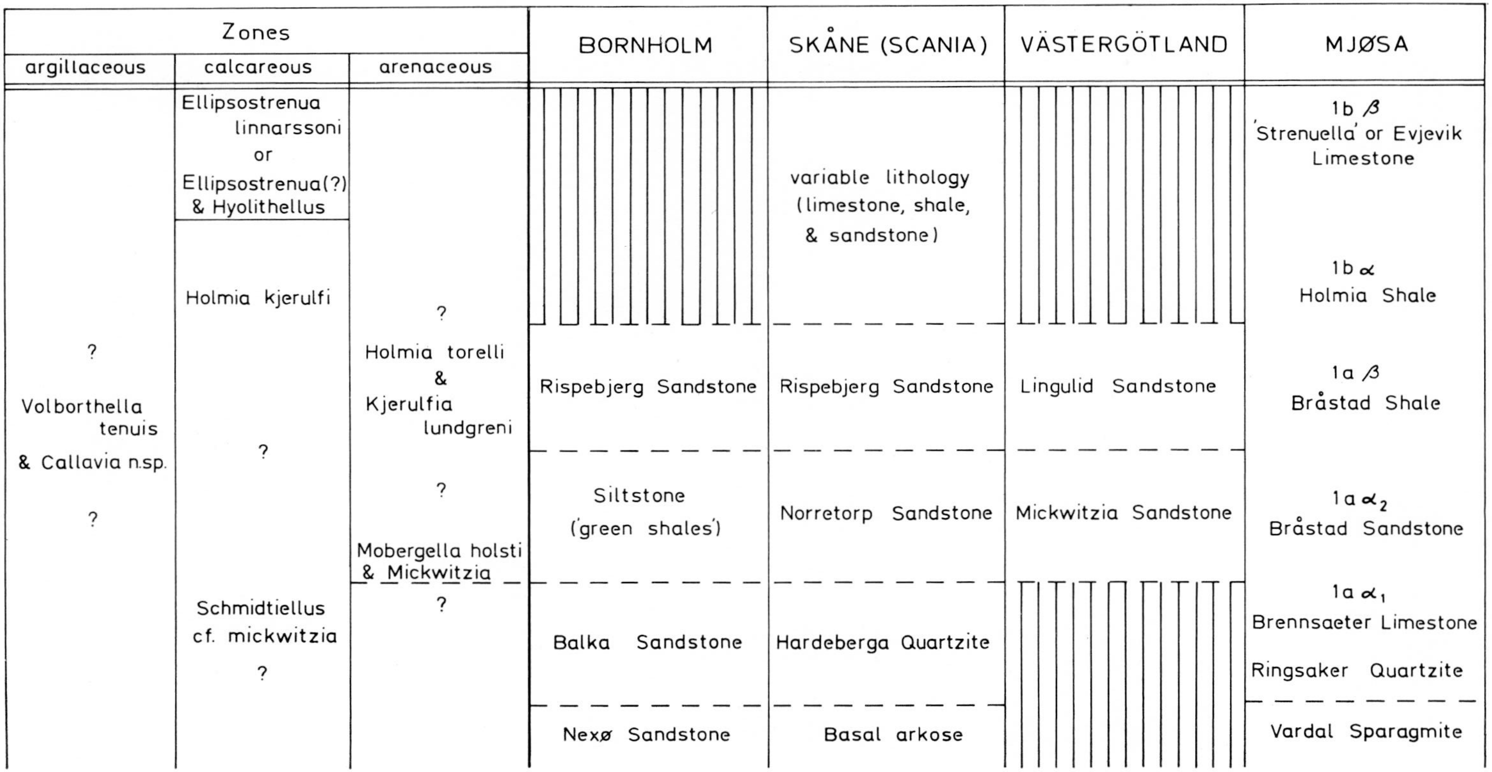

Zones (argillaceous)	Zones (calcareous)	Zones (arenaceous)	BORNHOLM	SKÅNE (SCANIA)	VÄSTERGÖTLAND	MJØSA
	Ellipsostrenua linnarssoni or Ellipsostrenua(?) & Hyolithellus			variable lithology (limestone, shale, & sandstone)		1b β 'Strenuella' or Evjevik Limestone
?	Holmia kjerulfi	Holmia torelli & Kjerulfia lundgreni	Rispebjerg Sandstone	Rispebjerg Sandstone	Lingulid Sandstone	1b α Holmia Shale
						1a β Bråstad Shale
Volborthella tenuis & Callavia n.sp.	?	?	Siltstone ('green shales')	Norretorp Sandstone	Mickwitzia Sandstone	1a α₂ Bråstad Sandstone
?	Schmidtiellus cf. mickwitzia	Mobergella holsti & Mickwitzia	Balka Sandstone	Hardeberga Quartzite		1a α₁ Brennsaeter Limestone / Ringsaker Quartzite
	?	?	Nexø Sandstone	Basal arkose		Vardal Sparagmite

Fig. 3. Possible correlation of Lower Cambrian strata in Denmark, Sweden, and Norway.

D

Acknowledgments. I am much indebted to Mr. Bo Arvidsson of Hardeberga and Dr. Lars Nilsson of Lund for providing the material and all available information about its provenance. Thanks are further due to Dr. L. R. M. Cocks of London for correcting the English, Mrs. Siri Bergström for preparing the figures, and Mr. Anders Ullman for making the photographs. The work and presentation of the results was made possible by funds from Kungl. Fysiografiska Sällskapet and Svenska Naturvetenskapliga Forskningsrådet.

References

ANGELIN, N. P. 1877. Geologisk öfversigts-karta öfver Skåne med åtföljande text, på uppdrag Malmöhus och Christianstads läns. *Kongl. Hushållnings Sällskap utarbetad.* Lund.

BERGSTRÖM, J. 1968. Eolimulus, a Lower Cambrian xiphosurid from Sweden. *Geol. För. Stockh. Förh.* **90**, 489.

—— 1970. Distinction of Lower Cambrian formations in Scania. *Geol. För. Stockh. Förh.* In preparation.

CASTER, K. 1938. A restudy of the tracks of *Paramphibius. J. Paleont.* **12**, 3.

HADDING, A. 1929. The pre-Quaternary sedimentary rocks of Sweden. *Lunds Univ. Arsskr* N. F. Avd. 2. **25**, no. 3, 1.

MARTINSSON, A. 1965. Aspects of a Middle Cambrian thanatotope on Öland. *Geol. För. Stockh. Förh.* **87**, 181.

ÖPIK, A. A. 1958. The Cambrian trilobite *Redlichia:* Organization and generic concept. *Bull. Bur. miner. Resour. Geol. Geophys. Aust.* **42**, 1.

RADWAŃSKI, A. and RONIEWICZ, P. 1967. Trace fossil *Aglaspidichnus sanctacrucensis* n. gen., n. sp., a probable resting place of an aglaspid (Xiphosura). *Acta Palaeont. pol.,* **12**, no. 4, 546.

REGNÉLL, G. 1960. The Lower Palaeozoic of Scania. *Int. Geol. Congr.* 21. *Copenhagen. Swedish geol. guide-books.* d, 1.

SEILACHER, A. 1955. Spuren und Lebensweise der Trilobiten. In *Beiträge zur Kenntnis des Kambriums in der Salt Range (Pakistan),* by O. H. Schindewolf and A. Seilacher. *Abh. naturw. Kl. Akad. Wiss. Mainz.* Jahrg. 1955, no. 10, 257.

—— 1956. Der Beginn des Kambriums als biologische Wende. *Neues Jb. Geol. Paläont. Abh.* **103**, 155.

J. Bergström, Paleontologiska Institutionen, Sölvegatan 13, 223 62 Lund, Sweden.

On bryozoan borings from the Danian at Fakse, Denmark

G. J. Boekschoten

Oyster shells from the Danian at Fakse, Denmark, showing diminutive bryozoan borings, are described. Difficulties concerning the taxonomy of boring bryozoa are discussed. It emerges that this new type of shell boring also necessitates a new generic name.

1. Introduction

The limestone from the quarry near Fakse (formerly Faxe), Denmark, is famous for its many fossils. Calcitic fossils have been preserved in their original state while aragonitic fossils (such as snail-shells) are found as internal and external moulds or with calcitized shells. Traces of boring organisms are well preserved in calcitic shells, particularly oysters.

In 1933 Professor A. Rosenkrantz collected some oyster-shells with such borings in the Middle Danian Naesekalk at Fakse (Rosenkrantz and Rasmussen 1960 p. 9, facies 1). The author is indebted to Professor Rosenkrantz for the loan of this material, deposited in the collections of the Mineralogical Museum of the University of Copenhagen.

Under the microscope the oyster-shells from Fakse show some cavities excavated by clionid sponges. Besides these there are also pores, connected with tunnels, very similar to the cavities made by Recent boring bryozoans. Such bryozoan tunnels were previously noticed in Pliocene, Pleistocene and Recent calcareous strata (Boekschoten 1966; 1967), but the author is not aware of any name available for these trace fossils.

2. Nomenclature

From the literature on recent and fossil boring Bryozoa, it is clear that there are two radically different interpretations of the systematic importance of the traces left by these animals. The early authors, like d'Orbigny (1841), Fischer (1866), Jullien (1880) and Norman (1907) described Recent genera and species founded solely on the strength of the morphology of the tunnel system excavated by the bryozoan. In fact, none of these authors had seen a living zoarium at all. Consequently, the systematic place of these trace fossils was in doubt. Busk (1852), for instance, considered the boring Bryozoa to belong to the Cheilostomata, whereas Ehlers (1876) thought that *Terebripora* (d'Orbigny 1841) could be a cheilostome while *Spathipora* (Fischer 1866) was certainly a ctenostome. Jullien (1880) and Calvet (1912 a, b) thought that these borings were not bryozoan but hydrozoan.

Marcus (1938) was the first to observe the living zooids of ctenostome bryozoa in these tunnel systems. To the animals he gave names created by earlier authors for the tunnel systems, because he thought that the borings were good diagnostic features. Subsequently Silén (1946; 1947; 1956), Soule (1950 a, b) and Soule and Soule (1968; 1969a) described the zooids of boring bryozoans. Recently Soule and Soule (1969b) gave evidence that not all boring bryozoans are ctenostomes. These zoologists discarded the former subdivision based solely on borings. It is appropriate to quote Soule (1950a) here: "Silén pointed out the futility of basing the specific classification of burrowing Bryozoa entirely upon their zoarial tracings made in the shells of molluscs. In so far as superficial external appearances are concerned, determination of the genera and the species is hopeless."

Since, however, the names were based precisely on these superficial external appearances, the type material of these ichnospecies consists solely of borings in shells. The only way to translate these trace fossil names into soft-body names would be to collect topotype material of the trace fossil species, and to investigate whether there are any zooids living in borings showing all features used in both classifications. Although Soule continued to use the old trace fossil names, he did not attempt this time-consuming approach. Soule should have considered the old generic and specific names as unrecognizable taxonomic entities. As he did not do so, a paradoxical situation has arisen. Soule (1950b) described a new species of boring bryozoan as *Terebripora comma* on the strength of its soft-body morphology, despite the fact that *Terebripora* was designated as a group of trace fossils.

When the tunnel-system of *Terebripora comma* Soule is inspected it is clear from the figures that this *Terebripora* should be called *Spathipora* because of the shape of its tunnel system. Curiously enough, *Terebripora comma* was reported by Gautier (1955) from the Mediterranean coast of France. Fischer (1866) recorded his *Spathipora sertum* from the same region, and it therefore seems probable that the bryozoan *Terebripora comma* excavates the tunnel system *Spathipora sertum*. But in several publications (for instance Bobin and Prenant 1954) the biospecies and the ichnospecies are placed on an equal footing as different species of bryozoan animals. It is clear that this practice leads to utter confusion, and it is therefore desirable to apply ichnogeneric names like *Terebripora* and *Spathipora* solely to trace fossils. On the other hand, Silén (1946) created the genera *Immergentia* and *Penetrantia* on the strength of the soft-body morphology of these boring bryozoans. Trace fossils, therefore, should not be called *Immergentia* or *Penetrantia*.

Both of these genera, nevertheless, inhabit a characteristic system of tunnels and pores. As yet, however, there is no trace fossil name for this pattern of borings. They have been noticed already in the fossil state. In previous publications (1966; 1967) the author referred to such Pliocene and Quaternary trace fossils as "*Penetrantia*", between inverted commas. There exists also a report of a Jurassic *Immergentia*-like fossil—*Immergentia? lissajousi* Walther 1965. However, it seems doubtful if this fossil has anything to do with *Immergentia*. Instead of a boring system, it looks much more like the zoarium of the cyclostome bryozoan *Stomatopora* externally encrusting an annelid tube.

3. The Danian Borings

The borings in the Danish oyster shells are of the same "*Penetrantia*"-type. It is the oldest occurrence so far recorded and it is desirable to designate an appropriate name for this trace fossil. It is proposed to give it the ichnogeneric name *Iramena*.

Ichnogenus IRAMENA nov.

Derivation of name. After Annemarie Boekschoten-Van Helsdingen, who helped the author throughout this trace fossil research.

Type ichnospecies. Iramena danica ichnosp. nov.

Other ichnospecies. It is possible that *Terebripora antillarum* Fischer (1868 p. 300) belongs to the same ichnogenus; its original description is vague and unillustrated, and the ichnospecies does not appear to have been cited since.

Diagnosis. Borings of probably ctenostome bryozoa, consisting of long (stolon) tunnels in an irregular network, with round to reniform (zooid cavity) apertures situated in alternating positions laterally to and close by the tunnels.

Stratigraphic range. Lowermost Tertiary (Danian)—Recent.

Remarks. Iramena differs from *Spathipora* in the round shape of the apertures (reniform or circular in the new genus, slitlike in *Spathipora*) and in the closeness of the apertures to the main (stolon) tunnel. It differs from *Terebripora* which consists of diamond-shaped apertures situated directly above the tunnel.

Iramena danica ichnosp. nov.

Figure 1.

Holotype. Trace fossils in the outer surface of an oyster (deposited in the Mineralogical Museum, Copenhagen) from the Middle Danian Naesekalk at Rosenkrantz locality C in the limestone quarry at Fakse, Denmark.

Paratypes. Trace fossils in pycnodont oyster shell and in coral branch (Mineralogical Museum, Copenhagen) from the same locality as the holotype.

Other material. Trace fossils in oyster shells from the Middle Danian (Naesekalk) at Rosenkrantz locality B, Fakse, limestone quarry, Denmark. Trace fossils in *Ostrea edule* Linnaeus, Pliocene, Tielrode (Belgium); in *Buccinum undatum* Linnaeus, Recent Schiermonnikoog beach, Netherlands and Arcachon, France; in a limestone pebble, Recent, Red Bay, Donegal, Eire; and other trace fossils in the collection of the Geological Institute, State University of Groningen (Netherlands).

Diagnosis. A bryozoan trace fossil consisting of a network of stolon tunnels with round to reniform apertures situated alternatively to the left or to the right of the tunnel (at a distance from 0·01 to 0·1 mm from the tunnel), between 0·5 and 2·5mm apart from each other. The diameter of a single aperture varies from 0·03 to 0·1 mm.

Description. The holotype shows borings at the outside of a partly defective juvenile shell of *Ostrea* cf. *reflexa* Ravn (Ravn 1902 pp. 115-116 pl. 3, fig. 12-14; Ravn 1934 p. 23). The diameter of the zoarium is about 11 mm, the width of the stolon tunnels is 0·003 mm. Most apertures are reniform, with diameters of about 0·05 mm; their distance from the stolon tunnel ranges from 0·03 to 0·08 mm. The distance between the more regularly spaced apertures is about 1 mm.

The paratype shows the same apertures as the holotype, but the stolon tunnels are hardly visible as these are deeply imbedded in the substratum.

The nine fragments of oyster shells from Rosenkrantz locality B were all attacked by boring organisms. Three specimens have traces of a boring sponge and two show algal borings. Five specimens contain *Iramena*. One of these shows many reniform apertures (diameter 0·054–0·062 mm) and one diamond-shaped aperture; stolon tunnels were not observed. Another fragment shows reniform and circular

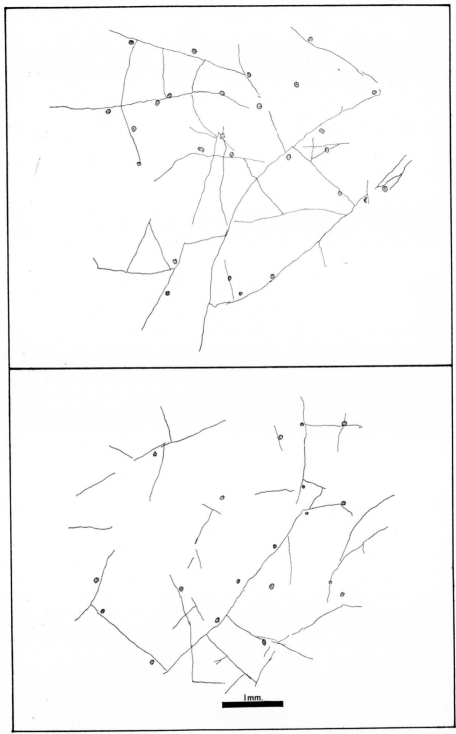

Fig. 1. Camera lucida tracings of two parts of the type zoarium borings of *Iramena*.

apertures (diameters between 0·062 and 0·075 mm). Some apertures are apparently 0·45 mm apart, measured along the rarely clearly visible stolon tunnels.

Remarks. All specimens of *Iramena* were found in calcareous sub-strata from the littoral to neritic zone of the marine environment. The author could not find any difference between the Danish fossils and the abundant material from the Pliocene and the Quaternary. No Cretaceous examples are yet known.

4. Conclusions

Like the ichnogenera *Terebripora* and *Spathipora*, *Iramena* is a trace fossil name and should be used for borings alone. By contrast, names such as *Immergentia* and *Penetrantia* refer to the bryozoan animals and cannot be directly applied to bryozoan borings.

References

BOBIN, G. and PRENANT, M. 1954. Sur un Bryozoaire perforant, *Terebripora comma* (Soule) trouvé en Méditerranée. *Arch. Zool. exp. gén.* **111**, 130.

BOEKSCHOTEN, G. J. 1966. Shell borings of sessile epibiontic organisms as palaeoecological guides. *Palaeogeogr. Palaeoclimatol. Palaeoceol.* **2**, 333.

—— 1967. Palaeoecology of some mollusca from the Tielrode sands (Pliocene, Belgium). *Ibid.* **3**, 311.

BUSK, G. 1852. An account of the Polyzoa and Sertularian Zoophytes collected in the voyage of the Rattlesnake. In *Narrative of the Voyage of H.M.S. Rattlesnake . . . during the years* 1846-1850. **1**, Appendix no. 4, 1.

CALVET, L. 1912a. Sur un Bryozoaire Cténostome (*Watersia paessleri* n.g., n. sp.) parasitant le cormus d'une Synascidie (*Polyzoa gordiana* Michaelsen). *C.R.hetd.Séanc. Acad. Sci. Paris* **154**, 243.

—— 1912b. A propos de *Watersia paessleri.*, Bryozoaire parasite. *Ibid.* **154**, 395.

EHLERS, E. 1876. *Hypophorella expansa.* Ein Beitrag zur Kenntnis der minierenden Bryozoen. *Abh. K. Ges. Wiss. Göttingen* **21**, 1.

FISCHER, P. 1866. Étude sur les Bryozoaires perforants de la famille des Térébriporides. *Nouv. Archs Mus. Hist. Nat., Paris* **2**, 293.

GAUTIER, Y. 1955. Bryozoaires des Gastéropodes de l'herbier de Posidonies. *Vie Milieu* **6**, 335.

JULLIEN, J. 1880. Description d'une nouvelle espèce de Bryozoaire perforant du genre *Terebripora* d'Orbigny. *Bull. Soc. zool. Fr.* **5**, 142.

MARCUS, E. 1938. Bryozoarios perfuradores de conchas. *Archos Inst. biol., Sao Paulo* **9**, 273.

NORMAN, A. M. 1907. On some British Polyzoa. *Ann. Mag. nat. Hist.* (7), **20**, 207.

ORBIGNY, A. d' 1841. Zoophytes. In *Voyage dans l'Amérique Méridionale* **5** (4) Levrault, Paris and Strasbourg.

RAVN, J. P. J. 1902. Molluskerne i Danmarks Kridtaflejringer. *K. danske Vidensk. Selsk. Skr.* naturw. math. Afd. (6) **11**, 69, 205.

—— 1934. Étude sur les Pélécypodes et Gastropodes daniens du Calcaire de Faxe. *Ibid.* (9) **5**, 1.

ROSENKRANTZ, A. and RASMUSSEN, H. W. 1960. South-eastern Sjaelland and Mön, Denmark. Guide to excursions A42 and C37, Part 1. *Int. Geol. Congr.*, 21 Copenhagen.

SILÉN, L. 1946. On two groups of Bryozoa living in shells of molluscs. *Ark. Zool.* **38B**, 1.

—— 1947. On the anatomy and biology of Penetrantiidae and Immergentiidae. *Ark. Zool.* **40**, 1.

—— 1956. On shell-burrowing bryozoa and *Phoronis* from New Zealand. *Trans. R. Soc. N.Z.* **84**, 83.

SOULE, J. D. 1950a. Penetrantiidae and Immergentiidae from the Pacific. *Trans. Am. microsc. Soc.* **69**, 359.

—— 1950b. A new species of *Terebripora* from the Pacific. *J. Wash. Acad. Sci.* **40**, 378.

SOULE, J. D. and SOULE, D. F. 1968. A new species of *Terebripora* (Ectoprocta, Ctenostomata) from Antarctic *Cephalodiscus*. *Bull. Sth. Calif. Acad. Sci.* **67**, 178.

—— and —— 1969a. Three new species of burrowing bryozoans (Ectoprocta) from the Hawaiian Islands. *Occ. Pap. Calif. Acad. Sci.* No. 78, 1.

—— and ——1969b. Systematics and biogeography of burrowing bryozoans. *Am. Zoologist* **9**, 791.

WALTHER, B. 1965. Un Bryozoaire perforant de l'Oxfordien: *Immergentia ? lissajousi* nov. sp. (Ctenostomata). *C. R. Somm. Séanc. Soc. géol. Fr.* fasc. 9, 286.

G. J. Boekschoten, Geological Institute, University of Groningen, Netherlands.

Borings as trace fossils and *Entobia cretacea* Portlock, as an example

R. G. Bromley

The paper comprises three sections. Firstly, the concept of fossil organic borings as trace fossils in hard substrates is discussed. Borings are distinguished from the related phenomena of burrows (in soft substrates), embedment cavities (in growing skeleton) and other forms of destruction of hard substrates by life processes of organisms. The importance of distinguishing ichnotaxa from zoological taxa is emphasized, and the value of borings as tools in palaeoecology is indicated.

Secondly, a survey is made of the present knowledge of living boring organisms from the point of view of the geologist. While the zoologist is chiefly concerned with the anatomy of boring organisms, data regarding their borings is largely lacking, and the geologist has often to make his own observations on living borers in order to interpret fossil borings. Considered here are the borings produced by algae, fungi and lichens; bryozoans, phoronids, sipunculids and polychaete annelids; piercing of shells by a turbellarian, brachiopods, cephalopods and gastropods; and rock, wood and shell borings of gastropods, chitons, bivalves, isopods, amphipods, various cirripeds, echinoids and sponges.

Finally, a sponge boring abundant in the European Cretaceous, and much quoted under the name *Cliona cretacea*, is redescribed, and a lectotype designated, under its original trace fossil name *Entobia cretacea* Portlock 1843.

1. Introduction

With the advance of palaeoichnology the definition of trace fossils has become increasingly restricted. As indicated by Ehrenberg (1954), definitions accepted today even exclude borings of organisms except where they are made in hard sediment. For example: "Lebensspuren are structures in the sediment left by living organisms" (Häntzschel 1962 p. 178), and "Traces are sedimentary structures resulting from biological activity" (Seilacher 1964 p. 296).

It is generally agreed, however, that borings, as excavations made by organisms in hard substrates, are trace fossils. Their definition thereby becomes "Hard substrate trace fossils".

The boring habit necessarily has gradational boundaries with other ways of life which cause cavities in, or the destruction of, hard materials. Before discussing borings themselves, therefore, it is important first to cross the limits of the defined area.

2. Definition and limitation of the term boring

2a. Boring/burrowing

Most authors describing borings use the nouns "boring" and "burrow" (and their related verbs and adjectives) indiscriminately as synonymous. This is confusing, particularly in environments of progressive hardening of the sea floor, where separate ichnocoenoses corresponding to soft and hard sediment are found together in one bed (Perkins 1966; Bromley 1968). The processes of boring in hard substrate and burrowing in soft were defined long ago by Krejci-Graf (1932 p. 31). Nevertheless, there are some groups of organisms which represent boundary cases, e.g. bivalves which bore or burrow by physical means into substrates which range in hardness from soft rocks to stiff clay.

2b. Boring/embedding

Many organisms come to live in hard substrates, not by boring, but through becoming overgrown by the skeleton of the animal or plant producing the substrate. Once embedded, the organism may employ genuine boring processes in order to enlarge its abode, so that the final cavity may have mixed origins. In fossil condition the origin of the cavity may not be easy to determine.

A variety of organisms allow themselves to be overgrown by coral as an easy way of obtaining protection. In the coral reef environment, such organisms include cirripeds such as *Creuzia* (Nilsson-Cantell 1921 p. 352) and *Pyrgoma* (Darwin 1854 p. 358; Utinomi 1953 p. 535), haplocarcinid crabs, eunicid annelids, sipunculids (Utinomi *loc. cit.*), and gastropods such as *Magilus* and some vermetids.

Another common form of embedment occurs within bivalve shells. No one will consider the fish which has accidentally become caught beneath the mantle of an oyster and coated over with pearly shell (e.g. Stearns 1889) a boring organism, even though its fossilized skeleton will be found within a cavity in the shell. Many animals, however, deliberately place themselves under the mantle of bivalves and allow themselves to be incorporated in the shell. Some species of the polychaete annelid genus *Polydora* do this today, for example, living in "pseudoborings" or blister-like cavities, particularly in oyster shells (Whitelegge 1890; Korringa 1951; 1952). Some of these worms live in a pad of mud within the shell which allows them to grow without boring. Others resort to true boring processes to enlarge the cavity, and long, U-shaped borings may result (Douvillé 1908 fig. 7). The same oyster shells are usually bored by *Polydora ciliata* (Johnston), the cavities of which do not originate by embedment, and so are randomly distributed and oriented. The embedding form, however, entering only at the margin of the shell, tends as a result to be oriented with the entrance of its cavity on a growth-line and the vertex of the U lying towards the umbo from this point. The cavity also lies parallel with and is incorporated in the laminar structure of the shell. Moreover, it is common that several individuals settle simultaneously, in which case their openings will all be connected with the same growth-line of the shell.

Thus there is a basis on which embedment cavities can be distinguished from pure borings in fossil shells. It is worth quoting some examples. In his original description of *Caulostrepsis taeniola,* Clarke (1908 p. 169) considered these cavities in Upper Devonian brachiopods to be true borings. However, in his specimens, the cavities all radiate inwards from the commissure towards the umbo in the manner of embedment cavities. Similar cavities in Pennsylvanian bivalves were described as *Caulostrepsis dunbari* by Condra and Elias (1944 p. 548) in terms of "pseudo-borings" or embedment structures.

Small pouch-like cavities in Cretaceous bivalves were named *Specus* by Stephenson (1952 p. 51) and considered by him borings, but these also show a distribution and orientation like embedment structures.

Another example of quite a different nature has been described by Biernat (1961) under the name *Diorygma atrypophilia*. This consists of a long V-shaped tubular cavity embedded in and deforming the shell in the interior of a single species of *Atrypa*.

The lodgment of a non-boring parasite in the calcareous skeleton of a host organism can cause great deformity of the skeletal material. The resulting cavity therefore can be distinguished easily from a boring. Such cavities have been described by Voigt (1959; 1967a) in Cretaceous octocorals as the work of parasitic ascothoracican cirripeds. One final example of rather similar nature also should be mentioned. The gastropod *Mucronalia* characteristically lives within the spines of certain living echinoids, causing the otherwise slender radiole to swell monstrously into subglobular form and engulf the gastropod in a central cavity (Koehler 1924). These cavities have been mistakenly compared by Tasnádi-Kubacska (1962 p. 95) with true borings which are common in the naturally globular radioles of *Tylocidaris* spp. in the Danian and Maastrichtian of Denmark (Grönwall 1900); the originator of these borings is still unknown.

2c. Borings and other forms of hard substrate destruction

Many animals destroy hard substrates as a result of their life processes, producing traces which cannot be considered borings, but which are allied to hard substrate trace fossils through the nature of the process, or the behaviour pattern producing it. Predation involves crushing shell or coral with chelae, biting with jaws, rasping with radulae. True borings in this group must include penetrations of shells by predatory gastropods, cephalopods and a turbellarian (see below). Furthermore, when certain bryozoans (MacGinitie and MacGinitie 1949 p. 298) and actinians (Chun 1900 p. 146) completely cover shells inhabited by hermit crabs, these shells may be completely dissolved. In the former case the crab is said to dissolve the shell, in the latter the sea anemones. Such a shell, partly dissolved, in fossil state, would present traces which the hard-substratum palaeoichnologist would be required to interpret.

3. Borings as trace fossils

Unlike other trace fossils, which are confined to soft sediments, borings occur not only in hardened sediments but also in igneous rocks, in pebbles and in organic skeletons such as mollusc shells, coral, bones, teeth, fish scales and wood, etc. It therefore serves no useful purpose to attempt to transfer to borings the stratinomic or toponomic classification designed for soft-sediment trace fossils. In its place, a description of the substrate (and if organic, whether dead or alive) is important in any description of a boring, since differences in substrates play a significant role in the form of the boring.

The ethological classification of trace fossils is also of restricted use in application to borings. Most borings are constructed for shelter and protection and fall within the domichnia. But the borings of fungi might be classed as fodinichnia, while the structures hollowed out in wood by certain crustaceans, insects and bivalves are a combination of the two.

As Seilacher (1953 p. 443) has pointed out, borings, like body fossils and unlike soft-sediment trace fossils, are most conveniently classified on the basis of zoological taxonomy. There are two chief reasons for this:

(i) Hard substrate is difficult to penetrate, and so specialized means of boring have to be developed. The various taxonomic groups of animals are differently pre-adapted to permit of such specialization. Thus the methods used and the holes produced bear characteristic indications of the nature of the originators.

(ii) Unlike the case with soft-sediment traces, the "fossilization barrier" (Seilacher 1967 p. 413) is no obstacle in the classification of borings. Indeed, on the contrary, modern examples are easily studied, and the hard substrate not only provides "ready-made fossils" capable of resisting most destructive tendencies of diagenesis; but in many cases the cavity also offers a microenvironment of high fossilization potential for the skeleton of the organism which bored the cavity.

However, it is also on account of their resemblance in this way to body fossils that fossil borings have been largely described by palaeontologists and neglected by palaeoichnologists, and this has resulted in great confusion in their names.

3a. Naming and description of borings

Description of borings by palaeontologists has resulted, in numerous cases, in confusion between the borer and the boring, with the result that cavities have been given the names of organisms. For example, owing to the application of the name of a living genus of boring sponge, *Cliona,* to Devonian borings (e.g. by Thomas 1911) this genus has now been quoted as having the range Devonian-Recent (De Laubenfels 1955 p. E40; Müller 1963 p. 120).

On the other hand, Häntzschel (1962 p. W228) dealt exclusively with ichnotaxa. This resulted in the omission of all reference to the majority of borings described in the literature, including all bivalve borings, since the majority have not been named as trace fossils.

According to their resemblance to body fossils, borings are most conveniently named with binominal ichnotaxa. However, among the plant and "worm" borings, which are not easily assigned a particular originator, some authors have used a system of letters to distinguish different borings (e.g. Joysey 1959; Jux and Strauch 1965). In some cases authors have chosen to offer no name at all, but to rely on illustration to distinguish the boring (e.g. Rodda and Fisher 1962). Indeed, the simplicity and irregularity of form of many borings defy accurate verbal description. For example, in an attempt to describe the shape of a sponge boring, Stephenson (1941 p. 55) stated that "in some specimens the channels are turnip-shaped, flattish jug-shaped, or irregularly ovate" which, without his excellent illustrations, would not serve to differentiate this boring from many other sponge borings. It must therefore be emphasized that illustration of every aspect of a boring is essential to its description.

Conversely, the borings of bivalves not only commonly have a shape characteristic in themselves, but in many cases also contain the shells of the originator. This has led to a lack of names for the borings themselves. However, it should be emphasized here that even if the originator is preserved, the borer and the boring should not be confused by giving body fossil and trace fossil the same name.

4. Ecological importance of borings

Trace fossils are absolutely autochthonous (Seilacher 1964 p. 301). While this is as true for hard substrate trace fossils as for soft, the fact that borings can easily be reworked together with their matrix confuses the situation. Although an extensively bored shell or pebble may be more likely to be destroyed by reworking than transported, nevertheless the literature contains reports of transported borings. For example, *Cliona celata* Grant does not live in the Wadden Sea (Holland), but shells containing its borings are swept into the area by flood currents (Boekschoten 1966 p. 351). It has also been shown that borings in shells on the Cadzand beach

(Holland) are of Eocene age (Boekschoten 1966 p. 347). The majority of fossil borings, however, would appear to occur at approximately their place of origin, and with this assumption they are of great importance to the palaeoecologist.

4a. Destruction by borers

The destructive effect of borers in wood, rock and shell has been emphasized for different reasons by many workers. Recent borings have been described from an economic standpoint (Calman 1919; Ray 1959) and from the point of view of the geographer (Jehu 1918). They have been especially studied as erosive agents of coral reefs (Gardiner 1902; 1903; Otter 1937; Utinomi 1953; Yonge 1963b), of carbonate coasts (Ginsburg 1953; Neumann 1965) and submarine rocks (Warme and Marshall 1969). By geologists their erosive effect has been noted in rudist reefs (Zapfe 1937) and hardgrounds (Bromley 1968). Emphasis has been placed by some workers on the destruction by particular groups of organisms, especially the sponges (Goreau 1965; Neumann 1966), the boring algae (Duerden 1902; Nadson 1927a; 1932; Hessland 1949; Ginsburg 1957) and the polychaete annelids (Ebbs 1966).

Boring organisms are directly destructive simply by replacing solid substrate with empty cavities. By weakening the substrate in this way they are indirectly responsible for its destruction by wave activity.

In another way the borers are responsible indirectly for rock destruction, by encouraging predation. Rasping by gastropods and chitons browsing on endolithic and epilithic algae produces considerable erosion of rock and shell surfaces in shallow water. Certain brachyuran crustaceans with powerful claws may also contribute to this destruction. On coral reefs, fish with powerful jaws cause much erosion through feeding directly on living coral, on organisms encrusting the coral, and also on organisms boring and hidden within the hard substrate (Cloud 1959; Bakus 1964; 1966). Results obtained by Bakus (1964 p. 18) indicated that fish were less interested in eating the boring sponge *Cliona* than another, encrusting, sponge. In the English Cretaceous chalk, however, Bromley (1970) described a clionid sponge boring which had been extensively damaged by a predator feeding on the sponge.

4b. Borers and the $CaCO_3$ cycle

Several authors have emphasized the importance of organisms which bore by chemical means in returning calcium carbonate to seawater (Mägdefrau 1937; Kühnelt 1951; Revelle and Fairbridge 1957), particularly in the case of boring algae (Nadson 1927b; 1932; Wetzel 1938; Hessland 1949). In the Black Sea, Nadson (1927a) suggested that the cement which bound a conglomerate of bored shells and debris was the result of the release of calcium carbonate by algae boring in the shells. This may possibly also apply to the apparently brittle "micrite envelopes" (Bathurst 1966) produced by boring algae on carbonate grains in shallow water.

4c. Borers as producers of sediment

Scraping and biting of rock by browsing and predatory animals produces much sediment (Cloud 1959 p. 398), and for this, boring organisms are indirectly responsible. Clionid sponges, however, are directly responsible for the production of sediment. The special manner in which these sponges bore disintegrates the substrate into large quantities of small chips. The importance of these chips as a source of fine sediment on coral fore-reefs was shown by Goreau and Hartman (1963). In the case of *Cliona lampa,* Neumann (1966) has estimated that this sponge produces nearly 6 kg fine sediment from 1 m² limestone per 100 days.

4d. Borings as environmental indicators

Borings have been used from early times for the interpretation of past environments (e.g. Lyell 1830 p. 453). Their great value in this field has been demonstrated
by Boekschoten (1966; 1967). However, the more precisely the boring organism
can be identified the more useful is the fossil boring as an environmental indicator.
Several general works have been written on borers by zoologists (e.g. Yonge
1963a; 1964) and on borings by geologists (e.g. Dacqué 1921 p. 427; Abel 1935
p. 374, 481; Elias 1956; Häntzschel 1962; Fatton and Roger 1968), but they cover
the field incompletely. There is still a need for a survey, from the point of view of
the geologist, of the borings produced by living organisms. This is attempted in the
following section.

5. Survey of boring organisms

5a. Penetrative Thallophyta

The very fine, mainly branched, borings of algae, fungi and lichens were initially
considered to be part of the intrinsic shell structure (e.g. Carpenter 1843). They
were first recognized as the borings of plants by Kölliker (1860a, b), who observed
them in a large number of organic calcareous substrates. Subsequently, a large
botanical literature on boring plants has materialized but is of limited use to the
geologist.

Although botanists acknowledge that it is often difficult to distinguish between
living boring algae and fungi and that it may be impossible to discriminate between
them in fossil material (Pia 1937 p. 341) several palaeontologists have made such a
distinction. Their interpretations, often reinforced by a binominal nomenclature
(the generic name often signifying the type of boring and the trivial name the type
of substrate) have been reassessed by other workers. For example, although
Schindewolf (1962 p. 213) proposed that the ichnogenus *Mycelites* Roux (1887)
should be used collectively for all branched fungal borings, Bernhauser (1962)
concluded that *Mycelites* was an alga or group of algae and that it was possible to
distinguish between marine and brackish-water forms. However, such trivial names
as *ossifragus* (Roux 1887), *conchifragus* (Schindewolf 1962; 1963; 1967) and
ammoniticus (Wetzel 1964) are useful as no origin is assumed.

While it may be hazardous to be too dogmatic in differentiating between fossil
boring algae and fungi, a combination of observations (mainly based on living
material) may enable one to make a reasonably satisfactory identification. The
following characteristics of thallophyte borings may be diagnostic, to some degree,
of borings of algae and fungi.

(i) *Bathymetry*. Marine boring algae normally flourish in the littoral zone and
may be abundant to a depth of about 20–25 m (Nadson 1927a p. 898). In the Black
Sea, bored shells are not found deeper than 50 m (Nadson 1927b p. 1016) but they
occur at 80 m in the Gulf of Naples (Nadson 1932 p. 848). Boring algae also abound
in fresh water (Chodat 1898). However, whereas boring fungi are also commonest
in the littoral zone (Bonar 1936) they have been recorded from as deep as 2,000 m
(Pia 1937 p. 370).

(ii) *Size of boring*. An examination of both living and fossil material suggests that
fungal borings are generally smaller than those of algae (Wetzel 1938), the
diameter of some rhizoids being almost as narrow as many bacterial cells. There is
an overlap between fungi and algae in the size range 4–25μ but borings larger than
50μ in diameter are usually algal (Pl. 1a). Regular swellings for reproductive cells
can occur in both, but gentle dilations in thin, vegetative hyphae appear to typify fungi.

(iii) *Course of borings*. There is a tendency for fungal hyphae to be straight or gently curved, while algal threads can produce contorted borings (Pl. 1a). There are perhaps too many exceptions for this rule to be generally applied, although Boekschoten (1966 p. 344) made a similar observation.

(iv) *Mode of branching*. Algae sometimes show "false ramification", individual threads comprising the main "trunk" departing from it at various points. The trunk thereby becomes narrower where a thread leaves it and thicker where one joins it. This feature is not typical of most fungi, where true branching generally results in a rather constant diameter of the hyphal borings. Considerable variation in diameter from branch to branch may therefore be indicative of an algal boring (Pl. 1a).

(v) *Angle of branching*. There is again a slight tendency for fungi to produce side branches at regular angles (60°–90°) from the main hypha, or to fork dichotomously with similar angles. In algae, the branching of the borings is often highly irregular, sometimes producing bundles which show false ramification elsewhere.

(vi) *Choice of substrate*. Algae probably bore for protection, not for food. Fungi bore for food, digesting organic material in the substrate. Borings of thallophytes are common in nutritive substrates such as dentine (Sognnaes 1963), bone (Roux 1887), fish scales (Rose 1855; Kölliker 1860a; Mägdefrau 1937) and the integument of arthropods (Rolfe 1962 p. 48). Most of these workers have therefore considered these borings to be fungal, which is generally supported by the other characteristics of the borings. Likewise, borings in a limestone pebble or reworked shell might be considered to be algal.

(vii) *Location in substrate*. Since most algae are dependent upon light, the position of the borings in relation to illuminated surfaces may be indicative of an algal or fungal origin. Where borings occur in dark or semidark areas of a substrate, as in the columella of a gastropod (see also Boekschoten 1966 p. 344) or in the septa of a cephalopod, they are probably fungal in origin. However, as some algae send long, exploratory threads into the dark interior of a substrate, the possibility of the borings being algal cannot be excluded.

(viii) *Association with iron*. Whereas some algae appear to have a chemotactic affinity for iron (Ellis 1914 p. 119), fungi have no such associations, although ferrous or ferric ions are essential to their growth. Several types of algae (mainly Cyanophyceae) deposit iron in or upon their filaments and penetrating forms often occur abundantly within iron oolites (B. J. Taylor, personal communication).

None of the above "rules" is diagnostic on its own, but combined they may be of some significance. For example, many belemnites from the Upper Cretaceous chalk of Europe contain *Chaetophorites* which were thought to be algal borings (Pratje 1922; Mägdefrau 1937 p. 59). However, their mode of branching, course, diameter and distribution on all surfaces of the substrate, combine to indicate that they were bored by a fungus.

Within a particular species, algae may produce many types of boring as a response to different environments or owing to an alternation of generations. Partially endolithic forms may produce no more than densely spaced, minute pin-prick holes 0·05–0·08 mm in diameter in a shell surface (Santesson 1939 p. 49). Such holes are common in fossil shells.

Lichens also form pits in carbonate substrates. The most important boring marine species, *Arthopyrenia sublitoralis* (Leighton), forms pits similar to but larger than those of algae in shells and limestone in the littoral zone (Santesson 1939 p. 46; Boekschoten 1966 fig. 4). Lichens, however, are more active in the terrestrial environment where boring forms represent an important agent of erosion of limestone outcrops (e.g. Fry 1922).

Finally, algae and fungi attack wood. Fungi are most important in this respect, since in addition to destroying the wood themselves, they also render it prone to attack by wood-boring bivalves and crustaceans (Meyers and Reynolds 1957) and constitute a major part of the food of those borers. Kohlmeyer (1969) found on the contrary, however, that it was the presence of animal borings which gave the fungus access to the interior parts of the wood which it could not otherwise infest.

5b. Boring Bryozoa

Borings most easily confused with those of thallophytes are those of Bryozoa. These are usually superficial, slender, branching stolons partially or wholly sunken into the carbonate matrix, and communicating repeatedly with the surface at points where zooids are developed. The zooids themselves may also be housed within the substrate (Fig. 2a), or be free and deciduous on the surface and leave no boring trace (Fig. 1).

The taxonomy of living boring bryozoans was greatly altered by the discovery of two families by Silén (1946): the Immergentiidae and Penetrantiidae. The former belongs to the Order of Ctenostomata, but Soule and Soule (1969) have removed the Penetrantiidae to the Cheilostomata. Before this there was but one family, the Terebriporidae (Ctenostomata), with two genera, *Terebripora* d'Orbigny and *Spathipora* Fischer, to which most Mesozoic and Tertiary borings were ascribed

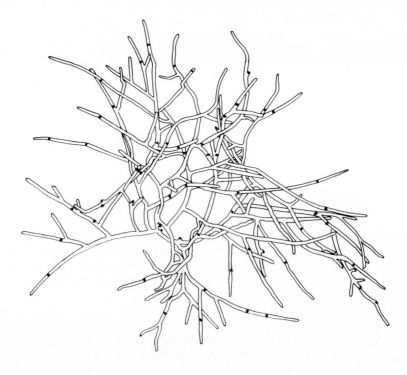

Fig. 1. Complete boring of a bryozoan in the shell of *Pecten maximus*. Surface apertures black. From a radiograph. × 4.

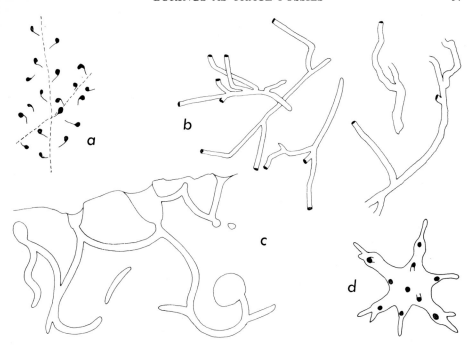

Fig. 2. Branching borings.   a   *Terebripora comma* Soule. Surface apertures to zooid borings black, course of stolon (sometimes visible at the surface) dotted. × 20. Modified after Soule (1950a);   b   Branching pattern shown by *Phoronis ovalis*. Surface apertures black. × 6. Modified after Harmer (1917) and Brattström (1943);   c   Branching boring of the polychaete *Marphysa* in soft rock. The apertures to the surface open into empty bivalve borings. × 1. After Morton and Miller (1968);   d   Boring of a juvenile clionid sponge in *Mytilus* shell from the Kattegat. Surface pores black. From a radiograph. × 10.

(Fischer 1866). But both these genera are in reality ichnogenera, since they were erected for empty borings, and they therefore rightly belong to the ichnologist rather than to the zoologist. Since most recent species of *Terebripora* and *Spathipora* have likewise been described from their traces alone (ichnospecies), while a few are based on soft parts of the animals themselves (species), there is confusion in their taxonomy (Silén 1948 p. 37). Silén wrote: "Several different types of Bryozoa have invaded shells, even members of such different groups as the Stolonifera and the Carnosa. This fact shows the danger of trying to identify the boring forms only on the traces in shells" (Silén 1946 p. 7). "I have found it extremely difficult, not to say impossible, to decide with any certainty upon the systematic position of a boring Bryozoan on these characters only. This is even more evident if we consider that the structure of the zoarium and consequently its traces in the shell changes considerably with its increasing age . . . and, to some extent, with the structure of the invaded shells". "A direct comparison between recent, anatomically researched species and fossil ones will possibly never give satisfying results" (Silén 1948 p. 37). However, it is worth mentioning that useful illustrations of borings of Recent Ctenostomata are given by Fischer (1866), Silén (1946; 1948), Soule (1950a, b) and Boekschoten (1966). Recent and fossil bryozoan borings have been surveyed by Soule and Soule (1969).

E

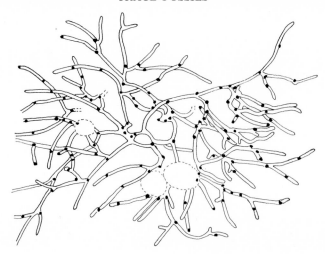

Fig. 3. A bryozoan boring, *Talpina ramosa,* in a Campanian belemnite from Frettenham, Norfolk, U.K. Apertures black. The branching pattern is obscured in places by other borings (dotted). The boring covers three-quarters of the circumference of the belemnite (alveolus towards left). Camera lucida drawing. ×2·5.

Some older fossil examples have received trace fossil names. European Cretaceous belemnites in many cases show the boring known as *Talpina ramosa* Hagenow (Fig. 3) which is most probably a bryozoan boring (Morris 1851 pl. 4 fig. 4 and 5; Lessertisseur 1955 p. 81).

In the Palaeozoic, particularly, many borings have been ascribed to bryozoans (see especially Ulrich and Bassler 1904; Condra and Elias 1944). There is a possibility that thallophyte borings have been confused in some of these forms, but most are quite clearly bryozoan and have trace fossil names. In the case of *Bascomella gigantea* Morningstar 1922, the borings of Carboniferous acrothoracican cirripeds were mistaken for zooid cavities since they are associated with thread-like borings which resemble bryozoan stolon borings. This species was discussed by Condra and Elias (1944 p. 539), but the mistake was not rectified until later (Elias 1957) and the name transferred to the cirriped boring. However, Stephenson (1952 p. 52) has given the name *Graysonia bergquisti* to a similar mixture of acrothoracican borings and thread borings in Cretaceous shells. The mixture even appears to include, as "modified forms of vesicles", worm borings or embedment traces described separately in the same paper under the name *Specus*. With emphasis on the stolon-like part of this compound genus, Casey (1961 p. 573) has named an Aptian form *Graysonia anglica*.

Bryozoa bore by chemical means. Silén (1946 p. 1) found evidence to suggest that the agent is phosphoric acid in *Penetrantia* and possibly in other forms also.

The cheilostome bryozoan *Electra* also produces superficial etching of shell surfaces in conditions of reduced salinity. Boekschoten (1966 fig. 10) gives a clear illustration of the trace.

5c. Boring Phoronidea

This small phylum contains two very small species which bore into calcareous substrates: *Phoronis ovalis* Wright and *P. hippocrepia* Wright. The animals usually occur in large numbers in "pseudocolonies" within the substance of shells: Marcus (1949 p. 158) recorded a density of 150 borings per cm² of *P. ovalis* in an exceptionally crowded example

The borings are irregularly winding tubes some 0·2–0·3 mm in diameter and of variable length, ending blindly and fitting the animal. However, owing to the well-developed powers of regeneration, new individuals bore their way out from the sides of older borings so that a complex, tangled branching pattern results (Fig. 2b). A whole interconnected pseudocolony results from budding from one original individual (Harmer 1917 pl. 8, 9; Brattström 1943 fig. 8, 9). Two adjacent pseudocolonies do not fuse together, although their boundaries may become intricately interwoven. In *P. ovalis* the branching tubes become very long and complicated. The pseudocolonies of *P. hippocrepia,* on the other hand, are simpler but irregular (Silén 1954 p. 221, 248, 254).

Phoronids are often accompanied by clionid sponges in the same shell. Boring presumably is effected by chemical means (Brattström 1943 p. 7).

Geological records of boring phoronids are few. Joysey (1959 p. 398), however, has suggested phoronid originators for borings in an Upper Cretaceous chalk echinoid.

5d. Boring Sipunculidea

The boring habit is well developed within this phylum. Sipunculids have been reported as agents of erosion of coasts in Britain (Jehu 1918 p. 6) and in coral reefs (e.g. Otter 1937 p. 332). Coral rock may contain within it many species of sipunculids living together (Shipley 1902). Some of these may become incorporated partly through the process of embedment, since they prefer living coral. They produce tubes lying parallel to the growing surface of the coral, but may cut a number of new openings to that surface at intervals (Utinomi 1953) and thus augment embedment by true boring processes. Other authors have considered that sipunculids use only boring processes to produce the cavities, which they snugly fit and Cloud (1959 p. 400) also indicates the importance of sipunculids in weakening coral rock.

Of the boring method Gardiner (1902 p. 336) believed that they use physical processes and Hyman (1959 p. 667) also doubted if chemical secretions are used. Rice (1969), however, found evidence for the employment of chemical means. The resulting borings may be straight or exceedingly sinuous and winding and typically have a single entrance, which is oval or circular and usually narrower than the boring; in coral rock they may penetrate more deeply than any other boring (Rice 1969 p. 806). The wall is smooth or shows slight scratch marks (Seilacher 1969 pl. 1). Therefore, chances of identification of sipunculid holes in fossil conditions appear to exist.

Certain members of the Echiurida also bore (Jehu 1918 p. 6), for example *Thalassema*. However, too little is known of the cavities to be of use to the geologist, beyond the fact that they do not interconnect, are accurately filled by the worm and can honeycomb limestone (Farran 1851). Joysey (1959 p. 398), nevertheless, made a tentative identification of a boring of an echiurid in a Senonian echinoid test.

5e. Boring Polychaeta

Despite the importance of the boring habit in this order of annelids, there is a general lack of information in zoological literature on the form of borings. Some of the most useful information on boring of living worms is found in the literature on oyster culture (particularly Korringa 1951; 1952), but worm damage in oyster shells is largely the work of spionids, and other families are neglected.

Thus the best known boring polychaete is the spionid *Polydora ciliata* (Johnston).

The small, pouch-like borings of this species, accommodating the worm in a U-posture (Fig. 4i), are well described and illustrated in the literature (Douvillé 1908; Söderström 1923; Korringa 1951; Hempel 1957; Dorsett 1961). There are also several other species of *Polydora* which bore, in shell and limestone in temperate waters (e.g. Colman 1940; Blake 1969) and in coral reefs (e.g. Hartman 1954 p. 621), but details of the form of their cavities are poorly known. The borings of *P. concharum* Verrill and *P. socialis* (Schmarda) are longer and more tortuous than those of *P. ciliata* (Blake 1969 p. 816; Evans 1969 fig. 2–4). Other species, particularly *P. hoplura* Claparède, gain access to shells through embedment, though this species seems to be capable also of boring rock.

Owing to the celebrity of *Polydora*, borings in the fossil record have been compared with, and in some cases placed directly in this genus (Richter 1928 p. 224). Comparable U-shaped borings in Upper Cretaceous belemnites have received the name *Polydora biforans* from Gripp (1967). Larger U-borings in Jurassic hardgrounds have been placed in the ichnogenus *Polydorites* Douvillé 1908 by Hölder and Hollmann (1969). Borings reminiscent of those of *Polydora*, in Turonian bivalves, have been named *Meandropolydora* by Voigt (1965). And as stated above, for fossil embedment cavities somewhat resembling those of *Polydora hoplura*, the ichnogenera *Caulostrepsis* Clarke (1908) and *Ostreoblabe* Voigt (1965) are available.

Despite this wide comparison with *Polydora*, it is well known that polychaetes of many genera and several families bore in calcareous substrates (e.g. Hartman 1954 p. 621; Boekschoten 1966 p. 352). The borings of the cirratulid *Dodecaceria concharum* Ørsted have been shown by Evans (1969 fig. 5 and 6) to resemble those of *Polydora* but to have an oval, not a dumb-bell shaped cross section.

The long, winding, tubular borings of the sabellid *Pseudopotamilla reniformis* (Müller) have been used for comparison with fossil borings, for example in the Miocene of Poland (Radwański 1964; 1968), in a Campanian hardground in the Paris Basin (Ellenberger 1947 p. 266 fig. 7) and in Jurassic hardgrounds in Switzerland and England (Hölder and Hollmann 1969). Comparable borings, but with a characteristic Y-shaped branching are produced in soft rocks in New Zealand by the eunicid *Marphysa* (Morton and Miller 1968 p. 232) (Fig. 2c).

Many examples of fossil vermiform borings have been described, but most of them show so few characteristic features that they have received no names, and have merely been ascribed to worms. Slender, vertical borings in Muschelkalk hardgrounds were named *Trypanites* by Mägdefrau (1932 p. 151), however, and the name has been used for borings in Devonian hardgrounds by Hekker (1965). Slender, branching, tubular borings attributed to worms in Permian brachiopod shells have been named *Conchotrema* by Teichert (1945), while unbranched worm borings in Palaeozoic shells have been named *Vermiforichnus* by Cameron (1969a, b). Single tubular borings into Cretaceous belemnite calcite from a circular orifice bear the name *Nygmites solitarius* (Hagenow) (Mägdefrau 1937 p. 56).

The method of boring involves different means in different annelids. In some (including *Polydora*), mechanical means are said to be important, involving jaws or setae (McIntosh 1868; 1908; Hartman 1954 p. 621; Hempel 1957). In the case of *Polydora ciliata*, Dorsett (1961 p. 588) concluded that a chelating agent might be used. However, in another species acid has been detected (Haigler 1969). Hartman (*loc. cit.*) believed that the sabellid *Hypsicomus* also bores by chemical means. A close study of the walls of fossil borings might not, therefore, provide much helpful information for distinguishing polychaete from other borings, since the boring method is so variable.

The palaeoecological significance of *Polydora* borings and pseudoborings in shells has been thoroughly discussed by Boekschoten (1966 p. 352; 1967).

5f. Drilling Turbellaria

In the fossil state, holes drilled right through shells are usually ascribed to predatory gastropods. There are, however, several different groups of organisms which pierce shells and produce a hole superficially comparable with those made by gastropods.

For example, a flat-worm, *Pseudostylachus ostreophagus,* bores through the valves of young oysters to eat the animal within. The hole produced is keyhole shaped (Yonge 1964 p. 108)

5g. Boring Brachiopoda

The ability of the pedicle to bore calcareous substrates appears to have evolved separately in three orders of brachiopods.

The living terebratulid, *Terebratulina retusa* (Linnaeus) possesses a pedicle which divides into fine branches on, or immediately after, emerging from the pedicle foramen. The branches appear to bore through skeletal fragments in the soft bottom sediment, producing a secure anchor (Schumann 1969). This habit is better developed in the closely related, living, deep-water form, *Chlidonophora chuni* Blochmann, dredged from *Globigerina*-ooze at 2,253 m. The long pedicle is finely divided at the distal end, the branches surrounding or boring through foraminiferan tests in the soft sediment (Blochmann, in Chun 1900 p. 404; Blochmann 1906 p. 695). No details of the form of the holes are available to assist in distinguishing these from those made by juvenile predatory gastropods in ostracod valves (Reyment 1966 p. 53).

Schumann (1969) also implied that the holes in the umbo of the pedicle valve in the Permian strophomenid *Kiangsiella* and the Devonian spiriferid *Uncites* may be due to self-boring. He believed that in these cases the pedicle divided up before emerging from the shell, the branches passing out of the shell through the many small holes.

5h. Drilling Cephalopoda

When *Octopus* is unable to open bivalve prey or dislodge a gastropod by force, it may resort to rasping with its radula a small hole in the shell through which to inject venom (Pilson and Taylor 1961; Wodinsky 1969). The holes drilled in *Haliotis* shell described by Pilson and Taylor (1961 fig. 1 and front cover) have a very characteristic form consisting of sub-hemiellipsoidal pits rasped into the shell to penetrate the inner surface. However, the holes attributed to *Octopus* and illustrated by Carter (1968 pl. 1 fig. 8 and 9) are quite different, having a jagged, irregular outline. *Octopus* rasp-holes studied by Arnold and Arnold (1969 fig. 2) were on average smaller and deeper than those measured by Pilson and Taylor, and were variable in size, shape and position on the shell. It would appear, therefore, that different forms of hole result from different species of *Octopus* and different substrates.

5i. Drilling Gastropoda

The drill-holes produced by gastropods are known through the work of several authors (e.g. Fischer 1922; Martin 1932; Carriker 1961). The morphology of the holes and its terminology have been thoroughly discussed and illustrated by Carriker and Yochelson (1968).

Typical gastropod bore-holes are reported as the work of species of two mesogastropod families, Capulidae and Cymatiidae. The cymatiids are carnivorous, but the capulids are parasitic and insert their proboscis through the hole to take food from the food-gathering tracts of ciliary-feeding bivalves. Members of a pulmonate family, Oleacinidae, are said to rasp highly irregular patches in shell, some in order to obtain calcium, others to consume the prey within (Carriker and Yochelson 1968). Some helicid pulmonates also bore (Carriker 1961). Abbott (1968) stated that the Cassidae bore, and a nudibranch has been described by Young (1969) which produces smooth, round, bevelled holes in serpulid worm tubes.

Best-known and most commonly encountered, however, are the borings of the prosobranchiate families Muricidae (including Thaididae) and Naticidae, all species of which drill. The holes produced by muricids and naticids are each very characteristic and are easily recognisable in fossil material. Carriker et al. (1963) have made a thorough investigation of the boring method which involves a combination of chemical and physical means. The holes drilled by the two families can be distinguished morphologically, those produced by muricids being generally smaller, less bevelled and more cylindrical than those of naticids (Carriker et al. 1963; Carriker and Yochelson 1968). Reyment (1967) found the holes to be distinguishable also by statistical analysis of their dimensions. This distinction is of palaeoecological importance, since today the epifaunal muricids attack their prey on the sediment surface while infaunal naticids seek and drill theirs beneath the surface.

The rasped holes of the oleacinids today, and reports of similar holes with roughly rasped edges in fossil occurrences (Jensen 1951; Martin 1932 pl. 2 fig. 1) demonstrate the possibility of confusion of these with *Octopus* holes.

While gastropod holes are common in later Mesozoic and Tertiary shells (Sohl 1969), supposed Palaeozoic occurrences have also been reported (Fenton and Fenton 1931; Bucher 1938; Brunton 1966) and Cameron (1967) has produced controversy over the originators. Carriker and Yochelson (1968) indicated that in several points the morphology of the Palaeozoic drill-holes does not resemble that of holes of living gastropods.

Furthermore, Richards and Shabica (1969) showed that in one (Ordovician) case the boring continued through the sediment between the brachiopod shells; they cited examples of a single hole penetrating more than one shell where these overlapped on the sea floor. Buehler (1969) has more recently attributed further Palaeozoic borings to gastropods. However, the recent thorough discussion of fossil gastropod holes by Sohl (1969) shows that it is highly unlikely that any Palaeozoic borings can have been the work of predatory gastropods, since the drilling faculty probably did not appear in this group before Cenomanian times.

5j. Boring Gastropoda

It is well-known that considerable erosion is caused by radulae of gastropods browsing on algal coatings on rock (Ginsburg 1953; North 1954; Cloud 1959 p. 400; Neumann 1966 p. 92; Craig et al. 1969). The resulting traces, although potential pascichnian trace fossils, cannot be considered to be borings. However, in cases where browsing gastropods (e.g. limpets) "home" to the same place regularly, a depression of varying depth may develop as a boring and potential domichnian trace fossil (e.g. Cloud 1959 p. 378, 400).

As the next stage, several authors have noted that in littoral zone rocks gastropods nestle in cavities, formed by the metabolic processes of the organisms. Thus North (1954) and Emery (1960 p. 18) have described Californian periwinkles forming cavities in littoral calcareous rocks. The resemblance of these to karst features has led some authors (Boekschoten 1966 p. 368) to doubt if the holes are entirely the result of gastropod activity. However, Lamy (1930) cites many examples of similar phenomena from the older literature, including land snails living in and forming cavities in terrestrial limestone outcrops (see also Kühnelt 1932).

Other groups of gastropods in quite different environments produce cavities in

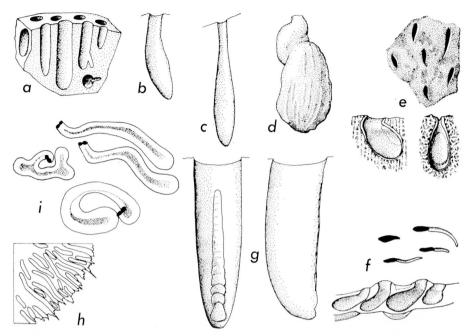

Fig. 4. Pouch-like borings.   a Sandstone with borings of *Sphaeroma* (isopod). × 1.;
b   Boring of *Stylarioides* (polychaete) in rock. × 1·5;   c   Boring of *Dendrostomum* (sipunculid) in rock. × 1·5. a–c modified after Morton and Miller (1968);   d   Artificial cast of boring
of *Magilopsis* (gastropod) in *Lobophyllia* from Eilat, Red Sea. The boring is unlined and the cast
therefore has ridges corresponding to spaces in the coral skeleton. × 1;   e   Borings of
Lithoglyptes indicus (acrothoracican) in surface view (in calcareous alga, aperture black) and
longitudinal and transverse section (in coral). The calcareous lining of the boring has a raised
disc anteriorly for the attachment of the animal. × 3. After Aurivillius (1894);   f   Borings of
Kochlorine hamata Noll (acrothoracican) in surface view and longitudinal section in *Haliotis*
shell. The aperture (black) is extended by a long anterior groove. In section it is seen that the
gastropod has added layers of shell locally where the borings have approached too close to the
internal surface. × 4. After Noll (1875);   g   Borings of *Lithotrya* (thoracican) in coral,
sectioned in two directions. The series of calcareous discs represent successive attachment
positions of the animal. × 1. After Reinhardt (1850);   h   *Limnoria* (isopod) borings in wood.
× 1·3. Modified after Menzies (1957);   i   Borings of *Polydora ciliata* (polychaete) in *Mytilus*
shell, surface apertures black. Kattegat. From a radiograph. × 5.

organic calcareous skeletons, some by embedding, others by true boring. Many
vermetid gastropods characteristically live embedded in living coral reefs. In the
case of certain vermetids, however, true boring processes are used to sink the shell
into calcareous substrates. This is the case in *Spiroglyphus annulatus* Daudin
(Pl. 1c) and *Veristoa howensis* Iredale, both of which grow on other shells, sinking
into them to form a groove which is lined and roofed by their own shell (Lamy
1930 p. 4; Wenz 1939 p. 677).

A further example should be mentioned. While *Magilus* is an embedding form,
two other magilids, *Magilopsis* and *Leptoconchus,* are thin-shelled coral-borers.
Magilopsis produces ellipsoidal cavities of the diameter of its shell but considerably
longer and with a very restricted opening to the exterior (Cloud 1959 p. 391 pl. 129d
and e) (Fig. 4d, Pl. 1b). Boring living coral, the length of the cavities depends on the
rate of growth of the coral. The wall is unlined, but in some cases it has ridges which

correspond to successive positions of the gastropod shell within the growing boring. The borings of *Leptoconchus,* on the other hand, are normally shorter and more globular (Soliman 1969 p. 891 fig. 4).

5k. Boring Amphineura

As in gastropods, browsing by chitons causes considerable erosion of rock surfaces and produces rasp marks preservable as trace fossils (Boekschoten 1966 p. 369). In "homing" forms, a depression of greater or lesser depth may be formed at the place of rest, probably by biochemical action (Otter 1937 p. 33; Cloud 1959 p. 378, 400; Kaye 1959 p. 89; Emery 1960 p. 17).

5l. Rock-boring Bivalvia

The borings of bivalves are of considerable importance to palaeoecologists for three reasons. Firstly, they are abundant in Mesozoic and Tertiary rocks (hard-grounds, boulders) and in shells; secondly, they commonly contain the body fossil of the borer; and thirdly, owing to detailed knowledge of modern forms, identification and palaeoecological interpretation of the ichnofossils is feasible. Indeed, bivalve borings have been used successfully for detailed environment interpretation from early times, as for example by Lyell (1830 p. 453) and Buckland and De La Beche (1835 p. 31).

Unlike the majority of boring organisms, the bivalves have been studied by zoologists with an eye also for their borings. Extensive work has been done by Kühnelt (1930; 1933), Otter (1937), Yonge (1932; 1936; 1951; 1955; 1963a), Hunter (1949), Purchon (1955a, b), Turner (1954; 1955), Ansell (1969) and Smith (1969).

Recently a new mytilid was described by Goreau *et al.* (1969) which lives commensally within the coelenteron of the coral *Fungia* and bores chemically into its septal skeleton.

The boring habit has been independently assumed in seven superfamilies of bivalves. Between and within these superfamilies the borings show great variety of form. This is useful, since the type of boring "is quite consistent for each species" (Turner 1954 p. 8). Furthermore, particularly in those bivalves which bore by chemical means, a deposit of calcium carbonate is laid down in some borings in a characteristic way in different species. In *Rocellaria* (*Gastrochaena*) this deposit may extend as a tube beyond the substrate surface (e.g. Purchon 1954). Kühnelt (1931), Itoigawa (1963) and Raynaud (1969) have made use of these calcareous deposits in the interpretation of fossil borings.

The preservation of bivalve shells within borings has to be treated with caution, since they need not necessarily be the valves of the borer. Many nestling bivalves today favour abandoned bivalve borings as a cranny in which to live, and adjust the shape of their valves to fit the boring (e.g. Kühnelt 1931 p. 247; 1951 p. 518; Yonge 1958).

The valves and borings of fossil boring bivalves have been described in detail by Turner (in Moore 1969). The oldest possibly boring bivalves are of Ordovician age (Kauffman in Moore 1969).

Rock-boring bivalves show a restriction to shallow water and are active in the littoral zone (Barrows 1917; Amemiya and Ohsima 1933; Turner 1954; Raynaud 1969). This fact has been used in environment interpretation in, for example, the Miocene of Poland (Radwański 1964; 1965; 1968), France (Raynaud 1969) and Japan (Itoigawa 1963).

The chemical reagent used in boring by *Lithophaga lithophaga* (Linnaeus) is not an acid, as often stated (e.g. Kauffman, in Moore 1969), but has been shown to be a calcium complexing secretion (Jaccarini *et al.* 1968). This restricts the chemical borers to calcareous substrates. The physical borers, however, penetrate a large variety of substrates, from soft clay to the hardest gneiss and granite. Turner (1954 p. 8) explained how the animal can bore physically into rock considerably harder than its own shell, through the accumulation of rock grains in mucous coverings of foot and shell until the shell is buried in them. "The result is that in such species as *Pholas dactylus* the stone in many cases is worn away with particles of the same hardness."

5m. Wood-boring Bivalvia

The Teredinidae (Pholadacea) and some genera of the Pholadidae bore wood so rapidly and abundantly today that, for economic reasons, they are the subject of a large literature. Much of this is listed in the annotated bibliography by Clapp and Kenk (1963). General aspects of these borers are dealt with in several papers in Ray (1959).

The teredinids are particularly well-known since they are shallow-water forms and the damage they cause to wooden ships (Betz 1967) and submerged marine woodwork is considerable. The borings they produce are therefore well described and illustrated: see Calman 1919; Edmondson 1953; Ricketts and Calvin 1962; Steenstrup 1968; Thorson 1968 p. 168. Wood is not infested until it is prepared for attack by boring fungi. The valves of teredinids are considerably reduced to small drilling tools at the anterior end of the body. At the base of the siphons at the other end of the long worm-like body, a pair of largely calcareous scales ("pallets") are used to adjust the boring at the opening to the sea and also to close this opening in the manner of opercula. The long body secretes a calcareous lining of varying thickness to the boring. This tube acts as a pseudoshell, since the siphonal muscles are attached to it, and it renders the boring an ideal subject for radiography (see Betz 1967 p. 311; Lane 1959 fig. 5).

In fossil material, the preservation of the pallets is essential for identification of species. These have been recorded from the Tertiary. Unfortunately, however, living species are distinguished on features of the soft anatomy which is not preserved fossil. Thus it would seem that ichnospecies, body fossil species and living species can never be compared. Turner (in Moore 1969 p. N722) deals in detail with the fossil forms.

While teredinid borings are extremely long, those of the pholadid *Xylophaga* are only 5–10 times the length of the shell, and lack the calcareous siphonal lining. This distinction is confused, however, by the recent discovery of a species of *Xylophaga* living in long borings with thin calcareous lining which, in fossil state, would be indistinguishable from *Teredo* borings (Turner 1965; and in Moore 1969 p. N721). The borings of *Teredo,* however, tend to follow the grain of wood and avoid other borings while those of *Xylophaga* are in many cases at right-angles to the grain, and cut other borings (Knudsen 1961 p. 204).

Generally, rock- and shell-borers are limited to shallow water by availability of suitable substrate. However, water-logged wood is present at all depths in such quantity as to provide abyssal and hadal niches to wood-borers. These deep-water niches are largely exploited by *Xylophaga,* which has developed an astonishing number of species of local distribution in isolated environments (Knudsen 1961; Turner 1965). However, there are a few littoral species and some common in floating timber (Purchon 1941), so that the bathymetric range of *Xylophaga* overlaps with that of teredinids (Turner *op. cit.*).

Another pholadid genus, *Martesia,* is important as a wood-borer. The borings of the genus are only slightly longer than the shell (e.g. Morris 1947 pl. 24). It is notable that while *Teredo* avoids crossing other borings in wood, *Martesia* may cut through them indiscriminately (Turner 1955 pl. 35). *Martesia* is less specific as to choice of substrate than other wood-boring bivalves. Annandale (1923) found *Martesia fluminalis* Blandford boring brick, although it normally bores wood and occasionally is found in soft argillaceous sandstone. *M. striata* (Linnaeus), normally a wood-borer, has been found in the lead sheath of cables lying off the Florida coast (Springer and Beeman 1960). *Xylophaga* has been found in manilla ropes (Turner *op. cit.*) and boring gutta-percha on submarine cables.

The valves of young *Martesia, Xylophaga* and teredinids can be indistinguishable in the fossil state (Turner in Moore 1969 p. N703).

5n. Wood-boring Arthropoda

The amphipod crustacean *Limnoria,* also produces considerable damage to submerged woodwork and is therefore treated by a large literature (see Clapp and Kenk 1963; Ray 1959). It, like *Teredo,* is dependent on the fungi in the wood it bores (Thorson 1968 p. 170). The discrete but densely crowded tunnels made by *Limnoria* (Fig. 4h) usually follow the grain of the wood. They contrast with borings of *Teredo* and *Xylophaga* through their smaller size and superficial position in the substrate, which produces flaking of the surface (Calman 1919 p. 19; Yonge 1949 p. 186; Yonge 1951 p. 166; Menzies 1957 p. 108; Traganza 1965). The bivalves, on the other hand, cause more deep-seated damage which is less visible at the surface. Comparison of various wood borings can be seen in the illustrations of Edmondson (1953).

The isopod crustacean *Chelura* has been considered responsible for borings similar to those of *Limnoria,* but Yonge (1949) believed that in most cases it lives within and slightly enlarges *Limnoria* borings.

In warm and southern seas, wood is bored extensively by the isopod *Sphaeroma* (Calman 1919 p. 21) where it may be a menace to harbour constructions. One species, *S. quoyana* Milne-Edwards bores in hard-wood and into clay and sandstone. In New Zealand it honeycombs these rocks so that they crumble (Chilton 1919 p. 11 fig. 12). Its long, tubular borings (Fig. 4a) are much larger than *Limnoria* borings, and even reach the size of those of *Teredo,* reaching 6–7 mm in diameter. The walls of the borings may be ornamented with scratch marks from the process of excavation (Morton and Miller 1968 p. 240). *Sphaeroma* has also been reported boring rock in California (Barrows 1919).

On land, wood is attacked extensively by insects. The variety of borings produced in wood and bark by beetles and ants is illustrated, for example, by Bejer-Petersen (1969). Fossil wood-borings ascribed to terrestrial insects have been described from the Trias by Linck (1949).

5o. Boring Echinoidea

Some regular echinoids which live on rock surfaces feed by browsing on the algae growing on the rock. As in gastropods and chitons with this habit, the teeth of the echinoid may leave characteristic scratch marks on the rock surface (Abel 1935 p. 372 fig. 310; Neumann 1966 fig. 7).

On rocky coasts subject to wave activity and lacking sufficient crevices to nestle in, echinoids show a well-developed ability to bore mechanically into rock for protection. Most of the literature is of the last century and has been reviewed by Otter (1932). Substrates of great variety are penetrated, including coral and oyster-shell, fine- and coarse-grained limestones, hard sandstone and mudstone, rotten and fresh granite, schist and basalt. Borings in wood have also been reported and Emery (1960 p. 147) suspected echinoids of attacking steel pilings. Tube feet, spines and especially teeth are used as boring tools. Granite is bored more rapidly than limestones since quartz and feldspar grains are prised out whole by pressure of the teeth after picking out the softer minerals round them.

Several unrelated species in many parts of the world are known to bore and the cavities which result cannot be easily differentiated (Otter 1932). The sea urchins leave the holes to feed and it is not known if they return to the same hole. It is clear, however, that several generations of echinoid may occupy the holes successively, and it is conceivable therefore that more than one species of echinoid might contribute to the excavation of the boring.

Otter (1932 p. 103) recognised three kinds of excavations distinguished only by depth of boring; they were all circular in cross section and only slightly wider than the diameter of the inhabitant.

(i) Shallow, hemispherical pits less deep than the height of the echinoid. J. W. Evans (personal communication) has seen these pits extended laterally over coral rock, producing grooves which branch in places (see also Kaye 1959 p. 89).

(ii) Borings of medium depth, in which the depth is the same as or slightly greater than the height of the echinoid.

(iii) Deep, flask-shaped borings reaching up to 10 cm depth in extreme cases, but usually much less.

Since the deeper borings commonly have narrow entrances it has been considered by most authors that the contained echinoid could not pass through them (e.g. Robert 1854; Yonge 1964) so that "the inhabitants of the very deep burrows are of course imprisoned within them" (Otter 1932 p. 103). However, Märkel and Maier (1966; 1967) have shown most convincingly that echinoids are able to squeeze through an exit to a boring which is only 3–4 mm wider than their test.

The floor of the boring may be polished through long habitation in some cases, but the walls normally remain rough and irregular, giving purchase for the spines so that the echinoid cannot be removed from its hole.

Illustrations of echinoids in their borings are given by Branner (1904 pl. 43, 50, 73), Abel (1935 fig. 406, 407), Kaye (1959 fig. 34) and Märkel and Maier (1967 fig. 2, 3, 4). The importance of echinoids as agents of erosion has been emphasized by Jehu (1918 p. 10), Ginsburg (1953), Kaye (1959 p. 89), Emery (1960 p. 16) and Neumann (1966); several authors have observed that the vacated borings are suitably shaped to initiate "pot-hole" activity (Otter 1932).

5p. Boring Cirripedia

Several different groups within this class show the boring habit to various degrees while others are embedders.

ASCOTHORACICA. As parasites, some ascothoracicans produce cavities in organic skeletons by causing deformation of the growth of the host. Voigt (1959; 1967a) has attributed deformity of this kind in Cretaceous octocorals to ascothoracican cirripeds but the cavities must be considered a result of embedment rather than of boring.

Species of the ascothoracican *Ulophysema* today parasitize various echinoids (Brattström 1936; 1937; 1947). Living inside the body of the host, the parasite bores a hole of about 1 mm diameter through the test to the exterior, invariably near the apical disc. On the basis of Brattström's work, Madsen and Wolff (1965) have ascribed holes in *Echinocorys* (Upper Cretaceous) to a similar ascothoracican parasite.

THORACICA. The least degree of boring is developed in some acorn barnacles. Darwin (1854 p. 512) notes that *Verruca* may hollow out the calcareous substrate beneath it as a very slight depression, and that such depressions can be observed also in fossils of Tertiary age.

It is not clear to what extent various species of *Pyroma* bore, but several of them embed in coral reefs (Darwin 1854 p. 354, 375). Utinomi (1953) denies that they bore, but Kühnelt (1931) gives a Miocene example of a species of *Pyrgoma* which bored into coral from the bottom of a vacant *Lithophaga* boring.

The thoracican *Lithotrya* bores sizable cavities in coral reefs (Gardiner 1902 p. 337; Otter 1937 p. 333) and beachrock (Ginsburg 1953). Darwin (1851 p. 336, 346) gave descriptions of this peculiar barnacle, but confused several species (Cannon 1935). The borings have an oval cross section up to or a little over 1 cm across and extending in some cases to over 7 cm into the substrate. They are slightly curved and taper to a rounded end (Fig. 4g). They are well illustrated by Reinhardt (1850 fig. 2, 3) and Darwin (1851 pl. 8).

The animal bores mechanically by means of calcareous and chitinous studs on the peduncle which are renewed with each ecdysis. While boring, a series of over-lapping disc-like calcareous plates are placed on one side-wall of the boring for attachment. After boring has ceased, an irregular, often thick cup of laminated calcium carbonate is secreted at the lower end of the boring beneath the base of the peduncle. Even if the scutes of the capitulum are lost in fossilization, there is a chance that the discs or cup in the hole would be preserved. Otherwise there is a possibility that these cavities in coral reefs will be confused with damaged borings of *Magilopsis* or of bivalves in the fossil state.

ACROTHORACICA. Since their first discovery (Hancock 1849b) many genera and species of these small, boring barnacles have been discovered in shallow seas. Emphasis has been placed, however, on soft anatomy and little is known of the differences between borings of the several species. In most cases they produce compact, shoe- or sack-like cavities with a narrow opening to the exterior (Fig. 4e, f). At the anterior end in some forms a slit-like extension gives the aperture the shape of a comma. However, comma-like apertures are also found in some bryozoan borings (Fig. 2a). The method of boring is physical, producing a "dust" of calcium carbonate (Aurivillius 1894 p. 75; Tomlinson 1955 p. 99; Seilacher 1969 p. 706). Chemical means may also be used subordinately (Seilacher 1969 p. 708), particularly at the first stages of boring (Tomlinson 1969). In the adult, after boring has ceased, the cavity is given a calcareous lining, particularly in porous substrates such as coral (Aurivillius 1894 p. 76) (Fig. 4e).

The Acrothoracica show a number of characteristic behavioural tendencies, some noted in living forms, some in fossil. Most remarkable, perhaps, is that both living species of *Trypetesa* are commensal with hermit crabs (Aurivillius 1894; Berndt 1903; Tomlinson 1953; 1955; Seilacher 1969 p. 715) and bore in the columella or inner wall of the last whorl of shells occupied by these crabs. *T. lampas* (Hancock), at least, is dependent on the presence of the crab and if the shell is discarded by the crab the barnacle dies (Genthe 1905). This may explain the large number of borings of juveniles observed in some shells by Boekschoten (1966 p. 374). The borings of this species (Berndt 1903 pl. 19; Kühnert 1935 p. 67; Boekschoten 1966 fig. 13; Seilacher 1969 pl. 4) are unlike most acrothoracican borings in that they are considerably widened beneath the anterior slit. The borings of *T. lateralis* Tomlinson are bent laterally and run parallel with the shell surface (Tomlinson 1955). A second exit, to the external surface of the shell, is constructed in this species (Seilacher 1969 p. 715 pl. 5). Association between acrothoracicans and hermit crabs should be recognisable in the fossil state owing to the traces which the crabs leave on shells which they inhabit (Ehrenberg 1931; Boekschoten 1966 p. 371).

Other genera of acrothoracican barnacles today show no commensal associations, but nevertheless are restricted in selection of substrate. For example, *Berndtia purpurea* Utinomi chooses two species of living coral (Utinomi 1949a; 1957) and *Balanodytes taiwanus* Utinomi bores the basal plates of *Balanus tintinabulum tintinabulum* (Utinomi 1949b). Again, *Cryptophialus minutus* Darwin "inhabits, in vast numbers, the shells of living *Concholepas peruviana* [Lamarck, a muricid gastropod] . . . the whole outside of the shell being sometimes completely drilled by its cavities, almost touching each other" (Darwin 1854 p. 567). Tomlinson (1969 fig. 3) illustrates *Cryptophialus minutus* in *Concholepas* shell, but also in *Fissurella,* while *Cryptophialus coronatus* Tomlinson occurs in the shell of *Haliotis tuberculata* Linnaeus (Tomlinson 1960 p. 402). On the other hand, *Lithoglyptes indicus* Aurivillius is found in calcareous algae, corals and mollusc shells (Aurivillius 1894). Other lithoglyptids also live in dead coral (Tomlinson and Newmann 1960 p. 525). Seilacher (1969 p. 711) states that acrothoracicans as a whole show a preference for living shells, but Tomlinson (1969) states the exact opposite.

Fossil examples of acrothoracican borings were not recognized for what they were until Zapfe (1936) described Miocene specimens. They had previously been mistaken for other things: for example, the form named *Rogerella mathieui* by Saint-Seine (1955) was mistaken for a sponge boring by Wetherell as early as 1852 and designated *Clionites mantelli*. In the last 15 years, however, many fossil acrothoracican borings have been described.

Ichnogenera and ichnospecies were erected by Saint-Seine (1951; 1954; 1955) for Mesozoic and Tertiary borings. These were then submitted to a biometric study (Codez and Saint-Seine 1957) and separated into two ichnofamilies. The Rogerellidae have an elliptical opening, rounded posteriorly but extended into a peduncular slit anteriorly as in the living *Lithoglyptes.* The boring is lined with secreted calcium carbonate which thickens towards the opening. It projects beyond the opening on one side, rarely on both, as a ridge or bourrelet. In contrast, the Zapfellidae have a more simple aperture, lacking the anterior slit, though nevertheless pointed at that end, and lacking the bourrelet. Further ichnospecies and ichnosubspecies have been added to the two families by Schlaudt and Young (1960), Taylor (1965) and Voigt (1967b).

Borings of Acrothoracica are not uncommon in the Palaeozoic (Rodda and Fisher 1962). It has been shown by Seilacher (1969 p. 709) that the morphology of fossil acrothoracican borings indicates an evolutionary development from Palaeozoic to Recent times. The earliest examples are deep and narrow, hardly wider than the aperture, the animal having bored almost exclusively in the sagittal plane. There was, however, a gradual increase in lateral boring in Mesozoic and Tertiary times, culminating in the broad borings of *Trypetesa.* The identification of a *Trypetesa* boring in the Upper Palaeozoic by Tomlinson (1963) was shown to be a mistake (Seilacher 1969 p. 709).

Fossil acrothoracican borings occur in a variety of substrates, some ichnospecies being specific, others occurring more generally. At first Saint-Seine (1955) considered that *Rogerella mathieui* was restricted to echinoid tests, but later she found these to be indistinguishable from borings in other substrates (Codez and Saint-Seine 1957).

The common fossil occurrence of acrothoracican borings in ambulacral pores of irregular echinoids led Seilacher (1969 p. 715) to suggest that there was a commensal relationship. In examples from the European Cretaceous chalk, however, the writer has seen no evidence to indicate that such borings were pre-mortal. Even if the epidermis of the echinoid were no hindrance to the settling of cirriped larvae, the lack of deformation of the test, the heavy infestation which in many cases closed a large number of pores, and the presence of demonstrably post-mortal borings, indicate that the cirripeds bored after the death of the echinoid. The attraction of the pores to the larvae was rather that of a cranny, as is seen in other substrates (Schlaudt and Young 1960; Seilacher 1969 p. 713). Recent acrothoracican borings have not been reported in echinoid calcite.

R. *mathieui* is recognizable also in Upper Cretaceous belemnites (Pugaczewska 1965), the aragonite of corals, bivalves and gastropods and the calcite of bivalves and brachiopods. This and other forms are also found in the cemented sediment of pebbles and hardgrounds of various ages (Maubeuge 1955; Radwański 1964; Jahnke 1966; Bromley 1968). In addition to calcium carbonate, phosphatized limestone pebbles have also been bored by acrothoracicans on Jurassic (Maubeuge 1955) and Cretaceous hardgrounds.

On the other hand, Schlaudt and Young (1960) found R. *cragini* S. and Y. only in the shells of a single species of gastropod, as a post-mortal boring, even though other apparently suitable substrates were available.

Acrothoracican borings are sensitive indicators of abrasion. Since Mesozoic and later borings have a narrow aperture, the slightest abrasion of the substrate exposes the conspicuously wider interior of the boring. In the Rogerellidae, the presence of an undamaged slit and a bourrelet are evidence that no abrasion has affected the substrate since the boring was excavated.

Seilacher (1968) has put acrothoracican borings in Jurassic belemnites to an original use. They show a strong orientation on certain species. He considered this to indicate that they were bored in the living belemnites, that the belemnites customarily swam head forward, and that if a mantle covered the guard of an adult belemnite, it was very thin.

5q. Boring Porifera

Sponge borings have received little attention as trace fossils, particularly those of the Mesozoic and Tertiary, which almost exclusively have been given the genus name *Cliona*. The type ichnospecies of the ichnogenus *Entobia* is redescribed in section 6.

Plate 1

a Thallophyte (probably algal) borings in *Dentalium* shell from a Turonian chalk hardground, Sparsholt, Berkshire, England. Borings preserved as phosphatized chalk casts exposed by natural dissolution of aragonite substrate. × 30.

b Cross section of boring of *Magilopsis* in *Lobophyllia* from Eilat, Red Sea. The boring cuts across the coral structure. At the far end of the hole the entrance is seen at top right. × 2.

c Shell of *Spiroglyphus* (gastropod) partly sunken into the surface of a *Tridacna* shell. A juvenile is seen at the bottom. Other holes are surface pores of sponge borings. × 1·3.

d Sculpture of the wall of the boring of a sponge (*Cliona* sp.) in *Haliotis* shell. Chip marks larger towards the right, in the floor of the gallery, than towards the left where the wall is curving up into a papillar pore. × 145.

e Same boring as **d**. Detail of fissures in the wall where chips were in process of being cut out. × 1400.

f Same boring as **d**. Opening to a small connecting canal between two parts of the boring is seen left of centre. Minute pin-prick holes, nature uncertain, also run into the wall. × 700.

d—f are scanning electron micrographs.

PLATE 1

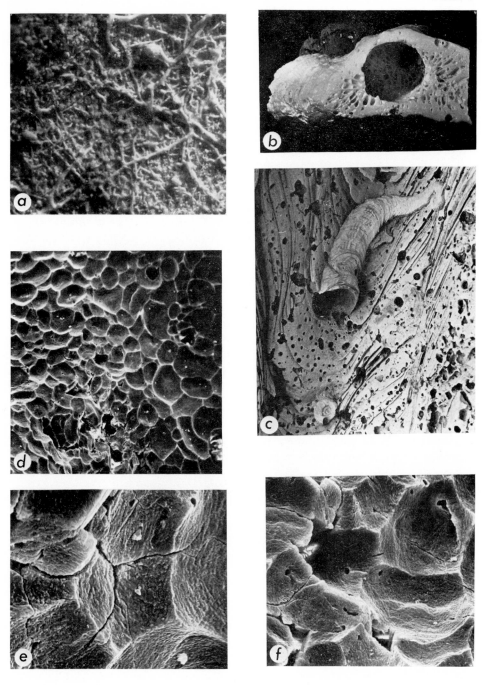

71

Owing to some taxonomic confusion, it is not clear if the family Clionidae (monaxonid Demospongia) comprises all sponges which today are capable of boring. References to other boring sponges (e.g. Gardiner 1902 p. 335; Burton 1934 p. 570) leave doubt either over their systematic position or over their true ability to bore. Thus it is probable that all boring sponges today belong to the Clionidae, and indeed, the ability to bore at some stage of life is an essential characteristic of the family (Old 1941).

These sponges are the subject of a very extensive zoological literature, to which the most important contributions are those of Topsent (e.g. 1887b; 1891; 1900; 1904; 1932). The Clionidae comprise about 100 species distributed among 14 genera, of which *Cliona* is the most important genus with 65 species (Goreau and Hartman 1963 p. 29). Genera and species are distinguished principally on the basis of spiculation (Pl. 2b, 3b) and secondarily on colour and histology of the soft parts. In most cases the characteristics of the boring have received little attention.

Spicules are rarely preserved in fossil sponge borings, and the geologist has to work mainly with evidence of borings alone. It is therefore necessary to study the borings of living sponges in order to attempt to identify zoospecies in fossil material. There is a great incentive for this study, since if this identification were possible, much ecological information would become available.

Various techniques have been applied to the study of Recent sponge borings. Hancock (1849a) picked away the surface of the bored shell to expose the boring system within, a laborious task which destroyed the papillar openings on one side of the shell. Warburton (1958a p. 557) prepared paraffin wax casts of empty borings (dissolving the shell in acid) but his only photograph of the result is poor (Warburton 1958b fig. 2). Ginsburg (1957 fig. 3) published a radiograph of sponge borings, but Warburton (1958a p. 557) criticized this technique on the grounds that a clear 3-dimensional picture could not be obtained. This drawback, however, is partly overcome by the use of thin shell (Pl. 2, 3) and by making stereopairs. While radiography is useless with thick matrices, it is useful in broadly distinguishing boring types. Time-lapse radiographs have been used with success by Evans (1969) to show the growth rate of *Cliona vastifica* Hancock.

Sponge borings consist characteristically of a series of galleries branching and anastomosing within the substrate, and communicating with the surface by numerous small, round pores which house the inhalent and exhalent papillae of the sponge (Pl. 2, 3).

(i) *Papillar openings.* Some authors have paid great attention to the size, density and distribution of the surface pores (Fischer 1868; Hartman 1957). However, such data should be used with caution, since the number and size of the papillae varies to some extent with the number of chambers to be served within the substrate. In a thin, dead mollusc shell, all chambers can be supplied directly by papillae on each surface of the shell. If the mollusc is still living, however, papillae can be formed only on the outer surface of the shell. But some clionids can bore to depths of several centimetres into calcareous rock (Ryder 1879; Neumann 1966). In such cases the number of the papillae must increase in response.

Nevertheless, in a given matrix and environment, the size, at least, of the surface pores of a given species is fairly constant. In many species the exhalent papillae are noticeably wider than the inhalent papillae.

(ii) *Galleries.* The general form of the galleries, best viewed in radiographs of shells, shows various characteristic types. In most species of clionids, the distal ends of the branches of the expanding sponge boring are fine, slender, and pointed. At a certain distance, varying with different borings, behind these ends the branches are enlarged irregularly by lateral boring on all surfaces. In some species, such as

PLATE 2

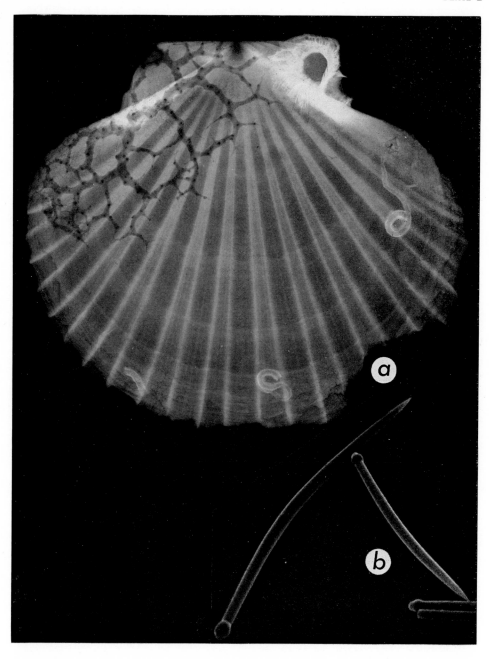

Plate 2

a Radiograph of *Pecten maximus* (Linnaeus) with palmate boring of *Cliona celata*. Slender borings of seven bryozoan colonies also visible. × 1.

b Scanning electron micrograph of spicules of *Cliona celata*. × 520.

Cliona celata Grant (Pl. 2a), the boring takes a form somewhat resembling a deer's antler, which may be called the "elk-horn" or "palmate" type. In most sponges, however, the branches are enlarged at regular intervals into a series of subspherical or sausage-shaped chambers, the "string-of-beads" or "camerate" type (Pl. 3a).

Volz (1939) has indicated another variable characteristic in borings of different species of sponge. Generally speaking, the advancing edge of the sponge boring may consist either of a few long, thin branches straggling out in exploratory fashion from the older part of the boring; or in other species, rapid swelling of numerous branches gives the impression that the sponge is advancing through the matrix with a "closed front". It follows, therefore, that the boring of a single sponge possesses different characteristics in different parts according to their age. In the youngest parts, slender canals with early stages of widening are found. In the "mature" regions the widening, whether camerate or palmate, reaches a typical maximum. In the oldest parts, new chambers and branches fill in interspaces where matrix is unused, bringing about great reduction of wall thickness between the chambers, or in other cases the branches or chambers are fused to eliminate the intervening matrix and produce large voids. Seven species of *Cliona* (including *Poterion*) continue to grow beyond the matrix, and become "free-living" sponges. In these cases the literature contains no mention of the appearance of the remnant matrix buried in the sponge.

Different substrates also influence the shape of the boring . Volz (1939 p. 14), for example, shows that the borings of *Cliona viridis* (Schmidt) are quite different in shell and in calcareous algae. Volz (1939 p. 44) offered an identification table of sponges living in the Adriatic Sea, based on characteristics of the borings alone (galleries and papillar pores). However, Boekschoten (1966 p. 349) failed to use this table successfully in the same locality.

(iii) *Wall ornament*. An aspect of sponge borings which has only recently received attention from geologists is the highly characteristic ornament which adorns the walls as a result of the mode of boring (Pl. 1d, e, f). It is clearly preserved in most fossil borings, even on their moulds (see Stephenson 1941 p. 55; 1952 p. 51).

The method of boring of clionid sponges is well understood, from the work of Nassonow (1883), Topsent (1887b), Cotte (1902), Nassonov (1924), Warburton (1958a), Goreau and Hartman (1963 p. 31) and Cobb (1969). The sponge tissue is closely applied to the wall of the boring, from which it cannot be pulled away easily. This is because the peripheries of surface cells pass as thin, sheet-like extensions into the calcareous matrix, producing narrow slits in the wall (Pl. 1e). These sheets advance in a curved manner through the substrate, so as to form part of a sphere and close on themselves, thus isolating chips of substrate with curved boundaries. The chip is passed through the tissue of the sponge and out of an exhalent papilla. Chips from *Cliona* in various substrates have been illustrated by Warburton (1958a fig. 1–3) and Cobb (1969) and from *Aka* by Johnson (1899 pl. 6, fig. 3). Sponges can penetrate conchiolin with difficulty, but the chemical boring agent has not been identified.

It is doubtful if study of the resulting wall ornament would have any taxonomic use. Size, shape and uniformity of chips vary in different borings and parts of borings (Pl. 1d), and would seem to vary with the microstructure of the matrix rather than the species of sponge.

(iv) *Spiculation*. The preservation of spicules in fossil sponge borings is rare. When found, however, they need not necessarily belong to the borer. However, without spicules, a fossil boring cannot be definitely ascribed to a living genus or species of sponge. Spicules found in the borings of *Entobia cretacea* are discussed below.

PLATE 3

Plate 3

a Radiograph of *Pecten maximus* with camerate boring of *Cliona vastifica*. × 1.

b Scanning electron micrograph of spicules of *Cliona vastifica*. × 1000.

(v) *Ecology*. Provided that zoospecies can be identified in ichnospecies, much valuable ecological data becomes available.

Salinity preferences have already been used. *Cliona vastifica* and its close relative *C. truitti* Old can tolerate brackish water (Annandale 1915a p. 8; 1915b p. 35; Old 1941 p. 10; Hopkins 1956a, b) and their borings are of the camerate type (Pl. 3a). Lawrence (1969) has shown that in an Oligocene channel the distribution of borings resembling those of *C. celata* (palmate) as opposed to those of *C. vastifica* type (camerate) indicates a similar tolerance of reduced salinity as do their modern counterparts. However, there is danger of over-generalization. It would seem, for example, that in Danish waters *C. celata* may penetrate as far as *C. vastifica* into the brackish water of the Baltic Sea, and that here *C. vastifica* appears to be restricted to deeper, more saline water (Hartman 1958 p. 135).

As bathymeters, clionid sponge borings may be particularly useful provided that zoospecies can be identified. Clionidae are entirely absent from the littoral zone but are most active and prolific in the uppermost 25 m of the sublittoral (Volz 1939; Hartman 1958 p. 137). Goreau and Hartman (1963) report flourishing activity of clionids on coral fore-reefs to a depth of 70 m, below which it becomes much reduced. Certain species, however, are recorded living at considerable depths, for example: *Thoosa investigatoris* Annandale and *Cliona annulifera* Annandale were dredged from 1280 m (Annandale 1915a), *C. abyssorum* Carter from 914 m (Carter 1874), *C. labyrinthica* Hancock from 1,424 m, *C. levispira* Topsent from 1,360 m, *Dotona pulchella* Carter from 880 m (Topsent 1904) and *Alectona millari* Carter from 664 m (Carter 1879) and 880 m (Topsent 1904). Nevertheless, a rich ichnocoenosis of sponge borings indicates a depth of less than 100 m and a very varied one should represent shallow sublittoral water.

One species, *Cliona viridis*, may have particular significance to bathymetry. The green colour of this sponge has been commented on by many workers (especially Volz 1939 p. 13), and it has now been shown that the soft tissues contain zooxanthellae (or, since they are green, zoochlorellae) living in symbiosis with the sponge (Sarà and Liaci 1964). Furthermore, this species has been reported living in association with calcareous algae (Cotte 1914). Volz (1939 p. 14, 49) found that in shallow water *C. viridis* bored in shells, but in deeper water it was restricted to coralline algae as a substrate. It would seem, therefore, that if the extremely camerate borings of this sponge in shells, and its broader, more extensive excavations in algal calcite in deeper water, can be recognized in fossils, a sensitive indicator of bathymetry would be available. It is encouraging that Radwański (1964) has identified Miocene borings with those of this species.

Boekschoten (1966; 1967) discusses clionid borings as indicators of sedimentation and the mode of life of the host shell. For example, it is easy to distinguish post-mortal borings from those made while the host shell was alive. If a species of mollusc contains only post-mortal borings while others in the sediment were bored during life, there is reason to believe that the first species was a burrowing form. On the other hand, shells with thick periostracum are normally not attacked until the mollusc is dead and the inner surface of the shell exposed.

(vi) *Agents of erosion and sedimentation*. Clionid sponges cause considerable destruction of calcareous rock. Goreau and Hartman (1963) considered them to exercise an important controlling influence on the form of coral reefs, and also to produce a significant proportion of the fine sediment of the fore-reef through their peculiar method of boring. Neumann (1966) investigated the remarkable rate at which *Cliona lampa* bored on the carbonate coast of Bermuda. While it destroyed the substrate at a rate of 6-7 kg per m² per 100 days, which is the equivalent of 1 m of calcarenite in 70 years, 90% of this material was removed in the form of chips as fine sediment. It is therefore not surprising that in many environments, sponge borers are the chief agent of erosion. On some Cretaceous chalk hardgrounds, for example, their activity largely controlled the sculpture of the sea-floor (Bromley 1968).

(vii) *Naming fossil sponge borings.* The oldest boring which has been attributed to a sponge is a small hole in a Lower Cambrian *Hyolithes* (Poulsen 1967). The ascription is based not on the form of the boring but on spicule-like bodies contained within it. The hole has not received a name.

Many varied, branching borings in shells have been described of Palaeozoic (chiefly Upper) age. They do not always bear a close resemblance to borings made today, and may have been made by sponges or "worms" (Clarke 1908; Fenton and Fenton 1932a; Solle 1938). The ichnogenera of Palaeozoic sponge borings now available are *Clionolithes* Clarke; *Filuroda* Solle and *Topsentopsis* de Laubenfels (see Teichert 1945; Häntzschel 1962; 1965). These borings resemble those of living sponges, rather than those of other living borers, chiefly in their radiating, branching habit. They are, however, much smaller, rarely possess chamber-like swellings of the branches, and pores for papillae are rarely distinguishable. The two such borings which most closely resemble Recent clionid borings were described by Elias (1957 p. 382) from the late Mississippian of Oklahoma. Unfortunately, Elias placed them in the Recent genus *Cliona,* despite lack of spicules and diminutive size. Even if such borings are the work of sponges, they cannot be placed with confidence in the Clionidae and their relationship to any living genus of sponges cannot be discussed until spicules are found.

Mesozoic sponge borings, certainly since Jurassic times, show a considerable resemblance to Recent ones and would appear to be the work of the Clionidae. Many "species" have been named in U.S.A. and Europe, and almost invariably placed in the genus *Cliona* (e.g. Fischer 1868; Fenton and Fenton 1932b; Stephenson 1941; 1952).

Entobia Bronn is the only ichnogeneric name available for the type of sponge boring which dominates in the Mesozoic and Tertiary, and resembles those of living clionids. This ichnogenus, redefined below, can simply take the place of *Cliona* in the names of Mesozoic borings.

In Tertiary borings the situation is more complicated. Using the scanty information available on the borings of living sponges, some workers (Roniewicz 1966; Radwański 1964; 1968; Boekschoten 1966; 1967) have recognized borings of living species in Eocene, Miocene and Pliocene beds. This crystallizes the problem of naming trace fossils. It is essential that the borer and the boring be distinguished with different names. A double taxonomy is unavoidable. The borings of clionid sponges of Tertiary age should be placed in the ichnogenus *Entobia*. Moreover, when more is known of the borings made by living sponges, they, too, should be grouped as ichnospecies of *Entobia*. The two series of names will not duplicate each other. Results so far indicate that several clionid species can produce indistinguishable borings which will receive a single entobian ichnospecies name while, on the contrary, there are individual clionid species which produce different borings under different conditions.

As a conclusion, therefore, the ichnogenus *Entobia* and its type ichnospecies *E. cretacea* Portlock are redefined as trace fossils.

6. Redefinition of *Entobia cretacea*

Ichnogenus ENTOBIA Bronn 1837

Borings attributable to sponges of the family Clionidae.

Type Species (by subsequent designation, Häntzschel 1962): *Entobia cretacea* Portlock 1843.

Discussion. The rank of taxon of a trace fossil need not be equivalent to that of the zoological taxon of the originating organism. We may therefore define an ichnogenus as covering traces produced by a zoological family. The result, a large number of ichnospecies equivalent in part to zoological species and in part to genera, cannot be avoided and is, indeed, desirable in palaeoichnology.

Entobia cretacea Portlock 1843

(Plates 4 and 5)

Selected synonymy. (Since 1854 generally known as *Cliona cretacea.*)

    1808. Bodies. Parkinson p. 75, 76, 151, pl. 8, figs. 8, 10, pl. 12, fig. 3.
    1814. Cavities. Conybeare pl. 14, figs. 1–8.
    1822. Parasitical bodies. Mantell p. 218, pl. 27, fig. 7.
    1837. *Entobia* Bronn pl. 34, fig. 12 inf.
    1838. *Entobia* Bronn p. 691.
    1843. *Entobia cretacea* Portlock p. 359, 360.
    1848. *Entobia conybeari* Bronn p. 462.
    1848. *Entobia cretacea* Portlock: Bronn p. 463.
    1850. *Clionites conybeari* Morris (in Mantell) p. 100.
    1851. *Clionites conybearei:* Morris p. 88, 89, pl. 4, figs. 8, 8a, 9, 10, 15.
    1851–1852. *Cliona conybearei* Morris: Bronn and Roemer p. 79.
    1852. *Entobia cretacea:* Morris (in Wetherell) p. 355.
    1854. *Cliona cretacea:* Morris p. 27.
    1856. *Cliona conybearei* Morris: Bronn pl. 281, figs. 15a, b.
    1856. *Cliona conybearei* Bronn pl. 34, fig. 12 inf.
    1868. *Cliona cretacea:* Fischer p. 167, pl. 25, figs. 5b, c. (pars).
    1872–1875. *Cliona conybearei* Bronn: Geinitz p. 233, pl. 36, figs. 6, 7.
    1883. *Cliona cretacea:* Hinde p. 21.
    1960. *Cliona celata micropora* Nestler p. 650, 655.
    1962. *Entobia cretacea:* Häntzschel p. 230.
    1965. *Entobia cretacea:* Häntzschel p. 34.
    1968. *Cliona cretacea* Fischer: Fatton and Roger p. 26.

Type material. Portlock designated no types and illustrated no examples. The only surviving specimen of Portlock's syntype series is housed in the Institute of Geological Sciences (London) with the number 9777. This specimen is chosen here as lectotype and figured in Plate 4a. It is preserved as a flint mould in belemnite (dissolved) in a flint nodule.

Locus typicus: Magilligan, Co. Londonderry, Northern Ireland

Stratum typicum: White Limestone, probably Campanian.

Other illustrated material. The first good illustrations of *E. cretacea* were given by Morris (1851). This material still exists and photographs are given here in Plate 4b, c.

Diagnosis. Clionid sponge borings showing extreme development of the camerate or "string-of-beads" form. Young parts of the boring extend in exploratory fashion as separate branches into the matrix. These are swollen at somewhat regular intervals into more or less spherical chambers which in the mature parts have diameters of about 1·5–4 mm. Interconnecting canals are slender (0·1–0·7 mm). In the oldest and most crowded parts of the boring, development of new and growth of old chambers restricted the substrate to thin partitions, and caused the shape of the chambers to become polygonal (Pl. 5c). Except between a few pairs of chambers, the thin partition walls remained intact and the chambers are not fused. The walls are penetrated not only by interconnecting canals but also by more slender, pin-

PLATE 4

Plate 4

a Lectotype of *Entobia cretacea.* × 1·5.

b *Entobia cretacea* in a belemnite moulded in flint, from the Campanian chalk of Norwich, England. The sponge boring is accompanied by the tubular *Nygmites solitarius* and in the upper part, superficial thallophyte borings. P 3041 Brit. Mus. (N.H.), figured by Morris (1851 pl. 4, fig. 9). × 2.

c *Inoceramus* with *Entobia cretacea,* in flint mould. 9778 I.G.S., London, figured by Morris (1851 pl. 4, fig. 8). × 1·5.

prick holes which in mould preservation appear as slender spines radiating from the chambers (Pl. 5b). Surface pores, one to four per chamber, are fine (0·13–0·7 mm). Wall ornament pits range from 25 to 65μ but are mostly about 50μ across.

Discussion. The most characteristic features of this boring are the globularity of the chambers, which are depressed in restrictively thin substrates, and become polygonal and irregular where crowded; the slender connections and small surface pores; and the closeness with which the chambers approach each other in crowded parts without fusion. In some specimens, including the lectotype, the interconnecting canals have been slightly enlarged except at the mid-point between the chambers, where the original diameter survives as a ring-like constriction. This may indicate the presence of a diaphragm in the sponge tissue at this point, as is found in some living clionids. In belemnite calcite the wall pits are deep, reaching the hemispherical (Pl. 5d), but in *Inoceramus* prismatic calcite they are shallow. It should be emphasized that the fine radiating pin-pricks are clearly part of the sponge, and are not analogous to the algal borings mistaken for extensions of the clionid by Nassonow (1883) and discussed by Topsent (1887a). The large-pored form with fusion of chambers occurring in belemnites, which was included by Fischer (1868 p. 167) in this ichnospecies, is quite different and is to be described elsewhere.

Spicules are generally not preserved and cannot be included in the diagnosis at this stage. Macroscleres (large monaxons) are enclosed in the sediment in the chambers in some cases but are reduced to hollow moulds in soft chalk or drusy fills of these in hard chalk.

Occurrence and stratigraphical range. *Entobia cretacea* occurs typically in the Turonian, Senonian and Maastrichtian White Chalk and Tuffeau of Europe. Substrates include all calcite and aragonite, including limestone. There is a tendency for valves of brachiopods to be attacked less than other shells in the same environment. Sponge borings in echinoid tests are usually of a different character, possibly owing to the stereome system in this substrate.

7. Conclusions

Fossil borings in shells and rocks may be defined as "hard substrate trace fossils". This definition also includes cavities produced by organisms which become embedded in living hard substrates (mollusc shell, coral). Unlike trace fossils in soft sediments, borings are most easily classified according to zoological taxonomy.

Plate 5

a Polished section of hard chalk pebble bored by *Entobia cretacea,* from a Turonian hardground, High Wycombe, Buckinghamshire, U.K. × 4.

b Fragment of large ammonite shell containing natural cast of *Entobia cretacea.* Chalk Rock (Turonian), from Hitch Wood, Hertfordshire, U.K. × 4.

c Thin, transparent shell of *Gibbithyris* showing *Entobia cretacea* within. Same locality. × 2·5.

d Scanning electron micrograph of the surface of a flint fill of a chamber of *Entobia cretacea,* showing crudely moulded, deep chip marks in the wall. Campanian White Limestone, Downhill Quarry, Co. Derry, U.K. × 325.

PLATE 5

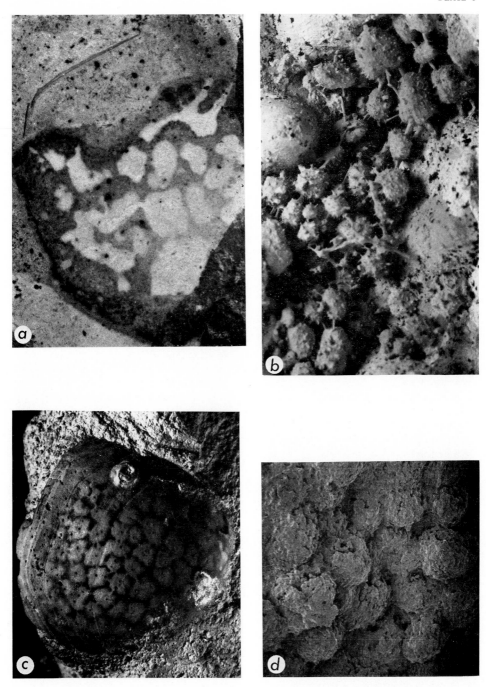

Nevertheless, they may be grouped in the following way according to the form of the boring.

(i) Shallow depressions to sizable pits are produced by certain chitons, gastropods such as *Patella,* a few thoracic barnacles such as *Verruca,* and several echinoids.

(ii) Single entrance, pouch-like borings (Fig. 4) are produced by some sipunculids, echiurids and polychaete annelids, all acrothoracican barnacles, the thoracican cirriped *Lithotrya,* the magilid gastropod *Magilopsis* (Pl. 1b), several echinoids, the boring bivalves, wood-boring isopod crustaceans and the rock-boring isopod *Sphaeroma.*

(iii) Tubular borings with two entrances, some with additional entrances are the work of some sipunculids and polychaete annelids.

(iv) Extensively branching borings (Fig. 1–3), with many surface openings in most cases, are produced by thallophytes (Pl. 1a), *Phoronis* pseudocolonies, bryozoans and clionid sponges (Pl. 2, 3).

(v) Small pin-prick holes result from the activity of some lichens and algae.

(vi) Discrete perforations of shells are the result of predation by a flat-worm, certain families of gastropods and *Octopus,* while certain brachiopods perforate tests of foraminifera with their pedicle for anchorage.

Particularly where borings of bivalves are concerned, it is possible in many cases to identify the borer accurately. In Tertiary borings it may be identified with a living genus, and in older examples a fossil borer is not uncommonly preserved within the boring. The opposite is the case, however, in "worm" and thallophyte borings, where not only is the soft borer hardly ever preserved, but even living forms produce borings which are neither well-known nor in many cases well-characterized.

Whether the borer can be identified or not, however, the boring should be designated by a trace fossil name and thus distinguished from the organism which made it. For example, nearly all fossil sponge borings have been placed in the genus *Cliona,* whereas the ichnogenus *Entobia,* redefined here, is available for these forms.

Acknowledgements. Thanks for advice, loan of material and assistance in the preparation of this paper are offered to Mr. C. J. Wood, Mr. S. Ware, Dr. J. W. Evans, Professor G. Thorson, Miss U. Asgaard, Professor T. Birkelund, Professor A. Rosenkrantz, Mr. B. Spiro, Mr. O. Tendal, Mrs. E. Nordmann, Mrs. H. Helbæk and Miss A. Andersen. Dr. B. J. Taylor critically read part of the manuscript (thallophytes) and gave valuable advice. The Electron Microscope Laboratory of the Institute of Historical Geology and Palaeontology, Copenhagen, is gratefully thanked for the production of the Stereoscan pictures.

References

ABBOTT, R. T. 1968. The helmet shells of the world (Cassidae). *Indo-Pacific Mollusca* **2,** 1.

ABEL, O. 1912. *Grundzüge der Palaeobiologie der Wirbeltiere.* Schweizerbart, Stuttgart.

—— 1935. *Vorzeitliche Lebensspuren.* G. Fischer, Jena.

AMEMIYA, I and OHSIMA, Y. 1933. Note on the habitat of rock-boring molluscs on the coast of central Japan. *Proc. imp. Acad. Japan* **9,** 120.

ANNANDALE, N. 1915a. The Indian boring sponges of the family Clionidae. *Rec. Indian Mus.* **11,** 1.

—— 1915b. Fauna of the Chilka Lake: Sponges. *Mem. Indian Mus.* **5,** 23.

—— 1923. Bivalve molluscs injuring brickwork in the Calcutta Docks. *J. Proc. Asiat. Soc. Beng.* **18,** 555.

ANSELL, A. D. 1969. A comparative study of bivalves which bore mainly by mechanical means. *Am. Zoologist* **9**, 857.

ARNOLD, J. M. and ARNOLD, K. O. 1969. Some aspects of hole-boring predation by *Octopus vulgaris. Am. Zoologist* **9**, 991.

AURIVILLIUS, C. W. S. 1894. Studien über Cirripeden. *K. svenska Vetensk-Akad. Handl.* **26**, 1.

BAKUS, G. J. 1964. The effects of fish-grazing on invertebrate evolution in shallow tropical waters. *Occ. Pap. Allan Hancock Fdn* no. 27, 1.

—— 1966. Some relationships of fishes to benthic organisms on coral reefs. *Nature, Lond.* **210**, 280.

BARROWS, A. L. 1917. Geologic significance of fossil rock-boring animals. *Bull. geol. Soc. Am.* **28**, 965.

—— 1919. The occurrence of a rock-boring isopod along the shore of San Francisco Bay, California. *Univ. Calif. Publs Zool.* **19**, 299.

BATHURST, R. G. C. 1966. Boring algae, micrite envelopes and lithification of molluscan biosparites. *Geol. J.* **5**, 15.

BEJER-PETERSEN, B. 1969. Hvirvelløse dyr som lever af traeerne. *Danm. Natur* **6**, 425.

BERNDT, W. 1903. Zur Biologie und Anatomie von *Alcippe lampas* Hancock. *Z. wiss. Zool.* **74**, 396.

BERNHAUSER, A. 1962. Über *Mycelites ossifragus* Roux und *Palaeomycelites lacustris* Bystrow in Vertebratenresten und ihre Deutung als Hinweise zur Fossilisationsgeschichte. *Mikroskopie* **17**, 187.

BETZ, J. J. 1967. Marine science and the Armada. *Sea Front.* **13**, 308.

BIERNAT, G. 1961. *Diorygma atrypophilia* n. gen., n. sp.—a parasitic organism of *Atrypa zonata* Schnur. *Acta palaeont. pol.* **6**, 17.

BLAKE, J. A. 1969. Systematics and ecology of shell-boring polychaetes from New England. *Am. Zoologist* **9**, 813.

BLOCHMANN, F. 1906. Neue Brachiopoden der Valdivia- und Gaussexpedition. *Zool. Anz.* **30**, 690.

BOEKSCHOTEN, G. J. 1966. Shell borings of sessile epibiontic organisms as palaeoecological guides. *Palaeogeogr. Palaeoclimatol. Palaeoecol.* **2**, 333.

—— 1967. Palaeoecology of some Mollusca from the Tielrode Sands (Pliocene, Belgium). *Ibid.* **3**, 311.

BONAR, L. 1936. An unusual ascomycete in the shells of marine animals. *Univ. Calif. Publs Bot.* **19**, 187.

BRANNER, J. C. 1904. The stone reefs of Brazil, their geological and geographical relations, with a chapter on the coral reefs. *Bull. Mus. comp. Zool. Harv.* **44**, 1.

BRATTSTRÖM, H. 1936. *Ulophysema öresundense* n. gen. et sp., eine neue Art der Ordnung Cirripedia Ascothoracica. *Ark. Zool.* **28A** (23), 1.

—— 1937. On the genus *Ulophysema* Brattström with description of a new species from East Greenland. *Meddr Grønland* **118** (7), 1.

—— 1943. Untersuchungen aus dem Öresund. 28. *Phoronis ovalis* Wright, eine für die Skandinavische Fauna neue Phoronide aus dem Öresund. *Acta Univ. Lund .N. F.*, Avd 2, **39** (2), 1.

—— 1947. Undersökningar över Öresund. 32. On the ecology of the ascothoracid *Ulophysema öresundense* Brattström. Studies on *Ulophysema öresundense* 1. *Acta Univ. Lund N. F.*, Avd. 2, **43** (7), 1.

BROMLEY, R. G. 1968. Burrows and borings in hardgrounds. *Meddr dansk. geol. Foren.* **18**, 247.

—— 1970. Predation and symbiosis in some Upper Cretaceous clionid sponges. *Ibid.* **19**, 398.

BRONN, H. G. 1838. *Lethaea geognostica.* Schweizerbart, Stuttgart. **2**, 545. (Atlas publ. 1837)

—— 1848. *Index palaeontologicus.* Schweizerbart, Stuttgart.

—— and ROEMER, F. 1851-1852. *Lethaea geognostica,* 3rd ed. Schweizerbart, Stuttgart. **2** (3), 1 (Atlas publ. 1850-1856).

BRUNTON, H. 1966. Predation and shell damage in a Viséan brachiopod fauna. *Palaeontology* **9**, 355.

BUCHER, W. H. 1938. A shell-boring gastropod in the *Dalmanella* bed of Upper Cincinnatian age. *Am. J. Sci.* (5) **36**, 1.

BUCKLAND, W. and DE LA BECHE, H. T. 1835. On the geology of the neighbourhood of Weymouth and the adjacent parts of the coast of Dorset. *Trans. geol. Soc. Lond.* (2), **4**, 1.

BUEHLER, E. J. 1969. Cylindrical borings in Devonian shells. *J. Paleont.* **43**, 1291.

BURTON, M. 1934. Sponges. *Scient. Rep. Gt Barrier Reef Exped.* **4**, 513.

CALMAN, W. T. 1919. Marine boring animals injurious to submerged structures. *Econ. Ser. Br. Mus. nat. Hist.* no. 10.

CAMERON, B. 1967. Oldest carnivorous gastropod borings, found in Trentonian (Middle Ordovician) brachiopods. *J. Paleont.* **41**, 147.

—— 1969a. New name for *Palaeosabella prisca* (McCoy), a Devonian worm-boring, and its preserved probable borer. *J. Paleont.* **43**, 189.

—— 1969b. Paleozoic shell-boring annelids and their trace fossils. *Am. Zoologist* **9**, 689.

CANNON, H. G. 1935. On the rock-boring barnacle, *Lithotrya valentiana. Scient. Rep. Gt Barrier Reef Exped.* **5**, 1.

CARRIKER, M. R. 1961. Comparative functional morphology of boring mechanisms in gastropods. *Am. Zoologist* **1**, 263.

——, SCOTT, D. B. and MARTIN, G. N. 1963. Demineralization mechanism of boring gastropods. In *Mechanisms of hard tissue destruction* (Ed. R. F. Sognnaes). *Publs Am. Ass. Advmt Sci.* **75**, 55.

—— and YOCHELSON, E. L. 1968. Recent gastropod boreholes and Ordovician cylindrical borings. *Prof. Pap. U.S. geol. Surv.* **593-B**, 1.

CARPENTER, W. B. 1843. General results of microscopic inquiries into the minute structure of the skeletons of Mollusca, Crustacea and Echinodermata. *Ann. Mag. nat. Hist.* (1), **12**, 377.

CARTER, H. J. 1874. Description and figures of deep-sea sponges and their spicules from the Atlantic Ocean, dredged up on board of H.M.S. "Porcupine". *Ann. Mag. nat. Hist.* (4), **14**, 245.

—— 1879. On a new species of excavating sponge (*Alectona Millari*); and on a new species of *Rhaphidotheca* (*R. affinis*). *J. R. microsc. Soc.* **2**, 493.

CARTER, R. M. 1968. On the biology and palaeontology of some predators of bivalved Mollusca. *Palaeogeogr. Palaeoclimatol. Palaeoecol.* **4**, 29.

CASEY, R. 1961. The stratigraphical palaeontology of the Lower Greensand. *Palaeontology* **3**, 487.

CHILTON, C. 1919. Destructive boring Crustacea in New Zealand. *N. Z. J. Sci. Technol.* **2**, 3.

CHODAT, R. 1898. Études de biologie lacustre. C. Recherches sur les algues littorales. *Bull. Herb. Boissier* **6**, 431.

CHUN, C. 1900. *Aus den Tiefen des Weltmeeres.* G. Fischer, Jena.

CLAPP, W. F. and KENK, R. 1963. *Marine borers, an annotated bibliography.* Office of Naval Research, Department of the Navy, Washington, D.C.

CLARKE, J. M. 1908. The beginnings of dependent life. *Bull. N.Y. St. Mus.* **121**, 146.

CLOUD, P. E. 1959. Geology of Saipan, Mariana Islands 4. Submarine topography and shoalwater ecology. *Prof. Pap. U.S. geol. Surv.* **280-K**, 361.

COBB, W. R. 1969. Penetration of calcium carbonate substrates by the boring sponge, *Cliona. Am. Zoologist* **9**, 783.

CODEZ, J. and SAINT-SEINE, R. 1957. Révision des cirripèdes acrothoraciques fossiles. *Bull. Soc. géol. Fr.* (6), **7**, 699.

COLMAN, J. 1940. On the faunas inhabiting intertidal seaweeds. *J. mar. biol. Ass. U.K.* **24**, 129.

CONDRA, G. E. and ELIAS, M. K. 1944. Carboniferous and Permian ctenostomatous Bryozoa. *Bull. geol. Soc. Am.* **55**, 517.

CONYBEARE, W. 1814. On the origin of a remarkable class of organic impressions occurring in nodules of flint. *Trans. geol. Soc. Lond.* (1), **2**, 328.

COTTE, J. 1902. Note sur le mode de perforation des Cliones. *C. r. Séanc. Soc. Biol.* **54**, 636.

—— 1914. L'association de *Cliona viridis* (Schmidt) et de *Lithophyllum expansum* (Philippi). *Ibid.* **76**, 739.

CRAIG, A. K., DOBKIN, S., GRIMM, R. B. and DAVIDSON, J. B. 1969. The gastropod, *Siphonaria pectinata:* a factor in destruction of beach rock. *Am. Zoologist* **9**, 895.

DACQUÉ, E. 1921. *Vergleichende biologische Formenkunde der fossilen niederen Tiere.* Borntraeger, Berlin.

DARWIN, C. 1851. *A monograph on the sub-class Cirripedia. The Lepadidae or pedunculated cirripedes.* Ray Society, London.

—— 1854. *A monograph on the sub-class Cirripedia. The Balanidae, the Verrucidae, etc.* Ray Society, London.

DORSETT, D. A. 1961. The behaviour of *Polydora ciliata* (Johnst.). Tube-building and burrowing. *J. mar. biol. Ass. U.K.* **41**, 577.

DOUVILLÉ, H. 1908. Perforations d'Annélides. *Bull. Soc. géol. Fr.* (4), **7** [for 1907], 361.

DUERDEN, J. E. 1902. Boring algae as agents in the disintegration of corals. *Bull. Am. Mus. nat. Hist.* **16**, 323.

EBBS, N. K. 1966. The coral-inhabiting polychaetes of the northern Florida reef tract. Part I. *Bull. mar. Sci. Gulf Caribb.* **16**, 485.

EDMONDSON, C. H. 1953. A survey of marine wood borers in the Pacific by the United States Navy. *Proc. pan-Pacif. Sci. Congr., 7*, **4** *Auckland* Zoology, 519.

EHRENBERG, K. 1931. Über Lebensspuren von Einsiedlerkrebsen. *Palaeobiologica* **4**, 137.

—— 1954. Zum Begriff "Lebensspuren" und sur Frage ihrer Benennung. *Neues Jb. Geol. Paläont. Mh.* 141.

ELIAS, M. K. 1956. Recent and ancient penetrants. *J. Paleont.* **30**, 1001.

—— 1957. Late Missisippian fauna from the Redoak Hollow Formation of southern Oklahoma, Part I. *J. Paleont.* **31**, 370.

ELLENBERGER, F. 1947. Le probléme lithologique de la craie durcie de Meudon. Bancs-limites et "contacts par racines": lacune sous-marine ou emersion? *Bull. Soc. géol. Fr.* (5), **17**, 255.

ELLIS, D. 1914. Fossil micro-organisms from the Jurassic and Cretaceous rocks of Great Britain. *Proc. R. Soc. Edinb.* **35**, 110.

EMERY, K. O. 1960. *The sea off southern California.* Wiley, New York.

EVANS, J. W. 1969. Borers in the shell of the sea scallop, *Placopecten magellanicus. Am. Zoologist* **9**, 775.

FARRAN, Dr. 1851. *Thalassema neptuni. Ann. Mag. nat. Hist.* (2), **7**, 156.

FATTON, E. and ROGER, J. 1968. Les organismes perforants: vue d'ensemble sur les actuels et les fossiles. *Trav. Lab. Paléont. Fac. Sci. d'Orsay, Univ. Paris*, Jan. 1968, p. 13.

FENTON, C. L. and FENTON, M. A. 1931. Some snail borings of Paleozoic age. *Am. Midl. Nat.* **12**, 522.

—— 1932a. Boring sponges in the Devonian of Iowa. *Ibid.* **13**, 42.

—— 1932b. A new species of *Cliona* from the Cretaceous of New Jersey. *Ibid.* **13**, 54.

FISCHER, P. 1866. Étude sur les bryozoaires perforants de la famille des Térébriporides. *Nouv. Archs Mus. Hist. nat., Paris* **2**, 293.

—— 1868. Recherches sur les éponges perforantes fossiles. *Ibid.* **4**, 117.

FISCHER, P. H. 1922. Sur les gastropodes perceurs. *J. Conch., Paris* **67**, 1.

FRY, E. J. 1922. Some types of endolithic limestone lichens. *Ann. Bot.* **36**, 541.

GARDINER, J. S. 1902. The action of boring and sand-feeding organisms. In *The fauna and geography of the Maldive and Laccadive Archipelagoes* (Ed. J. S. Gardiner) **1**, no. 3, 333.

—— 1903. The origin of coral reefs as shown by the Maldives. *Am. J. Sci.* (4), **16**, 203.

GEINITZ, H. B. 1872-1875. Das Elbthalgebirge in Sachsen. II, Der mittlere und obere Quader. *Palaeontographica* **20**, 1.

GENTHE, K. W. 1905. Some notes on *Alcippe lampas* (Hanc.) and its occurrence on the American Atlantic shore. *Zool. Jb.* **21**, 181.

GINSBURG, R. N. 1953. Intertidal erosion on the Florida Keys. *Bull. mar. Sci. Gulf Caribb.* **3**, 55.

—— 1957. Early diagenesis and lithification of shallow-water carbonate sediments in south Florida. *Spec. Publs Soc. Econ. Palaeont. Miner. Tulsa,* **5**. *Regional aspects of carbonate deposition,* p. 80.

GOREAU, T. F. 1965. Fore-reef slope of Jamaica: Structure, sediment, and community relationships. *Spec. Pap. Geol. Soc. Am.* **82**, 76.

——, GOREAU, N. I., SOOT-RYEN, T. and YONGE, C. M. 1969. On a new commensal mytilid (Mollusca: Bivalva) opening into the coelenteron of *Fungia scutaria* (Coelenterata). *J. Zool., Lond.* **158**, 171.

—— and HARTMAN, W. D. 1963. Boring sponges as controlling factors in the formation and maintenance of coral reefs. In *Mechanisms of hard tissue destruction* (Ed. R. F. Soggnaes). *Publs Am. Ass. Advmt Sci.* **75**, 25.

GRIPP, K. 1967. *Polydora biforans* n. sp., ein in Belemniten-Rostren bohrender Wurm der Kreide-Zeit. *Meyniana* **17**, 9.

GRÖNWALL, K. A. 1900. Borrade Echinidtaggar från Danmarks Krita. *Meddr dansk. geol. Foren.* **1** (6), 33.

HÄNTZSCHEL, W. 1962. Trace fossils and problematica. In *Treatise on invertebrate paleontology* (Ed. R. C. Moore). Univ. Kansas Press, Lawrence and Geol. Soc. Am., New York. Part W, p. W177.

—— 1965. Vestigia invertebratorum et problematica. *Fossilium catalogus,* 1 *Animalia* pars. 108, Junk, s'Gravenhage.

HAIGLER, S. A. 1969. Boring mechanism of *Polydora websteri* inhabiting *Crassostrea virginica.* *Am. Zoologist* **9**, 821.

HANCOCK, A. 1849a. On the excavating powers of certain sponges belonging to the genus *Cliona;* with descriptions of several new species, and an allied generic form. *Ann. Mag. nat. Hist.* (2), **3**, 321.

—— 1849b. Notice of the occurrence on the British coast of a burrowing barnacle belonging to a new order of the class Cirripedia. *Ibid.* (2), **4**, 305.

HARMER, S. F. 1917. On *Phoronis ovalis*, Strethill Wright. *Q. J. microsc. Sci.* **62**, 115.

HARTMAN, O. 1954. Marine annelids from the Northern Marshall Islands. *Prof. Pap. U.S. geol. Surv.* **260-Q**, 619.

HARTMAN, W. D. 1957. Ecological niche differentiation in boring sponges (Clionidae). *Evolution* **11**, 294.

—— 1958. Natural history of the marine sponges of southern New England. *Bull. Peabody Mus. nat. Hist.* **12**, 1.

HEKKER, R. F. 1965. *Introduction to paleoecology.* Elsevier, New York.

HEMPEL, C. 1957. Über den Röhrenbau und die Nahrungsaufnahme einiger spioniden der deutschen Küsten. *Helgoländer wiss. Meeresunters.* **6**, 100.

HESSLAND, I. 1949. Investigations of the Lower Ordovician of the Siljan District, Sweden. II. Lower Ordovician penetrative and enveloping algae from the Siljan District. *Bull. geol. Instn Univ. Upsala* **33**, 409.

HINDE, G. J. 1883. *Catalogue of the fossil sponges in the geological department of the British Museum (Natural History).* British Museum (Natural History), London.

HÖLDER, H. and HOLLMAN, R. 1969, Bohrgänge mariner Organismen in jurassischen Hart- und Felsböden. *Neues Jb. Geol. Paläont. Abh.* **133**, 79.

HOPKINS, S. H. 1956a. Notes on the boring sponges in Gulf Coast estuaries and their relation to salinity. *Bull. mar. Sci. Gulf Caribb.* **6**, 44.

—— 1956b. The boring sponges which attack South Carolina oysters, with notes on some associated organisms. *Contr. Bears Bluff Labs.* no. 23.

HUNTER, W. R. 1949. The structure and behaviour of *Hiatella gallicana* (Lamarck) and *H. arctica* (L.), with special reference to the boring habit. *Proc. R. Soc. Edinb.* **63B**, 271.

HYMAN, L. H. 1959. *The invertebrates* **5**: *Smaller coelomate groups.* McGraw-Hill, New York.

ITOIGAWA, J. 1963. Miocene rock- and wood-boring bivalves and their burrows from the Mizunami group, central Japan. *J. Earth Sci.* **11**, 101.

JACCARINI, V. BANNISTER, W. H. and MICALLEF, H. 1968. The pallial glands and rock boring in *Lithophaga lithophaga* (Lamellibranchia, Mytilidae). *J. Zool., Lond.* **154**, 397.

JAHNKE, H. 1966. Beobachtungen an einen Hartgrund (Oberkante Terebratelbank mu^{t2} bei Göttingen). *Der Aufschluss* **1**, 2.

JEHU, T. J. 1918. Rock-boring organisms as agents in coast erosion. *Scott. geogr. Mag.* **34**, 1.

JENSEN, A. S. 1951. Do the Naticidae (Gastropoda Prosobranchia) drill by chemical or by mechancial means? *Vidensk. Meddr dansk naturh. Foren.* **113**, 251.

JOHNSON, J. Y. 1899. Notes on some sponges belonging to the Clionidae obtained at Madeira. *J. R. microsc. Soc.* for 1899, 461.

JOYSEY, K. A. 1959. Probable cirripede, phoronid, and echiuroid burrows within a Cretaceous echinoid test. *Palaeontology* **1**, 397.

JUX. U. and STRAUCH, F. 1965. Angebohrte Spiriferen-Klappen; ein Hinweis auf palökologische Zusammenhänge. *Senckenberg. leth.* **46**, 89.

KAYE, C. A. 1959. Shoreline features and Quarternary shoreline changes Puerto Rico. *Prof. Pap. U.S. geol. Surv.* **317B**, 49.

KNUDSEN, J. 1961. The bathyal and abyssal *Xylophaga* (Pholadidae, Bivalvia). *Galathea Rep.* **5**, 163.

KOEHLER, R. 1924. Anomalies, irrégularités et déformations du test chez les échinides. *Annls Inst. océanogr.* n.s. **1**, 159.

KÖLLIKER, A. 1860a. Über das ausgebreitete Vorkommen von pflanzlichen Parasiten in den Hartgebilden niederer Thiere *Z. wiss. Zool.* **10**, 215.

—— 1860b. On the frequent ocurrence of vegetable parasites in the hard structures of animals. *Proc. R. Soc.* **10**, 95.

KOHLMEYER, J. 1969. The role of marine fungi in the penetration of calcareous substrates. *Am. Zoologist* **9**, 741.

KORRINGA, P. 1951. The shell of *Ostrea edulis* as a habitat: Observations on the epifauna of oysters living in the Oosterschelde, Holland, with some notes on polychaete worms occurring there in other habitats. *Arch. néerl. Zool.* **10** [for 1954], 32.

—— 1952. Recent advances in oyster biology. *Q. Rev. Biol.* **27**, 266 and 339.

KREJCI-GRAF, K. 1932. Definition der Begriffe Marken, Spuren, Fährten, Bauten, Hieroglyphen und Fucoiden. *Senckenbergiana* **14**, 19.

KÜHNELT, W. 1930. Bohrmuschelstudien. I. *Palaeobiologica* **3**, 53.

—— 1931. Über ein Massenvorkommen von Bohrmuscheln im Leithakalk von Müllendorf im Burgenland. *Palaeobiologica* **4**, 239.

—— 1932. Über Kalklösung durch Landschnecken. *Zool. Jb., Abt. System.* **63**, 131.

—— 1933. Bohrmuschelstudien. II. *Palaeobiologica* **5**, 371.

—— 1951. Contribution a la connaissance de l'endofaune des sols marins durs. *Année biol.* (3), **27**, 513.

KÜHNERT, L. 1935. Beitrag zur Entwicklungsgeschichte von *Alcippe lampas* Hancock. *Z. Morph. Ökol. Tiere* **29**, 45.

LAMY, E. 1930. Quelques mots sur la lithophagie chez les gastéropodes. *J. Conch., Paris* **74**, 1.

LANE, C. E. 1959. Some aspects of the general biology of *Teredo*. In *Marine boring and fouling organisms* (Ed. D. L. Ray). Univ. of Washington Press, Seattle. p. 137.

LAUBENFELS, M. W. DE. 1955. Porifera. In *Treatise on invertebrate paleontology* (Ed. R. C. Moore). Univ. Kansas Press, Lawrence and Geol. Soc. Am., New York. Part E, p. E21.

LAWRENCE, D. R. 1969. The use of clionid sponges in paleoenvironmental analyses. *J. Paleont.* **43**, 539.

LESSERTISSEUR, J. 1955. Traces fossiles d'activité animale et leur signification paléobiologique *Mem. Soc. géol. Fr. n.s.* **74**, 1.

LINCK, O. 1949. Lebens-Spuren aus dem Schilfsandstein (Mittl. Keuper km 2) NW-Württembergs und ihre Bedeutung für die Bildungsgeschichte der Stufe. *Jh, Ver. vaterl. Naturk. Württ.* **97-101**, 1.

LYELL, C. 1830. *Principles of geology.* **1**. John Murray, London.

MACGINITIE, G. E. and MACGINITIE, N. 1949. *Natural history of marine animals.* McGraw-Hill, New York.

MCINTOSH, W. C. 1868. On the boring of certain annelids. *Ann. Mag. nat. Hist.* (4) **2**, 276.

—— 1908. On the perforations of marine animals. *The Zoologist* (4) **12**, 41.

MADSEN, F. J. and WOLFF, T. 1965. Evidence of the occurrence of Ascothoracica (parasitic cirripeds) in Upper Cretaceous. *Meddr dansk. geol. Foren.* **15**, 556.

MÄGDEFRAU, K. 1932. Über einige Bohrgänge aus dem Unteren Muschelkalk von Jena. *Paläont. Z.* **14**, 150.

—— 1937. Lebensspuren fossiler "Bohr"-Organismen. *Beitr. naturk. Forsch. Südwdtl.* **2**, 54.

MÄRKEL, K. and MAIER, R. 1966. Über die Beweglichkeit von Seeigeln. *Naturwissenschaften* **53**, 535.

—— 1967, Beobachtungen an lockbewohnenden Seeigeln. *Natur. Mus.* **97**, 233.

MANTELL, G. A. 1822. *The fossils of the South Downs; or illustrations of the geology of Sussex.* Relfe, London.

—— 1850. *A pictorial atlas of fossil remains.* Bohn, London.

MARCUS, E. DU B. R. 1949. *Phoronis ovalis* from Brazil. *Zoologia* no. 14, 157.

MARTIN, H. 1932. Différents modes de perforation de la coquille chez les Mollusques. *P.-v. Soc. linn. Bordeaux* **84**, 84.

MAUBEUGE, P. 1955. Quelques remarques sur les cirripèdes du genre *Zapfella* et leur biotope. *C. r. Seanc. Soc. géol. Fr.* 67.

MENZIES, R. J. 1957. The marine borer family Limnoriidae (Crustacea, Isopoda). Part I: Northern and Central America: Systematics, distribution and ecology. *Bull. mar. Sci. Gulf Caribb.* **7,** 101.

MEYERS, S. P. and REYNOLDS, E. S. 1957. Incidence of marine fungi in relation to wood-borer attack. *Science, N.Y.* **126,** 969.

MOORE, R. C., Ed. 1969. Mollusca 6. *Treatise on invertebrate paleontology.* Univ. Kansas Press, Lawrence and Geol. Soc. Am., New York. Part N, p. N1.

MORNINGSTAR, H. 1922. Pottsville fauna of Ohio. *Bull. geol. Surv. Ohio* (4), no. 25.

MORRIS, J. 1851. Palaeontological notes. *Ann. Mag. nat. Hist.* (2), **8,** 85.

—— 1854. *A catalogue of British fossils.* 2nd ed. Morris, London.

MORRIS, P. A. 1947. A field guide to the shells of our Atlantic and Gulf coasts. Houghton Mifflin, Boston.

MORTON, J. and MILLER, M. 1968. *The New Zealand sea shore.* Collins, London.

MÜLLER, A. H. 1963. *Lehrbuch der Paläozoologie.* **II.** *Invertebraten. Teil 1, Protozoa-Mollusca 1.* G. Fischer, Jena.

NADSON, G. A. 1927a. Les algues perforantes de la Mer Noire. *C. r. hebd. Séanc. Acad. Sci. Paris* **184,** 896.

—— 1927b. Les algues perforantes, leur distribution et leur rôle dans la nature. *Ibid.* **184,** 1015.

—— 1932. Contribution à l'étude des algues perforantes. *Izv. Akad. Nauk SSSR* (7), math. nat. Classe, 1932, no. 6, 833.

NASSONOV, N. 1924. Sur l'éponge perforante *Clione stationis* Nason. et le procédé du creusement des galéries dans les valves des huîtres. *Dokl. Akad. Nauk SSSR (A)* p. 113.

NASSONOW, N. 1883. Zur Biologie und Anatomie der *Clione. Z. wiss. Zool.* **39,** 295.

NESTLER, H. 1960. Ein Bohrswamm aus der weissen Schreibkreide (Unt. Maastricht) der Insel Rügen (Ostsee). *Geologie* Jahrg. **9,** Ht. 6, 650.

NEUMANN, A. C. 1965. Erosion of carbonate coasts. *Spec. Pap. geol. Soc. Am.* **82,** 142.

—— 1966. Observations on coastal erosion in Bermuda and measurements of the boring rate of the sponge. *Cliona lampa. Limnol. Oceanogr.* **11,** 92.

NILSSON-CANTELL, C. A. 1921. Cirripeden-Studien. Zur Kenntnis der Biologie, Anatomie und Systematik dieser Gruppe. *Zool. Bidr. Upps.* **7,** 75.

NORTH, W. J. 1954. Size distribution, erosive activities and gross metabolic efficiency of the marine intertidal snails *Littorina planaxis* and *Littorina scutulata*. *Biol. Bull. mar. biol. Lab. Woods Hole* **106,** 185.

OLD, M. C. 1941. The taxonomy and distribution of the boring sponges (Clionidae) along the Atlantic coast of North America. *Publs Chesapeake biol. Stn* **44,** 1.

OTTER, G. W. 1932. Rock-burrowing echinoids. *Biol. Rev.* **7,** 89.

—— 1937. Rock-destroying organisms in relation to coral reefs. *Scient. Rep. Gt. Barrier Reef Exped.* **1,** 323.

PARKINSON, J. 1808. *Organic remains of a former world.* **II.** *The fossil zoophytes.* Whittingham, London.

PERKINS, B. F. 1966. Rock-boring organisms as markers of stratigraphic breaks. *Bull. Am. Ass. Petrol. Geol.* **50,** 631.

PIA, J. VON. 1937. Die kalklösenden Thallophyten. *Arch. Hydrobiol.* **31,** 264 and 341.

PILSON, M. E. Q. and TAYLOR, P. B. 1961. Hole drilling by *Octopus. Science, N.Y.* **134,** 1366.

PORTLOCK, J. E. 1843. *Report on the geology of the county of Londonderry, and parts of Tyrone and Fermanagh,* H.M.S.O., Dublin.

POULSEN, C. 1967. Fossils from the Lower Cambrian of Bornholm. *Mat.-fys. Meddr* **36** (2), 1.

PRATJE, O. 1922. Fossile kalkbohrende Algen (*Chaetophorites gomontoides*) in Liaskalken. *Zentbl. Miner. Geol. Paläont.* Jahrg. 1922, 299.

PUGACZEWSKA, H. 1965. Les organisms sédentaires sur les rostres des bélemnites du crétacé superieur. *Acta palaeont. pol.* **10,** 73.

PURCHON, R. D. 1941. On the biology and relationship of the lamellibranch *Xylophaga dorsalis* (Turton). *J. mar. biol. Ass. U.K.* **25,** 1.

—— 1954. A note on the biology of the lamellibranch *Rocellaria (Gastrochaena) cuniformis* Spengler. *Proc. zool. Soc. Lond.* **124,** 17.

—— 1955a. The functional morphology of the rock-boring lamellibranch *Petricola pholadiformis* Lamarck. *J. mar. biol. Ass. U.K.* **34,** 257.

—— 1955b. The structure and function of the British Pholadidae (rock-boring Lamellibranchia). *Proc. zool. Soc. Lond.* **124,** 859.

RADWAŃSKI, A. 1964. Boring animals in Miocene littoral environments of Southern Poland. *Bull. Acad. pol. Sci. Sér. Sci. géol. géogr.* **12,** 57.

—— 1965. Additional notes on Miocene littoral structures of southern Poland. *Ibid.* **13,** 167.

—— 1968. Tortonian cliff deposits at Zahorska Bystrica near Bratislava (southern Poland). *Ibid.* **16,** 97.

RAY, D. L., Ed. 1959. *Marine boring and fouling organisms.* Univ. of Washington Press, Seattle.

RAYNAUD. J.-F. 1969. Lamellibranches lithophages. Application à l'étude d'un conglomérat à cailloux perforés du Miocène du Midi de la France. *Trav. Lab. Paléont., Faculté Sci. d'Orsay, Univ. Paris.* p. 1.

REINHARDT, J. 1850. Om slaegten *Lithotryas* evne til at bore sig ind i steenblokke. *Vidensk. Meddr* d*ansk naturh. Foren.* for 1850 p. 1.

REVELLE, R. and FAIRBRIDGE, R. 1957. Carbonates and Carbon dioxide. In *Treatise on marine ecology and paleoecology,* 1. *Mem. Geol. Soc. Am.* **67**, 239.

REYMENT, R. A. 1966. Studies on Nigerian Upper Cretaceous and Lower Tertiary Ostracoda, 3: Stratigraphical, paleoecological and biometrical conclusions. *Stockh. Contr. Geol.* **14**, 1.

—— 1967. Paleoethology and fossil drilling gastropods. *Trans. Kans. Acad. Sci.* **70**, 33.

RICE, M. E. 1969. Possible boring structures of sipunculids. *Am. Zoologist* **9**, 803.

RICHARDS, R. P. and SHABICA, C. W. 1969. Cylindrical living burrows in Ordovician dalmanellid brachiopod beds. *J. Paleont.* **43**, 838.

RICHTER, R. 1928. Die fossilen Fährten und Bauten der Würmer, ein Überlick über ihre biologischen Grundformen und deren geologische Bedeutung. *Paläont. Z.* **9**, 193.

RICKETTS, E. F. and CALVIN, J. 1962. *Between Pacific tides.* 3rd. ed. Stanford Univ. Press, Stanford, Calif.

ROBERT, V. E. 1854. Action perforante d'une espèce d'Echinoderme. *C. r. hebd. Séanc. Acad. Sci.,* Paris **34**, 639.

RODDA, P. U. and FISHER, W. L. 1962. Upper Paleozoic Acrothoracic barnacles from Texas. *Tex. J. Sci.* **14**, 460.

ROLFE, W. D. I. 1962. The cuticle of some Middle Silurian ceratiocaridid Crustacea from Scotland. *Palaeontology* **5**, 30.

RONIEWICZ, P. 1966. New data on sedimentation of Eocene organodetrital limestones in the Tatra Mts. *Bull. Acad. pol. Sci. Sér. Sci. géol. géogr.* **14**, 165.

ROSE, C. B. 1855. On the discovery of parasitic borings in fossil fish scales. *Trans. microsc. Soc. London,* n.s. **3**, 7.

ROUX, W. 1887. Über eine in Knocken lebende Gruppe von Fadenpilzen (*Mycelites ossifragus*). *Z. wiss. Zool.* **45**, 227.

RYDER, J. A. 1879. On the destructive nature of the boring sponge, with observations on its gemmules or eggs. *Am. Nat.* **13**, 279.

SAINT-SEINE, R. DE 1951. Un cirripède acrothoracique du Crétacé: *Rogerella lecointrei* nov. gen., nov. sp. *C. r. hebd. Seanc. Acad. Sci., Paris* **233**, 1051.

—— 1954. Existence de cirripèdes acrothoraciques dès le Lias: *Zapfella pattei* nov. gen., nov. sp. *Bull. Soc. géol. Fr.* (6), **4**, 447.

—— 1955. Les cirripèdes acrothoraciques échinocoles. *Ibid.* (6), **5**, 299.

SANTESSON, R. 1939. Amphibious pyrenolichens. I. *Ark. Bot.* **29A**, no. 10.

SARÀ, M. and LIACI, L. 1964. Symbiotic association between zooxanthellae and two marine sponges of the genus *Cliona. Nature, Lond.* **203**, 321.

SCHINDEWOLF, O. H. 1962. Parasitäre Thallophyten in Ammoniten-Schalen. *Paläont. Z., H. Schmidt-Festband* p. 206.

—— 1963. Pilze in oberjurassischen Ammoniten-Schalen. *Neues Jb. Geol. Paläont. Abh.* **118**, 177.

—— 1967. Analyse eines Ammoniten-Gehäuses. *Abh. mat. naturw. Kl., Akad. Wiss. Mainz,* Jahrg. 1967, no. 8, 135.

SCHLAUDT, C. M. and YOUNG, K. 1960. Acrothoracic barnacles from the Texas Permian and Cretaceous. *J. Paleont.* **34**, 903.

SCHUMANN, D. 1969. "Byssus"-artige Stielmuskel-Konvergenzen bei artikulaten Brachiopoden. *Neues Jb. Geol. Paläont. Abh.* **133**, 199.

SEILACHER, A. 1953. Studien zur Palichnologie, I. Über die Methoden der Palichnologie. *Neues Jb. Geol. Paläont. Abh.* **96**, 421.

—— 1964. Biogenic sedimentary structures. In *Approaches to paleoecology* (Ed. J. Imbrie and N. Newell). Wiley, New York. p. 296.

—— 1967. Bathymetry of trace fossils. *Mar. Geol.* **5**, 413.

—— 1968. Swimming habits of belemnites—recorded by boring barnacles. *Palaeogeogr. Palaeoclimatol. Palaeoecol.* **4**, 279.

—— 1969. Paleoecology of boring barnacles. *Am. Zoologist* **9**, 705.

SHIPLEY, A. E. 1902. Sipunculoidea, with an account of a new genus *Lithacrosiphon.* In *The fauna and geography of the Maldive and Laccadive Archipelagoes* (Ed. J. S. Gardiner). **I**, 131.

SILÉN, L. 1946. On two new groups of Bryozoa living in shells of molluscs. *Ark. Zool.* **38B**, no. 1, 1.

—— 1948. On the anatomy and biology of Penetrantiidae and Immergentiidae (Bryozoa). *Ark. Zool.* **40A**, no. 4, 1.

—— 1954. Developmental biology of Phoronidea of the Gullmar Fiord area (West coast of Sweden). *Acta Zool., Stockh.* **35**, 215.

SMITH, E. H. 1969. Functional morphology of *Penitella conradi* relative to shell-penetration. *Am. Zoologist* **9**, 869.

SÖDERSTRÖM, A. 1923. Über das Bohren der *Polydora ciliata. Zool. Bidr. Upps.* **8**, 319.

SOGNNAES, R. F. 1963. Dental hard tissue destruction with special references to idiopathic erosions. In *Mechanisms of hard tissue destruction* (Ed. R. F. Sognnaes). *Publs Am. Ass. Advmt Sci.* **75**, 91.

SOHL, N. F. 1969. The fossil record of shell boring by snails. *Am. Zoologist* **9**, 725.

SOLIMAN, G. N. 1969. Ecological aspects of some coral-boring gastropods and bivalves of the northwestern Red Sea. *Am. Zoologist* **9**, 887.

SOLLE, G. 1938. Die ersten Bohr-Spongien im europäischen Devon und einige andere Spuren. *Senckenbergiana* **20**, 154.

SOULE, J. D. 1950a. A new species of *Terebripora* from the Pacific (Bryozoa Ctenostomata). *J. Wash. Acad. Sci.* **40**, 378.

—— 1950b. Penetrantiidae and Immergentiidae from the Pacific (Bryozoa: Ctenostomata). *Trans. Am. microsc. Soc.* p. 359.

—— and SOULE, D. F. 1969. Systematics and biogeography of burrowing bryozoans. *Am. Zoologist* **9**, 791.

SPRINGER, V. G. and BEEMAN, E. R. 1960. Penetration of lead by the wood piddock *Martesia striata. Science, N.Y.* **131**, 1378.

STEARNS, R. E. C. 1889. On certain parasites, commensals and domiciliars in the pearl oysters Meleagrinae. *Rep. Smithson. Instn* [1886], part 1, p. 339.

STEENSTRUP, E. 1968. Paeleorm. *Naturens Verd.* January 1968, 1.

STEPHENSON, L. W. 1941. The larger invertebrate fossils of the Navarro Group of Texas. *Univ. Tex. Publs* no. 4101.

—— 1952. Larger invertebrate fossils of the Woodbine Formation (Cenomanian) of Texas. *Prof. Pap. U.S. geol. Surv.* **242**.

TASNÁDI-KUBACSKA, A. 1962. *Paläopathologie.* G. Fischer, Jena.

TAYLOR, B. J. 1965. Aptian cirripedes from Alexander Island. *Bull. Br. Antarctic Surv.* **7**, 37.

TEICHERT, C. 1945. Parasitic worms in Permian brachiopod shells in Western Australia. *Am. J. Sci.* **243**, 197.

THOMAS, A. O. 1911. A fossil burrowing sponge from the Iowa Devonian. *Bull. Lab. nat. Hist. St. Univ. Ia* **6**, (2), 165.

THORSON, G. 1968. Epifaunaen. *Danm. Natur* **3**, 167.

TOMLINSON, J. T. 1953. A burrowing barnacle of the genus *Trypetesa* (order Acrothoracica). *J. Wash. Acad. Sci.* **43**, 373.

—— 1955. The morphology of an acrothoracican barnacle, *Trypetesa lateralis. J. Morph.* **96**, 97.

—— 1960. *Cryptophialus coronatus,* a new species of acrothoracican barnacle from Dakar. *Bull. Inst. fr. Afr. noire* (A) **22**, 402.

—— 1963. Acrothoracican barnacles in Paleozoic myalinids. *J. Paleont.* **37**, 164.

—— 1969. Shell-burrowing barnacles. *Am. Zoologist* **9**, 837.

—— and NEWMAN, W. A. 1960. *Lithoglyptes spinatus,* a burrowing barnacle from Jamaica. *Proc. U.S. natn. Mus.* **112**, 517.

TOPSENT, É. 1887a. Sur les prétendus prolongements périphériques des Cliones. *C. r. hebd. Séanc. Acad. Sci. Paris* **105**, 1188.

—— 1887b. Contribution à l'étude des Clionides. *Arch. Zool. exp. gén.* (2), **5**, Suppl., Mém. 4.

—— 1891. Deuxième contribution à l'étude des Clionides. *Ibid.* (2), **9**, 555.

—— 1900. Étude monographique des spongiaires de France III. Monaxonida. *Ibid.* (3), **8**, 1.

—— 1904. Spongiaires des Açores. *Résult. Camp. Scient. Prince Albert I.* Fasc. 25.

—— 1932. Notes sur des Clionides. *Arch. Zool. exp. gén.* **74**, 549.

TRAGANZA, E. D. 1965. *Limnoria,* termite of the sea. *Sea Front.* **11**, 164.

TURNER, R. D. 1954. The family Pholadidae in the western Atlantic and the eastern Pacific. Part 1—Pholadinae. *Johnsonia* **3**, 1.

—— 1955. The family Pholadidae in the western Atlantic and the eastern Pacific. Part 2—Martesiinae, Jouannetiinae and Xylophaginae. *Johnsonia* **3**, 65.

—— 1965. Some results of deep water testing. *Am. malacol. Un.* p. 9.

ULRICH, E. O. and BASSLER, R. S. 1904. Revision of the Paleozoic Bryozoa, I: Ctenostomata. *Smithson. misc. Collns* **45** [for 1903], 256.

UTINOMI, H. 1949a. A new remarkable coral-boring acrothoracican cirriped. *Mem. Coll. Sci. Kyoto Univ.* **19B**, 87.

—— 1949b. On another form of Acrothoracica, newly found from Formosa. *Ibid.* **19B**, 95.

—— 1953. Coral-dwelling organisms as destructive agents of corals. *Proc. pan-Pacif. Sci. Congr., Auckland* **4**, Zoology, 533.

—— 1957. Studies on the Cirripedia Acrothoracica I. Biology and external morphology of the female of *Berndtia purpurea* Utinomi. *Publs Seto mar. biol. Lab.* **6**, 1.

VOIGT, E. 1959. *Endosacculus moltkiae* n.g. n.sp., ein vermutlicher fossiler Ascothoracide (Entomostr.) als Cystenbildner bei der Oktokoralle *Moltkia minuta. Paläont. Z.* **33**, 211.

—— 1965. Über parasitische Polychaeten in Kreide-Austern sowie einige andere in Muschelschalen bohrende Würmer. *Ibid.* **39**, 193.

—— 1967a. Ein vermutlicher Ascothoracide (*Endosacculus* (?) *najdini* n. sp.) als Bewohner einer kretazischen *Isis* aus der UdSSR. *Ibid.* **41**, 86.

—— 1967b. Über einen neuen acrothoraciden Cirripedier aus dem Essener Grünsand (Cenoman). *Abh. Verh. naturw. Ver. Hamburg* N. F. **11** [for 1966], 117.

VOLZ, P. 1939. Die Bohrschwämme (Clionidus) der Adria. *Thalassia* **3** (2), 1.

WARBURTON, F. E. 1958a. The manner in which the sponge *Cliona* bores in calcareous objects. *Can. J. Zool.* **36**. 555.

—— 1958b. The effects of boring sponges on oysters. *Prog. Rep. Atlantic Ct Stns* **68**, 3.

WARME, J. E. and MARSHALL, N. F. 1969. Marine borers in calcareous terrigenous rocks of the Pacific coast. *Am. Zoologist* **9**, 765.

WENZ, W. 1939. Gastropoda. *Handb. Paläozool.* **6** (1), 481.

WETHERELL, N. T. 1852. Note on a new species of *Clionites. Ann. Mag. nat. Hist.* (2) **10**, 354.

WETZEL, W. 1938. Die Schalenzerstörung durch Microorganismen, Erscheinungsform, Verbreitung und geologische Bedeutung in Gegenwart und Vergangenheit. *Kieler Meeresforsch.* **2** (for 1937), 254.

—— 1964. Schalen-Parasitismus bei Ammoniten (aufgrund schleswig-holsteinischer Fund). *Meyniana* **14**, 66.

WHITELEGGE, T. 1890. Report on the worm disease affecting the oysters on the coast of New South Wales. *Rec. Aust. Mus.* **1**, 41.

WODINSKY, J. 1969. Penetration of the shell and feeding on gastropods by *Octopus. Am. Zoologist* **9**, 997.

YONGE, C. M. 1932. Giant clams and burrowing clams. *Nat. Hist. N.Y.* **32**, 244.

—— 1936. Mode of life, feeding, digestion and symbiosis with zooxanthellae in the Tridacnidae. *Scient. Rep. Gt Barrier Reef Exped.* **1**, 283.

—— 1949. *The sea shore.* Collins, London.

—— 1951. Marine boring organisms. *Research Lond.* **4**, 162.

—— 1955. Adaptation to rock boring in *Botula* and *Lithophaga* (Lamellibranchia, Mytilidae) with a discussion on the evolution of this habit. *Q. J. microsc. Sci.* **96**, 383.

—— 1958. Observations on *Petricola carditoides* (Conrad). *Proc. malac. Soc. Lond.* **33**, 25.

—— 1963a. Rock-boring organisms. In *Mechanisms of hard tissue destruction* (Ed. R. F. Sognnaes). *Publs Am. Ass. Advmt Sci.* **75**, 1.

—— 1963b. The biology of coral reefs. *Adv. mar. Biol.* **1**, 209.

—— 1964. Rock borers. *Sea Front.* **10**, 106.

YOUNG, D. K. 1969. *Okadaia elegans,* a tube-boring nudibranch mollusc from the central and west pacific. *Am. Zoologist* **9**, 903.

ZAPFE, H. 1936. Spuren bohrender Cirripedier in Gastropoden-Gehäusen des Miocäns. *Senckenbergiana* **18**, 130.

—— 1937. Paläobiologische Untersuchungen an Hippuritenvorkommen der nordalpinen Gosauschichten. *Verhandl. zool.-bot. Ges. Wien* Jahrg. 1936-1937, p. 73.

R. G. Bromley, Institut for Historisk Geologi og Palaeontologi, Øster Voldgade 10, 1350 Copenhagen K, Denmark.

Trace Fossils from the late Precambrian/ Lower Cambrian of East Greenland

J. W. Cowie and A. M. Spencer

Trace fossils are described from two formations. The older formation, which lies stratigraphic-ally beneath beds with the lowest early Cambrian body fossils, yields arthropod scratch marks, *? Diplichnites, Scolicia, Planolites, Skolithos* and *Phycodes*. The younger formation yields *Cruziana, Skolithos, Plagiogmus, Planolites* and *Diplichnites*. Present evidence on the positioning of the base of the Cambrian System in the East Greenland sequences is briefly reviewed.

1. Introduction

The trace fossil specimens described and illustrated here were collected from an unknown horizon in the Ella Island Formation of Strindberg Land (Fig. 1 and 2) by H. R. Katz and, nearly 20 years later, by A. M. Spencer from the Bastion Formation of Ella Island during the summer of 1968. The provenance of the material, though known with varying exactitude, is not in doubt, so that, in con-junction with earlier records, a composite, preliminary, picture of the Lower Cambrian trace fossils of East Greenland can be drawn.

2. The trace fossils

2a. Canyon, Spiral Creek and Kloftelv Formations

The algal stromatolites found in the Canyon Formation (Fig. 2) are the earliest described post-tillite organic traces (Cowie and Adams 1957 p. 169; Schaub 1950 p. 37) but pre-tillite algal stromatolites are well-known in East Greenland (Schaub 1950 p. 19). In the Lower Sandstones of the Kløftelv Formation, Spencer collected bottom structures, which may be due to organisms or desiccation, from near to Locality 2; in Hudson Land (to the north of Locality 3 in Fig. 1) 'possible worm-trails and casts' are recorded (Cowie & Adams 1957 p. 154). Quartzite boulders with *Skolithos linearis*, known from many parts of East Greenland, lithologically match the Kløftelv Formation but have not been found *in situ* (*op. cit.* p. 149).

2b. Bastion Formation

The Glauconitic Sandstones of the lower Bastion Formation contain, from near their base and top, grains, pellets and nodules of collophane-type phosphatic material. They may be organic, either coprolitic or accumulations of phosphatic hard parts of organisms during a period of non-deposition, or they may be in-organic (*op. cit.* p. 52, 86).

The new trace fossils from the Glauconitic Sandstones of Ella Island, which were collected rapidly (within three hours), mostly come from the outcrops above

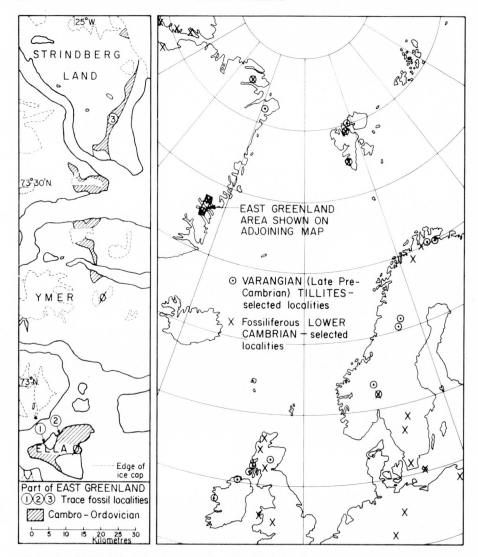

Fig. 1. Lower Cambrian trace fossil localities in East Greenland (left) and the relationship of the East Greenland area to selected North Atlantic tillites and fossiliferous Lower Cambrian localities (right). Trace fossils from Localities 1 and 2 were collected by Spencer, those from Locality 3 were collected by Katz.

Bastionbugt (Locality 1, Fig. 1) but a few are from an isolated outcrop above Solitaerbugt (Locality 2, Fig. 1). The strata consist of thinly interbedded glauconitic sandstones and siltstones and the trace fossils are believed to be almost all on the lower surfaces of the sandstone beds, but the specimens were not marked with their original orientation in the field before collection. Trace fossils have been noted previously at this horizon in Hudson Land (*op. cit.* p. 53 fig. 14).

The most noteworthy structures are probably arthropod scratch marks (Pl. 2a,

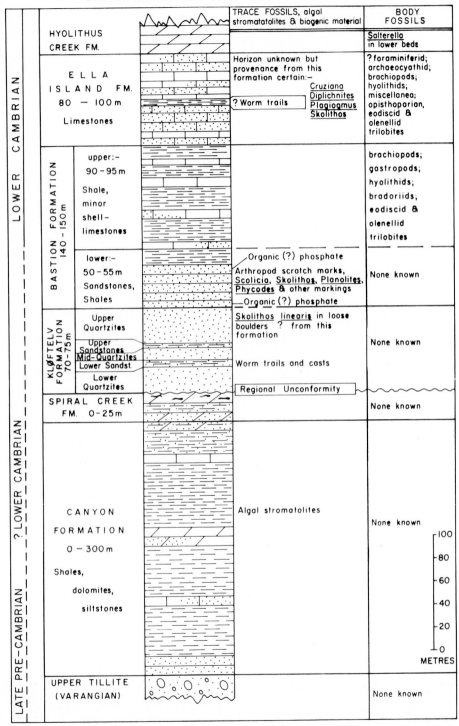

Fig. 2. Composite, conventionalized section of late Precambrian and Lower Cambrian rocks in East Greenland with summarized evidence of fossils and biogenic material. Faunal evidence of the "*Olenellus*" Zone is taken from Poulsen (1927; 1932) and Cowie and Adams (1957). Ichnofaunal evidence described below is supplemented by earlier records in Schaub (1950 p. 37) and Cowie and Adams (1957 p. 149).

b); of the two examples found, one shows that the animal responsible had a minimum of two "claws" per limb (Pl. 2b). One example of a possible arthropod walking track (*Diplichnites*) was also found. Three sinuous traces up to 15 mm wide and 300 mm long with a simple internal structure of smoothly curving, transverse segments may be the putative gastropod trace *Scolicia* (Häntzschel 1962). Seen in cross-section, the sandstone lamina immediately above one of these traces (Pl. 1a) thickens from 3 up to 6 mm, suggesting that it is a burrow. Another distinctive trail, of which only a single specimen was found (Pl. 2c), is smooth and has a minor longitudinal ridge along its centre which compares well with an illustration of a trace by Glaessner (1969 fig. 9c) which he ascribes to the activities of a mollusc-like animal.

Planolites traces are common. Frequently they are less than 5 mm wide but the widest measured 10 mm and was over 60 mm long. They lie approximately parallel to the bedding. Two small and simple examples of bundled sediment-filled burrows of *Phycodes* type were found. A third type of burrow, of which two or three examples were found, is similar to *Planolites* but is more sinuous on a smaller scale, and possesses a central groove in places. An example is seen 10 mm from the right margin of the slab in Plate 1a. A fourth type of burrow which lies parallel to the bedding, is small and resembles a "*Feather stitch trail*" (Häntzschel 1962).

Several examples of burrows in the sandstones are perpendicular to the bedding, from 3 to 5 mm in diameter and penetrate 50 mm or more. Some of the burrows are probably *Skolithos*, others (with the tubes 10 to 15 mm apart) may be *Arenicolites*.

2c. Ella Island Formation

Earlier records were of possible worm trails from one horizon in the Shaly Beds of the Formation in Hudson Land (Cowie and Adams 1957 p. 156) and of *Skolithos* (Poulsen 1932). Four of the specimens collected by Katz are described below.

An example of *Cruziana* sp. on the probable under-surface of a fine-grained quartzite with silty laminae (Pl. 2 d, e) shows a transition longitudinally from a relatively blunt V (130°), where the scratch marks extend right across and round the margins of the trace, to a sharper V (100°), where the scratch marks are confined to the axial portion of the trace, with smooth lateral areas (see discussion in Crimes 1970). Bunching of the V markings indicates at least two "claws" to a limb but there may be more; this feature strengthens the argument that this is a trilobite trace. The trilobites known from the Ella Island Formation are mainly opistho-parians, eodiscids and olenellids; of these only the olenellids could produce traces of this size. No body fossils have been found associated with these specimens of *Cruziana*, but species of *Olenellus* or *Wanneria* found in the formation in East Greenland match the traces in size (Poulsen 1932 pl. 9-13). In Plate 2e a section

---

Plate 1

a *Scolicia* and other trace fossils. Glauconitic Sandstones, lower Bastion Formation. Locality 1 (see Fig. 1); above Bastionbugt, Ella Ø. × 0·3 UBGM 20135 (UBGM: University of Bristol Geological Museum).

b *Cruziana* (C), *Plagiogmus* (P), *Skolithos* (S) and trilobite (?) scratch marks (X). Probable under surface of bedding lamina. Ella Island Formation. Locality 3 (see Fig. 1), Strindberg Land. × 0·5 UBGM 20142.

PLATE 1

across the end of the above specimen, where the V markings are at a more acute angle, shows that the sedimentary laminae extend straight across above the cast of the trace preserved on the undersurface of the overlying bed. This indicates that it was a surface furrow later covered by deposits with flat laminae. Laminations occur within the trace which are also relatively flat except near the margins and at the bottom where there have been slight modifications, possibly by compaction. The conclusion is drawn that the *Cruziana* specimen is a cast of an open furrow and not of an enclosed burrow (cf. Crimes 1970 fig. 6).

A lamina of hard, brittle, fine-grained siltstone was not orientated on collection, the probable bottom is shown in Plate 1b. *Skolithos* tubes penetrate the lamina and are seen in cross-section on both surfaces. On the bottom surface (Pl. 1b) two longer traces are seen—the narrower is *Cruziana* exhibiting no distinguishable "claw" pattern but the clear V form. This *Cruziana* is small enough to be matched in size with opisthoparian or olenellid trilobites known from the Ella Island Formation. The wider and longer trail is similar to *Plagiogmus* which may be a molluscan trace. The slightly pear-shaped spindly objects are noteworthy and one near the edge of the specimen has four ridges; these may be a random preservation of *Skolithos* at an angle to the bedding surface. At point X, markings suggest the impression which could be left by trilobites digging into the mud. There are paired shallow and faint impressions, suggesting that the trilobite had at least two claws per appendage: large and small.

The top of the lamina shows interfering wave forms of ripple-marks—probably of oscillation type. Larger, *Planolites*-type, worm tubes, flattened by compaction from their probable original circular cross-section, parallel the bedding; some forms show shallow longitudinal grooving which may indicate another taxon of animal but may equally be due to a change of behaviour of the same animal (cf. Glaessner 1969 fig. 9B and C). Smaller worm tubes which are similar to the large *Planolites* can also be seen.

The probable under-surface of a thin bed of dolomitic siltstone shows a trace (Pl. 2f) with transverse irregular markings which only go about one-third of the way across the trace leaving a gap down the middle. This is likely to have been caused by an arthropod and possibly by a trilobite which was not digging far into soft sediment; it is referred to *Diplichnites*. "Claw" patterns can be seen indicating two "claws"—one deeper than the other.

Plate 2

a, b Arthropod scratch marks. Glauconitic Sandstones, lower Bastion Formation. Locality 1 (see Fig. 1), above Bastionbugt, Ella Ø. a: × 1, b: × 0·5. The fine striae in the specimen in (**a**) are due to excessive wire-brushing. UBGM 20136 and 20137.

c Organic mark. Glauconitic Sandstones, lower Bastion Formation. Locality 1 (see Fig. 1), above Bastionbugt, Ella Ø. × 1. UBGM 20138.

d *Cruziana*, Ella Island Formation. Locality 3 (see Fig. 1), Strindberg Land. × 1 UBGM 20139.

e *Cruziana*, cross-section of **d**. above × 1.

f *Diplichnites*, Ella Island Formation. Locality 3 (see Fig. 1), Strindberg Land. × 0·66. UBGM 20140.

g *Plagiogmus*, Ella Island Formation. Locality 3 (see Fig. 1), Strindberg Land. × 0·5. UBGM 20141.

PLATE 2

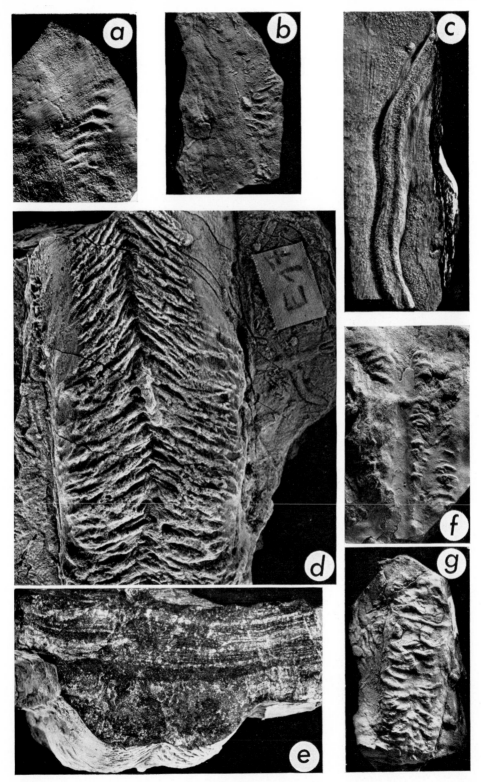

The under-surface of a thin bed of dolomitic siltstone, with cross-bedding which indicates the original orientation, shows a trail with transverse irregular ridges which in some cases go right across the trail but fail to extend to its sides (Pl. 2g). This is here assigned to the genus *Plagiogmus* which has recently been discussed by Glaessner (1969 p. 383). The single ridges are coarser than in *Cruziana* and show no "claw" or limb scratch-marks and no bunching in pairs or triplets. A particular feature which makes this trail unlikely to have been formed by an arthropod with paired bilaterally symmetrical appendages is the continuous nature of the ridges from one side to another. Glaessner (1969 p. 385) referred his new material of *Plagiogmus* to endichnial burrows of an ancestral mollusc, with a foot and a mantle, which fed on organic matter in sand (or silt?) and backfilled its partly mucus-lined trail with rejected sediment.

3. Stratigraphical discussion

Consideration of the stratigraphical significance of the body fossils, trace fossils, lithologies and depositional relationships so far known from the late Precambrian to Lower Cambrian succession in the East Greenland region—summarized in Figure 2 —is an aspect of global considerations and difficulties in arriving at an agreed and widely accepted Precambrian/Cambrian boundary. Many geologists think this world-wide problem can best be solved, or at least reduced, by international discussion and investigation leading to selection of an international stratotype section with a selected point for the base of the Cambrian; this would then be a stimulus to, and a working basis for, further research into regional and inter-continental correlations at this stratigraphic level.

Current and future work on microfossils, tillites (e.g. Spencer 1970) and radio-metric dates could also make a significant contribution. Previously the regional unconformity (which involves no discernible angular discordance) at the base of the Kløftelv Formation has been used as the most suitable regional level for the base of the Cambrian System (Cowie 1961 p. 28). This may only be a temporary criterion to be superseded as research progresses.

Accelerated collection and description of trace fossils in areas with Lower Cambrian body fossils and underlying presumed late Precambrian deposits (including, preferably, Varangian tillites) may lead to elucidation of the concept of a Phanerozoic/Cryptozoic transition with further evidence regarding the incoming of skeletalized organisms and the possible origin of the metazoa at or near these times. The absence of trace or body fossils is an unsatisfactorily negative criterion for suggesting a stratigraphical position with reference to the base of the Cambrian but should be considered, at least, if unfossiliferous lithologies are present which appear to be suitable for the preservation of fossils. Such a lack of finds of trace and body fossils in the Spiral Creek and Canyon Formations, in spite of prolonged search, is an example of this and may be significant. The presence or absence of trace and body fossils in late Precambrian and early Lower Cambrian strata may well, of course, be due to original ethological (behavioural) and ecological factors so that trace and body fossils should, perhaps, not be expected to be preserved together; this appears to be the case in the upper Bastion Formation. Absence of both could, of course, be due to unfavourable facies.

The sedimentology of the Spiral Creek Formation and also, to a certain extent, the Canyon Formation (Schaub 1950 pl. 1) indicates that marine conditions were replaced by terrestrial or littoral conditions with fresh or brackish water, which may explain the absence of trace and body fossils because (i) these non-marine environments may not anywhere at that time have been colonised by faunas, and/or (ii) the preservation potential was too low. The variation of lithology from the Kløftelv through the Bastion to the Ella Island Formation, suggesting changing marine conditions with decreased influx of clastics and increase of carbonate sedimentation, is probably reflected in the variation in the faunal characteristics and palaeoecology, with worms in the lowest formation followed upwards by a more varied assemblage including trilobites in the upper formations. The whole discussion is greatly complicated at this stratigraphical level, however, by the relatively rapid evolutionary changes which were probably taking place in the biosphere and which may have been associated with and related to the evolution of the physico-chemical framework of the hydrosphere, atmosphere and lithosphere.

Poulsen (1932 p. 62) suggested that the fossils from the Bastion Formation did not indicate the earliest Lower Cambrian Zone. This has been supported by recent work and if the basal Lower Cambrian of the world is truly without trilobites but yields other diagnostic body fossils, as seems to be the case in Europe and Asia (Rozanov 1967 p. 428), although the position in North America is not at present clear, then in East Greenland the base of the Cambrian defined on the basis of body fossils should lie, presumably, some considerable way below the upper Bastion Formation and may be as far down as the Spiral Creek or Canyon Formations.

New discoveries of Lower Cambrian fossils in Ellesmere Island, Arctic Canada (Kerr 1967; Cowie 1968), in conjunction with lithological and faunal correlations (including tillites) across northern Greenland and southwards to East Greenland suggest, in a speculative way, that the Spiral Creek and Canyon Formations may be, at least in part, assigned with question to the Lower Cambrian (Cowie 1970).

At the present time and in the context of this short contribution it is premature to draw conclusions; the Precambrian/Cambrian boundary is presumably bracketed between the Bastion Formation and the Varangian tillites. It may be nearer to the latter than the former. The known trace fossils in East Greenland are probably Lower Cambrian in age.

Acknowledgements. The authors wish to thank Dr. T. P. Crimes for encouragement and considerable help in describing the material. Spencer acknowledges with thanks a grant from the Royal Society which enabled him to collect the Bastion Formation trace fossils as a member of the 1968 Cambridge East Greenland Expedition under the leadership of Dr. P. F. Friend. Michael Parr is thanked for help. The energy and discernment of H. R. Katz in collecting the Ella Island Formation trace fossil fauna from Strindberg Land whilst he was a member of Lauge Koch's Danish East Greenland Expeditions, 1947-1958, is gratefully recalled.

References

COWIE, J. W. 1961. Contribution to the geology of North Greenland. *Meddr. Grønland*, **164**, no. 3.
—— 1968. Contributions to Canadian palaeontology. Lower Cambrian faunas from Ellesmere Island, District of Franklin. *Bull. geol. Surv. Can.* **163**, 1.
—— 1970. The Cambrian of the North American Arctic regions. In *The Cambrian of the New World* (Ed. C. H. Holland). Interscience, London.
—— and ADAMS, P. J. 1957. The geology of the Cambro-Ordovician rocks of Central East Greenland. Pt. 1. Stratigraphy and structure. *Meddr. Grønland*, **153**, no. 1.
CRIMES, T. P. 1970. Trilobite tracks and other trace fossils from the Upper Cambrian of North Wales. *Geol. J.* **7**, 47.
GLAESSNER, M. F. 1969. Trace fossils from the Pre-Cambrian and basal Cambrian. *Lethaia*, **2**, 369.

HÄNTZSCHEL, W. 1962. Trace fossils and problematica. In *Treatise on invertebrate paleontology* (Ed. R. C. Moore). Geol. Soc. Am., New York and Univ. of Kansas Press, Lawrence. Part W, p.W177.

KERR, J. W. 1967. Stratigraphy of central and eastern Ellesmere Island, arctic Canada. Pt. I. Proterozoic and Cambrian. *Geol. Surv. Pap. Can.* **67-27,** Pt. I.

POULSEN, C. 1927. Cambrian, Ozarkian and Canadian faunas of N.W. Greenland. *Meddr. Grønland*, **70**, no. 2, 237.

—— 1932. The lower Cambrian faunas of East Greenland, *Meddr. Grønland*, **87**, no. 6.

ROZANOV, A. Y. 1967. The Cambrian Lower boundary problem. *Geol. Mag.* **104,** 415.

SCHAUB, H. P. 1950. On the Pre-Cambrian to Cambrian sedimentation in NE-Greenland. *Meddr. Grønland*, **114**, no. 10.

SPENCER, A. M. 1970. Late Pre-Cambrian glaciation in Scotland. *Mem. geol. Soc. Lond.* **6.**

J. W. Cowie, Department of Geology, The University, Bristol, U.K.

A. M. Spencer, The Geological Society, Burlington House, Piccadilly, London, W.1., U.K.

The significance of trace fossils in sedimentology, stratigraphy and palaeoecology with examples from Lower Palaeozoic strata

T. P. Crimes

Firstly, the concept of trace fossils communities is examined and it is shown that they are often, but not always, depth controlled. Traces of the *Nereites* community, which have only been found in association with deep water turbidites, appear to be the most depth dependent. The particular members of this community present in a sequence are also shown to relate to the distance from source, thus suggesting the possibility of distinguishing proximal and distal turbidites by their contained ichnofaunas. Secondly, some trace fossils occurring in faunally dated successions, including species of *Cruziana, Rusophycus, Oldhamia* and *Phycodes,* are shown to have restricted time ranges. They are then used to determine the age of other unfossiliferous successions. Finally, the usefulness of trace fossils in palaeoecology, particularly for the study of the habits of 'live' populations, is briefly discussed and as an example Cambro-Ordovician trilobite traces are used to show that the trilobites which made them probably altered their behaviour patterns several times in the course of their life cycles.

1. Introduction

In the past five years trace fossils have been recorded, often in abundance, from many parts of Wales, the Welsh Borderlands and Leinster (Crimes 1968; 1969 a, b; 1970a, b, c; Crimes and Crossley 1968; Seilacher and Crimes 1969). Detailed descriptions of these ichnofaunas, together with locality lists, have already been given in the papers cited above or are in preparation. The trace fossils have proved to have wider application than might have been suspected and the purpose of the present paper is to show how they can assist in such problems as environmental interpretation, dating of otherwise unfossiliferous successions, investigation of behaviour patterns, and "live" population studies of extinct phyla.

2. The use of trace fossils in sedimentology

In a series of papers, Seilacher (1963; 1964; 1967) suggested that trace fossils do not occur in random combinations but in depth controlled communities. Much recent interest in trace fossils has, therefore, centred around their possible use as depth indicators in the marine environment.

2a. The concept of trace fossil communities

Trace fossils reflect the behavioural responses of animals. These responses are controlled by energy conditions at the depositional interface, substrate type, and availability of food. In general, the deeper the water, the finer the sediment and the greater the amount of food incorporated in it. These changes in conditions are reflected in the ichnofauna, consequently Seilacher (1964; 1967) was able to suggest that a relatively small number of distinct, depth controlled, communities recurred throughout Phanerozoic time. These communities, each of which he named after a characteristic trace fossil, are in order of increasing water depth: *Glossifungites* (littoral zone), *Skolithos* (littoral zone), *Cruziana* (littoral zone to wave base), *Zoophycos* (wave base to zone of turbidite deposition) and *Nereites* (turbidite zone). According to this concept the occurrence of one or more members of a community can be used to indicate the palaeobathymetric level.

2b. Communities in the Lower Palaeozoic of Wales and Leinster

In Wales *Skolithos* has been found immediately above known surfaces of disconformity or unconformity, at or near the base of the Lower and Middle Cambrian successions (Crimes 1970a) and the Arenig succession (Crimes 1970c). *Cruziana* and other traces belonging to the *Cruziana* community, such as *Rusophycus* and *Teichichnus,* occur more commonly a few metres above the basal Arenig unconformity associated with well sorted sandstones and siltstones which, on sedimentological evidence, appear to have been deposited above wave base but below the littoral zone (Crimes 1970c). Representatives of the *Nereites* community are found in association with deep water turbidites in the Lower Silurian at Aberystwyth (Wood and Smith 1958) and the Arenig at Courtown, Leinster (Crimes and Crossley 1968). Also, on a regional scale, good correlation has been found between water depths determined from trace fossil communities and those deduced from inorganic sedimentary structures both in the Cambrian and the Arenig of Wales (Crimes 1970a, c).

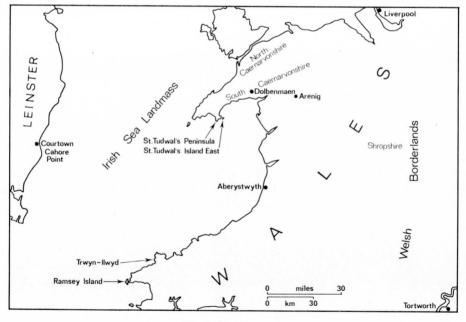

Fig. 1. Locality map.

The most striking example, however, is the contrast between the ichnofauna of the Lower Arenig rocks of Leinster and that of Wales and the Welsh Borderlands. These successions were deposited on either side of a landmass and are known from the sedimentological and tectonic evidence to have been deposited in very different environments. To the northwest of the landmass, in Leinster, there was rapid accumulation of distal turbidites in a rapidly subsiding trough (Crimes and Crossley 1968). To the southeast, in Wales, sediment accumulated slowly in a stable epicontinental sea (Crimes 1970c). The Leinster rocks contain five genera typical of the deep water *Nereites* community (Pl. 1): *Bifasciculus, Nereites, Helminthopsis, ?Lorenzinia* and 'scribbling grazing traces'. None of these genera were found in Wales but *Cruziana, Rusophycus, Phycodes, Bergaueria* and *Teichichnus,* all representatives of the *Cruziana* or *Skolithos* communities and absent in Leinster, are common and *Skolithos* occurs abundantly at some localities (Pl. 2).

In some cases, however, water depths deduced from trace fossil communities do not agree with those inferred from other evidence, and members of different communities are sometimes found in the same strata. In both the Upper Cambrian and the Arenig, traces belonging to the *Skolithos* community including *Skolithos* itself, occur locally in the same beds as *Cruziana* community traces such as *Cruziana, Rusophycus* and *Phycodes. Cruziana* also occur locally within a few centimetres of the base of the transgressive Arenig sequence as at Trwyn-llech-y-doll, St. Tudwal's Peninsula, without the intervention of beds containing examples of the *Skolithos* community. Also, nearby at Muriau, *Skolithos* bearing sandstones occur locally interbedded with siltstones yielding *Phycodes* and *Teichichnus,* the last two genera being members of the *Cruziana* community. Such examples could be multiplied. It would obviously be imprudent to infer alternate rise and fall of sea level to account for the repeated juxtaposition of beds of two different "depth zones". It is more likely that sand and silt sedimentaion alternated at a constant water depth and the trace fossils reflect the differing behavioural responses of the animals which colonised the two distinct habitats. Further anomalies of this type can be deduced from Figure 2 which shows that in the Lower Palaeozoic strata of this area at least, only the deeper water *Nereites* community is strictly facies controlled. Few traces amongst the shallow water forms are restricted to a single ichnofacies or community and, in all, three types of trace fossil can be recognised:

(i) *facies-independent,* occurring with similar frequency in all ichnofacies.
(ii) *facies-influenced,* occurring much more commonly in sediments of one ichnofacies.
(iii) *facies-specific,* restricted to one ichnofacies.

From the evidence presented in Figure 2, *Planolites* and *Sinusites* appear to be facies-independent, *Rusophycus* and *Diplichnites* are facies-influenced and *Paleodictyon* and *Helminthopsis* are facies-specific. Facies-influenced traces are the most common and facies-specific the least.

The lack of facies specificity and the break-down of the community concept within some shallow water sediments is presumably because the traces are controlled by both the surface environment and substrate and while as a generality these parameters are depth controlled this is not always the case. The complexities of shallow water sedimentation can result locally in the development in a given depth zone of conditions and, or, substrate type more commonly associated with another depth zone. For example, extensive deposits of mud capable of supporting a population of sediment feeders, and normally found below wave base, can occur in the littoral zone, particularly in association with estuaries (see Sly 1966). Trace fossils of one community can therefore occur locally in rocks deposited outside the normal depth limits of that community.

PLATE 1

LEINSTER: DEEP WATER ARENIG

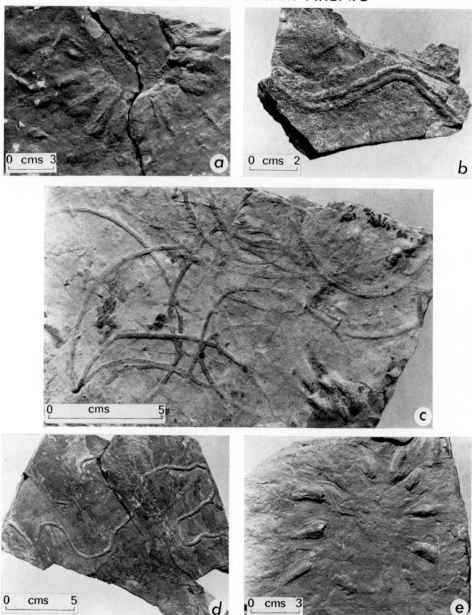

Plate 1

Ichnofauna of deep water Arenig turbidites of Leinster. See Crimes and Crossley (1968) for all localities except (e) which is Seamount Formation, Breanoge Head.

a *Bifasciculus radiatus* Volk.

b *Nereites* sp.

c 'Scribbling grazing traces.'

d *Helminthopsis* sp.

e *?Lorenzinia* sp.

PLATE 2

WALES:SHALLOW WATER ARENIG

0 cms 3

0 cms 3

Plate 2

Ichnofauna of shallow water Arenig sediments of Wales.

a *Cruziana furcifera d'Orb.*, Trwyn Llech-y-Doll, St. Tudwal's Peninsula.
b *Phycodes circinatum Mägdefrau*, Wig, Aberdaron.
c *Skolithos* sp. Porth Cadlan, Aberdaron.
d *Bergaueria* sp. Porth Cadlan, Aberdaron.
e *Teichichnus* sp. road cutting 2·5 km W. of Arenig.

	facies independent		Skolithos facies	Cruziana facies						Nereites facies				
	Planolites	*Sinusites*	*Skolithos*	*Cruziana*	*Rusophycus*	*Diplichnites*	*Dimorphichnus*	*Phycodes*	*Teichichnus*	*Helminthopsis*	*Bifasciculus*	*Nereites*	*Paleodictyon*	*Oldhamia*
Planolites (facies independent)		1	2	4	4	4	4	3	3	5	5	5		12
Sinusites	1		3	3				3	3					12
Skolithos (Skolithos facies)	2	3		6	6	7	7	9	9		10			
Cruziana (Cruziana facies)	4	3	6		8	8	8	9	9					
Rusophycus	4		6	8		8	8	9	9					
Diplichnites	4		7	8	8		8	8						
Dimorphichnus	4		7	8	8	8		8						
Phycodes	3	3	9	9	9	8	8		9					
Teichichnus	3	3	9	9	9			9						
Helminthopsis	5										5	5		
Bifasciculus	5		10							5		5		
Nereites (Nereites facies)	5									5	5		11	
Paleodictyon												11		
Oldhamia	12	12												

Fig. 2. Facies control of trace fossils at the ichnogeneric level. The numbers refer to localities at which ichnogenera of the appropriate vertical and horizontal columns occur in the same bed or in beds separated stratigraphically by less than 5 metres. The localities, with map references, are as follows.
1   Middle Cambrian, St. Tudwal's Peninsula, SH 297232;   2   Arenig, Porth Cadlan, Aberdaron, SH 200262;   3   Arenig, St. Tudwal's Peninsula, SH 302238;   4   Upper Cambrian, Cwm Graianog, SH 624628;   5   Arenig, coast south of Courtown, Leinster; 6   Arenig, Pembrokeshire, SM 878366;   7   Upper Cambrian, near Arenig Station, SH 782388;   8   Upper Cambrian, Cwm Graianog, SH 625630;   9   Arenig, St. Tudwal's Peninsula, SH 305247;   10   Arenig, coast south of Courtown, Leinster;   11   Llandoverian, Aberystwyth, SN 582828;   12   ? Lower Cambrian, Cahore Point, Leinster.

The influence of overall environment, rather than simply water depth, on a trace fossil assemblage, can be seen in the Welsh Upper Cambrian succession. In both north and south Caernarvonshire (Fig. 3) the Ffestiniog Stage sequence consists of sediments with large scale cross-bedding and symmetric, asymmetric and flat topped ripple marks, suggesting deposition between wave base and intertidal level, that is within the limits of the *Cruziana* facies (for sedimentological details see Crimes 1970a). In north Caernarvonshire, however, the sediments are mostly locally derived conglomerates and sandstones deposited in a high energy environment while in south Caernarvonshire they are mainly distantly derived siltstones

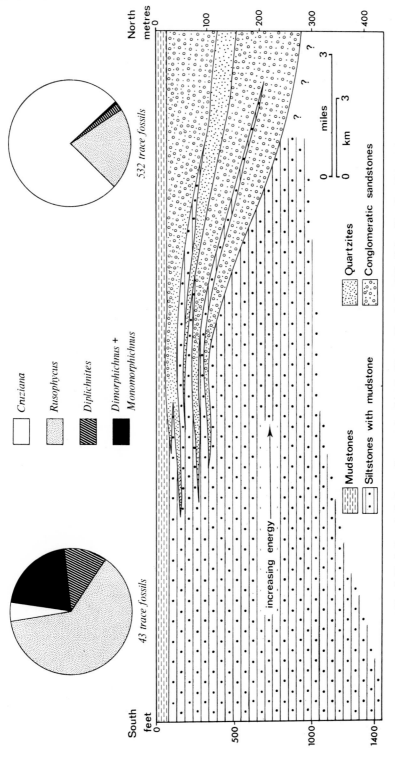

Fig. 3. Variations in facies and energy level in the Upper Cambrian (Ffestiniog Stage) sediments of Caernarvonshire with (above) proportional numbers of the different traces collected from the south and north of the area. Section from Pentrefelin to Cwm Graianog.

and mudstones deposited under low energy conditions. Although the same trace fossils have been recorded from both areas, there are marked differences in the relative frequency of occurrence of the traces in the two areas (Fig. 3). The deposits of the high energy environment include far more trilobite furrows (*Cruziana*), but far fewer walking and surface grazing traces (*Dimorphichnus, Diplichnites, Monomorphichnus*). This anomaly might be the result of varying preservation potential of the different traces in the different environments and substrates. In the high energy environment, *Cruziana,* being traces furrowed into the sediment surface, would be expected to have a higher preservation potential than the lightly impressed surface traces. In the lower energy environment, however, *Cruziana* should also have a preservation potential at least equal to that of the other traces. It is therefore unlikely that the rarity of *Cruziana* in the sediments of the low energy environments is entirely the result of preservational factors. Also, *Rusophycus* (resting excavations) are relatively more common in sediments of the low energy environment. Since they are excavated to a depth roughly equal to the *Cruziana,* they should have an equally high preservation potential in both environments. The differences in the ichnospectra cannot therefore be a function of preservation potential alone. Apparently, the animals were seeking protection, and perhaps food hunting, by furrowing in the higher energy environment, but either grazed the surface or were content to excavate resting places in the quiet water, lower energy, environment. In this case therefore the control on the ichnospectrum is not simply depth but overall environment of which depth is but one parameter. The best approach to determination of the palaeobathymetry would therefore appear to be the complete facies analysis as has been attempted for the Lower Palaezoic of the Oslo region by Seilacher and Meischner (1964), and the Cambrian and Arenig of Wales (Crimes 1970a, c).

From Figure 2 it is also apparent that the *Nereites* community shows the closest facies and depth control, it is therefore proposed now to investigate this community more closely.

2c. The *Nereites* community

Trace fossils belonging to the *Nereites* community, such as *Helminthopsis, Bifasciculus, Nereites* and *Paleodictyon,* have only been found by the writer in turbidite sequences. These occur at many stratigraphic levels within the Welsh and Leinster successions from the Lower Cambrian to the Silurian. The different turbidite sequences, however, show significant variations in trace fossil content. Some of the traces are known to have a limited time range. For example, *Oldhamia radiata* Forbes occurs within the early Cambrian Cahore Group and "Bray Series" in Leinster but at no other stratigraphic horizon in this area, and has never been recorded anywhere above the Middle Cambrian. Other cosmopolitan *Nereites* community traces (e.g. *Nereites, Helminthopsis, Paleodictyon*) are known to have a wide time range and yet are absent from many of these turbidite sequences. In these cases the control is unlikely to be stratigraphical. Other factors likely to influence trace fossil distribution are: depositional environment, substrate, and in the case of traces preserved as sole markings, the sediment type of the overlying bed. These factors are themselves often interrelated and it thus possible that some members of the *Nereites* community may be restricted to a particular type of turbidite. To pursue this further it is necessary to consider the deposition and environment of turbidites in greater detail.

It is known that as they travel further from the source area turbidity currents decelerate and deposit sediment of overall progressively finer grain size. The resultant turbidites are often distinguished as near source (proximal) and far from source (distal). Each type is therefore characteristic of a separate environment, one receiving coarse sediment from fast flowing turbidity currents, the other finer sediment from turbidity currents travelling at lower velocities. Thus the lowest, graded, division (A) of the typical turbidite sequence (Bouma 1964), representing conditions of high flow regime, will normally only be deposited in proximal environments. In more distal environments with lower flow velocities, deposition will normally commence with finer grained sediment of the lower division of parallel lamination (B) or the division of ripple drift (C). Walker (1967) suggested that a measure of the proximality or distality of a turbidite sequence can, therefore, be gained from the P value where:

$$P = A + \tfrac{1}{2}B$$

and A and B represent the percentage of beds in the sequence commencing with division A or B respectively.

Turbidites deposited in proximal environments will, in general, have high P values while low P values will be associated with distal environments. Also proximal turbidites will normally include coarser grained sediment and occur in thicker beds than distal ones. Thus, by consideration of regional palaeogeography, bed thickness, grain size, and P values, it is possible to closely define the environment of each turbidite sequence and then analyse the relationship between this and the trace fossil content. In Figure 4 the Lower Palaeozoic turbidite sequences of Wales and Leinster have been arranged in what is thought most likely to be an order of increasing distality (for additional sedimentological details see Crimes 1970a; Crimes and Crossley 1968; Wood and Smith 1958). Arranged in this way there appears to be a relationship between trace fossils present and distance from source. The most proximal sequences (the Cilan and Hell's Mouth Grits) have few surface trails or near surface burrow systems but simple sediment-stuffed burrows (*Planolites*) and ramifying burrows are present (see Crimes 1970a fig. 7). In general, however, trace fossils are rare in these deposits. The more distal and variable sediments of the Cahore Group have a greater abundance and variety of traces. Simple sediment-stuffed and ramifying burrows occur but they are less common than radiating traces (*Oldhamia*). Trails are also occasionally preserved and U burrows (*Arenicolites*) and trumpet burrows (*Histioderma*) also occur (see Crimes and Crossley 1968). The distal turbidites of the Ribband Group (Arenig) have an abundance of trace fossils. Surface and near surface grazing traces such as *Nereites, Helminthopsis* and also radiating traces such as *Bifasciculus*, all occur in the lowest and probably deepest water part of the succession. In the higher, slightly shallower water, sediments *Nereites* disappears from the ichnospectrum to be followed by *Helminthopsis* until, of the diagnostic forms, only the radiating traces of *Bifasciculus* type occur (see Crimes and Crossley *op. cit.* for details).

The most distal sequence here considered—the Lower Silurian Aberystwyth Grits—has the greatest abundance of traces, in particular of surface and near-surface types. *Nereites* is common and there are also near-surface burrow networks (*Paleodictyon*), some of which appear to have been exposed by the turbidity currents, the burrow infillings washed out and the furrows refilled with sediment. Complex feeding burrows such as *Dictyodora* have also been recorded from this area (Seilacher 1964). Radiating traces are notably absent; their place in the ichnospectrum appears to have been taken by more complex feeding burrow networks such as *Paleodictyon*.

Thus, in general, the proximal turbidites have relatively few traces, with a marked absence of surface or near surface grazing types and complex feeding burrows. In progressively more distal turbidites, radiating traces (*Oldhamia, Bifasciculus*) appear in the ichnospectrum to be followed by meandering grazing traces (e.g.

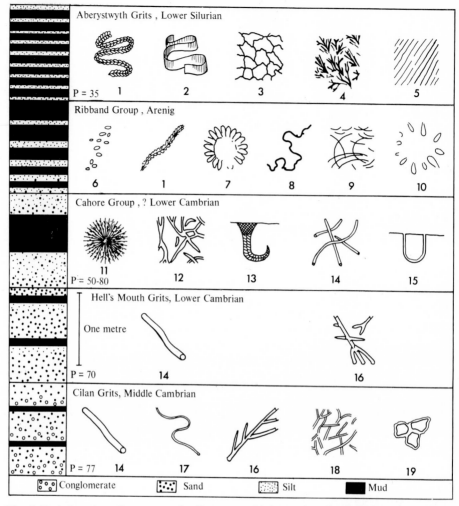

Fig. 4. Variations in sediment trace fossil content with increasing distality of the depositional environment. Average bed thickness, and approximate proportion of sediment of different grades shown in left hand column. Units arranged with increase in distality upwards.
    Trace fossils: 1   *Nereites*;   2   *Dictyodora*;   3   *Paleodictyon*;   4   *Chondrites*;   5   Graptolite drag-marks;   6   *Tomaculum*;   7   *Bifasciculus*;   8   *Helminthopsis*;   9   "scribbling grazing traces";   10   *?Lorenzinia*;   11   *Oldhamia*;   12   Irregular trails;   13   *Histioderma*;   14   *Planolites*;   15   *Arenicolites*;   16   Bifurcating burrows;   17   *Sinusites*; 18   Intertwining burrows;   19   Burrow network (cf. *Paleodictyon*)
    Localities: Aberystwyth Grits, coast north of Aberystwyth except traces 2 and 4 which are recorded in Seilacher (1964); Ribband Group, coast south of Courtown, Leinster; Cahore Group, around Cahore Point, Leinster; Hell's Mouth Grits, Trwyn-y-ffosle, St. Tudwal's Peninsula; Cilan Grits, south of Trwyn-Llech-y-doll, St. Tudwal's Peninsula.

Nereites, Helminthopsis, "scribbling grazing traces"). Finally in the most distal, deepest water environments, radiating traces disappear from the ichnospectrum and complex feeding burrow networks (*Paleodictyon*) take their place.
    This apparent relationship between the trace fossils and proximality or distality is undoubtedly at least partially controlled by preservational factors. In

proximal environments, most surface or near-surface traces will be removed by the fast flowing erosive turbidity currents, while any that are left exposed are unlikely to be adequately preserved as sole markings on the base of the coarse grained beds which are typical of this environment. Thus the preservation potential of traces of this type will increase with increasing distality. In proximal environments only burrows which are deep, or formed between beds, are likely to be preserved. The absence of radiating traces from the most distal environments and complex burrow networks from slightly more proximal environments cannot, however, readily be ascribed to preservational factors and may be a reflection of faunal distribution on the sea floor.

Thus the distribution of different members of the *Nereites* community may be a function of distance of the depositional environment from the shore. If this is confirmed by more extensive investigation, trace fossils may, conversely, be used as an additional criteria in distinguishing between proximal and distal turbidites.

3. The use of trace fossils in stratigraphy

To produce traces of stratigraphical value an animal should ideally be widely distributed, lead an active benthonic life, belong to a rapidly evolving group and be facies-independent. Few trace fossils are facies-independent; they also tend to occur most abundantly in shallow water sandstone-shale sequences, the *Skolithos* and *Cruziana* facies of Seilacher. It is, however, precisely these sequences which most commonly lack body fossils and in which a trace fossil stratigraphy is of the greatest potential value. Such a stratigraphy would need to be erected at the few localities where these sediments occur within successions having good faunal control. In Wales, intensive stratigraphical study over the past one hundred and fifty years has provided a good faunally controlled stratigraphical framework. Recent investigations (Crimes 1968; 1969a, b; 1970a, b, c; Seilacher and Crimes 1969) have also revealed an abundance of trace fossils some of which have proved to have a restricted time range and merit further consideration.

3a. *Cruziana*

Trilobite furrows (*Cruziana*) are common in Lower Palaeozoic strata all over the world. Crimes (1968) was able to demonstrate from material collected within faunally zoned strata in Caernarvonshire, North Wales, that one species (*Cruziana semiplicata* Salter) is common in the Upper Cambrian but does not range into the Arenig, while another (*Cruziana furcifera* d'Orbigny) occurs abundantly in the Arenig but does not range down into the Upper Cambrian.

Recently, more *Cruziana* localities have been found in the Upper Cambrian of Wales (Crimes 1969a), the Arenig of South Wales and Shropshire, and the Lower Tremadoc of Tortworth (Curtis 1968). Trace fossils from the Upper Tremadoc of Shropshire collected by the Geological Survey in the 19th century have also now been confirmed as *Cruziana*.

Within the Upper Cambrian (Ffestiniog Stage) sediments, almost all the *Cruziana* can be referred to *C. semiplicata* (Pl. 3a), none to *C. furcifera* (for localities see Crimes 1968; 1969a, b; 1970a, b).

In the overlying Dolgelly Stage no *Cruziana* has yet been found, but the succeeding Lower Tremadoc strata have yielded more than twenty *Cruziana* to Dr. Curtis and the author at Tortworth. Some of these *Cruziana* (Pl. 3b) have claw markings associated in twos or threes, occasional fine lateral lineations or wisps and genal spine ridges, and can therefore be assigned to *C. semiplicata*. Others (Pl. 3c) are more deeply sculptured with acute V-angles and normally without fine lateral lineations or wisps but nevertheless with claw markings associated in twos and threes. The first three features occur in *C. furcifera* but the bunching of the claw markings in twos and threes does not occur in this species but is a characteristic of *C. semiplicata*. These specimens therefore appear to have affinites with both species. Finally, some specimens (Pl. 3d) appear to show bunching of claw markings in sets of two or more but lack the genal spine ridges generally present in *C. semiplicata*. The scratches are also far more regular than is normal in traces of that species; however, they lack the deep sculpturing present in most specimens of *C. furcifera*. Also the individual claw markings appear to have greater relief and show steeper sides, suggesting excavation by stronger more pointed claws than normally occurs in either *C. semiplicata* or *C. furcifera*. Thus the Lower Tremadoc *Cruziana* include specimens of *C. semiplicata* and other probably new species with some features of both *C. semiplicata* and *C. furcifera*.

The Upper Tremadoc *Cruziana* (Pl. 3e) are poorly preserved and fragmentary but appear to show claw markings in sets of 10 or more, and to lack genal spine ridges, and are probably referrable to *C. furcifera*.

The mean width of the Tremadoc *Cruziana* is slightly greater than that of the Upper Cambrian form (Fig. 8). A further increase in mean width occurs in specimens from a very low Arenig horizon at Trwyn Llwyd, South Wales. These rocks have yielded abundant *C. furcifera* and also *C. goldfussi* Rouault and *C. rugosa* d'Orbigny. Neither *C. semiplicata* nor specimens the same as the two last described Lower Tremadoc forms have been found.

At a higher Arenig horizon (*D. extensus* Zone) on St. Tudwal's Peninsula (Localities 8 and 10 of Crimes 1969a) *C. furcifera, C. goldfussi* and *C. rugosa* also occur and the mean width of the *Cruziana* is even greater. Equally wide *Cruziana* (*C. furcifera* and probably a new species (Pl. 3h)), including the widest specimen yet found in this study, occur at what is probably the highest Arenig horizon, near the top of the Stiperstones Quartzite at Pontesbury, Shropshire. Thus not only is there a gradual increase in mean width of *Cruziana* in passing from the Upper Cambrian to the top of the Lower Arenig, but also the *Cruziana* are of different species. *C. semiplicata* apparently ranges from the Lower Tremadoc to the Upper Cambrian; *C. furcifera* from the Arenig probably to the Upper Tremadoc and intermediate forms occur in the Lower Tremadoc; *C. rugosa* and *C. goldfussi* have so far only been recorded from the Arenig and certainly do not range down to the Upper Cambrian.

Thus Upper Cambrian, Tremadoc and Arenig strata can be distinguished by their *Cruziana,* an observation which is likely to prove particularly useful because of the widespread occurrence of *Cruziana*-bearing, but otherwise unfossiliferous, Arenig successions from Newfoundland to the Far East.

Plate 3

Stratigraphic distribution of *Cruziana*. All figures *c.* ×0·5.

a *Cruziana semiplicata* Salter, Cwm Graianog, North Wales.

b *Cruziana semiplicata* Salter, Bushy Grove stream, Breadstone, Gloucestershire.

c-d *Cruziana* sp. (probably new species). Locality as (b).

e *Cruziana ?furcifera* d'Orb., Geological Survey specimen, Shropshire, exact locality uncertain.

f *Cruziana furcifera* d'Orb,, Trwyn-Llech-y-Doll, St. Tudwal's Peninsula.

g *Cruziana rugosa* d'Orb., Trwyn-Llwyd, South Wales.

h *Cruziana* sp. (probably a new species), Quarry *c.* 1 km SSW of Pontesbury, Shropshire.

PLATE 3

3b. *Rusophycus*

Trilobite resting excavations (*Rusophycus*) often occur in the same sequence and even on the same bedding planes as *Cruziana*. There is at the moment no satisfactory division of this ichnogenus into ichnospecies (see Crimes 1970b p. 55). Nevertheless, four characteristic forms can be recognised in these sequences, shown to have restricted time ranges, and used stratigraphically but the writer would at the present time hesitate to erect new species for these forms. They are:

Form A. This resembles in shape two coffee beans placed side by side, often slightly divergent, and with only a small gap separating them (Pl. 4a, b). Traces of segmentation often occur in the gap between the beans, particularly in larger specimens, but are not normally seen within the outlines of the beans. The length divided by the breadth (here defined as the shape factor) closely approximates to 1·5, regardless of overall size (see Crimes 1970b fig. 3). The mean width of traces of this form is about 1·5 cm. These traces occur abundantly in the Upper Cambrian of North Wales (Localities 1–3 of Crimes 1968, and 1–5, 7–8 of Crimes 1970b) and South Wales (Ramsey Island), also a single specimen has been found in the Lower Tremadoc of Tortworth.

Form B. These traces also resemble two coffee beans but the beans are generally parallel and come closer together along the central line, sometimes occurring fused. Some specimens show traces of segmentation. The shape factor (*c.* 2·0) is significantly higher than in Form A and the mean width is also greater. *Rusophycus* Form B (Pl. 4c) occur in the Arenig of North Wales (Localities 8–11 of Crimes 1969a), South Wales (Trwyn Llwyd, Pembrokeshire) and Shropshire (Pontesbury). One specimen from the Lower Tremadoc of Tortworth is also probably of this type.

Form C. This is similar to Form B except that there is a raised platform around the trace (Pl. 4). This corresponds to a depression around the original trace and may have resulted from pressing down of the doublure below the flattened border which occurs in some trilobites such as *Ogygiocaris*. This type, which is generally smaller than Form B, has so far only been found in Arenig strata and occurs in South Wales (Trwyn Llwyd), North Wales (Localities 8, 10 and 11 of Crimes 1969a) and Shropshire (Pontesbury).

Form D. This is characterised by well developed cross-ridges and sometimes lacks the coffee bean appearance, being almost half cylindrical in shape. It has a larger mean width than Form A and a more variable shape factor, which, nevertheless, is normally greater than 1·5 and averages about 2. *Rusophycus* of this form (Pl. 4e, f) have only been found in the Arenig of Shropshire (Pontesbury). Elongate traces of this form, however, appear to be the result of slow forward movement by the trilobite which was digging deeply in the sediment; the length of the trace is, therefore, not exactly the same as that of the trilobite and they are transitional with *Cruziana*.

Thus there appear to be differences in the time ranges of these forms. Form A occurs commonly in the Upper Cambrian and has also been found in the Lower Tremadoc but definitely does not extend up to the Arenig. Forms B-D all occur in the Arenig, B may extend down to the Lower Tremadoc but none of them range down into the Upper Cambrian. Strata with *Rusophycus* Form A alone can therefore be assigned to the Upper Cambrian; Arenig rocks may contain Forms B-D but never A, while the Tremadoc appears to contain a mixed assemblage

PLATE 4

Plate 4

Variations in *Rusophycus*.
All figures *c.* ×0·5.

a-b Form A, Cwm
Graianog, North Wales.

c Form B, Quarry *c.* 1 km
SSW of Pontesbury,
Shropshire.

d Form C, Pared Mawr,
St. Tudwal's Peninsula.

e-f Form D, same locality
as in (c); **e** complete
specimen, **f** part of trace
with very prominent
crossridges.

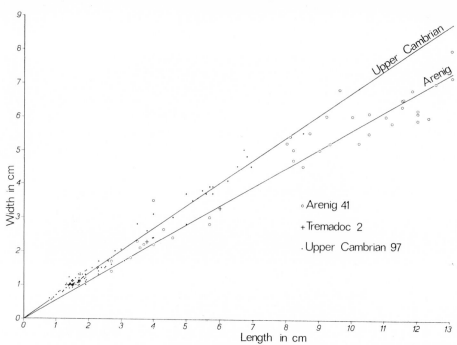

Fig. 5. Graph of length against width for *Rusophycus* from Upper Cambrian, Tremadoc and Arenig strata. Data from all *Rusophycus*-bearing localities mentioned in text and in Crimes (1969a; 1970b).

including Form A and probably also Form B. Following these changes in form there are gradual increases in mean width and mean shape factor in ascending from Upper Cambrian to high Lower Arenig (Fig. 5). Thus, as with *Cruziana, Rusophycus* can be used to distinguish between Upper Cambrian, Tremadoc and Arenig strata in otherwise unfossiliferous sequences.

3c. Other trace fossils

Trilobite walking traces (*Diplichnites*), sideways grazing traces (*Dimorphichnus*) and swimming grazing traces (*Monomorphichnus*) from the Upper Cambrian of Wales (Crimes 1970b) all appear to have been made by trilobites with two or three clawed limbs. A similar claw pattern occurs in traces of these genera from the Lower Cambrian of Pakistan (Seilacher 1955) and Middle Cambrian of Sweden (Martinsson 1965). Neither these genera nor this claw pattern have yet been recorded from Arenig strata thus their occurrence can be used as evidence of a Cambrian rather than Arenig age.

There are also many non-trilobite produced traces which appear to be useful stratigraphically. For example, *Oldhamia radiata* and *O. antiqua* (Andrews) appear to be restricted to Lower and Middle Cambrian strata and occur most commonly in Lower Cambrian turbidite successions (see Crimes and Crossley 1968 p. 190). The producers of these traces are unknown but their restricted time range still allows them to be used stratigraphically. Similarly, *Phycodes circinatum* Mägdefrau is restricted to Ordovician strata (Mägdefrau 1934) and in Wales is particularly common in the Arenig and can be used to distinguish strata of that age from lithologically similar Upper Cambrian strata (Crimes 1969a).

3d. Examples of the stratigraphical use of trace fossils

In some parts of Wales Upper Cambrian (Ffestiniog) and Arenig strata consist of confusingly similar lithologies, and often occur in juxtaposition without any marked unconformity. In some sections the beds lack body fossils and differentiation into Upper Cambrian and Arenig has proved difficult. Fortunately these rocks have abundant trace fossils some of which are known to have restricted time ranges. For example, the Plas-y-Nant beds of Snowdonia were regarded by Williams (1927) as Arenig but by Shackleton (1959) as Upper Cambrian. The discovery of *C. semiplicata* within them, however, allows an Upper Cambrian age to be preferred (Crimes 1969a). Similarly, the Upper Pennant Quartzite at Dolbenmaen, south Caernarvonshire, was considered by Shackleton (1959) to be Upper Cambrian or Arenig but by Roberts (1967) to be Llanvirn. The presence within it of *Phycodes circinatum* precluded an Upper Cambrian age while the common occurrence of this trace fossil locally in the Arenig rocks, but not the Llanvirn, allowed an Arenig age to be preferred.

The way in which ichnofaunas can help in stratigraphically dating successions without index fossils can best be seen by reference to the Cambro-Ordovician strata of Ramsey Island and St. Tudwal's Island East (Fig. 6). During the initial mapping by the Geological Survey (one-inch map sheet 40 and Ramsay 1866) the presence of a significant sub-Arenig break within both these sequences was overlooked, undoubtedly because of the lithological similarities of the successions on either side of the break and the absence of any significant difference in dip. Later work suggested the presence of a break mainly because of a slight change in lithology within the St. Tudwal's succession (Nicholas 1915) and the discovery of an apparent discordance of a few degrees beneath a bed of conglomeratic sandstone on Ramsey Island (see Cox *et al.* 1930).

Trace fossils, in places in abundance, allow stratigraphical dating of both of these sequences and unequivocal recognition of a stratigraphical hiatus within them (Fig. 6). On St. Tudwal's Island East the lower strata (Locality 1) contain typical Cambrian forms of *Diplichnites, Dimorphichnus, Monomorphichnus* and *Rusophycus* Form A. A few metres above the slight lithological change recognised by Nicholas (*op. cit.*), *Cruziana furcifera, C. goldfussi* and *Phycodes circinatum* occur (Locality 2). None of these species are found in the Upper Cambrian but all are common in the Arenig. Thus the lower strata can be referred to the Upper Cambrian and the higher to the Arenig, leaving the Tremadoc absent at the hiatus.

Similarly on Ramsey Island, specimens of *Diplichnites, Dimorphichnus* and *Monomorphichnus,* closely resembling the Upper Cambrian specimens from North Wales, and also *Rusophycus* Form A, occur a few metres below the alleged break (Locality 3). About a metre above, *Phycodes circinatum* appears and is common in the overlying strata. Again the trace fossils indicate an Upper Cambrian age for the lower strata and an Arenig age for the higher beds.

Thus the common presence of trace fossils in precisely those successions which lack body fossils will undoubtedly result in their making a significant contribution to stratigraphy.

4. Trace fossils in palaeoecology

In the past, the habits and modes of life of extinct animals and their relationship to the surroundings, have been deduced almost exclusively from the evidence of body fossils and the enclosing sediments. Body fossils are, however, only produced

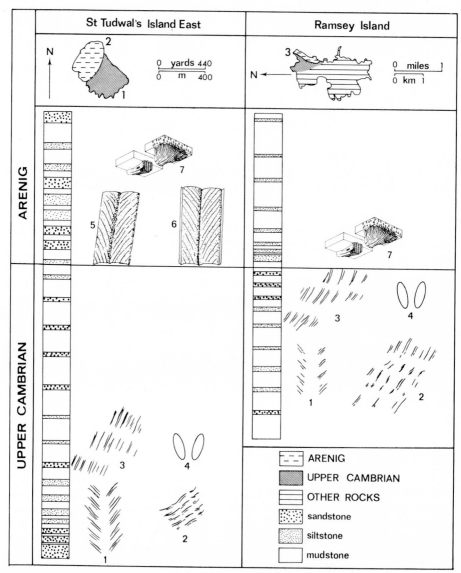

Fig. 6. Contrast in ichnofauna in similar lithologies on either side of the Upper Cambrian—Arenig junction on St. Tudwal's Island East and Ramsey Island. Trace fossils: 1   *Diplichnites*; 2 *Dimorphichnus*;   3   *Monomorphichnus*;   4   *Rusophycus* Form A;   5   *Cruziana furcifera*;   6   *Cruziana goldfussi*;   7   *Phycodes circinatum*.   All except 7 drawn from specimens or pencil rubbings.

on the death of individuals or communities. Trace fossils reflect the life rather than the death of animals and for this reason their study can be more rewarding. They can be used to investigate animals habits in relationship to their environment and also for size-frequency studies on pre-existing live communities. This approach has proved particularly appropriate to the study of trilobites because, being active creatures, they leave abundant traces, many of which have a high preservation potential. Therefore, as an example of the usefulness of trace fossils in palaeoecology, this section will attempt to show how trilobite produced traces can be used to investigate the habits and modes of life of trilobites and changes in behaviour patterns during the course of their life cycles.

There are three common trilobite produced trace fossils which can be used to determine the size (width) of individuals within the pre-existing live population: *Cruziana, Rusophycus* and *Diplichnites*.

Cruziana (Pl. 5a) is produced by the furrowing of the trilobite through the sediment, the V-markings being dug by the endopodites with a movement inwards and behind (Seilacher 1955; Crimes 1970b). The lateral ridges, which occur in many *Cruziana,* result from the dragging of the genal spines in the sediment (Crimes 1968; 1970b). No trace of a V-marking has ever been found by the writer outside the lateral genal spine ridges thus demonstrating that, as with modern arthropods, the trilobites only dug within the limits of the carapace (Crimes 1970b). Thus the distance between lateral genal spine ridges or, if absent, the full width of the trace, should correspond to the maximum width of the live trilobite.

Rusophycus are produced by trilobites digging in the sediment to rest temporarily on the sea floor (Radwański and Roniewicz 1963). Well preserved examples of *Rusophycus* (Pl. 5b, c) sometimes show impressions of the resting trilobite's segments, headshield, appendages, pleura, pleural spines and pygidium (Radwański and Roniewicz 1963 and this volume; Crimes 1970b). From these it is clear that measurement of the maximum width and length of *Rusophycus* corresponds closely to width and length measurements on the exoskeleton of the live trilobite.

Diplichnites (Pl. 5d) is normally interpreted as the track produced by a trilobite walking or striding across the sediment surface (Radwański and Roniewicz 1963; Crimes 1970b). The trace reflects the limbs touching the sediment surface rather than digging in. During movement of this type, the width of the trace will depend on the size of the animal and how far its limbs are extended outside, or contained within, the limits of the body. This depends on the speed of the animal: the faster the movement the more the appendages are likely to be tucked in (see Crimes 1970b). Thus the width of the trace can in this case only be used to give an approximation to the width of the live trilobite.

Two or all of these ichnogenera have been reported from the same or adjacent beds within Lower Palaeozoic sequences in many parts of the world (Fenton and Fenton 1937; Seilacher 1955; Radwański and Roniewicz 1963; Martinsson 1965; Crimes 1970a, b, c). This suggests that, at a given horizon, the same trilobites were probably producing all three traces. Within the Upper Cambrian of North Wales this has been confirmed by intensive collecting at several localities (Crimes 1970b). Specimens have been found in which a *Rusophycus* passes into a *Cruziana* (Pl. 5e). Additionally, specimens intermediate between *Cruziana* and *Diplichnites* (Crimes 1970b pl. 9) and a specimen in which *Diplichnites* emerges from a *Rusophycus* have been found. Thus it is clear that these morphologically distinct traces simply reflect different life activities of the same tribolites. From morphological details revealed by some of the specimens of *Rusophycus* it appears that these Upper Cambrian traces were produced by olenids. Thus there is a record of the types of life activity of olenid trilobites but, more important, these traces allow measurement of the

PLATE 5

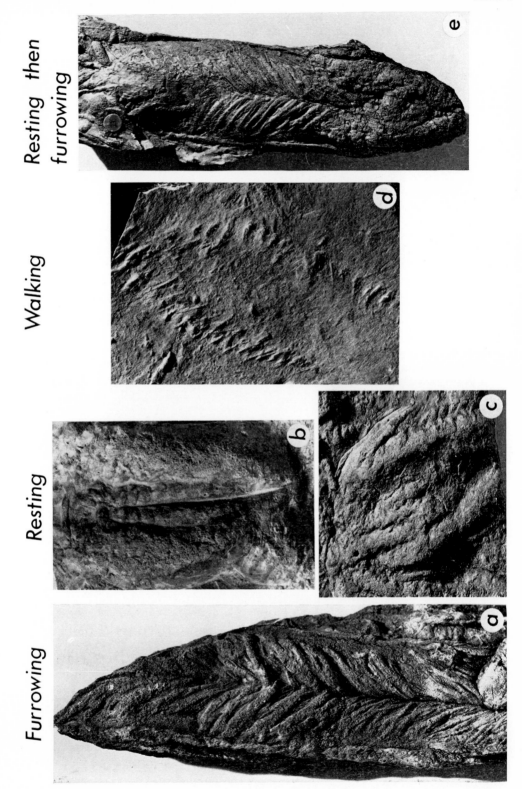

Resting then furrowing

Walking

Resting

Furrowing

120

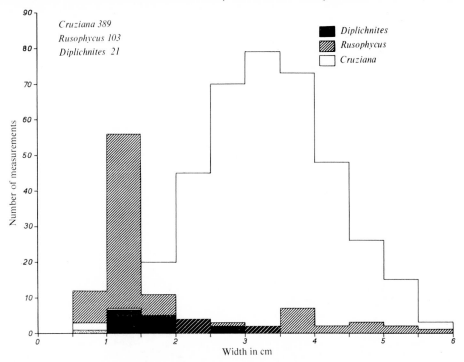

Fig. 7. Size: frequency histograms for *Cruziana, Rusophycus* and *Diplichnites* from the Upper Cambrian of Cwm Graianog, Caernarvonshire, SH 625630.

width of the live trilobites, accurately from *Cruziana* and *Rusophycus* and approximately from *Diplichnites*.

Measurement of the width of specimens of these three ichnogenera taken from a two metre thickness of lithologically similar sediment over a distance of about 100 metres, and therefore probably representing the deposits of a single environmental setting, are summarized as a size-frequency histogram in Figure 7. From this the following conclusions can be made:

(i) None of the traces found were made by trilobites smaller than 0·5 cm in width.
(ii) The size range of the *Cruziana* is the same as that of the *Rusophycus*.
(iii) The mean width of the *Cruziana* is about 2 cm greater than that of the *Rusophycus*.

Plate 5

Trilobite traces probably produced by Olenids and useful for size-frequency studies on the pre-existing live community. For localities see Crimes (1970).

a *Cruziana semiplicata* Salter.
b *Rusophycus* showing trilobite shape and impressions of coxae.
c *Rusophycus* showing trilobite outline and impressions of genal spines and pleurae.
d *Diplichnites.*
e *Cruziana semiplicata* Salter continuous with *Rusophycus.*

J

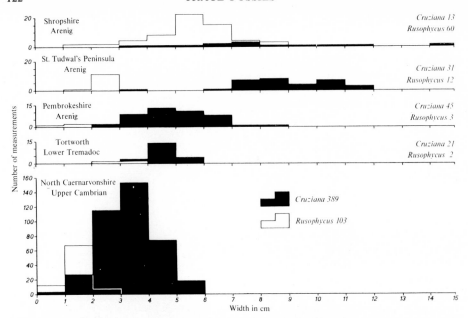

Fig. 8. Size: frequency histograms for *Cruziana* and *Rusophycus*. Localities: Upper Cambrian (Ffestiniog Stage), Cwm Graianog, North Caernarvonshire, SH 625630; Lower Tremadoc (Breadstone Shales), loose blocks in stream along northern boundary of Bushy Grove, Tortworth, Gloucestershire; Arenig, Pembrokeshire (Trwyn Llwyd Quartzites) Trwyn Llwyd; Arenig, St. Tudwal's Peninsula (St. Tudwal's Sandstones), localities 8, 10, 11 of Crimes (1969); Arenig, Shropshire (Stiperstones Quartzite), Quarry *c.* 1 km SSW of Pontesbury.

(iv) The mean width of the *Diplichnites* appears to be intermediate between the other two.

(v) *Cruziana* are more common in this environment than *Rusophycus*.

The absence of any traces less than 0·5 cm in this sample could mean: (a) the trilobites hatched at about this size, (b) smaller trilobites lived benthonically outside this environment, (c) traces made by small trilobites were too delicate to be preserved or (d) small trilobites lived planktonically.

It is known that adult trilobites are from 50 to 300 times larger than newly hatched forms (Whittington 1959). Since the maximum width of these traces is about 5 cm, the mean width of the adults must be less than this and is probably the same as the mean width of the *Cruziana*. Nevertheless, taking the largest width (5 cm) and the smallest factor of size increase (× 50) these trilobites cannot have been wider than 0·1 cm on hatching and probably were considerably less. This population should therefore have included many trilobites less than 0·5 cm wide. The possibility that the young trilobites lived benthonically in deeper water, or under lower energy conditions in shallow water, is also unacceptable because traces of their activity are not found in deeper water sediments and although in sediments of nearby low energy environments the traces tend to be smaller, with *Rusophycus* predominating over *Cruziana,* none of width less than 0·5 cm have been found (Crimes 1970b). The hypothesis that traces of such small trilobites were too delicate to be preserved can also be rejected because at least some of the *Cruziana* and *Rusophycus* produced by such trilobites would be at least one or two millimetres deep and many impressions far more delicate than this are preserved in these sediments. Thus, it appears that while some of the smaller trilobites may have preferred a quiet water environment, the absence of traces that would be produced by trilobites less than 0·5 cm wide can only be satisfactorily explained by assuming that after hatching these trilobites behaved planktonically and rarely if ever touched the bottom.

The difference in mean width of the *Rusophycus, Diplichnites* and *Cruziana* could be ascribed to production of the traces by different species of trilobites or to a change in habits during the life cycles of a single species such that with growth they changed from resting to walking and then furrowing.

The observation that the size range of the *Cruziana* and *Rusophycus* is the same, and similar to that of the *Diplichnites*, militates against their being produced by different species. Also the discovery of specimens showing *Cruziana* continuous with *Rusophycus*, the latter continuous with *Diplichnites* and intermediate forms between *Cruziana* and *Diplichnites* (Crimes 1970b pl. 9) implies that the same trilobites made all three ichnogenera. Furthermore, all the specimens of *Rusophycus* are morphologically similar irrespective of size and all have a shape factor closely approximating to 1·5, thus suggesting that they were most or all produced by trilobites of the same or very similar species (Crimes 1970b).

Further evidence in favour of a change in trilobite habits with growth comes from investigation of trilobite traces at stratigraphically higher horizons. Traces of this type occur in the overlying Tremadoc rocks and also at several horizons within the Arenig. Measurements of mean widths of *Cruziana* and *Rusophycus* at these horizons are shown in Figure 8, with the Upper Cambrian results also included for comparison. The histograms show:

(i) No trilobite traces of width less than 1 cm have been found in post-Upper Cambrian ichnocoenoses.

(ii) There is a general increase in mean width of both *Cruziana* and *Rusophycus* stratigraphically.

For the absence of very small traces to be ascribed to non-preservation, the minimum size of the traces in each population would need to be the same. The minimum size however, increases stratigraphically with increase in mean size of both *Cruziana* and *Rusophycus*.

It is also very unlikely that the trilobite populations from several different stratigraphical levels would consist of small species producing *Rusophycus* and proportionally larger species producing *Cruziana* as in these cases. These facts are, however, consistent with the production of these traces by trilobite populations which included a proportion of smaller and larger forms behaving differently.

Thus, although the traces from the different horizons were not produced by the same trilobite species (see section 2) all these species changed their behaviour pattern during their life cycles and passed from a planktonic stage to one of resting on the sea floor, later sometimes walking and finally furrowing (Fig. 9). The only difference between the Upper Cambrian and the stratigraphically younger trilobites investigated here, appears to be in the absence of walking traces (*Diplichnites*) in the latter cases. The trilobites would probably be more vulnerable to attack during walking; their temporary reduction or abandonment of this habit may be the result of increased competition after the domination of the Upper Cambrian seas by the olenids.

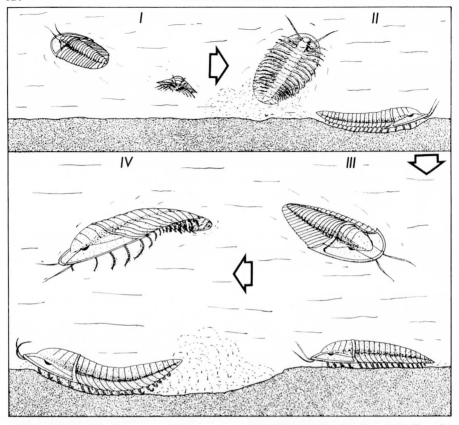

Fig. 9. Main trilobite activities at different stages in the life cycle. I swimming stage; II resting and swimming; III walking and swimming; IV adult furrowing and swimming stage.

This pattern of evolution of behaviour in the course of the life cycle is consistent with what is known of the morphological development of trilobites and other arthropods. During the stages immediately after hatching, their musculature would be weak and probably unable to adequately support the body on the sediment surface. Also, they would be more agile and less susceptible to attack as plankton. With further development of the musculature they would be able to colonise the ocean floor but at first were content to settle and make resting excavations from which they could swim away. During the early stages of development trilobites are known to moult frequently: after moulting when they would be at their most vulnerable they may have been content to rest and enjoy the protection of the resting excavation or indulge in filter feeding. Only after further growth, and presumably the development of stronger musculature, did they take to walking on the sediment surface and finally to furrowing. The occurrence of swimming grazing traces which appear to have been made by trilobites up to the adult size, indicates, however, that they continued to indulge in swimming throughout their life cycle.

It is therefore clear that trace fossils are useful not only in sedimentology and stratigraphy but also in palaeoecology where they can provide information on fossil-animal behaviour and can also provide a means of undertaking population studies on pre-existing live communities.

Acknowledgements. I am grateful to Dr. M. L. K. Curtis for assistance in collecting specimens from Tortworth and for placing his own collection at my disposal; Miss B. Dickinson for drawing my attention to the occurrence of *Cruziana* at Trwyn-Llwyd and for the loan of specimens from that locality; Dr. A. Rushton for locating trace fossils in the collections of the I.G.S., and Dr. J. C. Harper for critically reading this manuscript. I would also like to thank Mr. J. Lynch for redrawing the diagrams, Mr. D. Smart for photographing the specimens and students of the Department of Geology for assistance in collecting the many hundreds of specimens on which this paper is based.

References

BOUMA, A. H. 1964. Ancient and recent turbidites. *Geologie Mijnb.* **43,** 375.

COX, A. H., GREEN, J. F. N., JONES, O. T. and PRINGLE, J. 1930. The St. David's district. *Proc. Geol. Ass.* **41,** 412.

CRIMES, T. P. 1968. *Cruziana:* A stratigraphically useful trace fossil. *Geol. Mag.* **105,** 360.

—— 1969a. Trace fossils from the Cambro-Ordovician rocks of North Wales, U.K. and their stratigraphical significance. *Geol. J.* **6,** 333.

—— 1969b. *The stratigraphy, structure and sedimentology of some of the Precambrian and Cambro-Ordovician rocks bordering the southern Irish sea.* Ph.D. Thesis, Univ. Liverpool.

—— 1970a. A facies analysis of the Cambrian of Wales. *Palaeogeogr. Palaeoclimatol, Palaeoecol.* **7,** 113.

——1970b. Trilobite tracks and other trace fossils from the Upper Cambrian of North Wales. *Geol. J.* **7,** 47.

—— 1970c. A facies analysis of the Arenig of Western Lleyn, North Wales, U.K. *Proc. Geol. Ass.* **81,** 221.

—— and CROSSLEY, J. 1968. The stratigraphy, sedimentology, ichnology and structure of the Lower Palaeozoic rocks of part of northeastern County Wexford. *Proc. R. Ir. Acad.* **67B,** 185.

CURTIS, M. J. K. 1968. The Tremadoc rocks of the Tortworth Inlier, Gloucestershire. *Proc. Geol. Ass.* **79,** 349.

FENTON, C. L. and FENTON, M. A. 1937. Trilobite "nests" and feeding burrows. *Am. Midl. Nat.* **18,** 446.

MÄGDEFRAU, K. 1934. Über *Phycodes circinatum* REINH. RICHTER aus dem thuringischen Ordovicium. *Neues Jb. Miner.* **72,** 259.

MARTINSSON, A. 1965. Aspects of a Middle Cambrian Thanatotope on Oland. *Geol. För. Stockh. Förh.* **87,** 181.

NICHOLAS, T. C. 1915. The Geology of the St. Tudwal's Peninsula. *Q. J. geol. Soc. Lond.* **71,** 83.

RADWAŃSKI, A. and RONIEWICZ, P. 1963. Upper Cambrian trilobite ichnocoenosis from Wielka Wisniokwa (Holy Cross Mountains, Poland). *Acta palaeont. pol.* **8,** 259.

RAMSAY, A. C. 1866. The Geology of North Wales. *Mem. Geol. Surv. U.K.* **3.**

ROBERTS, B. 1967. Succession and structure in the Llwyd Mawr syncline, Caernarvonshire, North Wales. *Geol. J.* **5,** 369.

SEILACHER, A. 1955. Spuren und Fazies im Unterkambrium. In *Beitrage zur Kenntnis des Kambriums in der Salt Range (Pakistan)* by O. H. Schindewolf and A. Seilacher. *Abh. mat. naturw. Kl. Acad. Wiss. Mainz, Jahrg.* 1955, 373.

—— 1960. Lebenspuren als Leitofossilien. *Geol. Rdsch.* **49,** 41.

—— 1963. Kaledonischer Unterbau der Irakiden. *Neues Jb. Geol. Paläont. Mh.* **10,** 527.

—— 1964. Biogenic sedimentary structures. In *Approaches to Paleoecology* (Ed. J. Imbrie and N. D. Newell) Wiley, New York, 296.

—— 1967. Bathymetry of trace fossils. *Mar. Geol.* **5,** 413.

—— and CRIMES, T. P. 1969. "European" species of trilobite burrows in Eastern Newfoundland. *Mem. Am. Ass. Petrol. Geol.* **12,** 145.

—— and MEISCHNER, D. 1964. Fazies-analyse im Palaeozoikum des Oslo-Gebietes. *Geol. Rdsch.* **54,** 596.

SHACKLETON, R. M. 1959. The stratigraphy of the Moel Hebog district. *Lpool Manchr geol. J.* **2,** 216.

Sly, P. G. 1966. *Marine geological studies in the eastern Irish sea and adjacent estuaries, with special reference to sedimentation in Liverpool Bay and River Mersey.* Ph.D. Thesis Univ. Liverpool.

Walker, R. G. 1967. Turbidite sedimentary structures and their relationship to proximal and distal depositional environments. *J. sedim. Petrol.* **37**, 25.

Whittington, H. B. 1959. Ontogeny of trilobites. In *Treatise on Invertebrate Paleontology* (Ed. R. C. Moore) Part O *Arthropoda.* Univ. of Kansas Press, Lawrence and Geol. Soc. Am., New York.

Williams, H. 1927. The geology of Snowdon. *Q. J. geol. Soc. Lond.* **83**, 346.

Wood, A. and Smith, A. J. 1958. The sedimentation and sedimentary history of the Aberystwyth grits (Upper Llandoverian) *Q. J. geol. Soc. Lond.* **114**, 163.

T. P. Crimes, Department of Geology, The University, P.O. Box 147, Liverpool L69 3BX, U.K.

Palaeontological implications of a biological study of rock-boring clams (Family Pholadidae)

J. W. Evans

Biological and ecological studies of Recent rock and shell boring bivalves of the Family Phola-didae have yielded information which can help to identify the borers and aid in deducing something about the ecological conditions under which the animals lived.

The pholadids are important for the following reasons: (i) fossil pholadid beds provide evidence of disconformity wherever present. The older layer must have been solid and exposed to the sea for some time prior to the deposition of the overlying sediment. (ii) the time at which the borers were killed, either by sedimentary burial or uplift of the bed from the intertidal zone, can be established by radio-dating techniques, if shell remnants are present in the burrows. (iii) the state of preservation of the pholadid burrows indicates whether the terminal population was killed suddenly by sedimentation, while still submerged, or by gradual emergence from the intertidal zone, prior to sedimentation. (iv) the hardness of the substrate at the time of boring can be estimated by an examination of the shell and burrow morphology. (v) because of the large number of nestlers which live in empty pholadid burrows, well preserved pholadid beds may yield information about the fossil fauna inhabiting the otherwise poorly preserved rocky intertidal zone.

1. Distribution of fossil and living pholadids

Rock-boring bivalves of the Family Pholadidae are potentially of interest because of the intimate relationship between the pholadid and the rock into which it bores.

The family is globally distributed in rocks of marine origin. Numerous Japanese workers, including Amemeya and Oshima (1933), Uozumi and Fujie (1956), Masuda and Takezawa (1961) and Masuda (1968), have described extensive fossil pholadid beds from Japan. They refer to the sand-filled burrows as "sand-pipes". Evans (1968a) reported the presence of widespread pholadid beds (probably Pleistocene or Recent) in the Coos Bay area of Oregon. Fossil pholadid burrows from California have been described by Bradley (1956), Addicott (1963) and Adegoke (1966; 1967). Von Ihering (1907) reported pholadids from Eocene beds in Patagonia. Raynaud (1969) claimed that they are the most common of the litho-phagous fossils and described a formation in the south of France which contains many rock and shell borers of the genus *Aspidopholas* Fischer.

Modern genera of the Family Pholadidae are also widely distributed. Their principal ecological requirement is the presence of a suitable rocky substrate. Relatively soft limestones, greywacke and even schists are bored, but non-homogenous conglomerates and hard igneous rocks are usually avoided. Turner (1954; 1955) stated that the greatest development of the family is in the eastern Pacific, which has 13 genera including 23 species, while in the western Atlantic there are only 8 genera with 13 species.

Barrows (1917) made the generalization that most borers are open coast, littoral forms. This is not entirely true in the case of pholadids which are found on the open coast and in protected bays, wherever suitable rocky substrate is exposed. Forms like *Zirfaea* which bore softer substrates are most commonly found in estuaries or bays because such substrates rarely survive very long under open coast conditions. Raynaud (1969) reviewed the depth distribution of a number of rock-borers. He observed that littoral forms are best known because of their ease of collection but that exposed rocks in deeper water are also subject to attack by many species. Warme and Marshall (1969) observed *Lithophaga* and *Penitella penita* in the Scripps and La Jolla submarine canyons at depths of greater than 20 fathoms. *Xylophaga* is primarily a wood borer but it occurs at great depths. *X. abyssorum* bores into mud, sand and soft rock and has been dredged in the western Atlantic at depths of 1,342 fathoms (Turner 1955). I have observed *Nattastomella rostrata* boring in boulders, from approximately 40 fathoms, off the Oregon coast. Turner (1955) reported this same species collected from Baja, California in 55 fathoms.

Turner (1954) showed a chart of the probable geological range of the genera of this family. The sources of her information are published in Bivalvia (Vol. 2) in the *Treatise on Invertebrate Paleontology*. Raynaud (1969) also discussed the stratigraphical distribution of the group and claimed that some genera existed at the end of the Palaeozoic but that most appeared at the end of the Mesozoic.

Palaeoecological observations and conclusions about pholadids have been made by a number of authors. Barrows (1917) was one of the first to note that a knowledge of living borers would assist in determining the depositional history of formations in which fossil borers are found. He implied in his discussion that when a rocky coast is being covered by a layer of sediment the normal epifauna either moves away or is destroyed. Only the borers, imprisoned within the rocky substrate, remain as an *in situ* indicator of the community ecology prior to its destruction.

Bradley (1956) used the presence of fossil borers to establish the approximate date of the emergence of a marine terrace at Santa Cruz, California by assuming that these animals were killed at the time when the emergence began, and ascertaining their age from Carbon-14 analysis.

Adegoke (1966) described silicified sand-pipes from the late Miocene of California and drew certain conclusions about (i) the change of burrow shape with age and (ii) the ability of these animals to bore hard siliceous chert. On the basis of studies of living animals, Evans (1967a) contested some of Adegoke's conclusions.

Addicott (1963) reported the presence of fossilized nestling bivalves in burrows that probably were originally formed by *Penitella penita* or *Zirfaea pilsbryi*. Evans (1967b) listed 30 species of nestling organisms found to inhabit vacated *P. penita* burrows on the Oregon coast. Of these 15 have a shell or exoskeleton and thus could be preserved by fossilization. Since this was not an exhaustive collection, the actual list is probably longer. Certainly in other areas different infaunas would occur.

2. Summary of the biology of pholadids

Yonge (1951) considers that pholadids have evolved from deep mud and clay-burrowing bivalves. Their peculiar morphological features are viewed as adaptations which enable the animal to cope with hard substrates. As with other deep-burrowing bivalves, the burrow is merely a habitation. Food is obtained by filter feeding and reproduction is achieved by the shedding of gametes or larvae into the seawater.

When larval pholadids settle they measure less than 0·5 mm in diameter. They immediately penetrate the surface, growing in size as they bore deeper into the rock. This results in a conical burrow, the angle of which depends on the relative rates of penetration and growth in diameter.

The boring is executed mechanically by a rotary motion. This action has been described by Lloyd (1897) and Turner (1954). Under uncrowded conditions the burrow of *Penitella penita* penetrates straight into the substrate at an angle more or less perpendicular to the surface. Under crowded conditions the burrows may twist repeatedly. This is an indication of the animal's remarkable ability to detect and avoid neighbouring burrows. The avoidance reaction occurs when the intervening wall is about 1 mm thick. If *P. penita* is surrounded in such a way that it cannot avoid entering another burrow, it ceases boring entirely.

Penitella penita and all other members of the Subfamily Martesiinae have two distinct forms while in the rock, an actively boring form which metamorphoses into a non-boring form. The large round pedal gape of the active animal is closed at metamorphosis by the "callum", an accessory shell plate on the anterior ventral aspect of each valve. This renders the animal inactive within the burrow. Two types of non-borer are recognized, the "adult" and the "stenomorph". The adult is a full-grown animal that appears to have spontaneously metamorphosed upon reaching a certain size range. This range is determined by the species involved, substrate hardness, burrow entrance size and possibly other unknown factors. For any given circumstance, adult size is fairly predictable. A stenomorph is smaller than normal metamorphosed forms. In one intensively studied population of *P. penita*, where the adult population averaged 25·5 mm in height, I observed that stenomorphs ranged from about 1 mm to 21 mm. In all cases it appeared that crowding was the factor causing stunting or premature metamorphosis.

The anatomy and systematics of the pholadids have been extensively dealt with by Turner (1954; 1955) and Purchon (1955). In a series of recent studies of living *Penitella penita* from the Oregon coast, the author has described a number of morphological variations in features of the valves and burrows which appear to be directly related to the substrate hardness (Evans 1968a, b, c, d). These relationships and the conclusions derived from them can probably be applied to fossil forms.

3. Variations in shell morphology

Three populations of *Penitella penita* were collected from three types of greywacke on the Oregon coast. The rocks were graded as to hardness (Evans 1968a) as 1, 2 and 4 (4 being twice as hard as 2, and 2 being twice as hard as 1). A casual examination of *P. penita* from the three areas showed that there are considerable differences in the form and weight of the valves. Most of the features which will be described in the next paragraphs can be seen in Plates 1 and 2.

As rock hardness increased, the ratio of valve length to valve depth decreased and the weight of a valve of given size increased (Evans 1968b).

The growth bands (a growth band is the layer of shell between two growth interruption lines) of *Penitella penita* are potentially one of the most instructive features of the valves. I have suggested (Evans 1968c) the following sequence of activity in connection with their formation. Each band represents a period of active mechanical boring during which the base of the burrow is enlarged, followed by a quiescent period during which a new growth band is deposited. A growth interval is the time that is taken to complete these two periods.

The duration of the growth interval has been calculated for *Penitella penita*. It was shown that the interval increased as the animal increased in size, the earliest bands being deposited every six days, while in the older animal a period of approximately sixteen days was observed. The width of the growth bands is directly related to the amount of space available within the burrow after the boring period. Since

PLATE 1

Plate 1

Valves of active *Penitella penita* from different substrates. Relative hardness **a** = 4; **b** = 2; **c** = 1. ×2.

PLATE 2

Plate 2

Average sized adult *Penitella penita* from different substrates. Relative hardness **a** = 4; **b** = 2; **c** = 1.   ×1·2.

the duration of the growth period is considerably longer in the older animals it would be expected that growth band width would increase with age. This has been shown to be true of all animals examined (Evans 1968c). The duration of the growth interval of two populations of similar sized animals from rocks of hardness 1 and 2 were compared and found to be similar. However, the growth bands were significantly narrower in the animals from the harder rock. This demonstrated that in a given period of boring less enlargement was possible in the hard than in the soft rock. This pattern of growth is quite unlike that of mud-dwelling clams such as *Mercenaria mercenaria* which grows continuously (Pannella and MacClintock 1968).

The mechanical boring at the base of the burrow is effected by the grinding teeth that are located on the anterior ventral margin of the valve. A new set is secreted with the formation of each new growth band, the teeth being lateral scalloped extensions of the band. The size of the freshly secreted teeth was largest in animals from the hardest rock and the amount of wear increased as rock hardness increased.

The morphological variations listed above appear to be the logical results of the mechanical borer penetrating into progressively harder rock. In all cases it can be seen that unless the tool is made stronger, the wear and tear is greater or the growth is slower. This kind of rationalization cannot be used to explain why adult animals are larger in hard rock than in soft rock (Pl. 2). All features except tooth wear were tested by statistical analysis and proved significantly different (P <0·01). The numerical values of these features are listed in Table 1.

In an effort to discover if the observations made on *Penitella penita* could be generalized to other pholadids, two populations of *Zirfaea crispata* were collected from Port au Port Bay in western Newfoundland. One population was from clay and the other from relatively hard sandstone. All of the variations in features described for the valves of *P. penita*, as related to rock hardness, were repeated in *Z. crispata* (Table 1; Pl. 3).

Table 1. Valve and burrow parameters as related to substrate hardness

Parameter	Penitella penita from Oregon			Zirfaea crispata from Newfoundland	
Substrate Hardness	1	2	4	Clay	Sandstone
Mean ratio: valve length/valve depth of active animal.	2·10	1·75	1·45		
Valve depth of adult	25·5 mm (mean)	32·5 mm (mean)	40·0 mm (mean)	14·3 mm (max)	28·9 mm (max)
Mean weight of an active animal with a valve area of 1,200 mm².	1·66 g	3·95 g	5·07 g	1·14 g	3·80 g
Degree of grinding tooth wear.	little	moderate	great	little	moderate
Mean ratio: height/width of un-truncated conical burrow.	6·5	3·4	2·4	not measured	

PLATE 3

Plate 3

Zirfaea crispata from different substrates: **a** Sandstone (hard);   **b** Clay (soft).   ×4·5

PLATE 4

Plate 4

Plastic moulds of *Penitella penita* burrows from different substrates. Relative hardness, left to right, 1, 2, 4.   ×1.

4. Variations in burrow morphology

The pholadid burrow, unlike that of mud or sand burrowers, is of special interest in that it does not collapse and disappear with the death of the animal. It may be destroyed by erosion but if the rock is covered by sediment it remains as a permanent record of the borer's presence.

Most pholadid burrows are basically conical in shape with a small entrance and a large rounded bottom; in cross section they are circular (Pl. 4). There are, however, a number of species-specific variations in this standard pattern which may be of use to the palaeontologist in his attempt to identify the species responsible for a fossil burrow. Differences of burrow shape with environmental change have also been observed within a given species.

(i) *Species-specific variables.* Most pholadids bore into easily worked sandstone, shale, peat, etc. This includes all members of the Subfamilies Pholadinae and Jouannetiinae and most of the Martesiinae. In some cases, a knowledge of the composition of the substrate will aid in identification of the species involved. For example, the genera *Martesia* and *Xylophaga* are almost entirely restricted to wood, the genus *Lignopholas* also bores into wood but is unique in that it is the only pholadid that is found in fresh and brackish waters (Turner 1955), *Diplothyra smithii* and *Penitella conradi* bore into shells.

Sometimes the usual conical shape of the burrow is distorted. That of adult *Nettastomella rostrata* is atypical because of the bulbous expansion of its base (Pl. 5). Adegoke (1966) identified a number of "spherical" sand-pipes as the burrow of young *Chaceia ovoidea*. However, Evans (1967a) pointed out that these burrows were identical in shape to those of living *Nettastomella rostrata*. In some cases, the upper part of a pholadid's burrow is narrowed by a "chimney" composed of agglutinized particles from the animal's borings (Turner 1955). Raynaud (1969) described calcareous chimneys in the upper part of the burrow formed by *Aspidopholas*. Purchon (1941) claimed that *Xylophaga dorsalis* forms a chimney of faecal pellets. In *Penitella penita* I have noted similar but smaller chimney-like narrowings of the burrow composed of fine sand and clay bound together with mucus.

Typically, the cross section of the burrow is circular. An exception is *Diplothyra smithii* which bores into bivalve shells on the southeast and Gulf coasts of North America. The burrow of the active animal is a broad short cone with a round entrance (Pl. 6). Around the outside of this entrance is a very delicate upright wall of calcium carbonate deposited by the animal. The adult burrow is very distinctive in that the entrance is no longer round but is a broad figure eight shape. Apparently, when the rotary boring movement stops at metamorphosis, one of the siphons enlarges the original entrance thus forming a perfectly shaped hole from which the two fused siphons emerge. The delicate wall is also present around this entrance (Pl. 6). These features would help to distinguish this species from other shell-boring pholadids.

(ii) *Intraspecific variables.* The burrow of *Penitella penita* is basically a simple cone which can be described by the parameters: entrance diameter, maximum diameter and length (from entrance to maximum diameter). With these the angle of the cone can be calculated. In a given substrate, the angles of uncrowded burrows were found to be relatively constant (Evans 1968a). However in different substrates, the angle increased as rock hardness increased ($P > 0.01$) (Pl. 4). Masuda (1968) provides sufficient information to test the difference in burrow shape between location A: Minami—Akaishi and location B: Kita-Akaishi. The burrows from location A have a smaller angle than those from location B ($P > 0.05$) suggesting that at the time of boring the latter substrate was harder than the former.

PLATE 5

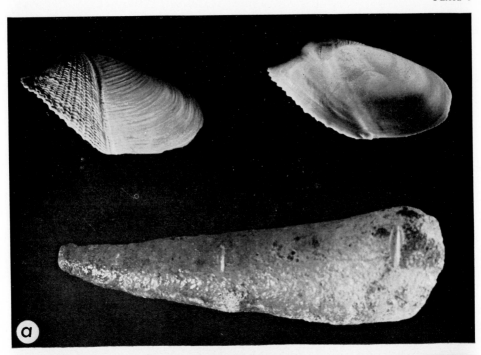

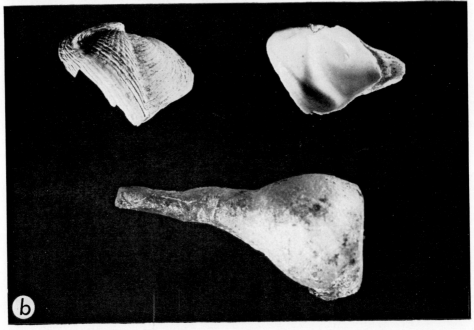

Plate 5

Burrow moulds of: **a** *Penitella penita*; **b** *Nettastomella rostrata*. Note atypical bulbous expansion of base of burrow of *N. rostrata*. ×2.3.

PLATE 6

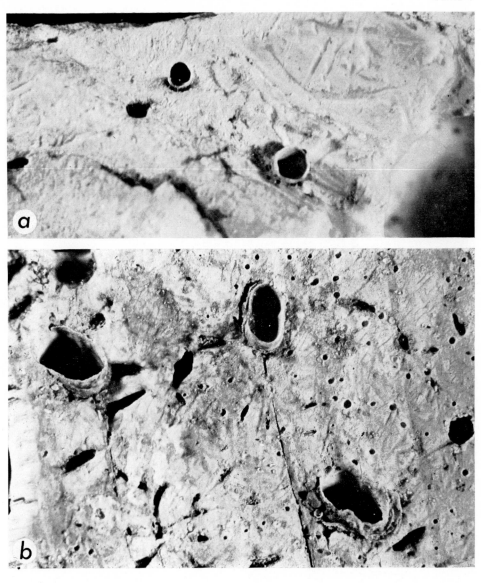

Plate 6

Entrances to the burrows of: **a** active and **b** adult *Diplothyra smithii* boring into *Mercenaria mercenaria* shells. Note the delicate calcareous wall secreted by the clam. ×8.

PLATE 7

Plate 7

Rock crowded with *Penitella penita* showing A stenomorph forced to stop boring due to crowding; E burrow of adult, twisted to avoid neighbouring burrows, this burrow has not been truncated by erosion; C adults in burrows truncated by erosion, this indicates that they are several years older than burrow B.

138

Other variations may occur within a given substrate (Evans 1968a), (Pl. 7). Crowding caused otherwise straight burrows to twist and elongate for short distances without increasing in diameter, thus reducing the normal burrow angle. Erosion of the surface rock caused shortening of the burrows and concomitant enlarging of their entrances.

The condition of the fossil pholadid bed gives some indication of the sequence of events between the death of the last population of borers and sedimentation. The Oregon beds described by Evans (1968a) which were bored into soft sandstone, showed little sign of erosional truncation. It is probable that this bed was buried by sand while still in the intertidal zone. Beds that are found to be extensively truncated were probably killed by emergence and suffered a considerable period of erosion in the upper intertidal zone prior to sedimentation.

5. Discussion

The rocky coast community is the most varied and interesting in the marine environment. It is, however, one of the most poorly preserved in the fossil record. During the process of deposition, prior to fossilization, the community living on or attached to the rocky shore is probably driven off or destroyed. The only *in situ* remnants are the borers and the nestlers inhabiting their burrows. The Pholadidae are probably the most widespread and obvious of the borers both in recent and fossil conditions. Knowledge of living pholadids should be of considerable help in identifying the fossil species. Even in the absence of the valves, details of the burrow morphology, substrate bored, and distribution could aid in identifying the borer.

The close relationship between substrate hardness and morphology of the valve and burrow, makes it possible to estimate the hardness of the substrate at the time of boring. The cherty mudstone described by Adegoke (1966) was probably much softer in the Miocene when the boring took place. The presence of beds of fossil pholadids can be used to indicate the presence of a disconformity. The older substrate must have been solid and located in the marine intertidal or subtidal zone when the boring took place. Furthermore, the age and sequence of sedimentary and isostatic changes can, under the right conditions, be interpreted from pholadid beds.

Acknowledgements. This paper is Studies in Biology from the Memorial University of Newfoundland No. 180; contribution No. 48 from the Marine Sciences Research Laboratory.

References

ADDICOTT, W. O. 1963. An unusual occurrence of *Tresus nuttalli* (Conrad 1837) (Mollusca: Pelecypoda). *Veliger* **5**, 143.

ADEGOKE, O. S. 1966. Silicified sand-pipes belonging to *Chaceia*(?) (Pholadidae: Martesiinae) from the late Miocene of California. *Veliger* **9**, 233.

—— 1967. New and oldest records of Pelecypod *Mya* from west North America, south of Alaska. *Nautilus* **80**, 91.

AMEMEYA, I. and OSHIMA, Y. 1933. Note on the habitat of rock-boring molluscs on the coast of central Japan. *Proc. Imp. Acad. (Japan)* **9**, 120.

BARROWS, A. L. 1917. Geological significance of fossil rock-boring animals. *Bull. geol. Soc. Am.* **28**, 965.

BRADLEY, W. C. 1956. Carbon-14 date for a marine terrace at Santa Cruz, California. *Bull. geol. Soc. Am.* **67**, 675.

Evans, J. W. 1967a. A re-interpretation of the sand-pipes described by Adegoke. *Veliger* **10**, 174.
—— 1967b. Relationship between *Penitella penita* (Conrad, 1837) and other organisms of the rocky shore. *Veliger* **10**, 148.
—— 1968a. The effect of rock hardness and other factors on the shape of the burrow of the rock-boring clam, *Penitella penita*. *Palaeogeogr. Palaeoclimatol. Palaeoecol.* **4**, 271.
—— 1968b. Factors modifying the morphology of the rock-boring clam, *Penitella penita* (Conrad, 1837). *Proc. malac. soc. Lond.* **38**, 111.
—— 1968c. Growth rate of the rock-boring clam *Penitella penita* (Conrad. 1837) in relation to hardness of rock and other factors. *Ecology* **49**, 619.
—— 1968d. The role of *Penitella penita* (Conrad, 1837) (Family Pholadidae) as eroders along the Pacific coast of North America. *Ecology* **49**, 156.
Lloyd, F. E. 1897. On the mechanisms in certain lamellibranch boring molluscs. *Trans. Acad. N.Y. Sci.* **16**, 307.
Masuda, K. 1968. Sand-pipes penetrating igneous rocks in the environs of Sendai. Japan. *Trans. Proc. palaeont. Soc. Japan*, N.S., No. 72, 351.
—— and Takezawa, R. 1961. On an interesting sand-pipe from the environs of Sendai, Myagi Prefecture, Northeast Honshu, Japan. *Rese. Bull. Saito Ho-on Kai Muse.* No. 30, 39.
Pannella, G. and MacClintock, C. 1968. Biological and environmental rhythms reflected in molluscan shell growth. *J. Paleont. Paleont. Soc. Memoir* **2**, 64.
Purchon, R. D. 1941. On the biology and relationships of *Xylophaga dorsalis,* (Turton) *J. mar. biol. Ass. U.K.* (NS) **25**, 1.
—— 1955. The structure and function of the British Pholadidae (Rock boring Lamellibranchia). *Proc. zool. Soc. Lond.* **124**, 859.
Raynaud, J. F. 1969. Lamellibranchs lithophages application a l'étude d'un conglómerat a cailloux perforés du Miocène du Midi de la France. *Trav. Lab. Palaeont. Orsay.*
Turner, R. D. 1954. The Family Pholadidae in the western Atlantic and in the eastern Pacific Part I—Pholadinae. *Johnsonia* 3 (33), 1
—— 1955. The Family Pholadidae in the western Atlantic and the eastern Pacific. II Martesiinae, Jouannetiinae and Xylophaginae. *Johnsonia* 3 (34), 65.
Uozumi, S. and Fujie, T. 1956. The sand-pipe created by the Pelecypod: *Platyodon nipponica* n. sp. and *Pholadidea* (*Penitella*). Kamakurensis (Yokoyama) *Fac. Sci., Hokkaidô Univ.,* Ser. IV, **9**, 351.
von Ihering, H. 1907. Les mollusques fossils. *An. Mus. nac. Hist. Nat. B. Aires* (3) 7,1.
Warme, J. E. and Marshall, N. F. 1969. Burrowing marine invertebrates in calcareous terrigenous rocks of the Pacific coast. *Am. Zoologist.* **9**, 765.
Yonge, C. M. 1951. Structure and adaptations for rock boring in *Platyodon cancellatus* (Conrad). *Univ. Calif. Publs. Zool.* **55** (7), 401.

J. W. Evans, Department of Biology, Memorial University of Newfoundland, St. John's, Newfoundland, Canada.

Comparison of Upper Cretaceous ichnofaunas from siliceous sandstones and chalk, Western Interior Region, U.S.A.

R. W. Frey and J. D. Howard

Trace fossils are abundant in the Lower Coniacian of west-central Kansas (Fort Hays Limestone Member, Niobrara Chalk) and in the Lower Campanian of east-central Utah (Blackhawk Formation and Panther Sandstone Tongue, Star Point Formation). Utah trace fossils are found in terrigenous detrital sands representing nearshore, shallow water deposition, whereas Kansas forms are found in finely crystalline, allochemical carbonates representing offshore, deeper water deposition. The presence of several congeneric burrows in both lithotopes thus obscures the facies significance of the ichnoassemblages.

Sedimentological and ichnological analyses suggest that the distribution of many of the trace-making animals was affected chiefly by factors such as substrate stability, type of food supply, and current strength, and that, in terms of these factors, the two depositional regimens were not especially different. Animals adapted to such conditions thus appeared in both places, leaving notably similar lebensspuren in conspicuously different sediments. Organisms less broadly adapted were restricted either to Utah or to Kansas, although the lebensspuren of few of these animals are judged to be widespread environmental indicators in the Upper Cretaceous of the Western Interior (knobby textured *Ophiomorpha* and tabular *Zoophycos* excepted).

1. Introduction

Trace fossils are being studied increasingly as possible facies indicators in the rock record. Seilacher (1958) used these criteria with considerable success in delimiting flysch and molasse deposits, and Farrow (1966) and Howard (1966a; 1969) have correlated local trace fossil distributions with particular depositional conditions. Similar relationships have also been demonstrated among extant trace-making organisms along the western Atlantic coast (Frey and Howard 1969; Frey 1970a). On the basis of such studies, the general conclusion has been that numerous lebensspuren are good facies indicators.

However, investigations such as that by Henbest (1960) have revealed the presence of supposedly deep water trace fossils in a shallow water environment, and Hattin and Frey (1969) have suggested that other forms may be facies-crossing types. In addition, Frey (1970b) described recently an ichnofauna from offshore micrites that resembles in many respects the ichnofauna described by Howard (1966a) from nearshore siliceous sands; this overlap in trace fossil distributions is even more pronounced when one considers that the assemblage from the nearshore clastics exhibits within itself strong facies control on a local scale. The overall facies significance of such assemblages thus requires additional analysis, which forms the basis for this report.

The assemblage described by Howard (1966a; 1969) was studied among Lower Campanian rocks in east-central Utah and that by Frey (1970b) among Lower Coniacian rocks in west-central Kansas. These strata and their respective ichnofaunas are discussed at greater length below. Additional information on the Lower Coniacian of Kansas may be obtained from publications by Loetterle (1937),

141

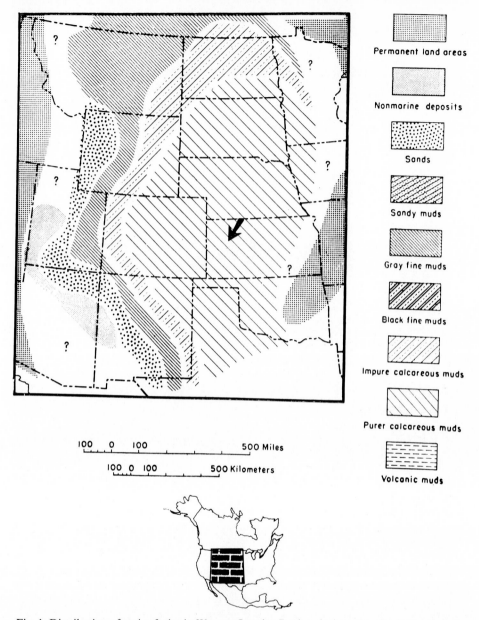

Fig. 1. Distribution of major facies in Western Interior Region during early Coniacian deposition. Study area in Kansas indicated by arrow. (From Reeside 1957 fig. 14, by permission of the Geological Society of America.)

Runnels and Dubins (1949), Cobban and Reeside (1952), Reeside (1957), Merriam (1957; 1963), Hattin (1964; 1965), Kauffman (1967), Frey (1970 b), and Kauffman and Hattin (in preparation). Similar information on Lower Campanian rocks in Utah is contained in papers by Spieker (1931; 1946; 1949), Cobban and Reeside (1952), Young (1955; 1957), Weimer (1960), Sabins (1962), Howard (1966a, b; 1969), and Maberry (1968).

2. Early Coniacian deposition in west-central Kansas

2a. Stratigraphic setting

Coniacian strata are represented in Kansas by the Niobrara Chalk, which consists of two parts: the Fort Hays Limestone Member, overlain conformably by the Smoky Hill Chalk Member. The Fort Hays ranges in thickness from about 15 to 25 m and the Smoky Hill from about 125 to more than 200 m. Only the lower 4m or so of the Smoky Hill have been studied closely ichnologically, but other investigations (e.g., Hattin 1965) indicate that sedimentary structures—both inorganic and biogenic—are considerably less diverse and abundant here than in the Fort Hays.

Niobrara sediments comprise part of a large-scale cyclothem found throughout the Western Interior Region. The Fort Hays represents maximum transgression, although the waters were deeper during parts of Smoky Hill deposition. The shoreline was far removed from west-central Kansas during Fort Hays deposition (Fig. 1), and very little terrigenous detritus reached this area. Sediments thus consisted predominantly of relatively pure carbonate muds, which graded laterally into coarser clastics nearer the western shore.

2b. Sedimentology

Lower Coniacian (Fort Hays) strata in west-central Kansas consist mainly of thick to very thick beds of yellowish gray to grayish orange chalky limestone, separated by very thin to thin beds of light gray chalky shale. These strata are remarkably uniform both laterally and vertically in the section, attesting to a stable, geographically widespread depositional regimen. The basal bed in this sequence contains considerable terrigenous detritus reworked from the disconformably underlying Carlile Shale.

Chalky limestones comprise more than 90 per cent of the total volume of Fort Hays rock. They constitute a soft, porous, somewhat friable, low-density micrite, made up predominantly (about 85 per cent) of cryptocrystalline to microcrystalline grains of calcium carbonate, including coccolith debris and whole and fragmentary planktonic foraminiferal tests; other constituents consist mostly of whole and fragmentary bivalve shells (about 11 per cent), authigenic iron compounds, and miscellaneous grains. The chalky shales, which are commonly thinly laminated, consist chiefly of clay and other very fine grained argillaceous detritus, containing subordinate quantities of chalk. Microfossils are considerably less abundant than in chalky limestones but the abundance of macro-skeletal remains and orthochemical minerals are generally similar. Insoluble residues among chalky limestones are typically 2 to 11 per cent whereas among chalky shales they are 60 to 70 per cent.

The chalky limestones are extensively burrow mottled (Pl. 1a) and reflect sediment reworking by different generations of burrowing organisms. Small-scale stratification features have thus been obscured or obliterated in most places, although distinct burrow structures referable to several ichnogenera are observed commonly. Thin to very thin scour zones that truncate burrows are present at numerous stratigraphic levels, and small channel structures are found locally. Bioturbation is considerably less intense, and current-influenced inorganic sedimentary structures less abundant, in the thin beds of chalky shale; primary stratification is thus generally well preserved, although obscured in places by bedding compaction. Only two distinct burrow types are found consistently in this lithotype: *Planolites* and pyrite and limonite filled burrows.

These sediments reflect essentially continuous but very slow, offshore, carbonate

PLATE 1

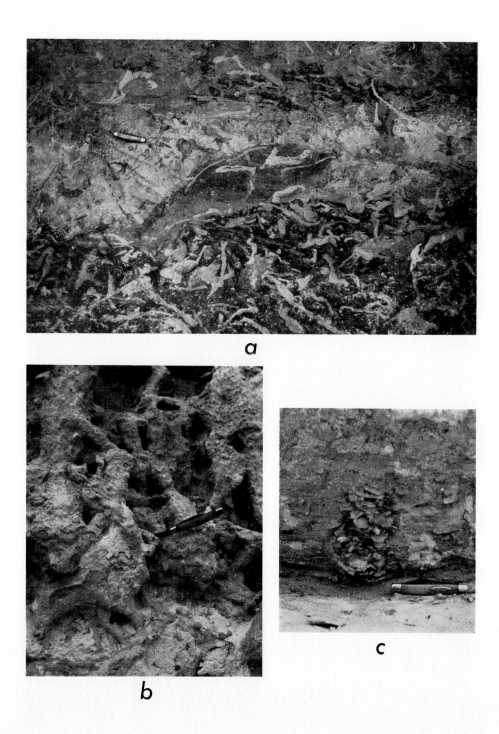

a

b

c

bank deposition; the relatively pure chalky sediments (now chalky limestone) were diluted periodically by brief influxes of very fine grained terrigenous detritus (now chalky shale). At the beginning of Coniacian deposition the water was relatively shallow (below wave base but within the inner or middle part of the *Cruziana* facies), and it deepened gradually but perceptibly with successive intervals of time (to the outer part of the *Cruziana* facies or the inner part of the *Zoophycos* facies). Biogenic and current-type inorganic structures became progressively less abundant and diverse during later episodes of deposition, evidently correlative in part with this increase in water depth and a corresponding decrease in current energy and sediment aeration.

2c. Ichnology

Trace fossils are diverse and abundant, although generally poorly preserved, in the Lower Coniacian of west-central Kansas. Distinctive ichnogenera include *Asterosoma* (two or three forms), *Chondrites, Laevicyclus, Planolites, Teichichnus, Thalassinoides* (two forms), *Trichichnus, Zoophycos,* and possibly *Arthrophycus*. Burrow structures not given formal designations include Scaphopod-Shaped Tubes, Mechanically Filled Burrows, Cylindrical Shafts, Secondary Feeding Burrows that course along primary burrows, and various calcite-, limonite-, and pyrite-filled tubular burrows. Tracks, trails, and other surficial traces were not observed. This ichnofauna is described briefly in Section 6a and is illustrated in Figures 2 and 3 and in Plate 1. Small borings in bivalve shells, attributable to acrothoracican barnacles and clionid sponges, have been omitted from this discussion because the structures are independent of the substrates.

The ichnofauna reflects a large, mixed assemblage of deposit- and suspension-feeding organisms. Diversity and abundance within this assemblage far exceeds that within the contemporaneous epibenthic assemblage (composed essentially of inoceramids and pycnodonteinid oysters), suggesting that environmental conditions were more favourable to mobile endobenthos than to sessile epibenthos, probably because of water turbidity and soft, watery substrates. The structure of the ichnoassemblage changed gradually with successive intervals of time (Fig. 4), correlative in part with slowly changing environmental conditions.

Ichnological evidence (supported by stratigraphical, sedimentological, and palaeontological evidence) indicates that (i) except for brief influxes of terrigenous detritus, the nearly pure carbonate muds of the early Coniacian accumulated very slowly, (ii) the organic-rich substrate was soft and yielding to considerable depth, and remained so until late in diagenesis, (iii) both the sediments and the overlying water were relatively well aerated, (iv) currents capable of substrate scour and shell-fragment transport were common, especially during earlier episodes of deposition,

---

Plate 1

Biogenic sedimentary structures from the Lower Coniacian of West-Central Kansas (Fort Hays Limestone Member, Niobrara Chalk). (Handles of knife used for scale in these illustrations are 6·6 cm long.)

a Bioturbate textures in chalky limestone. Teichichnian "ghost" near centre of photograph. Oblique surface; upper part inclined gently away from viewer.

b *Thalassinoides* cf. *paradoxica* (Woodward) Oblique surface; upper part of exposure inclined toward viewer.

c Mechanically Filled Burrow. Structure contains shell fragments from the bivalve *Inoceramus*. Vertical exposure.

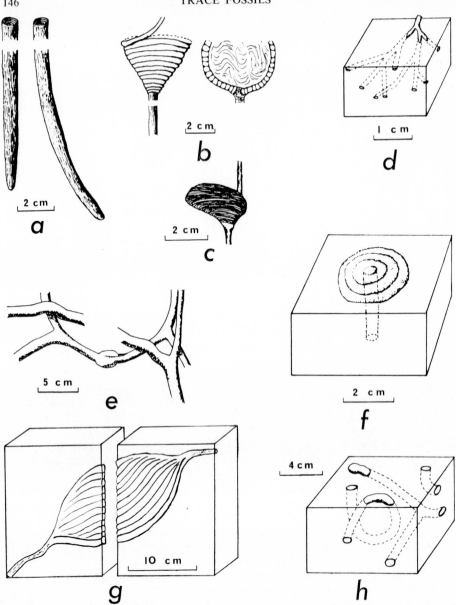

Fig. 2. Trace fossils from the Lower Coniacian of west-central Kansas (Fort Hays Limestone Member, Niobrara Chalk).   a   *Asterosoma* Form Cylindrichnus;   b, c   *Asterosoma* Form Helicoid Funnel;   d   *Chondrites* sp.;   e   *Thalassinoides* sp.;   f   *Laevicyclus* sp.;   g   *Teichichnus* sp.;   h   *Planolites* sp.

and (v) the sediments accumulated initially in relatively shallow water, which deepened gradually with successive intervals of time. Dearth of trace fossils and current-influenced inorganic structures in conformably overlying Coniacian rocks (Fig. 4) reflects the inception of a different depositional regimen, including in-creased deposition of terrigenous detritus, increased water depth, decreased current agitation, and decreased aeration of sediments.

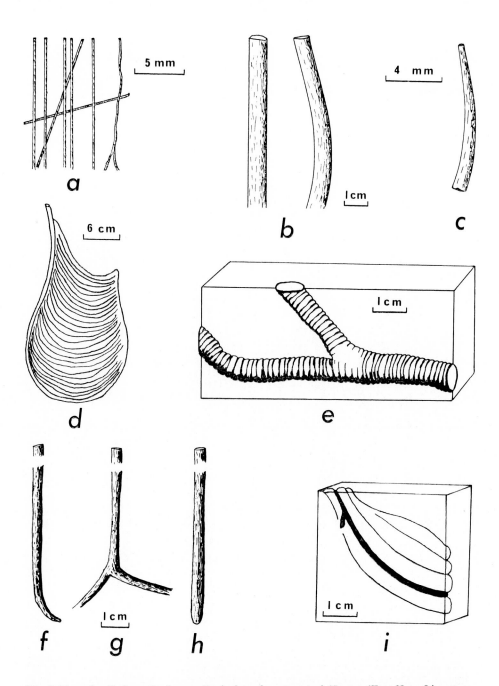

Fig. 3. Trace fossils from the Lower Coniacian of west-central Kansas (Fort Hays Limestone Member, Niobrara Chalk).   a   *Trichichnus* sp.;   b   Cylindrical Shafts;   c   Scaphopod-Shaped Tube;   d   *Zoophycos* sp.;   e   *Arthrophycus(?)* sp.;   f-h   Mineral-Filled Tubular Burrows;   i   Mineral-Filled Secondary Burrow coursing along Primary Burrow (teichichnian).

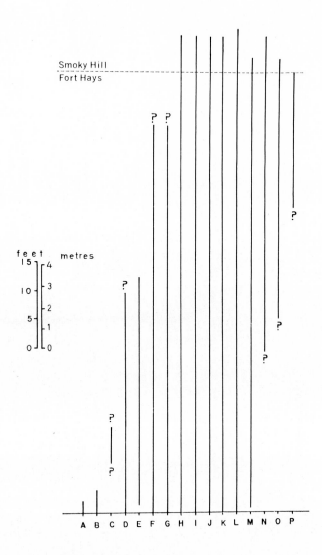

Fig. 4. Stratigraphic ranges of trace fossils from the Lower Coniacian of west-central Kansas.
Although several forms range through the Fort Hays Member into the overlying Smoky Hill
Member, their ranges terminate abruptly a few feet above the contact between members; this is
evidently due in part to decreased aeration of sediments.   A   *Arthrophycus*(*?*) sp. burrows;
B   Scaphopod-Shaped Tubes;   C   Mechanically Filled Burrows;   D   *Thalassinoides* cf.
paradoxica;   E   *Laevicyclus* sp.;   F   *Asterosoma* Form Cylindrichnus   G   Cylindrical
Shafts;   H   *Asterosoma* Form Helicoid Funnel (type in Fig. 2);   I   *Chondrites* sp.;
J   *Planolites* sp.;   K   *Trichichnus* sp.;   L   Mineral-Filled Burrows;   M   *Teichichnus*
sp.;   N   *Zoophycos* sp.;   O   *Thalassinoides* sp.;   P   *Asterosoma* Form Helicoid Funnel
(type in Fig. 2b).

3. Early Campanian deposition in east-central Utah

3a. Stratigraphic setting

Lower Campanian strata examined in the Book Cliffs and Wasatch Plateau areas of Utah are comprised by the Blackhawk Formation and the Panther Sandstone Tongue of the Star Point Formation. Both units were deposited as near-shore facies (Fig. 5) of the major cyclothem mentioned previously. Overall, the sea had begun its retreat from the Western Interior Region by early Campanian times, but smaller scale transgressive-regressive pulses remained prominent in east-central Utah (e.g. Weimer 1960 fig. 3); these imparted additional cyclicity to the depositional regime.

The Panther Sandstone Tongue is interpreted as part of a deltaic sequence, and the Blackhawk Formation evidently represents part of a barrier island-lagoonal complex. In spite of their different origins, however, they exhibit very similar ichnofaunas and general physical characteristics, including three distinct facies of terrigenous detrital silts and sands.

3b. Sedimentology

Most Lower Campanian sediments in east-central Utah may be grouped within three broad lithotypes (Fig. 6), which are repeated cyclically in the stratigraphic section. In ascending order, these include: (i) a basal gray, thin bedded, burrow mottled, clayey, quartzose siltstone, (ii) horizontal to gently inclined, laminated to cross-laminated beds of buff, poorly sorted, very fine grained, clayey, quartzose sandstone, and (iii) large- and small-scale cross beds of buff, very fine to medium-grained, locally calcitic, quartzose sandstone, alternating in places with thin beds of poorly sorted, organic-rich, shaly siltstone.

The gray siltstone (Fig. 6a) is so profusely burrow mottled that very little original stratification is preserved and distinctive burrow structures are uncommon. Mottling consists of abundant, irregular, discontinuous blebs and isolated small pockets of primary siltstone, intermixed with dense, interpenetrating sediment castings and strings of faecal pellets. The clays remain rich in particulate organic matter. Stratigraphic position and the inorganic and biogenic sedimentary structures reflect offshore, quiet-water deposition (middle part of the *Cruziana* facies).

Sands of the second lithotype (Fig. 6b) contain numerous, well defined burrows and distinct burrow mottles. Primary stratification is only locally obscured or obliterated by biogenic structures. These sediments and structures indicate nearshore (sublittoral) deposition in relatively more turbulent water (inner part of the *Cruziana* facies).

The sands of the third lithotype (Fig. 6c) are relatively cleaner and better sorted than sediments of the two underlying types. They contain abundant ripple marks of various sizes and locally a diverse suite of sole marks. These sediments contain many distinctive trace fossils but relatively little indistinct burrow mottling. The sediments were deposited near shore (littoral and shallow sublittoral) in moderately turbulent waters (essentially the *Skolithos* facies).

3c. Ichnology

Trace fossils from Lower Campanian rocks in east-central Utah are abundant and diverse, and they are generally much better preserved than in the Lower Coniacian of Kansas. Distinctive ichnogenera include *Arenicolites, Arthrophycus, Asterosoma* (three forms), *Chondrites, Ophiomorpha* (two forms), *Planolites, Scolicia, Teichichnus,* and *Thalassinoides*. Informally named traces include Chevron Trails, Large Tubes, Plug-Shaped Burrows, Plural Curving Tubes,

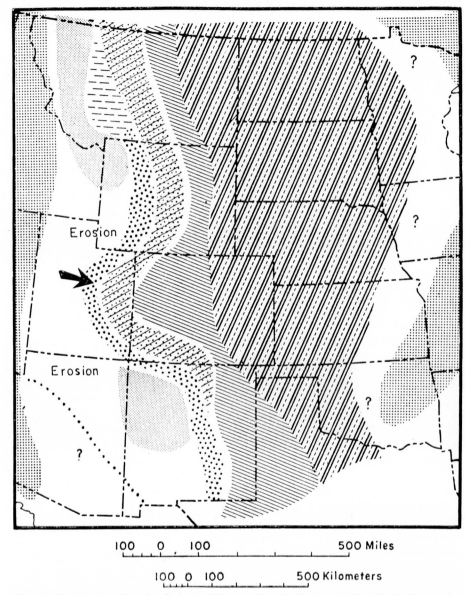

Fig. 5. Distribution of major facies in Western Interior Region during Early Campanian deposition. Study area in Utah indicated by arrow. See Fig. 1 for key to sediment types. (From Reeside 1957 fig. 17, by permission of the Geological Society of America.)

Ruhespuren, and "Snail Trails", The assemblage is illustrated in Figures 7 and 8 and is described briefly in Section 6b.

The "labyrinth castings" reported by Howard (1966a) represent *Teredo*-like borings in ancient wood are thus independent of detrital substrates. An ecological equivalent in Lower Coniacian strata of Kansas are the pholadid borings in wood (Miller 1968).

The distribution and abundance of these trace fossils is strikingly correlative with distinct lithotypes (Table 1), which are related in turn to a progressive change

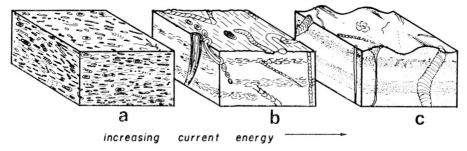

increasing   current   energy ————————➤

Fig. 6. General facies present in Lower Campanian rocks of east-central Utah (Blackhawk Formation and Panther Sandstone Tongue, Star Point Formation);   a   highly burrow-mottled grey siltstones containing very few distinctive trace fossils, representing offshore deposition;   b   very fine-grained sandstones containing larger but less abundant burrow mottles and many distinctive trace fossils, representing nearshore deposition;   c   fine to medium grained sandstones containing little burrow mottling but numerous distinctive trace fossils, representing nearshore and shore deposition.

from offshore, low energy conditions to nearshore, high energy conditions in the depositional environment.

The basal siltstone (Fig. 6a) represents a quiet-water environment dominated by deposit-feeding organisms, which thoroughly reworked the organic-rich sediments. These small, mobile animals evidently moved back and forth through the substrate several times, pillaging the sediment mostly in a horizontal direction, but generally left little evidence of their own morphology or identity. Their activity probably kept pace with the rate of sedimentation.

Coarser sediments overlying the siltstone (Fig. 6b) were deposited in slightly more turbulent waters and supported a mixed assemblage of deposit- and suspension-feeding animals, which were generally somewhat larger in size. Bioturbation by mobile animals was restricted to particular layers of sediment that were rich in organic detritus. Suspension-feeders, which dominated the assemblage, burrowed more deeply but caused relatively less destruction of primary stratification. Crawling and resting animals also left traces at the sediment-water interface in these (and the overlying) sands.

Above these sediments are still coarser sands (Fig. 6c) that were inhabited mostly by suspension-feeding organisms. Many of these animals constructed strong, deep burrows, partly in an effort to combat loose sediments that were shifted about frequently by strong currents in shallow water. Very little bioturbation was produced so that inorganic and biogenic sedimentary structures were well preserved.

These distributions parallel the models proposed by Sanders (1958), Purdy (1964), Seilacher (1964 p. 307; 1967 p. 421), and Rhoads (1967 p. 475). Shallow, horizontal burrows of deposit-feeding animals tend to dominate in quiet water deposits, where large quantities of organic matter settle from suspension, and deep, vertical burrows of suspension-feeding animals tend to dominate in turbulent water deposits, where organic matter is held in suspension. The distributions are related indirectly to bathymetry in that wave and current energy generally decrease with increasing depth of water, and they may be modified locally by other environmental conditions such as especially unstable substrates.

4. Comparison of the trace fossil assemblages

As indicated above, most of the distinctive trace fossils from Utah are found in siliceous, very fine to medium grained, terrigenous detrital sands (Fig. 6 b, c) that

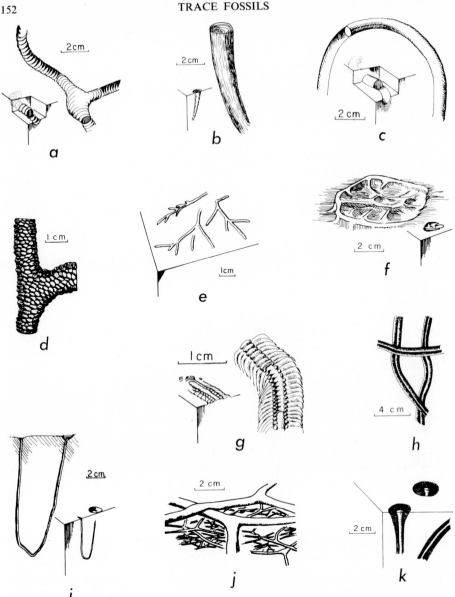

Fig. 7. Trace fossils from the Lower Campanian of east-central Utah (Blackhawk Formation and Panther Sandstone Tongue, Star Point Formation); a *Arthrophycus* sp.; b *Asterosoma* Form Cylindrichnus; c *Planolites* sp.; d *Ophiomorpha* sp. A; e *Chondrites* sp.; f "Rühespuren"; g *Scolicia* sp.; h "Snail Trails"; i *Arenicolites* sp.; j *Thalassinoides* sp.; k *Asterosoma* Form Rod-Shaped Burrows.

represent nearshore, shallow water deposition. Those from Kansas are found in crypto- to micro-grained allochemical carbonate sediments that reflect far offshore, generally deeper water deposition. Considering the possible influence of bathymetry and substrate texture and composition on the distribution of benthonic organisms, as well as the strict facies segregation of trace fossils in Utah (Table 1), a

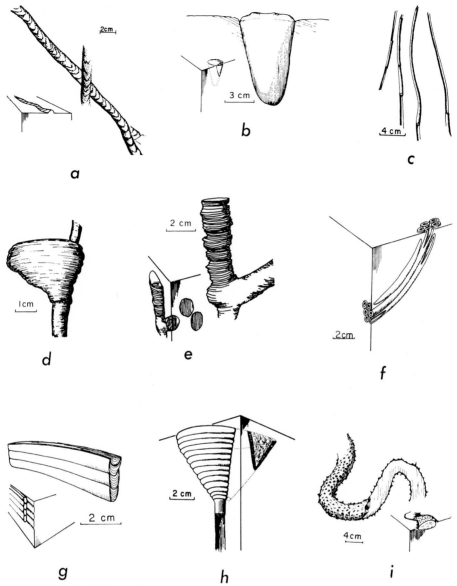

Fig. 8. Trace fossils from the Lower Campanian of east-central Utah (Blackhawk Formation and Panther Sandstone Tongue, Star Point Formation).   a Chevron Trails;   b Plug-Shaped Burrows;   c *Asterosoma* Form Rod-Shaped Burrows;   d, h *Asterosoma* Form Helicoid Funnel;   e Large Tubes;   f Plural Curving Tubes;   g *Teichichnus* sp.; i *Ophiomorpha* sp. B.

surprisingly large number of ichnogenera or morphological forms appears in both depositional environments (Table 2). The overall regional environmental significance of such trace fossils thus requires additional evaluation.

4a. Comparison at the generic level

The presence of certain ichnogenera in both Utah and Kansas rocks was anticipated. *Chondrites* and *Planolites* are well known facies-crossing forms, for example;

Table 1. Characteristic Facies Distribution of Trace Fossils in Lower Campanian rocks of east-central Utah

Biogenic Sedimentary Structures	Facies*		
	A	B	C
Arenicolites			X
Asterosoma Form Helicoid Funnel			X
Asterosoma Form Rod-Shaped Burrows			X
Large Tubes			X
Ophiomorpha sp. A.			X
Plug-Shaped Burrows			X
"Ruhespuren"			X
Chondrites		X	X
Teichichnus		X	X
Thalassinoides		X	X
Arthrophycus		X	
Asterosoma Form Cylindrichnus		X	
Chevron Trails		X	
Plural Curving Tubes		X	
Scolicia		X	
"Snail Trails"		X	
Planolites	X	X	
Ophiomorpha sp. B.	X		
profuse biodeformational structures	X		

*These categories are geared alphabetically to the rock types illustrated in Figure 6.

the latter is found even in non-marine deposits (Seilacher 1963 fig. 1). Because of such ambiguities, our attention was drawn first to those forms that are restricted either to Utah or to Kansas.

Of the 18 basic kinds of trace fossils observed in Utah, 8 to 10 were not found in Kansas (Table 2). Failure to observe such forms as Chevron Trails and "Ruhespuren" in Kansas is not surprising, because the carbonate muds of the early Coniacian were evidently too soft to support and preserve definite surficial traces (Frey 1970b). Bedding plane components of Laevicyclus (Fig. 2f) are an exception, yet this ichnogenus is common only in the basal sediments of the Fort Hays, which contain larger quantities of terrigenous detritus and which were thus probably more coherent. Even if such traces had been preserved, however, their facies significance would remain uncertain; the trail Scolicia, for example, commonly appears in rocks representing different depositional environments (e.g. Seilacher 1964 table 1).

On the other hand, the absence of such forms as *Arenicolites* and *Ophiomorpha* from the Coniacian is evidently important; in general, *Ophiomorpha* has proved to be a good indicator of shallow, nearshore areas in the Western Interior Region (e.g. Toots 1961 p. 168; Hoyt and Weimer 1965), and *Arenicolites* has been reported mainly from such deposits.

Of the 5 to 7 basic Kansas forms not observed in Utah (Table 2), two types—the Scaphopod-Shaped Tubes and the Mineral-Filled Burrows—are conceivably a simple matter of preservation; carbonate- and sulphide-filled burrows were observed rarely in the sandstones of Utah. Furthermore, certain vertical calcite-filled burrows in Kansas are very abundant locally and in sandstones would probably be called *Skolithos. Laevicyclus* has been found in shallow water, siliceous sands elsewhere in North America (e.g. Henbest 1960), hence, had it been observed in Utah, its presence would not have been surprising. *Trichichnus* ("*Pyrit-Stengel*") is apparently more common in marly or argillaceous sediments than in sandstones, yet its real importance also remains poorly known. Among the various trace fossils from Kansas, therefore, *Zoophycos* seems to have the most significance; flat, non-spiralled varieties are generally thought to be good indicators of offshore deposition (e.g. Seilacher 1964 table 1; 1967 fig. 2).

We thus concluded that, among these two ichnofaunas, burrows such as *Ophiomorpha* and *Zoophycos* have the greatest overall environmental implications. Their respective connotations of shallow water, nearshore deposition and somewhat deeper water, offshore deposition are also supported by local stratigraphical, sedimentological, and palaeontological evidence. Nevertheless, these two ichnogenera do not have unequivocal significance on a widespread geographical or temporal basis. *Ophiomorpha* has been found elsewhere in brackish to fresh water deposits (Hillmer 1963; Keij 1965), for example, and tabular forms of *Zoophycos* have been observed in shallow water siliceous sandstones (Henbest 1960; Bandel 1967 p. 9).

Distributions such as those discussed above thus show that checklists of trace fossil genera, like checklists of body fossil genera, cannot in themselves impart much information that is fundamental to the reconstruction of depositional environments, unless used in conjunction with other criteria.

4b. Comparison at the subgeneric level

In principle, ambiguities such as those outlined above can be offset to some extent by giving increased emphasis to detailed morphology rather than accepting the general generic characteristics of trace fossils. *Teichichnus* in Utah is predominantly retrusive whereas that in Kansas is predominantly protrusive, for example, and the Kansas form of *Chondrites* more nearly resembles a *Chondrites* from the English Chalk (Kennedy 1967 pl. 2, figs. 2-4; pl. 9, fig. 1) than specimens from Utah. Indeed, among the various genera or forms that appear in both ichnofaunas (Table 2), few Kansas types closely duplicate their Utah counterparts. On this basis the overall resemblance between the two assemblages is decreased while the local character of individual trace fossils is increased.

The major problem here is deciding which structural features are or are not environmentally significant. Variations in trace fossil morphology can reflect important ethological and ecological differences, but they may also result simply from the vagaries in preservation imposed by various sedimentological and diagenetic regimes.

Lithological and preservational differences must be considered especially when comparing ichnofaunas from siliceous and carbonate rocks, such as the sandstones of Utah and the chalks of Kansas. Kansas specimens of *Asterosoma* Form

Table 2. Comparison of Ichnofaunas from the Lower Coniacian of Kansas and the Lower Campanian of Utah

Inferred ecological and (or) ethological equivalents are linked by dashed lines

Utah Trace Fossils	Kansas Trace Fossils
Chevron Trails	— trails
"Ruhespuren"	— and resting
Scolicia	— traces not
"Snail Trails"	— preserved
Arenicolites	—
Ophiomorpha sp. A	—
Ophiomorpha sp. B	—
Plural Curving Tubes	—
Large Tubes————————??———————Thalassinoides cf. paradoxica	
Plug-Shaped Burrows————————??—————Mechanically Filled Burrows	
Arthrophycus————————————Arthrophycus(?)-like Burrows	
Asterosoma Form Cylindrichnus—————————Asterosoma Form Cylindrichnus	
Asterosoma Form Helicoid Funnel—————————Asterosoma Form Helicoid Funnel	
Asterosoma Form Rod-Shaped Burrows—————Cylindrical Shafts (in part)	
Chondrites————————————————Chondrites	
Planolites—————————————————Planolites	
Teichichnus—————————————Teichichnus	
Thalassinoides——————————————Thalassinoides sp.	
—	Laevicyclus
—	Mineral-Filled Burrows
—	Scaphopod-Shaped Tubes
—	Trichichnus
—	Zoophycos

Cylindrichnus differ from those of Utah primarily in wall texture and composition, for example. In specimens from Utah the walls consist of alternate layers of coarser and finer grained sediment. Particles of different grain size were not generally available to the *Asterosoma* organism of Kansas, and the wall layering within its burrows is detected chiefly through concentrically layered discontinuities in sediment fabric; these are enhanced by concentrations of diagenetic iron sulphide, probably representing mucus secreted by the organism. Such differences in composition and preservation were noted also among specimens of spreiten structures, e.g. *Teichichnus* and *Asterosoma* Form Helicoid Funnel.

Superimposed on these differences is the wide range in morphologic variability exhibited within certain populations of burrows. We have concluded that—allowing for preservational differences between these two ichnofaunas and for exceptional genera such as *Teichichnus* and *Chondrites*—the morphological variability found within a given population of burrows is generally about as great as that observed between Kansas and Utah populations of the same ichnogenus. Comparison of these assemblages at the subgeneric level is thus difficult and very subjective, and, as with the generic characteristics, is apt to yield little information that is unequivocally useful on a regional scale. We submit further that the unwavering use of binomial nomenclature in such cases could conceivably result in a unique group of ichnospecies for each suite of rocks examined; such taxonomies, as among body fossils (e.g. Boltovskoy 1965), tend to obscure the picture more than to clarify it.

4c. Comparison of "trace spectra"

An ethological analysis of the trace fossils—the "trace spectra" of Seilacher (1958)—also indicates a general similarity between these two ichnoassemblages (Table 3A). Bioturbate textures found commonly in the Coniacian of Kansas (Pl. 1a) resemble closely those of the offshore facies of Utah (Fig. 6a), but because distinct identifiable burrows are generally rare in these Utah rocks they were not included in the ethological analysis. Considering the gradual change in structure of the Kansas fauna (Fig. 4) and the facies segregation of trace fossils from Utah (Table 1), an overall comparison of this kind is imprecise, however.

The greatest similarity between the two assemblages is seen, perhaps surprisingly, when the lower part of the Kansas stratigraphic section is compared with the Utah facies deposited closest to shore and having the coarsest sediment (Table 3B, 2).

Table 3. Ethological Analysis of trace fossils from the Lower Coniacian of Kansas and the Lower Campanian of Utah

A. Total Assemblages

Location of Sample	Approximate Percent Composition			
	Dwelling Burrows	Combined Feeding– Dwelling Burrows	Feeding Burrows	Crawling and Resting Traces
Kansas	44	19	37	—
Utah	50	6	22	22

B. Selected Parts of the Assemblages: Stratigraphic Levels

1. Kansas (upper part, Fig. 4)	36	9	55	—
Utah (Fig. 6b)	40	—	30	30
2. Kansas (lower part, Fig. 4)	50	17	33	—
Utah (Fig. 6c)	50	10	30	10

The distribution of burrow types are enumerated further in the following tabulation, which discloses (i) a dominance of dwelling and feeding-dwelling burrows over
feeding burrows among trace fossils not found in both areas, and (ii) a marked
balance between burrow types common to both areas.

Trace Fossil Distribution	Percent Feeding Burrows	Percent Feeding– Dwelling Burrows	Percent Dwelling Burrows	Percent Crawling and Resting Traces
Forms found in Kansas only	29	29	42	—
Forms found in both places	50	—	50	—
Forms found in Utah only	—	25	50	25

In the upper part of the Kansas section and in the intermediate Utah facies, the
predominance of dwelling and feeding burrows is reversed (Table 3B, 1). Here, as
shown in the tabulation below, feeding burrows dominate among forms found only
in Kansas and also among burrow types observed in both areas, whereas dwelling
burrows are present to the exclusion of feeding burrows among those trace fossils
restricted to Utah rocks.

Trace Fossil Distribution	Percent Feeding Burrows	Percent Feeding– Dwelling Burrows	Percent Dwelling Burrows	Percent Crawling and Resting Traces
Forms found in Kansas only	50	17	33	—
Forms found in both places	60	—	40	—
Forms found in Utah only	—	—	40	60

Table 3B, and the above tabulations, considered in the light of such palaeoecological factors as food supply, current regimes, and substrate coherence, evidently
reveal some singularly important clues as to why several named ichnogenera should
appear in both nearshore, terrigenous-detrital sands and offshore, allochemical
carbonate muds. As indicated previously, unstable substrates (whether soft muds or
shifting sands), dominantly suspended food supplies, and substantial currents were
present during both early Coniacian deposition in Kansas and early Campanian
deposition in Utah; they thus constitute important common denominators between
the two depositional environments. We suggest that the distribution and
abundance of many of these trace-making organisms were effected less by bathymetry and the texture and composition of sediments than by currents, type of food
supply and capacity for exploiting loose sediments. In terms of these factors, the
two depositional regimes were evidently not too different; organisms that were able
to tolerate such conditions thus appeared in both environments, leaving conspicuously similar lebensspuren in grossly different sediments.

  Trace fossils restricted either to Kansas or to Utah, on the other hand, probably
do reflect the influence of sediment texture or composition, or other environmental
factors; the *Arenicolites* and *Ophiomorpha* organisms of the Utah environment

were apparently better adapted to life within these nearshore siliceous sands than in the offshore carbonate muds of the Kansas environment, for example. Furthermore, the large proportion of crawling traces in the very fine grained sands of Utah (Table 3B, 1), relative to the medium grained sands (Table 3B, 2), suggest a less unstable substrate and thus an important environmental difference between this and Kansas facies.

During later episodes of Coniacian deposition in Kansas, the waters deepened, the currents diminished in strength and persistence, and larger quantities of organic detritus were deposited with the sediment. This shift in conditions caused a conspicuous change in the endobenthic fauna (Fig. 4; Table 3B), especially including the increased importance of deposit feeders and the appearance of the *Zoophycos* organism. This assemblage bears slightly less resemblance to Utah assemblages, but the change was not so great that the organisms producing *Asterosoma, Chondrites, Planolites, Teichichnus,* and other burrows were eliminated from the Kansas environment.

5. Conclusions

Our study suggests that Coniacian and Campanian trace fossils in the Western Interior Region, and probably many trace fossils of other ages and geographic distributions, must be studied primarily in terms of specific depositional sites and secondarily in terms of their regional environmental implications.

Checklists containing trace fossil names, unless accompanied by considerable additional information, are not generally adequate criteria for delimiting facies—at least those facies defined partly on the basis of texture and composition of host sediments. Trace-making organisms, like all other organisms, are subject to a wide array of ecological parameters, and the factor(s) critical to their distribution may or may not be reflected lithologically.

On the other hand, checklists help reflect the diversity of ecological niches exploited by various trace-making organisms, and this, used with other criteria, is valuable in reconstructing local depositional conditions. It is thus important in environmental studies that the morphology, ethology, and stratigraphic-sedimentologic relationships of trace fossils be described and illustrated in detail, in order to present a maximum of information from particular depositional sites that will be most useful in comparative studies elsewhere.

6. Systematic descriptions

6a. Trace fossils from the Lower Coniacian of Kansas

(Fort Hays Limestone Member of the Niobrara Chalk)

Ichnogenus ARTHROPHYCUS Hall 1852

Arthrophycus(*?*) sp.

Figure 3e

Dominantly horizontal, branching burrows 0·5 to 3·0 cm in diameter, having an irregular or closely annulated exterior; annulated specimens closely resemble arthrophycids from Utah (Fig. 7a) whereas irregularly walled specimens more nearly resemble *Palaeophycus arthrophycoides* (Wilckens 1947 pl. 9, fig. 3). Full reliefs.

Ichnogenus ASTEROSOMA von Otto 1854

Figure 2a-c

Form Cylindrichnus: Kansas specimens (Fig. 2a), very similar to those from Utah (Fig. 7b), are dominantly vertical, 0·5 to 1·5 cm in diameter, and at least 30 cm long. Full reliefs.

Form Helicoid Funnel: These (Fig. 2b, c), also very similar to Utah specimens (Fig. 8d, h), have maximum diameter of 3 to 20 cm. Full reliefs.

Ichnogenus CHONDRITES Sternberg 1833

Chondrites sp.

Figure 2d

Irregularly branched, plant-like burrows 0·8 to 2·0 mm in diameter, resembling *Chondrites* sp. Kennedy (1967 pl. 2, figs. 2-4; pl. 9, fig. 1). Full reliefs.

Ichnogenus LAEVICYCLUS Quenstedt 1879

Laevicyclus sp.

Figure 2f

Vertical, approximately cylindrical shafts 0·6 to 0·7 cm in diameter, "capped" at upper end by concentric furrows 1·3 to 4·3 cm in overall diameter, on bedding surfaces. Full reliefs and epireliefs.

Ichnogenus PLANOLITES Nicholson 1873

Planolites sp.

Figure 2h

Irregularly sinuous, branched or unbranched, horizontal or randomly inclined burrows 0·5 to 1·2 cm in diameter. Full reliefs and convex hyporeliefs.

Ichnogenus TEICHICHNUS Seilacher 1955

Teichichnus sp.

Figure 2g

Protrusive spreiten, biconvex in vertical plane; typical spreiten are 12 to 35 cm in length, 0·4 to 0·9 cm wide, and 4 to 27 cm in height. Otherwise similar to specimens from Utah (Fig. 8g). Full reliefs.

Ichnogenus THALASSINOIDES Ehrenberg 1944

Thalassinoides cf. *paradoxica* (Woodward)

Plate 1b

Unornamented, very irregular burrows and branching burrow systems 0·8 to more than 5·0 cm in diameter; branching is three-dimensional, producing non-planar polygons; branches Y-shaped and enlarged typically at point of bifurcation. Burrow systems thus resemble *T. paradoxica* (see Kennedy 1967 p. 142). Full reliefs.

Thalassinoides sp.

Figure 2e

Horizontal burrow systems 0·5 to 2·0 cm in diameter; very similar to thalassinoids from Utah (Fig. 7j), except for absence of very small burrows. Full reliefs, convex epireliefs, and convex hyporeliefs at lithologic interfaces.

Ichnogenus TRICHICHNUS Frey 1970

Trichichnus sp.

Figure 3a

Branched or unbranched, hair-like, cylindrical burrows 0·1 to 0·3 mm in diameter and as much as 3·5 cm long, oriented at various angles. Burrow walls commonly lined with diagenetic iron sulphides. Equivalent to *"Pyrit-Stengel"* of German marly and argillaceous sediments (Walter Häntzschel 1968 personal communication). Full reliefs.

Ichnogenus ZOOPHYCOS Massalongo 1855

Zoophycos sp.

Figure 3d

Tabular, protrusive, spreiten structures 10 to 23 cm in width and 0·3 to 0·6 cm thick, morphologically duplicating *Glossophycus* (Lessertisseur 1955 fig. 41c). Plane containing spreite may be oriented randomly. Full reliefs.

Cylindrical Shafts

Figure 3b

Heterogeneous group of unbranched, vertical or steeply inclined, poorly preserved burrows 0·4 to 1·0 cm in diameter and at least 40 cm long, having more or less smooth, distinct walls. Equivalent in part to *Asterosoma* Form Rod-Shaped Burrows from Utah (Fig. 8c). Full reliefs.

Mechanically Filled Burrows

Plate 1c

Subcylindrical, straight to gently curved burrows 2·5 to 4·5 cm in diameter and 9 to 10 cm long, which acted as sediment traps for shell fragments upon demise of burrowing organism. Burrows generally inclined to bedding at angles of 45 to 55 degrees. Specimens observed invariably at lithologic interfaces, extending into overlying and underlying beds.

Mineral-Filled Burrows

Figure 3f-i

Various vertical to horizontal, branched or unbranched, tubular burrows 0·1 to 0·7 cm in diameter and 10 to 30 cm long, having distinct walls and (or) cores of calcite, pyrite, limonite, or mixtures of these. Subtle differences among these burrows are elaborated elsewhere (Frey 1970b); they are treated here as a unit, except to mention that the group consists of both feeding and dwelling burrows and that one form consists of secondary burrows that penetrate and course along primary burrows (Fig. 3i), suggesting a possible coprophagous relationship. Full reliefs.

Scaphopod-Shaped Tubes

Figure 3c

Vertical, trumpet-shaped tubes 0·6 to 1·3 mm in maximum diameter and as much as 1·6 cm long; small end oriented upward. Tube walls consist of microcrystalline calcite. Full reliefs.

6b. Trace fossils from the Lower Campanian of Utah

(Blackhawk Formation and Panther Sandstone Tongue of the Star Point Formation)

Ichnogenus ARENICOLITES Salter 1857

Arenicolites sp.

Figure 7i

Vertical, broadly U-shaped burrows 0·5 to 0·6 cm in diameter, extending downward approximately 1 m. One limb of burrow commonly terminates upward in a funnel-shaped, oval depression 2·0 to 3·0 cm in diameter. Full reliefs.

Ichnogenus ARTHROPHYCUS Hall 1852

Arthrophycus sp.

Figure 7a

Horizontal, annulated, conduit-like, branched or unbranched burrows 0·5 to 1·5 cm in diameter, some having a median furrow. Branched burrows enlarged slightly at point of bifurcation. Full reliefs or convex epireliefs.

Ichnogenus ASTEROSOMA von Otto 1854

Figures 7b, k; 8c, d, h

Three distinct but intergradational forms, each having specific ethological and environmental significance. Nomenclature presently in state of flux, hence the informal field designations used by Howard (1966a) are retained informally.

Form Cylindrichnus: Vertical to nearly horizontal, circular to oval, cylindrical burrows (Fig. 7b) 1·0 to 2·0 cm in diameter, having a central core 0·2 to 0·4 cm in diameter. Burrow walls consist of multiple, concentric layers. Full reliefs. The name "Cylindrichnus" Howard (1966a p. 45) is not to be confused with the name *Cylindrichnus* Bandel (1967 p.6) given subsequently to an altogether different trace fossil.

Form Helicoid Funnel: Funnel-shaped spreiten structures 4 to 24 cm in maximum diameter, grading downward into a cylindrical stem. Funnels consist of a laminated to bioturbated core and an outer wall, up to 1·0 cm thick, of feeding burrows arranged in helicoidal whorls. Centre of funnel sparsely (Fig. 8h) to intensely (Fig. 8d) bioturbated. Full reliefs.

Form Rod-Shaped Burrows: Unornamented, vertical to nearly vertical, slightly sinuous, rod-shaped burrows (Fig. 8c) 0·3 to 0·6 cm in diameter and approximately 1 m long. Some are branched upward, and some (Fig. 7k) are surrounded by bioturbate haloes, grading into *Rosselia* (Häntzschel 1962 fig. 131-2). Full reliefs.

Ichnogenus CHONDRITES Sternberg 1833

Chondrites sp.

Figure 7e

Asymmetrically ramifying, dominantly horizontal burrows in very plant-like, dendritic pattern. Branches short and 0·2 to 0·3 cm in diameter. Concave epireliefs.

Ichnogenus OPHIOMORPHA Lundgren 1891.

Ophiomorpha sp. A

Figure 7d

Straight, cylindrical, dominantly vertical, branched or unbranched burrows 1·5 to 2·5 cm in diameter, having a knobby exterior surface. Branches form acute angles. Full reliefs.

Ophiomorpha sp. B

Figure 8i

Sinuous, horizontal, branching burrows having an irregular to knobby exterior surface; specimens are oval in cross section and are 2·0 to 5·0 cm in width and 1·0 to 2·0 cm high. Convex epireliefs, concave hyporeliefs, and full reliefs.

Ichnogenus PLANOLITES Nicholson 1873

Planolites sp.

Figure 7c

Sinuous, smooth-walled burrows 0·8 to 1·5 cm in diameter, oriented at various angles. Full reliefs or convex epireliefs.

Ichnogenus SCOLICIA de Quatrefages 1849

Scolicia sp.

Figure 7g

Closely annulated, trilobed, bilaterally symmetrical trails 1·0 to 1·5 cm in width, having a median furrow 0·4 to 0·5 cm wide. Concave epireliefs.

Ichnogenus TEICHICHNUS Seilacher 1955

Teichichnus sp.

Figure 8g

Vertical, retrusive, straight to sinuous spreiten structures 0·8 to 1·6 cm wide and 5·0 to 15 cm high; some exceed a length of 30 cm. Within vertical plane, inclination of the spreiten ranges from horizontal to vertical. Individual burrows within spreite interlayered with silty laminae. Full reliefs.

Ichnogenus THALASSINOIDES Ehrenberg 1944

Thalassinoides sp.

Figure 7j

Unornamented, horizontal, branching burrows typically about 1·4 cm in diameter. Branches Y-shaped. Associated locally with similar although much smaller burrows. Convex hyporeliefs at lithologic interfaces.

Chevron Trails

Figure 8a

Linear series of nested chevrons, 1·0 to 1·5 cm wide. Except for absence of median furrow, this trail resembles *Gyrochorte* (Häntzschel 1962 fig. 122-1). Convex epireliefs.

Large Tubes

Figure 8e

Vertical, isolated, tubular burrows, or dense, horizontal, branching networks; individual burrows oval in cross section and 1·0 to 3·5 cm in diameter. Full reliefs.

Plug-Shaped Burrows

Figure 8b

Vertical, thin-walled, conical structures, oval in cross section. Diameter of upper end ranges from 3·0 by 4·0 cm to 6·0 by 8·0 cm; structures 12 to 20 cm long, tapering downward nearly to a point. Interior consists of nested, concave-upward laminae. Full reliefs.

Plural Curving Tubes

Figure 8f

Groups of parallel, open-ended, gently curved tubes having distinct walls, generally arranged in vertical planes. Individual burrows typically about 0·7 cm in diameter, including a wall thickness of 0·1 to 0·2 cm; tubes commonly 10 to 15 cm long. Full reliefs.

"Ruhespuren"

Figure 7f

Slightly elongate, subhorizontal depressions typically 5 by 6 cm having a raised, marginal rim; inner side of rim adjoined by a shallow trough 1·5 to 2·0 cm wide. Concave epireliefs.

"Snail Trails"

Figure 7h

Sinuous, unbranched, bilobate trail about 1 cm wide, having a narrow median furrow. Trails pass over or under one another but do not intersect. Probable affinity with *Gyrochorte* or *Aulichnites* (Häntzschel 1962 figs. 110, 4 and 122-1). Convex epireliefs.

Acknowledgments. We are grateful to Donald E. Hattin, Indiana University, and Robert J. Weimer, Colorado School of Mines, who reviewed the manuscript and offered critical comments.

Parts of this study were supported by National Science Foundation Grant GA-719 and by grants-in-aid of research from the Geological Society of America, the Society of the Sigma Xi, and Indiana University. This is contribution number 197 from the University of Georgia Marine Institute, Sapelo Island, Georgia 31327.

References

BANDEL, K. 1967. Trace fossils from two Upper Pennsylvanian sandstones in Kansas. *Paleont. Contr. Univ. Kansas* Paper 18.

BOLTOVSKOY, E. 1965. Twilight of foraminiferalogy. *J. Paleont.* **39**, 383.

COBBAN, W. A. and REESIDE, J. B., jun. 1952. Correlation of the Cretaceous formations of the Western Interior of the United States. *Bull. geol. Soc. Am.* **63**, 1011.

FARROW, G. E. 1966. Bathymetric zonation of Jurassic trace fossils from the coast of Yorkshire, England. *Palaeogeogr. Palaeoclimatol. Palaeoecol.* **2**, 103.

FREY, R. W. 1970a. Environmental significance of Recent marine lebensspuren near Beaufort, North Carolina. *J. Paleont.* **44**. In press.

—— 1970b. Trace fossils of Fort Hays Limestone Member of Niobrara Chalk (Upper Cretaceous), west-central Kansas. *Paleont. Contr. Univ. Kansas*. Article 53.

—— and HOWARD, J. D. 1969. A profile of biogenic sedimentary structures in a Holocene barrier island-salt marsh complex, Georgia. *Trans. Gulf Cst Ass. geol. Socs* **19**, 427.

HÄNTZSCHEL, W. 1962. Trace fossils and problematica. In *Treatise on invertebrate paleontology* (Ed. R. C. Moore). *Geol. Soc. Am., New York and Univ. of Kansas Press*. Part W, p. W177.

HATTIN, D. E. 1964. Cyclic sedimentation in the Colorado Group of west-central Kansas. *Bull. Kansas geol. Surv.* No. 169 (1), 205.

—— 1965. Upper Cretaceous stratigraphy, paleontology, and paleoecology of western Kansas. *Geol. Soc. Am. ann. Meet. Kansas City, Mo., Fld Conf. Guidebk*.

—— and FREY, R. W. 1969. Facies relations of *Crossopodia* sp., a trace fossil from the Upper Cretaceous of Kansas, Iowa, and Oklahoma. *J. Paleont.* **43**, 1435.

HENBEST, L. G. 1960. Fossil spoor and their environmental significance in Morrow and Atoka Series, Pennsylvanian, Washington County, Arkansas. *Prof. Pap. U.S. geol. Surv.* No. 400-B, B383.

HILLMER, G. 1963. Zur Ökologie von *Ophiomorpha* Lundgren. *Neues Jb. Geol. Paläont. Mh.* **3**, 137.

HOWARD, J. D. 1966a. Characteristic trace fossils in Upper Cretaceous sandstones of the Book Cliffs and Wasatch Plateau. *Bull. Utah Geol. miner. Surv.* No. 80, 35.

—— 1966b. Sedimentation of the Panther Sandstone Tongue. *Bull. Utah Geol. miner. Surv.* No. 80, 23.

—— 1969. Trace fossils as criteria for recognizing shorelines in the stratigraphic record (abs.). *Bull. Am. Ass. Petrol. Geol.* **53**, 723.

HOYT, J. H. and WEIMER, R. J. 1965. The origin and significance of *Ophiomorpha* (*Halymenites*) in the Cretaceous of the Western Interior. *Guidebks a. Fld Confs Wyo. geol. Ass.* **19**, 203.

KAUFFMAN, E. G. 1967. Coloradoan macroinvertebrate assemblages, central Western Interior, United States. In *Paleoenvironments of the Cretaceous seaway—a symposium*. Colorado School of Mines, Golden, Colorado. p. 67.

—— and HATTIN, D. E. Stratigraphic revision of the "Colorado Group" in Kansas and Colorado. In preparation.

KEIJ, A. J. 1965. Miocene trace fossils from Borneo. *Paläont. Z.* **39**, 220.

KENNEDY, W. J. 1967. Burrows and surface traces from the Lower Chalk of southern England. *Bull. Mus. nat. Hist. Geol.* **15**, 127.

LESSERTISSEUR, J. 1955. Traces fossiles d'activité animale et leur signification paléobiologique. *Mem. Soc. géol. Fr.* **34** (4), n.s. No. 74.

LOETTERLE, G. J. 1937. The micropaleontology of the Niobrara Formation in Kansas, Nebraska, and South Dakota. *Bull. geol. Surv. Neb.* 2nd ser. No. 12.

MABERRY, J. O. 1968. *Sedimentary features of the Blackhawk Formation (Cretaceous) at Sunnyside, Carbon County, Utah*. Unpublished Ph.D. Thesis, Colorado School of Mines.

MERRIAM, D. F. 1957. Subsurface correlation and stratigraphic relation of rocks of Mesozoic age in Kansas. *Oil Gas Invest. Kans.* No. 14.

—— 1963. The geologic history of Kansas. *Bull. Kans. Univ. geol. Surv.* No. 162.

MILLER, H. W. jun. 1968. Invertebrate fauna and environment of deposition of the Niobrara Formation (Cretaceous) of Kansas. *Fort Hays Studies*, new ser. *Sci. Ser.* No. 8.

PURDY, E. G. 1964. Sediments as substrates. In *Approaches to paleoecology* (Ed. J. Imbrie and N. D. Newell). Wiley, New York. p. 238.

REESIDE, J. B. jun. 1957. Paleoecology of the Cretaceous seas of the Western Interior of the United States. *Mem. Geol. Soc. Am.* **67** (2), 505.

RHOADS, D. C. 1967. Biogenic reworking of intertidal and subtidal sediments in Barnstable Harbor and Buzzards Bay, Massachusetts. *J. Geol.* **75**, 461.

RUNNELS, R. T. and DUBINS, I. M. 1949. Chemical and petrographic studies of the Fort Hays Chalk in Kansas. *Bull. Kans. geol. Surv.* No. 82 (1).

SABINS, F. F. 1962. Grains of detrital, secondary, and primary dolomite from Cretaceous strata of the Western Interior. *Bull. geol. Soc. Am.* **73**, 1183.

SANDERS, H. L. 1958. Benthic studies in Buzzards Bay. I. Animal-sediment relationships. *Limnol. Oceanogr.* **3**, 245.

SEILACHER, A. 1958. Zur ökologischen Charakteristik von Flysch und Molasse. *Eclog. geol. Helv.* **51**, 1062.

—— 1963. Lebensspuren und Salinitätsfazies. *Fortschr. Geol. Rheinld West.* **10**, 81.

—— 1964. Biogenic sedimentary structures. In *Approaches to paleoecology* (Ed. J. Imbrie and N. D. Newell). Wiley, New York. p. 296.

—— 1967. Bathymetry of trace fossils. *Mar. Geol.* **5**, 413.

SPIEKER, E. M. 1931. The Wasatch Plateau coal field, Utah *Bull. U.S. geol. Surv.* No. 819.

—— 1946. Late Mesozoic and Early Cenozoic history of central Utah. *Prof. Pap. U.S. geol. Surv.* **205-D,** D117.

—— 1949. Sedimentary facies and associated diastrophism in the Upper Cretaceous of central and eastern Utah. *Mem. geol. Soc. Am.* **39**, p. 55.

TOOTS, H. 1961. Beach indicators in the Mesaverde Formation. *Guidebks a. Fld Confs Wyo. geol. Ass.* **16,** 165.

WEIMER, R. J. 1960. Upper Cretaceous stratigraphy, Rocky Mountain area. *Bull. Am. Ass. Petrol. Geol.* **44**, 1.

WILCKENS, O. 1947. Paläontologische und geologische Ergebnisse der Reise von Kohl-Larsen (1928-29) nach Süd-Georgien. *Abh. senckenb. naturforsch.Ges.* **474.**

YOUNG, R. G. 1955. Sedimentary facies and intertonguing in the Upper Cretaceous of the Book Cliffs, Utah and Colorado. *Bull. Geol. Soc. Am.* **66,** 177.

—— 1957. Late Cretaceous cyclic deposits, Book Cliffs, Utah. *Bull. Am. Ass. Petrol. Geol.* 41, 1760.

R. W. Frey and J. D. Howard, University of Georgia, Marine Institute, Sapelo Island, Georgia 31327, U.S.A.

Comparative study on some Jurassic and Recent endolithic fungi using scanning electron microscope

Michael Gatrall and Stjepko Golubic

Fossil borings preserved in limonitic casts were extracted by decalcification from the Twinhce Beds of the Upper Bathonian (Jurassic, England). Recent borings from carbonate rocks and bivalve shells were prepared by using Epon-812 for penetration into the boring tunnels and for formation of hard resin casts. These casts were subsequently extracted by decalcification. Both fossil and Recent casts were metal coated under vacuum and studied by scanning electron microscopy for comparison. Several different types of borings were observed and described. Some fossil and recent forms show striking similarity. Borings within bivalve shells show that a part of their morphology is influenced by the substrate. Arrangement of carbonate crystals of the shell is reflected on the surface of the boring casts. Dissolution of crystals is found to be the dominant boring process which advances faster than the disintegration of the organic inter-crystalline lamellae.

1. Introduction

The occurrence of tubes a few microns across which penetrate the margins of fossil shells has long been known. They were first reported by Carpenter (1845) who believed them to be part of the shell structure. By analogy with similar tubes in Recent shells, they are generally referred to as boring algae or endolithic algae (Dangeard 1930; Hessland 1949; Rioult 1962; Davies 1966; Bathurst 1966). Recent endolithic algae were extracted from their substrates by decalcification and were studied by Bornet and Flahault (1889), Ercegovic (1932) and Frémy (1936).

It has been pointed out that some of the endolithic tubes might be fungal rather rather than algal (Hessland 1949). Direct study of endolithic fungi was performed on thin sections, transparent shells, and fungal materials extracted by decalcification (Zebrowski 1937; Porter and Zebrowski 1937; Frémy 1945; Newell *et al.* 1960; Schindewolf 1963; Höhnk 1969). The most recent contribution and review of previous work is that of Kohlmeyer (1969).

Generally the organisms themselves are not preserved as fossils. More or less well preserved endolithic tubes revealing the specific boring patterns of the organisms are all that remain. Such boring patterns are the only characteristics available for comparison which are common to fossil and Recent forms. Fossil tubes are usually infilled with some opaque material which renders them visible in the shell. As seen in conventional thin sections or even in serial peels, the spatial arrangement of the endolithic tubes is difficult to reconstruct.

Direct three-dimensional studies, with a scanning electron microscope, of the casts of fossil borings in limonite, and of recent borings cast in polymerizing resins are reported in this paper. This publication originates from independent studies by the authors. Gatrall studied exceptionally well preserved limonite casts of fossil endolithic fungi, extracted by decalcification. Golubic worked with Recent materials using a casting-embedding procedure in Epon-812 (Golubic *et al.* in press.) to prepare comparable specimens. Among the Recent specimens only those which are comparable to fossils described by Gatrall are dealt with here. For the purposes of comparison, illustrations on each of the three plates are arranged so that photographs on the left represent fossil forms and those on the right recent forms.

2. Occurrence of fossil borings

Limonitic filaments of the type referred to, were noted penetrating shell fragments in thin sections of limestones from the Twinhoe Beds (Upper Bathonian, Jurassic) of Bath, England. Identification of the shell fragments is difficult, they are completely "micritised" like those described by Bathurst (1966), but they are probably molluscan. The lower part of these beds is composed of "ironshot" limestone, which can be described as a limonitic biomicrite. This bed, which grades upwards from an ironshot limestone to a more or less iron-free oncolitic limestone, is interpreted as being deposited in shallow water, probably just subtidal (Green and Donovan 1969; Gatrall 1969).

3. Preservation and extraction

During the examination of polished and etched blocks of limestone by the scanning electron microscope many filaments, which have been etched out in full relief from the surrounding calcite, were found running through the shell fragments. The limonite coating of the tubes models the exact form of the borings and because of this coating, etching with dilute acid reveals their form. Small blocks of limestone were polished (using carborundum powder) and etched for 30–40 seconds using $2 \cdot 5 \%$ HCl. The etched blocks were mounted on stubs, coated with gold or aluminium under vacuum, and examined by a scanning electron microscope. It was possible to extract and mount individual shell fragments which could then be etched under a binocular microscope. This allowed controlled etching, together with possible complete removal of the calcite. Under the light microscope, the filaments are seen to be lined with a thin film of limonite which, in place, completely fills the tube. Similar observations can be made with the Stereoscan microscope (Pl. 1e). The preservation of such tubes in ironstones and in ferrugineous limestones is widespread. They have been reported in the Bajocian of France (Cayeux 1922; Dangeard 1930), from the Frodingham Ironstone of the Middle Lias (Hallam 1963), in the Upper Lias Cephalopod Bed (Davies 1966), and in the Twinhoe Beds (Gatrall 1969).

Davies (1966) attributed the limonite to precipitation in the tubes after the decay of the organic matter. Frémy (1945) described limonite in Recent fungal borings and attributed its formation to precipitation by fungal hyphae. Frequently, the filaments are most common around the margin of the shell fragments; this recalls the micrite envelopes of Bathurst (1966).

4. Description

From the specimens examined, several different types of endolithic structures were distinguished. For convenience they will be classified here as follows: Type A—will apply for larger tubes, possibly of algal origin; Type B—for filaments of different sizes of, presumably, fungal origin; Type C—for "swellings" and rounded, more or less isodiametric bodies; Type D—for structures of different shapes and origins which exhibit the imprints of the surrounding substrate in a recognizable manner.

Among boring tubes found in the fossil shell fragments from Twinhoe Beds, Type A is represented by relatively thick, mostly straight, filaments of very uniform diameter of 6–8μ, (Pl. 1c).

Type B-1 refers to the most common filament, a thinner type, around 2·5μ in diameter. These filaments branch frequently, mostly dichotomously. They intermingle between the filaments of type A and support and interconnect the rounded structures of type C. They correspond to the thinner branchlets of the B-2 type filaments (Pl. 1c, e, 2a, c, e, 3a).

Type B-2 filaments are thicker, of varying size, and irregularly and intensively branched, giving rise to finer branches of the B-1 type. At the junctions filaments often fuse into knob-like, or flat membrane-like, structures (Pl. 1e).

Type C-1 refers to spindle-like "swellings" around 10μ diameter occurring on filaments of B-1 type (Pl. 2a).

Type C-2 refers to sphaerical "swellings", single or in rows, interconnected by thin B-1 type filaments. The latter are often broken and reveal their tubular character (Pl. 2c).

Type C-3 refers to large (20×40μ) bulbous side branches attached to larger filaments of types A or B-2. These swellings vary in shape, some being roughly spherical, some tending to be more elongated or pear-shaped. Filaments may arise from these swellings (Pl. 2e, 3a).

Type D are "striped" structures, found in shell fragments not heavily infested by the other types. Usually they are filamentous with an average diameter of 2·4μ (1·3–2·9), however, at constrictions the diameter ranges from 0·9–2·4μ. The average length of the "segments" is 0·6μ (0·4–0·7). Less frequent among the filaments are "swellings" and isodiametrical bodies averaging 4·8μ (3·5–5·4) in diameter. All the stripes show unusual regularity. They run parallel to each other across the entire field regardless of the orientation of the filaments. The latter are therefore "striped" either across or obliquely (Pl. 3 c, e).

5. Occurrence of Recent borings

In order to supply material for comparison with the fossil fungi described by Gatrall, specimens from different shallow water marine habitats were investigated. The most sedimentologically similar material was chosen from the oolitic limestone along the supratidal and intertidal zones of Little Abaco Island in the Bahamas. This sediment is relatively soft, crumbling, and porous. Oolitic grains, as well as the carbonate cement connecting them, are heavily bored by endolithic algae and fungi. The boring activity was, however, limited to a surface layer not exceeding 2 mm (Pl. 1b).

Skeletons of living corals are known to be a substrate for endolithic algae. The preparation in Plate 2b was extracted from the interior of a coral head from the Caribbean Sea. It contained algal as well as fungal borings.

Preparations were isolated from the lower spray zone and also from the intertidal zone of the Mediterranean carbonate coast near Sorrento (Italy). Hard carbonate sediments were bored only at the surface. The algal and fungal components were equally well represented (Pl. 1d, 2d).

Recent bivalve shells from intertidal salt marsh pools of the non-carbonate Connecticut coast were a substrate heavily bored by endolithic fungi, with no evidence of the presence of algae.

M

6. Preservation and extraction

In most of the Recent borings the tubes are still occupied by boring organisms. In order to obtain a picture of boring patterns comparable to those of the fossils cast in limonite, Recent boring tubes must be filled with a penetrating substance suitable for study under the scanning electron microscope. An embedding-casting technique with Epon-812 developed by Golubic et al. (in press) was used. Specimens were fixed, dehydrated in acetone, and exposed to slow Epon-812 penetration under refrigeration. They were subsequently cured at 60°C for 2–3 days. The resulting Epon-blocks were cut open and exposed to dilute HCl in order to dissolve the carbonate substrate. The remaining casts contained the embedded organisms and reflected the outlines of the borings in their original spatial arrangements. The cast preparations were mounted, coated with carbon and gold-palladium under vacuum, and examined with a scanning electron microscope.

7. Description

The following types of structures were observed from the Recent endolithic specimens:

Type A-1 refers to thick filaments, 17–24μ in diameter, which penetrate perpendicular to the surface, straight into the substrate to a depth of about 150μ. The outlines of the casts are smooth and indicate slight constrictions where crosswalls may be expected. Branching is rare, usually single, lateral and short (Pl. 1d).

Type A-2 filaments are long with relatively constant diameters of 9–$11\cdot5\mu$, and without constrictions. They grow in semicircular curves composing characteristic nest-like or basket-like figures around grains of the substrate. Branches are lateral, short, and usually, irregularly curved (Pl. 1d).

Type A-3 filaments are shorter and irregularly curved. They form carpets of uniform density but never the "basket-figures" of type A-2. The filaments are $9\cdot5$–$12\cdot0\mu$ thick in medial parts and are slightly "inflated" terminally to a diameter of 12–15μ producing a club-shaped appearance (Pl. 1f).

Type B-1 refers to thin filaments spanning between larger, A-type filaments. They are attached to the latter directly or by short lateral branchlets. Branching is frequent, and usually dichotomous. Filament diameters vary between $1\cdot5$ and 3μ.

Plate 1

All illustrations on the left side of the plates refer to fossil material, the ones on the right side to Recent material. All scale bars 10 microns unless stated.

a Polished and etched surface of shell fragment and oncolite bearing ironshot from the Twinhoe Beds (Jurassic) at Bath showing full profiled limonite casts of endolithic tubes.

b Epon-embedded, open cut, and etched surface of the oolitic limestone from the Intertidal of Little Abaco Island (Bahamas) bored heavily by Recent algae and fungi.

c Accumulation of two types (A and B-1) of endolithic limonite filaments.

d Accumulation of three types of filaments (A-1, A-2 and B-1) from the intertidal zone of the Mediterranean carbonate coast. The thin filaments represent fungal hyphae parasitizing on the larger algal filaments.

e Branched tubes lined with limonite (B-2), and lamellar structures connecting the tubes.

f Club-shaped algal filaments from the spray zone of Little Abaco Island parasitized by fungal hyphae.

PLATE 1

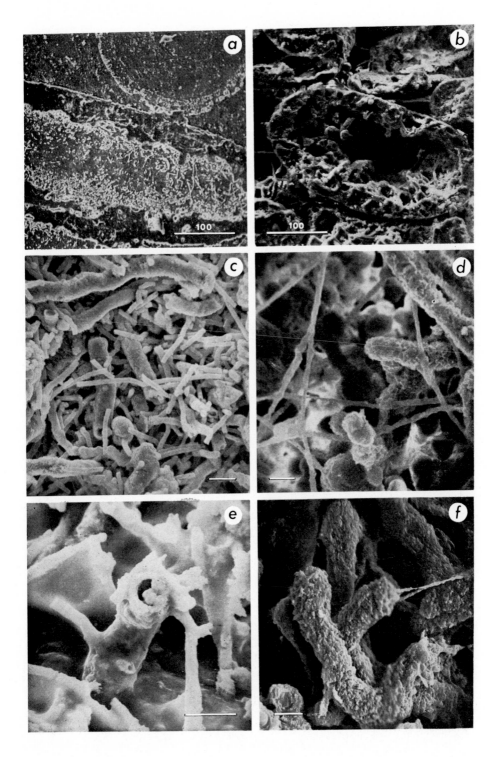

171

When dominant, they cover all other filaments with a dense interwoven mesh (Pl. 1d, f).

Type B-2 filaments are of similar growth and branching pattern, but of more variable size, normally $3–5\mu$. Wider filaments give rise to smaller branchlets, which again frequently bifurcate. These filaments sometimes bear spindle-shaped swellings of the C-1 type (Pl. 2b).

Type B-3 filaments are short and very thin. They vary from $0\cdot4–1\cdot0\mu$ in diameter and interconnect bag-like bodies of C-2 and D types (Pl. 2d, 3d, f).

Type C-1 consists of spindle-shaped swellings $22 \times 35\mu$, which sometimes occur along filaments of the B-2 type (Pl. 2b).

Type C-2 refers to accumulations of rounded, elongated and club-shaped bodies averaging $6\cdot6\mu$ $(4\cdot5–9\cdot0)$ in width and $9\cdot4\mu$ $(5\cdot0–13\cdot0)$ in length. They are often arranged in rows connected to each other directly through minor constrictions or indirectly by thin short filaments of B-3 type (Pl. 2d).

Type C-3 comprises large bulbous or pear-shaped swellings, $20–30\mu$ in diameter, attached laterally to $3–5\mu$ wide filaments. They often appear collapsed (Pl. 2f).

Type D refers to bag-like swellings "hanging" from the surface of the bivalve shells into the interior of the calcareous matrix. They differ widely in size ranging from a couple of microns in younger stages to a full size of 20–40 microns. They occur singly or in accumulations, attached to the shell surface by several "bottle-neck" tubes. Very thin filaments of the B-3 type also grow out from the swellings. Inverted, as they appear in the preparations, these bodies have the shape of a miniature octopus (Pl. 3b). In several larger bodies, the interior surfaces carry groves running parallel across the entire field regardless of the orientation of the swelling. The groves bifurcate and fuse again outlining elongated fields with pro-truded rough surfaces (Pl. 3b, d, f).

8. Discussion

From the materials studied, different morphological types of filaments were distinguished which in thin section could all be termed "boring algae". The comparison of fossil and Recent borings, using scanning electron microscopy, offered more certainty in their identification and revealed that most, if not all, of the filaments from the Twinhoe Beds were fungal.

The ecological importance of the distinction between endolithic algae and endolithic fungi is in their different requirements for life, and consequently, their different value as palaeoecological indicators. Using studies of Recent materials as a basis, the following considerations seem to have general validity:

Plate 2

a Spindle-shaped pair of swellings (C-1) among thinner filaments (B-1).

b Large spindle-shaped swelling (C-1) within the filament network (B-2) extracted from a Recent coral skeleton.

c A series of fossil globular swellings (C-2).

d Accumulation of rounded and club-shaped swellings (C-2) connected in series by very thin filaments (B-3) (lower right).

e Fossil bulbous lateral swelling (C-3) with collapsed upper wall.

f Recent bulbous lateral swelling (detail from Plate 1b). The lower left bulbs have impressed walls.

PLATE 2

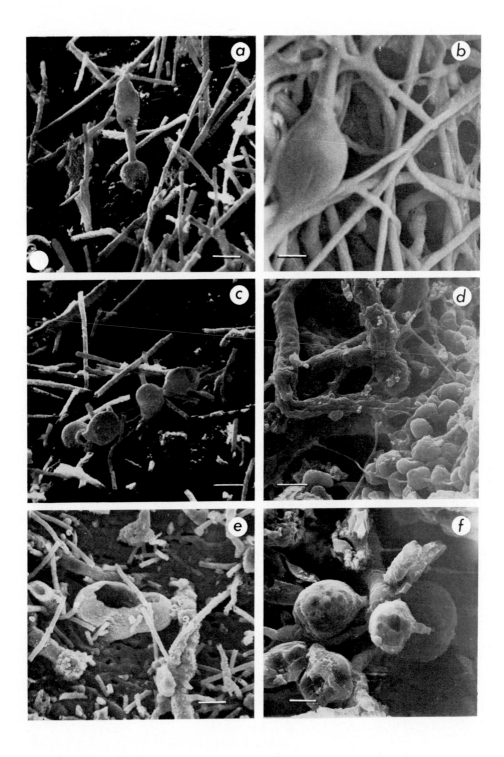

Algae are basically light dependent, but they are independent of organic matter in the substrate. They are able to colonize inorganic carbonate rocks or even pure calcite crystals (LeCampion-Alsumard 1969; Golubic 1969), as well as shells and skeletal fragments which are rich in organic matter. They stay, however, close to the substrate surface—within the photic zone. As such, boring algae can be considered indicators of illuminated shallow water environments.

Fungi are basically light independent, but they are dependent on organic matter for food. They can colonize deep into the darkness, provided that the substrate contains usable organic matter. Such is the case in fungae colonizing and boring into the shells of molluscs and other hard tissues. In inorganic carbonate rocks fungi occur only secondarily. They usually follow the boring algae to parasitize upon them (Pl. 1f).

Wendt successfully applied similar considerations in his interpretation of fossil borings in the Jurassic of Germany, where the borings were present only on the upper, presumably illuminated, surfaces (Wendt 1969). In cases, however, where the original orientation of the outcrop cannot be determined, a direct recognition of the boring organism is required.

Type A filaments found in the Recent materials were all identified as algal. The largest filaments in Plate 1d, termed here A-1, belong to a green alga of the family Cladophoraceae. The A-2 type filaments in the same photograph belong to *Mastigocoleus testarum* Lagerh. (Cyanophyta). None of these algal filaments was recognized in the fossil material with which it was compared. Their greatest similarity is with the slightly narrower filaments of the A type in Plate 1c. We do not consider this similarity sufficient for identification. The same situation is true for the algal filaments of the A-3 type in Plate 1f. They were identified as *Hyella caespitosa* Born. et Flah. (Cyanophyta). No similar filaments were found among the fossil tubes.

Connections between filaments of different sizes may be interpreted either as branchings (Pl. 1e) or as the attachments of smaller parasitic fungal hyphae on their larger algal hosts (Pl. 1f). Both cases were found in Recent materials and should be taken into account as possible sources of confusion.

The majority of filaments in the fossil material as well as in many of the Recent specimens belongs to B-1 type. The latter are identified as fungal hyphae, and there is little doubt that this identification also holds for the fossils with which they are compared (Pl. 1c, d, 2a, c, e).

Spindle-shaped swellings of the C-1 type are very rare in the Recent material. The one shown in Plate 2b, printed in scale with its fossil counterpart (Pl. 2a), obviously

---

Plate 3

a Large globular swelling with two connecting tubes visible (C-3).

b A side view of "Octopus"-like fungal sporangial swellings within a bivalve shell (D). Surface relief indicates the imprinted groves and fields.

c "Striped" limonite filaments from fossil shell fragments showing deep imprints of the internal shell structure (D).

d Vertical view of a group of sporangial swellings of different ages. The larger ones show distinct groves (D).

e "Striped" filaments (as in Plate 3c) in overall view (D).

f "Striped" Recent endolithic fungus (D) showing the arrangement of smooth groves and rough fields as well as the thin connecting hyphae (B-3). The scale is comparable to Plate 3e.

PLATE 3

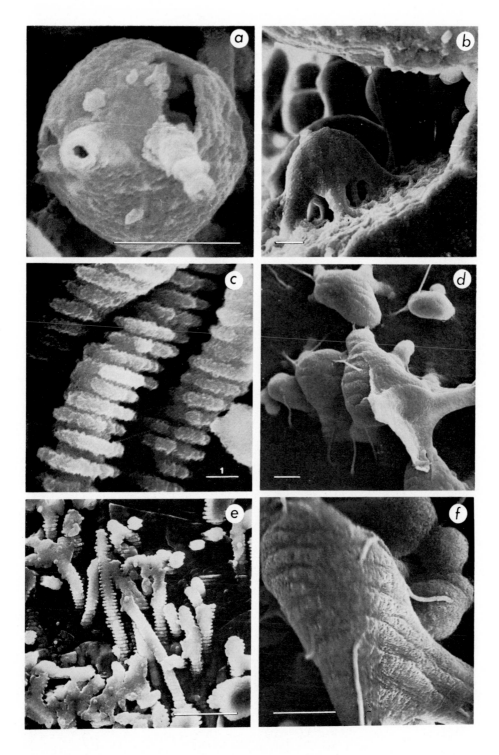

175

belongs to a larger organism. This same remoteness applies to the comparison of serial swellings (Pl. 2c, d). In this case the Recent C-2 type form is smaller and is characterized by a more common occurrence of swelling aggregations.

Surprisingly close comparison applies for the bulbous lateral swellings of the C-3 type (Pl. 2e, f). The size of the large pear-shaped body with a collapsed wall in Plate 2e falls within the size range of the identified fungal sporangia in Plate 2f. Both are photographed at the same magnification and in nearly the same position. The spherical body in Plate 3a is also strikingly similar to the Recent fungal sporangium in the centre of Plate 2f. In the two sporangia in the lower left hand corner of Plate 2f a depression is visible; this is probably due to a spore discharging mechanism. This might explain why the wall in its fossil counterpart collapsed. Frémy (1945) extracted similar spherical and ovoid dilatations from modern shells of France and similar bladders were noted by Wetzel (1938).

The bag-like forms of the D-type found in Recent bivalve shells (Pl. 3b, d, f) could not be recognized in the fossils studied. They have been identified as *Dodgella inconstans* Zebrowski (Archimycetes). The "bottle neck" connections between the fungal bodies and the shell surface are thought to serve for the discharge of spores.

At first sight, the "striped" appearance of the fossil D-type filaments, in Plate 3c and e, resembles the cellular structures in blue green algae (Oscillatoria). The orientation of the stripes, however, is not perpendicular to the longitudinal axes of the tubes. The stripes all have the same orientation and seem to be superimposed upon the boring material regardless of the direction of filament growth. The same phenomenon was encountered on Recent *Dodgella* borings in bivalve shells (Pl. 3b, d, f).

In the studies of endolithic algae penetrating calcite crystals (Golubic 1969; Golubic *et al.* in press) it was found that mineralogical properties of the substrate may be reflected in the shape and surface sculpturing of the boring tunnels. We interpret the "stripes" in shell-penetrating fungal borings as a mark of the crystalline arrangement within the shell. The character of relief of these marks in the Recent borings shows that the distintegrating process is faster at the crystal surfaces (protruded fields) than along the intercrystalline organic lamellae (impressed groves). This indicates that carbonate dissolution is the dominant boring mechanism. The shells compared in fossil and Recent materials do not have identical structures, neither are they bored by the same organisms. This becomes clear from Plate 3e and f printed at the same magnification for comparison. Nevertheless, they seem to illustrate the consequences of the same mechanism, as well as the possible complications involved in the interpretation of the morphology of the borings.

Acknowledgements. We thank Professor Seilacher of the University of Tübingen, West Germany and Professor Erben of the University of Bonn, West Germany, as well as many colleagues at the University of Leicester, U.K., who helped with advice and technical equipment. Part of this research was supported by Grant GB-6543 of the National Science Foundation to Yale University.

References

BATHURST, R. G. C. 1966. Boring algae, micrite envelopes and lithification of molluscan biosparites. *Geol. J.* **5,** 15.

BORNET, E. and FLAHAULT, C. 1889. Sur quelques plantes vivant dans le test calcaire des mollusques. *Bull. Soc. bot. Fr.* **36,** 147.

CARPENTER, W. 1845. On the microscopic structure of shells. *Rep. Br. Ass. Advmt Sci.* for 1844.

CAYEUX, L. 1922. *Études des gites mineraux de la France. Les minerais de fer oolithique de la France. Fasc. 2, minerais de fer secondaires.* Imprimerie Naturale, Paris.

DANGEARD, L. 1930. Recife et galet d'algues dans l'Oolithe ferrugineuse de Normandie. *C.r. hebd. Séanc. Acad. Sci., Paris* **190,** 66.

DAVIES, D. K. 1966. *The sedimentary petrology of the Upper Lias Sands, and associated deposits in Southern England.* Unpublished Ph.D. Thesis, Univ. of Leicester.

ERCEGOVIC, A. 1932. Études écologiques et sociologiques des Cyanophycées lithophytes de la côte adriatique de la Dalmatie. *Bull. int. Acad. yougosl. Cl. Sci. mat. nat.* **26,** 33.

FRÉMY, P. 1936. Les algues perforantes. *Mem. Soc. natn Sci. nat. math. Cherbourg* **42,** 275.

—— 1945. Contribution à la physiologie des Thallophytes marine perforant et cariant les roches calcaires, et les coquilles. *Annls Inst. océanogr., Monaco* **22,** 107.

GATRALL, M. 1969. *The depositional environment of some Middle Jurassic ironshot limestones of Southern England.* Unpublished Ph.D. thesis, Univ. of Leicester.

GOLUBIC, S. 1969. Distribution, taxonomy and boring patterns of marine endolithic algae, *Am. Zoologist.* **9,** 747.

——, BRENT, G. and LeCAMPION, T. Scanning electron microscopy of endolithic algae and fungi using a multi-purpose casting-embedding technique. *Lethaia,* in press.

GREEN, G. W. and DONOVAN, D. T. 1969. The Great Oolite of the Bath area. *Bull. geol. Surv. Gt. Br.* **30,** 1.

HALLAM, A. 1963. Observations on the ecology and ammonite sequence in the Frodingham Ironstone (Lower Jurassic). *Palaeontology* **6,** 554.

HESSLAND, I. 1949. Investigation of the Lower Ordovician of the Siljan District, Sweden, Pt. 2 Ordovician penetrative algae. *Bull. geol. Instn Univ. Upsala* **33,** 409.

HÖHNK, W. 1969. Über den pilzlichen Befall kalkiger Hartteile von Meerestieren. *Ber. dt. Wiss. Komm. Meeresforsch.* **20,** 129.

KOHLMEYER, J. 1969. The role of marine fungi in the penetration of calcareous substances. *Am. Zoologist.* **9,** 741.

LeCAMPION-ALSUMARD, T. 1969. *Contribution a l'étude des cyanophycées lithophytes des étages supralittoral et médiolittoral (Région de Marseille). Tethis* **1,** 119.

NEWELL, N. D., PURDY, E. G. and IMBRIE, J. 1960. Bahamian oolitic sand, *J. Geol.* **68,** 481.

PORTER, C. L. and ZEBROWSKI, G. 1937. Lime-loving molds from Australian sands. *Mycologia* **29,** 252.

RIOULT, M. 1962. *Le stratotype du Bajocien; Colloque sur le Jurassique.* Luxembourg, p. 239.

SCHINDEWOLF, O. H. 1963. Pilze in oberjurassischen Ammoniten-Schalen. *Neues J.B. Geol. Paläont. Abh.* **118,** 177.

WENDT, J. 1969. Stratigraphie und Paleogeographie des Roten Jurakalks in Sonnwendegebirge (Tirol, Österreich). *Neues Jb. Geol. Palaeont. Abh.* **132,** 219.

WETZEL, W. 1938. Die Schalenzerstörung durch Mikroorganismen, Erscheinungsform, Verbreitung und geologische Bedeutung in Gegenwart und Vergangenheit. *Kieler Meeresforsch.* **2**, 255.

ZEBROWSKI, G. 1937. New genera of Cladochytriaceae, *Ann. Mo. bot. Gdn* **23**, 553.

M. G. Gatrall, Abu Dhabi Petroleum Company, P.O. Box 270, Abu Dhabi.

S. Golubic, Biology Department, Paterson State College, Wayne, New Jersey 07470, U.S.A.

Did *Micraster* burrow?

R. Goldring and D. G. Stephenson

It is suggested that the Chalk echinoid *Micraster* did not burrow to a depth which necessitated a respiratory tube. This suggestion is based on morphological evidence, together with evidence from the manner of preservation and the associated epizoans and trace fossils.

1. Introduction

Nichols (1956; 1959a, b), in now classic work on the Upper Cretaceous spatangoid *Micraster,* concluded that the observed evolutionary changes originally recognised by Rowe (1899), could be interpreted as ecological adaptations independent of variation in the habitat; the principal resulting difference being the ability of later forms to burrow more deeply. Nichols determined the function of various structures in *Micraster* and based his arguments on comparative functional morphology. Recent work on some other spatangoids, and search for structures in the Chalk that could have been due to the activity of *Micraster,* has prompted us to inquire how deep *Micraster* burrowed.

2. Lack of trace fossils in the Chalk

The Upper Chalk is generally relatively pure and homogenous in southern Britain and, unlike the Lower Chalk, displays little obvious evidence of bioturbation. However, if cut or ground surfaces are stained with methylene blue solution, the clay and organic matter is picked out and shows that the *Micraster* Chalk is in fact strongly bioturbated. Sampling at many localities where *Micraster,* and especially *M. coranguinum,* is relatively common has failed to show any spatangoid burrows, nor have flint casts that could represent spatangoid burrows been found (cf. Bromley 1967). The type of structure which has been looked for is one resembling the traces left by *Echinocardium* as figured by Reineck (1968). The additional presence of associated sanitary burrows would, of course, be welcomed. Exactly what the consistency of Chalk was at the time of deposition is still a problem but the soft chalks may be regarded as coccolith-oozes (Hancock and Kennedy 1967), rather than as silts as envisaged by Nichols (1959a p. 419). The question is therefore posed: did *Micraster* burrow, and if it did why can we find no evidence of its activity?

The Upper Cretaceous Chalk of northwest Europe is generally regarded as representing a period of continuous sedimentation. It is now clear that sedimentation was not unbroken, as indicated by hard grounds (Bromley 1967). Nevertheless, the extraordinary detail in which the evolutionary succession of *Micraster* can be

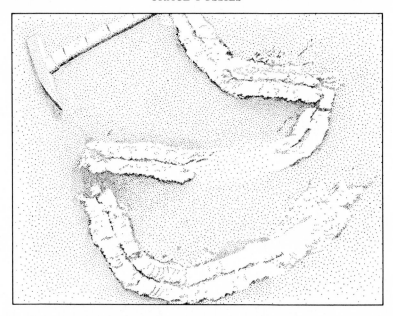

Fig. 1. Probable echinoid burrows from the Eocene of Maslin Bay, Willunga Basin, South Australia. Attributable to a lovenid or brissid. Hammer graduated in 5 cm intervals. Drawn from a photograph.

observed must imply that sedimentation was unusually continuous. This should favour the preservation of trace fossils and Bromley (1967) and Kennedy (1967) have described bioturbation structures from the Chalk. Nevertheless, they observed no structures that could be attributed to the activities of burrowing spatangoids.

Kennedy, in discussion of Bromley's paper, noted that the *Thalassinoides* burrows were often only horizontal, and vertical tubes were less common. In his reply, Bromley thought that this might be explained because horizontal burrows represented the basal parts of the network so that structures nearer to the surface would be obscured by later reworking from a higher level. However, it is unlikely that the clear structures produced by deeply burrowing spatangoids would be completely obscured and stained surfaces frequently show vertical burrows.

The activity patterns of the modern deeply burrowing spatangoid *Echinocardium cordatum* in the southern North Sea have been described by Schäfer (1962) and Reineck (1963; 1968). The banded and laminated sands, silts and muds are ideal for recording the progress of this echinoid through the sediment but the pattern is equally clear in uniform sand. Even in strongly bioturbated sediment the large backfilled burrows are very conspicuous. The sanitary tube does not preserve as an open tube but it is possible that its trace may show in fossil material. Fossil spatangoid burrows have been described by Reineck (1968) from the Lower Cretaceous of Germany. One of us (RG) has also observed what appear to be spatangoid burrows in the Eocene of the Willunga Basin, South Australia (Fig. 1).

The only structures thought by Nichols (1959a p. 424) to be due to the movement of *Micraster* through the sediment were a pair of parallel tubes 7·5 mm long and 5·0 mm apart, from White Nothe (Dorset), which he thought closely resembled a fallen-in sanitary tube. Nichols noted that the distance between the tubes should have been greater (13·0 mm) and he attributed the reduction to lateral compression. The specimen was not preserved.

Nichols did not give any figures as to what depth he considered the most advanced form of the *Micraster* lineage, *M. coranguinum,* burrowed. However, he gave diagrams showing the relative and inferred depths of burrowing of three modern spatangoids and three species of the *Micraster* group. *M. (Isomicraster) senonensis* is shown ploughing through the sediment to a depth similar to that of *Spatangus raschi; M. coranguinum* is shown burrowing to about twice its height and to a depth slightly less than that shown for *S. purpureus* (5–6 cm). We see no reason why *Micraster* should have burrowed deeply in the chalk sediment, which was not forming in the turbulent beach zone.

To explain the apparent absence of spatangoid burrows we have considered the manner in which *Micraster* is preserved and the functional efficiency of *Micraster* when compared with modern spatangoids.

3. Preservation of *Micraster*

Fossil off-shore burrowing echinoids might be expected to be preserved in position of life, and are less likely to be encrusted with epizoans than are surface-dwelling forms. Craig (1966) wondered whether higher zonal forms had less epizoans than low zonal forms. Unfortunately, observations on the Chalk do not support this. It is uncommon to find *Micraster* in a dorsal uppermost position and they are generally tilted or overturned, often with broken tests and often with a substantial epifauna of serpulids, bryozoans and oysters, all clearly indicating a period when the dead test was free on the sediment surface and subject to erosional forces.

It might be expected that the spines of a burrowing echinoid would often be preserved in association with the test. In fact, tests of *Micraster* with spines adhering are no more common in the Chalk than tests of non-burrowing echinoids with similar spines present. The rare *Micraster* with spines adhering have them dominantly on the underside. Hoffman (1914) figured spatulate spines from the plastron of *Micraster* and described pointed ones from the ambitus. Forbes (1850) figured both spatulate and pointed spines without mentioning their position on the test. We know of no specimen of *Micraster* with spines preserved on the apical part of the test, although spines preserved on the apical part of the test of *Echinocorys* are known (Stephenson 1963; and undescribed material). This implies that *Micraster*, a burrowing form, lost spines from the top of the test more easily than *Echinocorys* which lived on the sediment surface.

4. Functional morphology of *Micraster*

Nichols (1959b) considered that 'the Micrasters built respiratory funnels as do such living forms as *Echinocardium,* though probably not as deep'. The conclusion that *Micraster* did not burrow very deeply is strengthened by the work of Chesher (1963) on *Moira atropos,* which is described as burrowing to a depth of 15 cm in 'liquid mud'. This spatangoid is widely separated taxomically from *Echinocardium,* but is likewise much more advanced morphologically than *Micraster.*

Arguments from the functional morphology of *Micraster* alone are unlikely to be useful, but the following considerations suggest comparisons with modern spatangoids:

(i) *Micraster* has no tuft of enlarged spines ('primary spines' of Fischer 1966) on the dorsal surface which could be used to help the tube feet construct a respiratory funnel as in *E. cordatum* (Nichols 1959a), or could be used alone to keep a passage through the sediment open as in *E. flavescens* (Gandolfii-Hornyold 1910). *Brissopsis lyrifera* and *Meoma ventricosa* have fewer and smaller 'primary spines'.

(ii) In *Micraster* the upper part of the anterior ambulacrum evolved considerably. In *M. cortestudinarium* this part of the ambulacrum is sunken, with pore pairs emerging along the walls of the depression and smooth along the bottom. This resembles the anterior ambulacrum of *Meoma ventricosa*. In *M. coranguinum* this part is less depressed with pore pairs on the horizontal surface and their peripodia are more ornamented. This resembles those modern spatangoids in which this part of the ambulacrum carries extensile and penicillate tube feet. *M. coranguinum* has 30-40 pore pairs in this area, which is about the same as in *Brissopsis lyrifera*.

(iii) *Micraster* changes in shape as it evolves. In early forms (*M. cortestudinarium* zone and below) the highest point of the test is at the apical disc; the carina (or keel) along the posterior ambulacrum is non-existent or slight, and the profile is 'gibbous' to 'flat-arched' (Rowe 1899). This shape, especially the gibbous forms, resembles the somewhat streamlined upper surface of *Meoma ventricosa* (Kier and Grant 1965). In the final form (*M. coranguinum*) the highest point of the test is much more posteriorly situated and the test usually has a marked posterior rise and a strong posterior keel. These features are also found in *Brissopsis lyrifera*.

These comparisons may allow informed guesses about the depth of burrowing. The comparison of *M. cortestudinarium* with *Meoma ventricosa* is not exact because this echinoid is about three times as long as *Micraster* and usually burrows in sand. Its normal habit is to 'keep the uppermost part of the dorsal surface nearly at the surface of the sand' (Kier and Grant 1965). The comparison of *M. coranguinum* with *Brissopsis lyrifera* is more exact because the latter is similar in size and burrows in mud, similar in grade to the Chalk. Forbes (1850) compared the mode of life of *M. coranguinum* to that of *B. lyrifera* but his account of the latter (Forbes 1841) does not explain its ecology. *B. lyrifera* is a very shallow burrower with its aboral surface usually no more than 1·0 cm under the sediment (Buchanan, personal communication). Other species of the genus burrow to greater depths and construct respiratory funnels (Chesher 1969).

It is deduced therefore that *M. cortestudinarium* probably burrowed with the top of its test at about the level of the sediment surface and *M. coranguinum* probably had the top of its test a centimetre or so below the sedimentary surface. This depth was probably insufficient for the movement pattern to be preserved in such poorly consolidated sediment. At such depth it was also likely to be destroyed by subsequent burrowing. At the same time this is consistent with the increase in the depth of burrowing from *M. cortestudinarium* to *M. coranguinum* demonstrated by Nichols.

In spite of this tentative conclusion that *Micraster* was a very shallow burrower there is a possible alternative explanation which must be mentioned; that *Micraster* found in the Chalk is not in its optimal habitat but represents populations which have settled and grown with a different ecology in a less than optimal environment. Buchanan (1966) noted that offshore populations of *E. cordatum* living in a very silty sand burrowed only to a depth of 2·0 cm or less. They grew very slowly and do not appear to have bred. The statistical results of Nichols (1959a) and Kermack

(1954) were based on the assumption that they were dealing with a breeding population.

4. Conclusions

The absence of trace fossils which could be attributed to *Micraster* in the Chalk, is explained by the deduction that *Micraster* was only a very shallow burrower. Traces of movement could only have been made to depths at which the sediment was not consolidated enough to preserve them. Any traces which might be preserved would be destroyed later by the activities of animals which burrowed to greater depths.

Acknowledgements. We are grateful to Professor D. Nichols, Dr. R. M. Kier and Mr. C. J. Wood for reading the manuscript and for helpful comments, and to Dr. J. B. Buchanan for unpublished information on *Brissopsis lyrifera.*

References

BROMLEY, R. G. 1967. Some observations on burrows of thalassinidean Crustacea in chalk hardgrounds. *Q. J. geol. Soc. Lond.* **123**, 157.

BUCHANAN, J. B. 1966. The biology of *Echinocardium cordatum* (Echinodermata: Spatangoidea) from different habitats. *J. mar. biol. Ass. U.K.* **46**, 97.

CHESHER, R. H. 1963. The morphology and function of the frontal ambulacrum of *Moira atropos* (Echinoidea: Spatangoida). *Bull. mar. Sci. Gulf Caribb.* **13**, 549.

—— 1969. The Systematics of sympatric species in West Indian Spatangoids. *Stud. trop. Oceanogr. Miami* **7**.

CRAIG, G. Y. 1966. Concepts in palaeoecology. *Earth Sci. Revs* **2**, 127.

FISCHER, A. G. 1966. Spatangoids. In *Treatise on invertebrate paleontology* (Ed. R. C. Moore). *Part U Echinodermata 3* Geol. Soc. Am., New York and Univ. Kansas. Press, Lawrence. **2**, p. U543.

FORBES, E. 1841. *A history of British starfishes and other animals of the class Echinodermata.* van Vorst, London.

—— 1850. Figures and descriptions illustrative of British organic remains. *Mem. geol. Surv. U.K.* Decade 3, plate 10.

GANDOLFI-HORNYOLD, A. 1910. Beiträge zur Biologie und Anatomie der Spatangiden. *Mém. Soc. fribourg. Sci. nat.* (Schweiz) **1** (2), 25.

HANCOCK, J. M. and KENNEDY, W. J. 1967. Photographs of hard and soft chalks taken with a scanning electron microscope. *Proc. geol. Soc. Lond.* No. 1643, 249.

HOFFMAN, B. 1914. Über die allmähliche Entwicklung der Verschieden differenzierten Stachelgruppen und der Fasciolen bei den fossilen Spatangoiden. *Paläont. Z.* **1**, 216.

KENNEDY, W. J. 1967. Burrows and surface traces from the Lower Chalk of southern England. *Bull. Br. Mus. nat. Hist.* Geology **15**, 127.

KERMACK, K. A. 1954. A biometrical study of *Micraster coranguinum* and *M.* (*Isomicraster*) *senonensis*. *Phil. Trans. R. Soc.* **237B**, 375.

KIER, R. M. and GRANT, R. E. 1965. Echinoid distribution and habits, Key Largo Coral Reef Preserve, Florida. *Smithson. misc. Collns* **149**, No. 6.

NICHOLS, D. 1956. The palaeoecology of the Chalk. *Proc. Dorset nat. Hist. archaeol. Soc.* **77**, 192.

—— 1959a. Changes in the Chalk heart-urchin *Micraster* interpreted in relation to living forms. *Phil. Trans. R. Soc.* **243B**, 347.

—— 1959b. Mode of life and taxonomy in irregular sea-urchins. In *Function and taxonomic importance* (Ed. A. J. Cain). *Publ. Syst. Ass. Publ.* No. 3, 61.

REINECK, H. E. 1963. Sedimentgefüge in Bereich der südlichen Nordsee. *Abh. senckenb. naturforsch. Ges.* **505.**

—— 1968. Lebensspuren von Herzigeln. *Senckenberg. leth.* **49**, 311.

ROWE, A. W. 1899. An analysis of the genus *Micraster*, as determined by rigid zonal collecting from the zone of *Rhynchonella cuvieri* to that of *Micraster coranguinum*. *Q. J. geol. Soc. Lond.* **55**, 494.

SCHÄFER, W. 1962. *Aktuo-paläontologie, nach Studien in der Nordsee*. Kramer, Frankfurt-am-Main.

STEPHENSON, D. G. 1963. The spines and diffuse fascioles of the cretaceous Echinoid *Echinocorys scutata* Leske. *Palaeontology* **6**, 458.

R. Goldring, Sedimentology Research Laboratory, Department of Geology, University of Reading, Whiteknights, Reading, U.K.

D. G. Stephenson, Department of Geology, The University, Keele, Staffordshire,. U.K.

Rosetted trace fossils: a short review

Aleksandar Grubić

Rosetted trace fossils are briefly reviewed and their origins discussed. It is suggested that they can result from the activities of a number of very different animals but in only a limited number of cases can their genesis be satisfactorily demonstrated.

1. Introduction

Rosetted trace fossils are common, and their unusual form has attracted much attention; many types have been found in rocks of various ages from Cambrian to Tertiary.

In the past they were usually classified as *Atollites* or *Lorenzinia* and considered to be medusae. More recent research, carried out on better preserved material, has, however, shown that there are many different types of rosetted trace fossils.

2. Types of rosetted traces and their origins

Fossil rosetted forms, described as *Atollites zitteli* Maas and *A. minor* Maas (Maas 1902) are undoubtedly true fossil medusae, although types identical to *Lorenzinia* were later included in this group (*Atollites carpathicus* Zuber, according to Kuźniar 1911). Other rosettes, however, were shown to be true fossil plants, as in the case of forms from the *Gyrophyllites* Glocker group (Häntzschel 1930 p. 262). Also, specimens from the Caucasus originally referred to *Atollites* have more recently been interpreted as impressions of ammonite shell ornament by Grossgeym (1959).

It has also been suggested that some rosetted traces are of mechanical origin and Häntzschel (1935) has pointed out that in winter ice crystals are found in a rosetted form on North Sea beaches.

We are concerned here with rosetted forms originating from the life activity of animals. Such rosettes originate from the activities of worms, molluscs, crabs, starfish and unknown organisms. It is clear from the literature that these traces can be classified into a number of groups on the basis of their mode of origin.

2a. Rosetted traces probably resulting from the activity of worms

It is probable that fossil rosettes described by Nowak (1957 p. 213) from the Lower Cretaceous of the Polish Carpathians originated from the activity of worms. In Nowak's paper these traces, which are up to 30 cm in diameter are lettered A and C-I. They are characterised by dichotomous ramifications of their radial rays. Only the principal rays reach from the centre to the rosette periphery. The rays are cylindrical in shape, straight or convoluted, of unequal width and noticeably unequal length. In the middle of the rosette there is a convexity of 8 to 10 cm diameter. These features suggest that the rays are traces produced by the movement of worms.

The star-like B-type trace of Lucas and Rech-Frollo (1964 fig. 5) could perhaps also be included in this group. The fossil description is, however, incomplete and the photograph too small to reach any firm conclusions. The photograph gives the impression that the rays are convoluted and divide dichotomously.

The fossil rosette trace "*Spongia ottoi*" Geinitz from the Cenomanian of Germany consists of 6 to 10 cylindrical radially disposed rays, spreading from a convex centre. Its characteristic is that on each specimen there are a few radial rays which divide dichotomously. Rosettes of this type are about 5 cm in diameter, irregular and usually unilaterally developed. Geinitz (1849–50) considered that they were fossil sponges but Häntzschel (1930) has shown that they are trace fossils. Recently, Häntzschel (1962 p. w 217) has suggested that they are "probably feeding burrows made by crustaceans or worms". On the basis of the irregular construction of the rosettes and the branching of the radial rays it can be assumed that it is more probable that trace fossils of the "*Spongia ottoi*" type originated from life activity of worms.

2b. Rosetted traces probably produced by the activity of a siphon

Lucas and Rech-Frollo (1964) have described rosettes of diameter 30 to 50 cm from the Eocene flysh of Jaca (Aragon). These star-like fossils have oval contours and the number of radial rays is from 25 to 30. The rays which are straight or weakly curved vary in length on individual specimens. Their uneven expression is very characteristic. Furrows which separate neighbouring rays are better shown in sectors on the same axis, and are less apparent on the other two sectors the axis of which is perpendicular to the first one. In the middle of the trace fossil there is a prominent cone 2 cm in diameter. The print of the fossil trail is on the lower surface of the layer. Lucas and Rech-Frollo (*op. cit.*) think that the rosetted fossil trail of the A-type originates as a trail of the activity of a siphon of some large bivalve, such as *Mya,* similar to the trails left by the siphons of *Scrobicularia* (Häntzschel 1930; 1934).

2c. Rosetted traces attributed to the activity of dibranchiate cephalopod tentacles

According to Häntzschel (1962 p. w 184) trails of activity of tentacles of dibranchiate cephalopods have been preserved in the form of rosettes of the type *Asterichnites octoradiatus* Brown and Vokes, from the Cretaceous of North America. These are fine rosettes of eight very evenly distributed radial furrows. They are 13-18 mm long and have the form of a wedge. In the middle of the trail there is a featureless disc.

2d. Rosetted traces probably made by crabs

Fossil rosettes probably originating from the activity of crabs include *Lorenzinia apenninica* Gabelli. Rosette trails of *Lorenzinia* type consist of 16 to 24 rays of equal length and identical shape. For this reason they are very regular and the whole fossil has a circular form. The middle part of the rosette is also circular, flat or weakly concave. In detail, however, such fossil trails may differ between themselves considerably (Grubić 1961 fig. 3). Sometimes the rosette consists only of a circular set of small uneven knobs (Nowak 1957 pl. 18 fig. м, top right hand corner). In more complicated rosettes there are sometimes two circular series: external and internal ones. The internal series consists of small knobs while the external circle consist of large round or oval knobs. This is the form which was described by Renz (1925) as *Bassaenia morae*. The rosette, then, can consist of spaced ribs of a spindle-like or cylindrical shape (Nowak 1957 pl. 17 fig. J and pl. 18 fig. N). The typical rosettes of *Lorenzinia* have concentric rays of cylindrical or spindle-like shape. It was thought for a long time that *Lorenzinia* were fossil medusae (Gabelli 1900; Gortani 1920; Renz 1925; 1930; Mitzopoulos 1938; Harrington and Moore 1956; Dimitrieva 1962). Nowak (1957) suggested that they are the fossil traces of the life activity of crabs. This is now generally accepted (Grubić 1961; Ślączka 1964; Lucas and Rech-Frollo 1964). *Lorenzinia* is best known from flysch sediments of the Upper Cretaceous and Eocene of the Alps.

2e. Rosetted traces produced by brittle stars

The origin of five-rayed traces referred to *Asteriacites lumbricalis* Schlotheim (1820) has been reliably ascertained. These are undoubtly traces of brittle stars, auluroids and asteroids and are known from the Silurian to the Tertiary in Europe and North America. Some specimens show how the organism moved, with traces of former positions preserved in the fossil state.

2f. Rosetted traces of uncertain origin

In addition to the star-like traces already discussed, the origin of which has been resolved with a reasonable degree of certainty there are also some fossil rosettes of less certain origin. Indeed no attempts have even been made to explain the origin of some of them.

Astropolithon hindii Dawson is particularly mysterious. It consists of an oval depression surrounded by radially disposed rays. With some forms the rays bifurcate, while in smaller specimens they are weakly developed. These oval rosettes, described by Dawson (1890), were found in the Lower Cambrian of Nova Scotia.

A particularly interesting rosette trace of unknown affinities was described by Książkiewicz (1960 p. 746, pl. 3 fig. 10) without any special name or designation. This "rosetted trail" was found on the lower surface of one sandstone layer in the Upper Cretaceous flysch of the Polish Carpathians. The star-like fossil is not fully preserved, but appears to consist of eight short and regular rays of almost equal lengths and thickness. In the middle they are interconnected into a central cone. At the cone apex there is a small hole in the form of a crater and Książkiewicz supposes that "The trail might have been formed by an organism living in a hole on the sea floor, grazing around and thus scooping out the central crater (now the cone) and the furrows (now ribs) in all directions". The regularity of the fossil trail is, however, very obvious, and no conclusion could be reached as to what group of animals made it.

The origin of the trace fossil "*Atollites kulczinskii*" Kuźniar from Inoceramian beds of the Polish Carpathians is also problematical. This rosette resembles traces of the *Lorenzinia* type. On the interior face the radial rays are, however, connected by a narrow ring. This is what clearly distinguishes Kuźniar's (1911) "*Atollites*" from *Lorenzinia*. It obviously must also have a different origin. The specimen "L" described by Nowak (1957 pl. 17 fig. L, p. 216) from the Upper Cretaceous of the Polish Carpathians probably has a similar origin but, this specimen also differs from the trail of the "*Atollites kulczinskii*" type in the width of its ring.

3. Conclusions

(i)   Rosette fossil traces (biohieroglyphs) can be classified into groups on the basis of their morphology.

188   TRACE FOSSILS

(ii)   Of all the described rosetted fossil traces it is clear that the five-rayed star form of *Asteriacites* represents a trace of a starfish and it is very probable that some of the forms, described by Nowak (1957) from the Upper Cretaceous of the Polish Carpathians originated from the activity of worms.

(iii)   The origin of all other star-like trails is not yet sufficiently clear. There are still many uncertainties in their genetic interpretation. Thus, new material and further research are needed to determine their origin.

(iv)   Star-like fossil trails have practically no stratigraphical significance. They generally reflect the wealth of an organic world which has disappeared and of which no skeletal remains were preserved. Also they tell us about the ecology of these organisms and the palaeogeographic characteristics of the sedimentary environment; even here their significance is greatly reduced by the fact that the origin of most of them is still uncertain.

References

DAWSON, J. W. 1890. On burrows and tracks of invertebrate animals in Palaeozoic rocks, and other markings. *Q. J. geol. Soc. Lond.* **46**, 595.

DMITRYEVA, E. V., ERSHOVA, G. I. and ORESHNIKOVA, E. I. 1962. *Structures et textures des roches sédimentaires. Partie 1. Roches clastiques et argileuses.* Gosgeoltekhizdat, Moscow.

DOOR, J. W. and KAUFMAN, E. 1963. Rippled toroids from the Napoleon Sandstones member (Mississipian) of southern Michigan. *J. sedim. Petrol.* **33**, 751.

GABELLI, L. 1900. Sopra un interessante impronta medusoide. Il pensiero Aristotelico nelle science naturali. *Riv. Filos. natur.* **1**, 74.

GEINITZ, H. B. 1849–1850. *Das Quadersandsteingebirge oder Kreidegebirge in Deutschland.* Freiberg.

GORTANI, M. 1920. Osservazioni sulle Medusoidi del Flysch (Lorenzinia e Attolites). *Rivis. Ital. Paleont. Stratigr.* **26**, 56.

GROSSGEYM, V. A. 1959. K voprosu proishozdenii iskopayemih meduz. *Trudy krasnodar. Fil. vses. neftegaz. nauchno-issled. Inst.* **2**, 38.

GRUBIĆ, A. 1961. Lorenziniae from Eocene flysch of Montenegro. *Sedimentologija* **1**, 51.

HÄNTZSCHEL, W. 1930. *Spongia ottoi* Geinitz, ein sternformiges Problematikum aus dem sachsischen Cenoman. *Senckenbergiana* **12**, 261.

—— 1934. Sternspuren erzeugt von einer Muschel: *Scrobicularia plana* Da Costa. *Ibid* **16**, 325.

—— 1935. Rezente Eiskristalle in meerischen Sediment und fossile Eiskristalle Spuren. *Natur Volk* **65**, 151.

—— 1962. Trace fossils and problematica. In *Treatise on invertebrate paleontology* (Ed. R. C. Moore). Geol. Soc. Am., New York and Kansas Univ. Press, Lawrence. Part W, W117.

HARRINGTON, H. J. and MOORE, R. C. 1956. Scyphomedusae. In *Treatise on invertebrate paleontology* (Ed. R. C. Moore). Part F.

KSIĄŻKIEWICZ, M. 1960. On some problematic organic traces from the flysch of the Polish Carpathians. *Kwart. geol.* **4**, 735.

KUŻNIAR, W. 1911. Kilka problematycznych skamielin z fliszu karpackiego. Sur quelques fossiles problematiques du flysch des Carpathes. *Kosmos Warsz.* **36**.

LUCAS, G. and RECH-FROLLO, W. 1964. "Traces en rosette" du flysch eocene de Jaca (Aragon). Essai d'interprétation. *Bull. Soc. géol. Fr.* **6**, 163.

MAAS, O. 1902. Über Medusen aus den Solenhofener Schiefer und der unteren Kreide der Karpathen. *Paleontographica* **48**, 319.

MITZOPOULOS, M. 1938. Ein Medusen-Vorkommen in Eozänflysch des Peloponnes. *Praktika Akad. Athenon* **14**, 258.

NOWAK, W. 1957. Quelques hiéroglyphes étoilés des Karpathes de Flysch extérieures. *Annls Soc. géol. Pol.* **26**, 187.

RENZ, C. 1925. Problematische Medusenabdrücke aus der Olonos-Pindos-Zone des West-peloponnes. *Verh. naturf. Ges. Basel* **38**, 220.

—— 1930. Ein Medusen-Vorkommen im Alttertiär der Insel Cyprien. *Eclog. geol. Helv.* **23**, 295.

ŚLĄCZKA, A. 1964. *Kirklandia multiloba* n.sp.—a jellyfish from the Carpathian Flysch. *Annls Soc. géol. Pol.* **34**, 479.

A. Grubić, Faculty of Mining and Geology, Belgrade, Djušina 7, Yugoslavia.

Gyrochorte and other trace fossils in the Forest Marble (Bathonian) of Dorset, England

A. Hallam

Trace fossils in the Forest Marble formation of Dorset, and associated faecal pellets, probably signify the activity of a number of worms, crustaceans and bivalves. A detailed description is given of the ichnogenus *Gyrochorte*, which occurs abundantly on the surface of thin sandstone beds. It is characterised by long winding ridges with a plaited structure on the upper surfaces of the sandstones, and by biserial grooves on the under surfaces. The interpretation of *Gyrochorte* is discussed but no definite conclusions as to the nature of the organism responsible are arrived at. Associated trace fossils include a new ichnogenus consisting of horizontal burrows with an imbricated structure. Other occurrences of *Gyrochorte* in the English Jurassic are noted and the likely environment of deposition of the Forest Marble is briefly discussed.

1. Introduction

The Forest Marble formation of Dorset is excellently exposed on the coast at Watton Cliff, between West Bay and Eype (SY 453908), and moderately exposed on the shore at Herbury Point, facing the Fleet (SY 612808). While fallen blocks can be examined with ease at Watton Cliff, a recent landslip has made it impossible to measure an accurate section.

The following section was measured by the Geological Survey (Wilson *et al.* 1958):

		Ft.	In.
8.	Clay with thin sandy calcareous tiles	8	0
7.	Clay-shale with sandy calcareous leaves and thin shelly limestone bands	20	0
6.	Massive shelly current-bedded limestone	7	0
5.	Blue clay	1	6
4.	Creamy hard cementstone		11
3.	Buff laminated sandy shale, clayey at top	6	0
2.	Blue-grey shales with leaves of brownish calcareous sandstone	40	0
1.	*boueti* Bed: fossiliferous whitish calcareous marl	1	2

The formation thus consists of two units of clay or shale containing thin bands of sandstone, separated by a massive cross-bedded limestone (bed 6) (a similar sequence is present at Herbury Point). This limestone is largely composed of complete or fragmented shells, of which the most abundant are those of *Liostrea hebridica*. Other bivalve genera include *Chlamys*, *Camptonectes* and *Pseudolimea*, while brachiopods, echinoid spines and ossicles of *Apiocrinus* also occur. Calcitic ooliths are abundant, as are fragments of wood. Clay galls, calcilutite pebbles and fish teeth are found locally.

The sandstones range up to about 3 cm in thickness; they are fine to medium grained with a matrix of calcite cement and, in some beds, finely comminuted shell fragments. The upper surfaces of the sandstones frequently exhibit slightly asym-metrical ripple marks and trace fossils; the undersurfaces show load casts and groove casts together with distinctive trace fossils and a number of indistinct markings and filled burrows parallel to the bedding. The thicker sandstones may be composite, consisting of two or more units of ripple cross-laminated sediment with thin bioturbated layers at the base. Some casts of faecal pellets have also been found. These are empty casts of smooth cylindrical rods with abrupt terminations, ranging up to 3.0×0.5 m in size. This shape is characteristic of the faecal pellets of many types of crustacean.

The features of greatest interest are the trace fossils, which have been studied both at Watton Cliff and Herbury Point and form the principal subject of this paper. They include *Gyrochorte, Pelecypodichnus, ?Palaeophycus, Planolites* and a new ichnogenus.

2. Systematic descriptions

Ichnogenus GYROCHORTE Heer 1865

Gyrochorte comosa Heer

Plate 1 a-f; Figures 1, 2

Description. Low, winding ridges with a plaited structure on the upper surface of bedding planes (positive epirelief) composed of biserially arranged, obliquely aligned pads of sediment. The ridges range up to 4 mm in width and average about 3 mm. The pads or 'plaits', averaging 2 mm long and 1 to 2 mm high, tend to dip in the direction of acute intersection of the intervening furrows at an average of 30°. Locally they disappear, leaving a smooth bilobate ridge (Pl. 1 a-c). Such a ridge may end abruptly (Pl. 1a, b). In a few specimens, a sharp change of direction of a plaited ridge is associated with a triangular flat zone with thin radiating or parallel ridges on the convex side of the bend (Pl. 1d).

The ridges, which often cross each other (Pl. 1a), are only found on the upper surface of the thin sandstone beds. On the under surface of these beds one often finds winding, biserial 'tramline' grooves (negative hyporelief), i.e. two smooth grooves separated by a median ridge, of a similar width to the plaited ridges (Pl. 1e). In a few instances the grooves are seen directly to underlie the latter and have clearly been produced by the same organism.

Plate 1

Specimens of *Gyrochorte* and *Planolites,* Forest Marble, Watton Cliff, Dorset. Author's collection. Specimens **a** to **d** and **f**, *Gyrochorte.*

a Positive epirelief, $\times 0.5$.

b Positive epirelief, $\times 1$.

c Positive epirelief, $\times 0.75$.

d Positive epirelief, specimen showing fan structure at sharp bend, $\times 1$.

e Positive and negative hyporelief, $\times 1$. *Gyrochorte* structure in lower part of photograph (A), *Planolites* in upper and central part (B).

f Negative hyporelief, $\times 0.75$.

PLATE 1

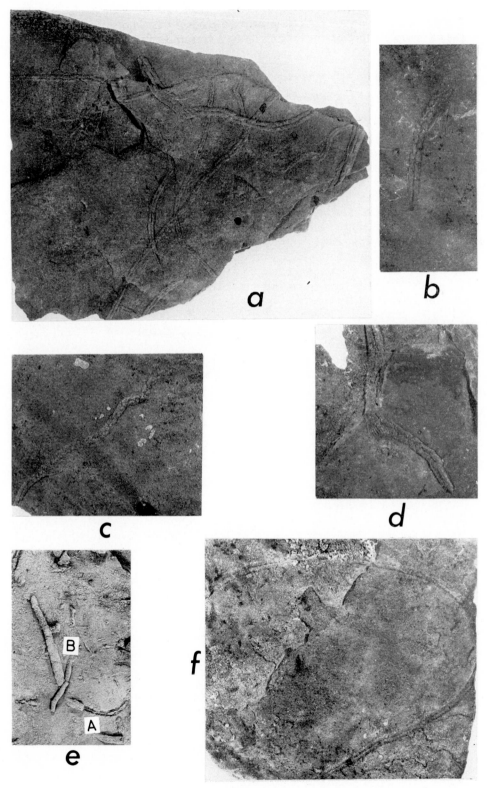

Strictly speaking the grooves should be assigned a different name but this appears to be unnecessary. Occasionally the grooves pass into smooth or slightly ridged cylinders of sediment ranging up to 2 mm in diameter and ending bluntly (positive hyporelief, Pl. 1f). These are normally short in extent.

Locality and horizon. Abundant throughout the sandstone-shale facies of the Forest Marble at Watton Cliff and Herbury Peninsula. They seem to characterise this facies throughout southern England because specimens have been found both in North Dorset and Oxfordshire. They also occur less commonly in the Cornbrash of the latter county, as at Long Hanborough. Wright (1968) records *Gyrochorte* from the Callovian of Yorkshire.

Interpretation. Gyrochorte is a well-known trace fossil on the European continent, and ranges in age from the Carboniferous to the Lower Tertiary. Its interpretation has been the subject of considerable dispute, partly because of a reliance on museum material in which the upper and lower surface of sandstone slabs was not known. In the absence of such diagnostic structures as ripple marks and load casts it is quite natural to assume that the tramline grooves signify the upper surface and the plaited ridges the lower surface. This mistake was made by Heer, the original describer of the ichnogenus, who considered that the plaited ridges (*Zöpfe*) were produced by crawling molluscs or worms, and also by Quenstedt, who took them for the impressions of ophiuroids.

Fuchs (1895) was the first to recognise that the plaited ridges of *Gyrochorte* signified tunnelling structures and drew attention to the observations of Hancock (1858) on amphipods tunnelling in intertidal sand flats in County Durham. He also compared the plaited structure to surface crawling traces of the amphipod *Corophium* in plaster of Paris, as recorded in the experiments of Nathorst (1881). Subsequently a certain amount of confusion was introduced by Abel (1935). On pages 222 and 241 of his work *Gyrochorte* is listed amongst traces attributable to gastropod trails but on page 274 *et seq.* the *Zöpfe* structures, which are in fact *Gyrochorte,* were considered, following the observations of Hancock and Nathorst, to be the result of amphipod activity. Unfortunately most of the *Zöpfe* were thought to occur on the bed undersurface and a clear distinction between subsurface tunnelling and surface crawling activity was not made. This led Häntzschel (1939) to point out that, while amphipods were by no means to be excluded, comparison with *Corophium* tracks was not justified because this genus apparently does not tunnel horizontally through the sediment.

This point was again raised by Weiss (1940), who gave a very thorough description of *Gyrochorte* in Lower and Middle Jurassic sandstones of southern Germany. Amphipods were dismissed as causative agents because *Corophium* produces surface tracks but not tunnels, but the allusions of earlier authors to Hancock's important observations were ignored. Weiss (1941) preferred to attribute *Gyrochorte* to a polychaete-like worm, but failed to produce supporting evidence or discuss the possible mechanism of formation. Seilacher (in Schindewolf and Seilacher 1955) also thought that a worm was responsible, and his interpretation will be discussed subsequently.

It is now clear that Quenstedt's interpretation is only of historical interest and that *Gyrochorte* could only have been produced by the movement through the sediment of some organism such as a gastropod, crustacean or worm.

A number of gastropods are known to produce winding surface trails with transverse markings, some of which may be obliquely oriented with respect to the axis of movement. None are known for certain to tunnel systematically beneath the sediment surface, however. Even if this were so, it is difficult to conceive how a trailing spire would produce the plaits.

With regard to crustaceans, it is important to consult the work of Hancock

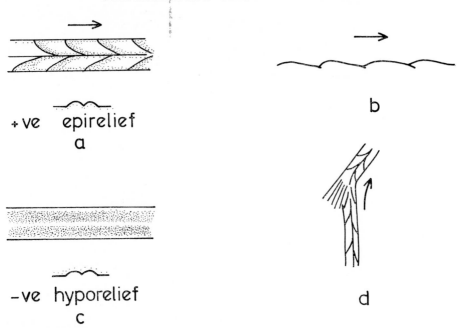

Fig. 1. Diagrams to illustrate structure of *Gyrochorte*. a upper surface; b lateral view, arrows indicate inferred direction of movement; c under surface tunnel; d structure at sharp bend of plaited ridges, arrow indicating inferred direction of movement.

(1858). He observed that species of the amphipod genera *Sulcator* and *Kröyera* produced tunnels immediately below the surface of sand in the intertidal zone. The structure produced by *Sulcator arenarius* was described in some detail. As the creature tunnels, an arch, up to 7·5 mm wide, is raised above the sediment surface. This arch collapses in the middle after the animal has passed because of lack of support, resulting in the formation of a median groove. Bilobate ribbon-like ridges are the end product; they may extend for several metres and exhibit intricate winding patterns. Occasionally Hancock was able to observe arched transverse ridges inclined at an acute angle to the axis of movement (pl. 14 fig. 1). Movement of the amphipods appeared to be intermittent rather than continuous. Lessertisseur gives an illustration of a bilobate ridge produced by the tunnelling amphipod *Haustorious* (1955 pl. 3 fig. 1). Tunnelling is, in fact, quite a common activity among burrowing amphipods and has also been recorded for certain isopods (e.g. Tait 1927).

A weakness of the tunnelling amphipod interpretation for *Gyrochorte* is that the vertical separation of the plaited ridge and underlying groove can extend up to 1 cm. Weiss (1940) claims instances of a 1·5 cm separation. Experiments with wet sand indicate that whereas superficial tunnelling of no more than a few millimetres may effect the creation of an overlying ridge, given a reasonably compacted sand, tunnelling at a depth of 1 cm or more apparently does not. It was presumably to account for this fact, and Weiss' (1940) claim that the ridges sometimes show a more irregular course than the grooves to which they appear to be related, that Seilacher in Schindewolf and Seilacher (1955 p. 380) proposed a worm-like burrower whose anterior end was raised above the general axis of movement of the body and could

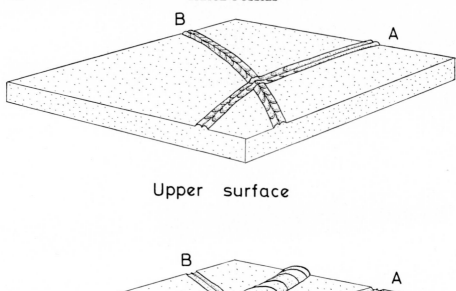

Upper surface

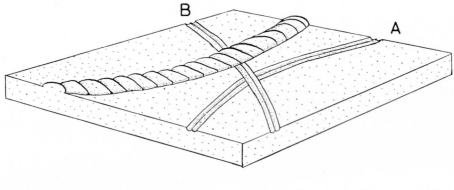

Lower surface

Fig. 2. Oblique view of sandstone bed with *Gyrochorte* (upper and lower surfaces) and *Imbrichnus* (lower surface).

move around to left and right of the hind part. The evidence supporting this conclusion was not, however, brought forward.

Any interpretation must take into account three important matters. Firstly, when two ridges cross each other (e.g. Pl. 1a, Fig. 2), which is the younger? In Seilacher's diagram (*op. cit.* 1955 p. 380) the topographically higher ridge is shown to be the younger, but it is difficult to see how this can be so, because the sand which forms the ridges has been displaced from below and the presumed older ridge would have been scythed through by the activity of the organism, most of whose body would have been up to a centimetre or more below the sediment surface. I consider, on the contrary, that, for instance in Figure 2, ridge B is younger than ridge A, which has in consequence been displaced upwards at the point of crossing.

Secondly, in which direction did the organism move? Seilacher has argued (personal communication) that this is given by the direction of lateral displacement of the older ridge at cross-over points, and always indicates movement opposed to the direction of acute intersection of the transverse minor ridges. Since we disagree about the relative age of such ridges I cannot accept this as valid, nor moreover does material from the Forest Marble convincingly show displacements of the kind mentioned.

Evidence that the direction of movement was in the sense opposite to that deduced by Seilacher, comes from specimens of the sort illustrated in Plate 1d, and Figure 1d. The triangular zone with fine radiating-to-subparallel ridges suggests marks made by limbs or parapodia, related to the sharp change in direction of movement. This, however, seems plausible only if the animal moved in the direction of acute intersection of the transverse ridges. Curiously, this is the interpretation illustrated in Seilacher's figure, in contradiction to his conclusion based on ridge intersection.

Thirdly, can Weiss' claim that *Gyrochorte* ridges may show a sinusoidal oscillation with respect to underlying grooves be clearly demonstrated? This cannot be done with the Forest Marble material I have studied but may be possible with the much more abundant material available to Professor Seilacher. It is earnestly to be hoped that he will publish the evidence supporting his 1955 interpretation.

From the foregoing discussion it is apparent that no definite conclusion can here be arrived at concerning the nature of the *Gyrochorte* organism, or about the precise mechanism of formation of the structures. Whereas some reasonable but not wholly satisfactory actualistic comparisons can be made with tunnelling amphipods, burrowing worms are known at present only to produce irregular, branching smooth-walled tubes at varying angles to the sediment surface (e.g. Nathorst 1881; Lessertisseur 1955). In all fairness to Seilacher's interpretation, however, it must be admitted that analysis of many familiar trace fossils has led to the deduction of activity programmes that cannot yet be matched in Recent sediments.

Ichnogenus PELECYPODICHNUS Seilacher 1953

Pelecypodichnus sp.

Description. Almond-shaped or pod-like trace fossils on the undersurface of sandstones, up to 1 cm in maximum dimension. The orientation appears to be random. They are not generally abundant but isolated slabs have been found in which they are quite common.

Locality and horizon. Forest Marble Formation, Watton Cliff.

Interpretation. Following Seilacher, the structures are interpretated as the resting traces of small bivalves. No body fossils corresponding to the trace fossils have been found, as is the usual situation.

Ichnogenus PALAEOPHYCUS Hall 1847

Palaeophycus(?) sp.

Plate 2a

Description. One specimen on the undersurface of a sandstone shows smooth, cylindrical subhorizontal sediment-filled tubes, 2·5 mm wide, which branch and pursue a sinuous course. This appears to correspond closely to Hall's description of *Palaeophycus* from the Ordovician of New York State (1847 p. 7 pl. 2 figs 1, 2, 4, 5). That part of the specimen between the two branchings reaches a height of 4 mm and shows laminations parallel to the bedding.

Locality and horizon. Forest Marble Formation, Watton Cliff.

Interpretation. Smooth, branching cylindrical tubes with a sinuous course are

PLATE 2

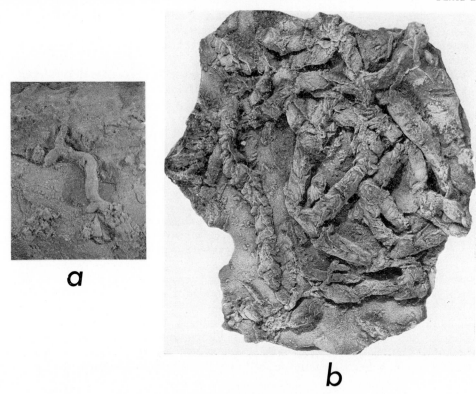

a

b

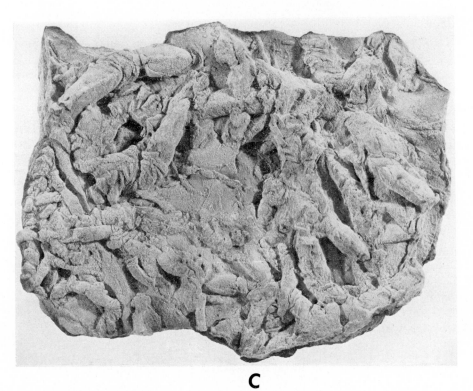

c

characteristic of annelids and this seems the most probable interpretation of the figured specimen. The laminations parallel to the bedding in one place and the fact that the tube is here slightly higher than long are reminiscent of *Teichichnus* and suggest an adaptation to sedimentation with the burrow rising slightly to keep pace.

Ichnogenus PLANOLITES Nicholson 1873

Planolites sp.

Plate 1f

Description. Subcylindrical, smooth-walled sediment-filled tubes, up to 4 mm diameter, running more or less parallel to the bedding planes on the undersurface of sandstones. They pursue a course which varies from straight to slightly sinuous.

Locality and horizon. Forest Marble Formation, Dorset and Oxfordshire.

Interpretation. These moderately abundant trace fossils have few distinctive morphological characteristics. *Planolites* has been applied rather loosely to a variety of comparable structures, which are commonly attributed to the burrowing activities of worms. This attribution would be difficult to demonstrate conclusively but is perhaps the most probable interpretation.

Ichnogenus IMBRICHNUS ichnogen. nov.

Imbrichnus wattonensis ichnosp. nov.

Plate 2 b, c, Figure 2

Holotype. Oxford University Museum J28228

Diagnosis. Sediment-filled burrows, with semi- or full-relief, parallel or sub-parallel to the bedding and with imbricate structure.

Description. The undersurface of one or more of the sandstone beds shows a great abundance of a distinctive type of trace fossil which requires a new name. The structures in question consist of winding, sediment-filled tubes, from 0·5 to 1·0 cm in diameter, aligned more or less parallel to the bedding (positive hyporelief). They grade from structures in semi-relief which resemble filled troughs to subcylindrical tubes affixed to the undersurface of the sandstone, in full or almost full relief. There is some variation in the horizontal plane, with locally slight ascent or descent, as when the structures cross each other. Generally they pursue a fairly sinuous course and may bend back on themselves. The most characteristic feature is the imbrication of the sediment fill, which consists of successive pads of sandstone from 1 to 3 mm thick, inclined on each other at 60° or less to the horizontal. Locally the visible evidence of imbrication, in the form of differential weathering, is lost and the trace

---

Plate 2

a *?Palaeophycus*, Forest Marble; Watton Cliff, Dorset. Author's collection, ×1.

b *Imbrichnus wattonensis* ichnogen. et ichnosp. nov. Forest Marble; Watton Cliff, Dorset. Author's collection, ×0·5.

c *Imbrichnus wattonensis* ichnogen. et ichnosp. nov. Forest Marble; Watton Cliff, Dorset, Holotype, Oxford University Museum J28228, ×0·75

fossil may pass into an apparently smooth-walled structure. This signifies that the imbrication is only a superficial structure. At sharp bends the imbrication tends to splay out.

Locality and horizon. Forest Marble Formation, Watton Cliff.

Interpretation. The imbricate structure rules out the possibility that a vacated burrow system has subsequently been filled in by sediment in the manner of, for example, *Thalassinoides* or *Ophiomorpha*. Such a structure could only have been created by the organism itself in the course of its progression along or just below the sand-mud interface. For those structures in semirelief, one can visualise an organism ploughing a furrow into which sand falls, to be pushed back intermittently in discrete 'packets' to form the imbrication. It is difficult to envisage this process accounting for the structures in full relief, however. If they truly represent burrows within the underlying mud how did the sand enter at a sufficiently early stage to be reworked by the organism? As preservation in semirelief is the more usual, it may be that burrowing (or tunnelling) was confined to small areas a slight distance below the sediment surface, into which sand fell immediately.

With regard to the identity of the organism, it is known that imbricate markings can be produced by a variety of crustaceans, either through irregular burrowing movements or by touching bottom periodically between bouts of swimming (Hancock 1858 pl. 14; Nathorst 1886 pl. 3 figs 5, 6). None of these structures correspond closely, however, with *Imbrichnus*. On the other hand, Bandel (1967) has described structures comparable to *Imbrichnus* associated with *Pelecypodichnus*, from the Carboniferous of Kansas. As illustrated best in his plate 5 fig. 1 these consist of forked ridges on the undersurface of bedding planes branching from a median ridge, and appear to represent the trails produced by the bivalves which left *Pelecypodichnus* as resting traces. Bivalves commonly move by extending their foot into the sand; the tip of the foot swells to produce an anchor and then the foot muscles contract, thereby drawing the body forward. It is tentatively suggested that the imbricate markings of the trace fossil in question might have been produced by periodic extensions of the foot of a small bivalve during locomotion, while the non-imbricate core marks the movement of the shell. Unfortunately, although *Pelecypodichnus* of a suitable size does occur in the Forest Marble no association, on the same bedding planes with *Imbrichnus* has been observed.

3. Environment of deposition of the Forest Marble Formation

Shallow, agitated marine conditions are signified by the central limestone, which is in effect an accumulation of shells and shell fragments, notably oysters, associated with scattered ooliths, from which no doubt fine particles have been winnowed out by wave action. The presence of clay-galls and occasional limestone pebbles also signifies a certain amount of erosion of consolidated rock.

There are several indications, however, that the terrigenous clastic sediments might have been deposited in water of slightly reduced salinity. Firstly, although there is a considerable amount of finely comminuted shell material in the sandstone together with occasional more complete shells, this has clearly been reworked and transported. Shallow marine deposits in the British Jurassic are usually strongly bioturbated, with an abundance of such trace fossils as *Diplocraterion, Chondrites, Rhizocorallium,* and *Thalassinoides,* whereas bioturbation of this type is absent from the sandstones of the Forest Marble Formation. The abundance of land-derived plant material suggests the proximity of a freshwater influx. It may be significant that the deposit that seems to resemble most closely the central Forest Marble limestone in the whole of the Jurassic of the Dorset coast is the Cinder Bed of the Purbeck Formation, which is generally held to represent a marginal marine transgression in a variable hypersaline or hyposaline lagoonal environment. A further comparison can be made with beds of approximately the same age in western Scotland. The Bathonian Upper Ostrea Beds of the Great Estuarine Series of the Inner Hebrides contain abundant *Liostrea hebridica* together with marine bivalves and are interpreted by Hudson (1963) as marginal marine, with a salinity of perhaps 30‰ (the presence of echinoderms and brachiopods in the Forest Marble probably signifies a slightly higher salinity).

The environment of the deposits containing *Gyrochorte* and its associated trace fossils is therefore interpreted as shallow marginal marine, probably a coastal lagoon with slightly lowered salinity due to the influx of freshwater from a nearby river or system of rivers. The other trace fossils are consistent with this interpretation. The alternations of sandstone and shale might possibly signify variations in stage of the river but a likelier interpretation is that given to a comparable sequence in the inner part of the German Bay south of Heligoland. Thin beds of fine sand in a mud sequence can here be shown to be the consequence of heavy storms (occurring about once every 25 or 50 years) which have transported sand from the nearby tidal flats (Reineck *et al.* 1967). The paucity of untransported body fossils in the terrigenous clastic facies of the Forest Marble might partly be a consequence of a high rate of sedimentation.

Gyrochorte has recently been reported from a rather similar facies in the Hettangian of Lower Saxony, in association with a variety of other trace fossils including *Chondrites*, *Rhizocorallium* and *Thalassinoides*, interpreted as shallow marine (Häntzschel and Reineck 1968). It is not clear from the description whether or not *Gyrochorte* occurs on the same bedding planes as the other cited trace fossils. If the latter is the case, this would signify that the organism responsible for *Gyrochorte* was adapted to normal marine conditions (as also suggested by its occurrence in the Callovian of Oxfordshire and Yorkshire and in deposits of different ages from other countries) and that its absence from most marine Jurassic beds was a function of conditions of preservation.

From the British occurrences, there is a strong suggestion that a superficial burrower such as *Gyrochorte*, disturbing only the top centimetre or so of sediment, would stand little chance of preservation in a shallow marine environment with a high diversity of burrowing forms and a low rate of sedimentation. These two factors would normally have combined to effect intense superficial bioturbation and possibly a high degree of fluidity, so that only deeper-burrowing structures such as *Chondrites*, *Thalassinoides*, *Rhizocorallium* and *Diplocraterion* would have survived. It is noteworthy in this regard that Tertiary examples of *Gyrochorte* are found in flysch facies.

Gyrochorte is also abundant in the non-marine, low salinity portions of Upper Carboniferous cyclothems in the Ruhr, occurring in association with *Planolites* (Jessen and Kremp 1954). The only other Jurassic *Pelecypodichnus* found by me occurs in the Rhaeto-Lias coal measures of southern Sweden and in the non-marine Bathonian of Elgol, Skye.

Acknowledgments. I wish to thank Dr. H. S. Torrens for first drawing my attention to the trace fossils and Professor A. Seilacher, Dr. W. J. Kennedy and Mr. B. W. Sellwood for stimulating and critical discussions.

References

ABEL, O. 1935. *Vorzeitliche Lebensspuren*. Gustav Fischer, Jena.

BANDEL, K. 1967. Trace fossils from two Upper Pennsylvanian sandstones in Kansas. *Paleont. Contr. Univ. Kansas* Paper 18.

FUCHS, T. 1895. Studien über Fukoiden und Hieroglyphen. *Denkschr. Akad. Wiss. Wien, Math. nat. Kl.* **62,** 369.

HALL, J. 1847. *Paleontology of New York* **1,** Albany.

HANCOCK, A. 1858. Remarks on certain vermiform fossils found in the mountain limestone districts of the North of England. *Ann. Mag. nat. Hist.* (3) **2,** 443.

HÄNTZSCHEL, W. 1939. Die Lebensspuren von *Corophium volutator* (Pallas) und ihre paläonto-logische Bedeutung. *Senckenbergiana* **21,** 217.

—— and REINECK, H.-E. 1968. Fazies-Untersuchungen in Hettangium von Helmstedt (Niedersachsen). *Mitt. geol. StInst. Hamb.* **37,** 5.

HUDSON, J. D. 1963. The recognition of salinity-controlled mollusc assemblages in the Great Estuarine Series (Middle Jurassic) of the Inner Hebrides. *Palaeontology* **6,** 318.

JESSEN, W. and KREMP, G. 1954. Feinstratigraphisch-mikrofaunistische Profilbeschreibung mit Fundstücken von *Gyrochorte carbonaria* im Oberkarbon (Westfal A) am Niederrheim. *Neues Jb. Geol. Paläont. Mh.* p. 284.

LESSERTISSEUR, J. 1955. Traces fossiles d'activité animale et leur signification paléobiologique. *Mém. Soc. géol. Fr.* **34** (4), n.s. No. 74.

NATHORST, A. G. 1881. Om Spar af Nagra evertevrevade djur m.m. och delas paleontologiska betydelse. *K. svenska Vetensk. Akad. Handl.* **18,** 1.

—— 1886. Nouvelles observations sur les traces d'animaux et autres phenomènes d'origine purement mecanique decrits comme "Algues fossiles". *Ibid.* **21,** 1.

REINECK, H. E., GUTMAN, W. F. and HERTWECK, G. 1967. Das Schlickgebiet südlich Helgoland als Beispiel rezenter Schelfablagerungen. *Senckenb. leth.* **48,** 219.

SCHINDEWOLF, O. H. and SEILACHER, A. 1955. Beiträge zur Kenntnis des Kambriums in der Salt Range (Pakistan). *Abh. mat. naturw. Kl. Akad. Wiss. Mainz* No. 10, 261.

SEILACHER, A. 1953. Studien zur Palichnologie. II. Die fossilen Ruhespuren (*Cubichnia*). *Neues Jb. Geol. Paläont. Abh.* **98,** 87.

TAIT, J. 1927. Experiments and observations on Crustacea: part vii. Some structural and physiological features of the valviferous isopod *Chiridotea*. *Proc. R. Soc. Edinb.* **46,** 334.

WEISS, W. 1940. Beobachtungen en Zopfplatten. *Z. dt. geol. Ges.* **92,** 333.

—— 1941. Die Entstehung der "Zopfe" im schwarzen und braunen Jura. *Natur. Volk* **71,** 179.

WILSON, V., WELCH, F. B. A., ROBBIE, J. A. and GREEN, G. W. 1958. Geology of the country around Bridport and Yeovil. *Mem. geol. Surv. U.K.*

WRIGHT, J. K. 1968. The stratigraphy of the Callovian rocks between Newtondale and the Scarborough coast, Yorkshire. *Proc. Geol. Ass.* **79,** 363.

A. Hallam, Department of Geology, The University, Parks Road, Oxford OX1 3PR, U.K.

Star-like trace fossils

Walter Häntzschel

Star-like trace fossils are known from the Cambrian to the Recent. The recognition of their ecological significance and their producers has been facilitated by observations in modern seas. They belong to grazing and feeding traces (combined with a dwelling burrow), resting and swimming traces. Worms, amphipods, decapods, bivalves, holothurians, and even fish produce recent star-shaped traces. Large star-like traces with many rays have been found in flysch deposits of Spain and Poland. Recent counterparts of them have been photographed on the deep ocean floors but their producers are unknown. Problematic star-like fossils from the Jurassic of Germany have generally been interpreted as Hydro- or Scyphomedusae, but were also considered as trace fossils. This problem is briefly discussed. The genera of true star-like ichnofossils, those of doubtful interpretation (medusae or other body fossils), and descriptions of unnamed star-like trace fossils are listed in an appendix.

1. Introduction

Star-like trace fossils (*"traces en étoile"* or *"traces en rosette"*, in French; *"Sternspuren"* in German) represent a group of morphologically well characterized fossils. In Vialov's system of traces, which is mainly founded on shape, they have been named "Asterichnidii" (Vialov 1968a p. 127). They are widely distributed all over the world, mostly on bedding planes of sedimentary rocks of marine origin. They range in age from Cambrian to Recent. Star-shaped trace fossils have attracted the attention of palaeontologists for a long time. As an example *"Spongia ottoi"* may be mentioned; it was described for the first time in 1849 by H. B. Geinitz from Cenomanian sandstones of Saxony. However, he considered it to belong to the Porifera as is shown by the assignation to the name of a Recent sponge genus. Some forty years ago the present author concluded that it was a grazing trace rather than a sponge (Häntzschel 1930). Meanwhile, many names for "genera" of star-like trace fossils have been erected on purely morphological criteria. They were listed as an appendix to that paper and some never used again. Those should therefore be cancelled as *"nomina oblita"* according to the International Rules of Zoological Nomenclature. Other generic names have been given to star-shaped fossils considered by several authors to be true body fossils belonging to Scyphomedusae or Hydromedusae. At least some of them are indeed more probably radiating feeding or grazing traces surrounding a vertical dwelling burrow. Nowak (1957) and Seilacher (1955; 1962 p. 229) have already published such views, for instance for the flysch fossil *Lorenzinia* Gabelli. This paper will contribute to the interpretation of such genera still in doubt (see p. 206). Other generic names on my list will possibly be recognized as synonyms after thorough investigation of many well preserved specimens of similar genera. Difficulties arise when searching for type specimens for the revision of ichnogenera published many decades ago. Thus an entirely satisfactory review of all star-like trace fossils is not possible at the present time.

o

2. Ecological significance of star-like traces

In spite of their regular shape, star-like traces cannot be ascribed solely to one of the five groups of Seilacher's system of lebensspuren which is based on behavioural aspects of the animal producing the trails, tracks and burrows (Repichnia, Domichnia, Pascichnia, Fodinichnia, Cubichnia). Observations on Recent forms, mainly in such shallow water biotopes as tidal flats, have facilitated the recognition of the ecological significance of star-like ichnofossils. Most of them belong to the grazing traces (Pascichnia). They are, however, generally combined with a dwelling burrow pertaining to the Domichnia, its opening often being visible in the centre of the star. Modern examples are the star-like traces made by the long flexible in-current siphon of the bivalve genus *Scrobicularia,* extended to the surface of the tidal flat deposits, or those produced by polychaete worms like *Nereis* or others, around the mouth of their vertical dwelling burrows.

However, the Recent star-like traces around the openings of the burrows of the amphipod *Corophium* should be considered as feeding traces. The rather short radiating trenches are produced by the second pair of antennae of the amphipod. These little stars differ distinctly from the patterns of grazing trails like the ramified ones of *Nereis* or *Scrobicularia* which intensely utilize the available surface. The radiating trenches scooped out by tropical crabs (e.g. *Scopimera*) can similarly be considered as feeding traces. These trenches may be observed around the entrance of the burrows occupied by the crabs and are excavated for food. This is demons-trated by the presence of numerous tiny pellets of sifted sand arranged behind the narrow trenches.

Stellate resting traces are easily recognizable as moulds of the body of certain animals. They are generally produced by asteroids and ophiuroids which dig themselves into the sediment near the surface in order to hide. They can be dis-tinguished from bodily preserved asteroids or ophiuroids by the occasional occurrence of overlapping and horizontal repetitions of the same trace. This is caused by a slight displacement of the animals in the sediment. Another feature of these traces is their vertical repetition on two or more planes of the sediment layer.

Difficulties arise in ascribing to one of the five ecological groups the peculiar star-like traces made by the present-day fish *Gobius*. These traces were observed on the coast of the Baltic Sea where the very shallow water near the beach was once driven back by a violent storm blowing seawards (Häntzschel 1935). In order to hide its "nest"—a shell of the bivalve genus *Mya,* on whose inner side the fish's eggs are fixed—the animal covers it with sand. Several times it swims radially in the direction of the shell, thereby "shovelling" sand over it by the movement of its pectoral fins and its tail. The star-like patterns originating in such an unusual and curious manner can be considered as swimming traces (Natichnia A. H. Müller, a subgroup of his Movichnia).

Another special kind of trace not to be ascribed to one of the ecological groups are the stellate imprints named *Asterichnites* Brown and Vokes 1944 from the Upper Cretaceous of Montana and Wyoming (U.S.A.). The authors published a very interesting and surprising interpretation of these ichnofossils based on observa-tions with the Recent cephalopod *Loligo.* They suggested that these star-like traces, which are arranged in rows, each consist of an unmarked central disc and 8 radiating grooves, were made by a dibranchiate cephalopod. Apparently it bounced over the bottom of the sea on the tips of its tentacles while the animal's body was turned into a nearly perpendicular position. Such an origin of a stellate imprint is certainly unexpected, but this could also be a very rare kind of Movichnia.

3. Producers

As proved by present day observations of Recent star-like traces described in the foregoing section, worms (particularly polychaetes), crustaceans (amphipods and decapods), bivalves, and even fish may produce such patterns on the sediment surface by various kinds of activity.

A further group of animals must still be mentioned. In very shallow water (zone of *Zostera*) off the coast of Brittany even a very narrow holothurian (*Leptosynapta inhaerens* T. O. Müller) produces star-like traces (Lessertisseur 1955 p. 32, pl. 4 fig. 6). A radiating pattern, with a diameter of about 4 cm, surrounds the anterior end of the animal which is dug in the sediment. The observer considered that form as "exceptional", but certainly it is not very surprising that such a narrow worm-like sediment feeding and inhabiting animal is able to make such traces.

To these six groups we should add dibranchiate cephalopods, provided that Brown and Vokes' interpretation of the ichnogenus *Asterichnites* is correct.

In some cases, however, we do not know the animals which produce Recent star-like traces. For instance, the large radiating grooves photographed from very deep ocean floors and discussed below are of unknown affinities. New methods remain to be developed for extracting blocks of undisturbed samples of sediment with their infauna from such parts of the bathyal depths where these traces have been photographed.

4. Large star-like flysch ichnofossils and their Recent counterparts from the deep-sea floor

From Eocene flysch sediments of the southern slope of the Pyrenees (near Jaca, northern Spain) G. Lucas and M. Rech-Frollo (1965) described large *traces en rosette*. They are characterized by very numerous straight rays (about 25 to 30) and by diameters from 30 to 50 cm.

In Polish flysch deposits of Upper Jurassic age (region of Bielsko, Carpathian mountains) W. Nowak (1957 p. 213 pl. 13, see also Pl.1b) has found in a sandstone a similar star-like trace of diameter nearly 30 cm. Some rays of this specimen bifurcate, partly near the centre, partly distally. Occurrences of similar smaller specimens (diameter about 15 cm) were also described and figured by the same author.

Furthermore, a sketch of a smaller star-like ichnofossil, previously unnamed, has been figured by A. Seilacher (1955 fig. 5 no. 89) in his general sketch summarizing fossil ichnocoenoses from different habitats. The size of this fossil, found in the flysch deposits of the Carpathian mountains, is about 15 cm in diameter. In 1968 it was named *Glockeria* by Książkiewicz (1968 p. 15) and the author chose it as the type species of that new ichnogenus.

Lucas and Rech-Frollo, Nowak, and Seilacher, rejected these "stars" as bodily preserved fossils and compared them with modern star-shaped lebensspuren made by various animals. The French authors excluded crabs as well as amphipods, annelids, and fishes as producers of these traces and also discounted an inorganic origin. They suggested bivalves as the producers of these star-like traces but *"de grande taille, comme une Mye ou une Lutraire, sans doute à coquille très mince"* (Lucas and Rech-Frollo 1965 p. 169). Contrary to this view Nowak (1957 p. 218) excluded—in my opinion rightly—crustaceans and bivalves. Although no modern counterparts of such large trace fossils have hitherto been observed as undoubtedly made by worms, Nowak interpreted his radiating traces as grazing trails of this group of animals. The specimen figured by Seilacher was classified as a feeding trace.

The still unsolved question of the producers must surely be of interest but cannot be discussed here at length. I disagree with the French authors. Even large bivalves cannot be considered able to make radiating traces of such dimensions. This would require bivalves with unusually long siphons of considerable flexibility as these are the only bivalve organs which could produce star-like traces by grazing the surface of the sea floor, as shown for example by the Recent *Scrobicularia* on the surface of tidal flat deposits. It is much more probable that worms or at least worm-like animals made these traces. Even if star-like traces made by Recent polychaetes on tidal flats are characterized by relatively few rays and small size these features are insufficient reasons for excluding worms as producers.

Recent counterparts of the large star-like traces in the flysch have been found and published after the appearance of the French and Polish papers mentioned above. Great "stars" with many rays radiating from a centre were observed by submarine photography on the Indian and Pacific Ocean floors, for the most part in depths from 2000 to 5700 m and in latitudes from 28°N to 35°S (Ewing and Davis 1967 p. 280-282 figs 24-53 to 24-60, see also Pl. 1a). Some of them have narrow grooves 40 cm in length radiating from a small central hole or, rarely, from a small central lump. According to Mrs. G. Hartmann-Schröder (Zoological Institute Hamburg) polychaetes with a tuft of very many tentacles, as in some terebellids, are most likely to produce such large traces.

Other photographs, taken from the same depths and localities, yielded pictures of the same patterns whose rays were only 10 or 15 cm in length. They also mostly radiate from central holes or lumps. In some cases the radiating groove pattern is incomplete or the furrows are concentrated into bunches.

From the Atlantic Ocean floor southeast of the Bermudas L. Dangeard and P. Giresse (1968 pl. 12 fig. 37) figured *"traces organiques en rosette"* seen on the *Globigerina* ooze at a depth of 4,050 m. As far as discernible on the photograph, these star-like traces show about 12 or more radiating furrows, but absence of a scale prevents determination of their size.

From the head of the submarine Wilmington Canyon (east-southeast of the mouth of the Delaware Bay, U.S.A.) Stanley and Kelling (1968 pl. 10D) figured asteroid lebensspuren photographed at a depth of about 730 m in silty mud. The precise size of them is unknown but the authors believe (*in litt.*) that the diameter of these structures is about 15 to 25 cm. They suspect burrowing worms or any other benthic animals as the producers.

Following the investigations of Ph. H. Kuenen on turbidites and modern turbidity currents, many flysch-sequences are now regarded as deposited in bathyal depths of the ancient oceans. In general true flysch sediments are ichnologically

Plate 1

a Large Recent star-like trace. Pacific ocean (17° 00′ S, 114° 32′ W; 3,147 m). 40 cm long narrow grooves, radiating from a small central elevation. (From Ewing and Davis 1967 p. 281, fig. 24-59. Photograph courtesy of Dr. Ewing, Palisades, N.Y., U.S.A.).

b Large fossil star-like trace. Region of Bielsko, Polish Carpathians, Flysch (Lower Ciesczyn shales), ? Kimmeridgian—Lower Tithonian. (From Nowak 1957 pl. 13. Photograph courtesy of Dr. Nowak, Kraków.)

PLATE 1

a

b

characterized by ichnocoenoses consisting mainly of surface sediment-grazers which produce Pascichnia. Networks, meanders of various forms, spirals, and similar patterns, but also smaller regular star-like traces (as for example the ichnogenus *Lorenzinia* Gabelli) belong to that group of trace fossils.

Large radiating grooves undoubtedly to be ascribed to grazing trails, and now detected in depths from about 2000 to 5700 m, are of great sedimentological as well as palaeontological significance. Thus the discovery of Recent large star-shaped traces, readily comparable to similar fossil ones, can be considered as new bathymetric evidence that true flysch sediments were deposited in bathyal depths. In this connection we also recall that recent giant spirals and meanders have been photographed on the Pacific and Indian Ocean floors, mostly on depths of more than 4000 m (Seilacher 1967).

However, it should never be forgotten that the same kind of tracks and trails of marine animals can exist in very different depths in the oceans. For instance, *Zoophycos* spreite burrows are known as trace fossils from sandy and obviously shallow water sediments, namely Middle Jurassic sandstones in South Germany. On the other hand, recent spreite burrows of the *Zoophycos* type have been found in a deep sea core from a depth of 3800 m in the southeastern Pacific where unknown animals excavated them in a fine ooze (Seilacher 1967 p. 424 pl. 1 fig. E).

Therefore, quick and premature generalizations on the bathymetric significance of trace fossils from actualistic observations on recent lebensspuren should be avoided. No general conclusions can be drawn on the bathymetric significance of star-like trace fossils in ancient sediments. We know them in various forms in recent marine sediments from the tidal flats to the deep sea. In this case, however, I consider the comparison of very similar traces from recent and ancient deposits justifiable, particularly since it conforms well with our conception of the sedimentation of the flysch-sequences.

5. Jurassic medusae or star-like ichnofossils?

From the Middle Jurassic of South Germany rosette-like fossils about 5 cm in diameter have been described several times as medusae or at least as problematical fossils of medusoid affinities. They are characterized by a rosette of 10 to 12 pillowy sectors sharply defined by grooves. However, the first interpretation of such a fossil described and named as *Medusina geryonides* by F. v. Huene (1901) was contested by Th. Fuchs (1901). He considered it to be related to the genus *Gyrophyllites* Glocker or *Discophorites* Heer, genera belonging to his "family" Alectoruridae in which he united all kinds of spreiten burrows. Subsequently, new specimens of the same *"Medusina"* or very similar fossils were again detected in Middle Jurassic sediments of Swabia and Franconia. They were named *Palaeosemaeostoma geryonides* by Rüger and Rüger-Haas (1925) who assigned them to sessile Scyphomedusae. After the appearance of that paper several German authors (Adam, Kiderlen, O. Kuhn, Lörcher) investigated a few specimens of that fossil but none of them contested the interpretation as medusae. Only Kieslinger (1939), a specialist in scyphozoans, clearly expressed doubt as to whether these fossils are true medusae (1939 p. A81, A101). In the American *"Treatise"* Harrington and Moore (1956 p. F76) assigned *Palaeosemaeostoma* with some doubt to the order Trachylinida of the Hydrozoa. In 1955 Seilacher considered that genus as a feeding burrow. He based this opinion on reconstructions of specimens of the Tübingen collection (1955 fig. 5 no. 53). As already suggested by Th. Fuchs (1901), he referred it again to the ichnogenus *Gyrophyllites*.

On most of these South German *Palaeosemaeostoma* a "pedicle" starting from the centre of the rosette and descending downwards has been found and was at first considered as the "mouth pedicle". Because of its position, different from that expected for that organ on a medusa embedded with its exumbrella convex-down, Rüger and Rüger-Haas interpreted the pedicle as "pedunculus umbrellae". Thus they assigned *Palaeosemaeostoma* to the sessile medusae which are fixed in the sediment by a "pedicle" as can be seen with recent Stauromedusae. However, several auxiliary hypotheses became necessary in order to explain the fossilization and preservation of such soft-bodies and—as could be learned from actualistic observations—very transient organisms.

In my opinion the interpretation of these radiating patterns as the product of feeding activities of animals living in the sediment is more convincing. The "pedunculus" is then to be regarded as the burrow occupied by the animal producing the star-like patterns on the surface of the sediment or sometimes possibly even in it.

The problematical *Palaeosemaeostoma* has not yet been recorded in Jurassic sediments in North Germany, but there are two interesting star-like fossils from the Lower Lias of Lower Saxony in the collections of the Geological-Palaeontological Institute of Hamburg. Though they are not to be assigned to *Palaeosemaeostoma* I will discuss them briefly in connection with the question: medusa or trace fossil?

The first specimen (Pl. 2a, c) was collected (by Professor Voigt, Hamburg) in the pit of a brick-yard 1 km southwest of Olber (Geological Map 1: 25000, no. 3927, Ringelheim, Lower Saxony). It lies on the surface of a flattened 3 cm thick calcareous and argillaceous concretion. The rosette consists of flat radiating grooves narrowing towards the centre. The diameter is about 5 cm. Owing to the incomplete preservation of the pattern it is not possible to state exactly how many radiating grooves are developed (about 10?). In the centre a low ringlike elevation can be seen, 1 cm in diameter and about 4 mm wide. I have cut across this specimen (Pl. 2c) and surprisingly, but not unexpectedly, a burrow 3 mm in diameter was to be seen cutting somewhat obliquely through the rock in its entire thickness. The sediment infilling is darker than the surrounding sediment, but the wall of the burrow is lighter than the filled burrow.

The second star-like fossil from the Lower Lias of North Germany (Pl. 2b) has been collected by Mr. K. Wiedenroth (Peine) who kindly presented it to the Geological-Palaeontological Institute of Hamburg University. It was found in the pit of the brick-yard Gretenberg near Sehnde, southeast of Lehrte (Map 1: 25000 No. 3625, Lehrte) in the Lias gamma (Lower *centaurum* zone). It was found in a fine-grained calcareous and argillaceous rock, the surface of which shows the rather well preserved impression of the rosette-like pattern which is somewhat more regular than that described from Olber. About 10 club or pear-shaped depressions, of varying size, are arranged radially. The diameter is 5 cm. The centre of the rosette is not surrounded by a narrow low-relief ring as observed in the other specimen but it is somewhat deepened and a little plug 2-3 mm wide is visible there. I have not sectioned this specimen but it seems certain that the plug is the upper end of a burrow starting from here and passing into the rock, as observed with similar fossils described above.

In spite of their low fossilization potential, jellyfish may be preserved under particular circumstances. However, all authors interpreting these Middle Jurassic problematic fossils as medusae have been forced to suggestions which were either improbable or without proof. Thus in order to prove the preservation of sessile medusae in their biotope it was supposed that the animals died by desiccation after a rapid, tectonically controlled, retreat of the sea. Very different opinions have been expressed concerning the systematic position of these problematica of medusoid affinities. It was uncertain whether they were to be referred to the Hydromedusae or Scyphomedusae (see also the note on p. 210), not to mention their reference to some order or family of these taxonomic units. The Hydromedusae and Scypho-medusae are based on tetrameral radial symmetry and four or some multiple of four is characteristic of several main parts of them. Although exceptions from this plan are known from recent medusae, as with several specimens of *Palaeosemaeostoma* where 9 to 10 lobes may be observed; in others 8 or 12 pillow-like sectors but of rather different width are seen.

Following Kieslinger 1939 (also Seilacher 1955; 1962; Nowak 1957; Grubić 1961; and Vialov 1968b) for the star-like flysch problematica like *Atollites, Bassaenia* and *Lorenzinia,* I must express considerable doubt as to the true nature of these presumptive jellyfish. An interpretation as trace fossils leads to no difficulties, although we do not yet have well documented recent counterparts of such stellate imprints as discussed here. It is to be hoped that more and thorough observations from biotopes of all modern marine environments and a better knowledge of the biology of the sessile medusae will help us solve these problems.

6. Appendix

The following list of star-like fossils has been divided into three groups: (i) genera of fossil star-like traces, (ii) genera possibly representing star-like traces, but mostly interpreted as medusae or other body fossils, (iii) descriptions of unnamed star-like trace fossils.

Pseudo fossils of star-like form are discussed in (iv).

The quotation of the age and occurrence of a "genus" refers to its first description, the reference to which may be found in Häntzschel 1965 (with the exception of *Asterichnus* Nowak 1961, *Asterichnus* Bandel 1967, *Dactylodiscus* Ślączka, *Fascisichnium, Glockeria,* and *Sublorenzinia* Książkiewicz 1968 and *Volkichnium* Pfeiffer 1965; for those see the list of references of this paper).

Plate 2

a Star-like fossil. Lower Lias, Ölber (Lower Saxony). (Discussion of the interpretation see p. 207.) Geol.-Palaeont. Inst. Univ. Hamburg, type specimen catal. no. 1337.

b Star-like fossil. Lower Lias, near Sehnde (Lower Saxony). (Discussion of the interpretation see p. 207.) Geol.-Palaeont. Inst. Univ. Hamburg, type specimen catal. no. 1338.

c The same specimen as in Pl. 2a, cut across and showing the burrow starting from the centre of the "star". Geol.-Palaeont. Inst. Univ. Hamburg, type specimen catal. no. 1337.

PLATE 2

a

b

c

(i) *Genera of fossil star-like traces*

Acanthus Grossheim 1946. L. Tert., U.S.S.R. (invalid name).
Asteriacites v. Schlotheim 1820. L. Juras., Germany.
Asterichnites Brown and Vokes 1944. U. Cret., U.S.A.
Asterichnus Bandel 1967. Pennsylv., U.S.A.
Asterichnus ("n.f.") Nowak 1961. Flysch, Poland. (nomen nudum).
Asterophycus Lesquereux 1876. Carbonif., U.S.A.
Asterosoma v. Otto 1854. U. Cret., Germany.
Astropolithon Dawson 1878. L. Cambr., Nova Scotia.
Bifasciculus Volk 1960. Ordovic., Germany.
Capodistria Vialov 1964. L. Tert., Jugoslavia.
Discophorites Heer 1877. L. Tert., Switzerland (synonym of *Gyrophyllites*).
Fascisichnium Książkiewicz 1968. L. Tert., Poland.
Glockeria Książkiewicz 1968. L. Tert., Poland.
Gyrophyllites Glocker 1841. U. Cret., Czechoslovakia.
Haentzschelinia Vialov 1964. U. Cret., Germany (for *Spongia ottoi* Geinitz.)
Heliophycus Miller and Dyer 1878. U. Ordovic., U.S.A. (synonym of *Asteriacites*).
Lennea Kräusel and Weyland 1932. L. Devon., Germany (not star-like trace *sensu stricto*).
Oldhamia Forbes 1849 (?). L. Cambr., Ireland.
Palaeocrista Hundt 1941. Ordovic., Germany (invalid name).
Petaloglyphus Vialov, Gorbatsch and Dobrowolskaja 1964. L. Cret., USSR.
Scotolithus Linnarsson 1871. L. Cambr., Sweden.
Spongaster Fritsch 1908. L. Silur., Czechoslovakia (invalid name).
Spongia ottoi Geinitz 1849. U. Cret., Germany (= *Haentzschelinia* Vialov 1964).
Stellascolites Etheridge 1876. L. Ordovic., England.
Stelloglyphus Vialov 1964. U. Cret., USSR.
Sublorenzinia Książkiewicz 1968. U. Cret., Poland.
Volkichnium Pfeiffer 1965. L. Ordovic., Germany.

(ii) *Genera possibly representing star-like traces but mostly interpreted as medusae or other body fossils*

Atollites Maas 1902. L. Cret., Czechoslovakia (very probably synonym of *Lorenzinia*).
Bassaenia Renz 1925. U. Cret., Greece.
Brooksella Walcott 1896. M. Cambr., U.S.A.
Dactyloidites Hall 1886. L. Cambr., U.S.A.
Dactylodiscus Ślączka 1965. Flysch, Poland (nomen nudum).
Duodecimedusina King 1955. U. Pennsylv., U.S.A.
Kirklandia Caster 1945. L. Cret., U.S.A.
Laotira Walcott 1896. M. Cambr., U.S.A.
Lorenzinia Gabelli 1900. L. Tert., Italy.
Medusina Walcott 1898. (Caster 1945 p. 196: "form-genus of highly questionable designation".
    M. tergestina Malaroda 1947 by Seilacher 1958 p. 1070 considered as feeding burrow).
Nimbus Bogatschew 1930. L. Tert., USSR. (invalid name).
Palaeosemaeostoma Rüger and Rüger-Haas 1925. M. Juras., Germany.
Rotamedusa Simpson 1969. L. Tert., Poland.
Solicyclus Quenstedt 1879. L. Juras., Germany.
Staurophyton Meunier 1891. Ordovic., France.

Note: The very divergent opinions concerning these genera may be demonstrated by the genera *Atollites* and *Lorenzinia*. Kieslinger (1939 p. A88) suggested that both of them are perhaps medusae and that *Atollites* is a synonym of *Lorenzinia*. Contrary to this Harrington and Moore (1956 p. F43, F73) considered *Lorenzinia* as belonging to the Scyphomedusae and *Atollites* to the Hydrozoa—not to mention their interpretation as trace fossils (Seilacher, Nowak, Grubić, Vialov, see p. 208).

(iii) *Descriptions of unnamed star-like trace fossils*

In several geological and palaeontological papers, star-shaped ichnofossils have only been described and/or figured but not named. Therefore it may be useful to put them together here as supplement to the preceding list of genera of such fossils. The writer is well aware of the probability of having overlooked some of these descriptions hidden in the worldwide palaeontological literature.

The quotations to the papers listed below may be found among the references of this paper Missing page quotations in a reference of the following table mean that the paper deals with star-like trace fossils exclusively. Otherwise I have quoted the passage in which the description and discussion of the star-shaped ichnofossil may be found.

Author	Age	Locality	Remarks
F. Prantl 1946 p. 6-9, pl. 2	Ordovician (U. Llandeilo)	Chrustenice (?) Bohemia (Czechoslovakia)	Diameter of the stars from 6 to 10 cm; number of rays from 9 to 25.
Rud. Richter 1927 p. 199, pl. 1 fig. 3	Ordovician	Beraun, Bohemia (Czechoslovakia)	Only 5 rays, diameter from 1 to 3 cm.
J. M. Clarke 1924	a. Silurian b. U. Devonian (Chemung)	a. Mt. Joli, Peninsula of Gaspé (Canada). b. Southwestern New York (U.S.A.)	a. 18 cm in diameter, about 35 rays. b. "Chrysanthemum-like tufted casts", from 3 to 5 cm in diameter.
H. Weyland and E. Budde 1932 p. 260-268, figs. 1-7, 12, 13	Middle Devonian	Elberfeld (West Germany)	Diameter of the stars from 3 to 4 cm, from 8 to 20 rays; identical traces from Gaspé ex parte = *Annularia laxa* Dawson 1871.
J. F. N. Delgado 1910 pl. 18 fig. 1-3, pl. 19, pl. 20 fig. 3	? L. Carbonif. ("schistes a Néréites")	San Domingos, Alentejo (SE-Portugal)	Not described, only figured
V. van Straelen 1938 p. 3-5, figs. 1-3	L. Carbonif. (Visean)	Eclaibes, Dépt. du Nord (France)	Very small, diameter 0·7 cm, made by crustaceans?
S. van der Heide 1955 p. 78-79, pl. B fig. 16	U. Carbonif.	Boring in Limburg, Netherlands	Diameter from 7 to 10 cm.
G. C. Lewarne 1964	U. Carbonif. (Namurian)	County Clare (Ireland)	Five-branched fossils; resting traces of ophiurans.
D. J. Jones 1935	Pennsylvan.	Seminole, Oklah. (U.S.A.)	Resting traces? Interpreted as young starfish.
O. Abel 1935 p. 391, fig. 327	Permian (Ecca slates)	Calvinia (South Africa)	Very small stars named by Vialov 1968 p. 335 *Stelloglyphus abeli*.
H.-G. Kupfahl 1965 pl. 4 fig. 1	L. Triass. (Middle Bunter)	Fraurombach, near Schlitz, Hessen (West Germany)	No description, only figured; small stars of about 2 cm in diameter.
A. Seilacher 1955 fig. 5 no. 55	L. Lias (Jurassic)	Hüttlingen, Swabia (South Germany)	Only sketched, irregular pattern, rays of varying length and branched, 1 cm in diameter.
H. Furrer 1939 p. 94-95, fig. 3	L. Cretac. (Valanginian)	Bernese Highlands (Switzerland)	No detailed description, only a few rays, about 5 cm in diameter.
W. Nowak 1957 p. 213-215, pl. 13-16	L. Cretac. (or U. Jurass.?) Flysch	Region of Bielsko, Carpathians (Poland)	See p. 203 and Pl. 1b of this paper!
W. Häntzschel 1964 p. 301-302, pl. 4 figs. 1-2	U. Campan. (U. Cretac.)	Beckum, Westphalia (West Germany)	Many narrow rays, diameter from 3 to 8 cm, central hole deep and wide.
M. Książkiewicz 1960 p. 740-741, 746, pl. 3 fig. 10	U. Cretac. (Godula beds, Flysch)	Polish Carpathian Mountains	Only a few rays, no complete star-like pattern.

Author	Age	Locality	Remarks
B. Zahálka 1957	U. Cretac. (Maastricht.) (Istebna sandstone)	Beskids (Poland)	Similar to *Palaeosemaeostoma*, 4 cm in diameter, detailed description only in Czech language.
J. Lessertisseur 1955 pl. 7 fig. 7	U. Cretac. ("Sénonien inférieur")	Region of Mauléon, Dépt. Basses Pyrenées (South France)	Only figured, diameter of about 6 cm, rays rather regular and straight.
A. Seilacher 1955 fig. 5 no. 89	Flysch	Carpathian Mountains	See p. 203 later on named by Książkiewicz 1968, p. 15 *Glockeria*.
J. Gomex de Llarena 1949 p. 125, fig. 7	L. Tert. ("Molasa mumulitica")	Pamplona (North Spain)	No detailed description, somewhat similar to *Lorenzinia*.
G. Lucas and M. Rech-Frollo 1965	Eocene (Flysch)	Jaca (North Spain)	See p. 203 of this paper.
H. Vetters 1910	Oligocene (L. Tert.)	Capo d'Istria (Yugoslavia)	Incomplete and irregular star-like pattern, named *Capodistria* by Vialov 1964.
H. Fuchs 1961 p. 75-76, fig. 6	Middle Miocene	Environs of Cluj (Roumania)	Irregular and incomplete star-like pattern.

(iv) *Star-like pseudofossils of inorganic origin*

It should not be forgotten that stellate imprints on bedding planes of sedimentary rocks often resembling plants like *Annularia* or *Asterophyllites* may be of inorganic origin. In some cases such pseudofossils have unnecessarily been named, for instance *Sewardiella* Fucini 1936 and *Gothaniella* Fucini 1936 from the Verrucano of Mt. Pisani near Pisa, Italy. Both of them were considered as impressions of true plants by Fucini though he described and figured in the same paper numerous rosettes of crystals of various minerals for comparison with his "plants" (Fucini 1936 pl. 12 figs. 1-6, 9-11). *Sewardiella* and *Gothaniella* are undoubtedly impressions of crystals which grew in radiating patterns on the surface of the still unconsolidated sediment and were probably later dissolved. Their original mineralogical composition, however, is unknown.

From Mesozoic, probably Jurassic, sandy shales Yabe (1950) described similar rather regular stellate pseudofossils of diameter from 8 to 15 cm. Their numerous narrow needles radiating from a central node are solid and consist of small crystals of calcite.

Acknowledgments. The writer is greatly indebted to Professor M. Ewing (Palisades, N.Y., U.S.A.), Dr. M. Rech-Frollo (Toulouse, France) and Dr. W. Nowak (Kraków, Poland) for photographs and also wishes to thank Dr. J. Hülsemann (San Diego, Calif., U.S.A.) and Dr. D. W. Fisher (Albany, N.Y., U.S.A.) for information and other help. I am most grateful to Dr. P. Crimes (Liverpool) for revising the manuscript and to Mr. W. Hähnel (Hamburg) for photographic work.

References

ABEL, O. 1935. *Vorzeitliche Lebensspuren.* Gustav Fischer, Jena.

BANDEL, K. 1967. Trace fossils from two Upper Pennsylvanian sandstones in Kansas. *Paleont. Contr. Univ. Kansas* Paper **18.**

BROWN, B. and VOKES, H. E. 1944. Fossil imprints of unknown origin. II. Further information and a possible explanation. *Am. J. Sci.* **242,** 656.

CASTER, K. E. 1945. A new jellyfish (*Kirklandia texana* Caster) from the Lower Cretaceous of Texas. *Palaeontogr. am.* **3,** 173.

CLARKE, J. M. 1924. Rosetted trails of the Paleozoic. *Bull. N.Y. St. Mus.* **251,** 128.

DANGEARD, L. and GIRESSE, P. 1968. Enseignements géologiques des photographies sous-marines. *Bull. Bur. Rech. min. Alger. Sér.* 2 Sect. IV, no. 2, 1.

DELGADO, J. F. N. 1910. Terrains paléozoiques du Portugal. Étude sur les fossiles des schistes à Néréites de San Domingos et des schistes à Néréites et à Graptolites de Barrancos. *Comunçoes Comm. Trab. Serv. geol. Port.* **56.**

EWING, M. and DAVIS, R. A. 1967. Lebensspuren photographed on the ocean floor. In *Deep-sea photography* (Ed. J. B. Hersey). *Johns Hopkins oceanogr. Studies* **3,** 259.

FUCHS, H. 1961. Fossile Lebensspuren aus der Litoralzone des transsylvanischen Mittelmiozän-Meeres. *Földt. Közlön.* **91,** 73.

FUCHS, T. 1901. Uber *Medusina geryonoides* von Heuene. *Zenthl. Miner. Geol. Palaont.* p. 166.

FUCINI, A. 1936. Problematica Verrucana. Parte I. *Paleontogr. ital.* Append. 1.

FURRER, H. 1939. Geologische Untersuchungen in der Wildstrubelgruppe. *Mitt. naturf. Ges. Bern* for 1938, 35.

GEINITZ, H. B. 1849/50. *Das Quadersandsteingebirge oder Kreidegebirge in Deutschland.* Freiberg.

GOMEZ DE LLARENA, J. 1949. Datos paleoicnologicos. *Notas Comun. Inst. geol. min. Esp.* **19,** 115.

GRUBIĆ, A. 1961. Lorencinije iz eocenskog flisa Crne Gore. (Lorenziniae from the Eocene flysch of Montenegro). *Sedimentologija* **1,** 51.

HÄNTZSCHEL, W. 1930. *Spongia ottoi* Geinitz, ein sternförmiges Problematikum aus dem sächsischen Cenoman. *Senckenbergiana* **12,** 261.

—— 1935. Ein Fisch (*Gobius microps*) als Erzeuger von Sternspuren. *Natur. Volk* **65,** 562.

—— 1964. Spurenfossilien und Problematika im Campan von Beckum (Westf.) *Fortschr. Geol. Rheinld Westf.* **7,** 295.

—— 1965. *Vestigia invertebratorum et problematica.* (*Fossilium Catalogus I. Animalia* pars 108).

HARRINGTON, H. J. and MOORE, R. C. 1956. Scyphomedusae. In *Treatise on invertebrate paleontology* (Ed. R. C. Moore). Geol. Soc. Am., New York, Univ. of Kansas Press, Lawrence. Part F, p. F38.

—— and —— 1956. Trachylinida. In *Treatise on invertebrate paleontology* (Ed. R. C. Moore). Geol. Soc. Am., New York, and Univ. of Kansas Press, Lawrence. Part F, p. F68.

HEIDE, S. VAN DER. 1955. Vestiges fossiles de vie dans le Carbonifère supérieur du Limbourg (Pays-Bas). *Publs Ass. Étude Paléont. Stratigr. houill.* no. **21** (hors série), 73.

HUENE, F. v. 1901a. Kleine paläontologische Mittheilungen. I. *Medusina geryonides. Neues Jb. Miner Geol. Paläont.* **1,** 1.

—— 1901b. Nochmals *Medusina geryonides* v. Huene. *Zenthl. Miner. Geol. Paläont.* p. 167.

JONES, D. J. 1935. Some asteriaform fossils from the Francis Formation of Oklahoma. *Am. Midl. Nat.* **16,** 427.

KIESLINGER, A. 1939. Scyphozoa. *Handb. Paläozool.* (Ed. O. H. Schindewolf) **2A,** 69.

KSIĄŻKIEWICZ, M. 1960. On some problematic organic traces from the Flysch of the Polish Carpathians. *Kwart. geol.* **4,** 735.

—— On some problematic organic traces from the Flysch of the Polish Carpathians (part III). *Annls Soc. géol. Pol.* **38,** 3.

KUPFAHL, H.-G. 1965. *Erläuterungen zur Geologischen Karte von Hessen* 1: 25 000 *Blatt No.* 5323, *Schlitz.* Wiesbaden.

LESSERTISSEUR, J. 1955. Traces fossiles d'activité animale et leur signification paléobiologique. *Mém. Soc. géol. Fr.* n.s. no. **74.**

LEWARNE, G. C. 1964. Starfish traces from the Namurian of County Clare, Ireland. *Palaeontology* **7,** 508.

LUCAS, G. and RECH-FROLLO, M. 1965. "Traces en rosette" du flysch écoène de Jaca (Aragon). Essai d'interpretation. *Bull. Soc. géol. Fr. Sér* **76,** 163.

MALARODA, R. 1947. Segnalazione di nouve impronte nelle arenarie del Flysch eocenico della Conca di Trieste. *Atti Mus. civ. Stor. nat. Trieste* **16,** 57.

NOWAK, W. 1957. Quelques hiéroglyphes étoilés des Karpates de Flysch extérieures. *Annls Soc. géol. Pol.* **26,** 187.

—— 1961. Z badań nad hieroglifami fliszu karpackiego. I. Niektóre hieroglify z warstw cieszyn-skich i grodziskich. *Sprawo. z Posiedzen Komiji Oddzialu Pan w Krakowie* p. 226.

PFEIFFER, H. 1965. *Volkichnium volki* n.gen., n.sp. (Lebensspuren) aus den Phycoden-Schichten Thüringens. *Geologie* **14,** 1266.

PRANTL, F. 1946. Two new problematical trails from the Ordovician of Bohemia. *Bull. int. Acad. tchèque Sci.* (*sci. math.*) **46,** 49.

RICHTER, R. 1927. Die fossilen Fährten und Bauten der Würmer, ein Überlick über ihre biologischen Grundformen und deren geologische Bedeutung. *Paläont. Z.* **9,** 193.

RÜGER, L. and RÜGER-HAAS, P. 1925. *Palaeosemaeostoma geryonides* v. Huene sp., eine sessile Meduse aus dem Dogger von Wehingen in Württemberg und *Medusina liasica* nov. sp., eine Coronatenähnliche Meduse aus dem mittleren Lias von Hechingen in Württemberg. *Sber heidelb. Akad. Wiss., math.-naturw. Kl.* Jahrg. 1925. Abh. p. 15.

SEILACHER, A. 1955. Spuren und Fazies im Unterkambrium. In *Beiträge zur Kenntnis des Kambriums in der Salt Range (Pakistan)*, by O. H. Schindewolf and A. Seilacher. *Abh. math.-naturw. Kl. Akad. Wiss. Mainz,* Jahrg. 1955, 373.

—— 1959. Zur ökologischen Charakteristik von Flysch und Molasse. *Eclog. geol. Helv.* **51,** 1062.

—— 1962. Paleontological studies on turbidite sedimentation. *J. Geol.* **70,** 227.

—— 1967. Bathymetry of trace fossils. *Mar. Geol.* **5,** 413.

SIMPSON, F. 1969. *Rotamedusa roztocensis* gen. et sp. nov., a medusa from the Eocene flysch of the Carpathians. *Annls Soc. géol. Pol.* **39,** 697.

ŚLĄCZKA, A. 1965. Nowe problematyki radialne z flisu karpachiego. *Spraw. Posied. Kom. Pan Oddzialu W. Krakowie* p. 470.

STANLEY, D. J. and KELLING, G. 1968. Photographic investigation of sediment texture, bottom current activity, and benthonic organisms in the Wilmington submarine canyon. *U.S. Coast Guard oceanogr. Rep.* **22.**

STRAELEN, V. VAN. 1938. Sur des restes de crustacés fouisseurs du Viséen inférieur du Nord de la France. *Bull. Mus. Hist. nat. Belg.* **14,** no. 30.

VETTERS, H. 1910. Über ein neues Hieroglyph aus dem Flysch von Capodistria. *Verh. geol. Reichsanst. Wien* p. 131.

VIALOV, O. S. 1968a. Materials for classification of traces of fossils and vital activity of organisms. *Paleont. Sb.* **5** (1), 125.

—— 1968b. O Zvezdĉatych Problematikach. [On star-shaped problematica]. *Ezheg. vses. paleont. Obshch. [Year-book all-unionist palaeont. Soc. USSR]* **18,** 326. [In Russian]

WEYLAND, H. and BUDDE, W. 1932. Fährten aus dem Mitteldevon von Elberfeld. *Senckenbergiana* **14,** 259.

YABE, H. 1950. Pseudofossils from Fengning-hsien, Jeho, similar to "*Sewardiella verrucana* Fucini" from Mt. Pisani. *Proc. Japan. Acad.* **26,** 29.

ZAHÁLKA, B. 1957. [On the occurrence of a medusa-like form in the Cretaceous of the Beskidy.] *Praha Vest. ústred. Ust. geol.* **32,** 294. [In Czech with English summary.]

W. Häntzschel, 2 Hamburg 73, Brockdorfstrasse 31, West Germany.

Palaeoichnological research in the Palaeontological Institute of the Academy of Sciences of the USSR

R. Th. Hecker

The main types of palaeoichnological literature are defined and briefly discussed. Soviet palaeoichnological work, particularly on the Palaeozoic seas of the Russian Platform and the Palaeogene Fergana Gulf are reviewed and further details of some of the trace fossils given.

1. Introduction

In the USSR comparatively little palaeoichnologic research has been carried out although there is abundant material available. The chief reason is that much work still remains to be done on body fossils.

Palaeoichnologic literature is poor in the USSR. The character of the Soviet work is closely connected with one of the main peculiarities of our country— the vast extent of its territory.

2. The main types of palaeoichnological papers

Let us consider the different types of palaeoichnologic literature in existence up to the present time. Although some papers are of mixed content most can be conveniently placed in one of seven categories.

(i) Papers and short monographs about particular traces, with descriptions of new forms, sometimes of separate specimens, or of chance discoveries; often without any stratigraphic or sedimentologic data. Studies of this type are the most frequently encountered.

(ii) Summarising works in which the authors try to embrace all or the greater part of known traces to classify them, order the nomenclature and give them group names. Examples include the well known publications by Rud. Richter (1927), Krejci-Graf (1932), Abel (1935), Lessertisseur (1955), Seilacher (1953a, b; 1964), Häntzschel (1962; 1965; 1966), Müller (1962; 1963), Martinsson (1965) and Vialov (1966).

(iii) Papers on facial distribution of traces and of whole palaeoichnocoenoses, such as those by Seilacher (1955; 1958; 1963a; 1964).

(iv) Publications in which the authors consider the mode of formation of the traces and the animal's behaviour as inferred from the character of the traces, such as those of Rud. Richter (1928) and Seilacher (1953b; 1955; 1967a, b).

(v) Papers on general changes of traces and palaeoichnocoenoses during geological time, such as those of Seilacher (1955; 1956).

(vi) Papers in which changes in trace assemblages and sometimes also other animal and plant remains have been followed through a vertical section in connection with change of facies. There are few publications of this type: Seilacher (1963b), Seilacher and Meischner (1964) and Farrow (1966).

(vii) Papers on the environmental control of palaeoichnocoenoses, such as those of Seilacher (1963a; 1964; 1967a) who reached his conclusions only after studying trace fossil rich beds and their characteristic ichnocoenoses in deposits of many ages and countries. Seilacher's major contribution was to recognise a depth controlled sequence of traces and to draft them on a bathymetric curve.

Seilacher's diagrams are an example of what can be called a "facial sequence" of the palaeoichnocoenoses—their lateral changes on the sea floor. They are based on specific material, but the facts are not published here and the diagrams themselves are of a very general character. Also, the author only considers trace fossils—he does not say anything about the associated fauna and flora.

It is also possible to envisage investigations in which changes in facies over the sea bottom are traced and described on the basis of detailed field research, both in those facies that contain fossil traces and whole ichnocoenoses, and in those where they are absent. Research of this type has yet to receive due attention.

Such trace fossil investigations must be combined, supplemented and tested by tracing the change of facies and faunal assemblages through a vertical section, i.e. through time. In European and American literature there is only one recent paper (Farrow 1966), in which the author, while studying the vertical sections of near-shore Jurassic sediments of England, also reconstructed the change of facies on the sea bottom.

All the types of research listed above are necessary, they complement one another. It is to be particularly hoped that large-scale researches of the last type discussed will be made.

The USSR is well suited to such investigations; it is possible to study large ancient sea basins of every geological period, sometimes from one shore to the other. That is, it is possible to trace over a large area assemblages of organisms, including also the traces of extinct animals and sometimes rich ichnocoenoses, and their spatial changes associated with depth, the character of the sea bottom and other factors of habitat. There are also opportunities to trace the change of facies and assemblages of organisms through time. Such researches are in the main palaeosynecologic.

3. Palaeoichnological investigations in the USSR

For many years in the Laboratory of Palaeoecology of the Palaeontological Institute of the Academy of Sciences of the USSR we have studied one ancient basin after another; where possible on a large area and over the whole period of the existence of the basin. We choose seas of different geologic age and character (e.g. epicontinental, geosynclinal). The study of several basins from the same point of view ultimately allows a comparative analysis.

Not only the USSR, of course, possesses such "territorial potentialities" for investigations, but also other large countries such as the USA and Canada.

Combined palaeoecologic and lithologic researches on ancient sea basins are very time consuming and much more complicated than the work which is done by the majority of palaeontologists: that is studies on some one group of fossil organisms without investigation of the depositional environment.

For palaeoichnology, combined investigations of large ancient basins and their inhabitants have some disadvantages in that their object is not a special study of fossil animal traces, but places an equal emphasis on studying all organic remains together with the traces. During such work it is also necessary to study the geological sections and rocks in detail and other geological evidence (earth movements etc.). In consequence this type of research is long-term and relatively little can be accomplished in a single life span. On the other hand such research is particularly useful because it is then possible to study each trace fossil or palaeoichnocoenosis in relation to its facial distribution and its association with other animals.

If you live in Moscow or Leningrad you need not go far to start research on large ancient sea basins. Near the latter town there are outcrops of the renowned Baltic Ordovician, with its rich fauna of trilobites, brachiopods, nautiloids, cystoids and other invertebrates. These beds, which show little lateral facies variation, can be traced for 500 km—from Lake Ladoga on the east to the north-west corner of Estonia.

To the south, northeast and southwest of Leningrad lies the region of the so-called Main Devonian Field, a large well exposed structure of Middle and Upper Devonian sediments. The Middle Devonian deposits are mostly continental, the Upper Devonian ones—continental and marine. These sediments, extending over 1,200 km from SW to NE, are rich in ichthyofaunal remains of the Old Red Sandstone type at some localities and of marine invertebrates at others.

Still further south we come to the so-called northwestern flank of Lower Carboniferous deposits of the Moscow syneclise which contain also a rich marine fauna. Here formations can be traced for 400 km along many river valleys in the Novgorod and Leningrad districts. But all this area is only the northern part of a vast early Carboniferous epicontinental marine basin. Going south we reach the western flank of this ancient basin, and to the south of Moscow the southern flank. Those sediments which have been preserved extend meridionally for about 1000 km.

Immediately to the south of Moscow, Middle and Upper Carboniferous deposits with a very rich fauna are developed. These basins also extended to the north of the European part of the USSR—so again there is the possibility of tracing the changes in fauna and ichnofauna over a considerable distance.

The marine Permian sediments contain a specific Kazanian fauna and can be studied from the river Volga near Kazan along the river Kama, and also in the valleys on the northern rivers (North Dwina, Pinega and their affluents) which are discharged into the White Sea.

All the seas discussed (and also the Cambrian and Silurian seas not mentioned) have covered the greater parts of the Russian Platform. Here it is possible to study the epicontinental seas which covered the Platform with sediments that are still perfectly preserved with gentle dips and abundant fossils. The results of study on all these deposits can be compared so that the similarities and differences in the processes of sedimentation and life can be established.

Palaeoecological and palaeoichnological study of the Palaeozoic seas of the Russian Platform was the main task for the Palaoecological Laboratory. A series of monographs and many papers have been published. The experience obtained here has led to the compilation of textbooks and papers on palaeoecologic methods (Hecker 1955; 1960a; 1964a, b; 1965; 1969).

Palaeoichnologically, the most interesting sediments on the Russian Platform were deposited in the Lower and Middle Ordovician, Upper Devonian and Lower Carboniferous seas. We will now consider some examples.

Sediments of these seas in the north of the platform were dominantly calcareous. Clays accumulated in the near shore parts of the Upper Devonian sea. The calcareous sediments of the Ordovician and Devonian seas consolidated shortly

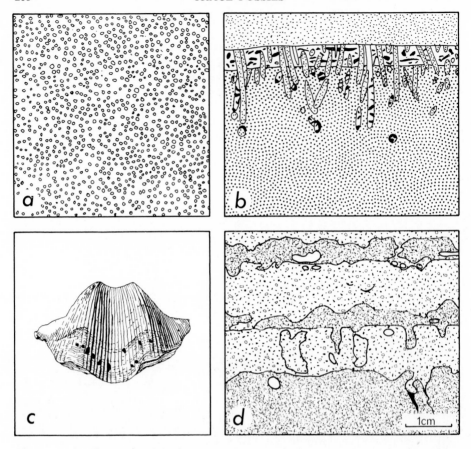

Fig. 1.   a, b   Traces of rock-boring worms *Trypanites* in limestones: a   view from above, Upper Devonian, Pskov Beds, Leningrad district,   b   longitudinal section, Upper Devonian, Chudovo beds, Pskov district;   c   Shell of *Cyrtosprifer rudkinensis* Ljasch., viewed from the side of the pedicle valve with *Palaeosabella's* borings produced along the margin of the valve while the brachiopod was still alive. Upper Devonian, Rudkino Beds, Don river.   d   Numerous burrowed disconformity and abrasion surfaces in the limestone, Middle Ordovician, Tallinn.

after accumulation and sometimes formed hard grounds, which were inhabited by a distinct biocoenose.

In general, the biocoenoses of the hard grounds contain organisms of several ethologic types. In such environments cemented, attached and boring organisms are normally present with traces of the last type having the highest preservation potential.

In the Lower Ordovician of the Baltic region and in the Upper Devonian of the Main Devonian Field it is possible to observe surfaces of hard ground, densely riddled by needle-form borings of *Trypanites* over large areas (Orviku 1940; Hecker 1960b, see also Fig. 1a, b). These surfaces have another peculiarity in that they are perfectly abraded and quite smooth. Sea abrasion first attacked the loose sediments and then carried away the particles. Subsequently, the currents worked through to the already hardened sediment and the hard bottom was perfectly polished by the movement of shell debris. At the same time these surfaces were penetrated by the burrows of *Trypanites* which were typical rock-borers, apparently belonging to the polychaetes. They could only bore in a hard substratum and the smooth flat rocky sea floor was an ideal habitat. In the Lower and Middle Ordovician sea this process was frequently repeated so that there are many such abraded surfaces in the limestones (Orviku 1940; see Fig. 1d).

In the Upper Devonian limestones of the Main Devonian Field smooth abraded surfaces with *Trypanites* borings are less abundant than in the Ordovician. But in the Devonian sea there existed at times, not far from the shore, a peculiar facies in which the bottom was covered with calcareous pebbles. Flat pebbles, up to 0·5 m across, were formed from thin layers of coquina limestones broken up by the waves. These pebbles are penetrated by *Trypanites* borings on all sides (Fig. 1a). Also the shells of dead molluscs (bivalves, gastropods and cephalopods) and brachiopods, and the shells of living brachiopods were inhabited by another boring animal—*Palaeosabella* (Hecker 1966; see Fig. 1c). This borer maintained a commensal relationship with the living animals which it infested.

During Devonian times, the hard surface of the sea floor and the pebbles provided a habitat for a varied fauna of cemented animals including brachiopods (a peculiar productoid *Irboskites*), bivalves (*Limanomia*), tabulate corals (*Aulopora*), echinoderms (Crinoidea, Edrioasteroidea) and worms (*Spirorbis, Serpula*) (Hecker 1960b).

In contrast to the abundance of *Trypanites* borings in the Ordovician and Upper Devonian, none have been found in the Carboniferous and Upper Permian of the Russian platform. This is an enigma! The creators of these burrows were not extinct in the Middle Palaeozoic, in fact they were initially described from the Triassic (Mägdefrau 1932). Their absence is, however, possibly to be ascribed to a lack of hard grounds here at this time.

Also, it is necessary to bear in mind that *Trypanites* represents the traces of rock borers, and fossil borings are in general rarer than most traces of burrowing organisms or mud-eaters and surface tracks and trails. The reasons for this are understandable: (i) it is much more difficult to penetrate through a rock or a shell than through loose ground and not many animals or plants can do it, (ii) there is little hard substratum in the seas, (iii) in loose sediment on the sea bottom one can look for shelter, and/or food but a hard substratum can give only shelter. Thus, in a hard substratum, the diversity of traces must be less and they will be rarer.

The limestone layers of the Ordovician and the Devonian, into which the borings of *Trypanites* penetrate, also often contain other invertebrate burrows, made before the sediment was lithified. These burrows are short, or form complexly curved channels (Fig. 2). They were first described by Mägdefrau (1932) from Triassic sediments in South Germany and provisionally ascribed to the Enteropneusta. Similar burrows were later described from the Triassic of Poland by Kázmierczak and Pszczółkowski (1969). Last autumn Kázmierczak visited the USSR, saw the burrows *in situ* in the Ordovician and Devonian sediments of the northern part of the Russian Platform, and confirmed that they were the same as the Triassic burrows in Poland and the burrows of Recent shallow water Enteropneusta. The habitats of these ancient animals, burrowing in ooze, fully coincide with their habitat today.

Other animal traces found in marine sediments of the Upper Devonian of the Main Devonian Field are generally encountered in nearshore sediments. In the lateral litho- and biofacies sequence of this sea and of the coastal continental

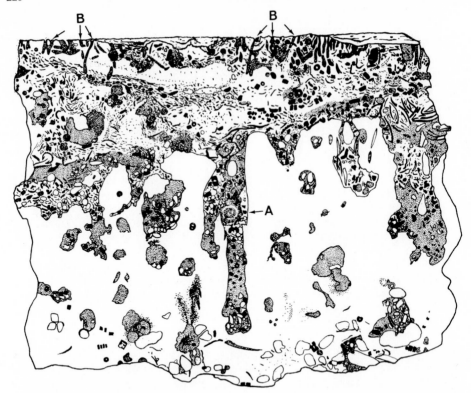

Fig. 2. Polished cut across the upper limestone layer of the Chudovo beds with Enteropneusta burrows: A   filled with pebbles and shell debris with calcareous cement, and with traces of boring worms *Trypanites*;   B   penetrating into a limestone layer from its abraded surface. Upper Devonian, Novgorod district, Shelon River.

sediments (facies 2 and 3 of Fig. 3) there are many different traces of marine invertebrates. They are generally found either in the form of pure ichnoceonoses or together with invertebrates with shells e.g. brachiopods, molluscs etc. One of the characteristic forms of this trace assemblage is *Rhizocorallium* (Hecker and Ushakov 1962). In deeper parts of the sea (facies 4 of Fig. 3) the diversity and abundance of marine animals with skeletons becomes much greater, and the number of traces is distinctly diminished. Towards the land to the east, in facies 1, there are no marine forms: here, in red micaceous and argillaceous sands one finds only the remains of continental fresh-water vertebrates (fishes and agnatha) and flora (trochiliscids).

In the Lower Carboniferous sea of the Russian Platform the sediments are generally of shallow-water type as in the Devonian. That is why, when studying the Lower Carboniferous, we constantly observe quick facial changes both in space and time. Such changes can be represented diagrammatically as in Figure 4.

The early Carboniferous sea contained a large fauna, the various traces of activity of which are preserved in the sediments as diversely curved simple tracks,

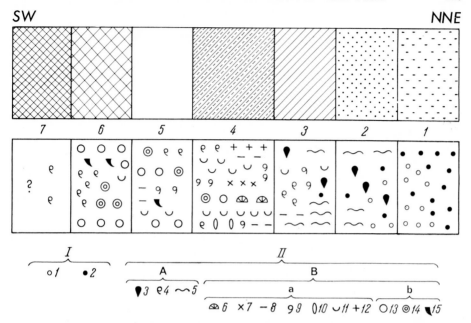

Fig. 3. Lateral facial sequence of rocks and associated assemblages of organisms in marine and near-shore continental deposits of Upper Devonian of Main Devonian Field from north-northeast to southwest (from sea shore to deep waters). Sediments:— 1 terrigenous red-beds; 2 white quartz sands; 3 clays; 4 argillaceous limestones and marls; 5 limestones; 6 dolomitic limestones; 7 dolomites.

Fauna and flora:—I *fresh-water forms:* 1 trochiliscids; 2 fishes and Agnatha of red-bed facies. II *marine forms:* A euryhaline forms: 3 *Lingula;* 4 *Platyschisma;* 5 worm traces. B stenohaline forms: a inhabitants of waters with normal salinity: 6 tabulate corals; 7 *Spirorbis;* 8 bivalves; 9 majority of gastropods; 10 nautiloids; 11 majority of articulate brachiopods; 12 crinoids; b inhabitants of waters with normal and a little above normal salinity: 13 blue-green algae (*Girvanella=Pycnostroma*); 14 stromatoporoids; 15 rugose corals.

Rhizocorallium, Corophioides, Teichichnus, Desmichnus, Chondrites and, most abundantly, *Zoophycos* (Hecker and Ushakov 1962). In the Upper Devonian only one trace could be referred to *Zoophycos s. l.* and that came from a single locality in near-shore marine sands. But in the early Carboniferous sea, as also in the middle and late Carboniferous seas of the Moscow syneclise, true *Zoophycos* was widespread. The animals which formed these traces inhabited seas of normal salinity, beginning from the intertidal zone. This is shown by the discovery of *Zoophycos* at the lower and the upper surfaces of limestone layers which pass up and down into continental sands. *Zoophycos* can also be found in near-shore marine sands within this area, but is much more abundant in the limestones, predominantly detrital ones. So, in the Carboniferous sea, as in the Permian (Kazanian) sea, the "creator" of *Zoophycos* burrows definitely lived in the shallows.

Figure 5 shows the distribution of the traces of some invertebrates and the remains of other organisms in the section of several horizons of marine sediments of the Lower Carboniferous in the northwestern flank of the Moscow syneclise. It is interesting to note the change of organic assemblages (including also the

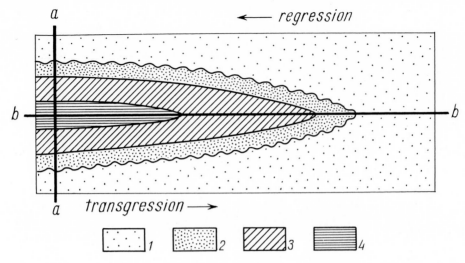

Fig. 4. General scheme of time- and space-migration of facies during transgression and regression.
1   continental sediments;   2   shallow-sea sediments;   3   comparatively deep-sea sediments;   4   deepest-sea sediments.
aa   alternation of sediments in vertical section;
bb   alternation of synchronous sediments in horizontal direction.

fossil traces) through the vertical section of "b" and "c" horizons—first in one direction then inversely. These sections are, in fact, equivalent to vertical cuts of Figure 4. When tracing at any one locality the change of separate organisms and assemblages of forms in the vertical direction in connection with facial changes in time it is not difficult to picture their areal distribution on the sea bottom.

My collaborators in this study of the Lower Carboniferous of the Moscow syneclise A. I. Ossipova and T. N. Belskaya have compiled a series of lithologic-palaeoecologic maps and diagrams showing the distribution and change of facial zones in these seas at different moments of their history. These diagrams also show the frequency of occurrence of traces and reveal that the greatest number of traces are always found in the most shallow nearshore part of the sea (Ossipova and Belskaya 1969).

The differentiated analysis of habitats of the trace fossil producers is also interesting and I am at present working on this in a collective work on ecology and the development of fauna in the early Carboniferous seas of the Moscow syneclise.

In conclusion, two further examples will be considered from our palaeoecologic and lithologic investigations on the basins of the geologic past and their inhabitants.

Work on the Fergana Palaeogene Gulf (Central Asia) is best known abroad through two papers (Hecker *et al.* 1962; 1963). In these publications there are facies maps, profile sections and lateral facies sequences through different parts of the Fergana Gulf on which the zonal distribution of faunal assemblages including the animal traces, are shown.

The Palaeogene is separated from the Palaeozoic, which we have studied, by a very long time interval. The benthonic marine fauna has completely changed

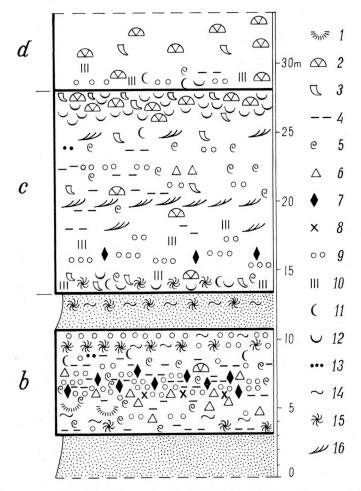

Fig. 5. Palaeoecological column of the "b", "c" and "d" horizons of Lower Carboniferous in the northwestern flank of the Moscow syneclise. Novgorod district, Msta River.
1 sponges, *Siderospongia;* 2 chaetetids and tabulate corals; 3 rugose corals; 4 bivalves; 5 gastropods; 6 cephalopods; 7 trilobites; 8 bryozoans; 9 various small brachiopods; 10 *Striatifera;* 11 *Gigantoproductus latissimus,* *G. latipriscus;* 12 *G. superior;* 13 crinoids.
Trace fossils: 14 simple tracks; 15 *Zoophycos;* 16 *Desmichnus.*

and those parts of the sea floor which were the most favourable as habitats for burrowing invertebrates have been occupied now for the most part by arthropods. Thus, in the near-shore shallow zone of the Fergana Palaeogene basin, we meet abundant burrows of *Callianassa* (Anomuran crustaceans) (Hecker 1956; Hecker et al. 1962). The most near-shore sand and clay facies with these burrows and also with oyster beds now formed the outer "bordering ring" in the Fergana Palaeogene Gulf.

Now the final example. This review of life in the seas of the geological past began with the traces of rock-borers in hard grounds: it will also finish with borings.

Where hard limestones were exposed they (as also in the Palaeozoic) could not avoid the activity of the rock-borers.

These limestone rocks were, of necessity, settled first of all by organisms of the same ethological groups—by cemented, attached and boring forms. So we find borings, this time belonging to the bivalve *Lithophaga*, along the shore of the Palaeogene Fergana Gulf (Hecker *et al.* 1962; 1963). The traces of the same rock-boring bivalves and the channels of the boring sponge *Cliona* also frequently occur on oyster shells.

Earlier, this area was the shore of the Cretaceous sea and in its rocky shore, formed also by Palaeozoic limestones, we find the borings of the same genus *Lithophaga*, and also of the worm *Potamilla*.

This zone of rocky shores can be best observed on the islands of the early Cretaceous (Aptian) sea in the same region—Central Asia—in the central part of the Kizil-Kum desert (Pianovskaya and Hecker 1966). These shores (cliffs) and the rocky bottom (bench) were formed of Palaeozoic limestones (Hecker 1962; 1963). The desert conditions of the present day result in perfect exposure and allow us to walk along these stone areas and ridges in the surf zone of the Cretaceous sea and observe how densely they were riddled by *Lithophaga* and *Cliona*. These rock-borers covered the surface of the coastal limestones and the bench so thickly that there remained no settling place for fixed forms, although these also existed in the Aptian sea. On the hard ground formed by the granite dykes which cut the Palaeozoic limestones one can see a complete crust of cemented oysters.

Here in the Kizil-Kum under our feet is the precisely delineated shore line of the Aptian sea. To one side of it there was an island, to the other (and also upward through the sequence, which formed over the hard ground) we can trace other facies adjacent to the rocky littoral zone. The delineating of the shore line of the ancient basin is of great importance as a datum line from which we can begin to enumerate the facies and zones of the sea bottom towards the deeper parts of the ancient sea.

References

ABEL, O. 1935. *Vorzeitliche Lebensspuren*. Gustav Fischer, Jena.

FARROW, G. E. 1966. Bathymetric zonation of Jurassic fossils from the coast of Yorkshire, England. *Palaeogeogr. Palaeoclimatol. Palaeoecol.* **2**, 103.

HÄNTZSCHEL, W. 1962. Trace fossils and problematica. In *Treatise on invertebrate paleontology* (Ed. by R. C. Moore). Geol. Soc. Am., New York and Univ. of Kansas Press, Lawrence. Part W, p. W176.

—— 1965. *Fossilium Catalogus I: Animalia, Pars* 108. *Vestigia invertebratorum et problematica* (Ed. F. Westphal). Junk, s' Gravenhage.

—— 1966. Treatise on invertebrate paleontology. Part W *Trace fossils:* comments and additions. *Paleont. Contr. Univ. Kansas* Paper 9.

HECKER, R. Th. 1955. Conseils pour les recherches. Paléoécologie. *Annls Cent. Étud. Docum. paléont.* No. 15.

—— 1956. Ecological analysis of crustacean decapods in Fergana Gulf of the Palaeogene sea of Central Asia. *Byull. mosk. Obshch. Ispyt. Prir.* **61**, ser. geol. **31**, 77 (In Russian).

HECKER, R. Th. 1960a. Bases de la paléoécologie. *Annls Servs Inf. géol. Bur. Rech. géol. géophys. min.*

—— 1960b. Fossil facies of smooth rocky sea-floor. (On types of rocky sea-floor). *Trudy geol. Inst. Akad. Nauk Est. SSR*, **5**, p. 199 (In Russian).

—— 1964a. Les recherches paléoécologiques et leurs importance. *Bull. trimest. Départ. Inf. géol.* No. 63, Avril, p. 1.

—— 1964b. Recent state in study of fossil invertebrate traces (palaeoichnology of invertebrates). *Problems of evolution of organic world. A Symposium. Trudy VII session All-Union Palaeontol. Soc.* "Nedra", Moscow. p. 178. (In Russian).

—— 1965. *Introduction to paleoecology.* Elsevier, New York.

—— 1966. On life-relations of organisms of the geological past. In *Organisms and environment in the geological past. A Symposium.* "Nauka", Moscow. p. 14 (In Russian).

—— 1969. Palaeoecological method in the service of detailed stratigraphy and its use for the study of deep-sea deposits. In *Cenozoic biostratigraphy, fauna and flora of the north-western part of Pacific mobile belt. A Symposium.* "Nauka", Moscow. p. 134 (In Russian).

——, OSSIPOVA, A. I., and BELSKAYA, T. N. 1962. *Fergana Gulf of Palaeogene sea of Central Asia, its history, sediments, fauna and flora, their environment and evolution.* **1** and **2**. Akad. nauk SSSR, Moscow (In Russian).

——, —— and ——. 1963. Fergana Gulf of Paleogene sea of Central Asia, its history, sediments, fauna, and flora, their environment and evolution. *Bull. Am. Ass. Petrol. Geol.* **47**, 617.

—— and USHAKOV, P. V. 1962. Vermes. In *Osnovy palaeontologii* (Principles of palaeontology). *Sponges, Archaeocyatheans, Coelenterates, Worms.* Akad. nauk SSSR, Moscow. p. 433 (in Russian).

KÁZMIERCZAK, J. and PSZCZÓŁKOWSKI, A. 1969. Burrows of Enteropneusta in Muschelkalk (Middle Triassic) of the Holy Cross Mountains, Poland. *Acta palaeont. pol.* **14**, 299.

KREJCI-GRAF, K. 1932. Definition der Begriffe Marken, Spuren, Fährten, Bauten, Hieroglyphen und Fucoiden. *Senckenbergiana.* **14**, 29.

LESSERTISSEUR, J. 1955. Traces fossiles d'activité animale et leur signification paléobiologique. *Mém. Soc. géol. Fr.,* n.s. **34** (4), no. 74.

MÄGDEFRAU, K. 1932. Über einige Bohrgänge aus dem Unteren Muschelkalk von Jena. *Paläont. Z.* **14**, 150.

MARTINSSON, A. 1965. Aspects of a Middle Cambrian thanatotope on Öland. *Geol. For. Stockh. Förh.* **87**, 181.

MÜLLER, A. H. 1962. Zur Ichnologie, Taxiologie und Ökologie fossiler Tiere. *Freiberger Forschritte* Heft C, 151.

—— 1963. Zur Ichnologie der Invertebraten. In *Lehrbuch der Paläozoologie.* II, *Invertebraten, Teil 3, Arthropoda 2—Stomochorda.* Gustav Fischer, Jena. p. 615.

ORVIKU, K. 1940. Lithologie der Tallinna—Serie (Ordovizium, Estland), I. *Tartu Ülik. Geol. Inst. Toim.* No. 5.

OSSIPOVA, A. I. and BELSKAYA, T. N. 1969. Use of combined palaeoecological and lithological investigations for analysis of facies and of the process of sedimentation (on the pattern of the Visean Sea of the Russian Platform). *Sixième Congrès Int. de Stratigraphie et de Géologie du Carbonifère. Compte rendu,* **2**.

PIANOVSKAYA, I. A. and HECKER, R. Th. 1966. Rocky shores and hard ground of the Cretaceous and Palaeogene seas in Central Kizil-Kum and their inhabitants. In *Organism and environment in the geological past. A Symposium.* "Nauka", Moscow. (In Russian).

RICHTER, R. 1927. Die fossilen Fährten und Bauten der Würmer, ein Überblick über ihre biologischen Grundformen und deren geologische Bedeutung. *Paläont. Z.* **9**, 225.

—— 1928. Psychische Reaktionen fossiler Tiere. *Palaeobiologica.* **1**, 225.

SEILACHER, A. 1953a. Über die Methoden der Palichnologie. (Studien zur Palichnologie, I). *Neues Jb. Geol. Paläont. Abh.* **96**, 421.

—— 1953b. Die fossilen Ruhespuren (Cubichnia). (Studien zur Palichnologie. II). *Neues Jb. Geol. Paläont. Abh.* **98**, 87.

—— 1955. Spuren und Fazies im Unterkambrium. In *Beitrage zur Kenntnis des Kambriums in der Salt Range (Pakistan)* by O. H. Schindewolf and A. Seilacher, *Abh. mat. naturw. Kl. Akad. Wiss. Mainz,* p. 342.

—— 1956. Der Beginn des Kambriums als biologische Wende. *Neues Jb. Geol. Paläont. Abh.* **103**, 155.

—— 1958. Zur ökologischen Charakteristik von Flysch und Molasse. *Eclog. geol. Helv.* **51**, 1062.

—— 1963a. Lebensspuren und Salinitätsfazies. *Fortschr. Geol. Rheinl. Westf.* **10**, 81.

—— 1963b. Kaledonischer Unterbau der Irakiden. *Neues Jb. Geol. Paläont. Mh.,* p. 527.

—— 1964. Biogenic sedimentary structures. In *Approaches to paleoecology* (Ed. J. Imbrie and N. D. Newell). Wiley, New-York. p. 296.

Seilacher, A. 1967a. Bathymetry of trace fossils. *Mar. Geol.* **5**. 413.

—— 1967b. Fossil Behaviour. *Scient. Am.* **217,** 72.

—— and Meischner, D. 1964. Fazies-Analyse im Paläozoikum des Oslo-Gebietes. *Geol. Rdsch.* **54,** 596.

Vialov, O. S. 1966. *Traces of life of organisms and their palaeontological significance.* "Naukova dumka", Kiev (In Russian).

R. Th. Hecker, Palaeontological Institute, U.S.S.R. Academy of Sciences, Leninsky prospect 33, Moscow V-71, U.S.S.R.

Some Jurassic trace fossils from Jameson Land (East Greenland)

C. Heinberg

Some trace fossils, chiefly endichnia, are described from the Middle Jurassic sandstones of Jameson Land, East Greenland. A U-tube with special structure is described. Forms also considered include other vertical burrows, *Curvolithus, Planolites,* meniscus tunnel-fills, *Gyrochorte, Teichichnus,* a spiral burrow and small meanders. Emphasis is laid on the orientation of mica in the fill. Some relationships are noted between trace fossils and sediment types.

1. Introduction

In the following study of trace fossils from Jameson Land, East Greenland (Fig. 1) it is attempted in most cases to relate the types of trace fossils to ichnogenera, while ichnospecies are not used. In certain cases names are not suggested, but instead descriptions are placed under morphological headings. Names indicating the nature of the originating organisms are used with much reluctance, since these imply an originator for which there is often no direct evidence.

Emphasis is laid on endogene creeping trails, while domichnia and fodinichnia are treated more briefly. The majority of trails were made within the sediment and are preserved in a three-dimensional manner, with sandstone above and below the original fill. Owing to the lack of alternation of clay and sandstone beds in this case, the traces are described in terms of endichnia (Martinsson 1965) and epirelief and hyporelief (Seilacher 1953) as shown in Figure 2. Thus "positive" and "negative" semirelief refers to topography, and also to the presence (positive) or absence (negative) of the fill.

The fills are recognisable as such through their intrinsic mica orientation. Some fills lack mica but are darker than the surrounding sediment, owing to the presence of allochthonous plant material.

The only previous descriptions of trace fossils from this area were made by Stauber (1942).

2. Stratigraphy and sedimentology

The material was collected from the "Yellow Series", which is the middle member of the Vardekløft Formation (see Table 1).

The "Yellow Series" is a well developed sand and sandstone series, of mixed coastal and deltaic origin, thinning southwards. The rock is well sorted sandstone, very variably cemented and with a greater or lesser muscovite content. In fresh section it is light grey but when weathered it becomes bright yellow or, more rarely, red or brown. In the area studied, there are four types of bedding:

227

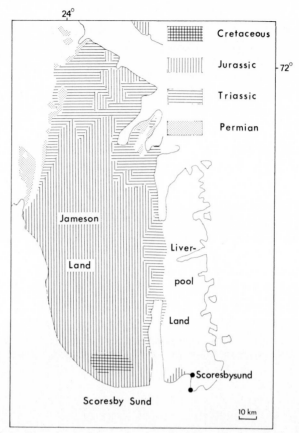

Fig. 1. Map. of the Scoresbysund area showing the Mesozoic deposits in simplified form. Partly after R. Trümpy, J. Callomon and D. T. Donovan (*Meddr. Grønland.* **168,** no. 3).

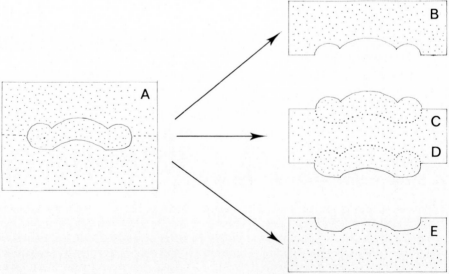

Fig. 2. Preservation types of endichnia.   A   Tunnel fill preserved in three dimensions in sandstone;   B   Negative endichnial hyporelief;   c   Positive endichnial epirelief;   D   Positive endichnial hyporelief;   E   Negative endichnial epirelief.

Table 1

Systems series and stages		Lithostratigraphical divisions	Approximate thickness in metres
Middle Jurassic	Lower Callovian	Upper Varde- kløft Member	170
	Upper Bathonian		
	Middle and Lower Bathonian	"The Yellow Series"	280–500+
	— — — ? — — —		
	Bajocian ?	Lower Varde- kløft Member	60–100

(After T. Birkelund and K. Perch-Nielsen, 1969)

(i) Massive layers of variably cemented sandstones without visible structures, individual beds reaching a thickness of 4–5 m.

(ii) Cross-bedded layers. The oblique individual beds separate easily as well cemented plates.

(iii) Horizontal, well-cemented, thin layers approximately 5–30 cm thick.

(iv) Platy to almost shaly sandstone in which the single thin plates (less than 5 cm) are well cemented.

Conglomerates also occur with either pebbles of well rounded quartzite, 1–10 cm in diameter, or broken belemnites.

Lateral and vertical variation is great. For example, in certain areas a massive sandstone, traced laterally, may be seen to develop strong cross-bedding. More or less regular vertical change among the four types of bedding occurs in most of the series. For example, between cross-bedded deposits with allochthonous plant remains and massive beds with U-tubes at the top, possibly indicating a change from limnic or brackish to marine environment.

3. Endichnial repichnia

Numbers of specimens refer to the collection of Grønlands Geologiske Undersøgelse (Geological Survey of Greenland).

Ichnogenus CURVOLITHUS Fritsch 1908

Type 1, Figure 3a. GGU 102678. This trail occurs very commonly as a positive epirelief (Fig. 3aв but in some cases the fill can be knocked out to expose the negative epirelief Fig. 3aᴀ). Widths range from 11 to 23 mm with 15–16 mm most common. Where mica occurs there is a concentration of vertical flakes along the sides, parallel with the trail. There is an indistinct orientation of mica within the side ridges of the trail, but its direction could not be determined.

The type occurs most commonly in a mica-rich grey sandstone weathering yellow. The trails run more or less straight but curve over and under each other in a vertical plane, crossing bedding. Solitary trails also cut bedding planes.

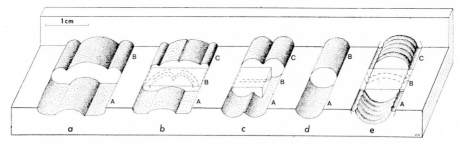

Fig. 3. Endichnial repichnia.   a   *Curvolithus* type 1,   A   negative epirelief,   B   positive
epirelief;   b   *Curvolithus* type 2,   A   negative epirelief,   B   horizontal section showing
mica orientation, the grains indicated at the sides belong to the zone between the fill and the
undisturbed sediment,   c   positive epirelief;   c   bilobate trail,   A   negative epirelief,
B   sections to show mica orientation in the fill,   c   positive epirelief;   d   *Planolites*
A   negative epirelief,   B   positive epirelief;   e   Meniscus tunnel fill,   A   possible
negative epirelief,   B   horizontal section showing mica orientation,   c   positive epirelief.

This type, together with *Curvolithus* type 2, is the most characteristic trace
fossil in the area and can dominate the sediment at certain levels.

Type 2, Figure 3b. GGU 102640. This trail occurs as positive epirelief (Fig. 3bC).
The negative epirelief (Fig. 3bA) has not been observed clearly, but the positive
hyporelief is known from a few samples. This shows that the under surface of
the trail is identical with *Curvolithus* type 1. Widths are from 10—20 mm, with
15 mm the commonest. The trail is distinguished from type 1 by a narrow median
furrow and in many cases clear mica orientation in the fill. The mica grains, which
are best seen on weathered examples, stand vertically and with a characteristic
orientation shown in Figure 3bB. Along the sides there is a concentration of
vertical grains parallel with the trail.
   This type occurs abundantly in a very mica-rich platy grey sandstone weathering
red-brown. Nevertheless, some examples have been found associated with *Curvolithus* type 1. At certain horizons, in mica-rich, almost shaly sandstone, the trails
dominate the sediment. The more or less straight course undulates slightly so
that trails pass over and under each other and cut bedding planes.

BILOBATE TRAILS

Figure 3c. GGU 102320. This trail occurs as a positive epirelief and badly
preserved positive hyporelief on the only specimen collected (evidence is supplemented by field photographs). In the fill there is an orientation of mica flakes
(Fig. 3cB). The flakes lie in a plane at right angles to the course of the trail and
oblique to the bedding plane. Along the sides the mica grains stand vertically and
parallel with the trail. On the collected sample two trails are present. One of them
passes through the fill of the other, destroying its structure. Both follow the
bedding plane except in one place where one dips a little downward. The trails
are 10 mm wide.
   On the specimen this trail is associated with two examples of *Curvolithus* type 2
in the grey, but red-brown weathered mica-rich sandstone, characteristic of the
Curvolithus type 2.

Ichnogenus PLANOLITES Nicholson 1873

Figure 3d. GGU 102351. The burrow occurs as positive epirelief (Fig. 3dB) and
negative epirelief (Fig. 3dA), often on the same specimen. In one case, in a 1 cm

thick plate of sandstone, the burrow occurs as positive epirelief, then dips down through the bed and appears as positive hyporelief on the under surface. Examples from 7 to 9 mm width occur, but 7 mm is most common. The burrows, which often occur together with *Gyrochorte,* curve gently from side to side; some cross bedding planes. Some of the burrows appear to branch, but in most of these cases it can be seen that a later fill is lying for a short distance within the fill of an earlier burrow. Likewise, it is common to see burrows which lie parallel, side by side, touching each other for a distance of a few centimetres.

Mica flakes along the sides of the fill lie vertical and parallel with the trail. The burrow is common and at certain horizons dominates the bedding planes. It occurs mainly in massive beds of yellow-weathering, mica-rich sandstone.

MENISCUS TUNNEL FILLS

Figure 3e. GGU 102324. These tunnels are found as positive relief (Fig. 3ec) and negative relief (Fig. 3eA). Way-up is uncertain and in the description all the tunnels are considered as epireliefs. Width 8–11 mm, most examples 10 or 11 mm. The course is slightly curved but often crosses bedding planes. The main characteristic is the watch-glass shaped meniscus structure which repeats with a distance of 3–4 mm in fills with a width of 11 mm. This structure is produced by upright orientation of mica flakes (Fig. 3eB). The whole structure weathers out as a central, meniscus-filled cylinder with a groove on either side into which the meniscus does not continue. In the groove the mica flakes are orientated at an angle to the mica in the meniscus. The groove would appear to represent loosely packed sediment surrounding the central cylinder. The surface of the cylinder is annulated. It is possible that this is a result of weathering of the meniscus structure, in which case the sculpture shown in Figure 3eA is doubtful. Based on the orientation of mica in the side grooves and the cylinder it must be considered that the meniscus is concave towards the direction of movement of the originator.

The structure occurs mostly in platy, red-weathering, mica-rich sandstone.

Ichnogenus GYROCHORTE Heer 1865

Figure 4a. GGU 102697. This trail occurs only as positive epirelief (consisting of two ridges with median groove, Fig. 4aA) and as negative hyporelief (Fig. 4aB). In many cases the negative hyporelief, which is most common, contains partial remains of the original "fill" (Fig. 4ac). Where the "fill" has been weathered down to bedding plane level it often shows a small median ridge, which may be due to tighter packing of the sediment in the middle. In a few cases there is a concentration of vertical mica flakes along the sides of the trail lying parallel with it. In some of the specimens collected the trail is seen to be a penetrative structure producing a negative hyporelief on successive bedding planes (Fig. 4a). These trails typically have a strongly winding course, crossing through themselves and others in many places. *Gyrochorte* occurs alone, or with *Planolites,* in a thick-bedded, grey, yellow-weathering sandstone.

4. Endichnial domichnia and fodinichnia

Ichnogenus TEICHICHNUS Seilacher 1955

GGU 102625. A single well-preserved example of this type of burrow was found. The stratigraphical horizon is rather uncertain but it is believed to have come from the lowermost part of the Yellow Series.

An 18 cm length of living tube is preserved, 20 mm wide and 10 mm high. The specimen appears to represent part of a horizontal, vertically retrusive burrow. The spreite beneath the tube widens upwards, the lowest preserved lamella measuring about 13 mm. The surface of the fill is indistinctly annulated.

The sediment is dark, sandy siltstone with a little fine mica.

Ichnogenus RHIZOCORALLIUM Zenker 1836

GGU 102682. Five specimens of *Rhizocorallium* were collected. In each the spreite is distinct as alternating arcs of light and dark sediment. In four of the specimens the tube wall is darker than the surrounding sediment. Width of the tubes ranges from 11 to 14 mm and the limbs are 16 to 30 mm apart. Four of the specimens occur in a yellow, micaceous sandstone, the other one in dark, micaceous, almost shaly sandstone containing plant material.

VERTICAL BURROWS

Vertical tubes (U-tubes and single shafts) of different types commonly descend from the upper surfaces of massive, coarse-grained sandstone layers. Cross-bedded and platy sandstones are also penetrated by vertical tubes but preservation is poor in these cases. The burrows fall into three groups:

(i) Narrow-U tubes of *Diplocraterion* type with long, parallel limbs. In most examples the presence of a spreite cannot be detected, however, possibly on account of the usual coarseness of the sediment. The dimensions of a typical example are: preserved length of limb, 15 cm; distance between limbs, 2 cm; diameter of tube *c.* 1 cm.

(ii) Wide-U tubes of *Corophioides* type with spreiten. The tube describes a wide arc in a vertical plane, the limbs are barely parallel. Many bedding planes show crescent-shaped vertical grooves (*Arenicoloides* form) produced by the weathering out or collapse of the spreite. The diameter of the tube is nearly 1 cm and the limbs are up to 8 cm apart.

(iii) *Tigillites* Rouault 1850. Single vertical tubes up to 30 cm long and with a diameter of *c.* 1 cm.

VERTICAL TO OBLIQUE, "MANTLED" U-TUBES

Figure 4b. GGU 103101. The most common orientation of these tubes is vertical, though oblique to almost horizontal pieces were found.

The structure has two parts:

(i) The central cylindrical fill. This is of yellow sandstone and is resistant to weathering. Its diameter is fairly constant, lying around 2·5 mm. Well preserved examples show slight annulation.

(ii) The "mantle". This is a primary dark layer surrounding the secondary fill. Its outside diameter is most commonly 6–7 mm; the largest measured 9 mm, the smallest 4 mm. The mantle has a looser structure than the surrounding sandstone. The dark colour is caused by the presence of mica and carbonaceous material. Grain orientation imparts to the mantle an appearance which resembles cones within cones (Fig. 4bA). The mica is orientated as shown in Figure 4bB. In cross section, the structure is easily recognizable through the circular orientation of mica grains around the upstanding central cylinder (Fig. 4bC). The tubes invariably occur in pairs with 9–14 mm between centres, indicating that they are U-tubes, but the vertex has not been seen. In the longest example the tubes run for 8 cm without reaching the vertex. There is no spreite between the limbs.

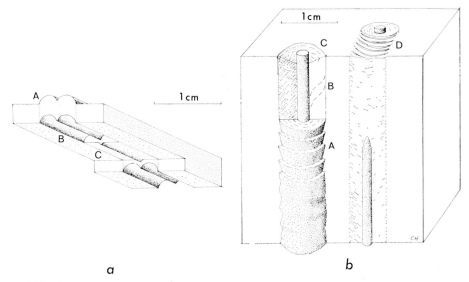

Fig. 4.   a   *Gyrochorte,* slab seen from below,   A   positive epirelief,   B   negative hypo-relief,   c   typical condition of fill after weathering;   b   "Mantled" U-tube,   A   Outer surface of "mantle" showing cone-in-cone structure (schematic),   B   mica orientation within "mantle",   c   weathered bedding plane showing upstanding central cylinder and circular orientation of mica in "mantle",   D   horizontal "spreite".

In one example, one of the two tubes has moved sideways through the sediment, producing a 2·5 cm long, horizontal "spreite" as seen on the bedding plane (Fig. 4bD).

These U-tubes are accompanied by *Planolites* and *Curvolithus* type 1. The sediment is hard, grey, yellow-weathering sandstone, rich in plant material.

SPIRAL BURROW

GGU 102668. A single specimen of a spiral burrow was collected in very poorly cemented, rather coarse, grey sandstone containing some mica. The spiral has a diameter of 8 mm and the whorls are 6 mm apart. Four whorls are preserved. Orientation is unknown.

Ichnogenus OPHIOMORPHA Lundgren 1891

GGU 102342. In a single specimen of massive sandstone (14 cm thick) there occur several vertical *Ophiomorpha* shafts. These penetrate through the whole thickness of the block and have diameters of 1–2 cm. On examples where the fill has weathered away, the knobbly wall structure is clearly visible. Besides the collected sample, *Ophiomorpha* was observed several times in the field, in one place together with vertical U-burrows, always in coarse, well-sorted sandstone.

5. Epichnia

SMALL MEANDERS

GGU 102656. This type occurs as positive epirelief. Width varies between 1 and 2·5 mm with 1·5 mm most common. The course is very winding and over short distances it meanders regularly with an amplitude of 3–5 cm. The trails do not cross bedding planes. In most specimens collected the meanders occur with

Q

Curvolithus type 2 in a platy to shaly, mica-rich sandstone. Usually no mica orientation is seen, but in some cases vertical mica grains lie parallel with the trail at the sides.

6. Conclusions

The following relationships were seen between sedimentary facies and ichno-coenoses:

(i) Massive, structureless, well-cemented, well-sorted, grey sandstone with or without mica, weathering yellow (high energy environment); vertical burrows descending from the top surface.

(ii) Platy to thick, micaceous, grey sandstone weathering red-brown; bedding planes rich in *Curvolithus* type 2, meniscus tunnels and bilobate trails.

(iii) Thick, bedded, micaceous, grey sandstone weathering yellow; *Curvolithus* type 1, *Planolites* and *Gyrochorte*.

(iv) Platy to shaly, red to dark grey, micaceous sandstones; small meanders, *Curvolithus* type 2 and penetration by vertical burrows.

Thus, there is some correlation between sediment type and some of the trace fossils in the Yellow Series.

Acknowledgements. The author is grateful to Dr. R. G. Bromley for advice and assistance and for the translation of this paper. The Geological Survey of Green-land is thanked for giving permission to publish.

References

BIRKELUND, T. and PERCH-NIELSEN, K. 1969. Field observations in Upper Palaeozoic and Mesozoics ediments of Scoresby Land and Jameson Land. *Rapp. Grønlands geol. Unders.* **21,** 21.

MARTINSSON, A. 1965. Aspects of a Middle Cambrian thanatotope on Öland. *Geol. För. Stockh. Förh.* **87,** 181.

SEILACHER, A. 1953. Studien zur Palichnologie. *Neues Jb. Geol. Paläont. Abh.* **96,** 421.

STAUBER, H. 1942. Die Triasablagerungen von Ostgrönland. *Meddr Grønland* **132,** no. 1.

C. Heinberg, Institut for Historisk Geologi og Palaeontologi, Oster Voldgade 10, 1350 København K., Denmark.

The animal community of a muddy environment and the development of biofacies as effected by the life cycle of the characteristic species

Günther Hertweck

Characteristic species of North Sea communities, in the sense of Petersen, have traditionally been chosen from members of the community that possess skeletal hard parts. The echiuroid *Echiurus echiurus* has, however, recently been designated the characteristic species of a community in the German Bay. This echiuroid produces a distinctive burrow, thus the "characteristic species" of the potential biofacies is a lebensspur.

Initial attempts to document the configuration, distribution, and environmental significance of these lebensspuren were only partly successful, mainly because subsequent observations revealed significant changes in burrow morphology. Systematic observations over a longer period of time showed that such changes were related to various stages in the life cycle of the echiuroid population. The burrows of juveniles were modified regularly, commensurate with the growth and maturation of the individuals. Burrows of adults were thus markedly different from those of immature animals.

Bioturbated zones, representing these cycles, are repeated vertically in sediment cores—thus attesting to the frequent occurrence of this phenomenon—although a given zone normally records only the final stage in that particular cycle.

The results of this study illustrate the need for additional documentation of life cycles and consequent burrowing behaviour among other Recent animals. The potential danger in basing palaeoecological reconstructions upon lebensspuren preserved at only one stage of their development is now equally obvious.

1. Concept of community and biofacies

A biofacies, as defined here, is the preserved record of all biogenic features imparted to the sediment by a community of organisms living within a particular set of environmental conditions. These biogenic features consist of body fossils and/or trace fossils (cf. Moore 1957 and Schäfer 1963).

Certain organisms found in a community are more sensitive to environmental parameters than others, so that the environmental significance of the various members of the community may differ considerably. Concepts and terms expressing the value of organisms as environmental indicators have resulted from studies of recent environments, such as those by Petersen (1913; 1924) who recognized and named communities by means of characteristic species.

The basis for erecting characteristic species of the 1st order (Petersen 1924; Thorson 1957) for definition of communities is derived essentially from the relationship between organisms and a substratum, i.e., for sediment-dwelling organisms, a close relationship exists between the characteristic species of the 1st order and a particular kind of sediment (Allen 1899; Ford 1923; Remane 1940; Reineck *et al.* 1968).

In the sequence of events leading from community to biofacies, upon death, burial, and preservation of organisms (including their bioturbation), the characteristic species of the community becomes the characteristic fossil of the biofacies (see Reineck *et al.* 1968 p. 291; cf. Petersen 1913 p. 27). The characteristic fossil can be a body fossil, a trace fossil, or both (related in life position), but it must first have been a characteristic species within the community.

Petersen (1913; 1915) relied principally upon molluscs and echinoderms as characteristic species for marine endobenthic communities; these animals are conspicuous because of their relatively large size and are usually easy to identify. He explicitly avoided the use of polychaetes in this context. At the same time, he considered palaeontological aspects of these two groups (1913 p. 27), because they contribute most of the "leading fossils" (ichnology did not play an important role in contemporary palaeontology). His characteristic species were thought to be the "leading fossils" of the present.

Certain aspects of the concepts propounded by Petersen and Thorson have been debated by some recent workers (see Mills 1969, and references therein). However, their concepts remain satisfactory for differentiating communities in the North Sea as well as in the Mediterranean Sea.

Assuming no *post-mortem* transport of skeletal remains, the close relationship between characteristic species and a certain kind of sediment in a recent environment, is reflected in a close relationship between characteristic fossil and host sediments in the palaeoenvironment. Lithofacies and biofacies are thus inseparable, and should be regarded as a unit within the facies in general.

2. The *Echiurus echiurus*-biofacies of the German Bay

Petersen's concept of the community and its characteristic species was followed later by other biologists, for example Ford (1923) in the English Channel, and Hagmeier (1925) in the German Bay. They obtained similar results, but were not able to apply Petersen's concept in every detail.

Petersen's *Abra alba* community partly overlaps (with respect to the distribution of the "characteristic species"—*Abra alba*) the *Macoma baltica* community (Hagmeier 1925). It also overlaps the *Amphiura filiformis* community (Ford 1923). Because of this overlapping, Hagmeier (in Hagmeier and Künne 1951 p. 222) named his former "*Abra alba* community", found in the muddy environment between the Elbe estuary and Helgoland (Fig. 1), as a "soft bottom variant of the *Venus gallina* community". However, this renaming violates the concepts of the community and characteristic species, because the sand-dwelling *Venus gallina* does not ordinarily live in this soft bottom environment. Occasionally, one finds a few valves of dead juvenile specimens (Reineck *et al.* 1967; 1968).

In contrast, Reineck *et al.* (1968 p. 282) found that *Echiurus echiurus* Pallas (Echiurida) is the characteristic species of the 1st order in this community of the muddy environment. He named it the *Echiurus echiurus* community. Distribution of this echiuroid, the characteristic species, conforms well with the clear cut boundaries of the environment.

In the eastern and southern parts of this region, toward the mainland, there are areas of fine grained sand with mud (Reineck 1963; Reineck *et al.* 1968); these areas are inhabited by the *Macoma baltica* community (Hagmeier 1925; Reineck *et al.* 1968). In the northwest, toward the open sea, there is an area of fine grained sand with medium grained sand and mud (Reineck 1963; Reineck *et al.* 1967) populated by the *Amphiura filiformis* community (Hagmeier 1925; cf. Hertweck and Reineck 1969). In the German Bay these two communities are normally separated by a belt of sandy sediments occupied by the *Venus gallina* community (Hagmeier 1925). In the muddy area the *Echiurus echiurus* community practically replaces the *Venus gallina* community. The mud deposited in this region has been

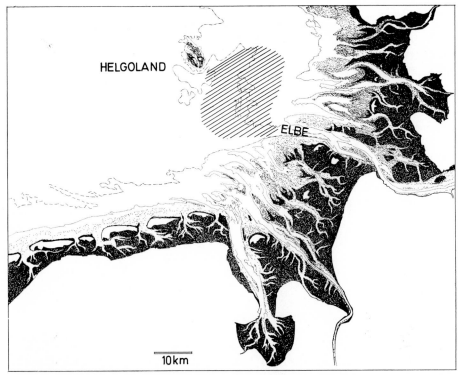

Fig. 1. Location map. The cross-hatched area represents the muddy environment populated by the *Echiurus echiurus* community. Dark hatching: intertidal flats; semi-dark hatching: depths to 6 m; isobaths: 10, 20, 30 m.

brought in by the rivers Elbe, Weser, and Eider (Pratje 1931 p. 65; Reineck 1963 p. 55; Lüneburg 1963).

The macrobenthic fauna of the *Echiurus echiurus* community is represented by about 40 species (Reineck *et al.* 1968 fig. 9). The more abundant species of living animals include:

Mollusca: *Nucula nitida* Sowerby, *Abra alba* S. Wood, *Corbula gibba* Olivi.

Polychaeta: *Pectinaria koreni* (Malmgren), *Notomastus latericeus* (Sars), *Scalibregma inflatum* Rathke, *Nephthys hombergi* Audouin and Edwards.

Cumacea: *Diastylis rathkei* Kröyer.

Echiurida: *Echiurus echiurus* (Pallas).

The last one is the characteristic species of the 1st order of this community. The bivalves *Nucula nitida* and *Abra alba* and the polychaete *Pectinaria koreni* may be considered as characteristic species of the 3rd order, that is they are found in more than one community, but in such large numbers and over such large areas that they necessarily belong to the characteristic animals of the community (Petersen 1924).

The most abundant dead Bivalvia are: *Nucula nitida* Sowerby, *Corbula gibba* Olivi, *Abra alba* S. Wood.

Less abundant dead bivalves are: *Montacuta bidentata* (Montagu), *Abra nitida* Müller, *Spisula subtruncata* Da Costa.

Dead gastropods were found only rarely, the most important species being *Lunatia nitida* (Donovan).

Other biogenic hard parts occurring in small quantities consist of: skeletal parts of Ophiuroidea, skeletal fragments and spines of *Echinocardium cordatum,* skeletal parts of Balanidae, and entire tubes and fragments of *Pectinaria koreni* and *P. auricoma.*

The taphocoenosis found in this depositional environment conforms well with the spectrum of living species. Practically all biogenic hard parts are autochthonous (Reineck *et al.* 1967 p. 233; 1968 fig. 14).

This taphocoenosis is quite characteristic for this muddy environment. However, one also finds these species in adjoining environments. In the eastern part of the bay, a region of fine-grained sand with medium-grained sand and mud exhibits the same spectrum of species as that of the muddy environment, but the relative abundance of individual species is different.

Molluscs, which constitute the most abundant animal group and which contribute two characteristic species of the 3rd order to this muddy environment community, are thus not potential characteristic fossils of this biofacies although their remains are well suited for preservation in the rock record.

In contrast, *Echiurus echiurus,* the only characteristic species of the 1st order of this community populating the muddy depositional environment southeast of Helgoland, does not leave behind any hard skeletal parts. It produces conspicuous and distinct lebensspuren, however, and thus provides an excellent example of the situation in which the characteristic fossil of a biofacies *in statu nascendi* is a lebensspur. This biofacies was named the *Echiurus echiurus*-biofacies (Reineck *et al.* 1968 p. 291).

Although in this special case a lebensspur is the "characteristic fossil," molluscs in adjoining environments retain their significance as characteristic species of 1st order of the communities. Later, in the preserved sediment-record they become characteristic fossils for their respective biofacies, for example—*Macoma baltica* in near shore environments, and *Venus gallina* in off shore sandy belts.

Recently, attempts have been made to use lebensspuren as general depth indicators (e.g. Seilacher 1967). Results of the present study suggest that this scheme can be generally successful only when the trace-making animals whose lebensspuren are used as environmental indicators are characteristic species of the 1st or 2nd order of the communities in which they live.

3. Morphology and development of trace fossils in the *Echiurus echiurus*-biofacies

The burrows of *E. echiurus* (cf. Reineck *et al.* 1967 p. 239) are U-shaped, having a broad lower part and narrower arms and surface openings (Pl. 1b). The lower part of the burrows of adult animals may be as much as 1·5 to 2 cm in diameter, and may extend to depths of 20 to 30 cm. The openings are usually about 0·5 cm in diameter. The walls of the burrow are reinforced by mucilaginous secretions.

Generally, the lower, curved, part of the U is surrounded above and below by spreiten. Concave-down spreiten are produced by growing juveniles during the process of shifting their burrows downward. Concave-up spreiten are generally produced when rapid sedimentation compels the animal to shift its burrow upwards (cf. Goldring 1964 fig. 1). This structure can also be produced when excessive sediment falls into the burrow, such as sand brought through storms (Reineck *et al.* 1967 p. 226; Reineck *et al.* 1968 p. 270, fig. 6; Gadow and Reineck 1969). The animal presses this sediment into the bottom walls of the burrow, thus shifting the burrow upwards. If a major part of the burrow is filled in by sand, the animal may re-excavate this part of the burrow, or less commonly, it may shift the position of its burrow by a few centimetres.

The polychaete *Notomastus latericeus* also produces conspicuous and distinctive burrows, 2 to 3 mm in diameter. Openings for ingestion and egestion are located about 8 to 10 cm apart, and may extend downward, more or less vertically, to depths of as much as 10 cm, where they are connected by a dominantly horizontal spiralled component. The polychaete *Scalibregma inflatum* produces irregular narrow burrows.

Based on these general types of individual lebensspuren Reineck *et al.* (1967 fig. 10-12) attempted to demonstrate the three-dimensional relationships of these lebensspuren in order to help characterize the biofacies of this muddy environment. However, this attempt was only partly successful, mainly because not enough emphasis was given to the relative abundance of the species of this community. Some of the species were over-emphasized with regard to their significance in producing bioturbated structures, and thus as environmental indicators. Another reason for the inadequacy of this interpretation as discussed below, is that the investigations were carried out during a rather exceptional stage in the development of the community.

In later investigations (Reineck *et al.* 1968 fig. 9) sufficient emphasis was given to the relative abundance of the species within the community. The bioturbation structures observed in this investigation (Reineck *et al.* 1968 fig. 11, 12) were somewhat different from those encountered previously (Reineck *et al.* 1967 fig. 10-12). Consideration of these differences led to the idea that developments in the life cycle of populations may produce important changes in their bioturbation structures. An attempt has been made below to compare the bioturbation structures observed during investigations conducted during several successive years.

The starting point for this succession was the very cold winter of 1962/63, when most of the animals inhabiting the muddy environment southeast of Helgoland were exterminated (Ziegelmeier 1964). When the area became repopulated, the community consisted predominantly of its 1st order characteristic species, *E. echiurus,* as observed in 1964 (Reineck *et al.* 1967). The dense juvenile population of this species—60 to 100 specimens per 0·2 m² (standard unit sample)—produced a completely bioturbated zone 10 to 13 cm in thickness. Within this zone, burrows of living *E. echiurus* were closely spaced, sometimes even interconnected. Below the lower surface of the U-curves, a few thin spreiten were generally observed (Pl. 1a). Although *Notomastus latericeus* was present, well developed burrows were found mostly below the bioturbation zone of *E. echiurus.*

In 1965, a marked decline in the population density of *E. echiurus* was evident. Although some minor changes in the bioturbated structures were observed, the general picture remained almost the same.

In 1967 the population declined further, moreover the population then consisted only of adult animals (Reineck *et al.* 1968), and some significant changes in the bioturbation structures could be recognised. The adult *E. echiurus* produced deep, broad burrows having many spreiten surrounding the lower curved parts of the structure. In places these deep burrows penetrated the lower surface of the bioturbation zone of 1964. The dense but distinct burrows within the 1964 zone had been completely destroyed by subsequent activity of the maturing juveniles. Simultaneously, *Notomastus latericeus* began constructing well developed burrows in the upper 10 cm of the sediment (Pl. 1b).

Observations in 1968 revealed that all individuals of the *E. echiurus*-population had died. Bioturbation structures were somewhat changed and were generally rather indistinct. Open burrows were absent; only incomplete sections of filled

Plate 1

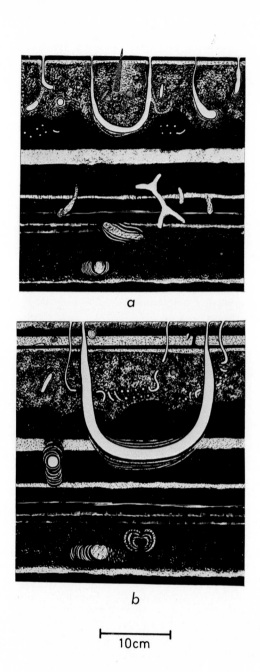

a

b

c

|———10cm———|

240

burrows, surrounded by spreiten were seen (Pl. 1c). This bioturbation zone is almost identical in appearance to older bioturbation zones in the deeper parts of the sediment (Pl. 1c). In cores up to 4 m in length, such bioturbation zones are repeated every 20 to 30 cm.

This series of bioturbated structures (Pl. 1) studied in successive years shows that the configuration of bioturbation structures observed at a given time depends mainly on the temporal stage of the life cycle of trace-making organisms. Only the completion of such life cycles produces the final configuration of bioturbation structures that may characterize the biofacies in general, and only this final configuration is usually comparable to the bioturbation structures observed in older horizons.

4. Conclusions

The results of this study prompt some comments on approaches to the investigation of bioturbation structures in Recent sediments:

(i) The series of bioturbation structures formed during intermediate temporal stages of the life cycle of animals is equally as important palaeoecologically as the final structures produced at the completion of the life cycle. Only the intermediate stages provide comprehensive information on the overall development of, and possible variations in, bioturbation structures.

(ii) Due to some calamity, such as the one reported herein, an animal population may be completely destroyed at a time when the population is only in some intermediate stage of development; the resulting record of bioturbation may be much different from that produced at the normal completion of the life-cycle.

(iii) Results of studies on recent lebensspuren would be more useful in interpreting the genesis of trace fossils if the whole spectrum of bioturbation features produced during a complete life-cycle of trace-making individuals and populations were to be included in the investigation. Otherwise one is apt to base palaeoecological models upon "by chance" observations of bioturbation structures *in statu nascendi* produced at a temporal stage in the life-cycle of the bioturbating population.

Acknowledgements. Financial help from Deutsche Forschungsgemeinschaft to carry out these investigations is gratefully acknowledged.

This paper is Senckenberg am Meer contribution number 287.

Plate 1

a Upper part of the diagram shows bioturbation structures produced by the juvenile population of *E. echiurus* of 1964.

b Bioturbation structures produced by the adult population of *E. echiurus* of 1967.

c The upper part shows bioturbation structures observed in 1968. They were left behind by the *E. echiurus* population after completion of its life cycle. The older horizons in the lower part of the picture show lebensspuren of *E. echiurus* which were produced and left behind by still older *E. echiurus* populations. This sequence can be regarded as a characteristic picture of the *E. echiurus*-biofacies.

References

ALLEN, E. J. 1899. On the fauna and bottom-deposits near the thirty-fathom line from the Eddystone Grounds to Start Point. *J. mar. biol. Ass. U.K.* n.s. **5**, 365.

FORD, E. 1923. Animal communities of the level sea-bottom in the waters adjacent to Plymouth. *J. mar. biol. Ass. U.K.* n.s. **13**, 164.

GOLDRING, R. 1964. Trace-fossils and the sedimentary surface in shallow-water marine sediments. *Devs in Sedimentol.* **1**, 136.

GADOW, S. and REINECK, H. E. 1969. Ablandiger Sandtransport bei Sturmfluten. *Senckenberg. maritima* **50**, 63.

HAGMEIER, A. 1925. Vorläufiger Bericht über die vorbereitenden Untersuchungen der Bodenfauna der Deutschen Bucht mit dem Petersen-Bodengreifer. *Ber. dt. wiss. Kommn Meeresforsch.* N.F. **1**, 247.

—— and KÜNNE, C. 1951. Die Nahrung der Meerestiere. IV. Beziehungen der Ernährung zur Verbreitung der Arten und der Gemeinschaften der Bodentiere. *Handbuch der Seefischerei Nordeuropas* **1** (5b), 177.

HERTWECK, G. and REINECK, H. E. 1969. Sedimentologie der Meeresbodensenke NW von Helgoland (Nordsee). *Senckenberg. maritima* **50**, 153.

LÜNEBURG, H. 1963. Wassermischvorgänge vor der Weser- und Elbmündung. *Veröff. Inst. Meeresforsch. Bremerh.* **8**, 111.

MILLS, E. L. 1969. The community concept in marine zoology, with comments on continua and instability in some marine communities. A review. *J. Fish. Res. Bd Can.* **26**, 1415.

MOORE, R. C. 1957. Modern methods in paleoecology. *Bull. Am. Ass. Petrol. Geol.* **41**, 1775.

PETERSEN, C. G. J. 1913. Valuation of the sea. II. The animal communities of the sea-bottom and their importance for marine zoogeography. *Rep. Dan. biol. Stn* **21**, 1.

—— 1915. On the animal communities of the sea bottom in the Skagerak, the Christiania Fjord and the Danish waters. *Rep. Dan. biol. Stn* **23**, 3.

—— 1924. A brief survey of the animal communities in Danish waters. *Am. J. Sci.* Ser. 5 **7**, 334.

PRATJE, O. 1931. Die Sedimente der Deutschen Bucht. Eine regional-statistische Untersuchung. *Wiss. Meeresunters.* N.F. **18**, 1.

REINECK, H. E. 1963. Sedimentgefüge im Bereich der südlichen Nordsee. *Abh. senckenberg. naturforsch. Ges.* **505**, 1.

——, GUTMANN, W. F. and HERTWECK, G. 1967. Das Schlickgebiet südlich Helgoland als Beispiel rezenter Schelfablagerungen. *Senckenberg. leth.* **48**, 219.

—— DÖRJES, J., GADOW, S. and HERTWECK, G. 1968. Sedimentologie, Faunenzonierung und Faziesabfolge vor der Ostküste der inneren Deutschen Bucht. *Senckenberg. leth.* **49**, 261.

REMANE, A. 1940. Einführung in die zoologische Ökologie der Nord- und Ostsee. *Tierwelt N. u. Ostsee* **1**, 1.

SCHÄFER, W. 1963. Biozönose und Biofazies im marinen Bereich. *Aufs. Reden senckenb. naturf. Ges.* **11**.

SEILACHER, A. 1967. Bathymetry of trace fossils. *Mar. Geol.* **5**, 413.

THORSON, G. 1957. Bottom communities (Sublittoral or shallow shelf). In *Treatise on marine ecology and paleoecology* **1**, Mem. Geol. Soc. Am. **67**, 461.

ZIEGELMEIER, E. 1964. Einwirkungen des kalten Winters 1962/63 auf das Makrobenthos im Ostteil der Deutschen Bucht. *Helgoländer wiss. Meeresunters.* **10**, 272.

G. Hertweck, Institut für Meeresgeologie und Meeresbiologie "Senckenburg", Wilhelmshaven, West Germany.

Burrowing patterns of haustoriid amphipods from Sapelo Island, Georgia

J. D. Howard and C. A. Elders

Haustoriid amphipods have long been known to be active burrowers in the intertidal zone. Using time lapse X-ray radiographic techniques and plexiglass aquaria connected to a flowing salt water system, the over-all burrowing patterns of seven species of haustoriid amphipods were studied. The burrowing pattern is considered to consist of burrowing rate, burrow width, bioturbation, concentration, burrow orientation, and burrow geometry. The burrowing pattern is found to be unique for each species studied, and in the case of such truly sympatric pairs as *Neohaustorius* and *Haustorius*, and *Parahaustorius* and *Acanthohaustorius*, the burrowing patterns are found to be complementary. This is considered effective in reducing competition, and the application of this to the Competitive Exclusion Principle is discussed briefly.

1. Introduction

A detailed study of niche diversity in sympatric species of intertidal amphipods was made by Croker (1967a). Results of that study and the finding of amphipod-produced bioturbation in Pleistocene sediments led the writers to investigate how the burrowing habits of co-existing species might differ and to determine if they could be differentiated on the basis of the structures which they formed.

The amphipods studied by Croker were observed in the laboratory by time lapse X-ray radiography to determine variations in burrowing pattern, depth and rate. These species were *Protohaustorius deichmannae* Bousfield, *Neohaustorius schmitzi* Bousfield, *Haustorius* sp., *Lepidactylus dytiscus* Say, *Acanthohaustorius* sp., *Parahaustorius longimerus* Bousfield and *Pseudohaustorius caroliniensis* Bousfield.

2. Habitat and burrowing of open beach amphipods, Sapelo Island.

Croker (1967a) demonstrated horizontal and vertical zonation of seven amphipod species. The areas he studied (Fig. 1) included (i) a part of the Sapelo Island beach exposed to the sea; (ii) Dean Creek beach, a protected beach in Doboy Sound; and (iii) Blackbeard Beach, a broad sand flat at the mouth of Blackbeard tidal-creek.

He sampled at various tidal levels throughout a year at each of the three localities. Figure 2 summarizes the horizontal density variations of the seven species of amphipods in the low, mid, and high tide positions on the three beaches. Throughout the year the principal animal-niche relationships remained relatively stable with only minor seasonal differences which he considered to be a reflection of recruitment and temperature tolerances. He also investigated vertical variation of amphipods on the beaches and these findings are summarized in Figure 3.

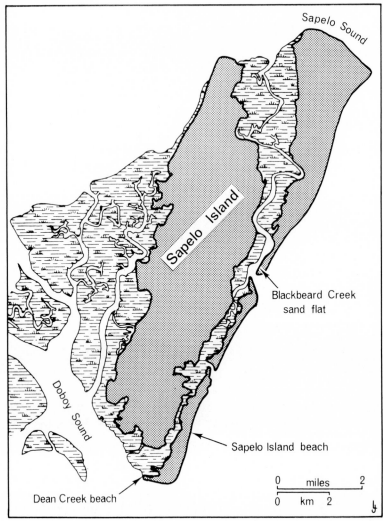

Fig. 1. Location of environments studied by Croker (1967a). Sapelo Island beach is exposed to the open sea and Blackbeard Creek sand flat and Dean Creek beach are protected from the direct effect of the sea.

Croker (*op. cit.*) summarizes his findings as follows: "*N. schmitzi* was generally distributed over the entire tidal range, with greatest abundance usually at higher levels. *Pa. longimerus* and *Acanthohaustorius* sp. were generally restricted to the lower half of the intertidal zone, while *L. dytiscus* was generally most abundant at mid-tide level with some extension both above and below this level. *Haustorius* sp. was generally restricted to the upper half of the intertidal zone, with some extension to lower levels. *Pr. deichmannae* and *Ps. caroliniensis* were restricted to either low tide level, or permanently wet tide pool areas." With respect to vertical zonation Croker noted that "at both habitats (Sapelo Beach and Dean Creek Beach) *N. schmitzi* was generally more abundant in the upper 2·5 cm sand layer, while *Haustorius* sp. was more abundant at deeper sand depths. This is particularly

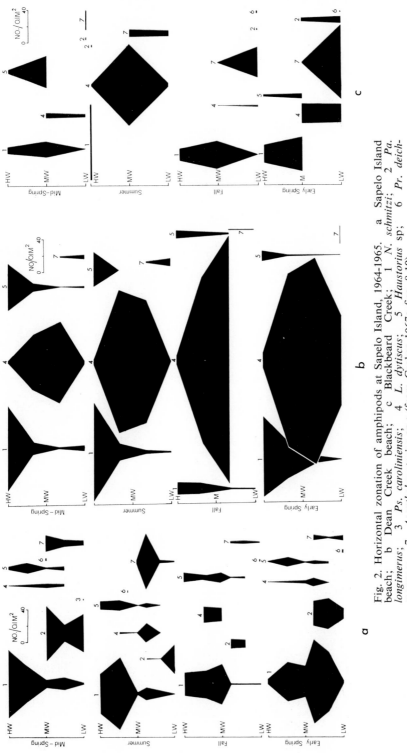

Fig. 2. Horizontal zonation of amphipods at Sapelo Island, 1964-1965.   a   Sapelo Island beach;   b   Dean Creek beach;   c   Blackbeard   Creek;   1   *N. schmitzi*;   2   *Pa. longimerus*;   3   *Ps. caroliniensis*;   4   *L. dytiscus*;   5   *Haustorius* sp;   6   *Pr. deichmannae*;   7   *Acanthohaustorius* sp.; (from Croker 1967a figs. 8-10).

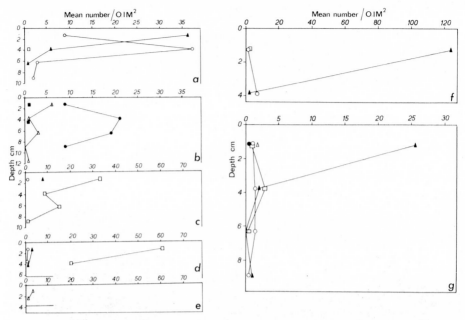

Fig. 3. Vertical zonation of amphipods. Summer 1965: a Sapelo beach, between high water and mean water; b Sapelo beach, between mean water and low water; c Dean Creek beach, high water; d Dean Creek beach, between mean water and high water; e Dean Creek beach, low water. Winter 1966: f Sapelo beach, high water; g Sapelo beach, between mean water and low water. Closed triangles *N. schmitzi*; open circles *Haustorius* sp.; closed rectangles *Pr. deichmannae*; open triangles *Acanthohaustorius* sp.; closed circles *Pa. longimerus*; open rectangles *L. dytiscus*. Short horizontal lines on ordinate in d and e indicate upper limit of black reduction layer (from Croker 1967a figures 11 and 12).

evident at Sapelo Beach during summer (Fig. 3a). There was a tendency for a similar distribution of *Acanthohaustorius* sp., and *Pa. longimerus* where they occurred together in abundance. *L. dytiscus* was more abundant in the upper sand layers at the protected Dean Creek Beach." A schematic presentation of these general features of zonation is given in Figure 4. A general separation of species is conspicuous both in lateral positions on the beach and by different depths of burrowing.

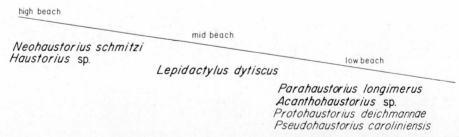

Fig. 4. Population distribution of the seven species of amphipods at Sapelo Island. This illustrates the general distribution although there is some overlap of all species as shown in Figure 2. *Protohaustorius deichmannae* and *Pseudohaustorius caroliniensis* are shown in lighter print because these species are much less abundant than the other species.

3. Procedures and description of burrowing patterns

Amphipods were collected from intertidal environments by sieving beach sands through a 1 mm mesh screen. Species identifications were made and individuals were placed in plexiglass aquaria. The aquaria were laminated with alternating layers of quartz and heavy mineral sand from the Sapelo Island beach (mean grain size 3 ϕ). It was necessary to layer the sediments in this manner to obtain maximum definition and contrast of the bioturbate textures. Since some of the species were known to show photonegative responses (Croker 1967a p. 188), the aquaria were made opaque by wrapping them with black tape. Aquaria used in this study were constructed of clear acrylic (plexiglass) sheets of 5 mm thickness. Dimensions of the aquaria were $20 \times 25 \times 3 \cdot 8$ cm so that the thickness of the laminated sand in the aquaria was 2·8 cm. Seven centimetres of salt water were maintained above the sand surface of the aquaria by a flowing salt water system. Two individuals of each species were placed in each separate aquaria and time lapse X-ray radiographs were made at designated time intervals. A more detailed discussion of X-ray radiography as a technique for the study of animal burrowing is given in Howard (1968).

Prints of the time lapse X-ray radiographs are illustrated in Plates 1–8. Time intervals between exposures for most of the radiographs illustrated in this paper were 6, 22, 48, 94 and 168 hours. Bioturbate structures formed by an individual animal consist of distinct, backfilled cylinders of shallow U-shaped laminae of light and heavy mineral sand. With time the cylindrical structures are crossed and recrossed many times. The sand becomes progressively more homogenized and evidence of primary lamination or individual burrowing gradually disappears.

Protohaustorius deichmannae (Pl. 1). During the first 48 hours the burrowing consisted of arcuate forays restricted to the upper 2·5 cm of the aquarium with the two individuals working on separate sides of the aquarium. The burrowing pattern indicates that the organism starting from just below the sediment-water interface, went down 1·0 to 2·5 cm, and then returned again to just below the sediment-water interface. Between 48 and 94 hours the amphipod which had been reworking the area on the left side of the aquarium made a deep foray to 11 cm below the surface concentrating most of its time in the heavy mineral layers. This deeper burrowing continued to 96 hours. It is not known if both individuals took part in the accelerated reworking because only one can be clearly identified on the radiograph print. From this and other radiographs made of *Pr. deichmannae* it appears that a shallow arcuate burrow is characteristic of its mode of burrowing.

Neohaustorius schmitzi (Pl. 2). The burrowing pattern of *N. schmitzi* is produced by numerous, nearly vertical, up-and-down movements to and from the sediment-water interface. The individuals worked on opposite sides of the aquarium. Between 22 and 48 hours the specimen on the right side of the tank made a foray to a depth of 4·5 cm below the surface and another to 6·5 cm depth between 48 and 96 hours. Otherwise both stayed in the upper 2·5 cm of the sand with most movements represented by short, nearly vertical marks. From the X-rays it appears that this species must break the sand surface often; this was verified by short "scratch-mark" trails seen on the sand surface, with small piles of sand at each end of the trail. It is interesting to note that *N. schmitzi* was the only haustoriid species which Croker (1967a p. 192) collected free in the water. Thus it is possible that this species utilizes the action of the surf across the beach for transport within

PLATE 1

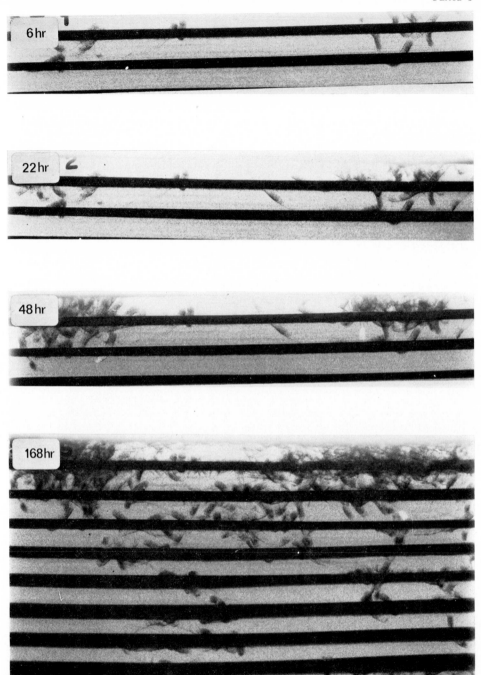

Plate 1

X-ray radiography study of burrowing by *Protohaustorius deichmannae*.

PLATE 2

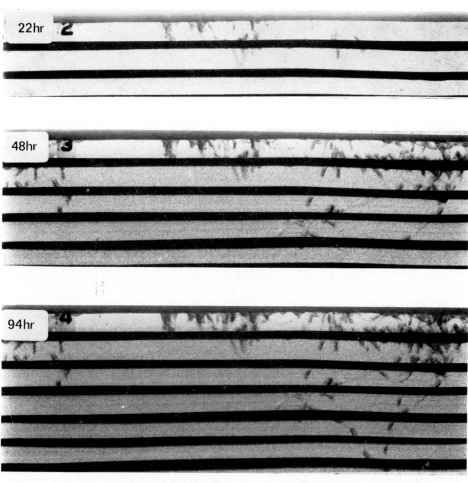

22hr

48hr

94hr

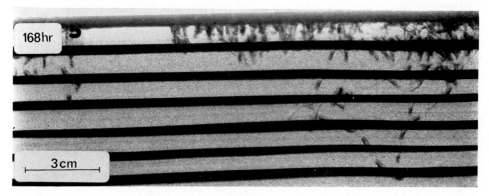

168hr

3cm

Plate 2

X-ray radiography study of *Neohaustorius schmitzi.*

PLATE 3

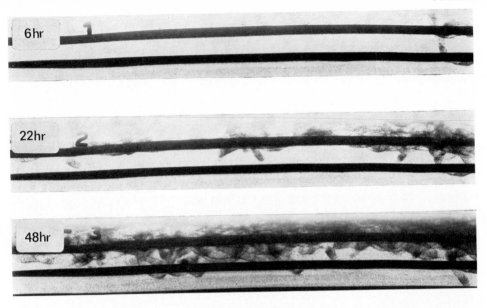

Plate 3

X-ray radiography study of *Haustorius* sp.

the habitat. Furthermore, this may be an explanation for its presence, to some extent, throughout the beach area.

Haustorius sp. (Pl. 3). Bioturbation produced by *Haustorius* sp., like that of *Pr. deichmannae*, consisted of shallow arcuate burrowing paths which began at the sediment-water interface and penetrated the aquarium to a depth of approximately 2·5 cm, but had a horizontal orientation. Almost all activity was restricted to the upper 2 cm until 48 hours. After this time some deeper burrowings were made to as much as 6·5 cm, but the same general arcuate pattern was maintained. Crokers' field sampling (1967a, p. 179) found *Haustorius* sp. more abundant below 2·5 cm.

Lepidactylus dytiscus (Pl. 4). Burrowing by *L. dytiscus* is very similar to that of *N. schmitzi* in that practically all movement is restricted to a vertical plane. However, with *L. dytiscus* the depth of penetration is greater; down to an average of 3 cm. Also, turns of 180° are often made so that the amphipod usually crosses over its own path. The reluctance of the organism on the left side of the aquarium to burrow until after 94 hours is unexplained, unless there happened to be sufficient food in the surface layers to sustain it for the first hours of the experiment.

Acanthohaustorius sp. (Pl. 5). A very characteristic deep burrowing pattern is produced by *Acanthohaustorius* sp. The legs of its traverse are marked by oblique angular movements, usually at angles approximately 60° from the sand surface, thereby producing a predominantly vertical orientation. In this experiment the similarity of the patterns produced by the two individuals is striking. This is most clearly seen in the burrowing pattern of the first 6 hour interval. When examined by stereo X-ray radiography (Pl. 9) it can be seen that this angular pattern results from the organisms moving from one side of the aquarium to the other as it moves downward. The obvious up-and-down movement displayed by this set of X-ray prints may be in response to tidal fluctuations following the initial burrowing, although the water level in the aquarium remained constant.

Parahaustorius longimerus (Pl. 6). The aquaria experiment with *Parahaustorius* sp. began with one individual making a burrow penetration to 10 cm below the sediment-water interface and then returning to the upper layers of the sand without further repetition of this activity. Subsequent burrowing by both individuals consisted of sediment reworking in the upper 3 cm of the aquarium. Most of the burrowing by this species consisted of up-and-down movement which followed an arcuate, somewhat swirling pattern oriented at about 45° from the sand surface. It is interesting to note that in other experiments with *Pa. longimerus*, in which the aquarium walls were not opaque, deep burrowing was its typical pattern.

Pseudohaustorius caroliniensis (Pl. 7). In several experiments conducted with *Ps. carolininesis* the organisms have immediately burrowed to depth in the aquarium, as they did in the example shown in Plate 7. The path followed is also very regular and consists of an angular, overall vertical path with turning points commonly approaching 45° angles. In this particular experiment only one amphipod was present and it made a burrowing foray from the surface to the bottom and back to the surface sometime in the first 22 hours. Based on other studies this probably occurred within the first two or three hours. The reason for this consistent method of movement is not known, but perhaps represents the search for a favourable feeding horizon. Following the initial deep burrowing, the animal showed little activity until 48 hours when the upper 3 cm were slightly reworked along a path also characterized by angular movements.

PLATE 4

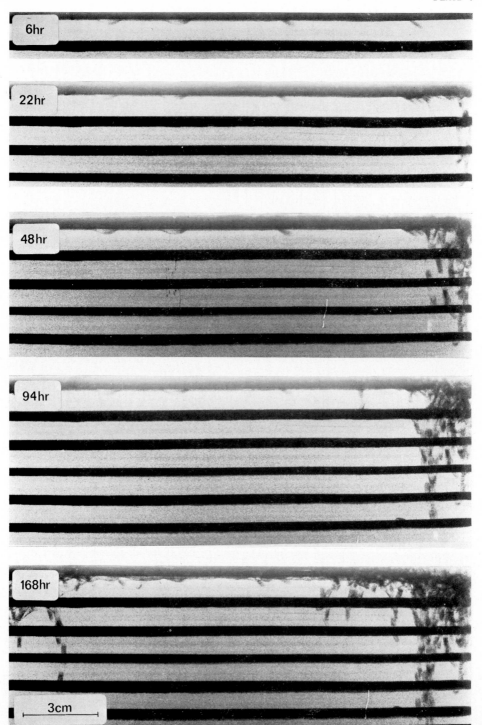

Plate 4

X-ray radiography study of *Lepidactylus dytiscus*.

PLATE 5

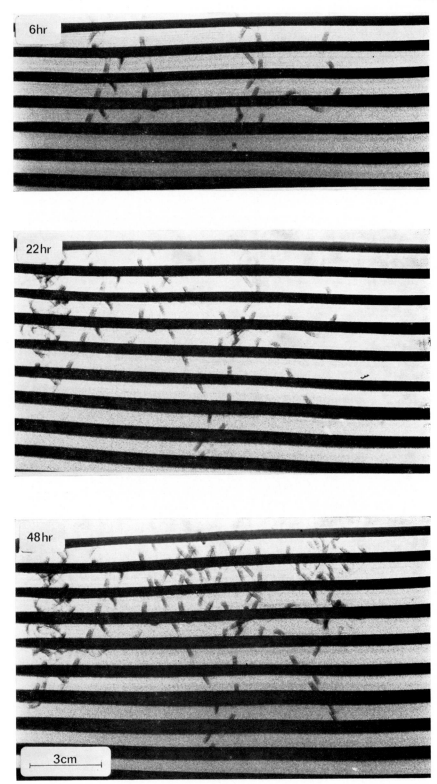

Plate 5

X-ray radiography study of *Acanthohaustorius* sp.

PLATE 6

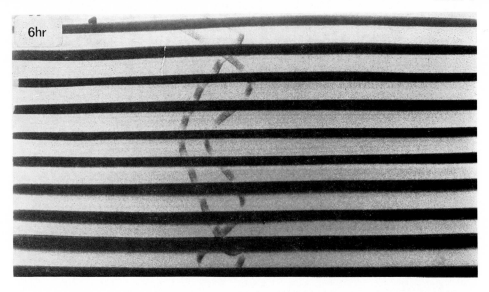

Plate 6

X-ray radiography study of *Parahaustorius longerimus*.

PLATE 7

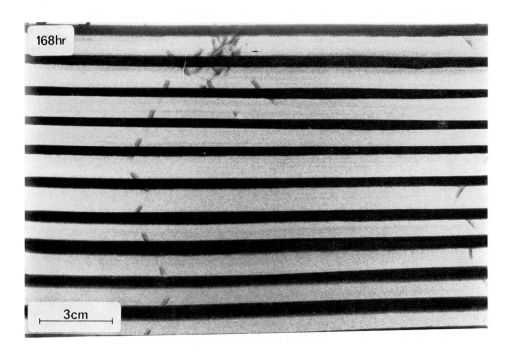

Plate 7

X-ray radiography study of *Pseudohaustorius caroliniensis*.

4. Summary of burrowing characteristics from aquaria studies

The writers have attempted to summarize some of the quantifiable data obtained from X-ray radiographs. These data are presented in Table 1 and are considered very general in their application. Much more study including replicate experiments would be necessary before this could be considered as applicable to haustoriid amphipods in general.

Rate. This is a measure of average movement through time. It is not the actual burrowing speed because the organism intermittently burrows and stops. Other experiments indicate that *Pa. longimerus* sp. can burrow at a maximum rate of 2·3 cm/min, while *Haustorius* sp. can burrow at 1·67 cm/min and *Acanthohaustorius* sp. at 0·47 cm/min.

Burrow width. This is measured from the radiographic prints and is a function of the size of the organism. The animal burrows through the sediment without building a permanent tunnel or tube and the width of the structure is approximately the same as the body width.

Bioturbation. The ability of amphipods to disturb the sediment is a function of the burrowing rate and the size of the burrow. The amount of burrowing that occurs over a long time interval appears to be at least in part related to the presence or absence of food. Plate 8 is a radiograph of an aquarium, one side of which contained sterile sand and the other side contained layers of sand mixed with (i) faecal material (ii) *Spartina* (marsh grass) detritus and (iii) mud. In the sterile sand the amphipods moved randomly through the sediment apparently in search of food. On the other side of the aquarium the organisms thoroughly reworked the portion mixed with *Spartina* detritus. Thus, it is difficult to arrive at a specific figure for the amount of bioturbation per unit time as this will vary with the nature of the substrate. Figures shown in Table 1 are average rates of bioturbation computed by squaring the width of the burrow measured on the radiographs, and then multiplying this figure by the average burrowing rate.

Concentration. This is an indication of the area of the aquarium in which most of the burrowing occurred and is based on experiments with two amphipods per aquarium. This is considered to be in uncrowded conditions. An increase in the number of amphipods or extended time causes the animals to burrow progressively deeper. It is assumed that this is in direct response to the availability of food and space available to the burrower. The effect of extended time can be seen in Plates 1 and 3, and other studies have shown the effect of increasing the number of amphipods.

Burrow pattern. This refers to burrow geometry in three dimensions and is determined by examining stereo X-ray radiographs (Pl. 9). Obviously this is significantly controlled by the artificiality imposed by using a laboratory aquarium which prohibits unlimited three-dimensional movement by the organism.

5. Phototaxic response and burrowing

Croker (1967a p. 188) tested various species of amphipods for phototaxic responses in fingerbowls that lacked detrital substrates, and found that while *Haustorius* sp., *N. schmitzi*, and *L. dytiscus* were phototaxically negative, a neutral response was given by *Pa. longimerus*, *Acanthohaustorius* sp. and *Pr. deichmannae*. These experiments were repeated and confirmed in the present work. However, results of burrowing patterns produced by these six species plus *Ps. caroliniensis*,

Table 1

	Acanthohaustorius sp.	Haustorius sp.	Parahaustorius longimerus	Protohaustorius deichmannae	Neohaustorius schmitzi	Lepidactylus dytiscus	Pseudohaustorius caroliniensis
Rate (cm/hr)	2·8	*	4·6	2·3	0·7	0·8	2·6
Burrow width (mm)	1	3	2	2	1	1	1
Bioturbation (cc/hr)	·07		·25	·23	·01	·01	·06
Concentration (cm)	above 10	above 1·5	above 3	above 6	above 2·5	above 3	above 5 (?)
Orientation	oblique, usually greater than 60° off sand surface	horizontal	more or less 45° off sand surface	variable	mostly vertical	vertical	oblique, usually greater than 45° off sand surface
Burrow type	usually straight, with some zig-zag; frequent cut-backs of almost 180°	somewhat like a sine curve	somewhat swirling	shallow arcuate pattern with occasional deeper penetration characterized by spiralling	down, 180° turn, then up again almost on same path; appears to break sand surface often	like Neo., except turn often greater than 180°, so that crosses over own path	vertically oriented burrow pattern with widely spaced spirals

* Average rate of burrowing for Haustorius could not be determined from available X-ray radiographs.

PLATE 8

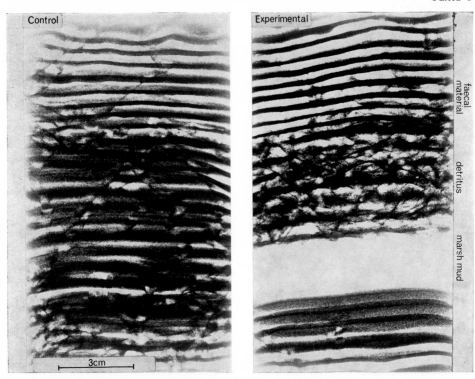

Control

Experimental

faecal material

detritus

marsh mud

3cm

Plate 8

X-ray radiography study of selective feeding by amphipods. Left side of aquarium contained sterile sand. Right side of aquarium contained sand mixed with faecal material from the beach, *Spartina* (marsh grass) detritus and marsh mud.

in both lighted and darkened aquaria indicate that this response by itself is not necessarily responsible for the preferred burrowing depth in substrates in all species. *Acanthohaustorius* sp. and *Ps. caroliniensis* tend to concentrate down to a depth at which the amount of light is too small to be a determinative factor. Thus the neutral phototaxic response displayed by *Acanthohaustorius* sp. is understandable. *Haustorius* sp. is phototaxically negative, yet our work showed that the majority of this species' burrowing occurred at a shallower depth than any of the other species studied. Thus one would conclude that in this case, the phototaxic response does not appear to play a part in determining the depth of burrowing, and this was indicated by the fact that *Haustorius* sp. did not burrow any deeper in a lighted aquarium relative to a darkened one. It is suggested instead that, with this species, the negative response must necessarily keep the amphipod from venturing out into the sand surface because of its shallow depth preference. The other four species had intermediate depth preferences, and so it is expected that light might be a determinative factor in these cases. Of the four, two were phototaxically neutral (*Pa. longimerus* and *P. deichmannae*) and two were negative (*N. schmitzi* and *L. dytiscus*), yet all four showed an effect of light on depth; *N. schmitzi* burrowed shallower in the light, while *L. dytiscus* burrowed deeper.

PLATE 9

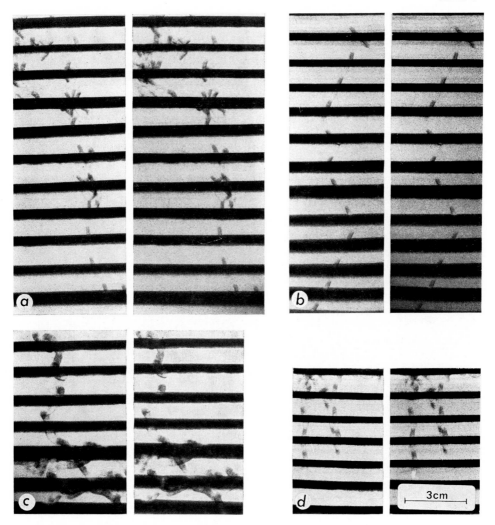

Plate 9

Stereo X-ray radiograph prints of burrow patterns to show the spatial geometry of various burrows. a *Acanthohaustorius* sp.; b *Pseudohaustorius caroliniensis;* c *Haustorius* sp.: d *Protohaustorius deichmannae.*

Here again, the phototaxic response itself is shown not to determine the preferred depth, although light is a determinative factor in these four species.

6. Relationships of density, species abundance and burrowing characteristics

Of the more than 8,000 individual amphipods examined and identified on Sapelo Island by Croker (1967a), *N. schmitzi* and *L. dytiscus* constituted 78·1 per cent of the total and *L. dytiscus* alone represented almost 50 per cent. *Haustorius* sp., *Pa. longimerus* and *Acanthohaustorius* sp. which were present in about equal abundance represented 21·6 per cent of the haustoriid fauna. *Pr. deichmannae* and *Ps. caroliniensis* made up less than 1 per cent of the total individuals examined by Croker.

One of the most important findings of this study is that the two most abundant species, *N. schmitzi* and *L. dytiscus* have almost identical burrowing patterns, and if these two species were placed in the same aquarium it would probably be impossible to differentiate one from the other based on the bioturbate textures which they produce. This similarity in burrowing probably accounts for the obvious reduction of one species or the other in situations where their habitats overlap as in the open beach and the protected beach (Fig. 2), in order to prevent interspecific competition either for the available food resources, or for space.

N. schmitzi and *Haustorius* sp., always co-dominated the upper tidal levels in the open beach and protected beach sands and during some seasons dominated the upper tidal levels in the tidal-creek sand flat. Both species show markedly different burrowing patterns as well as possessing different sizes and vertical zonations. Collectively these features must bear on the species ability to co-exist in the same parts of the beaches, i.e., their burrowing features have evolved complementarily, acting to reduce competition for space or food resources.

Pa. longimerus and *Acanthohaustorius* sp., which share the low tide area of the open beach and at times are found together in tidal-creek sand flat areas, also show considerably different sediment reworking patterns as well as differences in body size and choice of burrowing depth.

7. Discussion

Results of this study illustrate the principles which allow sympatric species to co-exist without violating Gause's Law, or the Competitive Exclusion Principle (Hardin 1959; 1960). MacArthur (1965) discusses it from the viewpoint of the "limiting similarity of co-existing species", offering a theory as to why this limit must exist for resource-limited species. He claims that this limiting similarity can be increased in a number of ways, one of which is by increasing the species specialization. It would seem to the writers, furthermore, that once this specialization has occurred, the problem of competition has, at least in part, been solved and the originally limiting resource need no longer be limiting.

Croker (1967a) has shown that the Sapelo Island species with which he worked fed with grossly similar behaviour. Furthermore, by examining gut contents of amphipods found on Cape Cod, Massachusetts, Sameoto (1969a, b) has shown that *Protohaustorius deichmannae, Acanthohaustorius millsi, Parahaustorius longimerus, Neohaustorius biarticulatus* and *Haustorius canadensis* feed on the same types of food.

Figures 2 and 3 clearly show that the spatial ranges of the Sapelo Island haustoriid amphipods do overlap. Thus, physical space and food are two of the main resources which are potentially limiting to these amphipods, and represent resources for which specialization exists, allowing a sympatric relationship to be maintained. This is not to say that actual competition must have been present between these particular sympatric species in order for the evolution of the specializations to have occurred. This could have happened separately in the species involved, and at the time could have been neutrally selected for. Positive selection for these specializations had to occur, however, when the sympatric relationship was set up, since co-existence demands such "niche diversification", as Hutchinson (1957) calls it. Note, however, that Hutchinson considers this "niche diversification" to be deliberate, whereas we consider it here, to be the result of natural evolutionary processes.

In some cases, as Croker (1967a) and Sameoto (1969a, b) have indicated, the separation is spatial (i.e., horizontal and vertical zonation) as in the case of *Haustorius* sp., *Pa. longimerus* and *Ps. caroliniensis* at Sapelo Island. But for pairs such as *Haustorius* sp. and *N. schmitzi* or *Pa. longimerus* and *Acanthohaustorius* sp. at Sapelo Island, there is definite horizontal overlap and, as the present work indicates, vertical overlap. Competition is reduced partly by size differences which may allow utilization of different food sizes (Sameoto 1969a, b; Croker 1967a) or food types (Croker 1967b). The use of X-ray radiography has enabled us to observe another way in which these sympatric pairs may avoid competition. This is a specialization in burrowing pattern, which may well play the most important role in maintaining the sympatric relationship. In these patterns, vertical separation is admittedly a part, but the burrowing velocity, type and orientation would appear to play at least as important a part. Examination of Plates 2 and 3, and of Table 1, show how the burrowing of *Haustorius* sp. complements rather than interferes with that of *N. schmitzi* in almost all the parameters investigated; the same can be seen with *Acanthohaustorius* sp. and *Pa. longimerus* in Plates 5 and 6. This allows more than one of the available niches in the area to be utilized, and thus represents the most important specialization as regards the minimization of competition. That this is true is supported by examination of *N. schmitzi* (Pl. 2) and *L. dytiscus* (Pl. 4). These two species show almost identical burrow patterns, as mentioned earlier. The fact that these species are not found to any great extent in the same area of the beach would appear to indicate that the failure of evolutionary differentiation of burrow patterns prevents a truly sympatric relationship to occur. Thus here, in contrast to the *N. schmitzi-Haustorius* sp. relationship, *L. dytiscus* and *N. schmitzi* have specialized in a different direction (i.e., horizontal zonation). This specialization again allows for co-existence on the same beach.

In summary then, evolution of specialized burrow patterns has, in the case of the two truly sympatric pairs mentioned above, served to allow for the sympatric relationship to be maintained. It has served to fill more than one niche within the same geographical area and thus minimizes the competition which might otherwise cause extinction of one of the species.

Acknowledgements. The writers wish to thank Dr. R. A. Croker of the University of New Hampshire for the use of several of his illustrations and for his critical remarks of the manuscript. Dr. E. L. Bousfield (National Museums of Canada) is thanked for his confirmation of amphipod species identification. The manuscript comments by Dr. R. Frey and Mr. K. L. Smith are also appreciated. Support for this study, which is University of Georgia Marine Institute Contribution 193, was provided by N.S.F. Grant GA-719.

References

CROKER, R. A. 1967a. Niche diversity in five species of intertidal amphipods (Crustacea: Haustoriidae). *Ecol. Monogr.* **37**, 173.

—— 1967b. Niche specifity of *Neohaustorius schmitzi* and *Haustorius sp.* (Crustacea: Amphipoda) in North Carolina. *Ecology* **48**, 971.

HARDIN, G. 1959. *Nature and man's fate.* Reinhart, N.Y.

—— 1960. The competitive exclusion principle. *Science, N.Y.* **131**, 1292.

HOWARD, J. D. 1968. X-ray radiography for examination of burrowing in sediments by marine invertebrate organisms. *Sedimentology* **11**, 249.

HUTCHINSON, G. E. 1957. Concluding remarks. *Cold Spring Harb. Symp. quant. Biol.* **22**, 415.

MACARTHUR, R. H. 1965. Patterns of species diversity. *Biol. Rev.* **40**, 511.

SAMEOTO, D. D. 1969a. Comparative ecology, life histories, and behaviour of intertidal sand-burrowing amphipods (Crustacea: Haustoriidae) at Cape Cod. *J. Fish. Res. Bd. Can.* **26**, 361.

—— 1969b. Some aspects of the ecology and life cycle of three species of subtidal sand-burrowing amphipods (Crustacea: Haustoriidae). *J. Fish. Res. Bd. Can.* **26**, 1321.

J. D. Howard, Marine Institute, University of Georgia, Sapelo Island, Georgia, 31327, U.S.A.

C. A. Elders, Department of Zoology, The University of Georgia, Athens, Georgia, U.S.A.

Trace fossils in the Chalk environment

W. J. Kennedy

Bioturbation is one of the most striking features of the English Chalk (Cenomanian-Maastrichtian). The following ichnogenera are recognisable: *Thalassinoides, Gyrolithes, Spongeliomorpha, Pseudobilobites* and *Zoophycos*. Faecal pellets are widespread, as are borings such as *Abeliella, Calcideletrix, Dendrina, Entobia* and *Nygmites*. The burrows form an assemblage broadly similar to that found in the marine Lower Cretaceous of England, and there are few changes seen across the transition from clays and sands into coccolith limestones. There are marked differences from Jurassic marine trace fossil assemblages of Southern England, possibly as a result of a general increase in water depth in this area from Jurassic to Cretaceous.

1. Introduction

The Cretaceous period is one of marine transgression in many parts of the world; the most important part of the transgression occurred in Mid- to Upper Cretaceous times. By the Cenomanian, retreat of shorelines and waning of supply of coarse clastic sediments resulted in the beginning of Chalk deposition in England. This continued for more than thirty million years—until terminated by the Maastrichtian regression.

In England, the Chalk is more than a thousand feet thick, and it is only in the Dorset and Devon Cenomanian that more marginal, non-Chalk facies appear.

Westwards, in Ireland, Chalk (the White Limestone) does not appear until the Campanian (*Marsupites testudinarius* Zone), resting unconformably on Hibernian Greensands (Cenomanian to Coniacian) (Hancock 1961). A similar sequence, of silicified Senonian Chalk resting on Cenomanian sands, is seen in Scotland (Lee and Bailey 1925).

Chalk sedimentation originally spread far to the west, in the approaches to the English Channel (Smith *et al.* 1965). In Europe, Upper Cretaceous chalks can be traced into Denmark, Holland, Belgium, Northern France, North Germany, Poland, European Russia, and south to the Caucasus (Wills 1951 pl. 18a). Upper Cretaceous chalks occur in the United States (Niobrara, Kansas) and Australia (Gingin). Black (1964) records Cretaceous and Tertiary chalks from the Galicia Bank, off the west coast of Spain.

For the present, however, attention will be confined to the English Chalk. Sediment, water-depth, and conditions of depositions are briefly discussed, and the main trace fossil occurrences reviewed.

2. The sediment

Chalk is essentially a coccolith limestone, contaminated by terriginous material and coarser organic debris. The composition was first noted by Ehrenberg in 1836, although he regarded coccoliths—'morpholiths' or 'crystalloids'—as inorganic. More recently, Black (1953; 1965), Black and Barnes (1959), Hancock (1963) and Hancock and Kennedy (1967) have given additional data, especially on the fine-structure of chalks.

The fine carbonate fraction is thus whole and fragmentary coccoliths. The coarser fractions consist of *Oligostegina,* foraminifera, and fragments of *Inoceramus,* echinoids, sponges and other organisms. The fine non-calcareous fraction consists of clay, recently discussed by Weir and Catt (1965), Jeans (1968), and others. Coarser material includes detrital silt and sand grade quartz, accompanied by authigenic minerals such as glauconite.

In general, insoluble residue is at a maximum in the Cenomanian (up to 40% in the Chalk Marl), falling to only a few per cent or less by the Turonian. A notable exception is the Blackband member of the *plenus* Zone in Yorkshire, a montmorillonite rock which is possibly a bentonite (Hallam and Sellwood 1969).

The coarse organic fraction is more variable in its distribution, and there are many horizons of winnowed shelly chalks.

Much of the Chalk has suffered little diagenetic change. Fine structure studies show that many soft chalks are even uncemented (Hancock and Kennedy 1967). Notable exceptions are: the hard northern chalks, the Irish White Limestone (Wolfe 1968), hardgrounds and nodular chalks.

3. Depth of deposition

The abundance of coccoliths in the Chalk suggests that the sea floor was below the maximum depth of coccolith abundance. Black (1965) indicates that this depth is about 50 m in present day Tropics, whilst off the British Isles it is shallower—from 10 to 20 m.

The most recent review of sponge distribution suggests that Chalk hexactinellid faunas need not necessarily indicate depths greater than 200 to 300 m (Reid 1968).

At the other end of the depth range, abundance of trochid gastropods in the Chalk Marl and Chalk Rock may suggest a depth of 50 m or less. Chalk Basement Beds in southwest England rest on erosion surfaces which in places bear what may be stromatolitic structures, and encrusting algae occur at the base of the transgressive Maastrichtian Chalk in Northern Ireland (Reid 1968).

Detailed studies on depth variation on the basis of foraminiferal spectra are given by Burnaby (1962) for the Cenomanian of Barrington (Cambridgeshire). Barr (1962) has suggested a shallowing to 30–50 m during *mucronata* Zone times in the Isle of Wight, using benthonic/planktonic ratios.

4. Bottom conditions

4a. Soft chalks

Bioturbation is intense throughout the whole of the Chalk (Pl. 1–2), and has destroyed most sedimentary structures. However, levels of coarse, winnowed chalk, drifted shell beds, scour hollows, development of encrusting epifaunas over burrowing echinoids, overturned sponges etc. all suggest periodic current activity.

Occurrence of large (up to 40 cm) epifaunal bivalves such as *Inoceramus*, large sponges, corals, serpulids and heavily armoured arthropods suggest that the sea-floor, although muddy, was firm.

4b. Hardgrounds

At many levels throughout the Chalk there are indications of hard, lithified, current-swept sea floors: hardgrounds.

Although studied in detail by continental workers (e.g. Ellenberger 1946; 1947; Voigt 1959a), it is only recently that chalk hardgrounds have received detailed study in Britain (Reid 1962; Bromley 1967; Kennedy 1967). The classic chalk hardground is a level of lithification and erosion formed soon after deposition. The hardground surface may have been phosphatised and glauconitised, bored by bivalves, cirripeds, sponges and other organisms, and penetrated by arthropod and perhaps other burrows, excavated in the sediment during early stages of hardground formation.

Nodular chalks represent the product of contemporaneous burrowing and cementation, as discussed by Bromley (1967). The upper parts of nodular horizons are often sharp, and there are transitions from nodular chalks (indicating burrowing, cementation, and perhaps slowing of sedimentation) to an undoubted hardground and rocky sea floor.

At many levels in the Middle and Upper Chalk, alternations of nodular chalks and/or hardgrounds with soft chalk (Pl. 2a) occur as distinct rhythms, indicating cyclical variations in sea floor conditions. Appearances of what may be intra-formational conglomerates at such levels suggests that nodules were sometimes washed out of their softer matrix.

5. Burrows

The chief previous accounts of burrows in English chalks are by Bather (1911), Bromley (1967) and Kennedy (1967).

In considering burrows, it must be stressed that the whole of the Chalk has been completely churned over many times (Pl. 1 and 2). Burrow fills are re-worked (Pl. 1c), and three, four, and perhaps more generations of disturbance are recognisable.

The various burrows preserved undoubtedly represent differing levels of penetration below the sediment/water interface; *Thalassinoides* is a deep burrow, *Chondrites* a shallow form. Thus, during sedimentation, it seems likely that the upper parts of most burrow systems were destroyed, and many systems found in soft chalks may represent only the basal networks of what were formerly more extensive systems (see also discussions in Bromley 1967 p. 181).

Ichnogenus THALASSINOIDES Ehrenberg 1944

Plate 1c, 2

Ehrenberg introduced this ichnogenus in 1944 for ramifying cylindrical burrows in Miocene sands which showed Y-shaped branching points, with swellings at the point of branching and elsewhere. Associations with callianassid remains noted by Ehrenberg (1938; 1944) and others leaves no doubt as to the organisms responsible. Other evidence of producers comes from the fossil association with arthropod faecal pellets and scratch marks on walls, whilst comparable structures have been described from Recent sediments.

s

In the Chalk, *Thalassinoides* is ubiquitous, but occurrences in soft chalks and hardgrounds are markedly different.

In soft chalks (especially the Cenomanian) several distinct types of *Thalassinoides* occur. The most striking is *T. saxonicus* Geinitz (Genitiz 1842; Kennedy 1967 p. 134), a giant form with horizontal burrows up to 20 cm in diameter, apparently connected to the surface by short shafts. No recent burrows of this size have been described.

Peculiar features of *T. saxonicus* are the mammillate ornament, and ridges, present on moulds. The mounds seem to be pellets pressed into the wall; the ridges are appendage marks. The presence of a pelletal lining recalls *Ophiomorpha* (Häntzschel 1952; 1962; Kennedy and Macdougall 1969), and Vialov (1966) has referred *T. saxonicus* to that ichnogenus.

Other, smaller, *Thalassinoides* lack such ornament, and again, are largely horizontal networks. Some (*T. ornatus* Kennedy) bearing a complex reticulum of scratch-marks, comparable to those seen on Recent crab burrows (Weigelt 1929; Shinn 1968), *Rhizocorallium* (Weigelt 1929; Shinn 1968) and *Ophiomorpha* (Kennedy and Macdougall 1969).

In hardgrounds two main types of system occur; *Thalassinoides paradoxica* (Woodward), prominent in the Cenomanian and Turonian, and larger, unnamed forms, occurring in higher hardgrounds (Bromley 1967; Kennedy 1967).

Hardground *Thalassinoides* differ markedly from soft chalk forms, especially in their irregular, 3-dimensional branching form (Pl. 2a). Tunnel dimensions are variable; a side-branch may be only 25% of the diameter of the parent passage. Many branches terminate in culs-de-sac. Distance between branching points is highly variable, and individual branches are often tortuous, whilst systems exist at several levels.

The peculiar features of systems in hardened chalks arises in part at least from their relations to the hardground or nodular chalk they are associated with. The burrowing animals were unable to penetrate hard objects, because echinoids and *Inoceramus* fragments are avoided, and left protruding into burrows. When multiple hardgrounds are developed, burrows arising from a higher hardground follow the surface of the subjacent one as a complex horizontal net—this is Bromley's (1967) imposed horizontality.

As a result of their inability to deal with hardened sediments, the animals were restricted in their living space as the hardground developed. At first restricted to the soft chalk between nodules, the burrows become increasingly confined as the nodules grow. Finally, no freedom of movement was available in a fully developed hardground, and to penetrate multiple hardgrounds, higher systems followed the soft fills of entombed burrows in the lower surface.

Plate 1

a Bed junction preservation of burrows, *Acanthoceras rhotomagense* Zone, Lower Chalk; Folkestone, Kent.

b Laminated structure, *Acanthoceras rhotomagense* Zone, Lower Chalk; Dover, Kent.

c *Thalassinoides* and other burrows at a marl/limestone junction, *Acanthoceras rhotomagense* Zone, Lower Chalk; Eastbourne, Sussex.

d Abundant *Chondrites* in *Calycoceras naviculare* Zone, Lower Chalk; Dover, Kent. ×1.

All photographs are of vertical sections.

PLATE 1

PLATE 2

These observations explain the irregularity of hardground *Thalassinoides* compared with those in soft chalks, but not the rarity of vertical elements in the latter. When, however, hardground burrows penetrated into soft chalk below the lower limit of nodules, 'normal' horizontal *Thalassinoides* developed (Bromley 1967 fig. 2). Soft chalk systems may represent basal networks, the upper, vertical portions having been destroyed by shallower burrowers churning higher layers of the sea-floor as sedimentation proceeded.

Irregular hardground burrows compare well with structures described by Shinn (1969) in Recent lime sediments of the Bahamas. Thus *Spongia paradoxica* (Kennedy 1967 pl. 8 fig. 5, pl. 9 fig. 2) closely resembles *Alpheus* burrows (Shinn 1968 pl. 109), whilst 'rooms' produced by *Callianassa* in the Recent environment are identical with the flat chambers present in *S. paradoxica*.

Shinn's observations that callianassid burrows can remain open and unfilled below up to 2·5 m of overburden for periods of 1,500–2,000 years suggest that open hardground burrows may have been preserved for long periods after the departure of the inhabitants.

THALASSINOIDES and 'Laminated Structures'

Laminated structures (Pl. 1c) are biogenic structures which appear in section as parallel-sided or semi-circular (convex downward) patches of layers of fine and coarse carbonate debris.

In plan, these may resemble *Thalassinoides saxonicus*, but indications that they lie in burrows of this type are lacking; in 1967 I suggested that they might result from the feeding activities of the *T. saxonicus* producer, without any available comparison in Recent sediments. Shinn (1968) has now provided such a comparison. Thus *Alpheus* (Shinn 1968 p. 882 *et seq.*; fig. 4), as it moves through its burrow, knocks sediment from the roof, producing an irregular surface, whilst sediment falling to the burrow floor is sorted by the water current maintained within the system. This 'internal sediment' is laminated, and has a smooth base, just like the Chalk occurrences.

Laminated floor sediments also occur in hardground and nodular chalk *Thalassinoides* systems, and dips of laminae are sometimes quite steep.

Ichnogenus GYROLITHES de Saporta 1884

Plate 3b, c

This ichnogenus covers spirally coiled cylindrical burrows with the axis of coiling normal to bedding. Burrows may be either dextral or sinistral and are usually several centimetres in diameter, and up to 40 cm high.

Plate 2

a *Thalassinoides* associated with nodular chalk (below) and a poorly developed hardground (above), *Holaster planus* Zone, Upper Chalk; South Foreland, near Dover, Kent.

b 'Banderkreide' with abundant *Zoophycos*, *Holaster planus*/*Micraster cortestudinarium* Zone junction, Upper Chalk; South Foreland, near Dover, Kent. Arrow indicates a hardground, with *Zoophycos* below this level confined to *Thalassinoides* burrow fills.

Both photographs are of vertical sections.

Several spiral structures preserved in flint, all probably of Senonian age belong here. They are undoubtedly burrows, although Dighton-Thomas (1935) dismissed them as concretions. Häntzschel (1934) records *Xenohelix* (= *Gyrolithes*) in association with *Thalassinoides* in the German Turonian, whilst a similar association is seen in the Lower Albian Folkestone Beds of Kent (Kennedy 1967). *Xenohelix* described by Keij (1965) and Killper (1962) are associated with, and have *Ophiomorpha*-like ornament. This suggests a decapod origin for *Gyrolithes*.

Ichnogenus PSEUDOBILOBITES Lessertisseur 1955

Plate 3a

The term "pseudobilobite" was used by Barrois (1882) for small oval masses of microfossils with lower surfaces covered in ridges which he described from the Turonian of the Ardennes. Use as a genus stems from Lessertisseur (1955). These structures range from Cenomanian to Senonian and probably higher, and are products of arthropod burrowing/feeding activities. They probably represent material accumulating at the bottom of burrow systems, although evidence of the burrow itself is lacking. Some Senonian examples reach a large size, and more closely resemble partial burrow fills, perhaps simple dwelling burrows (Pl. 3a).

Ichnogenus CHONDRITES Sternberg 1833

Plate 1d

Chondrites is abundant at many levels throughout the Chalk, giving rise to a characteristic sedimentary mottling (Pl. 1d).

It sometimes infests other burrows. Thus the fillings of *Thalassinoides* are often re-worked, *Chondrites* penetrating to far greater depths in burrow fills than in the surrounding sediment. When infestation is intense, burrow walls are coated by a felted mass of the smaller system. This is comparable to the examples of infested *Gyrolithes* figured by de Saporta (1884). Silicification frequently picks out *Chondrites* in burrow fills.

Sellwood (this volume) has stressed the variation in trace fossil type across small-scale calcareous cycles from the Lias. In the comparable cycles seen in the Lower Chalk, 1–2 mm diameter *Chondrites* are also most obvious at contacts where limestone is piped down into underlying marl.

Only small *Chondrites* have been recognised in the Chalk so far. It is possible that larger (5-10 mm) systems (Pl. 1a) may represent a larger form, but these are too poorly preserved for detailed study.

Plate 3

a *Pseudobilobites* from the Middle Chalk (?) of Dover, Kent (Bowerbank Collection). B.M. (N.H.) 55223. This specimen closely resembles a burrow fill. ×1.

b *Gyrolithes* preserved as a spiral flint, from the Upper Chalk; Dorset. B.M. (N.H.) Z906, ×0·5 approximately.

c *Gyrolithes* preserved as a flint, from the Upper Chalk; Norfolk. B.M. (N.H.) Z370. ×0·5 approximately.

d *Zoophycos* preserved as a flint, from the *Holaster planus/Micraster cortestudinarium* Zone junction; North Foreland, near Dover, Kent. The specimen is shown in side view, to show the helical form. Author's Collection. ×1 approximately.

PLATE 3

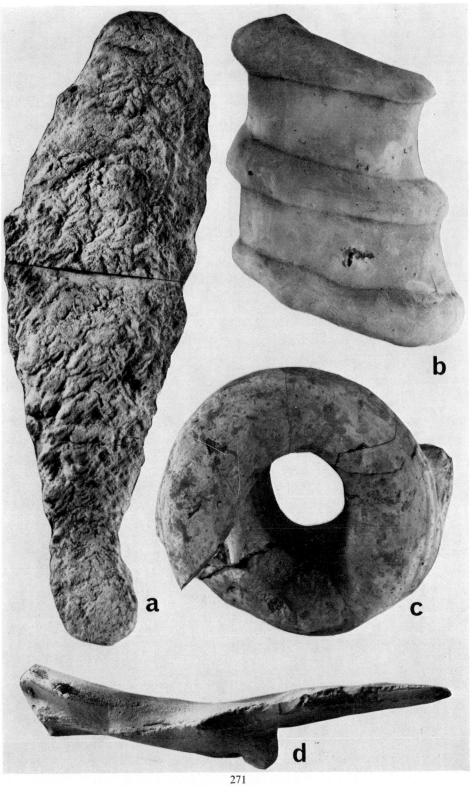

271

Ichnogenus SPONGELIOMORPHA de Saporta 1887

This is a rather unsatisfactory ichnogenus, available for irregularly branching burrow systems covered in reticulate ridges, interpreted as scratch-marks produced by the inhabitants. Some *Thalassinoides* fragments closely resemble the type species, *S. ibericiae,* but until its branching form is better known, the name must remain.

Spongeliomorpha annulatum Kennedy

This burrow system characterises glauconitic facies of the Chalk, and occurs in the Glauconitic Marl (Lower Cenomanian) abundantly. Its range can now be extended to Middle and Upper Cenomanian Chalk Basement Beds, and the Cenomanian and Senonian Hibernian Greensands. These burrows range down into Middle and Upper Albian greensands in southern England, and occur widely in Cretaceous greensands elsewhere.

"TEREBELLA"

Tubular structures, usually constructed of fish scales, but sometimes built of plant or echinoderm debris are widespread in the Chalk, ranging from Cenomanian to Campanian, and perhaps higher. They are flattened cylinders, usually 2–3 cm across, and up to 60 cm long. In some cases, a short side branch is present.

The history of study of these structures is complex. Mantell (1822 p. 232) considered them to be remains of an eel-like fish, *Muraena lewesiensis* Mantell, although subsequently referring them to *Dercetis elongatus* Agassiz (Mantell 1844) and producing a restoration of the animal (Mantell 1838 p. 309 fig. 39)! Davies (1897) and Bather (1911) suggested they might be dwellings of the polychaete *Terebella.*

These are lined dwelling burrows, the flimsy construction suggesting that there was no surface extension, unless lined by strong mud and mucilage coating. Reference to terebellids is purely speculative; there seems to be no reason why some other group of worms (or even arthropods) might not line their burrows in this way.

"Terebella" cancellata Bather

This is simply a convenient repository for burrows ornamented by fine longitudinal ridges and folds (Kennedy 1967). These range throughout the Chalk; 'worm' burrows seems the best interpretation. They probably account for much of the bioturbation present in the Chalk.

Ichnogenus ZOOPHYCOS Massalongo 1855

Plate 2b, 3d

Chalks characterised by the trace fossil *Zoophycos* are widely known in northern Europe: the Banderkreide of Voigt (1929), Voigt and Häntzschel (1956) and others. In Britain this facies is limited to beds only a few metres thick; the earliest occurrence noted is close to the Turonian/Coniacian boundary, the highest is in the Maastrichtian.

In the field (Pl. 2b), Banderkreide is characterised by grey bands, usually 1–3 cm thick, and up to 40 cm long. These run essentially parallel to bedding, although sometimes curved, undulating or quite strongly twisted (Pl. 2b) they are often branched. When cleaned of matrix, the bands are seen to be sections of sheet-like structures with irregular, sometimes sinuous margins; branched bands are sections of helical sheets, whilst many curved bands correspond to shallow cone-like sheets.

Detailed structure is not well-preserved, but in some cases fine parallel concentric ridges cover wide areas of these structures and are often visible on flint-preserved systems. These features, and comparisons with the excellent flint material figured by Voigt and Häntzschel (1956 pl. 6) leaves no doubt that these are helical, laminar and perhaps ribbon-like forms of *Zoophycos*.

Zoophycos is usually developed in soft chalks (i.e. in the *Porosphaera* Beds of the north Norfolk coast (Peake and Hancock 1961 fig. 7)). At Dover, close to the Turonian/Coniacian boundary, the burrows occur throughout a thickness of approximately 2 m, including part of a hardground and a nodular chalk (Pl. 2b). Close inspection shows *Zoophycos* extending through the nodular chalk, but only in the soft material between nodules. In the hardground, *Zoophycos* occurs in the basal 20 cm of nodular chalk, but not, it appears, throughout.

Häntzschel (1960; 1962), Seilacher (1967a, b) and others have interpreted *Zoophycos* as feeding traces. Plička (1968) has claimed that they are probably abandoned prostomial organs of sabellid worms, and this seems true of such forms as *Zoophycos caput-medusae* (Massalongo). Forms such as *Zoophycos briantius* (Villa) and less regular forms, as figured by Seilacher (1967a, b) and Taylor (1967) appear to be burrows as do all the Chalk forms. The producers remain unknown.

Other burrows. Recognisable burrow forms are exceptional. Most of the biogenic disturbance in the Chalk is so intense as to produce only a mass of interpenetrant burrows, usually with few distinctive features. One constantly recurring structure is the development of meniscus-filled burrows. Some of these are fragments of *Thalassinoides,* resembling recent structures figured by Shinn (1968 fig. 161). Others fill burrows completely and may also be due to arthropods; such fills occur in parts of *Ophiomorpha* systems (see Kennedy and Macdougall 1969). Similar structures may be produced by echiuroid worms and echinoids (Reineck *et al.* 1967), but no definite echinoid burrows have been recognised in the Chalk to date (Goldring, in discussion of Bromley 1967).

6. Borings

Borings are a neglected group of trace fossils in the Chalk. The principal descriptions are based on borings in belemnite guards, as given by Mägdefrau (1937) and Pugaczewska (1965).

Ichnogenus ABELIELLA Mägdefrau 1937

This (Mägdefrau 1937 p. 66, pl. 5, figs. 1-2) covers minute borings (the whole system being less than a millimetre across) consisting of dichotomously branching galleries 4–9 microns in diameter. These structures are best known from fish scales, and have been described from the Cretaceous, Jurassic and Oliogocene (Mägdefrau 1937). *Abeliella* is widespread in the Chalk, typically infesting fish-scales; the producers remain obscure, but they were probably algae or fungi.

Ichnogenus CALCIDELETRIX Mägdefrau 1937

This, like the last, probably represents the activities of penetrative thallophytes, and again, probably algae. The boring consists of irregularly branching, sometimes almost dendritic networks of tunnels from 0·02 to 0·1 mm in diameter. Mägdefrau recognised two species, *C. flexuosa* (1937 p. 57, pl. 4, fig. 4), a coarse form with tunnels 0·04 to 0·09 mm in diameter, and *C. breviramosa* (1937 p. 58, pl. 4, fig. 9) with tunnels 0·02 to 0·04 mm in diameter. These structures occur throughout the English Chalk, and are especially conspicuous infesting Senonian and Maastrichtian belemnite guards. *Calcideletrix* probably covers many of the fine borings which are so conspicuous in shells from the Basement Beds of the Chalk and the Chalk Rock (Pl. 4 c, d).

Ichnogenus CHAETOPHORITES Pratje 1922

This covers a distinctive group of straight branching tunnels best known in belemnite rostra. These have been recorded from the Jurassic to Pliocene, and were presumably produced by thallophytes. The borings are only a few tens of microns in diameter, and are common in the Chalk, especially in belemnite guards.

Ichnogenus DENDRINA Quenstedt 1849

Quenstedt introduced this name for the beautiful rosette-like borings which are so common in Upper Cretaceous belemnites. Morris (1851 p. 87, pl. 4 fig. 6 and 7) figured these structures as *Talpina dendrina* on the basis of material from Gravesend and Antrim, whilst Mägdefrau (1937) introduced further specific names, differences being based on size and complexity of branching. These structures are common in British Senonian and Maastrichtian belemnite guards. Interpretation of *Dendrina* is difficult. The most likely comparison at present available is with borings of the zygotic resting stage (*Codiolum*) of the recent alga *Gomontia polyrhiza* (Lagerheim) (Kornmann 1962 p. 195-202; Boekschoten 1966 p. 345). In this genus, however, the algal bore is connected to the surface by a series of apertures, absent in *Dendrina*.

Ichnogenus DICTYOPORUS Mägdefrau 1937

This is a series of net-like borings 0·06–0·08 mm in diameter, forming irregular polygonal networks. These borings are not open to the exterior. They commonly occur on belemnite guards, and are widespread in Britain and are also found in shells and pebbles. The range is from Cenomanian to Maastrichtian. The producer is unknown.

Plate 4

a A phosphatised type (i) faecal pellet from the *Holaster planus* Zone, Upper Chalk (just above the Chalk Rock); Hitch Wood, near Hitchin, Herts. Author's Collection. × 130.

b Type (i) faecal pellets preserved on a part silicified *Micraster* infilling, from the Upper Chalk; Upnor, Kent. B.M. (N.H.) Z672. × 2.

c, d Reticulate algal borings preserved as moulds attached to the internal mould of a pleurotomariid gastropod. From the *Acanthoceras rhotomagense* Zone, Chalk Basement Bed; Snowden Hill, Chard, Somerset. Author's Collection. **c** × 700; **d** × 250.

PLATE 4

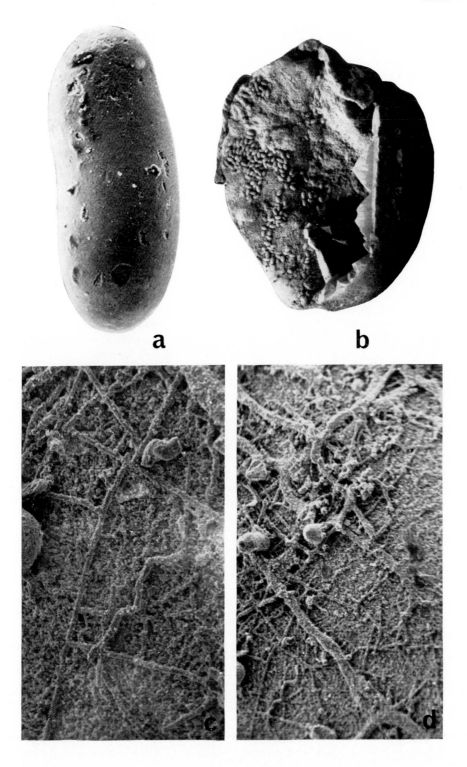

a

b

c

d

Ichnogenus ENTOBIA Bronn 1838

Plate 5b

Bronn (1838 p. 691) introduced this name for problematic fossils consisting of rounded, flattened bodies, a few centimetres across connected by fine, hair-like processes. Mantell (1822) and others had previously described these structures, which have passed into the literature as sponge borings, referred to the Recent genus *Cliona* Gray. There is little doubt that these are indeed sponge bores, but, unfortunately the taxonomy of recent clionids is based on soft-part anatomy and spicules (Hancock 1849; Fischer 1868), the nature and form of the crypts being, in part at least, a reflection of the form of the substrate infested. In addition, many other demosponge genera are known to bore (see Boekschoten 1966 p. 347). It would therefore seem safer to use *Entobia* for fossil crypts.

In addition to the type species *E. cretacea* Portlock and the Silurian *E. antiqua* Portlock, several other fossil names have been introduced, usually as *Cliona* species (Stephenson 1952), and differentiated on the basis of crypt form and dimensions.

In the Chalk *Entobia* is abundant, infesting every available type of hard substrate. The importance of this group of sponges in weakening and breaking up shells and rock fragments must have been considerable (Bromley 1968). *E. cretacea* is widespread; crypts are flattened in thin ammonite shells, but may become globular when a thick *Inoceramus* or a belemnite is attacked. Another widespread form has crypts several centimetres across, and may completely remove the core of a pebble (Bromley 1968 fig. 2). A small form (perhaps meriting a separate ichnogenus) sometimes completely removes all but a thin external layer of shells, so that moulds of the crypt are accurate casts of the species infested.

Entobia ranges throughout the Chalk.

Ichnogenus MYCELITES Roux 1887

This is a general name for what is probably a polygenetic assemblage of irregular borings only a few microns in diameter. It can be applied to many of the small undiagnostic borings which range throughout the Chalk. *Mycelites* is probably a thallophyte bore.

Plate 5

a *Rogerella* borings in a fragment of *Inoceramus* from the *Micraster cortestudinarium* Zone, Upper Chalk; Seaford Head, Sussex. B.M. (N.H.) P7305. ×2.

b *Entobia* crypts in an *Inoceramus* fragment, preserved as a silicified mould in a flint from the Upper Chalk (ex Chalk Drift); Southern England. B.M. (N.H.) P3626. ×1 approximately.

c *Nygmites solitarius* Von Hagenow in an *Echinocorys* test, preserved as a silicified mould in a flint from the Upper Chalk; Bromley, Kent. B.M. (N.H.) 57589. ×1 approximately.

d *Rogerella* borings in an *Inoceramus* fragment, preserved as silicified moulds in a flint from the Upper Chalk; Kent. B.M. (N.H.) P4165. ×2 approximately.

e *Talpina* in a belemnite guard from the *Belemnitella mucronata* Zone, Upper Chalk; Norwich. B.M. (N.H.) 5·8958 ×2·5.

PLATE 5

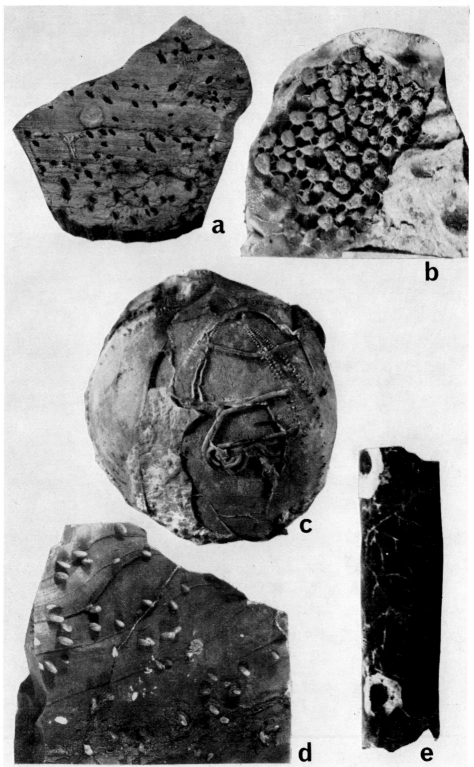

Ichnogenus NYGMITES Mägdefrau 1937

Plate 5c

Simple, cylindrical unbranched borings, open to the exterior. *Nygmites solitarius* Von Hagenow (1840 p. 671; Morris 1851 p. 87, pl. 4, fig. 6a; Quenstedt 1847 p. 470, pl. 30, fig. 37), in a large form (several millimetres in diameter and several centimetres long). It is common in Senonian and Maastrichtian belemnites and occurs at lower horizons. *Nygmites pungens* (Pugaczewska 1965 p. 77) is a smaller form 0·04–0·07 mm in diameter and about 1 mm long, also widespread in the English Chalk. The producers of both these borings is unknown. *Nygmites sacculus* Mägdefrau (1937 p. 57 pl. 5 figs. 3, 4) appears to be a cirriped bore.

Ichnogenus ROGERELLA Sainte-Seine 1951

Plate 5 a, d

The small, purse-shaped borings of acrothoracic cirripeds are well-known from Recent and fossil occurrences (Voigt 1959b) and a number of ichnogenera are recognised. *Rogerella* ranges from the Cenomanian Basement Beds of the Chalk in southwest England, through to the Maastrichtian, and forms an interesting addition to chalk ichnofaunas.

Ichnogenus TALPINA von Hagenow 1840

Plate 5e

Straight branching tunnel systems less than a millimetre in diameter, with many openings to the exterior. By comparison with Recent structures these can be identified as ectoproct bryozoan bores (Lessertisseur 1955). *Talpina* is widespread in Upper Chalk belemnites.

7. Faecal pellets

Recognisable faecal pellets have been recovered mainly in insoluble fractions of chalks, preserved as a result of glauconitisation or phosphatisation. They are rarely recognisable in hand specimens, although rod-like phosphatic pellets— categories (ii) and (iii) below—sometimes occur abundantly in burrows, whilst other forms may be recognisable as a result of freak preservation (Pl. 4b). Faecal pellets (or 'microcoprolites') were described by Hume (1893) and Jukes-Browne & Hill (1903; 1904) from washings and insoluble residues; occurrences in phosphatic horizons are noted by Strahan (1891; 1896) and, more recently, Wilcox (1953a, b). The main types present are briefly noted below; all range throughout the Chalk.

(i) Ovoid pellets, 0·3–0·75 mm long and 0·25–0·3 mm in diameter, tapering at each rounded extremity (Pl. 4a). These occur abundantly in glauconitic residues and also in phosphatic chalks. Surfaces smooth, pitted or wrinkled. Some contain foraminifera, others consist of fine-grained material, apparently altered sediment. These pellets were regarded by Strahan (1891) as fish coprolites, but they are probably of invertebrate origin. Studies on recent sediments (Moore 1939; Edge 1934) show that such pellets are produced by bivalves, gastropods, nudibranchs and worms. The general composition of the pellets suggest detritus feeding (Wilcox 1953a), whilst those enclosing one or more foraminifera may be the result of actual predation on these micro-organisms.

(ii) Cylindrical, rod-like pellets, 0·3–0·5 mm in diameter, and 2 mm long (ends are usually broken). Sections show that these are perforated by longitudinal canals. These are decapod faeces, and the name *Favreina* is available for such objects. The origin, structure and formation of these pellets in Recent animals is described by Moore (1932), fossil occurrences are discussed by Bronniman and Norton (1960), Elliot (1962), and Kennedy *et al.* (1969).

These pellets occur in many residues, and are sometimes common in *Thalassinoides* burrows (Kennedy 1967) although not confined to them (Bromley 1967 p. 172).

(iii) Rod-like pellets up to 0·75 mm in diameter and several millimetres long, without canals. Pellets of this type are produced by worms, arthropods and molluscs (Edge 1934). In the Lower Chalk specimens often occur in concentrated patches; one occurrence in the Midde/Upper Cenomanian of Lower Froyle, Hampshire was concentrated close to a terebellid burrow.

8. Discussion

Trace fossils are one of the most striking features of the English Chalk; bioturbation is intense throughout, and burrowing activity has influenced the development of nodular chalks and hardgrounds. The most obvious structures are arthropod feeding and dwelling burrows, as represented by *Thalassinoides, Gyrolithes, Spongeliomorpha, Pseudobilobites* and laminated structures. Equally widespread is *Chondrites,* also a feeding structure. The bulk of the remaining bioturbation is due to non-diagnostic vermiform burrows probably dwelling/feeding structures. The spreite burrow *Zoophycos,* probably a feeding trace, is abundant at a few restricted levels.

This general assemblage is comparable to that of other, lithologically dissimilar English Cretaceous marine sediments; *Thalassinoides, Chondrites, Spongeliomorpha* and *Zoophycos* occur associated in the Upper Greensand, whilst similar structures (less *Zoophycos*) occur in contemporary Gault Clay facies. *Thalassinoides, Gyrolithes* and *Chondrites* occur together in the Lower Greensand, but other vermiform burrows not seen in the Chalk are present, and *Palaeodictyon* occurs in the Folkestone Beds of East Kent.

The change from Lower Cretaceous sand and clay to Upper Cretaceous chalk sedimentation thus seems to have had little effect on trace fossil assemblages.

When compared with Seilacher's "Ichnofacies" (1955; 1964; 1967b) the general Chalk association suggests the shallow, *Cruziana* facies, the horizons with *Zoophycos* the intermediate, *Zoophycos* facies. This is somewhat surprising, since the former ichnofacies is regarded as littoral to sublittoral, and deposited above wave base (Seilacher 1964 p. 311).

In fact, many diagnostic forms of the *Cruziana* facies are lacking from the Chalk. There are no obvious septate burrows such as *Rhizocorallium* or *Diplocraterion,* and no obvious resting traces. In this respect there is a marked difference from British Jurassic shallow marine assemblages where *Thalassinoides* and *Chondrites* occur in a variety of facies, i.e. Liassic clays, sands, limestones and ironstones, Bathonian and Bajocian, Oxfordian and Portlandian limestones, and in Middle to Upper Jurassic clays and sands; in these sediments they are accompanied by *Rhizocorallium* and *Diplocraterion.* In a more restricted range of sediments they are associated with *Teichichnus, Phycosiphon* and *Asterosoma.*

The reduced assemblages from the Chalk support the sedimentary evidence that deposition took place in somewhat greater depths of water than the typical *Cruziana* facies.

The faecal pellets present in the Chalk belong largely to detritus feeders, as might be expected from the dominance of feeding burrows.

Borings present many problems, for most are of unknown origin. The presence of possible algal bores, taken with the evidence for the occurrence of non-boring algae (given by the common occurrence of trochid gastropods) suggests deposition may have been within the photic zone.

Acknowledgements. I thank Drs. A. Hallam and H. G. Reading for critically reviewing early versions of the manuscript of this paper, and am grateful to them and to Dr. R. G. Bromley, Mr. B. W. Sellwood, Professor W. Häntzschel and many others for useful discussions. Dr. J. M. Hancock has kindly allowed me to examine material in his private collections, whilst Mr. H. G. Owen and Mr. S. Ware have both aided me when working in collections under their care in the British Museum (Natural History).

References

BARR, F. T. 1962. Upper Cretaceous planktonic Foraminifera from the Isle of Wight, England. *Palaeontology* 4, 552.

BARROIS, C. 1882. Recherches sur les terrains anciens des Asturies et de la Galicie. *Mém. Soc. Géol. Nord* 2, 1.

BATHER, F. A. 1911. Upper Cretaceous Terebelloids from England. *Geol. Mag.* 8, 481.

BLACK, M. 1953. The constitution of the Chalk. *Proc. geol. Soc. Lond.* No. 1499, 81.

—— 1964. Cretaceous and Tertiary Coccoliths from Atlantic seamounts. *Palaeontology* 7, 306.

—— 1965. Coccoliths. *Endeavour*, 24, 131.

—— and BARNES, B. 1959. The structure of Coccoliths from the English Chalk. *Geol. Mag.* 96, 321.

BOEKSCHOTEN, G. J. 1966. Shell borings of epibiontic organisms as palaeontologic guides (with examples from the Dutch Coast). *Paleogeogr. Palaeoclimatol., Palaeoecol.* 2, 333.

BROMLEY, R. 1967. Some observations on burrows of thalassinidean crustacea in chalk hardgrounds. *Q. J. geol. Soc. Lond.* 123, 157.

—— 1968. Burrows and borings in hardgrounds. *Meddr dansk. Geol. Foren,* 18, 247.

BRONIMANN, P. and NORTON, P. 1960. On the classification of fossil fecal pellets and description of new forms from Cuba, Gautemala and Libya. *Eclog. geol. Helv.* 53, 832.

BRONN, H. G. 1838. *Lethaea Geognostica.* Schweizerbart, Stuttgart.

BURNABY, T. P. 1962. The palaeoecology of the Foraminifera of the Chalk Marl. *Palaeontology* 4, 599.

DAVIES, W. 1897. On some fish exuviae from the Chalk, generally referred to *Dercetis elongatus* Ag. and on a new species of fossil annelide, *Terebella lewesiensis. Geol. Mag.* 6, 145.

DIGHTON-THOMAS, H. D. 1935. On *Dinocochlea ingens* B. B. Woodward and other spiral concretions. *Proc. Geol. Ass.* 46, 1.

EDGE, E. R. 1934. Faecal pellets of some marine invertebrates. *Am. Midl. Nat.* 26, 78.

EHRENBERG, K. 1938. Bauten von decapoden (*Callianassa* sp.) aus dem Mioäzn (Burdigal) bei Eggenburg im Gau Nieder-Donau (Neiderosterreich). *Paläontz.* 20, 354.

—— 1944. Ergänzende Bemerkungen zu den seinerzeit aus dem Miozän von Burgschleinitz beschriebenen Gangkern und Bauten dekapoder Krebse. *Paläont. Z.* 23, 354.

ELLENBERGER, F. 1946. Observations nouvelles sur la craie jaune à tubulures de Meudon. *C. r. Somm. Séanc. Soc. géol. Fr.* No. 1946, 202.

—— 1947. Le problème lithologique de la craie de Meudon. *Bull. Soc. géol. Fr.* (5) 17, 255.

ELLIOT, G. F. 1962. More micro-problematica from the Middle East. *Micropaleontology* 8, 29.

FISCHER, P. 1868. Recherches sur les éponges perforantes fossiles. *Nouv. Archs Mus. Hist. nat. Paris* 4, 117.

GEINITZ, H. B. 1839–42. *Charakteristik der Schicten und Petrefacten des sächsich-böhmischen Kreidegebirges.* Dresden and Leipzig.

HAGENOW, F. VON, 1840. Monographie der Rügenschen Kreide Versteinerungen II. Abth. Radiarien u. Annulaten. *Neues Jb. Mineral, Geogn. Geol. Petrefaktenkd.* p. 631.

HALLAM, A. and SELLWOOD, B. W. 1969. Origin of Fuller's Earth in the Mesozoic of Southern England. *Nature, Lond.* 220, 1193.

HANCOCK, A. 1849. On the excavating powers of certain sponges, belonging to the genus *Cliona. Ann. Mag. nat. Hist.* (2), 3, 321.

HANCOCK, J. M. 1961. The Cretaceous system in Northern Ireland. *Q. J. geol. Soc. Lond.* 117, 9.

—— 1963. The hardness of the Irish Chalk. *Ir. Nat. J.* 14, 157.

—— and KENNEDY, W. J. 1967. Photographs of hard and soft chalks taken with a scanning electron microscope. *Proc. geol. Soc. Lond.* No. 1643, 249.

HÄNTZSCHEL, W. 1934. Schraubenförmige und spiralige Grabgänge in turonen sandstein des Zittauergebirges. *Senckenbergiana* **16**, 313.

—— 1952. Die Lebensspuren von *Ophiomorpha* Lundgren im Miozän bei Hamburg, ihre weltweite Vebreitung und Synonymie. *Mitt. geol. StInst. Hamb.* **29**, 95.

—— 1960. Spreitenbauten (*Zoophycos* Massal.) im Septarienton Nordwest-Deutschland. *Mitt. geol. StInst. Hamb.* **29**, 95.

—— 1962. Trace-fossils and problematica. In *Treatise on invertebrate palaeontology* (Ed. R. C. Moore). Geol. Soc. Am., New York and Univ. Kansas Press, Lawrence. Part W.

JEANS, C. V. 1968. The origin of the montmorillonite of the European Chalk, with special reference to the Lower Chalk of England. *Clay Minerals* **7**, 311.

JUKES-BROWNE, A. J. and HILL, W. 1903. The Cretaceous rocks of Britain. **2**. The Lower and Middle Chalk of England. *Mem. geol. Surv. U.K.*

—— and —— 1904. The Cretaceous rocks of Britain. **3**. The Upper Chalk of England. *Mem. geol. Surv. U.K.*

KEIJ, A. J. 1965. Miocene trace-fossils from Borneo. *Paläont.Z.* **39**, 220.

KENNEDY, W. J. 1967. Burrows and surface traces from the Lower Chalk of Southern England. *Bull. Br. Mus. nat. Hist. Geology* **15**, 127.

—— and MACDOUGALL, J. D. S. 1969. Crustacean burrows in the Weald Clay (Lower Cretaceous) of south-eastern England and their environmental significance. *Palaeontology* **12**, 459.

——, JAKOBSON, M. E. and JOHNSON, R. T. 1969. A *Favreina-Thalassinoides* association from the Great Oolite of Oxfordshire. *Palaeontology* **12**, 549.

KILLPER, K. 1962. *Xenohelix* MANSFIELD 1927 aus dem miozänen niederrheinischen Braunkohlenformation. *Paläont. Z.* **36**, 55.

KORNMANN, P. 1962. Die Entwiklung von *Monostroma grevillei*. *Helgoländer Wiss. Meeresunters.* **8**, 195.

LEE, G. W. and BAILEY, E. R. 1925. The Pre-Tertiary geology of Mull, Lochaline and Oban. *Mem. Geol. Surv. U.K.*

LESSERTISSEUR, J. 1955. Traces fossiles d'activité animale et leur significance paléobiologique. *Mem. Soc. geol. Fr.* (n.s.) **74**.

MÄGDEFRAU, K. 1937. Lebensspuren fossiler, Bohr "-Organismen. *Beitr. naturk. Forsch. SüdwDtl.* **2**, 54.

MANTELL, G. A. 1822. *The fossils of the South Downs*. Relfe, London.

—— 1838. *The wonders of geology*. Relfe, London.

MOORE, H. B. 1932. Faecal pellets of the Anomuran Crustacea. *Proc. R. Soc. Edinb.* **52**, 296.

—— 1939. Faecal pellets in relation to Marine deposits. In *Recent Marine Sediments, A symposium* (Ed. P. D. Trask). Murby, London, p. 516.

MORRIS, J. 1851. Palaeontological notes. *Ann. Mag. Nat. Hist.* (2), **8**, 85.

PEAKE, N. B. and HANCOCK, J. M. 1961. The Upper Cretaceous of Norfolk. *Trans. Norfolk Norwich Nat. Soc.* **19**, 293.

PLIČKA, M. 1968. *Zoophycos* and a proposed classification of sabellid worms. *J. Paleont.* **42**, 836.

PUGACZEWSKA, H. 1965. Les organismes sédentaires sur les rostres des belemnites du Crétace Supérieur. *Acta palaeont. pol.* **10**, 73.

QUENSTEDT, F. 1845–49. *Die Petrefaktenkunde Deutschlands. Die Cephalopoden*, Fues, Tübingen.

REID, R. E. H. 1962. Sponges and the Chalk Rock. *Geol. Mag.* **99**, 273.

—— 1968. Bathymetric distribution of Calcarea and Hexactinellida in the present and the past. *Geol. Mag.* **105**, 546.

REINECK, H. E., GUTMANN, W. F. and HERTWECK, G. 1967. Das Schlickgebiet südlich Helgoland als Beispiel rezenter Schelfablagerungen. *Senkenberg. leth.* **48**, 219.

SAPORTA, G. DE, 1884. *Les organismes problématiques des anciennes mers*. Paris.

—— 1887. Nouveaux documents relatifs aux organismes problematiques des anciennes mens. *Bull. Soc. Geol. Fr.* (3), **15**, 286.

SEILACHER, A. 1955. Spuren und Lebensweise der Trilobiten; Spuren und Fazies im Unterkambrium. In *Beiträge zur Kenntnis des Kambriums in der Salt Range* (*Pakistan*) by O. SCHINDEWOLF and A. SEILACHER. *Abh. mat. natur. Kl. Akad. Wiss. Mainz*. Jahrg 1955, No. 10, 86.

—— 1964. Biogenic sedimentary structures. In *Approaches to paleoecology* (Ed. J. Imbrie and N. D. Newell). Wiley, New York. p. 296.

—— 1967a. Fossil behaviour. *Scient. Am.* **217**, 72.

—— 1967b. Bathymetry of trace fossils. *Mar. Geol.* **5**, 413.

SHINN, E. A. 1968. Burrowing in recent lime sediments of Florida and the Bahamas. *J. Paleont.* **42**, 879.

SMITH, A. J., STRIDE, A. H. and WHITTARD, W. F. 1965. The geology of the Western Approaches of the English Channel. IV. A recently discovered Variscan granite north-west of the Scilly Isles. In *Submarine geology and geophysics* (Ed. W. F. Whittard and R. Bradshaw). Butterworth, London.

STEPHENSON, L. W. 1952. Larger invertebrate fossils of the Woodbine Formation (Cenomanian) of Texas. *Prof. Pap. U.S. geol. Surv.* **242**.

STRAHAN, A. 1891. On the phosphatic chalk with *Belemnitella quadrata* at Taplow. *Q. J. geol. Soc. Lond.* **47**, 356.

—— 1896. On a phosphatic chalk with *Holaster planus* at Lewes. *Q. J. geol. Soc. Lond.* **52**, 463.

TAYLOR, B. J. 1967. Trace fossils from the Fossil Bluff Series of Alexander Island. *Br. Antarct. Surv. Bull.* **13**, 1.

VIALOV, O. S. 1966. *Sledy zhiznedeyatelnosti; organismov i ikh paleontologichesko znachenie.* Akademiya Nauk, Kiev.

VOIGT, E. 1929. Die Lithogense den Flach-und Tiefwasser sedimente des jungeren Oberkreide-meeres. *Jb. hall. Verb. z. Erforsch. d. mitteldt. Bodenschätze* **8**, 1.

—— 1959a. Die ökologische Bedeutung der Hartgrunde (Hardgrounds) in der oberen Kreide. *Paläont. Z.* **33**, 129.

—— 1959b. *Endosacculus moltkiae,* n.g. n.sp., ein vermulicher fossiler Ascothoracide (Entomostr.) als cystenbildner bei der Oktokoralle *Moltkia minuta Paläont. Z.* **33**, 211.

—— and HÄNTZSCHEL, W. 1956. Die grauen Bander in der Schreibe-kreide Nordwest-Deutsch-lands und ihre Deutung als Lebensspuren. *Mitt. geol. StInst. Hamb.* **25**, 104.

WEIR, A. H. and CATT, J. A. 1965. The mineralogy of some Upper Chalk samples from the Arundel area, Sussex. *Clay Minerals* **6**, 97.

WEIGELT, J. 1929. Fossile Grabschächte brachyurer Decapoden als lokalgescheibe im Pommern und des *Rhizocorallium*-problem. *Z. Gescheibeforsch Flachld geol.* **5**, 1.

WILCOX, N. R. 1953a. Some coprolites from phosphatic chalks in S.E. England. *Ann. Mag. nat. Hist.* (12), **6**, 369.

—— 1953b. The origin of beds of Phosphatic Chalk with special reference to those at Taplow, England. *Int. geol. Congr.* 19, *Algiers, Comp. Rend.* p. 119.

WILLS, L. J. 1951. *A palaeogeographic atlas of the British Isles and adjacent parts of Europe.* Blackie, London.

WOLFE, M. J. 1968. Lithification of a carbonate mud: Senonian Chalk in Northern Ireland. *Sediment. Geol.* **2**, 263.

W. J. Kennedy, Department of Geology, The University, Parks Road, Oxford OX1 3PR, U.K.

Observations on the ichnofauna of the Polish Carpathians

M. Książkiewicz

About forty ichnogenera with several ichnospecies are described from flysch sediments of the Polish Carpathians. The abundance and the character of the ichnofauna depends to a great extent on lithology. Coarse flysch facies is poor in trace fossils, both in the number of types and individuals. The most abundant ichnofauna occurs in beds consisting of fine grained, thin-bedded sandstones alternating with light-coloured shales; similar beds with dark or black shale, contain much poorer and less diversified assemblages of trace fossils. This suggests that aeration of the bottom is also an influential factor.

Most of the trace fossils are burrows parallel to bedding at the shale/sandstone interface and they rework the sand. Therefore it is thought that the majority of the flysch trace fossils was post-depositional and psammophagous.

Three types of assemblages of trace fossils are distinguished; (i) composed of irregularly winding traces and helicoidal forms (*Zoophycos*), with very rare rosetted or patterned trails; (ii) composed of rosetted and helicoidal traces with some patterned forms; (iii) containing, in addition to irregularly winding traces numerous patterned types; helicoidal forms are rare and rosetted trails absent. The first group possibly indicates a smaller depth of water than the third assemblage, while the second association may be indicative of an intermediate environment.

The differences in the vertical distribution of the ichnofauna are mainly due to changing bottom conditions. There are, however, indications that several forms may have a stratigraphic value.

1. Introduction

The Carpathian flysch beds (Tithonian-Oligocene) are known for the abundance of trace fossils. Nearly all papers concerned with flysch beds of the Carpathians contain references to biogenic "hieroglyphs". Few papers, however, were specially devoted to the ichnofauna. Notes of Zuber (1910) and Kuźniar (1911) should be mentioned, while more recently Nowak (1956; 1959) and the present author (1960; 1961; 1968) have described several forms.

The present paper is based mainly on the author's collections and observations made during his field mapping both in the pre-war and post-war periods. In addition Miss Dr. J. Burtan, Professor S. Dżułyński, Dr. S. Liszka and Dr. J. Małecki provided him with some fine specimens. My daughter Mary Margaret has been very helpful in finding and collecting fossils during the last few years.

2. Review of the ichnofauna

More than forty genera of trace fossils are known from the Carpathians; each genus consists of several types which may be regarded as species. Based on the manner of winding, meandering and branching the trace fossils are classified in this paper into nine groups. All specimens figured in this paper are in the collections of

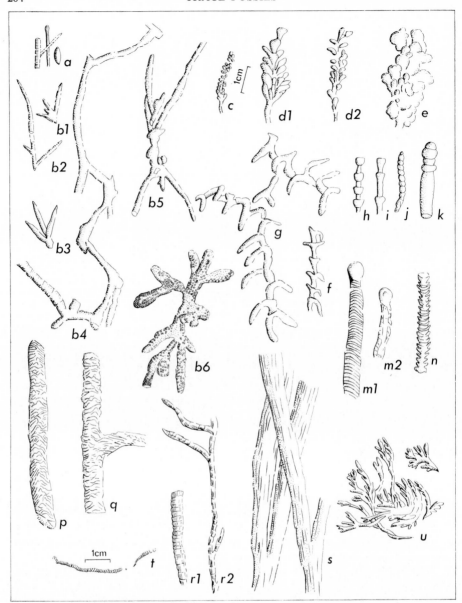

Fig. 1a. *Arthrophycus* sp. . Rzyki, Lgota Beds, Albian.
    b. *Granularia*.1, 2. Lipnica Mała, Inoceramian Beds, Senonian.
             3.   Goleszów, Cieszyn Limestone, Berriasian.
             4.   Zubrzyca Górna, Beloveza Beds, Lower Eocene.
             5.   Lipnica Mała, Beloveza Beds, Lower Eocene.
             6.   Osielec, Pasierbiec Sandstone, Middle Eocene.
    c. *Strobilorhaphe pusilla* Książkiewicz, Lipnica Mała, Beloveza Beds, Lower Eocene.
    d. *Strobilorhaphe clavata* Książkiewicz, Lipnica Mała, Beloveza Beds, Lower Eocene.
    e. *Strobilorhaphe clavata*, large form, Lipnica Mała, Beloveza Beds, Lower Eocene.
    f. *Rhabdoglyphus grossheimi* Vassoievitch. Gołebiówka, Lower Godula Beds, Cenomanian-Turonian.
    g. *Rhabdoglyphus* aff. *grossheimi*, Wisła, Lower Godula Beds, Cenomanian-Turonian (coll. Miss J. Burtan).
    h, i *Rhabdoglyphus* ichnosp. ind. Goleszów, Cieszyn Limestone, Berriasian.

the Department of Geology, Jagellonian University of Cracow, unless otherwise indicated.

Spelling of generic names follows that used by Häntzschel (1965).

Abbreviations: R—rare; F—frequent; VR—very rare; VF—very frequent. Asterisk * by stratigraphic terms denotes coarse flysch facies; terms without asterisk, fine grained flysch beds. L—Lower; M—Middle; U—Upper.

I. STRAIGHT, UNBRANCHED FORMS

Ichnogenus ARTHROPHYCUS Hall 1852
Arthrophycus sp.

Figure 1a

Description. Short tubes, 1-5 cm long, 1-3 mm wide, transversely striated. Some tubes consist of coarser grains. Sole trail; tubes often stick to the sole of thin-bedded sandstones.

Horizon. Albian (R); U. Senonian (R).

Ichnogenus RHABDOGLYPHUS Vassoievitch 1951
Rhabdoglyphus grossheimi Vassoievitch

Figure 1f

Description. Straight stem composed of thin (2-3 mm) calyx-like limbs with short branches; occurs on soles of thin-bedded (up to 4 cm) sandstones. Slightly larger than the form figured by Vassoievitch (1951 p. 219 pl. 6 fig. 4).

Horizon. Cenomanian—Turonian (R).

Rhabdoglyphus aff. *grossheimi* Vassoievitch

Figure 1g

Description. Sole trail similar to the preceding form, but the branches are longer and less regularly arranged. The trail consists of coarser grains than the adjacent sole and cuts across post-depositional traces.

Horizon. Cenomanian-Turonian (VR).

Rhabdoglyphus ichnosp. a

Figure 1 h-k

Description. Small straight tubes with regular swellings at varying intervals. Some

---

j. *Rhabdoglyphus* ichnosp. ind. Mucharz, Upper Godula Beds, Senonian.
k. *Rhabdoglyphus* ichnosp. ind. Mszana Dolna, Inoceramian Beds, Senonian.
m. Ex aff. *Rhabdoglyphus.* Sanok, Krosno Beds, Oligocene (coll. Prof. Dżułynski).
n. Ex aff. *Rhabdoglyphus.* Kobyle, Upper Istebna Beds, Palaeocene.
p. *Halymenidium oraviense* Książkiewicz. Lipnica Mała, Beloveza Beds, Lower Eocene.
q. *Halymenidium* cf. *sublumbricoides* (Azpeitia). Lipnica Mała, Beloveza Beds, Lower Eocene.
r. *Fucusopsis annulata* Książkiewicz. 1—Zubrzyca Górna, Beloveza Beds, Lower Eocene, 2—Sidzina, Beloveza Beds, Lower Eocene.
s. *Fucusopsis angulata* Palibin. Łodyna, Inoceramian Beds, Senonian.
t. *Helicorhaphe tortilis* Książkiewicz. Lipnica Mała, Beloveza Beds, Lower Eocene.
u. *Lophoctenium ramosum* (Toula). Lipnica Wielka, Variegated Beds, Lower Eocene.

All figures × 0·5 except where otherwise indicated.

of them resemble the form described by Bouček and Elias (1962) which is not
identical with the trail figured by Vassoievitch.

Horizon. Berriasian (F); U. Cretaceous (R); U. Eocene ?

Rhabdoglyphus ichnosp. b

Figure 1n

Description. Cylindrical sole trail, 8 mm wide, consisting of short calyces closely
spaced.

Horizon. Senonian*—Palaeocene* (F).

Rhabdoglyphus(*?*) sp.

Figure 1m

Description. Straight or nearly straight sole trails, 1 cm wide, transversely striated
with narrow furrows. At one end of the trail a club-like flattened termination
(Fig. 1m). Probably not ascribable to the ichnogenus *Rhabdoglyphus* and deserving a
separate denomination.

Horizon. Oligocene (R?).

Ichnogenus HELICORHAPHE ichnogen nov.

Type Species. H. tortilis ichnosp. nov.

Diagnosis: Sole trail spring-like twisted around a horizontal axis. In contrast to
Helicolithus Azpeitia it is nearly straight, not meandering and more tightly twisted.
   It has been described as *Helicoraphe* n.f. (Książkiewicz 1961 p. 885, 889);
nomen invalidum (no type species).

Helicorhaphe tortilis ichnosp. nov.

Figure 1t

Description. Comparable with specimen figured by Książkiewicz 1961 (pl. 2
fig. 1). Narrow sole trail, nearly straight, spring-like, tightly wound around a
horizontal axis.

Horizon. L. Eocene (VR).

II. STRAIGHT, BRANCHING FORMS

Ichnogenus FUCUSOPSIS Palibin in Vassoievitch 1932
Fucusopsis angulata Palibin

Figure 1s

Description. Straight ramifying tubiform strings, longitudinally striated; sole trail.

Horizon. Senonian (R).

Fucusopsis annulata ichnosp. nov.

Figure 1r

Description. Straight cylindrical strings, longitudinally densely striated, with
transverse breaks. Branching at a larger angle than the preceding form. Two types

with thicker (4-5 mm) and thinner (2 mm) strings. Strings adhering to, or tunnelling into, the sole.

Horizon. L. Eocene (F).

Ichnogenus HALYMENIDIUM Schimper 1879

Description. Tubes elliptical in cross-section, occurring usually on soles, but also tunnelling into sandy layers or adhering to upper surfaces. The trail is straight or only feebly bent, 0·5-1 cm thick. If it branches, the branching angle is large. The lower surface of the trail is ornamented with oblique narrow riblets, which either terminate in the axial region of the tube, or cross each other, producing a criss-cross pattern. This sculpture is less marked or absent on the upper surface of the trail.

Halymenidium sublumbricoides (Azpeitia)

Figure 1q

Description. Riblets chaotically winding, forming an irregular pattern.

Horizon. L. Eocene (VF).

Halymenidium oraviense Książkiewicz

Figure 1p

Description. The pattern formed by riblets approaches pigtail design, riblets more distinct and straight.

Horizon.L. Eocene (VF); similar but smaller trails are known from the Berriasian (R).

Ichnogenus GRANULARIA Pomel 1849

Description. To this group all unsculptured tubes composed of sand grains and clay pellets are assigned. There is a great range in the thickness of the tubes and the coarseness of the constituting material. The thickness varies between 2 and 15 mm; in some cases the infilling grains have a diameter of 1 mm. The fill is usually coarser than the nearby material. The tubes occur mainly on the soles of sandy layers, less commonly in shales (filled with sand and parallel to bedding); in some cases they run vertically or obliquely across sandy beds. There are also tubes occurring as convex semireliefs on top surfaces of sandy layers. Often they branch at various angles, are twig shaped and have irregular swellings and knots (Fig. 1b 1-3). There are also zigzag forms with knobs on turning points (Fig. 1b 4). Usually *Granularia* cuts across other traces; often it penetrates flutes.

Horizon. L. Cretaceous (R); Albian (R); U. Cretaceous (F); Palaeocene* (R); L. Eocene (VF); L. Eocene (R); M. Eocene (VF); M. Eocene* (R); U. Eocene* (F); Oligocene (R).

Ichnogenus LOPHOCTENIUM Reinh. Richter 1850
Lophoctenium ramosum (Toula)

Figure 1u

Description. Densely ramifying sole trail. Some specimens display a more delicate sculpture, approaching *L. comosum* Reinh. Richter.

Horizon. L. Eocene (F).

Ichnogenus STROBILORHAPHE Książkiewicz 1968

Description. Sole trail ramifying into knobs arranged in a cone-shaped form.

Strobilorhaphe clavata Książkiewicz

Figure 1d

Description. Short thin string, ending with knobs tapering into a cone, 3-4 cm long and 1-1·5 cm wide. Knobs of varying size.

Horizon. L. Eocene (VF); M. Eocene (R).

Strobilorhaphe pusilla Książkiewicz

Figure 1c

Description. Much smaller than *S. clavata*; the shape and size of knobs uniform.

Horizon. L. Eocene (R).

Ichnogenus CHONDRITES Sternberg 1833

Description. Very numerous traces, occurring in nearly all stratigraphic members, variable in size and shape. No attempt of classification has been made.

Horizon. Particularly frequent in the Berriasian and Senonian.

III. WINDING, UNBRANCHED FORMS

Three groups may be distinguished here: uni-, bi- and tri-lobate forms. Representatives of the first group are unnamed. They are all sediment filled strings of various thicknesses, on the whole rare. The second group is represented by *Gyrochorte* and *Taphrhelminthopsis* (*p.pt.*), the trilobate group by *Scolicia* and related forms.

Ichnogenus GYROCHORTE Heer 1865

Included here are the forms with pigtail-like sculpture; they do not correspond exactly to any described species. Two types are distinguished.

Gyrochorte ichnosp. a

Plate 1a

Description. Sole ridges, 1-2 cm wide, with transverse incisions obliquely and biserially arranged, joining in a median furrow. Usually the trail terminates with an oblong coniform extremity.

Horizon. Hauterivian (VR).

Gyrochorte ichnosp. b

Plate 1b

Description. Double-tracked, pigtail-like concave (negative) trail on the upper surface of sandstones. The trace consists of straight little furrows disposed obliquely to the axis of the trail.

Horizon. L. Eocene (R).

Ichnogenus SCOLICIA de Quartrefages 1849

Trilobed trails corresponding to *Subphyllochorda* and *Palaeobullia* of Götzinger and Becker (1932) are common in the Carpathian flysch. Similarly, as in the material of the authors mentioned (1932 pl. 9a), there are specimens uniting features of both forms. These occur both on lower and upper surfaces. In the first instance the lower convex side of the trail displays features of *Subphyllochorda,* while its upper side a relief similar to that of *Palaeobullia,* although not identical. In the second case the lower concave side is similar in its relief to *Palaeobullia,* and the upper convex side is trilobed and somewhat like that of the lower side of *Subphyllochorda.* The differences in sculpture and the manner of occurrence indicate that the traces have been formed by different, although no doubt closely related organisms. Therefore, following the example of Gomez de Llarena (1946 p. 134; 1954), the term *Scolicia* is used here only for the traces of *Palaeobullia* type, as de Quatrefages (1849) had this type of trail in mind, and the name *Subphyllochorda* is maintained in the meaning of Götzinger and Becker.

Scolicia prisca de Quatrefages

Plate 1d

Description. Top trail. As in Wienerwald, Guipuscoa (Kindelan 1919) and other places, *Scolicia* displays variability in morphology, to a certain extent due to influence of the material, compaction, mode of preservation and so on, but, nevertheless, there are also differences of specific nature. The specific name of de Quatrefages refers to various forms, and there is no other way as to limit it arbitrarily to one type. Following Häntzschel (1962 p. W 215, fig. 132-4a) the term *S. prisca* is used for the form with a relatively narrow and convex, strongly ribbed, median lobe (types 1 and 2, fig. 4. of Götzinger and Becker, phot. 7a, 8a, 9a of Kindelan). The width of the median ridge-like lobe is variable, 2-3 up to 5-6 mm. Lateral lobes are always larger than the central lobe.

Horizon. U. Cretaceous(?); L. Eocene (VF); M. Eocene (F); U. Eocene (R).

Scolicia plana ichnosp. nov.

Plate 1c

Description. Trilobed concave top trail. The median lobe is large, flat or slightly elevated, separated by narrow, deep, furrows from lateral lobes, which are of the same width as the median lobe. The ribbing is more delicate and denser and in the lateral lobes rather feebly marked. Types 3 and 4 of Götzinger and Becker (1932 fig. 4) correspond with this species, as well as *S. prisca* of Kindelan (1919 phot. 5a).

Horizon. Albian (F); Cenomanian-Turonian (R); Senonian (F).

Ichnogenus SUBPHYLLOCHORDA Götzinger and Becker 1932

Description. Sediment-stuffed flat tubes, mainly sole trails. According to the ornamentation, three species are distinguished.

Subphyllochorda granulata ichnosp. nov.

Plate 1g

Description. The median lobe feebly convex, ornamented with granules, limited by narrow ridges which often wane. Lateral lobes obliquely striated. The width of the trail is 2-2·5 cm, the three lobes being of nearly equal width.

Horizon. Senonian (F); Palaeocene (F); L. Eocene (VF); M. Eocene (R). The Cretaceous forms are somewhat smaller.

Subphyllochorda striata ichnosp. nov.

Plate 1f

Description. The median lobe is transversely striated. Slightly larger than the preceding form. Corresponds with types 8 and 9 of Götzinger and Becker.

When preservation is poor, the granulation and striation are feebly marked or absent, and then the two species are indistinguishable.

Horizon. L. Eocene (F).

Subphyllochorda laevis ichnosp. nov.

Plate 1e

Description. The median furrow flat or feebly concave, ridges bordering the median lobe strongly marked; no ornamentation. The width *c.* 3 cm.

Horizon. Albian (R); Cenomanian-Turonian (?); Senonian (R).

Ichnogenus TAPHRHELMINTHOPSIS Sacco 1888

Description. According to its author this genus includes (*pro parte*) bilobate forms consisting of two lateral ridges separated by a median furrow. He distinguished four species, none of them meandering. As the type species Andrews (1955) and Häntzschel (1962; 1965) chose *T. auricularis* Sacco. However, the figure given by Häntzschel (1962 fig. 136-3), who in this respect follows Seilacher (1954), is based on a specimen in the collection at Pisa; it shows a meandering bilobate form and does not correspond to the figure and description of Sacco (pl. 2 fig. 3) which depicts a freely winding form. In the Carpathian material there occur forms of similar relief both freely winding and meandering.

Freely winding bilobate forms, very common in the Carpathian flysch, exhibit a great variety of size and relief. They may be grouped around two species of Sacco, *T. recta* and *T. auricularis.*

Taphrhelminthopsis aff. *recta* Sacco

Plate 2a-d

Description. To this species, represented by *T. recta,* based by Sacco on a small fragment, are assigned all more or less straight bilobate trails. Their width is

---

Plate 1

a *Gyrochorte* ichnosp. a (1 and 2). Poznachowice, Grodischt Beds, Hauterivian (coll. Miss J. Burtan).

b *Gyrochorte* ichnosp. b (top trail). Lipnica Górna, Beloveza Beds, Lower Eocene.

c *Scolicia plana* ichnosp. nov. Sromowce Wyżne, Sromowce Beds, Lower Senonian.

d *Scolicia prisca* De Quatrefages. Zubrzyca Górna, Beloveza Beds, Lower Eocene.

e *Subphyllochorda laevis* ichnosp. nov. Rzyki, Lgota Beds, Albian.

f *Subphyllochorda striata* ichnosp. nov. Zubrzyca Górna, Beloveza Beds, Lower Eocene.

g *Subphyllochorda granulata* ichnosp. nov. Lipnica Wielka, Beloveza Beds, Lower Eocene.

All figures × 0·5.

PLATE 1

usually 2-4 cm, but specimens 5 cm wide also occur. The length of the trail may be up to 1 m. The median furrow is either concave and deep or shallow and nearly flat. On the Carpathian specimens no central ridge occurs within the furrow, as seen on Sacco's figure, but on some specimens lengthwise striation is visible, on others the striae are oblique. All trails of this group are sole trails (semi-hyporeliefs). Very seldom similar forms occur as convex (positive) epireliefs on the upper surface of sandy beds.

Horizon. Albian (F); U. Cretaceous (F); L. and M. Eocene (VF); U. Eocene (F); Oligocene (R).

Taphrhelminthopsis auricularis Sacco

Plate 2e-g

Description. Here belong forms corresponding with the description and figure of Sacco (1888 p. 172 pl. 2 fig. 3); freely winding, with bends reminiscent of the outline of the human ear. Although Sacco took the specific name from this feature he did not put much value to it, but in the Carpathian material trails actually bent in this way are not uncommon. Two groups, according to the size, may be distinguished; larger trails, 1·5 cm wide, and smaller ones, 6-7 mm wide. The median furrow is concave and deep. In addition there are several irregularly winding trails of various sizes (Pl. 2 f, g). No intermediate forms to *T. recta* have been found, but their existence cannot be precluded as the relief of trails of either groups is in several cases identical.

As in *T. recta* this species is represented by sole trails, filled either with much coarser grains than in the neighbouring parts of the sole, or with obliquely stratified sand.

Horizon. Albian (R); U. Cretaceous (R); Palaeocene (R); L. Eocene (F); M. Eocene (F); U. Eocene (F); Oligocene (?).

IV. MEANDERING FORMS

Ichnogenus COSMORHAPHE Fuchs 1895
Cosmorhaphe sinuosa (Azpeitia)

Figure 2a; Plate 3a

Description. Sole trail corresponding closely to the type of Azpeitia (1933 p. 45, pl. 14, fig. 24B). Strings 2 mm diameter, forming regular meanders of the first order consisting of loop-like meanders of the second order. The first order meanders are high (10-15 cm) but narrow (4-5 cm at the base). The filling of the cast is not

---

Plate 2

a *Taphrhelminthopsis* ex gr. *recta* Sacco. Variety with striation. Zubrzyca Górna, Beloveza Beds, Lower Eocene. × 0·5.

b *Taphrhelminthopsis* ex gr. *recta*. Large variety. Zubrzyca Górna, Magura Sandstone, Upper Eocene. × 0·25.

c *Taphrhelminthopsis* ex gr. *recta*. The most common variety. Sidzina, Beloveza Beds, Lower Eocene.

d *Taphrhelminthopsis* ex gr. *recta*. Trails partly filled with coarse sand. Sidzina, Beloveza Beds, Lower Eocene.

e *Taphrhelminthopsis auricularis* Sacco. Small form. Sidzina, Beloveza Beds, Lower Eocene.

f *Taphrhelminthopsis auricularis* Sacco. Large form, Lipnica Mała, Beloveza Beds, Lower Eocene.

g *Taphrhelminthopsis* ex gr. *auricularis*. Zubrzyca Górna, Beloveza Beds, Lower Eocene.

PLATE 2

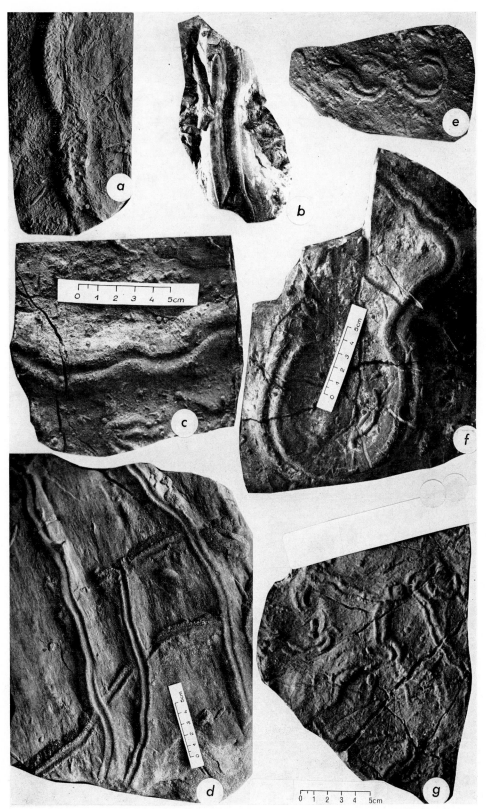

separated from the sole. In some specimens there is pronounced enrichment in mica and coarser grains.

Horizon. L. Eocene (R).

Cosmorhaphe helminthopsidea (Sacco)

Figure 2c

Description. Strings thinner, meanders of both orders also tightly compressed but not so regular. By this irregularity this type resembles the species of Sacco (1888 p. 180, pl. 2 fig. 7) and the trace figured by Paul (1898 pl. 3 fig. 1). This form has also been figured by the author (Książkiewicz 1958 pl. 3 fig. 2).

Horizon. U. Senonian (R); L. Eocene (R).

Cosmorhaphe fuchsi ichnosp. nov.

Figure 2b; Plate 3b

Description. The meanders of the first order are high but wide at the base, meanders of the second order are short, not compressed, and irregular. This form resembles the types figured by Fuchs (1895 pl. 6). In one case the trail is traversed by a drag-mark (Pl. 3b).

Horizon. L. Eocene (F); M. Eocene (R).

Cosmorhaphe (*?*) *tortuosa* ichnosp. nov.

Plate 3c

Description. Sole trail, Very thin ribs of nearly equal length parallel to each other are arranged so that a line joining centres of the ribs describes narrow meanders. Ribs are slightly arcuate, with a median bend. At a few points the neighbouring ribs join at their ends forming short arcs. This may indicate that the ribs are actually arms of second order meanders set out at right angles to the axis of the first order meanders. If so, the form should be assigned to *Cosmorhaphe* as this ichnogenus unites all meandering forms consisting of second order meanders. The height of the first order meanders is *c.* 5 cm, their width, 2·5 cm; the length of ribs 1-1·5 cm.

Horizon. U. Cretaceous? (VR).

Ichnogenus HELMINTHOIDA Schafhäutl 1851

Description. Following the current definition (Häntzschel 1962; 1965) all forms with obligatory parallel meanders belong here. The Carpathian forms may be

---

Fig. 2a. *Cosmorhaphe sinuosa* (Azpeitia). Lipnica Wielka, Variegated Beds, Lower Eocene.
   b. *Cosmorhaphe fuchsi* ichnosp. nov. Zubrzyca Górna, Łącko Beds, Middle Eocene.
   c. *Cosmorhaphe helminthopsidea* (Sacco). Łętownia Górna, Beloveza Beds, Middle Eocene.
   d. *Helminthoida crassa* Schafhäutl. Pieniny Mts., Sromowce Beds, Lower Senonian.
   e. *Helminthoida crassa.* Strings thinner. Rzyki, Lgota Beds, Albian.
   f. *Helminthoida crassa.* Strings very thin. Sidzina, Beloveza Beds, Lower Eocene.
   g. *Helminthoida labyrinthica* Heer. Lipnica Mała, Inoceramian Beds, Palaeocene.
   h. *Helminthoida labyrinthica,* f. *serrata.* Bieńkówka, Inoceramian Beds, Senonian.
   i. *Helminthoida labyrinthica,* f. *lata.* Poreba Wielka, Inoceramian Beds.
   j. *Helminthoida* (*?*) *molassica* Heer. Skrzydlna, Krosno Beds, Oligocene.

All figures × 0·5.

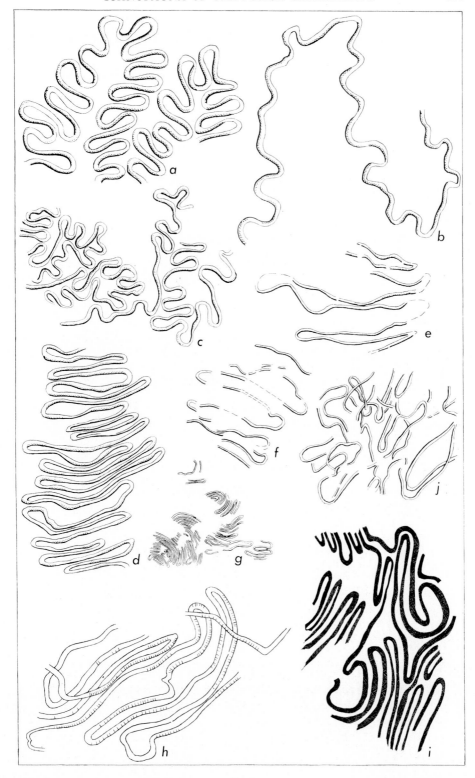

Fig 2.

grouped around the already known species, but as they exhibit much variability, the species names are used here rather as denomination of groups of related species than species in a narrow sense.

Group of *Helminthoida crassa* Schafhäutl

Description. Sole trails. This group consists of a few types differing only in the thickness of their trails which have in common closely spaced, not very regular meanders. By their irregularity the meanders are more like Seilacher's (1954) figure than that of Schafhäutl(1851 p. 142 pl. 9 fig. 11). All are sole trails, sometimes filled with coarser grains.

(a) Strings 2-3 mm thick, the height of the meanders up to 10 cm, the width *c.* 1 cm (Fig. 2d).

Horizon. Senonian (R).

(b) Strings very thin (1 mm and less), not so closely meandering (Fig. 2e, f).

Horizon. Albian (VR); Senonian (R); Palaeocene-L. Eocene (R).

Group of *Helminthoida labyrinthica* Heer

Description. Endopelitic traces, occurring as narrow meandering furrows.

Helminthoida labyrinthica Heer forma *typica*

Figure 2g

Description. Very narrow furrows concentrically meandering. Traces occur in marls and shales. Similar, but not identical trails occur very rarely on the soles of sandstones.

Horizon. U. Senonian (R); Palaeocene (VF). In the L. Eocene similar form, but less densely spaced and more irregular in meandering.

Helminthoida labyrinthica Heer forma *lata*

Figure 2i

Description. Identical in shape to forma *typica* but the meanders are larger.

Horizon. Senonian (F).

Plate 3

a *Cosmorhaphe sinuosa* (Azpeitia). Lipnica Mała, Variegated Beds, Lower Eocene.

b *Cosmorhaphe fuchsi* ichnosp. nov. Zubrzyca Górna, Łącko Beds, Middle Eocene. The trail cut across by a drag mark.

c *Cosmorhaphe(?) tortuosa* ichnosp. nov. Inoceramian Beds, Senonian-Palaeocene (coll. School of Mines, Cracow).

d *Spirophycus* ex gr. *involutissimus* (Sacco). Zawoja, Hieroglyphic Beds, Middle Eocene. The trail filled with tests of foraminifers (*Sphaerammina*). × 0·5.

e *Spirorhaphe minuta* ichnosp. nov. Kłodne, Kluszkowce Beds, Palaeocene. × 0·5.

f *Taphrhelminthopsis convoluta* (Heer). Sidzina, Beloweza Beds, Lower Eocene.

g *Taphrhelminthopsis plana* ichnosp. nov. Zubrzyca Górna, Beloveza Beds, Lower Eocene.

h *Taphrhelminthopsis plana* ichnosp. nov. Small form. Zubrzyca Górna, Beloveza Beds, Lower Eocene.

i *Helicolithus sampelayoi* Azpeitia. Homrzyska, Magura Sandstone, Upper Eocene.

PLATE 3

Helminthoida labyrinthica Heer forma *serrata*

Figure 2h

Description. Furrows 2 mm wide, divided by densely spaced transverse ridges.

Horizon. Senonian (F).

Helminthoida(?) aff. *molassica* Heer

Figure 2j

Description. Sole trail consisting of thin strings (<1 mm). Meanders are irregular and cut one another on the same level.

Horizon. Oligocene (R).

Ichnogenus HELMINTHOPSIS Heer *emend.* Sacco 1888

Description. This genus, as amended by Sacco (p. 174), comprising all irregularly meandering forms, may be divided into groups according to the thickness and sculpture of the trails. All are sole trails, often cutting across sedimentary structures (Książkiewicz 1968 pl. 4).

Helminthopsis sp.

Figure 3a

Description. Strings 2-3 cm thick.

Horizon. Berriasian (R); Albian (?); U.Cretaceous (R); L. and M. Eocene (R); U. Eocene (R); Oligocene (?).

Helminthopsis sp.
Description. Strings thinner than preceding species (0·5 cm).

Horizon. L. Eocene (R).

Fig. 3a. *Helminthopsis,* thick form. Sidzina, Magura Sandstone, Upper Eocene.
   b. *Helminthopsis tenuis* Książkiewicz, Goleszów, Cieszyn Limestone, Berriasian.
   c. *Helminthopsis granulata* Książkiewicz Goleszów, Cieszyn Limestone, Berriasian.
   d. *Paleomeandron elegans* Peruzzi. Lipnica Mała, Inoceramian Beds,.Senonian.
   e. *Paleomeandron rude* Peruzzi, Sidzina, Beloveza Beds, Lower Eocene.
   f. *Paleomeandron robustum* Książkiewicz. Lipnica Mała, Beloveza Beds, Lower Eocene.
   g. *Paleomeandron* aff. *robustum.* Podwilk, Łącko Beds, Middle Eocene.
   h. *Paleomeandron* aff. *robustum.* Lipnica Mała, Beloveza Beds, Lower Eocene.
   i. *Helicolithus sampelayoi* Azpeitia. Homrzyska, Magura Sandstone, Upper Eocene.
   j. Interrupted meander, unnamed form. Lipnica Mała, Inoceramian Beds, Senonian.

All figures × 0·5.

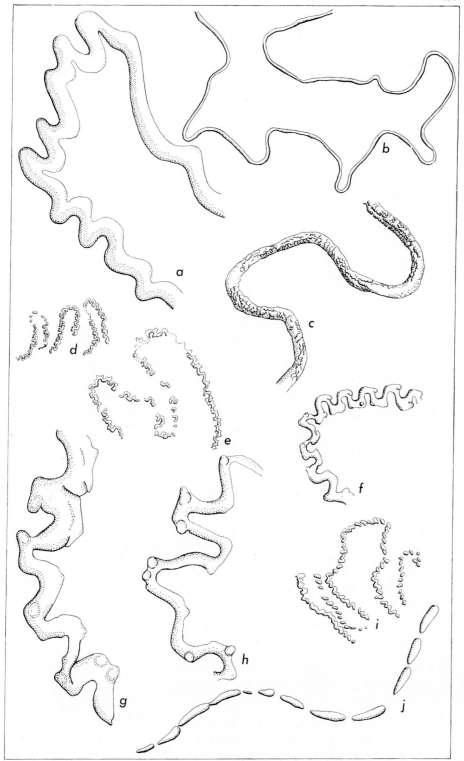

Fig. 3.

Helminthopsis tenuis Książkiewicz

Figure 3b

Description. Strings 1 mm thick. See Książkiewicz (1968 p. 7 pl. 4 fig. 1) ..

Horizon. Berriasian (R); L. Eocene (VR).

Helminthopsis granulata Książkiewicz

Figure 3c

Description. Cylindrical tubes, 5-7 mm thick, their lower surface covered with tubercles and ridges. See Książkiewicz (1968 p. 7 pl. 4 fig. 2).

Horizon. Berriasian.

Ichnogenus TAPHRHELMINTHOPSIS Sacco 1888 (*pro parte*)

Description. This group, which unites all meandering trails with a central furrow, should probably be separated as a distinct genus. "*Meanderfahrten*" of Götzinger and Becker (1932; 1934) belong here.

Taphrhelminthopsis convoluta (Heer)

Plate 3f

Description. Double meanders closely spaced and sometimes coiled. Central furrow deep and concave, the ridges large and prominent. The meanders are up to 15 cm amplitude. The trails, either filled with current bedded sand or with coarse sand, are pre-depositional, a view in conformity with the first interpretation of Götzinger and Becker (1932) ,and not with their later (1934) explanation.

Horizon. Albian (R); U. Cretaceous (?); L. Eocene (F); M. Eocene (R).

Taphrhelminthopsis plana ichnosp. nov.

Plate 3gh

Description. Double obligatory meanders, sometimes coiled. Median furrow large and flat ridges narrow, feebly jutting out. The width of the trail up to 2 cm, the amplitude of the meanders up to 15 cm, their width 4 cm. There are also smaller forms, not so closely meandering. On some specimens transverse striation. This form differs from *T. convoluta* by its subdued relief and more "obliged" meandering. It resembles that figured by Książkiewicz (1968 p. 15 pl. 6 fig. 3).

Horizon. L. Eocene (R).

Ichnogenus HELICOLITHUS Azpeitia 1933
Helicolithus sampelayoi Azpeitia

Figure 3i

Description. The trail, screw-like and meandering, corresponds exactly to the figure of Azpeitia (1933 p. 48, pl. 4 fig. 11). Often cuts across fluting.

Horizon. L. Eocene (F); M. and U. Eocene (R).

Ichnogenus PALEOMEANDRON Peruzzi 1881

Description. Meanders consisting of small second order meanders, with protuberances on their corners. A few species are distinguished, differing mainly by their size.

Paleomeandron elegans Peruzzi

Figure 3d

Description. Meanders of the first order 2-3 cm high, the secondary quadrangular meanders 1-2 mm.

Horizon. Senonian–Palaeocene (F); M. Eocene (?).

Paleomeandron rude Peruzzi

Figure 3e

Description. Meanders of the first order 3-6 cm amplitude, less regular than in *P. elegans.* Meanders of the second order 3-5 mm wide.

Horizon. L. Eocene (VR); M. and U. Eocene (R).

Paleomeandron robustum Książkiewicz

Figure 3f-h

Description. Thick (4-5 mm) trail, the second order meanders quadrangular or trapezoidal, much larger (12–14 × 12–14 mm) in comparison with the species described above. Trails penetrate and distort oblique lamination. Previously figured by Książkiewicz (1968 p. 4, 14, table 1, fig. 3).

Horizon. L. Eocene (F); M. Eocene (VR).

V. MEANDERING OR WINDING BRANCHED FORMS

Ichnogenus ACANTHORHAPHE ichnogen. nov.

Type Species. Acanthorhaphe incerta ichnosp. nov.

Diagnosis. Trail winding in curves of small amplitude, with lateral thorn-like branches on the convex side of the windings.

   Previously described by the author (1961 p. 883, 888) as *Acanthoraphe* n.f.; *nomen invalidum* (no type species given).

Acanthorhaphe incerta ichnosp. nov.

Figure 4a

Description. This form is identical with that figured by Książkiewicz (1961 p. 888 pl. 1 fig. 4). Sole trail 1 mm thick, irregularly winding, provided with short lateral thorn-like branches. The trail, apparently cuts across flutes. It is sometimes filled with coarser material.

Horizon. Berriasian (R).

Remarks. To the same ichnogenus should be assigned small bent rods with tiny often club-like appendices on one side (Fig. 4b) from the L. Eocene (VF).

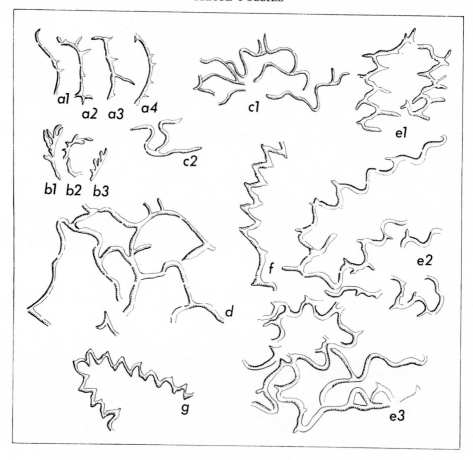

Fig. 4a. *Acanthorhaphe incerta* ichnosp. nov. Goleszów, Cieszyn Limestone, Berriasian.
  b. *Acanthorhaphe,* unnamed form. Zubrzyca Górna, Beloveza Beds, Lower Eocene.
  c. *Palaeophycus.* Przykrzec, Hieroglyphic Beds, Middle Eocene.
  d. *Palaeochorda submontana* (Azpeitia). Lipnica Mała, Beloveza Beds, Lower Eocene.
  e. *Protopaleodictyon incompositum* ichnosp. nov. Przykrzec, Hieroglyphic Beds, Middle Eocene.
  f. *Belorhaphe fabregae* (Azpeitia). Zubrzyca Górna, Łącko Beds, Middle Eocene.
  g. *Belorhaphe zickzack* (Heer). Sidzina, Beloveza Beds, Lower Eocene.

All figures × 0·5.

Ichnogenus PALAEOCHORDA McCoy 1848
Palaeochorda submontana (Azpeitia)

Figure 4d

Description. Sole trail, similar to that figured by Lessertisseur (1955) as *Palaeochorda marina* Emmons and identical with *Cylindrites submontanus* Azpeitia (1933 p. 44 pl. 10 fig. 21B). Strings thin (1-2 mm), irregularly winding and branching, regarded by Gomez de Llarena (1946) as a disordered *Paleodictyon* net.

Horizon. Cenomanian-Turonian (R); L. Miocene (VF); M. Eocene (R).

Ichnogenus PALAEOPHYCUS Hall 1847

Description. Irregularly meandering sole strings, irregularly and rarely branching. In comparison with the previous form, the meandering is more pronounced and branching less frequent (Fig. 4c).

Horizon. L. and M. Eocene (R).

Ichnogenus PROTOPALEODICTYON ichnogen. nov.

Type species. Protopaleodictyon incompositum ichnosp. nov.

Diagnosis. Meandering sole trail, with one or two appendices branching from the apices of the meanders. The meanders occur closely one near the other and therefore an irregular network is formed. The trail differs from *Cosmorhaphe* by the presence of lateral ramifications, from *Belorhaphe* by sinuous course of bendings and longer appendices, from *Paleodictyon* by the less regular and not polygonal network.

The new genus includes the trace described by the author (1960 p. 737,745, also 1958) as *Protopalaeodictyon* n.f.; *nomen invalidum* (no type species given).

Protopaleodictyon incompositum ichnosp. nov.

Figure 4e

Description. Meandering sole trail with ramifications on the apices of the meanders. Considerable variability in the shape of the meanders and the length of the appendices. Often densely spaced and forming irregular networks. Cuts fluting and current lineation.

Horizon. L. Eocene (R); M. Eocene (F); U. Eocene (R).

Ichnogenus BELORHAPHE Fuchs 1895
Belorhaphe fabregae (Azpeitia)

Figure 4f

Description. Sole trail; zigzag meanders and appendices thick. Meanders of the first order rarely preserved.

Horizon. Cretaceous (?); L. Eocene (F); M. Eocene (R); M. Eocene* (R).

Belorhaphe zickzack (Heer)

Figure 4g

Description. Trails and appendices thinner than in *B. fabregae*. Both these and the the previous species cut flutes and are evidently post-depositional traces.

Horizon. Berriasian (R); Hauterivian (R); Upper Cretaceous (?); L. Eocene (R).

VI. SPIRALS

Ichnogenus SPIRORHAPHE Fuchs 1895

Occurrence. Traces are found both on soles of sandstone and within shales. Those occurring on the lower surfaces of sandstones are probably mainly pre-depositional, as they occur on soles of thick-bedded sandstones. In one instance the spiral is interrupted by a narrow strip with small flutes and prods. In other cases, however, the spirals are undisturbed by fluting.

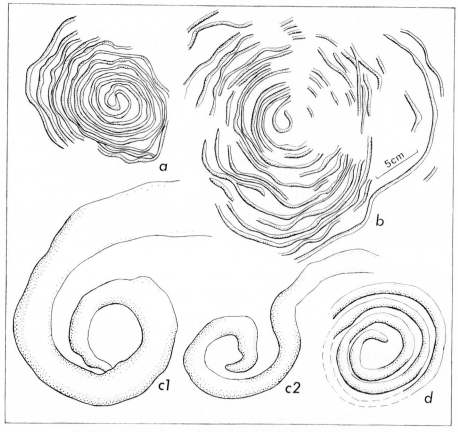

Fig. 5a. *Spirorhaphe involuta* de Stefani. Kobyle, Upper Istebna Beds, Palaeocene.
  b. *Spirorhaphe*. Large form. Lipnica Mala, Inoceramian Beds, Senonian.
  c. 1. *Spirophycus*. Zubrzyca Górna, Beloveza Beds, Lower Eocene.
  c. 2. *Spirophycus*. Łętownia Górna, Beloveza Beds, Lower Eocene.
  d. *Spirophycus* aff. *involutissimus* (Sacco). Zawoja, Hieroglyphic Beds, Middle Eocene.

All figures, except Fig. 5b, × 0·5.

Two types of trails can be distinguished on the soles of sandstone and are referred to below as *S. involuta* de Stefani and *S.* sp. The trace found inside shales is *S. minuta* ichnosp. nov.

Spirorhaphe sp.

Figure 5b

Description. Strings 2-3 mm thick; diameter of spiral 20-50 cm.

Horizon. Senonian (F); L. Eocene (VR); M. and U. Eocene (R).

Spirorhaphe involuta de Stefani

Figure 5a

Description. Strings 0·5-1 mm thick; diameter of elliptically elongated coil up to 8 cm.

Horizon. U. Senonian-Palaeocene* (F).

Spirorhaphe minuta ichnosp. nov.

Plate 3e

Description. Spiral exactly circular, consisting of tiny closely spaced furrows less than 1 mm wide. Diameter of spiral 5-8 cm.

Horizon. Palaeocene (F).

Ichnogenus SPIROPHYCUS Häntzschel 1962

This very common trace may be separated into two groups:
  (i) Thick strings 1-2 cm thick (Fig. 5 cd), the spiral usually simple.

Horizon. U. Senonian (R); Senonian* (R); Palaeocene* (R); L. Eocene (VF); M. and U· Eocene (R).

  (ii) Strings thinner (5-8 mm), the spiral usually multiple (Fig. 5d). Probably related to *Munsteria involutissima* Sacco (1888).

Horizon. L. Eocene (R); M. Eocene (F).

Spirophycus trails are often filled with current-bedded sand or lined with small foraminifera (Pl. 3d).

VII. NETWORKS

Ichnogenus DESMOGRAPTON Fuchs 1895

Very rare and imperfectly developed; Senonian and L. Eocene. Figure 6a.

Ichnogenus MEGAGRAPTON Książkiewicz 1961

Type species. Megagrapton irregulare Książkiewicz (1968 p. 14, fig. 3; see also 1961 p. 882 pl. 1 figs. 1-2.).

Description. Straight or feebly curved strings, branching at right angles and forming a network composed of irregular rectangles.

Megagrapton irregulare Książkiewicz

Figure 6b

Description. Cylindrical strings, 4-5 mm thick, adhering to the sole.

Horizon. L. Eocene (R).

Megagrapton tenue Książkiewicz

Figure 6c

Description. Strings very thin (1 mm), ramifying at irregular intervals and forming a network of irregular polygons and rectangles. See Książkiewicz 1968 p. 5. pl. 3 fig. 1.

Horizon. Berriasian (R); L. and M. Eocene (?).

Ichnogenus SQUAMODICTYON Vialov and Golev 1960
Squamodictyon squamosum Vialov and Golev

Figure 6d

Description. Net resembles large fish scales. Probably there are intermediate forms between *M. tenue* and this form. Species based on the specimen figured by Nowak

(1959 pl. 2 fig. a), and referred to *S. squamosum* by Vialov and Golev (1960 p. 178 fig. 1 d′ d″).

Horizon. Berriasian (R).

Ichnogenus PALEODICTYON Meneghini 1850

Description. The division into species, in accordance with previous workers, is based on the dimensions of meshes and the thickness of bordering strings. Nowak's (1959) classification, disregarding previously introduced specific names, is not followed here.

In a few cases it has been found that the bordering ridges are cylindrical. In one instance ridges of the net cut across a post-depositional *Helminthopsis* type trail (Pl. 4h), in another a *Fucusopsis* rod. In some cases an undisturbed net covers fluting, similarly as in several published figures (Kindelan 1919 fig. 11a; Gomez de Llarena 1954 pl. 50 fig. 2; Vialov and Golev 1964 pl. 4 fig 1). These facts would support the view that *Paleodictyon* nets are post-depositional burrows at the interface of clay and sandstone (cf. Wood and Smith 1959; Simpson 1967). On the other hand, on one specimen the net seems to be cut by a drag cast, as in the case figured by Dżułyński and Sanders (1962). In one specimen the strings are built of conspicuously coarser material than the neighbouring parts of the sole.

Paleodictyon minutissimum ichnosp. nov.

Plate 4ab

Description. Meshes smaller than 1 mm, strings thinner than 0·5 mm, but in relation to the size of the meshes comparatively thick.

Horizon. L. Eocene (VR).

Paleodictyon minimum Sacco

Plate 4c

Description. Meshes 1-1·2 mm, strings thinner than 0·5 mm.

Horizon. Senonian (VR); L. Eocene (R); M. Eocene (VR); Oligocene (R).

Paleodictyon latum Vialov and Golev

Plate 4d-f

Description. Meshes 1-1·2 mm, strings thicker, 0·5-0·7 mm. In certain specimens separation from *P. minimum* seems difficult, as the thickness of strings varies in one and the same specimen.

Horizon. Senonian (VR); L. Eocene (F); M. Eocene (VR).

Paleodictyon intermedium ichnosp. nov.

Plate 4g

Description. Meshes 1·5-2·5 mm, strings 0·5 mm. This form is intermediate between *P. latum* and *P. miocenicum*.

Horizon. Senonian (F); M. Eocene (R).

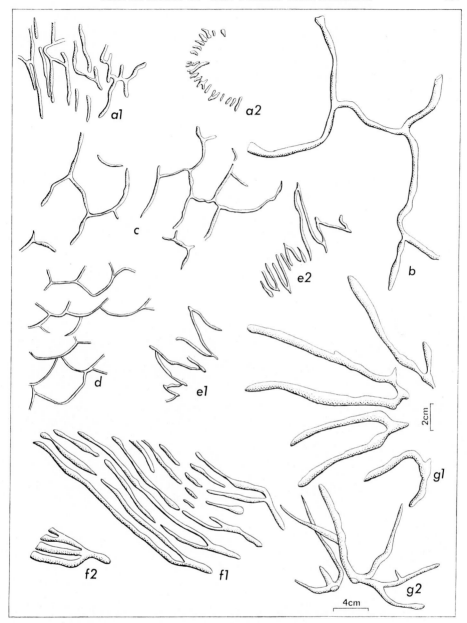

Fig. 6a. 1. *Desmograpton*. Sidzina, Beloveza Beds, Lower Eocene.
    a. 2. *Desmograpton*. Lipnica Wielka, Inoceramian Beds, Senonian.
    b. *Megagrapton irregulare* Książkiewicz. Zubrzyca Górna, Beloveza Beds, Lower Eocene.
    c. *Megagrapton tenue* Książkiewicz. Goleszów, Cieszyn Limestone, Berriasian.
    d. *Squamodictyon*. Goleszów, Cieszyn Limestone, Berriasian (cf. Nowak 1959).
    e. 1. *Urohelminthoida dertonensis* Sacco. Osielec, Beloveza Beds, Lower Eocene.
    e. 2. *Urohelminhoida dertonensis* Sacco. Kłodne, Kluszkowce Beds, Paleocene.
    f. *Urohelminthoida* aff. *appendiculata* (Heer). Lipnica Wielka, Inoceramian Beds, Senonian.
    g. 1. Unnamed trace, related(?) to *Urohelminthoida*. Sidzina, Beloveza Beds, Lower Eocene.
    g. 2. Unnamed trace, Podwilk, Beloveza Beds, Lower Eocene.

All figures, except Fig. 6g, × 0·5.

Paleodictyon strozzi Meneghini

Plate 4h

Description. Meshes 3-5 mm, strings very thin (up to 0·5 mm). See Peruzzi (1880).

Horizon. Senonian (R); Palaeocene (R); L. Eocene (F); M. Eocene (R).

Paleodictyon tellini Sacco

Plate 4m

Description. Meshes 4-7 mm, polygons less regular than at *P. strozzi,* strings even thinner.

Horizon. Berriasian (R); Senonian (R).

Paleodictyon miocenicum Sacco

Plate 4 i-k

Description. Meshes 2·5-4. 3-4 or 3-5 mm, often elongated; strings 1-1·2 mm thick.

Horizon. Berriasian (R); L. Senonian (R); Palaeocene (R); L. Eocene (R).

Paleodictyon carpathicum Matyasovszky

Plate 4 n-q

Description. Nets cover large areas, in one case nearly 1 m². Meshes 5×7 up to 7×9 mm, consisting of hexagons or pentagons, often irregular, elongated in one direc-

---

Plate 4

a *Paleodictyon minutissimum* ichnosp. nov. Sidzina, Beloveza Beds, Lower Eocene.

b *Paleodictyon minutissimum* ichnosp. nov. Slightly larger mesh. Sidzina, Beloveza Beds, Lower Eocene.

c *Paleodictyon minimum* Sacco. Lipnica Mała, Beloveza Beds, Lower Eocene.

d *Paleodictyon latum* Vialov and Golev. Sidzina, Beloveza Beds, Lower Eocene.

e *Paleodictyon latum* Vialov and Golev, Zubrzyca Górna, Beloveza Beds, Lower Eocene.

f *Paleodictyon latum* Vialov and Golev. Ridges thinner than in preceding specimens. Zubrzyca Górna, Beloveza Beds, Lower Eocene.

g *Paleodictyon intermedium* ichnosp. nov. Sromowce Wyżne, Sromowce Beds, Lower Senonian.

h *Paleodictyon strozzi* Meneghini. Przykrzec, Hieroglyphic Beds, Middle Eocene.

i *Paleodictyon miocenicum* Sacco. Lipnica Mała, Beloveza Beds, Lower Eocene.

j *Paleodictyon miocenicum* Sacco. More irregular meshes. Grzechynia, Inoceramian Beds, Palaeocene.

k *Paleodictyon miocenicum* Sacco. Ring-like arrangement of meshes. Istebna, Hieroglyphic Beds, Middle Eocene.

m *Paleodictyon tellini* Sacco. Koninka, Inoceramian Beds, Senonian.

n *Paleodictyon carpathicum* (Matyasovszky). Lubomierz, Variegated Beds, Lower Eocene (coll. Miss J. Burtan).

p *Paleodictyon carpathicum.* Ridges thicker than at the preceding specimen. Sidzina, Beloveza Beds, Lower Eocene.

q *Paleodictyon carpathicum.* Thickness of ridges variable. Ridges cut across a *Helminthopsis* trail. Lubomierz, Beloveza Beds, Lower Eocene.

r *Paleodictyon regulare* Sacco? Lipnica Mała, Beloveza Beds, Lower Eocene.

s *Paleodictyon majus* Meneghini. Lipnica Mała, Beloveza Beds, Lower Eocene.

All figures $\times$ 0·5.

309

tion. Some meshes 12 mm. wide. The smaller the size of meshes the more regular the network.

Horizon. L. Cretaceous (?); Palaeocene (R); L. Eocene (VF); M. Eocene (R).

Paleodictyon regulare Sacco (?)

Plate 4r

Description. The size of meshes like in the previous species, but bordering ridges thicker (1-2 mm, mostly above 1·5 mm). The separation from *P. carpathicum* seems to be doubtful, as the ridges in the both species are variable in thickness.

Horizon. L. Eocene (R).

Paleodictyon majus Meneghini

Plate 4s

Description. Meshes mainly 9-10 mm wide, with some smaller and larger (up to 10×11 mm). Strings 1 mm thick or slightly less. Other nets with meshes even larger than these occur sparingly but are too incomplete for specific determination.

Horizon. L. Eocene (R).

Ichnogenus UROHELMINTHOIDA Sacco 1888

Urohelminthoida dertonensis Sacco

Figure 6e

Description. Figured by Sacco (1888 p. 184 pl. 2 fig. 8). Thin (1 mm or less) forking strings, the angle of forking variable (10-40°). On one specimen small flutes are cut by strings.

Horizon. Palaeocene (R); L. Eocene (F).

Urohelminthoida aff. *appendiculata* Heer

Figure 6f

Description. Strings thick and long. Forking in two, as in the preceding species, but some initial strings are dichotomized in two strings, each of which branches again in two. This trace corresponds better with the figure of Fuchs (*Hercorhaphe,* pl. 5 fig. 3) than to that of Heer. Strings are enriched in coarser grains and mica. On the other hand in one specimen strings intersect a delicate ridge-and-furrow lineation.

Horizon. Senonian (R); L. Eocene (VR).

To this ichnogenus is assigned a trace (Fig. 6g), known only in a single specimen, it consists of thick (5 mm) dichotomous strings, 15 cm long radially disposed with no counterpart developed. L. Eocene.

VIII. ROSETTED TRAILS

Ichnogenus ASTERICHNUS Nowak 1961

Type species. Asterichnus nowaki ichnosp. nov.

Asterichnus nowaki ichnosp. nov.

Figure 7d

Description. This name was proposed by Nowak (1961) for star-like traces with long irregular rays, described by him previously (1956) It was proposed by the present

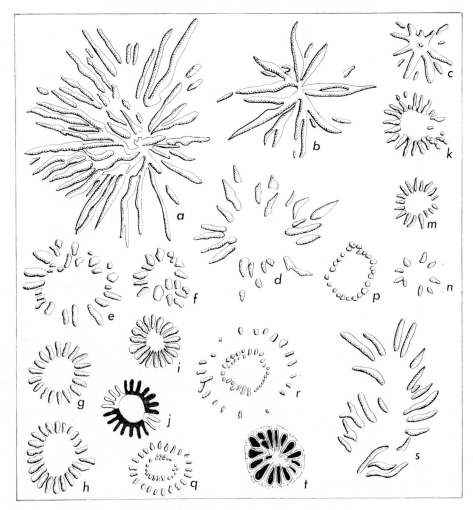

Fig. 7a. *Glockeria glockeri* Książkiewicz. Goleszów, Cieszyn Limestone, Berriasian.
 b. *Glockeria sparsicostata* Książkiewicz. Zawoja, Inoceramian Beds, Senonian.
 c. *Glockeria parvula* Kisążkiewicz. Lipnik, Upper Godula Beds, Lower Senonian.
 d. *Asterichnus nowaki* ichnosp. nov. Goleszów, Cieszyn Limestone, Berriasian.
 e, f *Sublorenzinia plana* Książkiewicz. Porabka, Lower Godula Beds, Cenomanian.
 g. *Lorenzinia carpathica* (Zuber). Lipnica Mała, Variegated Beds, Palaeocene.
 h. *Lorenzinia carpathica* (Zuber). Variety with more numerous ribs. Coll. School of
    Mines, Cracow, unknown locality.
 i. *Lorenzinia carpathica* (Zuber). Variety with compressed ribs. Wiśnicz, Senonian? (cf.
    Kuźniar 1911).
 j. *Lorenzinia*(?) *kulczynskii* (Kuźniar). Mordarka, Inoceramian Beds, Senonian or
    Palaeocene (cf. Kuźniar 1911).
 k. *Lorenzinia* aff. *apenninica* Gabelli. Coll. School of Mines, Cracow, unknown locality.
 m. *Lorenzinia apenninica* Gabelli. Poreba Wielka, Inoceramian Beds, Senian.
 n. *Lorenzinia* aff. *apenninica,* possibly intermediate to *Sublorenzinia.* Cieszyn Limestone,
    Berriasian.
 p. *Lorenzinia perlata* ichnosp. nov. Lipnica Mała, Variegated Beds, Paleocene.
 q. *Bassaenia morae* Renz. Limanowa, Inoceramian Beds, Senonian (coll. Miss J. Burtan).
 r. *Bassaenia* aff. *morae.* Lipnica Mała, Variegated Beds, Palaeocene.
 s. *Fascisichnium extendum* Książkiewicz. Lipnica Mała, Variegated Beds, Palaeocene.
 t. *Gyrophyllites kwassicensis* Glocker. Istebna, Upper Istebna Beds, Upper Senonian.
All figures × 0·5.

author (1968) to limit this term to the trails with fairly large ribless central field and aureole of long ribs, variable in length and shape, but always pointed outwards. Some types are provided with a central knob. Sole trail.

Horizon. Tithonian-Berriasian (VF); Valanginian (R); Hauterivian (F).

Ichnogenus GLOCKERIA Książkiewicz 1968

Description. Sole trails with numerous ribs radiating from the centre.

Glockeria glockeri Książkiewicz

Figure 7a

Description. See Książkiewicz 1968 (pl. 5 fig. 4). Ribs numerous, straight, long and pointed outwards, often dichotomous, run from the central field, more or less depressed. Several intercalated ribs. This is the largest rosetted trail in the Carpathian flysch (up to 15 cm).

Horizon. L. Cretaceous (F).

Glockeria sparsicostata Książkiewicz

Figure 7b

Description. See Książkiewicz 1968 (pl. 5 fig. 4). Ribs less numerous with few intercalated. Smaller than the preceding trace.

Horizon. Senonian-Palaeocene (R).

Glockeria parvula ichnosp. nov.

Figure 7c

Description. Comparable to form figured by Książkiewicz (1960 p. 746 pl. 3 fig. 10). Ribs short and regular, nearly equal in length, radiating from a central cone provided with a tiny pit. This very rare form is only provisionally assigned to *Glockeria.*

Horizon. Turonian-Senonian (R); Smaller, but not identical, traces occur also in U. Eocene.

Ichnogenus LORENZINIA Gabelli 1900

Description. Short ribs or knots disposed around a central empty area. Sole trails.

Lorenzinia carpathica (Zuber)

Figure 7g–i

Description. Ribs rounded on both ends. Some types correspond exactly to the figure of Zuber (1910); in others ribs are thicker and more tightly spaced (Fig. 7 g,h; cf. Kuźniar 1911 fig. E; Vassoievitch 1953 pl. 3 fig. b).

Horizon. Senonian (R); Palaeocene (R but in some layers occurs gregariously).

Lorenzinia apenninica Gabelli

Figure 7m

Description. Nail-like ribs, sharp at outer end. Ribs less regular in shape than in the figure of Gabelli (1920), more resembling the figure of Desio (1923 pl. 1). In some specimens ribs begin with a knob, seen also sometimes at the outer end (Fig. 7k). There are also forms with few ribs (Fig. 7n).

Horizon. Senonian (R). Related, but not identical, forms occur in L. Cretaceous.

Lorenzinia perlata ichnosp. nov.

Figure 7p

Description. Circular or elliptical ring of small knobs, *c.* 20 in number; diameter of the ring 1·5-2 cm. The specimen of Nowak (1956 pl. 18 fig. M, upper corner refigured by Grubić 1961 fig. 3) may also belong to this species.

Horizon. Palaeocene (R).

Lorenzinia(?) kulczynskii Kuźniar

Figure 7j

Description. See Kuźniar 1911 (p. 524, fig. F). Rays connected on the inner side. Possibly this form should be separated from *Lorenzinia.*

Horizon. Senonian (?).

Ichnogenus BASSAENIA Renz 1925

Bassaenia morae Renz

Figure 7q

Description. Inner circle composed of round knobs. Diameter of the circle *c.* 4 cm.

Horizon. Senonian (VR).

There are specimens of a larger form, in which the inner circle consists of double knobs (Fig. 7r) which occurs in Palaeocene beds on the same sole together with *Lorenzinia carpathica.*

Ichnogenus SUBLORENZINIA Książkiewicz 1968

Description. Sole trail similar to *Lorenzinia,* but with larger knobs, irregular in shape and arrangement.

Sublorenzinia plana Książkiewicz

Figure 7e, f

Description. Knobs variable in shape, round or elongated, irregularly spaced. Diameter of the rosette 3-6 cm. Traces cut by flutes or dragmarks. See Książkiewicz 1968 (p. 10, 15, pl. 5 figs. 1-2).

Horizon. Cenomanian-Turonian (R).

Ichnogenus FASCISICHNIUM Książkiewicz 1968

Description. Ribs arranged in bundles.

Fascisichnium extendum Książkiewicz

Figure 7s

Description. Large semi-rosetted trail, ribs long and pointed outward. See Książkiewicz 1968 (p. 10, 16, pl. 6 fig. 1).

Horizon. Senonian (R); Palaeocene (R).

V

Ichnogenus GYROPHYLLITES Glocker 1841
Gyrophyllites kwassicensis Glocker

Figure 7t

Description. Rosetted trail occurring in the upper silty part of sandy layers.

Horizon. Senonian* (F). Generally absent, but in some layers gregriously covers top surfaces.

IX. SPREITEN TRACES

Ichnogenus ZOOPHYCOS Massalongo 1855

Description. First described from the Carpathian flysch by W. Kuźniar (1911) under the name of *Spirophyton.* Very abundant, it has a great variety in shape, and in size is up to 1 m in diameter. Two groups may be distinguished: one with a cylindrical marginal string, and the other without it. No attempt has yet been made to identify the Carpathian specimens with the numerous species so far described.

Horizon. Tithonian (R); Berriasian (VR); Cenomanian-Turonian (VF); Senonian (F); Senonian* (VR); Palaeocene (R); L. Eocene (VR); M. Eocene (R); U. Eocene (VF); Oligocene (?). The forms occurring in younger bed as a rule are provided with the marginal rim.

Ichnogenus PHYCOSIPHON Fischer-Ooster 1858

Description. Tiny loops enclosing transversely striated areas, often branched. Occur on upper surfaces of sandy layers.

Horizon. Berriasian (R); Palaeocene (VR, but gregarious in some layers).

Ichnogenus RHIZOCORALLIUM Zenker 1836

Description. Two more or less parallel tubes filled with silt, between them 8-10 mm wide zone, feebly convex, transversely striated. Striation bent in one direction. The trace, straight or feebly bent, is parallel to bedding. So far no U-shaped termination, characteristic for *Rhizocorallium,* has been found and the reference to this genus is not certain. *Rhizocorallium* is recorded from flysch sediments (Papp 1962).

Horizon. L. Senonian (R); L. Eocene (VR); M. Eocene (R).

Ichnogenus CYLINDRICHNUS Howard 1966

Description. Howard (1966), following H. Toots (unpublished thesis) uses this name for vertical cylindrical funnel-shaped burrows consisting of concentric layers. The form described by Howard is small, 1-2 cm in diameter and 8 cm in height. A similar, but a much larger trace was described by the present writer (1958 p. 61 fig. 3) 1 m high and 25 cm wide at the upper end of the funnel (Fig. 8).

Horizon. U. Eocene (VR).

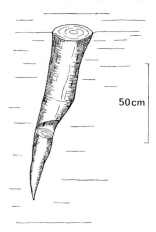

50cm

Fig. 8. *Cylindrichnus*. Grzechynia, Magura Sandstone, Upper Eocene.

3. Ecology

The nature of the trace, and the relationship between the trace and sedimentary structures, may give hints as to where the trace-making form lived and whether the trace is pre- or post-depositional.

A *post-depositional* origin is indicated by the following features:

a. Position of the trace within the sedimentary unit; traces occurring inside sandy layers or within shales are evidently post-depositional in relation to the sediment in which they occur.

b. Filling of the trace with material in such a way, that the trace is sharply separated on all sides from the enclosing sediment. Tubiform cylindrical trails on soles and inside sediments belong here, as well as tubiform trails attached to the sole or the top surface.

c. Intersection of sedimentary structures formed during the deposition of sediment (flutes, drag marks, current lineation etc) by the trace (Pl. 3i, also Książkiewicz 1968 pl. 4).

d. Intersection of a proven post-depositional trail by the trace (e.g. Pl. 4q).

e. Limitation to very thin sandy layers may also be taken into account as an indirect indicator.

Evidence for post-depositional origin has been found for the following traces (letters point to indicators found for the given trace, while the maximum thickness of layers with sole trails is given in cm):

Arthrophycus **b** 6
Belorhaphe **c, d** 25
Chondrites **a**
Cylindrichnus **a**
Fucusopsis **b** 5
Granularia **a, b, c** 18 for sole trails, up to 1·2 m for internal trails
Gyrochorte and aff. traces **a** 4
Gyrophyllites **a**

Halymenidium **a, b** 5
Helicorhaphe **a, b** 3
Helicolithus **c** 5
Helminthoida labyrinthica and related forms **a**
Helminthopsis tenuis, granulata **b, c** 15
Lophoctenium **a** 5
Megagrapton **b** 4
Paleodictyon **b, d** 6
Paleomeandron, probably all forms **b,** 4 for small forms, 5 for large forms
Phycosiphon **a**
Protopaleodictyon **c** 6
Rhabdoglyphus **b, c** 3
Rhizocorallium? **a**
Scolicia **a**
Subphyllochorda **b** 4
Strobilorhaphe **a, b** 3
Taphrhelminthopsis (very rare cases) **a**
Urohelminthoida **c** 3
Zoophycos **a**

A *pre-depositional* origin is indicated by such features as:

a. Dissection of the trace by current structures (flutes, drag marks) e.g. Pl. 3b. The value of this indicator must, however, be treated with caution, for it is possible that burrowing organisms constructing their traces below sandy layers could avoid irregularities of the interface, and either by-pass them or tunnel above (in sand) or below (in clay) any protrusion of the sole.

b. Filling of the trace with obliquely stratified sediment.

c. Filling with coarse grains and abundant mica. This may indicate that the pre-existing furrows cut by the trace-making organism acted as traps for the transported material. This indicator also has a limited value because some, surely post-depositional, traces (e.g. *Granularia*) are often filled with grains coarser than that occurring in the neighbouring parts of the sole. Probably, these organisms, when reworking the sand, could enrich it in coarser grains and mica flakes.

d. Filling of pre-existing furrows with organic material (detritus of Polyzoa, foraminiferal tests, Pl. 3d).

e. Occurrence at the base of very thick sandstone layers.

Based on these indicators the following traces may be regarded as pre-depositional:

Acanthorhaphe **a, c** 3
Cosmorhaphe (evidence only for *C. fuchsi*) **a** 5
Glockeria parvula **a** 4
Helminthoida aff. *labyrinthica* (no evidence, but the resemblance to the typical form suggests that the sole trail may be the fill of a pre-existing furrow)
Spirophycus **b, c, d** 10
Spirorhaphe **a** 120
Sublorenzinia **a**
Taphrhelminthopsis **b, c** 100 **c**

No evidence has been found for *Helminthoida crassa, Lorenzinia, Bassaenia, Fascisichnium, Glockeria, Asterichnus, Squamodictyon, Palaeochorda, Palaeophycus.* All these traces occur on the soles of very thin-bedded sandstones or siltstones. For *Paleodictyon* the evidence is conflicting, and the question whether it is pre- or post-depositional is still open to argument.

From the above given tabulations it is clear that post-depositional traces are much more numerous. This statement is further emphasised if one takes into consideration the fact that, within the post-depositional group, there are forms which usually occur in great numbers (*Chondrites, Granularia, Halymenidium, Scolicia, Subphyllochorda, Strobilorhaphe, Zoophycos*). The pre-depositional group is represented by a much smaller number of species, of which only *Spirophycus* and *Taphrhelminthopsis* occur in profusion.

The trace-making organisms may be divided into five groups on the basis of their site of activity.

(i) The most numerous group is represented by the species mining at the clay/ sand interface. Their traces occur on the lower surfaces of sandy layers. Some of them reworked sand and formed cylindrical tubes (*Arthrophycus, Granularia, Halymenidium,* most of *Helminthopsis, Megagrapton, Paleomeandron, Rhabdoglyphus, Subphyllochorda, Strobilorhaphe,* others tunnelled below sand and the sandy casts of the tunnels they made were formed by collapse of the roof of the tunnels (*Belorhaphe, Lophoctenium, Protopaleodictyon?, Urohelminthoida?*). Most of the organisms of this group must have been psammophagous.

(ii) Forms mining across sandy layers are on the whole scarce (certain *Granularia, Halymenidium, Cylindrichnus, Zoophycos*). Therefore, bioturbation in flysch deposits is only slight.

(iii) A large group is represented by the forms burrowing near the sand/clay junction. This is also a psammophagous group, but with predilection for silty material (*Scolicia,* some *Gyrochorte, Gyrophyllites, Phycosiphon, ?Rhizocorallium,* some *Taphrhelminthopsis*).

(iv) Pelophagous organisms burrowing inside clays or marly oozes. To this group belong some *Spirorhaphe* (*S. minuta*), *Helminthoida labyrinthica, ?Rhizocorallium, Chondrites.*

(v) Forms living on the bottom. This group may include all pre-depositional traces such as *Spirophycus, Taphrhelminthopsis, Spirorhaphe, Cosmorhaphe* and nearly all rosetted trails. Theoretically, following the hypothesis of Seilacher (1962), it may be thought that these traces belong to groups (iii)-(iv), and represent organisms living in clays, whose burrows, filled with faecal pellets, were stripped off by currents, washed and filled with sandy sediment. However, sole traces of this group have no counterparts in the pelofauna. Neither *Cosmorhaphe, Spirophycus, Spirorhaphe,* or rosetted forms, corresponding with *Glockeria* or *Lorenzinia,* have been found in shales. On the other hand, pelophagous forms, such as *Gyrophyllites, Chondrites, Spirorhaphe minuta, Helminthoida labyrinthica* have no counterparts among sole traces. Naturally, one may presume that compaction could obliterate these traces, but *Helminthoida labyrinthica* is perfectly preserved, and, although in some sections it is abundant in shales, intercalated sandy layers exhibit no traces of this form (actually a trace resembling *H. labyrinthica* is known as sole trail in a single specimen, but it is not identical with the form occurring in the shales).

4. Ichnofauna and lithofacies

The Carpathian flysch sequence is very thick (6,000 m) and both vertically and laterally differentiated, consequently the relationship between the ichnofauna and the lithologic development may be studied to good advantage. Generally, those flysch beds which consist of coarse-grained, thick-bedded sandstones and shales are poor in trace fossils. Similarly with thick intercalations of shales and marls. The richest ichnofauna is developed in sequences of alternating thin-bedded and fine-grained sandstones or siltstones, provided the shaly interbeds are not too thick.

The following main factors seem to be controlling the development of the ichnofauna:

Thickness of individual sandy layers. If the layers are above 20 cm thick, all psammophagous forms of the first group are absent, only second group may be represented. The sole assemblages consist of representatives of the fourth group (*Taphrhelminthopsis, Spirorhaphe, Spirophycus*), on the whole few and poorly preserved. If sandy layers are not too coarse, *Zoophycos* and the traces of the third group may be developed.

Grain-coarseness. The more fine-grained are sandy interbeds, the richer is the ichnofauna. This factor acts together with the first factor, as thick layers are usually coarser. If beds are fine-grained but thick-bedded, trace fossils are uncommon. When they are fine-grained and thin-bedded at the same time, the ichnofauna may be abundant.

Character of the sole. If the soles of sandy intercalations are covered with numerous flute casts and other current structures, post-depositional traces of the first group are scarce. Presumably the uneven junction clay/sand presented obstacles to their burrowing activities. *Granularia*, often tunnelling across flutes, is a notable exception. On the other hand, dense fluting destroyed pre-depositional trails.

Aeration of the bottom. This is shown to a certain extent by the colour of the sediments. In light-coloured (green, red, light-grey, blue) beds the ichnofauna is much richer, both in terms of number of species and individuals as compared with dark beds (black, dark-grey) in which the ichnofauna, if present, consists only of few forms, although these may be numerously represented. Poor aeration conditions of these beds are also indicated by impoverished benthonic foraminiferal assemblages.

For instance a member particularly rich in trace fossils in the Carpathian flysch is the Lower Eocene Beloveza Beds. Here all four factors discussed are favourable: sandy layers are thin (5-10 cm), intervening shales of the same thickness, grain size approaching silt grades, soles generally smooth, colours light. More than 25 ichnogenera with 44 species are known from these beds. The Middle Eocene Hieroglyphic Beds, similar in stratonomy, contain a much poorer assemblage of trace fossils. They are slightly darker and the flutes are abundant. The thin-bedded, dark, Albian Lgota Beds contain few trace fossils, but the upper surfaces of many sandstones are densely covered with *Scolicia*. The poorest member is represented by the Senonian-Palaeocene Istebna Beds, composed of coarse sandstones and dark shales. The ichnofauna is absent, excepting for some *Granularia*, few *Spirophycus* and *Gyrophyllites*.

5. Vertical distribution

As the information about the Carpathian ichnofauna is still limited and much work remains to be done in this field, it is certainly too early to present a final opinion on the stratigraphic value of trace fossils in the area.

The composition of the ichnofauna depends on many factors, and it is difficult to evaluate which changes in its vertical distribution are caused by changes in lithology and environmental conditions, and which are due to evolutionary trends of the trace-making organisms. Nevertheless several forms have a limited vertical distribution and may have a certain stratigraphic value. The possibility of using trace

Table 1. Vertical distribution of some trace fossils in the Carpathian flysch.

Ichnospecies	Tithonian	L. Cretaceous	Albian	U. Cretaceous	Palaeocene	L. Eocene	M. Eocene	U. Eocene	Oligocene
Asterichnus nowaki		×							
Bassaenia morae				×	×				
Belorhaphe fabregae						×	×		
Belorhaphe zickzack		×				×			
Cosmorhaphe sinuosa						×			
Cosmorhaphe helminthopsidea				×	×	×			
Cosmorhaphe fuchsi						×	×		
Fascisichnium extendum						×			
Fucusopsis angulata				×					
Fucusopsis annulata						×			
Glockeria glockeri		×							
Glockeria sparsicostata				×	×				
Glockeria parvula				×					
Gyrophyllites kwassicensis				×					
Halymenidium oraviense		×				×			
Helicolithus sampelayoi						×	×	×	
Helminthoida crassa type				×					
Helminthoida labyrinthica type				×	×				
Helminthoida labyrinthica (lata)				×					
Helminthoida(?) molassica									×
Helminthopsis tenuis		×				×			
Helminthopsis granulata		×							
Lophoctenium ramosum					×	×			
Lorenzinia div. sp.				×	×				
Megagrapton tenue		×							
Megagrapton irregulare						×			
Palaeochorda submontana						×			
Paleodictyon minutissimum						×			
Paleodictyon minimum						×	×	×	×
Paleodictyon latum					×	×			
Paleodictyon intermedium				×			×		
Paleodictyon strozzi				×	×	×	×		
Paleodictyon tellini		×		×					
Paleodictyon miocenicum		×		×	×	×			
Paleodictyon carpathicum		?				×	×	×	
Paleodictyon majus						×			
Paleomeandron elegans				×	×				
Paleomeandron rude						×	×		
Paleomeandron robustum						×			
Protopaleodictyon incompositum						×	×	×	
Rhabdoglyphus grossheimi				×					
Scolicia prisca					?	×	×		
Scolicia plana			×	×	×				
Spirophycus div. sp.				×	×	×	×	×	
Spirorhaphe div. sp.				×	×	×		×	
Strobilorhaphe clavata						×	×		
Strobilorhaphe pusilla						×			
Sublorenzinia plana				×					
Subphyllochorda granulata					×	×	×		
Subphyllochorda striata						×			
Subphyllochorda laevis			×						
Taphrhelminthopsis ex gr. recta		×	×	×	×	×	×	×	×
Taphrhelminthopsis ex gr. auricularis		×	×	×		×	×	×	
Taphrhelminthopsis convoluta		×				×	×	×	
Taphrhelminthopsis plana						×			
Urohelminthoida dertonensis					×	×			
Urohelminthoida aff. appendiculata				×	×	×			
Zoophycos div. sp.	×	×		×	×	×	×	×	

fossils for stratigraphy and correlation was discussed by Häntzschel (1962), Vialov (1966) and Crimes (1968).

The following forms have a limited vertical range (Table 1):

Asterichnus, Glockeria glockeri are limited to the lowest Cretaceous.

Lorenzinia to Upper Senonian and Palaeocene.

Gyrophyllites kwassicensis occurs only in the Upper Senonian.

Taphrhelminthopsis plana occurs only in the Lower Eocene, while *T. convoluta* seems to have a rather wider range.

Fucusopsis angulata occurs only in the Senonian. This form is recorded only from the Senonian of various areas (Vassoievitch 1932; Birkenmajer 1959; Vialov 1966). In the Lower Eocene it is replaced by similar *F. annulata*.

Rhabdoglyphus grossheimi in the shape figured by Vassoievitch (1951) from the Caucasian Cenomanian, also occurs in the Carpathians in beds of similar age (Cenomanian-Turonian).

Helminthoida labyrinthica occurs in the Senonian and the Palaeocene, var. *lata* being limited to the Senonian. *H. crassa* in its typical form occurs only in the Senonian.

Scolicia plana occurs in beds of Albian-Senonian age, replaced in younger beds by *S. prisca*.

6. Ichnofaunal assemblages

There are four groups of associations of trace fossils in the Carpathian flysch.

(i) Assemblages composed of abundant *Zoophycos, Granularia*, non-meandering *Taphrhelminthopsis* and a few rosetted forms, Meandering trails and *Paleodictyon* are absent, and in patterned trails only *Spirorhaphe* is represented and then rarely. These assemblages occur in the coarse flysch facies, e.g. Upper Eocene Magura Sandstone. If the beds are very coarse, as the Upper Senonian-Palaeocene Istebna Beds or Lower Eocene Ciężkowice Sandstone, only *Granularia* is present.

(ii) Assemblages containing *Zoophycos*, freely winding trails (*Taphrhelminthopsis, Scolicia, Subphyllochorda*), *Granularia*, some *Paleodictyon* and meandering trails, and fairly common rosetted traces. Such assemblages are characteristic of the Tithonian-Berriasian Cieszyn Limestone (detrital limestones, graded and alternating with shales), for the lower part of the Godula Beds (Cenomanian-Turonian) and the Senonian-Palaeocene "Inoceramian Beds". This association is connected with the flysch consisting of medium- and fine-bedded sandstones.

(iii) Assemblages consisting of abundant meandering trails (*Cosmorhaphe, Helminthoida*, meandering *Taphrhelminthopsis*) and *Paleodictyon* in addition to numerous winding forms (*Taphrhelminthopsis, Scolicia, Subphyllochorda*) and ubiquitous *Granularia*. *Zoophycos* is extremely rare and rosetted forms absent. These assemblages are characteristic of the thin-bedded flysch (Lower Eocene Beloveza Beds, Lower Senonian flysch of the Pieniny Klippen belt, Middle Eocene Hieroglyphic Beds).

As several factors control the composition of an ichnocoenosis, it is difficult to draw conclusions from the differences in the ichnofaunal associations. Beside the composition of beds and bottom conditions, depth of water and distance from the shore should also be taken into consideration. The first association is connected with thick-bedded, coarse flysch. It is believed that the coarse flysch is a proximal deposit, laid down in a more shallow water than the other flysch facies. If this be true, the first assemblage may be indicative of shallow water regions, the third—of deeper parts of the bottom, whilst the second points to intermediate depth. Such an inference would to a certain extent be in agreement with the view of Seilacher (1967), according to whom the abundance of *Zoophycos* indicates shallower water as compared with assemblages consisting of patterned burrows. The presence of numerous rosetted trails possibly points to intermediate depths. However, within this group *Lorenzinia* may represent a trace due to an organism living at a greater depth than other rosetted trail makers, because it occurs in sandy inter-beds of red shales (Variegated Beds) in which intercalations with *Cosmorhaphe* also occur.

References

ANDREWS, H. N. 1955. Index of generic names of fossil plants, 1820-1950. *Bull. U.S. geol. Surv.* **1013.**

AZPEITIA MOROS, F. 1933. Datos para el estudio paleontologico del Flysch de la costa cantabrica y de algunos otros puntos de Espana. *Boln Inst. geol. min.* **53,** 1.

BIRKENMAJER, K. 1959. *Fucusopsis angulata* Palibin (Problematica) from the variegated beds (Danian-Paleocene) of the Pieniny Klippen-Belt Mantle (Central Carpathians). *Annls Soc. géol. Pol.* **39,** 227. (In Polish, English summary.)

BOUČEK, B. and ELIAS, M. 1962. Ueber eine interessante Lebensspuren aus dem Palaogen der Tscheckoslovakischen Flysch-Karpathen. *Geol. Pr. Bratisl.* **25/26,** 145. (In Czech., German summary.)

CRIMES, T. P. 1968. *Cruziana:* a stratigraphically useful trace fossil. *Geol. Mag.* **105,** 360.

DESIO, A. 1923. Sopra una Lorenzinia del Flysch nei dintorni di Firenze. *Riv. ital. Palaeont. Stratigr.* **29,** 7.

DŻUŁYŃSKI, S. and SANDERS, J. E. 1962. Current marking on firm mud bottoms. *Trans. Conn. Acad. Arts Sci.* **42,** 57.

FUCHS, T. 1895. Studien über Fucoiden und Hieroglyphen. *Denkschr. Akad. Wiss. Wien Math.-nat. Kl.* **62,** 1.

GLOCKER, E. F. 1841. Ueber die kalkfuhrende Sandsteinformationen auf beiden Seiten der mittleren March, in der Gegend zwischen Kwassitz und Kremsier. *Nova Acta Acad. Leop.-Carol.* **22,** 309.

GOMEZ DE LLARENA, J. 1946. Revision de algunos datos paleontologicos del Flysch Cretaceo y Numulitico de Guipuzcoa. *Notas Comun. Inst. geol. min. Esp.* **15,** 113.

——1954. Observaciones geologicas en el Flysch cretacico-numulitico de Guipuzcoa. I. *Monografias Inst. "Lucas Mallada" Invest. Geol.* **13,** 5.

—— 1956. Observaciones geologicos en el Flysch cretacico-numulitico de Guipuzcoa. II. *Monografias Inst. "Lucas Mallada" Invest. Geol.* **15,** 1.

GORTANI, M. 1920. Osservazioni sulle impronte medusoidi del Flysch (Lorenzinia e Atollites). *Riv. ital. Palaeont. Stratigr.* **26,** 56.

GÖTZINGER, G. and BECKER, H. 1932. Zur geologischen Gliederung des Wienerwaldflysches. *Jb. geol. Bundesanst. Wien* **82,** 343.

—— and —— 1934. Neue Fährenstudien im ostalpinen Flysch. *Senckenbergiana* **16,** 77.

GRUBIĆ, A. Lorenziniae from Eocene Flysch of Montenegro. *Sedimentologija* **1,** 51. (In Serbian, English summary.)

HÄNTZSCHEL, W. 1962. Trace fossils and problematica. In *Treatise on invertebrate paleontology* (Ed. R. C. Moore). Geol. Soc. Am., New York and Kansas Univ. Press, Lawrence. Part W, p. 177W.

—— 1965. *Vestigia invertebratorum et problematica. (Fossilium Catalogus. I. Animalia,* pars 108.) Junk, 's-Gravenhage.

HEER, O. 1877. *Die vorweltliche Flora der Schweiz.* Frauenfeld, Zurich.

HOWARD, J. D. 1966. Characteristic trace fossils in Upper Cretaceous sandstones of the Book Cliffs and Wasatch Plateau. In *Central Utah coals. Bull. Utah geol. miner, Surv.* **80.**

KINDELAN, D. V. 1919. Nota sobre el Cretaceo y el Eocene de Guizpuzcoa. *Boln Inst. geol. min. Esp.* **20,** 163.

KSIĄŻKIEWICZ, M. 1958. Stratigraphy of the Magura Series in the Sredni Beskid (Carpathians). *Biul. Inst. Geol.* **135,** 43. (In Polish, English summary.)

—— 1960. On some problematic organic traces from the flysch of the Polish Carpathians. I. *Kwart. geol.* **4,** 735. (In Polish, English summary.)

—— 1961. On some problematic organic traces from the flysch of the Polish Carpathians. II. *Kwart. geol.* **5,** 882. (In Polish, English summary.)

—— 1968. On some problematic organic traces from the flysch of the Polish Carpathians. III. *Annls Soc. géol. Pol.* **38,** 3. (In Polish, English summary.)

KUŹNIAR, W. 1911. Sur quelques fossiles problématiques du flysch des Carpathes. *Kosmos Warsz.* **36,** 317. (In Polish, English summary.)

LESSERTISSEUR, J. 1955. Traces fossiles d'activité animale et leur signification paléobiologique. *Mém. Soc. géol. Fr.* **34,** n.s. **74,** 1.

Matyasovszky, J. 1878. Glenodictyum carpaticum Maty. *Természetr. Fuz.* p. 262.

Nowak, W. 1956. Quelques hiéroglyphes étoilés des Karpates de Flysch extérieures. *Annls Soc. geol. Pol.* **26**, 187. (In Polish, French summary.)

—— 1959. Palaeodictyum in the Flysch Carpathians. *Kwart. geol.* **3**, 103. (In Polish, English summary.)

—— 1961. Z badań nad hieroglifami fliszu karpackiego. *Spraw. Pos. Kom. Odd. PAN Kraków* (*Rep. geol. Comm. Pol. Acad. Sci.*) p. 226.

Papp, A. 1962. Das Vorkommen von Lebensspuren in einzelnen Schichtgliedern im Flysch des Wienerwaldes. *Verh. geol. Bundesanst. Wien* **2**, 290.

Paul, K. M. 1898. Der Wienerwald. *Jb. geol. Reichsanst. Wien.* **2**, 290.

Peruzzi, D. G. 1880. Osservazioni sui generi Paleodictyon e Paleomeandron dei terrani cretacei ed eocenici dell Appennino sett. e centrale. *Memorie Soc. tosc. Sci. nat. Pisa* **5**, 1.

Quatrefages de A. 1849. Note sur la Scolicia prisca (A. de Q.) Annelide fossile de la Craie. *Annls Sci. nat., sér. Zool.* **12**, 265.

Renz, C. 1925. Problematische Medusenabdrucke aus der Olonos-Pindoszone des Westpeloponnnes. *Verh. naturf. Ges. Basel* **36**, 220.

Sacco, F. 1888. Note di Paleoichnologia italiana. *Atti Soc. ital. Sci. nat.* **31**, 151.

Schafhäutl, K. E. 1851. *Geognostiche Untersuchungen des Sudbayrischen Alpengebirges.* Munich.

Seilacher, A. 1954. Die geologische Bedeutung fossiler Lebensspuren. *Z. dt. geol. Ges.* **105**, 214.

—— 1962. Palaeontological studies on turbidite sedimentation and erosion. *J. Geol.* **70**, 227.

—— 1967. Bathymetry of trace fossils. *Mar. Geol.* **5**, 411.

Simpson, F. 1967. Some morphological variants of Palaeodictyon. *Annls Soc. géol. Pol.* **37**, 509.

Vassoievitch, N. B. 1932. Some data allowing us to distinguish the overturned position of flysch sedimentary formations from the normal ones. *Trudy geol. Inst. Akad. Nauk SSSR* **2**, 47. (In Russian, English summary.)

—— 1951. *Uslowia obrazowania flisza.*

—— 1953. O niekotorych fliszewych teksturach (znazkach). *Trudy lvov. geol. Obshch.* **3**, 17.

Vialov, O. S. 1966. *Sledy zhiznedeyatelnosti organizmow i ikh paleontologicheskoe znachenie.* Akad. Nauk SSSR Kiev.

—— and Golev, B. T. 1960. K sistematike Paleodictyon. *Dokl. Akad. Nauk SSSR* **134**, 175.

—— and —— 1964. Paleodictyon Krima. *Izv. vyssh. ucheb. Zaved. Geologia i Razwiedka* **3**, 24.

—— and —— 1965. O drobnom podrazdeleni gruppy Paleodictyonidae. *Byull. mosk. Obsch. Ispyt. Prir. otdel geol.* **40**, 93.

Wood, A. and Smith, A. J. 1959. The sedimentation and sedimentary history of the Aberystwyth Grits (Upper Llandoverian). *Q. J. geol. Soc. Lond.* **114**, 163.

Zuber, R. 1910. Eine fossile Meduse aus dem Kreideflysch der ostgalizischen Karpathen. *Verh. geol. Reichsanst. Wien* p. 57.

M. Książkiewicz, Jagellonian University, Department of Geology, Cracow, Orleandry 2 A, Poland.

Toponomy of trace fossils

Anders Martinsson

Toponomy is the basic approach to the study of trace fossils. Not only palaeobiologists but also a very wide range of specialists in organic sedimentology, as well as field geologists, frequently need to record and describe fossils from a toponomic aspect. Palaeobiologists, too, are often incapable of a genetic interpretation of trace fossils. Comparatively seldom do they have a satisfactory basis for applying a nomenclature of the type used in biosystematics. Hence, there is a need for a toponomic nomenclature which does not require a genetic or functional interpretation or a systematic determination. This would also have didactic advantages.

With rare exceptions, if any (depending on definition), trace fossils are interface phenomena in sediments. By far the most common preservation is the casting of the traces along the interfaces between a coarser-grained bed and underlying or overlying finer-grained material. If terminology is based on the preserving medium, only four terms are needed for a basic toponomic classification, viz. *hypichnia, epichnia, endichnia,* and *exichnia* (and derivatives). In combination with commonplace vocabulary or well-known sedimentological or morphological terms they can be used for the detailed description of any trace fossil with terminological brevity but without a burden of specific terms.

1. The definition of "trace fossils"

"Trace fossils are structures in sediments, caused by animal activity."

To many palaeoichnologists this might seem to be a simple and adequate definition. However, it contains a number of restrictions, mainly connected with the words "sediment", "animal", and "activity", which all palaeoichnologists would probably not agree about. In the *Treatise on Invertebrate Paleontology* Häntzschel (1962) makes reference to one definition of "*Lebensspur*" and one of "trace fossil". The former one, by Haas (1954) and Seilacher (1955), excludes both "animal" and "activity" but mentions "living organisms". The latter, by Simpson (1957), considerably restricts the definition by requiring the animal to have moved on or in the sediment at the time of its accumulation. In the French term *trace d'activité* (Lessertisseur 1955), activity is implicit.

Simpson's addition to the definition excludes such important palaeoecological indicators as bivalve or echinoid borings in consolidated sediments. There is a general tendency to exclude borings from the concept of trace fossils. This is hardly motivated by their mode of origin, particularly since their delimitation from burrows is not very distinct. When not associated with a consolidated surface in a sediment, they commonly penetrate major sedimentary particles, such as shells and carbonate pebbles. On the other hand, algal borings are not much different in origin from borings made by the etching activity of animals, and there are fossil borings which are not associated with sediments at all, such as pholadid borings in submerged turf.

Even the word "structure" causes unnecessary restrictions of the concept of trace fossils. The trace fossil may consist of a distinctive textural pattern, or a stain pattern which does not appreciably change even the texture of the rock.

The great advantage of the ichnocoenosis in comparison with other fossil coenoses is that it reflects organisms which actually lived at the thanatotope. Hence, it would be of methodological interest to include all preserved evidence of such activity: "Trace fossils are structures, texture patterns, or stain patterns in sediments, caused by the action of living organisms." Unfortunately the evidence is not complete enough to tell us whether the environment reflected by the trace fossil was the ideal or normal one for the originator of the trace. Very frequently even the most ideally preserved trace fossils mark the trail to death in a foreign environment. There is a good and quite recent extreme example to illustrate the fallibility of trace fossils as palaeoecological indicators: man's tracks on the lunar surface do not reflect a very normal human coenosis.

It is very difficult, then, to find a brief and yet adequate definition of trace fossil— even in the latter definition above the word "sediment" was retained. For the special purposes of this paper the discussion will be based on a looser definition, in which the exceptions are obvious but rare enough to be unimportant:

"Trace fossils are mostly interface phenomena in sediments, caused by animal activity."

2. Approaches to trace fossils

Trace fossils have been spontaneously treated systematically and taxionomically like other fossils. It has seldom been clearly realized by the ichnosystematists that what is really classified are the traces of sundry functions of the same or very different animals. It is not very natural to other branches of biosystematics that a number of functions of the same animal should be attributed to different genera or paragenera and that the same function in animals of different families or higher units should be included in the same species or paraspecies.

Biosystematics and taxionomy are scientific tools, much neglected and under-estimated in the ecology of body fossils. A tool corresponds to a need. Palaeoichnology would indeed be refined if the originator of each series of trails could be determined as to species, following which normal biosystematic nomenclature would be available. Only very exceptionally have trace fossils been determined in this way. It would be realistic to disregard biosystematics as a tool for refined palaeosynecology which will have to concentrate on more generalized problems, such as the recognition of facies bodies of different magnitude, etc.

The tool needed is a terminology rather than names. The units needed are generally fairly close to the paragenera as hitherto applied in palaeoichnology. It would be wise to apply them in a vernacular construction when the form of the name allows this, as for example a vermiglyph, a spiroraph, a chondrite (!), a halopoan, a cruziana, a dimorphichnian, or a rusophycus (but not with the vernacular family ending -id!). These names already largely designate ecological groupings, without, however, interpreting the function which have caused their origin. Such terms could be formed directly, without a formal generic diagnosis and a designation of a type species, and they might to some extent be used according to convenience instead of according to priority.

In the first part of his "Studies on Palaeoichnology" Seilacher (1953) made a clear distinction between three kinds of interpretations of trace fossils, based on *taxionomy* (in the strict sense, not the paratataxionomy applied as discussed above), *ecology,* and *stratonomy,* respectively.

The importance of the last-mentioned "interpretation" is often overlooked. It includes the basic approach to the description and definition of trace fossils. The need of a clear and simple international terminology for this purpose is the main subject of this paper.

Since this approach does not essentially deal with the "science of strata" ("stratonomy" is an old synonym of "stratigraphy") but with the position of a trace fossil in relation to a certain bed, it is preferable to talk about the *toponomy* of trace fossils.

Even if it is the ecological (and very occasionally the taxionomical) interpretation which is the purpose of palaeoichnological studies, a descriptive terminology is badly needed which is non-interpretative with respect to the ecological functions of the originator of a particular trace fossil. It is often difficult to tell without profound biological knowledge or protracted analysis whether a trace fossil is a repichnion or a pascichnion, or in another case a domichnion or a fodinichnion according to Seilacher's (1953) widely applied ecological terminology. Many of the observations on trace fossils are made by students of inorganic sedimentary structures with little or no background in palaeontology, or by field geologists. A lack of understanding of the importance of trace fossils, and of a simple terminology for describing them, has often resulted in a complete omission of important ichnological evidence or a cursory remark on "worm trails" in geological as well as palaeontological papers.

A terminology for such descriptive purposes was presented by Martinsson (1965) in a paper of local character and in a very brief form. When this paper was in the press, another important reconsideration of the problem appeared, worked out by Seilacher (1964) for the Committee for the Nomenclature of Sedimentary Structures; this made the publication of Martinsson's terminology less timely. Since it has, nevertheless, received wide attention (and has been re-lettered in the supplement to Part W of the *Treatise* in a way which makes it less easy to understand), I feel motivated to present it internationally in a more exhaustive manner. It should be stressed that the approach presented here is on the lines of the Committee and emphasizes the tripartite treatment of trace fossils outlined by Seilacher in 1953 and 1964.

3. Terminology based on the main casting medium

This terminological system fulfils the following requirements: (i) It is based on the main "casting" medium, i.e. the more resistant substance in which the trace fossil is preserved when found in a stratigraphical sequence; (ii) hence the fossil is strictly regarded as an interface phenomenon; (iii) the number of specific terms for the description of these toponomic relationships is reduced to a minimum, are self-explanatory and mnemotechnically attractive if the two preceding requirements are borne in mind, and gives all essential data on the gross morphology of the trace fossil if combined with terms well known from general sedimentology or common-place vocabulary.

The influx of a coarser medium—silt or sand—into a muddy thanatotope results in the instantaneous casting of the trace found on the mud surface. Genetically, of course, an intercalating layer of mud also casts the traces provided in the under-lying harder surface. But as the ichnologist *recovers* the trace fossils along the more firmly consolidated bed (with extremely few exceptions the coarser-grained bed) there is no question that this bed is to be regarded as the main casting medium in a softer "matrix" substance.

Sedimentologists use the word "cast" in a way that is different from the usage in the metal industry. The two sides of a slab with trace fossils are of course each others opposite in genesis. When it is regarded as the "main casting medium" in the sequence, it takes the role of the lead soldier in its mould—the mould corresponding to the soft components in the sequence.

The interface relationships of the casting medium and the softer matrix may be very complicated. Animals work themselves down through the accumulating casting substance into the soft mud below or, more rarely, from the mud into the unconsolidated coarser substance. This mostly concerns comparatively large forms. A large proportion of the smaller animals are strictly adjusted either to the mud or the silty-sandy sediment and cause only textural phenomena in contrast to the structural phenomena just referred to. There are boundary cases between these categories, such as disturbance of lamination within the casting medium or the matrix. Those cases where the interface aspect has to be carried *in absurdum* ('no interfaces—no trace fossils") are of no practical importance. The extremes are different types of bioturbation and indistinct stain patterns.

Trace fossils in firm primary contact with the lower surface of the main casting medium are termed *hypichnia* and the corresponding structures on the upper surface are termed *epichnia*. Trace fossils within the casting medium are called *endichnia,* and trace fossils outside the casting medium, primarily not in firm con-tact with it along their lateral surfaces, are called *exichnia*. The singular forms are *hypichnion, epichnion, exichnion,* and *endichnion,* and recommended adjectives are *hypichnial, epichnial, exichnial,* and *endichnial*.

By adopting such a system one does not only indicate the position of a trace fossil in relation to the casting medium but also a rough definition of its mechanical origin and the nature of its relief. Exichnia and endichnia are by definition *Vollformen* (in full relief). Hypichnia and epichnia are by definition *Halbformen* (in semirelief). Also the terms "endogenic" and "exogenic" may be disposed of for all practical purposes. Both endichnia and exichnia are endogenic by definition (burrowed *within* the casting medium and its matrix, respectively), and both hypichnia and epichnia are exogenic (impressed or otherwise marked as tracks, trails, etc. *upon* muddy and sandy surfaces, respectively). Admittedly, there are cases when, for example, an epichnion has been formed endogentically by an animal burrowing along a sand-mud interface, and many of quite normal epichnia on sandstone beds seem to have been formed under a thin cover of mud. In those special cases where this is needed, the endogenic origin of false surface trace of course may be pointed out.

If the four terms mentioned are used in combination by common morpho-graphical terms, in the simplest case "ridge" and "groove", there is no need to indicate whether the trace is a negative or a positive ($-$ or $+$) feature. The ex-pressions "hypichnial ridge" automatically tells us that the feature referred to is in "positive semirelief" and situated at the lower surface of the casting substance, and furthermore that it has filled a corresponding groove of exogenic origin in the substratum on which the casting medium came to rest. By adding some more descriptive features like "a *c.* 3 mm broad, smooth epichnial ridge, forming irregular loops 10–25 cm in diameter, interrupted at ripple crests and traceable for a distance of at least 3 m until covered by the overlying bed" we arrive at a very

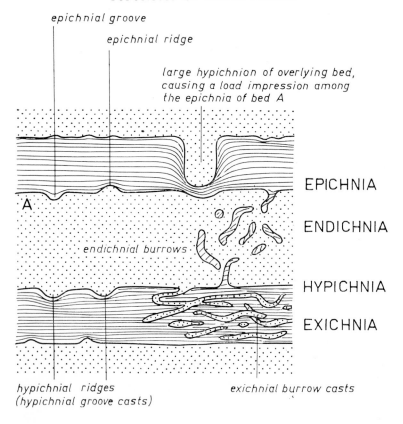

epichnial groove

epichnial ridge

large hypichnion of overlying bed,
causing a load impression among
the epichnia of bed A

EPICHNIA

A

ENDICHNIA

endichnial burrows

HYPICHNIA

EXICHNIA

hypichnial ridges
(hypichnial groove casts)

exichnial burrow casts

Fig. 1. Diagrammatic representation of a toponomic terminology, based on the main medium of
preservation (the "casting" medium). Siltstone beds (stippled) are seen in cross section, embedded in shales (ruled). The four key terms to the right of the diagram refer to bed A.
   The endichnia and exichnia are here drawn as mud-filled (or mineral-filled) burrows and silt-
filled burrow casts respectively. In sequences like the present one they are generally developed
more as a far-reaching textural reorganization of the sediment than as distinct projections from
a bed with another grain size—the little compacted endichnial bioturbation and the strongly
compacted exichnial bioturbation (mostly obsolete when no mixing of beds or laminae has
taken place) often form distinct units in logs of cores and sections.

accurate description which can be made by any recorder not knowing more about
palaeoichnology than the four terms mentioned but which nevertheless is very
informative even for the palaeoecologist.
   The mostly exogenic feature called "cleavage relief" (*Spaltrelief*) also marks an
interface in the sediment, which might be a hidden hiatus (marking, e.g., two

lithification units), a textural discontinuity, or an extremely thin mineral or clay coating, etc. The four-term terminology covers this special case too.

Borings in an indurated sediment may turn out either as endichnia (probably the more common case) or exichnia, depending on whether this consolidated sediment of the superimposed bed comes to play the role of main casting substance when the trace fossil is recovered. The four terms, however, are not applicable on borings in sediment particles (shells, pebbles, etc.). If a special term is needed at all, it could be *ichnidion* or *endichnidion* (plural *ichnidia*).

4. The trace types in the sequence

The main casting medium may dominate the sequence entirely. Nevertheless, if it is constituted by a sandstone or siltstone, the muddy intercalations, even if thin, may represent almost all the time represented in the sequence. Hence it is the hypichnia and the hypichnocoenosis and the exichnia which represent normal life conditions in the area during sedimentation. Epichnia and endichnia represent coenoses which could exploit the influx of the casting medium (occasionally organisms in these coenoses may penetrate the casting medium and form hypichnia).

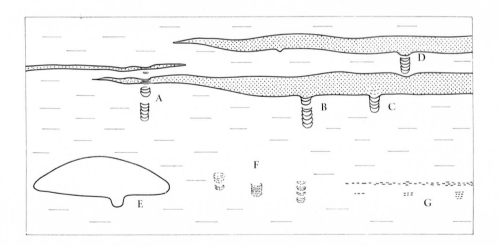

Fig. 2. Different types of preservation of teichichnian burrows in the Middle Cambrian (*Oelandicus* and *Paradoxissimus* Beds) of Öland. A Material from two siltstone beds has been involved. The main preservation is exichnial, but both epichnial and hypichnial structures are developed in the lower bed;   B and C   normal hypichnial preservation. Endichnial structures in connection with the teichichnia are rare;   D   a teichichnion in a higher bed leaving a load impression among the epichnia of the lower bed;   E   hypichnial preservation in connection with a limestone concretion;   F   mineralized, compacted exichnia in the shale;   G   exichnial preservation as strips of fossil fragments below a bed with such fragments.

The exichnocoenoses often do not seem to have much in common with the hypichnocoenoses. In the case of a coarser-grained casting medium in a normally muddy environment the similarity is masked by compaction. Compaction is the most important secondary change in the ichnocoenosis.

The teichichnians in the Middle Cambrian of Sweden may be taken as a single example. In normal hypichnial preservation they form high, wall-like structures, as their name suggests. The originator of the teichichnian was a repetitive burrower, and the hypichnia were formed by filling a burrow in the mud with silt from above. Was this animal a survivor of the normal mud community or an early colonizer of the casting medium?

Investigations show, however, that the originators of the teichichnia were present in the exclusively muddy environment. Teichichnia may be found in exichnial preservation of a few lamellae marking the passage of the originator through a thin patch of silt at the end of the burrow. In a shaly sequence without silt intercalations they may be found in hypichnial preservation at the lower side of calcareous concretions. They are also found impregnated with pyrite or iron oxides and then considerably compacted before consolidation. Finally, they may be recorded as a band of trilobite or brachiopod debris along one or a few shale laminae, marking the passage of their originator through such material at a higher level.

Compaction is a most efficient negative agent in the taphonomy of both body fossils and trace fossils. Like decalcified body fossils, trace fossils are very frequently "squeezed out of the fossil record" (Martinsson 1965; 1968) by strong compaction, destroying the interface conditions necessary for preservation. *Exichnial bioturbation* appears quite different from *endichnial bioturbation* and is probably totally eliminated by compaction much more frequently than generally realized. A homogenous dark shale with or without chitinous and phosphatic skeletal remains does not necessarily record the primary absence of considerable coenotic components of calcareous shells or traces of animals.

Differential compaction of the sequence may result in load impressions on the upper surface of the casting medium caused by the hypichnia of an overlying bed of the same medium, made through the muddy intercalation between the beds. On a smaller scale, and more frequently, this occurs from lamina to lamina in finely banded sediments. Depending on the lithification history of the sediment, load deformation of hypichnia and the orifice region of burrows in the exichnocoenosis may occur. Hypichnial load-casting may, like exichnial compaction, totally conceal the primary presence of an ichnocoenosis.

References

HAAS, O. 1954. Zur Definition des Begriffs "Lebensspuren". *Neues Jb. Geol. Paläont. Mh.* **8.**

HÄNTZSCHEL, W. 1962. Trace-fossils and Problematica. In *Treatise on invertebrate paleontology* (Ed. R. C. Moore). Geol. Soc. Am., New York and Univ. of Kansas Press, Lawrence. Part W, p. W177.

LESSERTISSEUR, J. 1955. Traces fossiles d'activité animale et leur significance paléobiologique. *Mém. Soc. Géol. Fr.* n.s. **74.**

MARTINSSON, A. 1965. Aspects of a Middle Cambrian thanatotope on Öland. *Geol. För. Stockh. Förh.* **87**, 181.

—— 1968. Cambrian palaeontology of Fennoscandian basement fissures. *Lethaia.* **1**, 137.

W

SEILACHER, A. 1953. Studien zur Palichnologie. I. Über die Methoden der Palichnologie. *Neues Jb. Geol. Paläont. Abh.* **96**, 421.

—— 1955. Spuren und Lebensweise der Trilobiten; Spuren und Fazies im Unterkambrium. In *Beiträge zur Kenntnis des Kambriums in der Salt Range (Pakistan)*. Ed. O. H. Schindewolf and A. Seilacher. *Abh. mat. naturw. Kl. Akad. Wiss. Mainz.* Jahrg. 1955.

—— 1964. Sedimentological classication and nomenclature of trace fossils. *Sedimentology.* **3**, 253.

SIMPSON, S. 1957. On the trace fossil *Chondrites. Q. J. geol. Soc. Lond.* **112**, 475.

A. Martinsson, Department of Palaeobiology, Box 564, S-751 22 Uppsala 1, Sweden.

Some palaeoichnological observations on the tube of *Diopatra cuprea* (Bosc): Polychaeta, Onuphidae.

A. C. Myers

Various morphological features of non-calcareous polychaete tubes are directly relatable to environmental forces and events. The feeding structure of *Lanice conchilega* is oriented across the direction of current flow; the exposed portion of the tube of *Diopatra cuprea* is oriented normal to the direction of current flow. This suggests the need for caution in the interpretation of fossil material with apparent directional properties. Both polychaetes provide morphological clues in their tubes about sedimentation rates prevailing at the time of formation. *Diopatra* accumulates materials, particularly shells, in current-swept areas where these materials otherwise would not occur. As a fossil occurrence, such tubes might be used to infer some characteristics of the up-current environment.

1. Introduction

Special feeding structures and reinforcing or decorating materials on non-calcareous dwelling tubes built in unconsolidated sediments by polychaetes are often affected by environmental forces or events, and therefore may be useful in the interpretation of some fossilized tubes.

Seilacher (1951) and Ziegelmeier (1969) have described the special feeding structure (Fransenkrone) which the polychaete *Lanice conchilega* (Pallas) builds at the mouth of its tube. This filtering device consists of two roughly planar branching structures which are parallel to each other and are oriented with the greatest surface area exposed to the direction of main current flow. Ziegelmeier (1969) has demonstrated that the orientation of the feeding structure becomes most uniformly perpendicular to current as the current velocity is increased from 15 mm to 60 mm per second. Thus if a fossilized group of such structures were found on a bedding plane, the statistical scatter of the orientations could give some indication of current strength. A second feature of *Lanice* tubes noted by Seilacher (1951) is that, as sediment accumulates, the worm adds on to its tube and builds a new feeding structure. The spacing between old feeding structures along the outside of the tube may be used to indicate the local rate of net sediment accumulation: narrow spacing indicates gradual net accumulation, while wide spacing indicates sudden or very rapid accumulation.

Tubes of *Diopatra cuprea* contain similar kinds of environmental information and because the tube is robust and is constructed with materials seldom found in the worm's local habitat, its chances of fossilization and recognition are much better than those of *Lanice*'s sand-grain tube or delicate Fransenkrone. *D. cuprea* ranges along the east coast of North America from Cape Cod to Florida, and from the intertidal zone—where it reaches its greatest population densities—to 150 m water depth (Mangum *et al.* 1968). The present discussion of palaeoichnological aspects of *Diopatra*'s tube is developed from a more comprehensive study of the tube-animal-sediment relationships of this worm (Myers, in preparation).

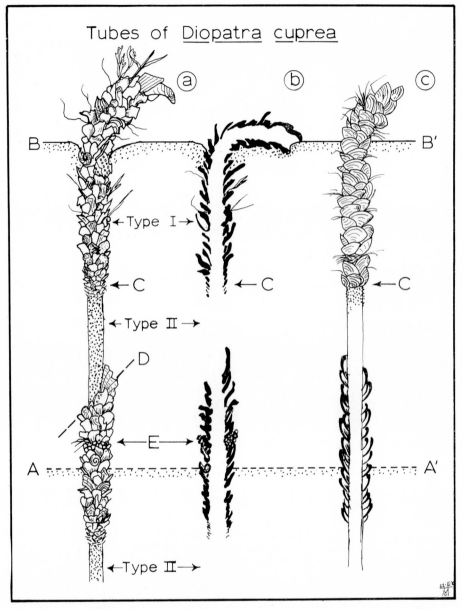

Fig. 1. Tubes of *Diopatra cuprea*. Schematic. For all tubes pictured, the current flow direction is normal to the plane of the paper.   a   Tube of a living worm;   b   Longitudinal section through a tube without the cementing and lining mucus sheets, and with the tube cap compressed as might occur during sediment compaction after final burial;   c   Tube of *D. cuprea* from Sapelo Island, Georgia (U.S.A.), to which only one major kind of reinforcing material—a small bivalve, *Mulinia* sp.—was available. Note in the longitudinal section beneath, that all the shells are attached by their ventral margins and are oriented concave upwards. Type I: reinforced tube. Type II: unreinforced tube.   A—A': A previous sediment surface, buried by sudden or rapid sediment accumulation forming the new surface B—B'.   C: the junction between Type I and Type II tubes is marked not only by lack of reinforcing materials on the latter, but also by a diminution in the size and amount of reinforcing materials at the base of Type I tube. C also marks the beginning of new tube built at surface B—B' and pulled down into the sediment as new tube was built at the surface. Before pulling down, Type II tube extended all the way from the old tube cap to the surface B—B'.   D: Because the mouth of a *Diopatra* tube generally faces

2. Observations on the tube of *Diopatra cuprea*

A *Diopatra cuprea* tube always shows two modes of construction (Fig. 1): *Type* I, characterized by camouflage-reinforcement—bits of shell, rock fragments, sediment, algae, or plant debris—which the worm carefully attaches to the tube wall in an imbricate-upward pattern; this type of tube is only built *at* or *above* the sediment surface; and *Type* II, characterized by a simple mucus-sheet wall to which adjacent sand grains adhere; this type of tube is only built *below* the sediment surface. The inner diameter of a *Diopatra* tube varies depending on the size of the occupant—the tube is large enough for the worm to double up in comfortably, and generally not more than 8 mm in diameter. The outside diameter varies with the amount and nature of the reinforcing materials.

The portion of the tube exposed above the sediment surface is called the tube cap (Mangum *et al.* 1968), and is generally one to two inches (2-5 cm) long—a length maintained by the worm either by trimming or adding on to the cap. The tube cap is built bent over so that the tube mouth obliquely faces the sediment surface: in this position, the tube cap is oriented normal to the main direction of current flow. When considering a group of *Diopatra* tube caps, consistency of current direction seems more important for determining uniformity of orientation than current velocity—although obviously in some situations the two factors are related. Only if the worm is dead and its tube is exposed 10 cm or more by erosion will the tube assume an orientation with the long axis down-current.

Materials used to reinforce the tube come from environments up-current from the worm's own habitat. In tidal situations two or more "up-current" environments may be involved. *Diopatra cuprea* prefers tabular materials, such as pieces of shell, when building Type I tube, but will use anything available, including sediment grains from its own habitat, as a last resort. The worm will use any materials it can catch and manipulate, including living animals such as small bivalves or gastropods, and thus the materials appearing in Type I tube are "selected" by the competence of the current carrying them past the tube. Because *Diopatra* is so often associated with strong current situations (Mangum *et al.* 1968), the tubes represent accumulations of materials not normally found in the immediate sedimentary environment. Also, the tubes are associated with various current structures both on and within the bed (ripple cross-bedding, tidal rhythmites, scour marks and lineations). A striking example of materials selection imposed by current and source of supply, and the meticulous care and consistency with which *Diopatra* builds reinforcing materials into its tube is shown by tubes collected at Sapelo Island, Georgia (U.S.A.), illustrated in Figure 1(c). Non-selectivity among reinforcing materials used in other *Diopatra* tubes found near-by in other areas around Sapelo Island indicates that the apparent selectivity in a large number of tubes whose only reinforcing materials were the shells of a small bivalve (*Mulinia* sp.) and plant debris

---

obliquely down towards the sediment surface, its orientation can often be detected even when the tube is straightened out: in the case of tube (a), the orientation of the tube mouth has changed 180° between the old and the new (upper) tube mouths—orientation to current, however, has not changed. E: Layers of coarse sand or other distinctive materials used in reinforcing record distinct small sedimentary episodes or events up-stream which resulted in the transport of these certain materials past the worm simultaneously with sediment accumulation around the tube which necessitated further tube construction.

was due to supply. In all *Mulinia*-reinforced tubes from this group studied, all the bivalve shells were affixed to the *Diopatra* tube wall along their ventral margins, and were oriented concave upwards.

Regardless of any interposed unreinforced sections (Type II tube), the total length of tube from the bottom of the lowest Type I section to the base of the tube cap represents net sediment accumulation. This does not generally exceed 30-40 cm for *Diopatra cuprea*. A long, uninterrupted Type I section generally indicates gradual sediment accumulation. If a Type II section is interposed between two Type I sections, a sudden sediment accumulation is indicated whose magnitude is at least equal to (i) the length of the Type II section plus (ii), the length of the old tube cap plus (iii), an additional amount which remains indeterminate because the worm pulls new Type I tube built at the surface down into the sediment as far as it can— generally not more than 6 cm.

During normal life activities, *Diopatra* may plug the lower parts of its tube with sediment. In the absence of the worm, the tube may fill with sand or other sediment. Also, small amounts of fine-grained materials may be incorporated into the mucus sheets of the inner walls during tube construction. These factors—plus the possible formation of pyrites during the diagenetic break-down of the sulphate-rich tube wall itself—would seem to give *Diopatra*'s tube good fossilization potential, producing features both on the bedding plane (the tube cap, probably somewhat flattened) and within the bed. Even if the tube were compressed and collapsed during sediment compaction and consolidation, the concentration into a roughly vertical band of materials not found in the surrounding sediments would be diagnostic for this general type of tube and the implied current conditions, and would enhance the chances of recognition by the palaeontologist.

Acknowledgements. I would like to thank Professor Nelson Marshall of the University of Rhode Island Graduate School of Oceanography for his support of the original project from which this discussion developed; also Drs. James D. Howard and Robert Frey of the University of Georgia Marine Institute at Sapelo Island for their encouragement; also Mr. Cuyler Feagles and Mr. Thomas Crowe of East Hill School for their technical assistance in the preparation of this manuscript.

References

MANGUM, C. P., SANTOS, S. L. and RHODES, W. R. jun. 1968. Distribution and feeding in the onuphid polychaete, *Diopatra cuprea* (Bosc). *Mar. Biol.* **2**, 33.

MYERS, A. C. Tube-animal-sediment relationships of *Diopatra cuprea* (Bosc) (Polychaeta: Onuphidae). (In preparation.)

SEILACHER, A. 1951. Der Röhrenbau von *Lanice conchilega* (Polychaeta). Ein Beitrag zur Deutung fossiler Lebensspuren. *Senckenbergiana* **32**, 267.

ZIEGELMEIER, E. 1969. Neue Untersuchungen über die Wohnröhren-Bauweise von *Lanice conchilega* (Polychaeta, Sedentaria). *Helgoländer wiss. Meeresunters.* **19**, 216.

A. C. Myers, Graduate, School of Oceanography, The University, ¦Kingston, Rhode Island, U.S.A.

A symbiotic relationship between *Lingula* and the coral *Heliolites* in the Silurian

G. Newall

Many specimens of *Heliolites interstinctus* from the Aymestry Limestone (Ludlovian) of the Welsh Borderlands contain borings: the most commonly associated coral, *Favosites gothlandicus*, does not. The only fossil preserved intact in the now sediment filled borings is *Lingula* sp., which occurs in life position in some 28 borings. It is concluded that in some cases the corals were still alive when the borings were occupied. It is inferred that *Lingula* was unlikely to have made the borings and from the morphology of the borings themselves, annelids, bivalves or cirripeds were the most likely borers. It is concluded that *Lingula* occupied preformed sediment filled borings, in some cases living symbiotically with the live *Heliolites*. It is suggested that the structure of *Heliolites* was less resistant to boring attack than that of *Favosites*.

1. Introduction

In the Upper Silurian (Ludlovian) Aymestry Limestone of the Welsh Borderlands, colonial corals are common. Within many of these colonies there are macroscopic borings. Borings are a well known feature of modern coral reefs and Mesozoic corals.

The Aymestry Limestone borings have a unique feature in that within several of them *Lingula* sp. is preserved in life position. It is not uncommon to find *Lingula* in life position in sedimentary rocks, but there is no other record of ancient or modern *Lingula* inhabiting borings in a hard substrate.

2. Occurrence of the borings

Tabulate corals are common within the Aymestry Limestone, especially in the main coral unit near the middle of the limestone member (Newall 1966). The corals are distributed as single colonies often in courses through the Aymestry Limestone and only at one locality (Leinthal Earls Quarry—Grid Ref. SO4421 6799) do the corals become amassed into a 2·5 m thick unit of reef-like form, where all the colonies are in growth position. Each course of corals is covered by a thin siltstone which seems responsible for the death of the corals. At Leinthal Earls borings are most abundant and there appears to be a correlation between abundance of corals and frequency of borings: borings are very scarce outside the main coral unit, even in corals of the same species. The most common species are *Heliolites interstinctus* (Linnaeus), and *Favosites gothlandicus* (Edwards and Haime); occasional *Halysites catenularius* (Linnaeus) and *Syringopora* sp. occur as well as stromatoporoids.

Of the total occurring coral genera only *Heliolites* contains borings, 75% of specimens of this genus being bored; even in juxtaposed colonies of *Favosites* borings do not occur.

335

3. Description of the borings

Borings occur only in the upper surface of the colonies, never in the edge or in the base. Inverted and overturned colonies may contain borings (Pl. 1a) but even here the borings enter the original upper surface suggesting that they were formed before the corals were overturned. As many as 28 borings were found in a single coral. The borings are usually sub-circular in transverse section, though some are ovoid. The transverse section varies little in general shape from aperture to base, though some-times the borings become more or less ragged along their length. The apertural diameters vary between 5 mm and 10 mm with a mean between 7-8 mm. In longi-tudinal section the borings are sub-parallel sided (Pl. 1 b, c, d), the diameter only changing as the borings become narrower towards the rounded closed end. The borings are sometimes straight and are radial to the coralla, being parallel to the direction of corallite growth: commonly they are radial for most of their length but become curved towards the closed end (Pl. 2a). The total length of the borings varies and is controlled by the height of the coral, since borings are never seen to pass right through the corallum, even when corals occur one on top of another. The average length of the borings is, therefore, c. 2·5—3·0 cm, the longest observed being 4·2 cm. Serial sectioning of the borings indicates that they never interconnect and are never 'U'-shaped.

The borings show no sign of a lining: their walls are of coral and the adjacent coral structure is usually damaged and broken, when on a small scale the wall appears ragged. The broken coral structure indicates that these are distinct borings and not just dead areas of coral, which themselves are common but do not penetrate the coral structure. The raggedness of the walls compared to the very smooth nature of many modern borings is attributable mainly to the lack of a lining. The borings now appear as sediment filled holes: usually the main part is filled with coarse grained terrigenous and bioclastic sediment, while the aperture may be filled with finer grained silt of the same type and continuous with that which overlies the whole colony.

4. Fauna within the borings

The majority of the borings contain only bioclastic debris, predominantly from brachiopods and crinoids. Complete fossils have been found in only 28 borings: here *Lingula* sp. occurs and in all cases the valves are still attached and the shells are oriented with their umbones directed into the borings. There is no sign of breakage or other damage. *Lingula* can be found in all parts of the boring (Pl. 2 c, d). The shells are filled either totally by drusy calcite or are geopetally infilled with sediment and calcite. In thin section (Pl. 2b) the normal linguloid laminated shell structure can be clearly seen and the boring shows an ovoid cross-section, matching that of *Lingula*.

5. Origin of the borings

5a. Introduction

Much is known of the boring and burrowing habits of a wide range of animals and plants, many of which commonly inhabit coral reefs. The Algae, Fungi, Porifera, Bryozoa, Arthropoda, Annelida, Echinodermata and Mollusca, all contain forms capable of boring into a hard substrate. The borings made by

PLATE 1

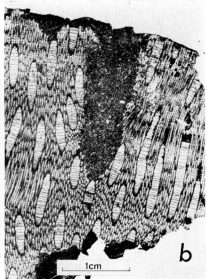

Plate 1

a Numerous borings in overturned *Heliolites, in situ* at Mocktree Quarry, Herefordshire.

b Sediment filled boring in *Heliolites* (enlargement of left hand boring in Plate 1c).

c Sediment filled borings in *Heliolites*.

d Sediment filled boring in *Heliolites* (enlargement of right hand boring in Plate 1c). Note divergence and reformation of coral structure in the upper part on the left.

members of some of these groups are morphologically very different from the Aymestry borings; Algae and Fungi make borings measured in microns (Clarke 1921; Frémy 1936; Hessland 1949; Bathurst 1966; Golubic 1969; Kohlmeyer 1969; Gattral and Golubic this volume) and Porifera usually make ramifying and cavity style borings (Lessertisseur 1955; Warburton 1958; Goreau and Hartman 1963; Neumann 1966; Cobb 1969). The borer into the Aymestry corals probably came from the other phyla, bearing in mind that the principal features of the Aymestry borings are:

  (i)   they are sub-parallel sided and rounded at the closed end, though they never taper towards the aperture.
 (ii)   their diameter is relatively constant at about 7 mm.
(iii)   they are usually nearly straight but may curve towards the closed end; they are never U-shaped.
 (iv)   they are up to *c.* 40 mm long.
  (v)   they never have any lining.
 (vi)   they sometimes contain *Lingula* in life position.
(vii)   no complete fossil other than *Lingula* is ever found in the borings.

5b. Brief review of possible boring organisms

LINGULA. The only animal found intact in the Aymestry borings is *Lingula* which, from all available evidence, seems to be incapable of attacking a hard substrate. The mode of life and burrowing activity of *Lingula* has been discussed by Craig (1952), Ferguson (1963) and Paine (1970). Its normal habitat is mud flats in tropical and sub-tropical regions where it makes burrows, up to 30 cm deep, in the soft sediment. The shell is attached by a long pedicle to a hard shell fragment or to hardened sediment at the base of the burrows. It can retract into or extend from the burrow by contraction or elongation of the pedicle.

General morphology and shell structure are similar in ancient and modern *Lingula* suggesting similar modes of life. Thus it seems most unlikely that *Lingula* made the borings in the Aymestry corals; they must have been produced by some other boring organism, *Lingula* then utilising the pre-existing holes.

ARTHROPODA. Several groups of Crustacea are capable of boring into solid substrates, though some can only attack wood. Cirripeds are commonly found boring into dead coral in reefs; in the Low Isles of the Great Barrier Reef, *Lithotrya valentiana* makes neat holes in dead coral (Otter 1937). The borings have apertural diameters of 10×7 mm and are up to 30 mm long. The borings taper to the closed end which is rounded. Boring species of barnacles are confined to the tropics.

Barnacles or supposed barnacles are known from the Ordovician, and acorn barnacles boring into *Favosites* have been described from the Lower Devonian of America (Clarke 1921). Clarke's figure (*op. cit.* fig. 51 p. 62) shows some resemblance to the Aymestry examples. Lessertisseur (1955) records cirriped borings (*Zapfella*) from the Lias, and Seilacher (1969) describes boring cirripeds from as far back as the Upper Palaeozoic, boring into calcareous shell material, with borings only a few millimetres in diameter; Tomlinson (1969) describes recent borings of similar type. Baluk and Radwański (1967) describe the cirriped, *Creusia*, from the Miocene of Poland, living symbiotically with the coral *Tarbellastraea;* the borings are much shorter and squatter than those of the Aymestry Limestone though they have similar sub-parallel sides and rounded bases. It is common to find overgrown sealed burrows within the coralla, a feature not seen in the Aymestry specimens.

The scale and general morphology of some cirriped borings e.g. *Lithotrya,* approximate to those in the Aymestry corals, but no cirriped fragments have been observed or recorded from the Aymestry Limestones.

ANNELIDA. Some Polychaetes can bore into a hard calcareous substrate: they are well-known in temperate waters and also in coral reefs (Yonge 1951; Blake 1969; Haigler 1969; Jones 1969). *Polydora* forms U-shaped burrows, which may be long and winding: the boring species are minute, forming burrows with a diameter of about 1 mm, and they usually occur in vast numbers. Some sipunculids make wider straight burrows (up to *c.* 4 mm in diameter), but these taper rapidly to their apertures (Rice 1969).

Body fossils of annelids are seldom found, but their traces are ubiquitous. Clarke (1921) indicates that symbiosis between worms and corals became established in the Silurian: he figures stromatoporoids and *Favosites* from American Silurian and Devonian localities, which are bored by *Gitonia sipho*. Although no scale is given on these figures, the borings appear to be about 1 mm or 2 mm in diameter (*op. cit.* fig. 8, 9, 10 and 11). Clarke also states that the tubes of *Sabella* and *Palaeosabella* are straight curved, or U-shaped and that these forms reached their acme in the Devonian; he also figures a Silurian stromatoporoid from the Niagaran of Ontario (*op. cit.* fig. 76) which he suggests to have been "bored by worms or sponges". This specimen shows, in upper surface view, the closest resemblance of any figured specimen to the Aymestry coral borings.

Records of supposed annelid burrows indicate that these vary in morphology; authenticated forms are usually long, narrow, winding and commonly U-shaped, features which are not seen in the Aymestry borings.

MOLLUSCA. This phylum contains a large number of hard rock borers, belonging mainly to the Classes Bivalvia and Gastropoda: some members of the Amphineura (chitons) make shallow borings and in the Great Barrier Reef *Acanthogostera gemmata* is sometimes found occupying old *Lithophaga* burrows (Otter 1937).

Boring gastropods make flask shaped borings into coral. The apertures are circular and have a calcareous lining though the borings themselves are unlined and up to 2 cm deep. Normally borings are made into dead coral but two genera, *Leptoconchus* and *Magilopsis,* make 'borings' into living corals in the Red Sea reefs: the 'boring' is initiated passively, the coral growing upwards around a young settled gastropod (Gohar and Soliman 1963a; Soliman 1969). These authors suggest, from examination of the structure of the shell and its modifications, that the 'boring' is later enlarged by mechanical means, the boring activity being directed upwards to keep pace with the growth of the coral colony (compare Aymestry borings). The aperture of these borings is small (2–3 mm), compared to the diameter inside the coral (up to 10 mm).

The mytilid genus *Lithophaga* is among the best known hard substrate borers. Bivalve borings have sub-parallel sides but taper to the aperture and usually have a rounded closed end. The aperture is either single and oval, sometimes with a median constriction making an hour-glass shape or is double. The diameter of the aperture, the boring and the length depend largely upon the size of the inhabiting shell (Gohar and Soliman 1963b). The borings usually contain a calcareous lining, which may be complete or only partial.

A few boring bivalves will attack living corals. Gohar and Soliman (1963c) describe three species of *Lithophaga* boring into living corals in the Red Sea and suggest that one of them, *L. hanleyana,* bores almost exclusively into living coral, only encrusting upon dead colonies. In live corals the borings have a circular aperture, and are usually longer than the corresponding borings in dead corals—a result of the shell having to bore upwards to keep pace with the growth of the coral. The borings become overgrown by coral when they become uninhabited.

Bivalves of other genera can bore into solid substrates including *Pholas, Saxicava, Modiolus, Botula* and *Rocellaria* (Kühnelt 1934; Otter 1937; Hunter 1949; Yonge 1951; 1955; 1963; Clapp and Kenk 1963; Gohar and Soliman 1963d; Ansell and Nair 1969; Evans this volume). All produce borings similar in form to those described for *Lithophaga*. Most of the important boring genera do not occur as early as the Silurian, though bivalve borings are well-known, for example, in the Corallian (Jurassic) of England, where their morphology compares very closely with that of modern forms.

The sub-parallel sides of the Aymestry borings makes them dissimilar to the modern and known fossil molluscan borings. Also the absence of any lining from the Aymestry borings is a further point of contrast. The only bivalve to occur in the same beds as the bored corals is *Orthonota* (*Fuchsella*) *amygdalina* but it is uncommon, never occurs in the borings, and there is no evidence elsewhere to suggest that it ever had a boring habit. In fact, no boring bivalves are known from the Silurian (T. Soot-Ryen and the late L. R. Cox—personnal communication).

5c. The Aymestry Limestone borings

Comparison of the features of the Aymestry borings with those of modern forms and other fossil forms indicates that no absolute match can be made in detailed morphology. Considering gross morphology, bivalve and cirriped borings bear the closest resemblance, but bearing in mind the total lack of any faunal evidence, a soft bodied organism, especially an annelid, becomes possible. H. A. F. Gohar (personal communication) suggests that the Aymestry specimens look most like modern *Lithotrya* borings.

Silurian boring organisms seem only poorly known and it is, therefore, possible that the direct uniformitarian comparison of modern forms and more recent fossils with Silurian forms is unjustified and that in the Silurian borings by familiar forms had a different aspect: the possibility that Silurian *Lingula* could bore into solid substrata cannot be totally discounted, though of all the possibilities this seems the most unlikely.

Thus, except that some form of cirriped, bivalve or annelid seems likely, no conclusion can be reached as to the boring organism in the Aymestry corals.

5d. The presence of *Lingula* in the borings

Lingula in the borings is always in life position: it is well preserved with articulated valves and umbones directed downwards. There is no modern equivalent. If *Lingula* did not make the borings it must have entered after vacation by the original borer. It is concluded that preformed borings are utilized by other organisms and that these later inhabitants may modify the boring.

In some cases (Pl. 1d, 2a) there is evidence that the corallites diverge from the boring and in the divergent, upper part the corallites and the intervening coenenchyma of *Heliolites* is intact. This suggests that the coral was alive when the borings were formed and inhabited. The presence of an animal within a live colony is known to distort the coral growth pattern (Gohar and Soliman 1963a, c). Baluk and Radwański (1967) illustrate the divergence of the corallites of *Tarbellastraea* away from cirriped borings (refer *op. cit.* fig. 4 and pl. II) The original borer must have been present in the live coral, but the occurrence of borings which are ovoid in cross-section in a sense which fits closely the *Lingula* shell (Pl. 2b) suggests that *Lingula* occupied the borings while the coral was still alive. In modern living corals inhabited holes fit closely the form of the animal e.g. crabs domiciled in *Fungia*.

PLATE 2

Plate 2

a Sediment filled boring in *Heliolites,* showing vertical section through articulated *Lingula* and also divergence of corallites from upper part of the boring.

b Transverse section through boring containing *Lingula.* The laminated shell structure of *Lingula* can be seen, as well as shell infilling of drusy calcite.

c *Lingula* in life position in boring.

d *Lingula* shells in borings, one showing longitudinal section with geopetal infilling.

The presence of *Lingula* is, therefore, explained as follows: planktonic *Lingula* larvae settled on the surface of living or dead coral. As these larvae can only become attached if the substrate is favourable, larvae landing on live coral would either be consumed or swept off the surface by ciliary action of the polyps. If, however the larvae settled upon a sediment filled boring they could attach normally and introduce their pedicles into the sediment, thereby utilizing an ideal protected niche for development. It is suggested that the movement of *Lingula* within the boring, its emergence and retraction, was a source of irritation to the coral and caused the corallites to deviate from their normal growth pattern (Pl. 2a). Colonies in which no deviation is seen were presumably dead. *Lingula* spat could also fall upon a dead sediment covered area of coral and may have initiated a 'boring' passively, the coral growing upwards around the settled larva (as in the case of symbiotic gastropods and bivalves (Gohar and Soliman 1963a, c). This latter explanation is considered unlikely since all the holes show evidence of active boring and destruction of coral structure for part of their length.

6. Restriction of borings to *Heliolites*

It has already been stated that only *Heliolites* contains borings whereas the other corals, including the other common form *Favosites,* do not. This selectivity on the part of the boring organism may be explained in terms of the different structures of these two genera.

Modern corals can clear themselves of sediment and other detritus accumulating on their upper surfaces but the efficiency of the clearing mechanism varies. The detritus is first entrapped in a mucous secretion and then the whole mass removed by ciliary action. Sediment accumulating from below and at the sides is not so easily dealt with and it is common to find fossil examples of coral colonies choked at their edges but still growing in the middle. This accumulation at the edges may be the reason for the lack of borings there. Marshall and Orr (1931) found that corals with larger polyps could clear sediment more efficiently: *Favia,* for example, removed sediment very quickly and completely whereas *Porites* removed it slowly or sometimes not at all, resulting in death.

The accumulation of sediment on the coral has an influence on the boring fauna; *Lithophaga* is prevented from boring by silt layers, even when adjacent silt-free colonies are heavily attacked (Otter 1937). Equally the texture of the skeleton affects mechanical borers, hard corals with thick corallite walls, coarse texture and large calices being less frequently attacked than the softer corals with thinner walls and compact soft calices. *Favia* is less affected by boring than *Porites* (Otter 1937). It is suggested that *Heliolites* and *Favosites* were analogous to *Porites* and *Favia* respectively.

Heliolites coralla are made up of two elements, larger corallites which contained the polyps and intervening porous coenenchyma which probably had only a thin cover of tissue over its surface during life (cf. modern *Heliopora*). *Favosites* coralla are more compact consisting of tight-packed corallites, each having contained a polyp, and well developed tabulae (better developed than those in *Heliolites*). It is suggested, by comparison with *Favia* and *Porites,* that *Favosites* may have been able to clean sediment from its surface more efficiently than *Heliolites*. Sediment accumulated on the *Heliolites* surface would have produced local dead areas and enabled the borer to initiate a burrow in the live colony. Also the softer *Heliolites* structure would have made it the more attractive substrate when the colonies were dead. It is therefore concluded that the nature of the

Favosites structure made it resistant to attack by borers, which could relatively easily attack the *Heliolites* skeleton.

7. Conclusions

Many specimens of *Heliolites* from the Aymestry Limestone are bored. *Lingula* is the only complete fossil preserved in the borings and from present knowledge of the life habits of *Lingula* it is inferred that the possibility that this Silurian form could attack hard substrates is remote. From dimensions of the borings and comparison with modern and other fossil forms, the borings could possibly be attributed to annelids, bivalves or cirripeds. It is therefore concluded that *Lingula* spat happened by chance upon preformed sediment filled borings, in which the settled larvae became established. Sometimes these borings were in live coral, where *Lingula* lived symbiotically with the coral. It is suggested that the presence of *Lingula* irritated the coral and caused some distortion of its structure; thus the upper part of some borings were formed by the coral growing upwards around the inhabiting *Lingula*.

    Heliolites alone contains borings while even adjacent *Favosites* colonies do not. By comparison with modern forms this appears to be due to the different styles of the two skeletons, that of *Heliolites* being the less resistant and more easily attacked.

References

ANSELL, A. D. and NAIR, N. B. 1969. A comparative study of bivalves which bore mainly by mechanical means. *Am. Zoologist* **9**, 857.

BALUK, W. and RADWÁNSKI, A. 1967. Miocene cirripeds domiciled in corals. *Acta palaeont. polon.* **12**, 457.

BATHURST, R. G. C. 1966. Boring algae, micrite envelopes and lithification of molluscan biosparites. *Geol. J.* **5**, 15.

BLAKE, J. A. 1969. Systematics and ecology of shell-boring polychaetes from New England. *Am. Zoologist* **9**, 813.

CLAPP, W. F. and KENK, R. 1963. *Marine borers: an annotated bibliography*. Office of Naval Res., Dept. of the Navy, Washington.

CLARKE, J. M. 1921. Organic dependence and disease: their origin and significance. *Bull. N.Y. Stn. Mus.* **221**, 1.

COBB, W. R. 1969. Penetration of calcium carbonate substrates by the boring sponge, *Cliona*. *Am. Zoologist* **9**, 783.

CRAIG, G. Y. 1952. A comparative study of the ecology and palaeoecology of *Lingula*. *Trans. Edinb. geol. Soc.* **15**, 111.

FERGUSON, L. 1963. The palaeoecology of *Lingula squamiformis* Phillips during a Scottish Mississippian marine transgression *J. Paleont.* **37**, 669.

FRÉMY, P. 1936. Les algues perprantes. *Mém. Soc. natn. Sci. nat. math. Cherbourg* **42**. 275.

GOHAR, H. A. F. and SOLIMAN G. N. 1963a. On the biology of three corallophyllid gastropods boring in living corals. *Publs mar. biol. Stn Ghardaqa (Red Sea)* No. 2, 99.

—— 1963b. On two mytillids boring in dead coral. *Ibid.* No. 12, 205.

—— 1963c. On three mytillids boring in living corals. *Ibid.* No. 12, 65.

—— 1963d. On the rock-boring lamellibranch *Rocellaria ruppelli* (Deshayes). *Ibid.* No. 12, 1.

GOLUBIC, S. 1969. Distribution, taxonomy and boring patterns of marine endolithic algae. *Am. Zoologist* **9**, 747.

GOREAU, T. F. and HARTMAN, W. D. 1963. Boring sponges as controlling factors in the formation and maintenance of coral reefs. *Mechanisms of hard tissue destruction* (Ed. R. F. Sognnaes) *Publs Am. Ass. Advmt Sci.* **75**, 25.

HAIGLER, S. A. 1969. Boring mechanism of *Polydora websteri* inhabiting *Crassostrea virginica*. *Am. Zoologist* **9**, 821.

HESSLAND, I. 1949. Investigation of the Lower Ordovician of the Siljan district, Sweden. II, Lower Ordovician penetrative and enveloping algae from the Siljan district. *Bull. geol. Instn Univ. Upsala* **33**, 409.

HUNTER, W. R. 1949. The structure and behaviour of *Hiatella gallicana* (Lamarck) and *H. arctica* (L.) with special reference to the boring habit. *Proc. R. Soc. Edinb.* **63B**, 271.

JONES, M. L. 1969. Boring of shell by *Casbangia* in fresh water snails of Southeast Asia. *Am. Zoologist* **9**, 829.

KOHLMEYER, J. 1969. The role of marine fungi in the penetration of calcareous substances. *Am. Zoologist* **9**, 741.

KÜHNELT, W. 1934. Bohrmuschelnstudier 2. *Palaeobiologica* **5**, 371.

LESSERTISSEUR, J. 1955. Traces fossiles d'activité animale et leur signification paléobiologique. *Mém. Soc. géol. Fr.* n.s. **74**, 1.

MARSHALL, S. P. and ORR, A. P. 1931. Sedimentation on the Low Isles Reef and its relation to coral growth. *Scient. Rep. Gt Barrier Reef Exped.* No. 5, 93.

NEUMANN, A. C. 1966. Observations on coastal erosion in Bermuda and measurements of the boring rate of the Sponge, *Cliona lampa*. *Limnol. Oceanogr.* **11**, 92.

NEWALL, G. 1966. *A faunal sedimentary study of the Aymestry Limestone and adjacent beds in parts of Herefordshire and Shropshire*. Ph.D. thesis, Univ. Manchester.

OTTER, G. W. 1937. Rock destroying organisms in relation to coral reefs. *Scient. Rep. Gt Barrier Reef Exped.* No. 1, 323.

PAINE, T. P. 1970. The sediment occupied by recent lingulid brachiopods and some palaeoecological complications. *Palaeogeogr. Palaeoclimatol. Palaeoecol.* **7**, 21.

RICE, M. E. 1969. Possible boring structures of sipunculids. *Am. Zoologist* **9**, 803.

SEILACHER, A. 1969. Palaeoecology of boring barnacles. *Am. Zoologist* **9**, 705.

SOLIMAN, G. N. 1969. Ecological aspects of some coral-boring gastropods and bivalves of the northwestern Red Sea. *Am. Zoologist* **9**, 887.

TOMLINSON, J. T. 1969. Shell-burrowing barnacles. *Am. Zoologist* **9**, 837.

WARBURTON, F. 1958. The manner in which the sponge *Cliona* bores in calcareous objects. *Can. J. Zool.* **36**, 555.

YONGE, C. M. 1951. Marine boring organisms. *Research, Lond.* **4**, 162.

—— 1955. Adaptation to rock boring in *Botula* and *Lithophaga* (Lamellibranchia; Mytilidae.) with a discussion on the evolution of this habit. *Q.J. microsc. Sci.* **96**, 383.

—— 1963. Rock-boring organisms. In *Mechanisms of hard tissue destruction* (Ed. R. F. Sognnaes). *Publs Am. Ass. Advmt Sci.* **75**, 1.

G. Newall, Department of Geology, The University, P.O. Box 147, Liverpool L69 3BX, U.K.

The trilobite ichnocoenoses in the Cambrian sequence of the Holy Cross Mountains

S. Orlowski, A. Radwański and P. Roniewicz

The Cambrian deposits of the Holy Cross Mountains (Central Poland), developed in the form of shales, siltstones and, more or less, quartzitic sandstones, make up a *c.* 2·2 km thick series in which the faunal assemblages occur at short intervals. The trilobites are the main components of these assemblages, while other animals (archaeocyathids, jellyfish, hyolithids, gastropods, brachiopods, eocrinoids) are of lesser importance. The fossiliferous parts of the profile as a rule bear evidence of the activity of animals, mostly trilobites. In comparing the morphology of trilobites and their traces, the genera *Kjerulfia* or *Holmia, Germaropyge, Paradoxides* and *Olenus* seem to be the trace-makers in successive ichnocoenoses which may, to some extent, be used in stratigraphy. The morphology of the traces allows one to conclude on the behaviour and mode of life of these genera. Other traces are indicative of the forms associated with the trilobite communities (sea anemones, polychaetes, aglaspids). The occurrence of ichnocoenoses and/or trilobite remains in a profile depends on environmental conditions which controlled the accumulation of fossils or preservation of their traces in some intervals of the Holy Cross Cambrian profile.

1. Introduction

The Cambrian deposits in the Holy Cross Mountains, comprising the most extensive occurrence area of the Palaeozoic core, crop out mostly in the Łysogóry anticline and Klimontów anticlinorium. In the former of these regions only the Middle and Upper Cambrian are present, while in the latter, only the Lower and Middle Cambrian (Fig. 1) are recorded. These deposits are almost exclusively fine clastic sediments, about 2·2 km (Fig. 2) in total thickness.

The observations which are the subject of the present paper are the result of studies on the Cambrian of the Holy Cross Mountains over an extensive period. These observations were made by the first of the co-authors during his stratigraphical and palaeontological studies (Orłowski 1959a, b, c; 1964a, b; 1965; 1968a, b) and by the remaining two during their sedimentological and ichnological investigations (Radwański and Roniewicz 1960; 1962; 1963; 1967).

2. Occurrence of organic assemblages

2a. Lower Cambrian

The Lower Cambrian deposits are mostly alternating thin-layered siltstones and shales; fine-grained sandstones are of lesser importance (Fig. 2). The deposits are monotonous, facially unified, with the upper surfaces of layers generally smooth and covered with muscovite flakes. Sedimentation took place under quiet conditions, well beneath wave base. Fossils (mostly trilobites) and trace fossils, appear only in some lithological sets and are described below in ascending stratigraphical order.

x

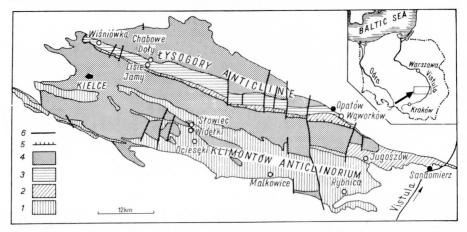

Fig. 1. Cambrian outcrops in the Holy Cross Mountains, with regional locality map inset. 1 Lower Cambrian; 2 Middle Cambrian; 3 Upper Cambrian; 4 Younger Palaeozoic deposits; 5 overthrust; 6 major faults.

(i) *Sub-Holmia horizon*. No trilobites and trace fossils have so far been found in the deposits of this horizon.

(ii) *Holmia horizon*. About 600 trilobite remains (including three complete exoskeletons) mostly assignable to the genera *Strenuaeva, Strenuella, Holmia,* and less frequently to *Kjerulfia* and *Termierella* were found at this horizon; hyolithids were also present (cf. Samsonowicz 1959a, b; Orłowski 1968b). The most prolific localities for trilobites are Ociesęki and Malkowice (Fig. 1), where they abound in some fine-grained, strongly lithified sandstones, occurring in shale complexes. Trace fossils are very frequent at this level.

(iii) *Protolenus horizon*. This horizon yielded about 120 trilobite remains (including 20 complete exoskeletons). The species of the genus *Germaropyge,* much larger than the remaining genera, are present in this horizon (mostly in the locality Widełki, Fig. 1). The genera *Protolenus, Strenuaeva, Strettonia, Serrodiscus* (Samsonowicz 1959c; Bednarczyk, *et al* 1965) are less frequent. Brachipods (Czarnocki 1927) and jellyfish (Stasińska 1960) are also found. The trilobite fauna is confined to sandstone layers intercalating with the shales; trace fossils are rare.

2b. Middle Cambrian

The Middle Cambrian deposits are differentiated facially. In the Łysogóry anticline, there are shales with thin sandstone intercalations and in the Klimontów anticlinorium—either thin-layered sandstones with shales (at Jugoszów), even with shales predominating locally (in the environs of Sandomierz), or thick-layered quartzitic sandstones at Słowiec). In the sandy deposits, thin, fine-gravel streaks appear along with shale intraclasts and current or wave structures on the topsides of layers. Sedimentation took place in a shallower environment, where various sediments were brought in and the bottom was remodelled by currents and/or wave action. The fossils and trace fossils occur only in some of the facies.

(i) *Oelandicus Stage*. This Stage is developed in two facies: either coarse-grained sandstones (Mt. Słowiec, Fig. 1; column S in Fig. 2), or siltstones with intercalation of sandstones and shales (Jugoszów, Fig. 1; column J in Fig. 2).

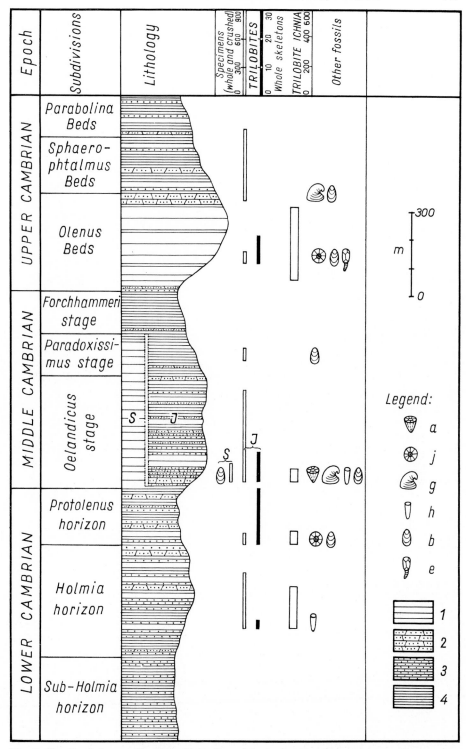

Fig. 2. The Cambrian profile of the Holy Cross Mountains (detailed explanation in the text)
a archaeocyathids;   j jellyfish;   g gastropods;   h hyolithids;   b brachiopods;
e eocrinoids;   1 quartzitic sandstones;   2 sandstones;   3 siltstones;   4 shales.

The Słowiec profile yielded about 200 disarticulated trilobite remains, mostly of the genera *Paradoxides, Ellipsocephalus* and *Strenuella*; brachiopods are also present (cf. Orłowski 1964a, b; 1965). The fossils occur scattered throughout some layers or in those parts which usually contain coarser clastic material. Trace fossils are unknown in this facies.

The Jugoszów profile yielded about 1,000 trilobite remains (including 11 complete exoskeletons), mostly assigned to the genera *Strenuella, Ellipsocephalus* and *Paradoxides*, less frequently to *Kingaspis* and *Protolenus;* archaeocyathids, gastropods, hyolithids and brachiopods are also present (cf. Orłowski 1959a, b, c; 1964a, b). The trilobite remains are common in glauconite-bearing siltstones and in sandstones alternating the shales. Trace fossils are infrequent.

(ii) *Paradoxissimus Stage.* This Stage yielded about 150 trilobite remains, all of them crushed and assigned to the genera *Paradoxides, Solenopleura, Jincella, Ptychagnostus* and *Agnostus;* brachiopods are also frequent (cf. Orłowski 1964a, b). The fossils occur only in a thin, lenticular intercalation of fine-grained sandstones in alum shales (Pepper Mountains near Sandomierz upon the Vistula, Fig. 1).

(iii) *Forchhammeri Stage.* In the deposits assigned to this Stage neither fossils nor trace fossils have so far been found.

2c. Upper Cambrian

The Upper Cambrian deposits consist mostly (Fig. 2) of thick-layered quartzitic sandstones, the complex of which reaches *c.* 350 m in thickness, including much of the Łysogóry anticline and forms the main range of the Holy Cross Mountains. In this complex, there are often intercalations of slightly lithified shales (claystones), as well as sets of thin-layered siltstones and claystones. Under the quartzitic-sandstone complex, as well as above it in the profile, there are complexes consisting of thin-layered shales, siltstones and sandstones. The quartzitic sandstones contain, on their topsides, various structures formed by currents and/or wave action. All these structures are indicative of very shallow marine sedimentation (Radwański and Roniewicz 1960; 1962; Dżułyński and Zak 1960). In the Upper Cambrian complexes, the fossils and trace fossils occur irregularly.

(i) *Olenus Beds.* These beds, outcropping at Waworków near Opatów, yielded about 120 trilobite remains (including five complete exoskeletons), as well as brachiopods and eocrinoids which occur in lenticular accumulations (Orłowski 1968a). In the strata observable in the large quarries known as Wielka (Great) and Mała (Little) Wiśniówka, only four, but more or less completely preserved, trilobites (see Pl. 3a, d; also Orłowski 1968a pl. 7 fig. 12) and rather problematical jellyfish (Orłowski 1968a) have been found. Of the trilobites the commonest is *Olenus*, and less so *Protopeltura* (Orłowski 1968a). The trace fossils are known only at Wiśniówka, where they were the subject of separate papers (Radwański and Roniewicz 1963; 1967).

Plate 1

All natural size.

a "*Cruziana rusoformis* ichnosp. nov.", Holmia horizon, Malkowice.
b "*Cruziana rusoformis* ichnosp. nov.", Holmia horizon, Rybnica.
c "*Cruziana rusoformis* ichnosp. nov.", Holmia horizon, Rybnica.
d *Cruziana* sp., trace cut by a synaeresis crack, Holmia horizon, Rybnica.

PLATE 1

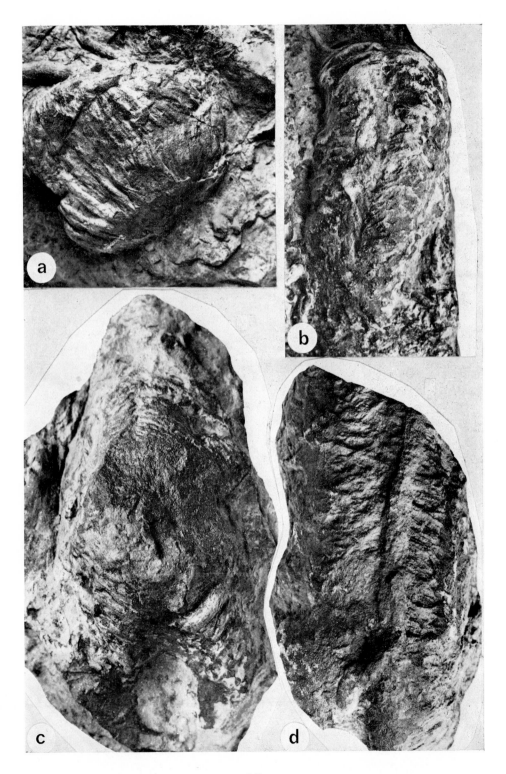

(ii) *Sphaerophthalmus Beds.* About 800 distintegrated trilobite remains of the genera *Sphaerophthalmus, Beltella, Peltura* and less common *Parabolina, Acerocare* and *Agnostus* have been found in these beds; brachiopods and gastropods also occur (Orłowski 1968a). The fossils occur in lenticular sandy layers in shales at Chabowe Doły and Lisie Jamy (Fig. 1). Trace fossils have not so far been found.

(iii) *Parabolina Beds.* These beds, pierced only in boreholes on the northern limb of the Łysogóry anticline (Fig. 1), are not considered in this paper.

3. Characteristics of the ichnocoenoses

The occurrence of trace fossils forming ichnocoenoses is confined to the parts of the Holy Cross Cambrian profile which yield fossils (see Fig. 2). The present state of knowledge of the Cambrian outcrops in the Holy Cross Mountains allows one to conclude that principal faunal groups, having skeletons or shells (archaeocyathids, hyolithids, gastropods, brachiopods, trilobites and eocrinoids) have already been recognized. In some localities, impressions of animals without skeletons, such as jellyfish, were preserved (Stasińska 1960; Orłowski 1968a). A few groups were recognized on the basis of the traces of their life activity (polychaetes, sea anemones, aglaspids—see below). Of these animals, trilobites are notably most common and the majority of traces can be ascribed to them (Pl. 1 to 4). Such traces are generally considered to have been left by trilobites (cf. Fenton and Fenton 1937; Seilacher e.g. 1955; 1959; 1962; Radwański and Roniewicz 1963; Martinsson 1965; Goldring 1967; Crimes 1968; 1969). Recently, however, suggestions have also been put forward that some of the traces of the type under study might be related to other arthropods, namely aglaspids (Bergström 1968). In the present writers' opinion, the fact that ichnocoenoses occur only in trilobite-bearing parts of the profile (see Fig. 2) is an important argument for relating these traces to trilobites. A morphological conformability of the traces, in particular those of resting, with the trilobites found in these same layers, additionally supports such an interpretation. This problem will be examined in section 4.

(i) *Holmia horizon.* Most of the traces are short forms whose morphological type is transitional between *Rusophycus* and *Cruziana* (Pl. 1a, b). Some of them are of relatively high relief which indicates that the animal dug itself in deeply in the bottom (Pl. 1c). Such forms are sometimes similar to either *Cruziana irregularis* Fenton and Fenton (Fenton and Fenton 1937; Martinsson 1965) or *Cruziana dispar* Linnarsson (Bergström 1968). Long *Cruziana* are less frequent (Pl. 1d, 2a). All these forms have visible imprints of walking legs, mostly perpendicular or subperpendicular to the axis of a given form.

(ii) *Protolenus horizon.* Wide (3-4 cm) *Cruziana* type traces with a wide ridge on the margin and widely spaced imprints of walking legs have been found in this horizon.

Plate 2

a *Cruziana* sp., Holmia horizon, Rybnica.

b "*Cruziana rusoformis* ichnosp. nov.", Oelandicus Stage, Jugoszów.

c A trace made by a crawling trilobite on the upper surface of a ripple-marked, thin layer of sandstone. The trace corresponds to the hieroglyph *Cruziana semiplicata* Salter which has been taken off; Olenus Beds, Wielka Wiśniówka.

PLATE 2

(iii) *Oelandicus Stage*. Short, wide traces of a type transitional between *Rusophycus* and *Cruziana,* and with clear imprints of walking legs perpendicular to the axis of the form (Pl. 2b) are here recorded.

(iv) *Olenus Beds*. Many and various traces have been found among which trilobite resting impressions (*Rusophycus*) are common and in which, depending on the degree of excavation of the sediment and on its consistency, more or less distinct imprints of segmentation are preserved (Pl. 3b, c; cf. Radwański and Roniewicz 1963 pl. 2). There are also various forms of *Cruziana*, mostly of the species *Cruziana semiplicata* Salter (Pl. 4), described in detail elsewhere (Radwański and Roniewicz 1963). There are, much less frequently, *Diplichnites* and *Dimorphichnus* (see also Dżułyński and Zak 1960; Radwański and Roniewicz 1963).

In the Olenus Beds, the traces are particularly abundant at Wiśniówka, where they occur either singly on the surface of layers (Pl. 2c), or in great quantities covering the entire surface with their intricate pattern. In this locality, conditions were undoubtedly very favourable for trilobites and their traces depict an extensive range of life activity, that is, resting, digging, walking or striding, crawling and swimming close to the bottom. Of the forms interesting morphologically, attention is attracted by *Rusophycus* with clear imprints of legs of the *Dimorphichnus* type situated posteriorly and on one side of the form. These forms should be interpreted as traces of a trilobite which left its resting place, getting out of it by means of its walking legs and, in principle, by a lateral movement (Pl. 3e). There are also *Rusophycus* with a trace of an animal which moved by a rather long forward push and apparently without employing its walking legs (Pl. 3f). Some trilobites covered relatively great distances to judge from their crawling traces which reach nearly 1·5 m in length (Pl. 2c).

Within the trilobite ichnocoenose at Wiśniówka, attention is also attracted by associated forms of traces left by other animals which accompanied trilobites and their biotopes. These include many *Diplocraterion* sp., related to the activity of polychaetes (cf. Radwański and Roniewicz 1963), *Bergaueria perata* Prantl, related to sea anemones (see also Radwański and Roniewicz 1963; Arai and McGugan 1968), as well as a strange form *Aglaspidichnus sanctacrucensis* Radwański and Roniewicz, a resting place left probably by an aglaspid (Radwański and Roniewicz 1967).

It is clear from these observations that, owing to the presence of the traces left only by trilobites or to the predominant share of such traces, the ichnocoenoses under study should be considered as trilobite ichnocoenoses. The composition and appearance of particular forms is variable in individual stratigraphic units (compare Pl. 1, 2 with Pl. 3). This was undoubtedly because the traces were formed by

---

Plate 3

All natural size.

a *Olenus rarus* Orłowski, Olenus Beds, Wielka Wiśniówka.

b "*Rusophycus polonicus* ichnosp. nov.", Olenus Beds, Wielka Wiśniówka.

c "*Rusophycus polonicus* ichnosp. nov.", Olenus Beds, Wielka Wiśniówka.

d A fragment of a bigger form *Olenus rarus* Orłowski, Olenus Beds, Wielka Wiśniówka.

e "*Rusophycus polonicus* ichnosp. nov." with traces of legs imprinted while the trilobite pulled itself aside out of the trace; Olenus Beds, Wielka Wiśniówka.

f "*Rusophycus cruziformis* ichnosp. nov.", Olenus Beds, Wielka Wiśniówka.

PLATE 3

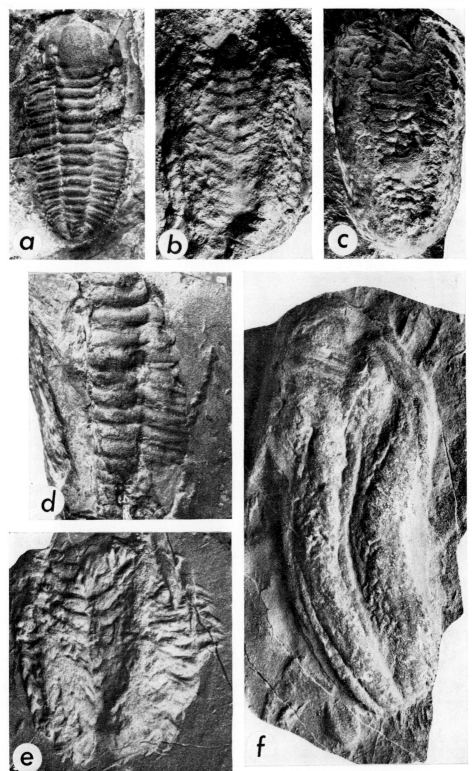

various genera of trilobites differing in morphology and even in their mode of life. This fact may in turn be used, to a certain extent, for stratigraphic purposes and for tentative correlations in newly discovered outcrops.

4. Trilobite genera suggested as trace-makers

Ichnocoenoses found in trilobite-bearing parts of the profile allow one to suggest definite genera of trilobites as responsible for making these traces. Within the trilobite assemblages, occurring in the same layers in which the ichnocoenoses have been found, only one or at most two genera can be pointed out which in their size or shape correspond to either resting traces of *Rusophycus* type, or to a general outline of the crawling trace of *Cruziana* type.

Among the trilobites, found in the Holmia horizon, the only forms which could leave the traces illustrated (Pl. 1, 2) are *Kjerulfia* or large individuals of the genus *Holmia*. The remaining trilobites are considerably smaller.

In the Protolenus horizon, the only forms which correspond in size to the traces are *Germaropgye*.

Among the forms from the Oelandicus Stage, only the genus *Paradoxides* can be responsible for making such traces as those presented here (Pl. 2b). The traces are 7–7·5 cm wide and only *Paradoxides* could reach this size. This is confirmed by single pleurae, cranidia and librigenae of various species of this genus, found in associated deposits (cf. Orłowski 1959b; 1964a, b).

Of the trilobites found in the Olenus Beds, especially those from the sedimentary environment of Wiśniówka, the species *Olenus rarus* Orłowski strongly corresponds in shape, size and number of segments to the resting traces of the *Rusophycus* type (comp. Pl. 3a with Pl. 3b, c). Since many forms transitional between resting and crawling traces have been preserved in this environment (e.g., Pl. 3f; cf. also Radwański and Roniewicz 1963), precisely this species seems to be responsible for making all the traces of the Wiśniówka ichnocoenose. Larger individuals of this species (Pl. 3d) formed wider traces, which were equally common as those presented (Pl. 3, 4) and, in the case of crawling traces, reached exceptionally great lengths (Pl. 2c). It is noteworthy that the conformability in shape and size of the resting place *Rusophycus* with its probable maker, *Olenus rarus* Orłowski, is here exceptionally conspicuous and should be used as a basis for the identification of trace-makers also in the case of other ichnocoenoses. In the literature, known so far, the trace-makers were usually suggested on the basis of general notions concerning the structure of a given trilobite in reference to the various traces studied of an animal,

Plate 4

All natural size.

a Two *Cruziana semiplicata* Salter crossing each other, the longer one being older; Olenus Beds, Wielka Wiśniówka.

b Short *Cruziana semiplicata* Salter, Olenus Beds, Wielka Wiśniówka.

c *Cruziana semiplicata* Salter of a diversified morphology resulting from various types of trilobite movement, Olenus Beds, Wielka Wiśniówka.

PLATE 4

moving or digging up the sediment (cf. Fenton and Fenton 1937; Seilacher 1955; 1962; Henningsmoen 1957; Martinsson 1965).

From examination of the richest trilobite ichnocoenoses from the Cambrian of the Holy Cross Mountains (Holmia horizon and Olenus Beds), some suggestions can be made concerning the behaviour of the tracemakers. Thus, *Kjerulfia* were probably benthonic forms which frequently stayed on the bottom and dug up the sediment probably in search for food and maybe also for shelter. *Olenus rarus* Orłowski probably led a more vagile life, frequently swimming over the bottom on which it either settled for a longer rest, sometimes digging itself in some depression, or roamed over it, maybe chasing its prey and, consequently, left behind *Cruziana* type traces of varying length. These traces were sometimes very short as if the animal only grazed the bottom and once again shot up (Pl. 4b).

5. Taxonomic remarks

Except for one (Pl. 2c), all the traces under study are filled with grooves left behind by trilobites and are therefore hieroglyphs (= sole markings). The ichnological names, so far used in literature, concern only hieroglyphs (cf. Radwański and Roniewicz 1963 table p. 264).

As regards the ichnological nomenclature, no consistent and uniform taxonomy has thus far been accepted. Attention has previously been drawn by the present writers (Radwański and Roniewicz 1963) to the fact that the traces which compose the ichnocoenose at Wielka Wiśniówka mostly do not comply with the taxonomic categories adopted. It seems that these problems even now should be the subject of a detailed discussion, since many old taxons in current use are of a questionable value, particularly where transitional forms are found (cf. Seilacher 1953; 1964; Häntzschel 1962).

As regards the traces presented from the Cambrian of the Holy Cross Mountains, the writers believe that the taxons under study should either be presented in an extensive range exclusively *sensu* ichnogenus (e.g. *Rusophycus* sp. and *Cruziana* sp. except for the generally accepted *Cruziana semiplicata* Salter), or new, detailed taxons should be erected which would emphasize rather morphological features of the form and at that given in a fairly extensive presentation. Thus, short forms from the Holy Cross Cambrian with the features of *Cruziana* but having the nature of a resting trace of the *Rusophycus* type, might be called "*Cruziana rusoformis*" (Pl. 1a-c; Pl. 2b). Analogous forms of long *Rusophycus,* having the general character of a trace of a resting trilobite which, however, moved forward (Pl. 3f), might be called "*Rusophycus cruziformis*". Finally, the forms of the *Rusophycus* type, having impressions of segments (Pl. 3b, c, e), might be called "*Rusophycus polonicus*" since this state of preservation is very characteristic of the ichnocoenoses of the Polish Cambrian under study. These names are not, however, designated formally as new ichnospecies at the moment.

6. Environmental conditions under which the trilobites lived

The relatively abundant trilobite remains, collected in the Holy Cross Cambrian sequence (about 3,000 specimens) comes from short intervals in the profile in which it accumulated, mostly in definite layers. In these layers, the trilobite remains occur abundantly. They are either scattered in definite, parallel layers, which only differ slightly lithologically from the adjoining ones in the profile (the localities

Ociesęki, Malkowice, Widełki—the Lower Cambrian; Słowiec, Jugoszów—the Middle Cambrian), or in lenticular layers, composed of a coarser material (Pepper Mountains—the Middle Cambrian; Waworków, Chabowe Doły, Lisie Jamy—the Upper Cambrian). It is of interest that complete exoskeletons of trilobites are found mostly in the first of the areas mentioned above (except for Słowiec, where the crushed remains are related to more coarse-grained streaks within the range of the continuous sandstone sequence). In addition, all traces of trilobites are connected with the sets of deposits in which complete or almost complete exoskeletons of trilobites may be found (Ociesęki, Malkowice, Widełki, Jugoszów). Traces of trilobites are also particularly abundant in a thick series at Wiśniówka, where only four complete or almost complete trilobite exoskeletons were found. These occurrences are the result of the environmental and taphonomic conditions.

The occurrence in some series of only disarticulated trilobite exoskeletons, frequently surrounded by a coarse-grained material of the type of lenticular layers and with the lack of complete exoskeletons and traces of trilobites, indicates that the remains of trilobites are an allochthonous material, transported, together with a coarser clastic material, by currents. Under such hydrodynamic conditions, live trilobites were probably capable of extricating themselves from the deposit. Driven by currents and destroyed during transport, the remains of exoskeletons probably came from dead individuals or from the accumulations of moults cast-off by large communities of trilobites which lived gregariously. In the Cambrian sequence of the Holy Cross Mountains, the localities in which trilobite remains are most abundant seem, therefore, to represent accumulations of moults periodically cast-off by trilobites. Thus, these accumulations are of the nature of merocoenose sensu Davitashvili (1945). It is most likely, that many other rich trilobite localities in the Cambrian of Europe are similar in character (e.g. *Acerocare ecorne* Angelin assemblages described by Henningsmoen 1957).

The localities in which, in addition to the disarticulated trilobite remains, complete exoskeletons are found but occur as a minority (cf. Fig. 2) and in which trilobite ichnocoenoses are preserved (Ociesęki, Malkowice, Widełki, Jugoszów), surely had quite different hydrodynamic conditions. In such localities, trilobite remains usually occur in thin layers which differ only slightly in development from the adjoining ones in the profile and which are composed only of a purer sandstone. The clastic material was deposited here in a much calmer way, in the form of regular, thin layers. Trilobite remains were not strongly reworked hydrodynamically, thus even the preservation of complete exoskeletons was possible. In the case of the deposition of a larger amount of sediment, some of the trilobites might be buried alive (e.g. enrolled specimens at Ociesęki and Jugoszów). On the whole, the assemblages of trilobite remains under study were, however, buried in sediment in the area of biotope or in its close neighbourhood. At the same time hydrodynamic factors did not lead to the erosion of the bottom and, therefore, different traces of trilobites' activity on the bottom could be preserved in these places.

From the viewpoint of the problem under study, Wielka Wiśniówka is a locality of a particular importance. Within a 400 m thick series of alternate quartzitic sandstones and claystones, the trilobite traces are very numerous and, on the surface of some layers, even occur in masses. Detailed sedimentological studies of this series (Radwański and Roniewicz 1960; 1963; Dżułyński and Zak 1960) allow one to state that the mobile character of the environment (ripple marks, bottom sweeping or scouring), recorded here during the periods of the sedimentation of the sandy material, made the preservation of light trilobite remains impossible. Crushed remains (moults) were swept from that area by wave action and currents, while live animals could actively oppose such conditions by getting out of the drifting sediment or leaving the unfavourable environment. The sweeping activity resulting from wave action and currents during the sedimentation of sand was not sufficiently intensive to destroy the traces of trilobites' activity on the firm mud of the bottom. The infillings (hieroglyphs) of these traces are excellently preserved thus making the locality of Wiśniówka particularly important to the ichnological studies of the European Cambrian. It should be emphasized that the preservation of grooves, made by trilobites on the upper surface of claystones, must have been caused by an appropriate consistency of the mud and considerable firmness (cf. Dżułyński and Sanders 1962). In the sand, which was a loose sediment for a longer time, all types of traces, made by trilobites on the surface of the bottom, were rapidly obliterated. Only exceptional conditions could enable their preservation (e.g. the specimen in Pl. 2c).

All the conditions discussed above explain the absence of mass accumulations of the remains (merocoenoses) from the sedimentary environment of Wielka Wiśniówka. Single, complete exoskeletons probably represent the conditions under which whole and, consequently, heavy organisms were buried either alive or shortly after their death.

7. Conclusions

The entire Cambrian profile of the Holy Cross Mountains is characterized by clastic sedimentation which took place in a relatively shallow and extensive sea, without any evidence of shoreline processes. The Lower Cambrian is marked by sedimentation in slightly deeper waters, while the subsequent members are indicative of gradually more and more shallow-marine conditions. The thickness of deposits in this profile, devoid of any gaps in sedimentation, indicates continuous subsidence and, consequently, the miogeosynclinal character of the basin, formed somewhere on the peripheries of the Caledonian geosyncline (cf. Henningsmoen 1957). The range of the Cambrian sea of the Holy Cross Mountains clearly exceeded the present geographical boundaries of this region. It should be emphasized that this sea was connected with the sea of Sweden (Czarnocki 1927; Henningsmoen 1957; Radwański and Roniewicz 1960; 1962) which was near-shore in character and was subject to the influence exerted by the oscillation of the shoreline (Westergård 1922; Hessland 1955; Henningsmoen 1957; Martinsson 1965). In addition the latter sea invaded, over a wide zone, the margin of the Fennosarmatian platform from Estonia through northeastern and eastern Poland to Podolya and Volhynia. On its other side, the Holy Cross geosyncline was connected, through the Sudetes, Lusatia and the Ardennes, with the Caledonian geosyncline of Wales.

Clearly, then, within the range of such an extensive basin, the assemblages of trilobites and associated fauna were distributed irregularly and the preservation of their remains in the deposits depended on local hydrodynamic conditions rather than on a general palaeogeographical situation. The preservation of the ichnocoenoses depended in turn on an appropriate type of sediment, its state of consolidation and calm conditions under which it was covered with sandy material. On the other hand, the places of occurrence of the ichnocoenoses were situated in the trace-makers' biotope or in its near neighbourhood (cf. Martinsson 1965).

References

ARAI, M. N. and McGUGAN, A. 1968. A problematical coelenterate(?) from the Lower Cambrian, near Moraine Lake, Banff area, Alberta. *J. Paleont.* **42**, 205.

BEDNARCZYK, W., JURKIEWICZ, H. and ORŁOWSKI, S. 1965. Lower Cambrian and its fauna from the boring Zaręby near Łagów (Holy Cross Mountains). *Bull. Acad. pol. Sci. Ser. Sci. géol. géogr.* **13**, 231.

BERGSTRÖM, J. 1968. *Eolimulus,* a Lower Cambrian xiphosurid from Sweden. *Geol. För. Stockh. Förh.* **90**, 489.

CRIMES, T. P. 1968. *Cruziana:* A stratigraphically useful trace fossil. *Geol. Mag.* **105**, 360.

—— 1969. Trace fossils from the Cambro-Ordovician rocks of North Wales and their stratigraphic significance. *Geol. J.* **6**, 333.

CZARNOCKI, J. 1927. Le Cambrien et la faune Cambrienne de la partie moyenne du Massif de Swiety Krzyż (Ste Croix). *Int. geol. Congr. 14, Madrid, 1926.*

DAVITASHVILI, L. S. 1945. Cenozi zhivih organizmov i organikheskih ostatkov. *Soobchch. Akad. Nauk. gruz. SSR. (Bull. Acad. Sci. Georgian SSR)* **7**, 527.

DŻUŁYŃSKI, S. and ZAK, C. 1960. Sedimentary environment of the Cambrian quartzites in the Holy Cross Mountains, Central Poland, and their relationship to the flysch facies. *Annls Soc. geol. Pol.* **30**, 213.

—— and SANDERS, J. E. 1962. Current marks on firm mud bottoms. *Trans. Conn. Acad. Arts Sci.* **42**, 57.

FENTON, C. L. and FENTON, M. A. 1937. Trilobite 'nests' and feeding burrows. *Am. Midl. Nat.* **18**, 446.

GOLDRING, R. 1967. The significance of certain trace-fossil ranges. In *The Fossil Record.* Geol. Soc. of London, London. p. 37.

HÄNTZSCHEL, W. 1962. Trace fossils and problematica. *Treatise on invertebrate paleontology* (Ed. R. C. Moore). Geol. Soc. Am., New York and Univ. of Kansas Press, Lawrence. Part W, p. W177.

HENNINGSMOEN, G. 1957. The trilobite family Olenidae with description of Norwegian material and remarks on the Olenid and Tremadocian series. *Skr. norske Vidensk-Akad. I. Mat. naturv. Kl.* **1**, 1.

HESSLAND, I. 1955. Studies in the lithogenesis of the Cambrian and basal Ordovician of the Böda Hamn sequence of strata. *Bull. geol. Instn. Univ. Upsala* **35**, 35.

MARTINSSON, A. 1965. Aspects of a Middle Cambrian thanatotope on Öland. *Geol. För. Stockh. Förh.* **87**, 181.

ORŁOWSKI, S. 1959a. Archaeocyatha from lower Middle Cambrian of the Holy Cross Mountains. *Bull. Acad. pol. Sci. III Cl.* **7**, 363.

—— 1959b. Paradoxididae from lower Middle Cambrian strata in the vicinity of Sandomierz (Central Poland). *Ibid.* **7**, 441.

—— 1959c. Ellipsocephalidae from the lower beds of the Middle Cambrian in the vicinity of Sandomierz (Central Poland). *Ibid.* **7**, 515.

—— 1964a. Middle Cambrian and its fauna in the eastern part of the Holy Cross Mountains. *Studia geol. pol.* **16**, 1.

—— 1964b. The Middle Cambrian in the Holy Cross Mountains. *Acta geol. pol.* **14**, 547.

—— 1965. A revision of the Middle Cambrian fauna from the Slowiec hill, Holy Cross Mountains. *Biuletyn geol.* (published by University of Warsaw) **6**, 3.

—— 1968a. Upper Cambrian fauna of the Holy Cross Mountains. *Acta geol. pol.* **18**, 257.

—— 1968b. The Cambrian stratigraphy in the Holy Cross Mountains (Poland). *Int. geol. Congr. 23, Prague* **9**, 127.

RADWAŃSKI, A. and RONIEWICZ, P. 1960. Ripple marks and other sedimentary structures of the Upper Cambrian at Wielka Wiśniówka (Holy Cross Mountains). *Acta geol. pol.* **10**, 371.

—— and —— 1962. Upper Cambrian sedimentation near Opatów (eastern part of the Holy Cross Mountains, Central Poland). *Ibid.* **12**, 431.

—— and —— 1963. Upper Cambrian trilobite ichnocoenosis from Wielka Wiśniówka (Holy Cross Mountains, Poland). *Acta palaeont. pol.* **8**, 259.

—— and —— 1967. Trace fossil *Aglaspidichnus sanctacrucensis* n. gen., n. sp., a probable resting place of an aglaspid (Xiphosura). *Ibid.* **12**, 545.

SAMSONOWICZ, J. 1959a. On the Holmia fauna in the Cambrian of the anticlinorium of Klimontów. *Bull. Acad. pol. Sci. Ser. Sci. chim. géol. géogr.* **7**, 447.

—— 1959b. On Strenuaeva from Lower Cambrian in Klimontów anticlinorium. *Ibid.* **7**, 521.

—— 1959c. On Strenuella and Germaropyge from the Lower Cambrian in the Klimontów anticlinorium. *Ibid.* **7**, 525.

SEILACHER, A. 1953. Studien zur Palichnologie, I-II. *Neues Jb. Geol. Paläont. Abh.* **96**, 421 and **98**, 87.

SEILACHER, A. 1955. Spuren und Lebenweise der Trilobiten. In *Beiträge zur Kenntnis des Kambriums in der Salt Range (Pakistan)*, by O. H. Schnindewolf and A. Seilacher *Abh. Acad. Wiss. Lit. Mainz. Mat. Nat. Kl.* Jahrg 1955, p. 342.

—— 1959. Vom Leben der Trilobiten. *Naturwissenschaften* **46,** 389.

—— 1962. Form und Funktion des Trilobiten-Daktylus. *Paläont. Z.* H. Schmidt-Festband, p. 218.

—— 1964. Biogenic sedimentary structures. In *Approaches to Paleoeclogy* (Ed. J. Imbrie and N. D. Newell). Wiley, New York. p. 296.

STASIŃSKA, A. 1960. *Velumbrella czarnockii* n. gen., n. sp.-Méduse du Cambrien inférieur des Monts de Sainte-Croix. *Acta palaeont. pol.* **5,** 337.

WESTERGÅRD, A. H. 1922. Sveriges olenidskiffer. *Sver. geol. Unders. Abh. Ser. Ca.* **18,** 1.

S. Orłowski, A. Radwański, P. Roniewicz, Institute of Geology, The University, Warsaw 22, Poland, Al. Zwirki-i-Wigury 93.

Zoophycos and similar fossils

M. Plička

Zoophycos and similar forms are interpreted as imprints of abandoned prostomial parts of sedentary polychaetes of the Family Sabellidae and a similarity is noted with the prostomium of *Spirographis*. The classification of sabellid worms is then discussed with particular reference to the fossil forms. Both modern and fossil forms appear to have been restricted to shallow water environments.

1. Introduction

Radiate forms with a spiral or planar arrangement (Pl. 1) have been widely recorded in the literature as *Zoophycos, Spirophyton, Taonurus* and *Cancellophycus*. Their variability in shape and regular structural arrangement has led to differing views on their origin and accidental similarities between these radiate forms and other forms of known origin has led to confusion. The first account of such a radiate form was by Brongniart (1828) who named it *Fucoides circinnatus* and suggested that it was a plant, a view supported by Barsanti (1902) and still held for similar structures by some recent authors (Venzo 1951; 1954; Cecioni 1957; Plumstead 1967). A mechanical origin has, however, been ascribed to *Zoophycos* by some writers. Nathorst (1882), for example, contended that they were traces produced either by water currents or the movements of marine organisms. He also tried experimentally to simulate forms similar to *Zoophycos* but failed. Later he again advocated an origin by animal movement (Nathorst 1883; 1886; 1889) and experimented with a worm but failed to produce a *Zoophycos*-like form (Barsanti 1902).

Recently the interpretation of *Zoophycos* as the burrow system of a marine animal has become common. This was first suggested by Th. Fuchs in 1893 and has recently been supported by other authors (Abel 1935; Seilacher 1954; Lessertisseur 1955; Scott Simpson this volume).

Investigation of radiate forms from the Miocene of New Zealand (Stevens 1968) and the flysch of the Czechoslovak Carpathians, has suggested that they are imprints of abandoned prostomial parts of sedentary marine polychaetes of the family Sabellidae, very similar to the recent *Spirographis spallanzanii* Viviani (Plička 1962; 1965a, b; 1966; 1968; 1969).

2. Morphology of *Spirographis*

The spiral, radiating imprints under discussion conform to the spirally arranged prostomium of the present day *Spirographis* Viviani 1805. This conformity is particularly evident in sections perpendicular to the bedding passing through the

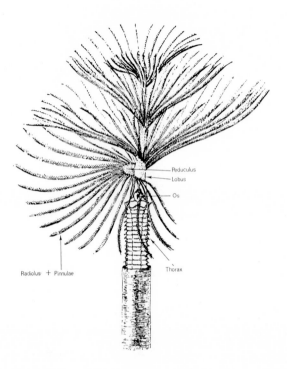

Fig. 1. *Spirographis spallanzanii* Viviani, the prostomial lobe with gill rays supporting fine, transverse filaments (pinnulae). At the base of the gill lobe there is a projection (peduculus), over the oral aperture. The segmented visible part of a worm is called the thorax, the remaining —the major part—abdomen (with pygidium) is concealed within a siphuncle. (According to H. M. Edwards and A. Lameere 1931.)

centre of the spiral (i.e. from a longitudinal section through the prostomium). To pursue these comparisons the morphology of *S. spallanzanii* Viviani will be described in detail (Fig. 1).

In the anterior portion of *Spirographis* the prostomium is formed by two gill lobes (lobus), one longer than the other. The gill rays (radiolus) are sinistrally or dextrally spiralled around the longer lobe in a 50:50 ratio. Their length becomes reduced towards the apical end of the gill lobe. The gill rays show fine cross furrows (pinnulae). A strong cuticle is developed over the surface of the rays, and the gill rays together with the pinnulae form the gill-organs. The gill rays are joined by a palm-shaped, imperfectly developed membrane. This membrane maintains regular spaces between the rays and serves for intercepting food, that is micro-organisms and plant detritus slowly sinking to the sea floor. At the base of the spiral, close to the oral aperture of the worm, the gill lobe is enlarged forming a calyx—a basal leaf (peduculus). Food is drawn into the centre of the spiral by the moving gill rays and after settling on the membrane it is moved in a spiral around the gill lobe towards the basal leaf and to the oral aperture.

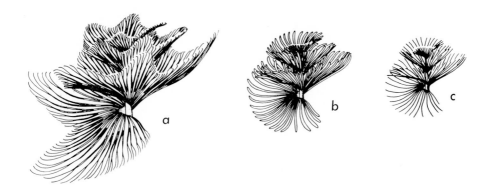

Fig. 2. Reconstructions of fossil prostomia of the genera: a *Zoophycos* Massalongo 1851; b *Palaeospira* Plička 1964; c *Spirographis* Viviani 1805. In order to simplify the drawing, pinnulae of the single gill rays are omitted.

The spiral consists of two to six or more whorls. The number of gill rays increases with the age of the worm. The prostomium can be regenerated after being discarded by the worms either when they are in danger, or, possibly during vegetative reproduction (Romanovski *et al.* 1953).

The anterior part of the cylindrical trunk terminates in a collar which consists of four lobes (two dorsal, two ventral).

The cylindrical part of the *Spirographis* body is composed of a peristomium which encircles the oral aperture (os) (Hempelmann 1931), a thorax of 6 to 14 segments, an abdomen of 100 to 300 segments and a pygidium.

The worms are hidden in a pellicular tube (siphuncle) attached to the sea floor. Only their gill apparatus (the spiral) is thrust out but this is retracted when danger threatens. They live either singly or grouped in colonies normally at depths reaching only a few metres but occasionally up to 30 metres.

3. The classification of sabellid worms

Following the recognition that the radiating and spirally arranged structures were the prostomia of sabellid worms a revised classification of such worms can be advanced on the basis of material from the Czech and Polish Carpathians and elsewhere.

So far three genera have been proposed: *Zoophycos* Massalongo 1851, *Palaeospira* Plička 1964, and *Spirographis* Viviani 1805. Two species have been referred to each of the genera *Zoophycos* and *Spirographis* and one to the genus *Palaeospira* (Plička 1968).

In the genus *Zoophycos*, the gill rays of the prostomium show repeated dichotomous branching (Fig. 2). Their mean length is 15–20 cm and there are 14 to 18 pinnulae per centimetre of ray length. On the basis of the different lengths of the gill rays in the spiral, two species have been established: *Zoophycos circinnatus* (Brongniart) and *Zoophycos massalongi* Plička.

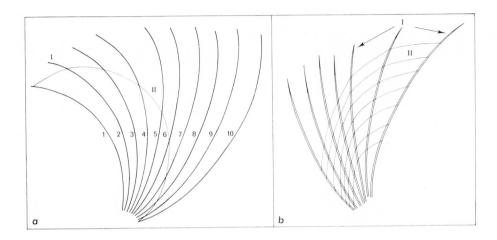

Fig. 3   a Schematic sketch: a secondary ray runs from the gill lobe and before it reaches the periphery of a gill ray surface, it covers about 10 primary rays;   b Schematic sketch: Secondary gill rays (II) are stretched when primary ones (I) are more separated. (See Stevens 1968 fig. 11.)

In *Zoophycos circinnatus* (Brongniart), the gill rays are of variable length, because the peripheries of individual gill ray surfaces are surmounted by projecting lobes. In *Zoophycos massalongi* Plička the peripheries are of circular shape. *Zoophycos circinnatus* (Brongniart) is distributed in the Cretaceous and Palaeogene throughout Europe (Pl. 1d), *Zoophycos massalongi* Plička ranges from the Ordovician (?) through the Palaeogene of Europe, Africa (?), and America (?).

The gill rays in *Palaeospira* are flattened, arcuately bent, unbranched and well defined (Pl. 1 e, f, Fig. 3). The average length of the gill rays is 7 to 13 cm. There are 11 to 15 pinnulae per centimetre of ray length. In *Palaeospira ensigera* Plička, the gill rays are flattened and sword-shaped, their curvature following the direction of the spiral coiling. This species has been reported from the Cretaceous and Palaeogene of Europe, and from the Permian of Asia.

Plate 1

a *Zoophycos circinnatus* (Brongniart), Eocene, Carpathian flysch, specimens viewed from above. Spec. No. 33108D–6/18, Central Geological Survey, Brno.

b *Zoophycos circinnatus* (Brongniart). Palaeocene, Carpathian flysch, a right hand spiralled specimen viewed from below. Spec. No. 3486D—12/3, C.G.S., Brno.

c *Zoophycos circinnatus* (Brongniart). Cretaceous, Carpathian flysch, Czechoslovakia. Planar imprint of gill rays. Spec. No. 3485B—14/1, C.G.S., Brno.

d *Zoophycos circinnatus* (Brongniart), flysch, Mt. Sporno (Parma), Italy. Spiral imprint of the gill organs, viewed from below, a sinistral specimen.

e, f *Palaeospira ensigera* Plička, Permian, NW of Chabarovsk (U.S.S.R.).   **e** sinistral specimen 4/23–1962–R.T.V.;   **f** dextral specimen, 4/25–1962–R.T.V. (T. V. Romanchuk, Museum of Chabarovsk.)

PLATE 1

365

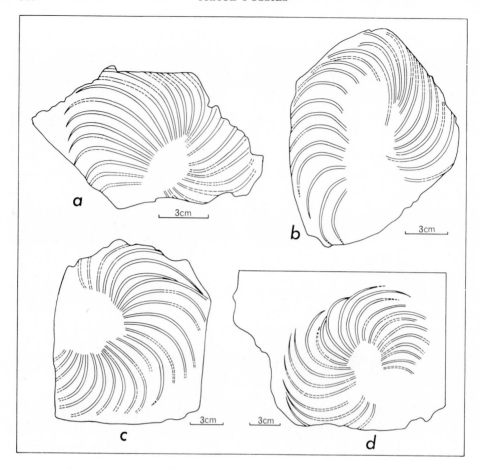

Fig. 4. *Palaeospira ensigera* Plička, Permian, flysch, NW of Chabarovsk (USSR), found by T. V. Romanchuk, deposited in Museum of Chabarovsk; a–4/25; b–4/8; c–N1; d–4/2: R.T.V.–1962.

Spirographis displays fine, unbranched gill rays of mean length 5 to 8 cm. Individual gill rays are well defined with 20 or more pinnulae per centimetre of ray length. By consideration of the shape of individual gill ray surfaces, two species

---

Plate 2

a "*Zoophycos*" dextral specimen, Gower River, probably derived from Upper Tongaporutuan beds (Upper Miocene). (Stevens 1968 fig. 11).

b "*Zoophycos*", Moki Road, near Rimuputa Junction, New Zealand. Note the preservation of secondary filaments between the large primary filaments (Stevens 1968 fig. 9). Viewed from below.

PLATE 2

have been established: *Spirographis carpatica* Plička and *Spirographis eifliense* (Kayser). *Spirographis carpatica* shows straight gill rays in individual surfaces when observed in a longitudinal section through the prostomium. They occur in the Cretaceous and Palaeogene of Europe. A longitudinal section through the prostomium of *Spirographis eifliense* shows that the ends of the gill rays are bent upwards with the palm-shaped membrane which joins the gill rays more developed.

New specimens showing prostomial imprints have been reported from New Zealand (Stevens 1968), and South Africa (Plumstead 1967); they may represent new genera, or at least species. The specimens from New Zealand are particularly large, being twice the size of *Zoophycos*, four times the size of *Palaeospira* and six times that of *Spirographis*. The "primary" (Stevens 1968) gill rays are very strong owing to the size of the prostomium (Pl. 2); they may represent a supporting element absent in the genera discussed above.

The presence of fine cross furrows (pinnulae) observed in filaments (rays) of fossil *Spirographis, Palaeospira* and *Zoophycos* is also apparent in the "secondary" filaments (see Stevens 1968 fig. 11).

The primary filaments are covered by the secondary ones from above and are joined with them. The filaments are also joined together without showing any spaces between them. The membrane, which is imperfectly developed between the gill rays of sabellid worms, may be developed along the whole surface of rays in the New Zealand forms, thus joining the primary and secondary rays. The secondary filaments (rays) and (?) pinnulae form the gill organs which diminish or enlarge the spaces between the primary rays and serve as an apparatus for breathing and intercepting food.

The New Zealand specimens conform to fossil sabellid genera so far known because their gill rays coil in a left-hand or right-hand spiral around a gill lobe; both the primary and secondary gill rays are arched following the direction of the spiral coiling. Some regularities are known between the primary and secondary rays: each of the secondary rays, which is arch-like, runs from the gill lobe and before it reaches the periphery of a gill ray surface, it covers about 10 primary rays (Fig. 4a).

In the New Zealand specimens of *"Zoophycos"*, a mechanical stress between the primary and secondary gill rays is evident, as with bird-feathers, Where greater spacing between the primary rays is shown, the angle between the primary and secondary rays is more obtuse, and vice versa (see Pl. 2a, Fig. 4b).

4. Ecology and Palaeoecology

Recent sedentary sabellid worms assigned to the genera *Spirographis, Sabella* and *Bispira* are usually restricted to a shallow-water marine environment, where they live either singly or in colonies. *Spirographis spallanzanii* lives in the Mediterranean Sea, near the coasts of Italy, Yugoslavia and France. *Bispira volutacornis* has also been reported from the Mediterranean area, where they are commonly found in association with *Spirographis*. *Sabella pavonina* is known to occur in the Baltic Sea, near the north coast.

The habitat of Recent sabellid worms is thus analogous to that of their fossil ancestors which occur widely in shallow water sandstones, marls, limestones and quartzites from the Ordovician onwards.

The preservation of soft, fleshy parts of worm prostomia with distinct gill ray structure also points to rapid sedimentation, during which the worms were covered by sediment particles.

6. Conclusions

The investigations already completed together with recently discovered material provide a basis for further detailed and systematic study of these fossils. The work carried out in the last few years, e.g. in New Zealand, may enable a detailed investigation of the morphology and structure of individual organs to be made. It appears that the misinterpretations and accidental similarities between these radiate fossils and trace fossils has already obscured the true origin of these forms for a long time. The recent investigations (Plička 1962; Plumstead 1967; Stevens 1968) show that these radiate organisms must be considered from a palaeozoological standpoint. The study of analogous fossil and living organisms thus allows inferences about the development and distribution of sedentary marine sabellids ranging from the Palaeozoic to the Recent. The observation here that these worms are restricted to shallow water, allows them to be used for deducing depositional conditions, the habitat and palaeogeography.

Addendum. Discussions held at the International Conference in Liverpool brought out many points bearing on the problems discussed above. Further knowledge of "*Zoophycos*" from the Mesozoic of Antarctica (Dr. Taylor) the Neogene of central Italy (Dr. Girotti) and other areas (Professor Simpson), presented to the conference, necessitates continued detailed study to allow its origin to be established unequivocally.

References

ABEL, O. 1935. *Vorzeitliche Lebensspuren*. Gustav Fischer, Jena p. 644.
BARSANTI, L. 1902. Considerationi sopra il genere *Zoophycos*. *Memorie Soc. tosc. Sci. nat.* **18,** 68.
BRONGNIART, A. T. 1828. *Histoire des végétaux fossiles*. **1.** Paris.
CECIONI, G. O. 1957 Cretaceous flysch and molasse in Departmento Ultima Esperanza, Magallanes Province, Chile. *Bull. Am. Ass. Petrol. Geol.* **41,** 538.
FUCHS, T. 1893. Beiträge zur Kenntnis der *Spirophyten* und *Fucoiden. Sber. Akcd. Wiss. Wien, Mat.-nat. Kl.* **102,** 552.
LESSERTISSEUR, J. 1955. Traces d'activité animale et leur signification paléobiologique. *Mem. Soc. géol. Fr.* **34,** n.s. **74,** 150.
NATHORST, A. G. 1882. Mémoire sur quelques traces d'animaux sans vertèbres etc. et de leur portée paléontologique. *K. svenska Vetensk-Akad. Handl.* **18,** no. 7, 61.
—— 1883. Quelques remarques concernant la question des Algues fossiles par M. A. Nathorst. *Bull. Soc. géol. Fr.* ser. 3, **11,** 452.
—— 1886. Nouvelles observations sur des traces d'animaux et d'autres phénomènes d'origine purement mécanique et décrits comme Algues fossiles. *K. svenska Vetensk.-Akad. Handl.* **21,** no. 14.
—— 1889. Ueber verzveigte Wurmspuren im Meeresschlamme. *Annln naturh. Mus., Wien* **4,** no. 2, 84.
PLIČKA, M. 1962. Verbreitung von *Palaeospirographis hrabĕi* n.g.n.sp. (Chaetopoda, Polychaeta) im Westgebiet von Magura-Flysch in der Tschechoslowakei (vorläufiger Bericht) (Summary of Czech text.) *Vest. ústred. Úst geol.* **37,** 359.
—— 1965a. New genus of fossil marine worms (Sabellidae) of Carpathian Flysch (Czechoslovakia). (Summary of Czech text.) *Zpr. Vlastivéd. ústavu v Olomouci* no. 122, 1963/1964.
—— 1965b. Origin of fossil "*Zoophycos*". *Nature, Lond.* **208,** 579.
—— 1966. Sedimentological approach to the recognition of the origin of "*Zoophycos*" casts (Summary of Czech text). *Čas. Miner. Geol.* **11,** 423.
—— 1968. *Zoophycos,* and a proposed classification of Sabellid worms. *J. Paleont.* **42,** 836.
—— 1969. Methods for the study of "*Zoophycos*" and similar fossils. *N. Z. J. Geol. Geophys.* **12,** 551.

PLUMSTEAD, E. P. 1967. A general review of the Devonian fossil plants found in the Cape System of South Africa. *Palaeont. afr.* **10,** 1.

ROMANOVSKY, V., FRANCIS-BOEUF, C. and BOURCART, J. 1953. *La mer.* Larousse, Paris. (Russian transl.-Moscow, 1960, p. 260.)

SEILACHER, A. 1954. Die geologische Bedeutung fossiler Lebensspuren. *Z. dt. geol. Ges.* **105,** 214.

STEVENS, G. R. 1968. The Amuri fucoid. *N. Z. J. Geol. Geophys.* **11,** 253.

VENZO, S. 1951. Ammoniti e vegetali albiano-cenomaniani nel Flysch del Bergamasco occidentale. *Atti Soc. ital. Sci. nat.* **90,** 175.

—— 1954. Stratigrafia e tettonica del Flysch (cretacico-eocene) del Bergamasco e della Brianza orientale. *Memorie descr. Carta geol. Ital.* **31,** 1.

M. Plička, Central Geological Survey, Brno 3, Kamenomlýnská 581, Czechoslovakia.

Dependence of rock-borers and burrowers on the environmental conditions within the Tortonian littoral zone of Southern Poland

A. Radwański

Along the littoral zone of the Tortonian sea in Southern Poland, traces of life activity of rock-boring sponges, polychaetes, bivalves, cirripeds and echinoids are mostly confined to, and indicate, the course of rocky seashores along the southern slopes of the Central Polish Uplands. The assemblages of borings (lithophocoenoses) vary considerably and depend on the local environmental conditions prevailing in individual habitats (lithophotopes) within the littoral zone. Burrows of callianassid decapods occur only in sandy facies locally developed on the southern slopes of the Holy Cross Mountains. The burrows, mostly *Ophiomorpha nodosa* Lundgren, are confined to very shallow water marine deposits which sometimes have diversified marine communities or may lack any body fossils. In the latter areas a supply of terrestrial plant detritus was once brought in and deposited as an allochthonous brown coal, the sedimentation of which stopped the succession of burrowing callianassids. The most suitable habitat for callianassid decapods occurred when the Tortonian basin shallowed and sedimentation and infilling of bottom depressions was progressing.

1. Introduction

During the Miocene epoch, after the Carpathian range was formed by Alpine orogenic movements, a marine transgression took place in Southern Poland (Fig. 1). The transgression, which is of Lower Tortonian age, was connected with the development of the fore-Carpathian depression (Fig. 1b) situated in front of the Carpathian folds. The depressed belt, which lay outside the entire Alpine-Carpathian orogenic range, had at that time been so deepened that it became a route of marine invasion from the internal-Alpine and Mediterranean regions. While the sediments of the southern margins of the Tortonian sea are overlain by the Carpathian nappes and are disturbed by overthrusts, the northern margins, which extended to the chain of the Central Polish Uplands, are undisturbed tectonically and exposed over large areas. The Tortonian littoral zone and its deposits, extending along the southern slopes of the Central Polish Uplands, give ample evidence of the life activity of the rock-borers (lithophages) in hard substrates and of the burrowers in soft sediments.

2. The rock borers and their life environment

The Lower Tortonian transgression entered the Central Polish Upland region through valleys which were transformed into bays or straits. The littoral zone extended along the sides of all the ancient valleys. When the more resistant, usually harder or weakly stratified, limestones were encountered at the seashore, rocky littoral structures were formed. In some places on the southern slopes of the Holy Cross Mountains tracts of the rocky seashores more than 1 km in

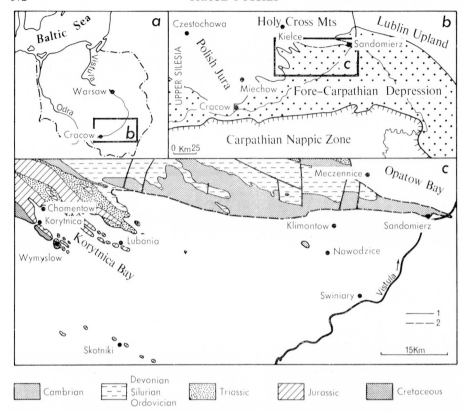

Fig. 1.   a   General map of Poland depicting the area discussed;   b   Extent of the Miocene (Tortonian) sea in Southern Poland;   c   Tortonian deposits on the southern and eastern slopes of the Holy Cross Mts.; in the Tortonian contours, the shoreline detected by littoral structures along the rocky seashores (1), and its probable extent (2) in the low lying eastern region are shown.

length (locality Lubania, Fig. 1c), are detectable in present-day morphology. If developed as abrasion surfaces, they may be easily recognized by the numerous traces of the activity of rock-borers. Likewise, their borings indicate the course of an ancient shoreline in scree-covered slopes of hills far away from the area of the Tortonian sediments now preserved.

The development of diversified rocky littoral features depended on the palaeo-geographical situation controlling local hydrodynamic conditions prevailing in the Tortonian sea. The author's detailed studies have shown to what extent these factors influenced the distribution and size of various features in the Cracow and Miechów Uplands (Radwański 1968b), as well as on the southern slopes of the Holy Cross Mountains (Radwański 1969). For the western part of the latter region it was even possible to draw a palaeogeographical map for the time of the transgression (Fig. 1c). Generally, in all the regions of the Central Polish Uplands under study, the cliffs and cliff conglomerates (boulder masses) were confined to the open sea areas, where they were developed as a result of the abrasion of rocky islands or cliffs facing the open sea. The abrasion surfaces and platforms were connected with broad bays or wider straits. Shore rubble adhered to the heads of the bays and also to some imperfectly swept abrasion surfaces, where it was trapped in clefts.

All the types of littoral habitats were occupied by lithophages. Their habitats, for which the term *lithophotope* is here introduced, were usually an extremely favourable environment for their life activities (Pl. 1-4). Sponges, polychaetes, bivalves, cirripeds and echinoids have been recognized and determined to a generic or specific rank (Radwański 1964; 1965; 1969) on the basis of their borings. The assemblages of such borings, i.e. the lithophocoenoses (Radwański 1964), vary greatly both in composition and state of preservation. Where preservation is good the openings of sponge chambers, cirripeds' sac-like holes or bivalves' siphonal necks, shaped as a figure-of-eight, are seen (Pl. 3a). The pits of echinoids are also remarkably preserved (Pl. 1a). Poorer preservation is sometimes the result of slight abrasion destroying the outlets of borings (Pl. 4a, b). Stronger abrasion is evident in the cases in which bivalve borings are cut halfway or more along their length (Pl. 2a, 4d). In such cases smaller borings of other lithophages may have been completely removed. Frequently, a partly abraded older lithophocoenose was followed by a younger one (Pl. 3c, 4c).

The composition of the lithophocoenoses is often diversified. Usually, two or at most three lithophages predominate in a lithophotope, which affects both fixed (abrasion surfaces, Pl. 1-3) and moveable substrates (pebbles, rubble, Pl. 4). In the latter case, the redeposition and accumulation of pebbles could lead to a concentration of the material inhabited by various lithophages. Thus, the lithophocoenoses of cliff conglomerates, whose material was redeposited (so-called allochthonous boulder masses), were obviously the richest ones (Radwański 1968a).

Of the rock-boring animals, sponges are the most frequent components of the lithophocoenoses. The occurrence of *Cliona celata* Grant, very abundant *Cliona vastifica* Hancock (Pl. 4c), *Cliona viridis* (O. Schmidt) (Pl. 4b) and *Cliothosa* sp. was inferred on the basis of the morphology of the borings (Radwański 1964; 1969).

Polychaetes have also been recognized from their borings (Radwański 1964; 1965; 1969) including *Potamilla reniformis* (O. F. Müller), *Polydora ciliata* (Johnston) which lived in some places in huge swarms (Pl. 3c) and *Polydora hoplura* (Claparède) in more dispersed colonies (Pl. 2b).

Next to the sponges, bivalves are the most frequent rock-borers. Most of their borings are preserved empty since the shells have been crushed and swept away by spray or abraded by littoral currents. In some borings, mostly where abrasion was slight, the shells, calcareous linings (in pholadids) or moulds are, however, preserved and allow specific determinations (Radwański 1964; 1965; 1968b; 1969). Since the borings were found by the present writer to correspond exactly in shape to individual bivalves, it was suggested (Radwański 1965) that the empty borings should be determined only to generic rank, while specific determinations should be restricted to borings which contain shells or moulds. Thus, *Gastrochaena* sp. (Pl. 3a, 4d), *Aspidopholas* sp., *Jouannetia* sp. and *Lithophaga* sp. (Pl. 4c) have been recognized on the basis of empty borings. The species *Gastrochaena dubia* (Pennant), *Aspidopholas rugosa* (Brocchi), *Jouannetia semicaudata* (des Moulins) and *Lithophaga lithophaga* (Linnaeus) respectively (Radwański 1965; 1969) are responsible for making the borings. Of these bivalves, *Gastrochaena* and *Lithophaga* were the most abundant and lived in large colonies (Pl. 3a, 4c), while both pholadids were either sparsely distributed or gathered in small groups.

PLATE 1

Plate 1

a Fragment of an abrasion surface bored by echinoids and *Polydora hoplura* (Claparède) on a hill at Lubania, Holy Cross Mountains.

b Marginal part of an abrasion platform at the foot of a hill, with various borings, mostly the same as those in the preceding figure. Same locality.

Cirripeds recognized on the basis of their borings (Radwański 1964; 1969), such as *Zapfella pattei* Saint-Seine, are the rarest lithophages, but in some litho-photopes they occasionally occur in great numbers, both in abrasion surfaces and pebbles (Pl. 4a). This species has so far been most frequently encountered in the Tertiary, mostly in the shells of dead molluscs (Radwański 1964).

Taxonomically undetermined echinoids have been recognized by Radwański (1965; 1969) on the basis of their shallow pits which frequently appear in some abrasion surfaces or platforms (Pl. 1a, b, 2b), which, were the only habitats of these shallow borers.

The distribution of the lithophages under study evidently depended on local environmental conditions. Sponges preferred clean and highly agitated waters as a lithophotope and here they are especially numerous. They disappear in places where Upper Cretaceous marls were being eroded to produce significant amounts of marly ooze. Such an environment was, however, preferred by pholadids (*Jouannetia*, less frequently *Aspidopholas*) and an associated polychaete, *Polydora ciliata*.

Polychaetes mostly inhabited abrasion surfaces, as for example *Polydora ciliata*, in densities amounting to 15-20 individuals per cm², which corresponds to popula-tions of 150,000-200,000 per m², similar to those on the present day English coasts. The species discussed has also very often gathered in clefts in surfaces formed under mild abrasion. The species *Polydora hoplura* inhabited zones affected by strong waves and currents. These conditions usually occurred on abrasion surfaces placed centrally along the longer bays or straits. Similar conditions were favourable for echinoids, thus both these lithophages occur together (Pl. 1a, b, 2b). In other environments polychaetes occur dispersed or sometimes collect in larger boulders quietly resting near or far from the cliffs.

Among bivalves, *Lithophaga* preferred abrasion surfaces and bigger boulders or cobbles (Pl. 4c) regardless of local hydrodynamic conditions, while *Gastrochaena* bored densely (Pl. 3a) only in quiet waters, usually in the terminal parts of bays or amidst thresholds in the marginal zones of bays. The pholadids also preferred rather quiet conditions and, as mentioned above, even penetrated niches avoided by other bivalves.

Finally, the cirriped *Zapfella pattei* clearly chose a littoral-rubble zone at the heads of bays as its habitat.

In analysing all the lithophocoenoses of the area investigated and their environments, it is clear that the distribution pattern of lithophages presented above should be regarded only as a generalised picture. Some lithophocoenoses appear to be the results of the life activity of two or more generations during which time the environmental conditions could have changed somewhat. It is also obvious that the lithophocoenoses preserved represent, and reflects, the life conditions existing just before the area was covered by sediment and when the action of littoral agents was ceasing. At this time, some lithophocoenoses might yet have been destroyed (Pl. 2a), although most of them are preserved in a state as if the life of the last generation of lithophages had just terminated. In fact, the time interval between the cessation of abrasion and the covering of the lithophotope by sediments, was probably long enough for the development of the red alga *Lithothamnium* sp. and various epizoans and endozoans living in borings vacated by shells or bodies. Corals (Pl. 3a, b), serpulids, the gastropod *Vermetus intortus* (Lamarck), and bryozoans, abundant in some places, belong to the first group of animals, while another gastropod, *Crepidula crepidula* (Linnaeus), and a bivalve *Sphenia anatina* (Basterot) are predominant in the second group. In some cases, a more complete succession of conditions may be traced, such as, for instance, habitation of borings by bivalves after a period of stronger abrasion, the sweeping of the shells out of the borings and, subsequently, abrasion of the lithophotope together with the bivalves domiciled inside (Pl. 2a); another example includes stronger abrasion after the formation of the older lithophocoenose and a lesser abrasion after the younger generation of rock-borers (Pl. 4b). All these examples indicate that the lithophocoenoses are sensitive indicators both of hydrodynamic conditions and the environment of rock-borers and associated littoral animals.

The lithophocoenoses under study extended over rocky parts of the shores in the Central Polish Uplands. The shores of almost the entire Cracow Upland (Upper Jurassic or Middle Triassic limestones) were rocky. This character, less conspicuous in the Miechów Upland (Upper Cretaceous marly limestones and marls) was once again prominent in the western part of the southern slopes of the Holy Cross Mountains (Upper Jurassic and Middle Devonian limestones and, locally, Upper Cretaceous marly limestones and marls—Fig. 1c). At the time of the transgression in these regions, morphological depressions were as deep as 40-60 m. These depressions were gradually filled with sediments either transported from the land, or spread from the littoral zone which contained, in addition to the abrasive material, abundant organic detritus consisting mainly of lithothamnians with some oysters and bryozoans. It is clear from successive organic communities that as the depressions were filled, the depth of the basin gradually decreased by the continual deposition of littoral material formed by the abrasion of higher parts of rocky shores. During that period, communities of rock-borers frequently spread from the eulittoral zone and settled in adjacent parts of the submerged bottom on all available hard objects, mostly on organic material such as corals and shells of dead molluscs.

In general, the Lower Tortonian lithophocoenoses of Southern Poland are similar to those of the present-day Mediterranean, especially to those of the Dalmatian coasts. The Lower Tortonian coasts, marked by longitudinal and parallel interconnected bays, are evidently morphologically of Dalmatian type. In fact, as revealed by an analysis of several faunal groups contained in the Lower Tortonian, climatic conditions in this marine basin were also comparable to or slightly warmer than the present Mediterranean (cf. Bałuk and Radwański 1967 p. 497). The Tortonian sea of Southern Poland was connected by wide zones with other peri-Carpathian and peri-Alpine basins and, through them, with the seas of the Mediterranean region. The rock-borers, many of which persisted in the Mediterranean basins from the Miocene up to the Recent, spread during that period over the entire part of Europe under study. Their occurrence was occasionally recorded in a few localities as, for instance, in the Vienna basin, along the coasts of which even quite large littoral features have been preserved with markedly developed lithophocoenoses (Radwański 1968a).

Plate 2

Fig. a natural size.

a Fragment of an abrasion surface bored by *Aspidopholas* sp. and *Lithophaga* sp. The borings partly abraded after inhabitation by other bivalves (arrowed) and infilling by fine-detrital oyster material. Bodzów, Cracow Upland.

b Fragment of an abrasion surface bored by *Polydora hoplura* (Claparède) and faintly pitted by echinoids (at centre and left margin). Lubania, Holy Cross Mts.

PLATE 2

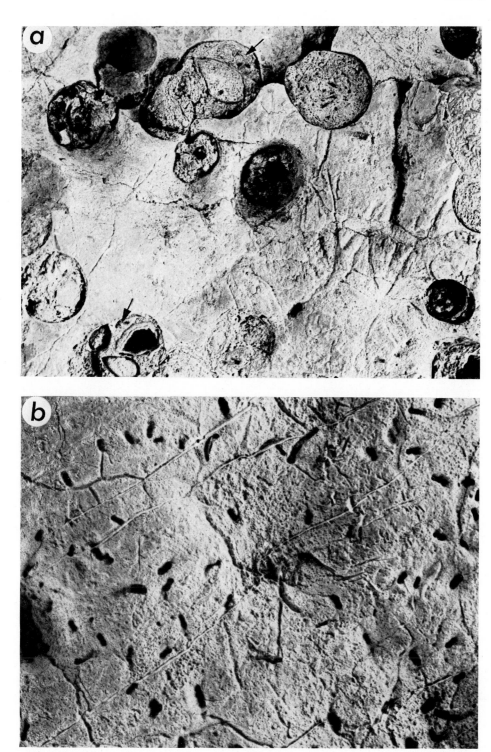

3. The burrowers and their habitat

Within the littoral zone of the Tortonian sea of Southern Poland, conditions favourable for a mass appearance of burrowers became prevalent only in the areas in which a sandy facies developed. This took place mostly in the eastern part of the southern slopes, and on the eastern slopes, of the Holy Cross Mountains where the transgression covered an area consisting mainly of fine-grained clastics of Lower and Middle Cambrian age (Fig. 1c). Here there were few surface features and the terrain was covered with rubble; more resistant elements were limited to small, local, occurences of the Devonian or Jurassic limestones. Shallow parts of the littoral zone were mostly covered with variously developed sandy deposits containing a variety of palaeontological material depending on the changing environmental conditions. This facies provided a suitable habitat for callianassid decapods, which produced burrows corresponding closely to *Ophiomorpha nodosa* Lundgren (Pl. 5a, b), for synonymy see Häntzschel 1952; Kennedy and Macdougall 1969. Their mode of occurrence is indicated in profiles (Fig. 2) of sand pits at Męczennice, Nawodzice and Świniary (Radwański 1967; Bałuk and Radwański 1968).

At Nawodzice, *Ophiomorpha nodosa* occurs infrequently in sands with a rich faunal assemblage (unit 2, in the profile) which overlies unfossiliferous sands (unit 1). Within unit 2, several indistinct layers contain diverse fossils, either in life position or redeposited (Fig. 3). The latter fossils usually occur in lenses which also contain many crushed remains. In other layers, most fossils (lithothamnians, veneridid or razor clams, branched bryozoans, starfish) are preserved in life position. The starfish are preserved as complete skeletons with the original arrangement of plates and dermal spines. It has been shown by a detailed palaeontological study (Bałuk and Radwański 1968) that deposition probably took place in the littoral or sub-littoral zone. The sandy material, stirred up in adjoining areas probably by storms and transported by wave-produced currents, rapidly settled here, covering various living organisms. Stronger currents led to the spreading of the material and traction of the organic detritus and gravels, which were then deposited in lenses. This activity resulted in a destruction of upper parts of *Ophiomorpha* burrows (Fig. 3 and Weimer and Hoyt 1964 pl. 123 fig. 4). The sedimentation of unit 2 was completed when storm agitation spread to this region, covering it with a mass of irregularly deposited large pebbles and cobbles, along

---

Plate 3

All natural size except **b**.

a Fragment of an abrasion surface bored by abundant *Gastrochaena* sp. Borings with preserved figure-of-eight openings visible right of centre, those destroyed by abrasion, in the remaining part. Also, many borings of *Potamilla reniformis* (O. F. Müller), *Polydora ciliata* (Johnston) and three large borings of *Lithophaga* sp.

b ×2 magnification of the part of **a** arrowed showing agglutinated siphonal chimney of *Gastrochaena* sp., of a new generation, projecting above the abraded boring of an older generation. Also an epizoic coral. Korytnica, Holy Cross Mountains.

c Fragment of an abrasion surface extensively bored by *Polydora ciliata* (Johnston). Strongly abraded borings of *Lithophaga* sp., partly infilled by fine-detrital oyster material, belong to an older generation of rock-borers. Cracow-Zwierzyniec, Cracow Upland.

PLATE 3

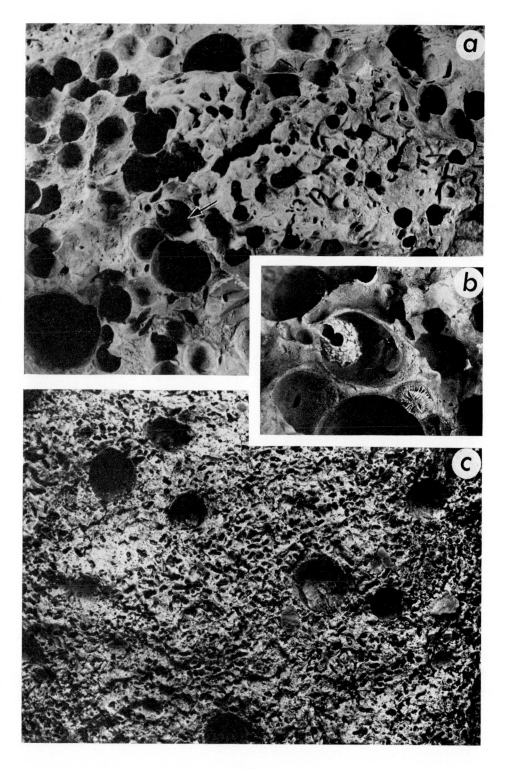

379

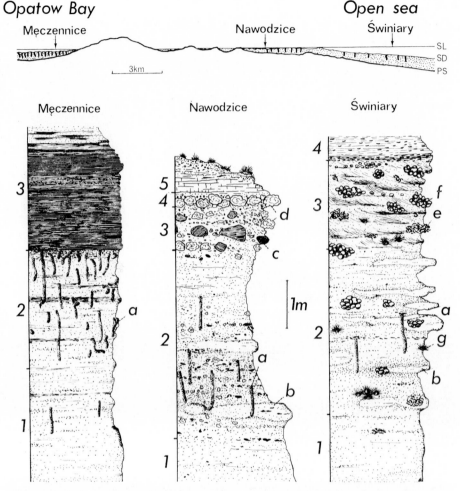

Fig. 2. *Ophiomorpha* bearing profiles and their palaeogeographical situation on the eastern slopes of the Holy Cross Mts. In the section, the extent of the probable pre-Tortonian surface of substratal rocks (PS), the surface of deposits during formation of *Ophiomorpha* (SD), and the sea level (SL) are shown. In the profiles the numbers denote the units discussed in the text, while the letters indicate some components of the deposits: a *Ophiomorpha nodosa* Lundgren; b calcitic cementations c pebbles and cobbles; d lithothamnian balls; e serpulid clusters; f oyster clusters; g echinoids.

Plate 4

All natural size.

a Pebble bored predominantly by *Zapfella pattei* Saint-Seine; the borings with abraded openings. Littoral rubble at Korytnica, Holy Cross Mountains.

b Pebble bored predominantly by *Cliona viridis* (O. Schmidt); the borings, with outlets subsequently abraded, belong to a younger generation of lithophages that have settled after abrasion of neighbouring bivalve borings. Allochthonous boulder at Skotniki, Holy Cross Mountains.

c Similar example to preceding one: a cobble with crowded borings of older *Lithophaga* sp., strongly abraded before colonisation by *Cliona vastifica* Hancock and *Polydora ciliata* (Johnson). Same locality.

d Pebble attacked by *Gastrochaena* sp. the borings of which have been strongly abraded, and by a single *Polydora ciliata* (Johnston). Littoral rubble at Wymysłów, Holy Cross Mountains.

PLATE 4

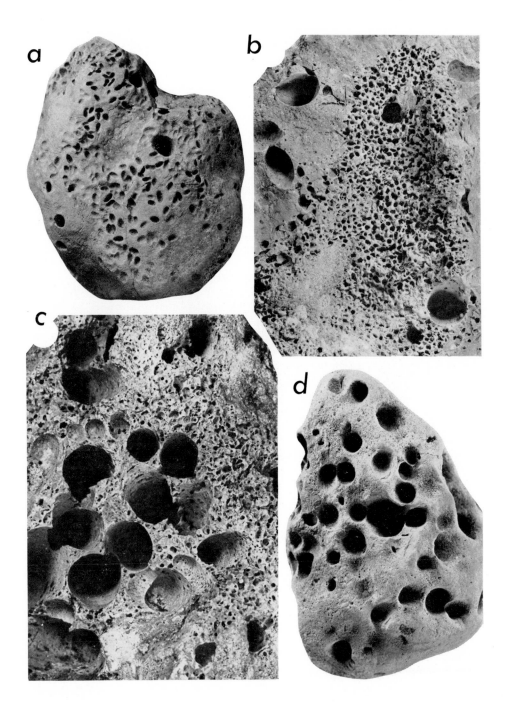

with lithothamnian balls and a comminuted strongly crushed fauna (unit 3). The sequence terminates with lithothamnians and a fine gravel (unit 4).

At Świniary, the sands are finer-grained and without gravel. In this profile, the first sands have a sparse fauna or are unfossiliferous (unit 1); higher up there are sands with sporadic *Ophiomorpha nodosa* (unit 2). In the latter unit, a relatively sparse and strongly selective fauna consists mostly of scallops and schizechinid(?) echinoids which sometimes occur in groups and are preserved as skeletons complete with spines and lantern; in addition, the serpulid *Serpula subpacta* Rovereto and the oyster *Pycnodonta leopolitana* (Niedźwiedzki), both occur in small clusters encrusted by bryozoans. Sedimentation took place under calm conditions far from the influences of the littoral zone and its rich organic life. A stronger influx of material led to the formation of unit 3 in which sands are cross-bedded and contain many large oysters and/or serpulid clusters sometimes crushed and spread in cosets. There are also solitary echinoids, sometimes fragmented.

The profiles of Nawodzice and Świniary display a consistent change in environment with increase in water depth from an initial stage high in the sublittoral zone. Towards Świniary, the sea was gradually deepening and the influence of the littoral zone gradually diminishing. During stronger storms (unit 3), the coarser clastic material and lithothamnians were no longer transported to this locality but echinoids and clusters of oysters and serpulids were introduced from somewhere in the mid-offshore zone. A reconstructed section (upper part of Fig. 2) shows the probable situation of the sea bottom during the activity of callianassid burrowers. These animals gradually disappeared towards the deeper waters of the open sea to the south. From cross-bedding orientation it is clear that the sandy material was drifted here by storms from the intermediate zone, situated nearer Nawodzice. This zone appears to have had an irregular substratum as shown in Figure 2 in which the vertical scale is exaggerated. During the transgression, the area north of Nawodzice, where the Tortonian deposits are preserved as thin erosional lenticles (Fig. 1c), was either thinly covered with sediment or emergent. These deposits occur once again in a large depression which was transformed during the transgression into an extensive, although not very deep, bay (Opatów Bay, Fig. 1c and the section in Fig. 2). Abundant sandy sedimentation and a habitat suitable for burrowing callianassids persisted in this area.

At Męczennice, *Ophimorpha nodosa* is abundant (Pl. 5a, b) in sands *c.* 2 m thick (unit 2), overlying sands with individual *Ophiomorpha* (unit 1) and underlying brown-coal layers (Unit 3). Limonitized *Ophiomorpha* is the only evidence of organic life in the sands. The limonitization of *Ophiomorpha* is here an epigenetic phenomenon, probably related to the dissolution of not only the primary material of the walls of burrows but also of other faunal remains. Since the *Ophiomorpha*-bearing layers are intercalated with laminated clay layers, which usually truncate some of the burrows, sedimentation in this area must have been turbulent. The next generation of callianassids has frequently burrowed through the previously deposited layers and consequently, in many places the burrows intersect the clay intercalations which truncate previous burrows (Pl. 5b). The richest development of callianassids took place in the top of the unit, which probably corresponded to a long period of non-deposition. The latter assemblage of burrows is, however, markedly truncated (Fig. 2) by brown coal layers rarely intercalated by sands. Interbedding of brown-coal and sand indicate that the coal is allochthonous and that it was probably transported by strong currents which, in the first phase, truncated the *Ophiomorpha*-bearing sands. Above the coal, the sandy sedimentation again appears but without *Ophiomorpha*. In higher parts of the profile, the sands gradually pass into fossiliferous, marly lithothomnian deposits. The appearance

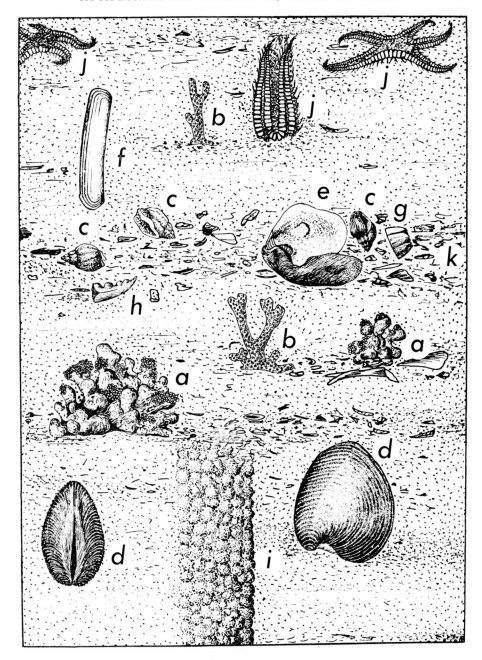

Fig. 3. Detail of part of the *Ophiomorpha*-bearing unit at Nawodzice showing alternation of fossils buried in life position or redeposited (natural size):   a red alga *Lithothamnium* sp. encrusted by bryozoans, mainly *Colletosia endlicheri* (Reuss), and by cirripeds *Verruca* sp.; b branched bryozoans *Porella cervicornis* (Pallas);   c gastropods *Nassa coarctata zboroviensis* Friedberg;   d bivalves *Chione subplicata orientalis* Friedberg;   e bivalve *Ostrea* sp. encrusting a pebble;   f bivalve *Ensis rollei* Hoernes;   g cirriped *Balanus* sp.;   h crab's claw;   i burrow *Ophiomorpha nodosa* Lundgren;   j starfish *Astropecten* sp., one of the specimens buried with upraised arms in its burrowing position; k shell detritus.

of brown coal is the result of the isolation of the wide and relatively shallow
Opatów Bay from the sea. Large amounts of plant detritus, either transported
fluvially from the land or derived from shore zone swamps, drifted to this bay.
The sudden appearance of this material suggests that violent storms attacked
shore zone swamps. This corresponds to similar violent changes in environment
and material supply recorded in the Nawodzice and Świniary profiles. In all the
profiles, these changes terminate the conditions favourable for callianassids,
and mark the onset of stronger current activity.

The persistence of the brown-coal material only in Opatów Bay was caused by a
ridge, which separated the bay from the Nawodzice-Świniary zone and hampered
the transport of this material towards the open sea. It was precisely from this
ridge that the clastic material, and from its margins that many lithothamnian
balls, were supplied during the deposition of units 3-4 at Nawodzice. During the
formation of the *Ophiomorpha*-bearing sands (unit 2), this ridge supplied much
smaller amounts of material. Organic material, swept from the ridge, was supplied
to the Nawodzice zone, e.g. the gastropods *Nassa* and *Potamides* which are not
wholly marine in character, and oysters (Fig. 3). Both these gastropods presumably lived in temporary lagoons or pools on or near the ridge where
brackish conditions prevailed within an extensive littoral zone in which the
oysters were also more numerous. The periodical sweeping out of all the
material from the lagoons either took place during violent storms, or might be
the result of tidal activity. Perhaps, the laminated clayey intercalations in the sands
of the Opatów bay should also be correlated with the activity of tides or resultant
water movement in the subtidal zone. The last-named possibility would also
explain the persistence of a high-energy environment in the bay and, consequently,
an abundant occurrence of callianassids whose burrowing habit is a result of
adaptation to such conditions. The Nawodzice zone, far away from the ridge
(Fig. 2), was always situated below the intertidal or shallow subtidal zone, thus
resulting in the infrequent occurrence of callianassids, as in Recent seas (Weimer
and Hoyt 1964). Possibly also, *Ophiomorpha* at Nawodzice indicates that during
the formation of the profile the sedimentation zone was temporarily included in
the intertidal environment. As shown by the Świniary profile such suggested
vertical changes did not lead, in deeper parts of the sea, to any major decrease in
depth or to a more abundant appearance of callianassids.

In all profiles under study, *Ophiomorpha nodosa* appears not in the bottom of
transgressive deposits but in a specific part of the profile overlying, often completely, unfossiliferous sands which are of variable character and thickness. It
is therefore concluded that in this area, the transgression rapidly flooded a terrain

---

Plate 5

a Burrows of *Ophiomorpha nodosa* Lundgren in a sandy layer at Męczennice, Holy Cross
Mountains.

b Unit with *Ophiomorpha nodosa* Lundgren at Męczennice; some burrows penetrate through
the clayey intercalations, others are truncated by the latter.

PLATE 5

of variable relief, whereas the conditions favourable to callianassids prevailed only when the depressions were being filled with sediment and the water was shallow (Fig. 2).

Faunal and sedimentological features of the Tortonian sands indicate that the callianassids inhabited the same environment as *Callianassa major* Say, found today along the coasts of Florida and Georgia (Weimer and Hoyt 1964). In the Tortonian burrows there are no skeletal remains of decapods and, therefore, no particular species of callianassids can be held responsible for making these *Ophiomorpha*. The features of the deposits with *Ophiomorpha nodosa* are also indicative of low littoral and shallow offshore conditions (Häntzschel 1952; Hecker *et al.* 1963; Weimer and Hoyt 1964; Gry 1968; Jux and Strauch 1968; Kennedy and Macdougall 1969). In this very zone, there was the possibility of an accumulation of a brackish fauna drifted from temporarily fresh-water parts of the littoral zone as for example at Nawodzice, as in the Weald Clay of southeastern England (Kennedy and Macdougall 1969). The occurrence of intercalations within the the allochthonous brackish fauna is not, therefore, evidence of brackish conditions in the sedimentary environment. Likewise, the appearance of the allochthonous brown-coal material in the Męczennice profile does not indicate a terrestrial environment in that area.

The Męczennice profile is particularly significant because in the European Tertiary, particularly in Germany, e.g. in the Eocene (Hillmer 1963), Oligocene (Baatz 1959; Jux and Strauch 1967) and Miocene (Häntzschel 1952; Seidel 1956; Lohmann 1959), *Ophiomorpha* often occur in sands of the brown-coal bearing profiles. On the basis of the presence of a marine fauna in associated deposits, these burrows have been considered by most authors to be indicative of a marine environment (Häntzschel 1952; Seidel 1956; Lohmann 1959; Baatz 1959; Jux and Strauch 1967). In the light of these facts, the conclusions of some authors on a nonmarine origin of at least some *Ophiomorpha* (Lüttig 1962; Hillmer 1963; Seilacher 1967) based on observation of these profiles, are not convincing. Furthermore, they cannot be sustained after a more detailed facial analysis of *Ophiomorpha*-bearing profiles containing nonmarine horizons (Jux and Strauch 1968; Kennedy and Macdougall 1969).

It is striking that *Ophiomorpha nodosa* from various localities and ages displays conspicuously similar shape characteristics and mode of occurrence, thus allowing one to consider it as a well defined ichnospecies. Its synonymy should also include the burrows from the Eocene of Hungary illustrated by Dudich (1962) and regarded as made by annelids (a view accepted by Häntzschel 1966).

Along the Tortonian seashores of the Holy Cross Mountains, burrows of another type appear in the terminal part of the Korytnica Bay (Fig. 1c), in which a transitory sandy facies occurred locally near the shores of the bay. This facies appeared after the period during which a pre-Tortonian valley was filled with the Korytnica clays (of the Baden type), containing numerous fossils, mostly gastropods and less frequently bivalves, chitons, corals and cirripeds (Radwański 1964; 1969; Bałuk and Radwański 1967). The Korytnica clays are overlaid (Radwański 1969) by sandy marls with an abundant fauna (unit 1 in the Chomentów section, Fig. 4) and yet higher up by marly sands with large shells of *Pinna pectinata brocchii* d'Orbigny and *Crassostrea gryphoides* (Schlotheim) usually encrusted by barnacles, serpulids and bryozoans, and with other fauna and burrows (unit 2). The burrows are cylindrical, straight or gently curving, 4-6 cm in diameter (canal 1·5-2·5 cm), smooth or sometimes grooved probably by synaeresis or desiccation cracks (Pl. 6a, b), their length amounts to *c.* 75 cm, although most of them are truncated (Fig. 4). They probably represent a new ichnological taxon, but it is not proposed to

PLATE 6

Plate 6

All natural size.

a Terminated fragment of a callianassid burrow from sands at Chomentów, Holy Cross Mountains.

b Fragment of another callianassid burrow from sands at Chomentów, with a grooved pattern on the surface.

c Underside view of the above, showing canal.

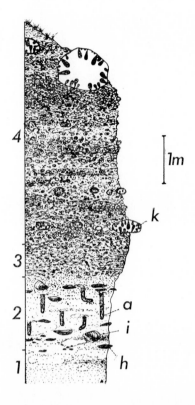

Fig. 4. Burrow-bearing profile at Chomentów. The numbers denote the units discussed in the text, while the letters indicate some components of the deposits: a   callianassid burrows, h segregated valves of *Crassostrea gryphoides* (Schlotheim), usually bored by lithophages and encrusted by various epizoans;   i   shells of *Pinna pectinata brocchii* d'Orbigny in their supposed life position;   k cobbles and boulders bored by lithophages and embedded in lithothamnian layers.

introduce a new name here. The general shape and the canal preserved (Pl. 6, Fig. 2a) suggest a large callianassid as the burrower. Segregated valves of encrusted oysters and truncated burrows indicate a high-energy environment, different from that which existed during the formation of the Korytnica clays. In this locality, the sedimentation of burrow-bearing sands also terminates abruptly and the sands are overlain by marls with redeposited lithothamnian balls (unit 3); they are followed by lithothamnian limestones containing, in a few layers, larger cobbles and boulders of Jurassic limestone (unit 4). The last-named, up to one metre in diameter, were derived from the rocky shores of the bay in which they were bored by lithophages, later on to be hurled by storms over a lithothamnian pavement which probably carpeted the basin up to sea level. Such transport from the shore (for *c.* 200-300 m) was similar to that over the surface of Recent coral reefs (Newell 1955 pl. 2A). The callianassid inhabited, therefore, the Korytnica Bay during the period when the bay shallowed to depths of a few metres as a result of the inflow of sands. The regularity in the appearance of these decapods is, therefore, the same here as in the eastern part of the Holy Cross Mountains, where there is also evidence of a considerable change in hydrodynamic conditions above burrow bearing units. These great, more or less contemporaneous changes can be related to the changes in palaeogeography caused by the uplift of the Carpathian range (Fig. 1b). These movements in the Carpathians took place when the depressions in the substratum on the slopes of the Holy Cross Mountains, flooded by the transgression, were already almost completely filled with sediment. Admittedly, these movements were followed by a conspicuous deepening of the fore-Carpathian basin, which facilitated further sedimentation (units 4 at Świniary and 5 at Nawodzice), but, owing to the Carpathian uplift, the Tortonian sea lost its connection with the Mediterranean region. During that period, the wholly-marine fauna and flora, that is the rock-borers and burrowers, disappeared, then there occurred either a gradual evaporation of the basin, combined with gypsum precipitation, or persistent clastic sedimentation in extensive lagoons, diluted by fresh water, in the upper parts of the Tortonian. The rock-borers and burrowers never returned to the territory of Southern Poland during the final stage of the development of this fore-Carpathian basin.

References

BAATZ, H. 1959. *Ophiomorpha* Lundgren, ein marines Spurenfossil, im Oberen Quarzitsand Niederhessens. *Notizbl. hess. Landesant. Bodenforsch. Wiesbaden* **87**, 168.
BAŁUK, W. and RADWAŃSKI, A. 1967. Miocene cirripeds domiciled in corals. *Acta palaeont. pol.* **12**, 457.
—— and —— 1968. Lower Tortonian sands at Nawodzice (southern slopes of the Holy Cross Mountains), their fauna and facial development, *Acta geol. pol.* **18**, 466.
DUDICH, E. 1962. Ein neues Anneliden-Wohnrohr aus dem helvetischen Schotterkomplex in der Nähe von Budapest. *Földt. Közl.* **92**, 107.
GRY, H. 1968. Callianassagange og Skolithorsrør i Robbedaleformationen. *Meddr dansk geol. Foren.* **18**, 205.
HÄNTZSCHEL, W. 1952. Die Lebensspur *Ophiomorpha* Lundgren im Miozän bei Hamburg, ihre weltweite Verbreitung und Synonymie. *Mitt. Geol. St. Inst. Hamb.* **21**, 142.
—— 1966. Recent contributions to knowledge of trace fossils and problematica. *Paleont. Contr. Univ. Kansas* Paper 9.
HECKER, R. Th., OSSIPOVA, A. I. and BELSKAYA, T. N. 1963. Fergana gulf of Paleogene sea of Central Asia, its history, sediments, fauna, and flora, their environment and evolution. *Bull. Am. Ass. Petrol. Geol.* **47**, 617.
HILLMER, G. 1963. Zur Ökologie von *Ophiomorpha* Lundgren. *Neues Jb. Geol. Paläont. Mh.* **3**, 137.
JUX, U. and STRAUCH, F. 1967. Zum marinen Oligozän am Bergischen Höhenrand. *Decheniana* **118**, 125.
—— and —— 1968. *Ophiomorpha* Lundgren 1891 aus dem Mesozoikum von Bornholm. *Meddr. dansk geol. Foren.* **18**, 213.
KENNEDY, W. J. and MACDOUGALL, J. D. S. 1969. Crustacean burrows in the Weald Clay (Lower Cretaceous) of south-eastern England and their environmental significance. *Palaeontology* **12**, 459.
LOHMANN, G. 1959. Zum Bau des Oberweserberglandes zwischen Hannoversch-Münden und Karlshafen. *Diss. Hamburg Geol. Inst.* for 1959, p. 44.
LÜTTIG, G. 1962. Das Braunkohlenbecken von Bornhausen am Harz. *Geol. Jb.* **79**, 565.
NEWELL, N. D. 1955. Depositional fabric in Permian reef limestones. *J. Geol.* **63**, 301.
RADWAŃSKI, A. 1964. Boring animals in Miocene littoral environments of Southern Poland. *Bull. Acad. pol. Sci. Sér. Sci. géol. géogr.* **12**, 57.
—— 1965. Additional notes on Miocene littoral structures of Southern Poland. *Ibid.* **13**, 167.
—— 1967. Remarks on some Lower Tortonian brown-coal bearing sediments on the southern and eastern slopes of the Holy Cross Mountains. *Ibid.* **15**, 33.
—— 1968a. Tortonian cliff deposits at Zahorska Bystrica near Bratislava (Southern Slovakia). *Ibid.* **16**, 97.
—— 1968b. Lower Tortonian transgression onto the Miechów and Cracow Uplands. *Acta geol. pol.* **18**, 438.
—— 1969. Lower Tortonian transgression onto the southern slopes of the Holy Cross Mountains. *Ibid.* **19**, 137.

SEIDEL, U. 1956. Ein Vorkommen von *Ophiomorpha* Lundgren im Miozän der Niederrheinischen
    Bucht. *Neues Jb. Geol. Paläont. Mh.* **10,** 489.
SEILACHER, A. 1967. Bathymetry of trace fossils. *Mar. Geol.* **5,** 413.
WEIMER, R. J. and HOYT, J. H. 1964. Burrows of *Callianassa major* Say, geologic indicators
    of littoral and shallow neritic environments. *J. Paleont.* **38,** 761.

A. Radwański, Institute of Geology, The University, Warsaw 22, Poland, Al. Zwirki-i-Wigury
93.

Mass properties, stability, and ecology of marine muds related to burrowing activity

D. C. Rhoads

Intensive burrowing of subtidal muds by deposit-feeding organisms in Buzzards Bay and Cape Cod Bay, Massachusetts produces a granular surface layer 5-10 mm thick. This uncompacted zone contains more than 60% water by weight and exhibits thixotropic properties. Less intensively burrowed muds lack the granular surface texture, contain less than 50% water, and have plastic properties. Burrowed muds experience resuspension rates of 35 mg/cm²/day in Buzzards Bay and 80 mg/cm²/day in Cape Cod Bay. Resuspension of the reworked granular layer is related to erosion by tidal currents.

The original near surface water content may be reconstructed for ancient sediments by observing features of biodeformational structures in thin-section.

Bivalved molluscs and articulate brachiopods show similar behavioural and morphologic adaptations for living on burrowed unstable muds: formation of epibioses, migration of adults to muds from solid surfaces of juvenile settlement, development of thin-compressed valves and formation of spines or frilly extensions. Infaunal bivalves are of low bulk density and display a high degree of vertical mobility.

1. Introduction

Burrowing activities of deposit-feeding organisms contribute significantly to the mass properties of bottom muds. These biogenic changes are commonly in the form of decreased compaction and increased water content of the sediment. In turn, the state of compaction of a mud bottom influences the species composition of populations capable of living on a mud surface. Analysis of animal-sediment interactions is necessary to understand the ecology and palaeoecology of fine-grained sediments.

Organisms living on, or in, a 'soft' mud bottom commonly differ in features of morphology, behaviour, and feeding type from species living on 'firm' mud bottoms. These biologic differences may exist although the two sediment types are comparable in organic content and grain size, differing only in water content. The purpose of this study is to: (i) investigate the relationship between burrowing activity, mass properties, and the physical stability of fine-grained sediments, (ii) demonstrate how the original surface water content may be inferred from preserved details of burrow structures in ancient sediments, and (iii) review those morphologic and behavioural adaptations of bivalves and articulate brachiopods that have allowed members of these two groups to populate successfully soft, unstable, muddy substrata.

Observations and measurements of animal-sediment interactions were made during the period 1967–1969 in Buzzards Bay and Cape Cod Bay, Massachusetts. Buzzards Bay is approximately 35 km long and 13 km wide. The centre of the bay is occupied by a silt-clay bottom at a depth range of 13-20 m. Shallower near-shore bottoms are composed of sandy muds, sands, and gravel. Data for Buzzards Bay was obtained from two sampling transects established earlier by Sanders (1958) and Rhoads and Young (1970). From these intensively studied transects, two stations

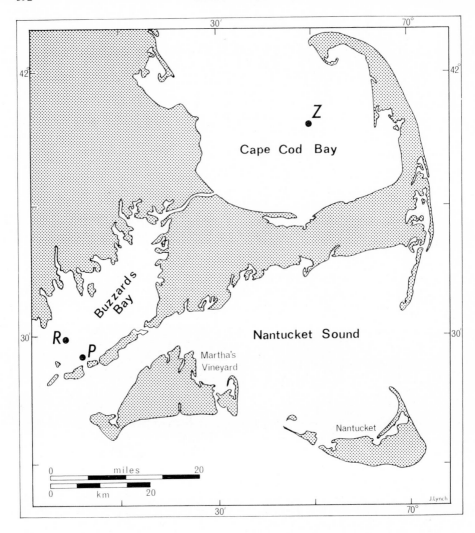

Fig. 1. Index map of sampling stations. Sts. P (13 m) and R (20 m), were established earlier by Sanders (1958). St. Z (34 m), Cape Cod Bay, was located for the present study.

are chosen for this study as they are typical of firm (St. P, 10m) and soft (St. R, 20m) bottom types. Comparative data on the structure and dynamics of a soft mud bottom located in 34 m of water in Cape Cod Bay (St. Z) are also included (Fig. 1).

2. Methods of investigation

The vertical distribution of Recent infaunal benthos living in muds was determined from X-radiographs of narrow aquaria maintained in laboratory tanks. Plexiglas

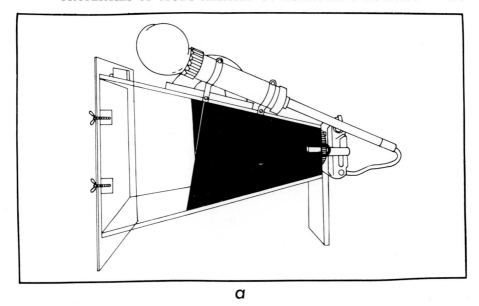

a

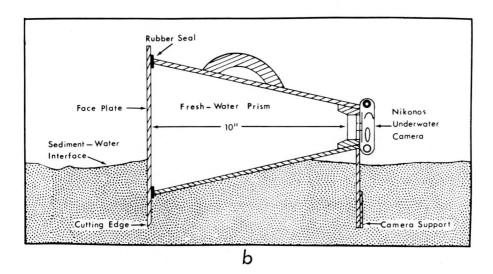

b

Fig. 2. Sediment-water interface camera.   a Lateral view showing the plexiglas pyramid attached to a Nikonos underwater camera, the apical part of the fresh-water prism, painted black to decrease backscatter of light, ar d Nikonos flash unit used to illuminate the sediment-water interface profile.   b Cross-section showing the camera placed in position (by a diver) to photograph the sediment surface in profile.

box cores of bottom muds taken by divers were also X-rayed to document the vertical distribution of infaunal species.

Small scale structures at the surface of the bottom were documented by divers operating a sediment-water interface camera designed by the author. This camera was used to obtain undisturbed photographs of the bottom in profile (Fig. 2). A plexiglas extension was constructed to fit on the front of an underwater Nikonos camera. The plexiglas chamber was filled with clean water to provide a clear optical path. The ventral edge of the transparent face plate was sharpened to permit insertion of the camera in the bottom with little resistance or deformation of the bottom.

Vertical gradients in sediment water content were determined from cores (4·7 cm in diameter) obtained by divers. The cores were rapidly frozen soon after recovery and then extruded for sectioning into 5 mm or 10 mm increments to a depth of 10 cm. Water content is expressed as percent weight loss after drying. Deposited salts were not removed from the samples before weighing. Sediment texture is given in Udden-Wentworth size terms.

A time-lapse movie sequence of the bottom at St. R, Buzzards Bay, Massachusetts was taken with a Bolex 16 mm camera in a Jubamarine 16 Mark IV underwater housing (J. R. Bailey Enterprises, Agincourt, Ontario, Canada). Light was provided with a Bosun quartz lamp. Timers in the underwater housing turned the camera and light on once each hour for a period of 4·5 sec. The camera was supported above the bottom on a pipe frame at an underwater focal length of 34 cm. All movie sequences were recorded at 18 frames-per-second on Kodachrome type A film.

Resuspension of bottom muds was measured by placing either a plastic box (19·9 cm long by 14·3 cm wide) or a one litre jar (with a mouth area of 50 cm²) on the bottom. In either case, a wire screen (12 mm mesh) covered the opening to exclude crustacea and fish. The openings of these traps were approximately 10 cm above the bottom. The traps were placed and recovered by divers.

3. Burrowing of subtidal muds

The vertical distribution of infaunal deposit-feeding organisms within the bottom closely controls sediment water content. The vertical distribution of deposit-feeders may extend several centimetres into the sediment but the greatest density of macrofaunal invertebrates in subtidal muds is found within the upper 10 cm of the bottom (Mare 1942; Moore 1931; Rhoads 1967). In Buzzards Bay, frequent lateral burrowing and grazing of the bivalves *Nucula proxima, Yoldia limatula,* and *Macoma tenta,* produce a faecal-rich surface layer. This surface has the appearance of a granular zone when viewed in profile (Pl. 1a). The same type of reworked surface structure is generated by the holothurian *Molpadia musculus* in Cape Cod Bay (Pl. 1b). Thickness of this uncompacted faecal zone ranges from 5-10 mm,

---

Plate 1

Surface texture and water content of intensively burrowed muds at St. R, Buzzards Bay and St. Z, Cape Cod Bay. Photographs were taken of the bottom in profile with the sediment-water interface camera shown in Fig. 2.

a Station R (20 m), Buzzards Bay. The granular surface is produced by *Nucula proxima,* a protobranch bivalve, burrowing through the upper 1 cm of the silt-clay bottom.

b Station Z, Cape Cod Bay, (34 m). The granular surface texture is formed by the accumulation of faeces of *Molpadia musculus* (holothurian) on the silt-clay bottom. Higher water content at depth at this station reflects a deeper depth of reworking by *M. musculus* than *N. proxima* at St. R.

PLATE 1

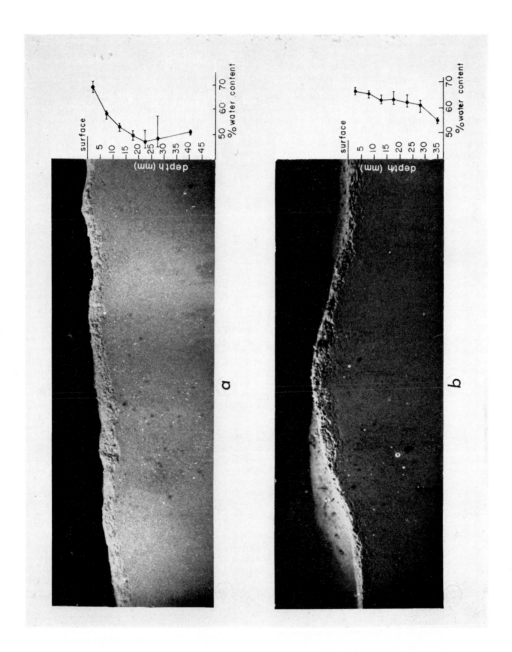

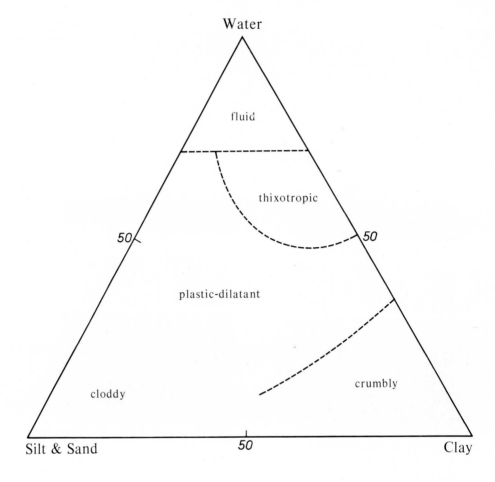

Fig. 3. Mass properties of sediments related to grain-size and water content (from Boswell 1961).

depending upon seasonal activity of the benthos. In Buzzards Bay, this zone reaches a maximum thickness in late summer and is minimal in late winter (Rhoads and Young 1970).

The near surface faecal zone exceeds 60% in water content and may approach 80% in highly reworked bottoms. Buzzards Bay muds, lacking the granular zone, have near surface water contents less than 50%. Biogenic modification of sediment water content indirectly influences the mechanical and rheologic properties of the bottom. The tendency for a muddy sediment to flow (display rheotropism) is linked to the transformation gel/more-fluid-gel/gel (Boswell 1961). This transformation is characteristic for high water content muds and is called false-bodied thixotropism. The rheotropic behaviour of non-calcareous muds at ambient surface temperature and pressure is given in Figure 3. The physical state of a sediment of fixed solid composition (clay-silt-sand) is directly related to water content, a parameter influenced

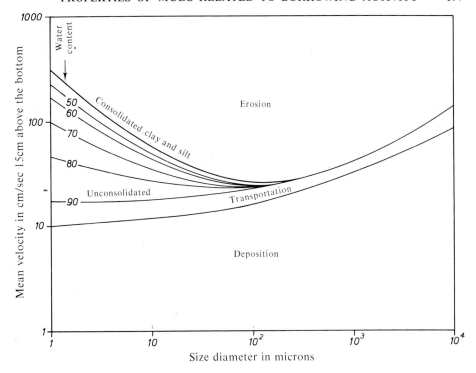

Fig. 4. The influence of water content on the critical erosion velocity in fine-grained ($<100\mu$) sediments (From Postma 1967).

by burrowing activity. High clay content muds containing greater than 50% water display false-bodied thixotropism or fluid properties. These same muds are potentially unstable in the presence of relatively weak bottom currents. The relationship between mean erosion velocity, sediment size, and water content is given in Figure 4. Postma notes that the critical values are not only determined by particle size and degree of consolidation but are also related to turbulence and bottom roughness. The granular surface produced by burrowers is important in this regard as the granular zone is a hydrodynamically 'rough' surface. (Pl. 1).

Physical instability of the bottom at station R, Buzzards Bay (Fig. 1) is documented by a time-lapse movie sequence made at this station over a 26 hour period. The level of turbidity near the bottom was observed to change hourly (Pl. 2 a-c). A white disc bearing a watch in the centre of the photographs was repeatedly covered and uncovered with sediment. This disc was elevated 2-3 cm above the bottom. The three hour sequence (Pl. 2 a-c) shows a dramatic change in bottom turbidity during the initial stages of flood tide. Turbulent eddies generated by tidal flow are probably responsible for resuspension of the bottom. Many of the suspended particles were observed to follow rotational flow paths in a horizontal or nearly horizontal plane, while other particles followed straight flow paths related to the mean tidal flow direction.

Instability of this bottom is also shown in an earlier part of the same movie sequence. Preserved specimens of the epifaunal bivalves *Placopecten magellanicus, Pandora gouldiana,* and *Crassostrea virginica,* and the shallow infaunal bivalve

PLATE 2

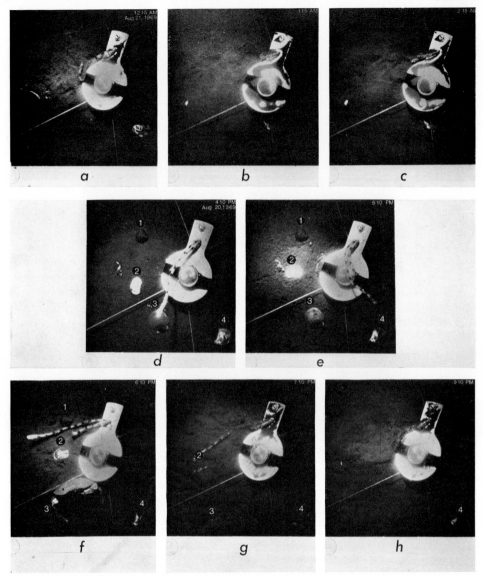

Plate 2

Change in bottom mud stability over a two hour period at St. R, Buzzards Bay. Photographs are enlargements of 16 mm movie film.

a Turbidity of the water is low during the final minutes of ebb tide. Note that the watch face and white disc are largely free of sediment.

b Initial stage of flood tide accompanied by high turbidity related to the resuspension of the burrowed surface. The watch and disc are covered with resuspended sediment.

c Return of relatively clear water conditions with the deposition of the suspended load.

In situ burial of four transplanted bivalve species during a five hour period at St. R, Buzzards Bay. Photographs are enlargements of 16 mm movie film.

d-e The dead preserved specimens of *Astarte castanea* (1), *Pandora gouldiana* (2), *Placopecten magellanicus* (3), and *Crassostrea virginica* (4), were placed on the bottom by divers.

f Portions of the shells of all of the species are covered with sediment after two hours.

g Small areas of the shells of (2-4) are still exposed by the third hour. Note the accumulation of sediment on the white disc.

h only *C. virginica* (4) remains at the surface after 5 hours on the bottom.

Astarte castanea, were placed on the bottom by divers within the camera's field of view (Pl. 2d). These species do not occur naturally at this station. The purpose of this transplantation was to see how long the shells would passively remain at the surface of an unstable thixotropic mud. After a period of three hours *A. castanea* (the thickest shelled species) was no longer visible at the surface and *P. gouldiana* and *P. magellanicus* were nearly covered with sediment (Pl. 2g). After a period of six hours, only *C. virginica* was still visible at the sediment surface (Pl. 2h).

Small parts of the shells were re-exposed in subsequent frames indicating that the shells were not transported laterally but, were buried in place by gravity settling and burial by resuspended sediment.

During the 26 hour period of photographic documentation, a resuspended sediment flux of 35 mg/cm²/day was measured 10 cm above the bottom by a trap located near the camera. The granular zone is probably resuspended with each ebb and flow of the tidal cycle, creating a very dynamic surface environment. Burrowed mud bottoms experience up to seven times more sediment resuspension (by volume) than less intensively reworked muds in Buzzards Bay (Rhoads and Young 1970).

4. Preserved evidence of syndepositional sediment properties

During the diagenetic processes of burial, compaction, dewatering, and cementation, the physical states of a mud undergo the deformational transition: fluid-thixotropic-plastic-solid or plastic-solid, depending upon the initial surface water content. These diagenetic changes are fortunately not destructive, i.e. the record of syndepositional or initial sediment states may be recorded and preserved in biodeformational or biokinematic structures (Elliott 1965). An example of this can be seen in a Recent core from St. R, Buzzards Bay (Pl. 3). The core had an original surface water content of 60%. This sediment falls within the thixotropic field of Boswell's diagram (Fig. 3). Grazing organisms moving through the mud deformed the sediment thixotropically. The zone of deformation adjacent to burrows underwent the transition gel/more-fluid-gel/gel as burrowers moved through the sediment. The zone of deformation surrounding each burrow is narrow as the water-lubricated grains slipped past each other in the loosely packed matrix to accommodate volume displacement. Burrows exhibiting this type of deformation have indistinct outlines and may be observed and studied only in thin section. Plate 3b shows a thin section of the Elk Butte Member of the Pierre Shale (Maastrichtian) showing similar thixotropic deformation.

An example of plastic deformation representing firm bottom conditions is shown for a 10 m deep station (P) in Buzzards Bay (Pl. 3c). This sediment is a clean, well sorted, very fine sand. Water content of this sediment was initially between 20-30%. Divers sampling this bottom have confirmed its firm dilatant properties. Evidence of the initially low water content and firm packing is preserved in burrow deformation. Deformation in this case is entirely plastic. Each burrow is surrounded by a wide zone of deformation extending several grain diameters away from the burrow wall. Shearing of the sediment by the burrower was transmitted from the immediate area of penetration to the surrounding matrix by intergrain friction and adhesion. A fossil example of plastic deformation is shown for the trail City Member of the Fox Hills Formation (Maastrichtian) (Pl. 3d).

Some sediments exhibit an intimate mixture of plastic and thixotropic burrow deformation. This is produced by thixotropic deformation of surface layers by shallow burrowers and plastic deformation of more compacted mud by deeper burrowing forms.

PLATE 3

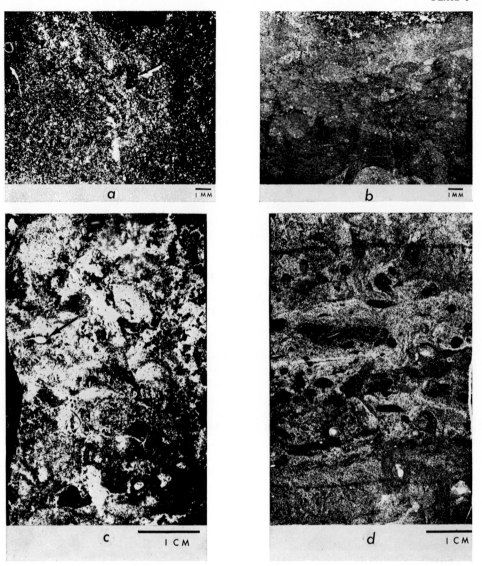

Plate 3

Burrow deformation of **a-b** thixotropic (high water content) muds, **c-d** plastic (low water content muds. Thin sections photographed with transmitted light.

a This Recent silt-clay bottom had a water content of 60% within the upper 1 cm of the surface. Burrows (arrow) have indistinct walls caused by mixing of the burrow filling with the thixotropic matrix.

b Thixotropic burrow deformation (arrow) of the Elk Butte Member of the Pierre Shale (Maastrichtian) indicates that this shale unit was initially of high water content when deposited.

c This Recent fine-sand bottom contained 20-30% water to a depth of 5 cm below the surface. Burrows (arrow) have sharp boundaries with the matrix and are surrounded by a region of plastic deformation.

d Plastic deformation in the Trail City Member of the Fox Hills Formation (Maastrichtian). This siltstone was a firm mud bottom when deposited.

5. The ecology and palaeoecology of high water content muds

The rapid *in situ* burial of epifaunal mollusc shells placed on the bottom at station R, Buzzards Bay, demonstrates the problem of living on, or in, an intensively burrowed mud. The problem of surviving in such an environment is especially critical for newly settled larvae and early juvenile stages. Early growth stages of macrofaunal organisms less than 1 cm in greatest dimension, must live within the unstable 1 cm thick granular surface zone or maintain periodic connection with it for purposes of respiration. These small individuals may experience, therefore, frequent resuspension and burial. Shell-bearing organisms living on soft muds display many morphologic and behavioural similarities related to adapting to this unstable environment. The convergence of form and behaviour is especially striking in mud-dwelling bivalves and fossil articulate brachiopods. The following examples, drawn from these two groups, are not intended to represent a comprehensive review but, a few examples have been chosen to point out striking similarities in adaptation.

Instability of the bottom is a major limiting factor for sessile invertebrates. The severity of the attachment problem depends upon the intensity and frequency of resuspension and individual species tolerance. At Buzzards Bay, St. R, a resuspension rate of 35 mg/cm²/day is sufficient to exclude all sedentary epifauna from this station. On more stable muds, colonization may be accomplished by attachment to dead or living shells exposed at the surface, benthic plants, or pieces of rock projecting above the surface of the mud. This type of attachment has been proposed for some brachiopod species by Rudwick (1961) and Ager (1965). The patchy or 'nested' occurrence of some brachiopod populations found in fine-grained lithologies may represent epibioses resulting from localized settling on solid objects projecting above an otherwise unstable bottom (Hallam 1961; Ager 1965; Ziegler *et al.* 1966; 1968; and Bray 1969). Oysters similarly form epibioses in muddy substrata creating, in some cases, extensive biostromal accumulations.

The problem of early ontogenetic stages attaching to, and surviving on, unstable muds has been solved in some species by a change in living habits and/or morphology during growth. Grant (1968) has proposed that the spat of the Permian productoid genera *Marginifera* and *Echinauris* from the Salt Range, West Pakistan, settled and metamorphosed on algae and bryozoans. After attaining spines, individuals dropped to the bottom initiating a free benthic stage. A similar behavioural adaptation has been cited for the Recent pectinid bivalve *Chlamys septemradiata* from the Clyde sea area (Allen 1953). Allen suggests that larvae of this bivalve settle and metamorphose nearshore. During the second year of growth, the clams detach and migrate to deeper soft mud bottoms. Once these epifaunal bivalves are established on the mud as adults, their shells provide firm settling surfaces for fourteen species of epizoans. Direct attachment to soft mud bottoms may have been possible for some articulate brachiopods with a pedicle divided into rootlet-like terminations (Rudwick 1961).

The maintenance of a stable position on periodically unstable mud bottoms requires special stabilization and orientation mechanisms in unattached organisms. A commonly encountered adaptation in the brachiopods relates to the 'snowshoe effect'. The weight of the shell is spread over a large cross-sectional area. The thin dorso-ventrally compressed valves commonly bear spinous or frilly extensions projecting beneath the shell margin to assist in anchoring and stabilizing the shell. Atrypids living on fine-grained muds of the shallow Devonian seas of northwestern Europe were characterized by these kinds of morphologic features (Copper 1966; 1967). Mesozoic brachiopods living on sublittoral muds were generally smaller and thinner-shelled than those living on more firm or stable bottom types. These species also tended to be dorso-ventrally compressed (Ager 1965). The development of extreme spinosity in the Permian productoids *Marginifera* and *Echinauris* is also interpreted as a stabilization device. The spines were apparently effective in elevating the commissure above the fine-grained bottom (Grant 1968). The posteriorly thickened shells of Silurian pentameroid brachipods may also have aided in stabilization (Ziegler *et al.* 1966).

Few bivalves have developed ornamentation to assist in stabilization on soft muds. Clams living on, or in, soft muds commonly have thin shells and are small, maintaining a large surface area to volume ratio to maximize support from the substratum per unit animal weight (Stanley 1970). Of particular interest is the adaptation to living on one valve in the families Tellinidae, Pandoridae, and Pectinidae. The latter two families are epifaunal or partially infaunal in habit while the tellinids are completely infaunal. The low bulk density and large surface area to weight ratios of members of these families make them particularly well suited to life on soft muds. Right-left valve symmetry has been lost in these families reflecting this unique mode of life. Several species of the Jurassic-Cretaceous bivalve *Inoceramus* were able to live on soft muds by distributing their large mass over a broad cross-sectional area. These disc-shaped shells commonly served as solid settling surfaces for epizoans such as *Ostrea* (Hattin and Cobban 1965).

Most bivalves living in soft muds are members of the deposit-feeding families Nuculidae, Nuculanidae, Tellinidae, and Semelidae. The problem of maintaining a position within the sediment is solved in these families by being rapid burrowers. These clams lack strong ornamentation and can burrow vertically through several centimetres of sediment dumped on them in the laboratory. Frequent readjustment to the sediment-water interface is necessary for species living in or on these bottom types. It is, in fact, the high mobility of members of these bivalve families that commonly contributes to bottom mud instability.

6. Discussion

The influence of benthic organisms on the compaction of sediments has been recognized by many workers (Schwartz 1932; Brinkmann 1932; Linke 1939; McMaster 1967; Chapman 1949). The significance of this phenomenon in the dynamics of the bottom and as a feed-back controlling benthic community structure has not however, received sufficient attention.

The degree of instability and thixotropy of the bottom described here for Buzzards Bay, St. R and Cape Cod Bay, St. Z represent an extreme case. Not all reworked muds exhibit this degree of instability. Horizontal gradients of bioturbation on the sea floor are largely related to the distribution and density of deposit-feeding organisms, rate of sedimentation, and water motion (Reineck 1967). The presence of benthic plants, domichnia (permanent dwelling) tubes, or bioclastic debris on the bottom contribute to bottom stability.

The relationship of water content to sediment 'state' is defined by Atterberg limits used in soil mechanics. The liquid limit of a sediment defines the rheotropic transition liquid-plastic determined by agitating the sample under standard laboratory conditions. The lowest moisture content that permits liquid behaviour is defined as the liquid limit. The plastic limit is defined as the water content at which the sediment undergoes the transition from the plastic to solid state and is determined by rolling a sample into an unbroken cylinder of standard thickness (Lambe 1962). The liquid limit is an ecologically important parameter as this limit closely defines the lower thixotropic limit (Boswell 1961). Boswell states that present-day silty-muds display properties of false-bodied thixotropy at a natural water content of about 52%. This value agrees well with the author's observations in Buzzards Bay and Cape Cod Bay, Massachusetts. A water content of approximately 50% appears to separate firm from soft muds.

A rheological and kinematical classification of sedimentary structures is very helpful in relating the deformational behaviour of a sediment to sedimentary structures (Elliott 1965), an approach subsequently employed by Coneybeare and Crook (1968). Elliott's statement that quasifluid deformation by organisms is incapable of being preserved may, however, be questioned in light of the thin section evidence of Plate 3. Orientation of shells at a high angle to the bedding has also been used to recognize soft muds, while shells lying parallel to bedding mark firm bottoms (Wobber 1968). The degree of compaction (compression) of burrows may also be used.

The ecologic importance of sediment mass properties in the distribution of Recent benthic organisms has been studied in Chesapeake Bay (Harrison *et al.* 1964; Harrison and Wass 1965). Although a cause-effect relationship was not established, water content was found to be a major controlling factor in the distribution of three species. The influence of bottom stability on trophic group distribution has been studied in Recent muds (Rhoads and Young 1970), in the Upper Cretaceous Fox Hills Formation and Pierre Shale of South Dakota (Maastrichtian) (Rhoads *et al.* in press), and in the Silurian of Nova Scotia (Levinton and Bambach 1969).

Conclusions presented here on the ecologic significance of burrowed muds have been based largely on Recent animal-sediment relations. Wobber has arrived at very similar conclusions from his palaeoecologic study of the Lias (Lower Jurassic) of South Wales (Wobber 1968).

Several comparable morphologic adaptations have been described for soft mud-dwelling species of bivalved molluscs and articulate brachiopods. The relative success of these two groups in colonizing this substratum type has been unequal however. I propose that the epifaunal mud habitat was exploited more successfully by Palaeozoic articulate brachiopods than by epifaunal suspension-feeding clams.

7. Summary

Intensive reworking of the upper 10 cm of the bottom by deposit-feeding organisms produces the following changes in the structure, mass properties, and stability of fine-grained muds: (i) generation of a granular faecal-rich surface containing greater than 60% water by weight, (ii) production of relatively high water content (> 50%) to the base of the intensively burrowed zone (usually 10 cm), (iii) biogenic modification of compaction and water content produces a sediment displaying mass properties of a false-bodied thixotropic medium, and (iv) such thixotropic muds are easily resuspended by weak tidal currents.

The original water content of a mud bottom may be inferred from biodeformational structures observed in thin sections of sedimentary rocks. Thixotropic, plastic, or solid deformation of near surface layers of the bottom may be determined from the relative thickness of the shear zone surrounding grazing burrows and by the degree of mixing of the burrow filling with the surrounding matrix.

The mass properties and stability of mud surfaces are important parameters in benthic ecology. The following morphologic and behavioural features, exhibited in Recent and fossil molluscs and brachiopods, are related to living on thixotropic burrowed muds: (i) formation of epibioses with attachment to solid objects projecting above an unstable interface. (ii) attachment to the bottom directly by a rootlet-like pedicle in some brachiopods, (iii) migration of adults from solid surfaces of juvenile attachment to soft mud surfaces, (iv) development of spines, frills, or posterior shell thickenings as stabilization structures in epifaunal species, (v) development of dorso-ventrally compressed (brachiopods) or laterally compressed (bivalves) valves (vi) infaunal bivalve species are commonly small and of low bulk density. These species also display a high degree of vertical mobility for maintaining a connection with the unstable surface.

The dynamic interactions of burrowing organisms, mass properties of the bottom, and bottom currents are important in understanding the ecology of marine muds. Gradients in original sediment-water content, determined from biodeformational features in ancient rocks, may be used to reconstruct these dynamic interactions for ancient sea floors. This palaeoecologic information may then prove useful in explaining observed patterns of fossil distribution and morphology.

Acknowledgements. Dr. David Young, resident ecologist of the Systematics-Ecology programme, Marine Biological Laboratory, Woods Hole, Massachusetts, assisted me in collecting much of the field data. Facilities of both the Marine Biological Laboratory and Woods Hole Oceanographic Institution, Woods Hole, Massachusetts, were made available to the author.

Many of the ideas presented here have benefited from criticism and discussions between the author and his students. I wish to especially credit the contributions of Charles Thayer and Jeffrey Levinton. Karl M. Waage read the manuscript and offered helpful suggestions.

This study was supported by a National Science Foundation Grant GB 7181.

References

AGER, D. V. 1965. The adaptation of Mesozoic brachiopods to different environments. *Palaeogeogr. Palaeoclimatol. Palaeoecol.* **1**, 143.

ALLEN, J. A. 1953. Observations on the epifauna of the deep-water muds of the Clyde Sea area, with special reference to *Chlamys septemradiata* (Müller). *J. Anim. Ecol.* **22**, 240.

BOSWELL, P. G. H. 1961. *Muddy sediments.* Heffer, Cambridge.

BRAY, R. 1969. *The paleoecology of some Middle Devonian fossil clusters, Erie Co., N.Y.* Unpublished M.S. thesis, Dept. of Geol. McMaster Univ., Hamilton, Ontario.

BRINKMANN, R. 1932. Über die Schichtung und ihre Bedingungen. *Fortschr. Geol. Palaeont.* **11**, 187.

CHAPMAN, G. 1949. The thixotropy and dilatancy of marine soil. *J. mar. biol. Ass. U.K.* **28**, 132.

CONYBEARE, C. E. B. and CROOK, K. A. W. 1968. Manual of sedimentary structures. *Bull. Bur. miner. Resour. Geol. Geophys Aust.* **102**.

COPPER, P. 1966. Ecological distribution of Devonian atrypid brachiopods. *Palaeogeogr. Palaeoclimatol. Palaeoecol.* **2**, 245.

—— 1967. Adaptations and life habits of Devonian atrypid brachiopods. *Palaeogeogr. Palaeoclimatol. Paleoecol.* **3**, 363.

ELLIOTT, R. E. 1965. A classification of subaqueous sedimentary structures based on rheological and kinematical parameters. *Sedimentology* **5**, 193.

GRANT, R. E. 1968. Structural adaptation in two Permian brachiopod genera. Salt Range, West Pakistan. *J. Paleont.* **42**, 1.

HALLAM, A. 1961. Brachiopod life assemblages from the Marlstone rock-bed of Leicestershire. *Palaeontology* **4**, 653.

HARRISON, W., LYNCH, M. P. and ALTSCHAEFFL, A. G. 1964. Sediments of lower Chesapeake Bay, with emphasis on mass properties. *J. sedim. Petrol.* **34**, 727.

—— and WASS, M. L. 1965. Frequencies of infaunal invertebrates related to water content of Chesapeake Bay sediments. *S. East. Geol.* **6**, 177.

HATTIN, D. E. and COBBAN, W. A. 1965. Upper Cretaceous stratigraphy, paleontology, and paleoecology of western Kansas. *Guidebk. geol. Soc. Am. Meet. Kansas City, Missouri.* St. Geol. Surv. of Kansas, Univ. of Kansas, Lawrence, Kansas.

LAMBE, T. W. 1962. *Soil testing for engineers.* Wiley, New York and London.

LEVINTON, J. and BAMBACH, R. K. 1969. Silurian and recent deposit-feeding communities. A comparative study. *Abstr. geol. Soc. Am. Meet. Atlantic City, New Jersey.* p. 134.

LINKE, O. 1939. Die Biota des Jadebusenwattes. *Helgoländer wiss. Meeresunters.* **1**, 201.

MCMASTER, R. L. 1967. Compactness variability of estuarine sediments: An *in situ* study. In *Estuaries* (Ed. G. H. Lauff). *Publs Am. Ass. Advmt Sci.* **83**, 261.

MARE, M. 1942. A study of a marine benthic community with special reference to the microorganisms. *J. mar. biol. Ass. U.K.* **25**, 517.

MOORE, H. B. 1931. The muds of the Clyde Sea area III: Chemical and physical conditions, rate of sedimentation; and fauna. *J. mar. biol. Ass. U.K.* new series **17**, 325.

POSTMA, H. 1967. Sediment transport and sedimentation in the estuarine environment. In *Estuaries* (Ed. G. H. Lauff). *Publs Am. Ass. Advmt Sci.* **83**, 158.

REINECK, H. E. 1967. Layered sediments of tidal flats, beaches, and shelf bottoms of the North Sea. In *Estuaries* (Ed. G. H. Lauff) *Publs Am. Ass. Advmt Sci.* **83**, 191.

RHOADS, D. C. 1967. Biogenic reworking of intertidal and subtidal sediments in Barnstable Harbor and Buzzards Bay, Massachusetts. *J. Geol.* **75**, 461.

—— WAAGE, K. M. and SPEDEN, E. Benthic molluscan trophic group distribution in the Upper Cretaceous (Maestrictian) of S. Dakota. *Bull. Am. Ass. Petrol. Geol.* (In press.)

—— and YOUNG, D. K. 1970. The influence of deposit-feeding organisms on sediment stability and community trophic structure. *J. mar. Res.* **28**. (In press.)

RUDWICK, M. J. S. 1961. The anchorage of articulate brachiopods on soft substrata. *Palaeontology* **4**, 475.

SANDERS, H. L. 1958. Benthic studies in Buzzards Bay. I. Animal-sediment relationships. *Limnol. Oceanogr.* **3**, 245.

SCHWARTZ, A. 1932. Der tierische Einfluss auf die Meeressedimente. *Senckenbergiana* **14**, 118.

STANLEY, S. M. 1970. Relation of shell form to life habits in the bivalvia mollusca. *Mem. geol. Soc. Am.* **125.** (In press.)

WOBBER, F. J. 1968. A faunal analysis of the Lias (Lower Jurassic) of south Wales (Great Britain). *Palaeogeogr. Palaeoclimatol, Palaeoecol.* **5,** 269.

ZIEGLER, A. M., BOUCOUT, A. J. and SHELDON, R. P. 1966. Silurian pentameroid brachiopods preserved in position of growth. *J. Paleont.* **40,** 1032.

—— COCKS, R. M. and BAMBACH, R. K. 1968. The composition and structure of Lower Silurian marine communities. *Lethaia* **1,** 1.

D. C. Rhoads, Department of Geology and Geophysics, Yale University, New Haven, Connecticut, U.S.A.

Late Devonian-early Mississippian ichnofossils from Western Montana and Northern Utah

J. Rodriguez and R. C. Gutschick

Shell borings, burrows, and other trace fossils occur within the Sappington Member (Famen-nian-Tournaisian) of the Three Forks Formation and overlying Lodgepole Limestone (Tour-naisian-late Kinderhookian) sequence of western Montana, and the Leatham (= Sappington) Formation of northern Utah. Four distinct types of well-preserved borings have been recognized on silicified invertebrate skeletons which are present within calcareous oncolites common to Sappington and Leatham strata. Two linear types are ascribed to the work of polychaete annelids and are interpreted as pre-depositional. The third boring type is slit-like and is attributed to the activity of acrothoracican barnacles. A fourth type, which is cylindrical, is thought to represent a post-depositional living burrow, probably of annelid worms. Middle Sappington shales and siltstones contain the striking double arrow-shaped *Bifungites* burrow. *Scalarituba* burrows are present in the middle Leatham and in both the upper Sappington and lower Lodgepole beds. *Zoophycos* occurs at the top of the Sappington, is characteristic of the Cottonwood Canyon Member (basal Lodgepole) and common in the upper Lodgepole Limestone. Double ribbon herring-bone trails, cylindrical burrow-fills, and fine, vermicular, meandering grazing trails are also present.

The succession of ichnofacies ranges from shallow littoral *Cruziana?* facies (Sappington and Leatham) to *Zoophycos* facies (upper Sappington and Lodgepole) with some alternation in the lower Lodgepole Limestone. Palaeoichnology supplements the modern carbonate analog model for interpretation of the environments of deposition.

1. Introduction

This paper presents a detailed case history of the palaeoichnology of transitional Upper Devonian-Lower Mississippian rocks of western Montana and northern Utah. Trace fossils reported include shell borings, trails and burrows. They occur in the Sappington Member of the Three Forks Formation; Cottonwood Canyon and Paine Members of the Lodgepole Limestone (Madison Group), of western Montana; and the Leatham Formation of northern Utah—the stratigraphic equivalent of the Sappington.

The Sappington sequence (Fig. 1) represents a series of transitional environmental changes which occurred between Late Devonian (Three Forks) and Early Mississippian (Lodgepole) time under normal marine conditions. These strata include the lower black shales (A-C) lacking recognizable trace fossils; an extensive oncolite biostrome (E) with a brachiopod-dominated but diverse community and a varied epibiontic assemblage with abundant examples of the work of boring organisms; and clastic shales and siltstones (F-G-H) showing infaunal burrowing activity. The exact position of the systemic boundary is uncertain.

The Sappington counterpart south of the Snake River volcanic plain of south-eastern Idaho is the Leatham Formation of northern Utah. The Leatham contains the oncolite biostrome and its shell borings along with some overlying clastic units which have a limited trace fossil fauna. An analysis of the type Leatham Formation was given by Holland (1952).

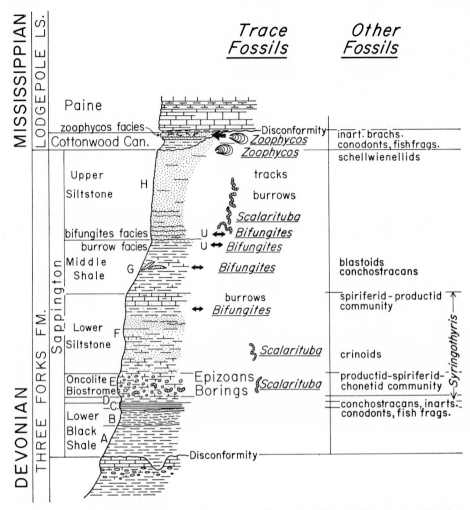

Fig. 1. Biostratigraphic summary and distribution of trace fossils in the Sappington Member

The Cottonwood Canyon Member of the Lodgepole Limestone is the basal clastic deposit of a transgressive Madison sea over an irregular erosion surface, which includes the top of the Sappington, in western Montana (Sandberg and Mapel 1967). Only the thin western edge of this stratigraphic unit has been examined for trace fossils for this report; however, there is persistent development of *Zoophycos* and burrow-fill layers as indicated in Figure 2.

Observations for trace fossils were made through 700 feet of the Paine Member of the Lodgepole Limestone. Two of these carbonate sections were closely scrutinized: the type section of the Lodgepole Limestone at Logan, Montana, and the Sacagawea Peak section in the Bridger Range north of Bozeman, Montana. More specific locations for these two outcrops are available in a Locality List at the end of this paper. The two sections are about 22 miles apart on an east-west line. Columnar sections are plotted in Figure 3 to facilitate comparison of lithologies and trace fossils. The localities are referred to by numbers in the text and detailed locations are given at the end of this paper.

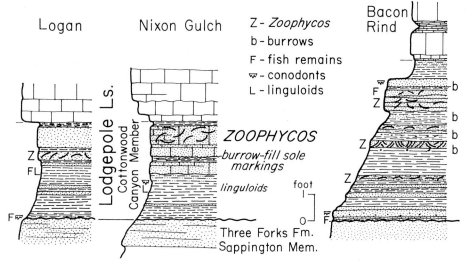

Fig. 2. Detailed key stratigraphic sections of Cottonwood Canyon Member of Lodgepole Limestone with the occurrence of *Zoophycos* and other burrows.

2. Borings

Numerous borings on the shelled population within the oncolite biostrome (Unit E) provide evidence that the shallow algal bank community was also inhabited by many boring epibionts capable of creating living quarters by penetrating calcareous invertebrate skeletal material. These excavations were probably valuable shelters in the high energy bank environment.

Four types of boring traces are recognized here: (i) cylindrical boreholes of an unknown burrower, and/or, as seems less likely, of predatory gastropods; (ii) large, elongate (*Vermiforichnus*) borings by unknown organisms, probably polychaete worms; (iii) fine tube-shaped borings assigned to the genus *Conchotrema*, also of probable worm origin; and (iv) the slit-like borings of acrothoracican barnacles. Evidence is presented to show that at least some, if not all of the cylindrical boreholes were formed after burial of the shells in which they are found, whereas the other boring types, with the possible exception of (ii), are regarded as having been excavated either during the life of the host, or of post-mortem, pre-burial origin. Description and analysis of the borings follows.

CYLINDRICAL BOREHOLES

Plate 1 a-e, g-i

Description. Approximately 10 per cent of almost 200 shells of the brachiopod *Rhipidomella missouriensis* (Swallow), collected from the algal nodule residues of the Sappington Member and Leatham Formation, bear cylindrical boreholes drilled perpendicular or nearly perpendicular to the shell surface. The *Rhipidomella* shells constitute about one-fifth the total number of individual brachiopod specimens recovered from the nodule horizon. No other brachiopod genus in the collection is bored extensively in this manner, although there are isolated bored individuals of other genera. No bivalves are present in the nodule faunas, although they are known from the underlying beds.

Most of the perforations have a circular or near-circular horizontal cross-section. However, the inner opening is occasionally less sharply defined than the outer opening and in some individuals the inner and outer borders of the holes are quite irregular. Oblique holes penetrating the shell at a low angle and leaving smooth, elliptical, bevelled holes are present but less common. Aligned holes of similar size and in similar locations on opposing valves of articulated *Rhipidomella* were observed.

Incomplete digestion of some oncolites, composed of aphanitic limestone, in a solution of dilute hydrochloric acid has allowed the recovery of gently curved cylindrical burrow fillings which penetrate the nodules. Prolonged exposure to the acid, or too strong a concentration, caused disaggregation of the easily destroyed burrow fills. In one case (Pl. 1h), however, it was possible to photograph a burrow penetrating both valves of a small strophalosiid brachiopod and continuing its open U-shaped path therefrom. Other burrows have been noted passing obliquely into *Rhipidomella* shells, although strikingly preserved specimens such as that above were not recovered. Thin sections of the oncolites (Pl. 1i) also demonstrate clearly the penetration of the brachiopod shells by the burrows.

Many of the boreholes have smaller inner openings than outer openings, but in other cases the diameter of the hole is constant from outer to inner shell surface. In a number of individuals the inner hole diameter cannot be measured because matrix fills the shell interior. The smooth walls of the boreholes are sometimes concave producing a parabolic (truncated spherical paraboloid) hole. Straight-walled untapered individuals are also encountered. None of the holes are countersunk and all appear to have sharp external rims. An incomplete hole is unbossed.

The location of the holes on the brachiopod shells is frequently, but not exclusively, posterior, in the umbonal region, often in a position which approximates the former location of the muscles internally. There is no apparent preference for either valve.

Interpretation. Past reports of this type of borehole in Palaeozoic skeletons have usually attributed the boring activity to predatory carnivorous marine gastropods (e.g. Hecker 1965; Brunton 1966; Cameron 1967a). However, in recent analyses of modern and fossil occurrences, Fischer (1962), Carriker and Yochelson (1968), and Sohl (1969) have suggested rejection of the gastropod predation hypothesis for pre-late Mesozoic boreholes of cylindrical shape on the basis of both morphologic and phylogenetic evidence. Buehler (1969) has described Devonian boreholes of this type and has agreed that they may not be of gastropod origin.

In this study the almost complete limitation of the boreholes to *Rhipidomella* shells is the most suggestive characteristic supporting a gastropod predation hypothesis. The concentration of borings in the posterior (umbonal) portion of the shell may also be significant since Siler (1965) and Reyment (1966) have indicated that some naticids tend to concentrate boring activity in the umbonal region of bivalves, and some muricids focus their attack on the area of the adductor muscles. Multiple borings are not rare with five such cases noted. Also, although the degree of predation is high among the total shells of the genus *Rhipidomella*, the number of bored shells represents a small fraction of the more than 1,000 brachiopods recovered from nodule residues in this study. While the evidence is apparently inconclusive, had the cylindrical holes been drilled by Palaeozoic gastropods, their umbonal location implies that the feeding habits would probably have been more similar to those of the modern Muricidae which feed through gaping valves, rather than to the naticids which feed through the excavations themselves (Cameron 1967a p. 148).

The suggestion that the coprophagous gastropod *Platyceras* was a borer (Fenton and Fenton 1931) has generally been rejected (Cameron 1967a p. 148), especially for early Palaeozoic boreholes (Carriker and Yochelson 1968 p. 19). However, its presence in the nodule faunas is recorded here. A more likely carnivore is a large, high-spired (probably loxonematacean) archaeogastropod which is somewhat less common than *Platyceras* in both the Sappington Member and the Leatham Formation.

Richards and Shabica (1969) have described cylindrical borings in the Ordovician dalmanellid *Onniella* in which the holes pass in perfect alignment through several shells. The borings were interpreted by those authors as the result of the burrowing activity of an unknown polychaete subsequent to deposition of the shells on the sea floor. Further evidence for this kind of post-depositional origin for cylindrical borings in shells of Palaeozoic age can be found in bored brachiopods from the Sappington and Leatham rock units. It seems likely that many of the perforations described above may be attributed to post-depositional burrowing activity of an animal which was able to burrow through the oncolite and its enclosed hard calcareous shells, probably at a time when the oncolite was only partially exposed or buried to a shallow depth. Following Richards and Shabica (p. 840) it seems probable that polychaetes burrowing and boring for protection rather than predation, were responsible for the construction of the living chambers described here. As habitation burrows are known to increase in diameter inwards, it may be that some of the boreholes with smaller inner diameters were bored from the inner shell surface to the exterior or outer shell surface.

A small number of circular and near-circular perforations (not illustrated) have also been observed in delicate silicified brachiopods described by Rodriguez and Gutschick (1968; 1969) from the lower Lodgepole Limestone at Brownback Gulch, Montana. The thin-shelled nature of the brachiopod material does not allow observations on the angle of penetration. As in the Sappington-Leatham occurrences, platycerid gastropod shells are common faunal associates.

Occurrence. Lower Lodgepole Limestone at Locality 6; Sappington Member, Localities 2 and 5; Leatham Formation, Locality 21.

VERMIFORICHNUS BORINGS

Plates 1f; 2a, b; 3d

Description. A distinctive elongate boring, usually straight or gently curving, is found on six Sappington *Rhipidomella* shells and on a single rare spiriferid. The borings have not been observed in Leatham brachiopods. The excavations are essentially open, roofless tunnels bored parallel to the shell surface to a depth of 0·3 to 0·4 mm. The maximum width of the tunnel is usually located 0·1 to 0·2 mm below the lateral rim of the excavation, producing an outline in vertical cross-section that is a truncated subcircular curve. The orientation of the boring may be in alignment with the radial ornamentation, or may cut obliquely across it (Pl. 2a, b). Extremities of the tunnels are smoothly rounded as are the walls and floor of the depression. Where tunnel floors are not present, this may be due to either collapse or shell penetration. Measurements of length yield an observed range of 5·3–16·7 mm with a mean value of 11·1 mm. Width values range from 0·3–1·5 mm with a mean of 0·9 mm.

Interpretation. Borings of this type have usually been attributed to the activity of polychaete worms. The spionid polychaete *Polydora* is an example of a present-day borer (Boekschoten 1966) and fossil excavations of a generally similar nature have been described recently from Cretaceous (Voigt 1965), Pliocene (Boekschoten 1967), Devonian (Cameron 1967b; 1969), and Mississippian strata (McKinney 1968). Illustrations of what are apparently similar borings have also been presented by Clarke (1908 pl. 5 fig. 2), and by Hecker (1965 pl. 3 fig. 2) from the Devonian.

Whether the borings described here represent the activity of a polychaete other than the form responsible for the cylindrical burrows is uncertain. The dimensions of the cylindrical boreholes and the diameter of the observed three-dimensional burrow fills are of similar magnitude and it is conceivable that the length of the cylindrical excavation may be related to the orientation of the shell in the oncolite when encountered by the burrower. Thus a near tangential low-angle approach may explain the longer borings described here, while a high-angle encounter would yield a hole more nearly circular in appearance.

Occurrence. Sappington Member, Unit E, Localities 2, 13 and 14.

CONCHOTREMA BORINGS

Plates 2a, c-f; 3a-f

Description. Conchotrema is a common boring encountered on many Leatham *Rhipidomella* shells, less frequently on Sappington specimens of that genus, on spiriferids, platycerid gastropods, and on rugose corals. Infestation on both external and internal skeletal surfaces was observed in some *Rhipidomella* and gastropod shells.

The "form genus" *Conchotrema* Teichert (1945 p. 203) includes narrow tubular borings of generally less than 0·2 mm diameter which communicate with the surface, but are otherwise completely buried in the shell. They are either straight, or only gently curved, and branching. Although Teichert suggests that species may be differentiated on the basis of tube thickness and distribution density, the present material indicates that at least the latter characteristic is variable on *Rhipidomella* shells and might be related to the degree of infestation or perhaps ease of boring. No new species are named here, but two or more types can be recognized on the basis of distribution density alone. The Leatham-Sappington material is very close to *C. tubulosa* Teichert from the Permian of Western Australia where excavations penetrate large productids, spiriferids, and pectinid bivalves. *C. canna* (Price) from the Pottsville and Conemaugh Series (Pennsylvanian) of West Virginia is also similar and was well illustrated by Cameron (1969 pl. 1 figs. A-B).

The tubular borings in the Leatham and Sappington shells are usually straight or gently curving with a diameter of 0·1 to 0·2 mm. Tunnels exposed through collapse of the shell vary considerably in length but usually do not exceed 10 mm. Many are apparently short. Branching is not rare but in some cases may be due to intersection of distinct tunnels. Tiny circular perforations (easily distinguished from rib-apertures where occurrence is in *Rhipidomella*) indicate the point of entrance to the tunnels. Although some tunnels are in alignment with costae in the brachiopod occurrences, no consistent pattern of this type emerges.

Interpretation. Restriction of *Conchotrema* borings to dorsal valves and to the edges and extremities of ventral valves led Teichert (1945 p. 198) to conclude that infestation of the Permian brachiopods he studied took place while the latter animals were alive. He also reasoned (p. 207) that the shell rested on the ventral valve which was largely embedded in the muddy substrate. In the present study, a survey of 25 *Rhipidomella* shells, two large spiriferids, and one syringothyrid, all articulated and bearing *Conchotrema* borings, does not allow the same conclusions. Twelve specimens of *Rhipidomella* were bored on both valves, seven were bored on the pedicle valve only, and six have excavations restricted to the brachial valve. The spiriferids and syringothyrid were bored extensively on both valves. Following Teichert's reasoning, this might be interpreted to suggest that those shells with borings in both valves were attacked while alive and positioned above the sea floor. The remaining shells were probably bored after death during which time the valve which happened to be lying uppermost on the substrate was exposed.

Lamont (1954 p. 190) has recognized *Conchotrema* borings in chonetids, spiriferids, and crinoid crowns from the Lower Carboniferous of Scotland. The Scottish forms, unlike those reported here, are said to be commonly U-shaped and open toward the shell margins. Cameron (1969 p. 692) reports the presence of similar but slightly larger forms in the Upper Devonian of New York State.

Occurrence. Leatham Formation, Locality 21: Sappington Member Unit E, Locality 2.

ACROTHORACIC BARNACLE BORINGS

Plate 3d-f

Description. Slit-like borings are present on the adapical portion of the epithecae of three solitary rugose corals and on both valves of an unidentified spiriferid brachiopod, all collected from the Sappington oncolite residues. Borings of the same type are present on several *Rhipidomella* valves from both Sappington and Leatham residues. In almost all of the brachiopod occurrences the floor of the depression is not present. The aperture of the boring is usually of the elongate-elliptical type described by Rodda and Fisher (1962 p. 472) and lacks a peduncular slit. In the better preserved coral specimens the excavations typically have steep lateral walls almost perpendicular to the skeletal surface and invariably inclined at a high angle. The extremities of the borings are either inclined steeply toward the deepest (posterior) part of the opening, or, as in some cases, the aperture is almost symmetrical and it is difficult to determine which extremity is the narrow anterior end. Dimensions of the apertures of 32 borings have a mean length of 1·3 mm and a mean width of 0·4 mm. In the spiriferid brachiopod occurrence one extremity of the borehole aperture is located in a depressed intercostal space. Although some of the borings are almost wholly situated in the intercostal depressions, most have their long axes oriented at an angle of deviation of less than 20° from the costae.

Interpretation. Borings similar to those described here have been identified as fossil barnacles of the cirriped Order Acrothoracica by a number of authors (*see* Rodda and Fisher 1962; Tomlinson 1963 for reviews). They are known from the Devonian to the present. The Sappington-Leatham occurrences are the first to be described as such from the clastic units that straddle the Devonian-Mississippian boundary in North America and may be the first reported from the Rocky Mountain region.

The observed relationship of the location of the borings to the intercostal depressions suggests that depressed areas of the shell may have provided some shelter for the cypris larva (Saint-Seine 1955; Schlaudt and Young 1960; Rodda and Fisher 1962). Septal grooves are not well preserved in the coral specimens, but it is probable that these served as areas of attachment on those forms.

While modern acrothoracicans bore only into shells of dead animals, Rodda and Fisher reported a Permian bivalve that might have been bored while alive, and Seilacher (1968; 1969) has suggested that this was generally true of the group because of the absence of these borings from shell interiors, and from shells of burrowers. The spiriferid (Pl. 3d-e) of the present study has borings in both valves. These are moderately numerous on the lateral flanks of the shell where feeding currents may have been located, but they are not restricted to that area. There is no indication that the host responded to the boring activity by secreting new shell material. The rugose corals must be assumed to have been bored after death if one assumes the former presence of an overfold at the growing lip of the skeletal wall.

Rodda and Fisher concluded that the shape and attitude of the barnacle boring are related as much to the position on the host and features of the host as to soft part morphology and manner of burrowing into a shell. However, Seilacher (1969) has described evolutionary trends in the attitude of the boreholes as well as changes in the rasping process with time.

Occurrence. Sappington Member, Three Forks Formation, Localities 2 and 17; Leatham Formation, Locality 21.

3. Ichnocoenoses of the Sappington-Leatham-Lodgepole succession

Trace fossil assemblages are described below in their stratigraphic order of appearance. Figures 1 and 3 summarize vertical distributions and Figure 4 the geographic occurrences. Boring traces are not included in Figure 4.

Sappington—Leatham Oncolite, Unit E. This assemblage, discussed in detail above, is one of borers and burrowers (domichnia) seeking protection against an environment which was, at times, hostile to unsheltered life. The predominance of suspension feeders such as brachiopods, sponges, bryozoans, and crinoids is suggestive of an intertidal or shallow sublittoral habitat.

Sappington Member, Unit F. The lower siltstone unit of the Sappington contains shales, thin-bedded siltstones, and calcareous beds with marine fossils; trace fossils, however, are limited in variety and number. *Scalarituba* feeding burrows and fine meandering traces (*Cosmorhaphe?*) occur in abundance in shales and siltstones of the unit at Bacon Rind Creek section and *Scalarituba* is present at Crown Mountain section. Tube-shaped burrow-fill structures have been found at the Logan and Sixteen Mile Creek sections, and *Bifungites* has also been found in the upper part of the unit. U-shaped burrows (*Arenicolites?*) occur at the upper boundary of the unit in the Bridger Range.

In the Leatham Formation there are shales and siltstones above the oncolite unit that contain the brachiopod *Syringothyris* and are equivalent to Unit F of the Sappington. These beds have *Scalarituba* and *Cosmorhaphe?* as in the corresponding Sappington unit, but no other ichnofossils were observed, possibly because of too few and very limited exposures.

Habitation burrows continue to dominate in this very sparse assemblage, but the first appearance of feeding burrows indicates that non-selective deposit feeders were present.

Sappington Member, Unit G. This dark greenish-grey, partly calcareous, slope-forming shale has occasional channel fill siltstones and silty shale intercalations, especially in the upper part. Unit G contains the Sappington "burrow facies" in which the shale is extensively perforated by cylindrical silt-filled burrows in vertical, inclined, and horizontal orientations (Pl. 4a-e; 5b; Fig. 5a, b). This unit also contains vertical U-shaped burrows with faint suggestion of spreiten (Pl. 4c). The upper part of this middle shale unit becomes more silty and transitional into the overlying upper siltstone unit. Thin, slabby siltstones in the upper part of the unit

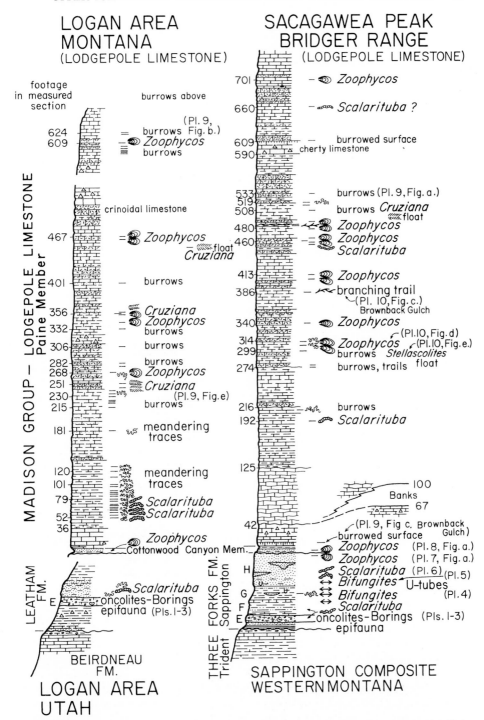

Fig. 3. Generalized diagram to show stratigraphic sections and distribution of trace fossils in the Sappington, Leatham, Cottonwood Canyon, and Paine Units. The Leatham Formation of the Logan area, Utah, is shown separately in the lower left corner. The Sappington section is generalized for western Montana; otherwise the Lodgepole sections are specific for their localities.

often contain *Bifungites*. Deposition appears to have been in a nearshore environment (Gutschick 1964).

The non-appearance of *Scalarituba*, which is present in both underlying and overlying beds, is probably related to the change in the nature of the sediments being deposited.

Sappington Member, Unit H. This upper siltstone unit, which is cliff-forming and weathers to a characteristic yellow-orange colour, contains the greatest diversity and abundance of trace fossils. It is also the best exposed unit in the Member. Sedimentary structures present include oscillation and current ripple marks, channel fill scours, ball and pillow, small scale cross-stratification, and parting lineation. *Bifungites* (Pl. 5a, c-f) is most common in the platy siltstone layers in the lower part of the unit, and is often associated with tubular burrow structures. *Scalarituba* (Pl. 6 a-d) is common in the middle portion of the unit, and *Zoophycos* (Pl. 7a) is present near the top. Other ichnofossils (Pl. 7b-e; Fig. 5d, e) occur as isolated specimens in the float of Unit H. These forms include *Planolites* (Pl. 7b) on soles(?); bilobate trails (Pl. 7c, d) and an unidentified form (Pl. 7e). It is probable that the trail in Plate 7c was made by a conchostracan. It closely resembles trails made by living *Cyzicus* (Tasch 1964). Also, *Cyzicus* (*Lioestheria*) sp. occurs in channel siltstones of Unit G at Antelope Valley. Fine meandering traces resembling *Cosmorhaphe* (Pl. 6a) are present as associates of *Scalarituba*.

The vertical change from abundant dwelling burrows and common shallow-water structures in the lower part of the unit, to the varied burrows of sediment feeders in higher beds (*Zoophycos* facies of Seilacher) signals at least a temporary change to somewhat deeper waters of the sub-littoral before a return to emergent conditions.

Lodgepole Limestone, Cottonwood Canyon Member. This study involves only the thin western edge of the Member (<6 feet thick), but where siltstones are present, there is persistent occurrence of *Zoophycos* throughout the beds (Fig. 2, 4; Pl. 8a-d). The organism probably "mined" the entire silt layer for food. Sole faces of the siltstone beds are intricately covered with tubular silt-filled *Chondrites* burrows (Simpson 1957; Goldring 1964) where the contact is with underlying shales, indicating that the organism burrowed into the shale and the tubes were later filled with silt.

The Cottonwood *Zoophycos* specimens are short spiral forms, suggesting the existence of intermediate subtidal depths during the deposition of the unit.

Lodgepole Limestone, Paine Member. Approximately 700 feet of carbonate beds overlying the Cottonwood Canyon Member are found in this unit. The strata are thin-bedded (<1 foot thick, most often 2-6 inches), micritic, crinoidal, and calcarenitic limestones with many calcareous shale interbeds.

Two related stratigraphic sections—Logan and Sacagawea Peak (Fig. 3), in western Montana—were examined for ichnofossils, compared, and correlated. An ordered succession of trace fossils was observed.

Basal Lodgepole carbonate beds are crinoidal, with vertical burrows (Pl. 9c). These are followed by numerous (e.g. 50 in 100 feet) alternations of fine-grained limestone and calcareous shale. Myriads of fine meandering traces and *Scalarituba* are present in the argillaceous layers at the Logan section, but are much less common in the Sacagawea Peak section. Bilobate, furrowed trails (*Cruziana?*, Pl. 9d; 10b) on sole faces of thin-bedded crinoidal limestones appear next at Logan and at Brownback Gulch in overlying layers. These were not found at Sacagawea Peak, however, although equivalent crinoidal beds crop out. In close succession, *Zoophycos* appears above the Cottonwood Canyon Member for the first time, and it persists almost to the top of the Paine Member. This ichnofossil is found on bedding planes of thin-bedded shaly limestone or calcareous shale layers. In one

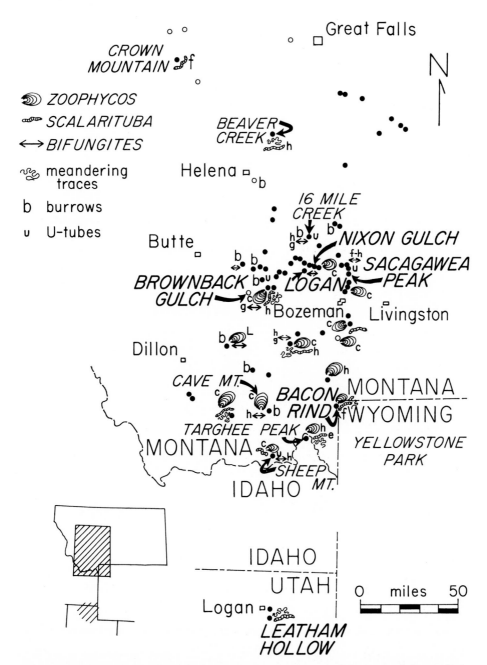

Fig. 4. Distribution of trace fossils in the Sappington, Leatham, and Cottonwood Canyon beds for western Montana and northern Utah. Designations e, f, g and h refer to subdivisions of the Sappington Member, c is Cottonwood Canyon Member, and L represents Lodgepole. Several key sections are shown and referred to in the text.

occurrence, *Zoophycos* was found in thin-bedded coarse-grained limestone within a fine-grained stratigraphic unit. In another case, at Sacagawea Peak, 486 feet above the base of the section, it occurs in argillaceous limestone directly atop large, symmetrical, sharp-crested ripple marks, similar to the situation in Plate 10a. The ripple marked layer is coarsely crinoidal.

Several other elements of the Paine ichnofauna occur within the *Zoophycos*-bearing sequence, some as direct associates in the same bed. The distinctive branching feeding trail of Plate 10c is separated from both overlying and underlying *Zoophycos* beds by 2 to 4 feet. As in the case of the figured specimen, the ichnofossils occur on sole faces in crinoidal limestone beds. The occurrence of *Scalarituba* within the *Zoophycos* zone was noted. In one example, at 457 feet above the base of the Sacagawea section, the two trace fossils are together along bedding planes in thin-bedded, fine-grained shaly limestone, 3 to 4 inches above a crinoidal limestone bed. A radial feeding burrow resembling *Asterophycus?* or *Stellascolites?* has been found in the float, probably derived from the basal part of the *Zoophycos*-bearing sequence at Sacagawea Peak section. The fine meandering traces (*Cosmorhaphe?*) were nowhere found in the same beds as *Zoophycos*, although they are present in adjacent beds. Burrows, burrowed surfaces, and burrow mottled beds occur throughout the two sections; however, no attempt was made to determine systematically the geometry and depth of burrows from bed to bed. In addition to the ichnofauna described above, the striking occurrence of horizontally protrusive rhizocorallid spreiten on an interference-ripple marked surface is noted here (Pl. 10a), and is indicative of mining activity along bedding planes.

4. *Bifungites, Scalarituba,* and *Zoophycos*

Because of their repeated occurrence and large numbers, three ichnogenera dominate the ichnocoenoses described above and merit additional comment.

Ichnogenus BIFUNGITES Desio 1940

The genus was first described from Late Devonian examples in Libya. Dubois and Lessertisseur (1964) found the ichnogenus to be cosmopolitan, with a geologic range of Cambrian to Devonian. The Sappington specimens are also of Late Devonian age. Dubois and Lessertisseur illustrate *Bifungites* on sole faces of silty and sandy beds in positive hyporelief.

Bifungites has been interpreted as the dumb-bell or arrow-shaped bedding impression which becomes detached from the U-shaped burrow with which it is connected. We have as many or more arrow-shaped specimens as of the dumb-bell type, and have noted a mode of occurrence which differs from that cited above. Although positive hyporeliefs are the most common occurrences in the Sappington Member, positive epireliefs are also common (see Pl. 5c and the field sketch (RG) Fig. 5a). The bedding position is known and confirmed by sharp crested oscillation ripple marks on which *Bifungites* is superposed.

Sappington *Bifungites* occur on bedding surfaces of slabby, thin-bedded siltstones, invariably associated with transversely circular burrows; however it is not always clear that the two are related to the same organism. The animal responsible for the trace remains enigmatic. *Bifungites* is found in intertidal or near-intertidal strata in the Sappington beds, and characterizes the first trace community to succeed the shallow water oncolite bank after its burial by clastic sediments.

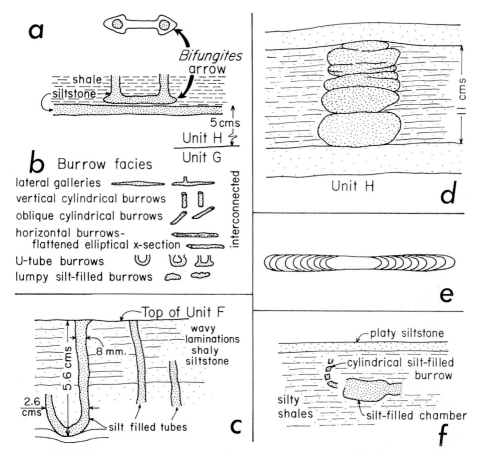

Fig. 5. Field sketches of trace fossils in the Sappington Member.   a   U-shaped burrow associated with *Bifungites*: in cross-section (below), view looking down the burrow (above). *Bifungites* may be connected with the underlying siltstone layer and preserved as a positive epirelief on the upper surface of that bed (see Pl. 5c). Locality 19;   b   Burrow types noted in upper part of Unit G, Locality 19;   c   Burrows (*Arenicolites?*) into top surface of Unit F observed in cross-section along a joint surface. About 500 feet to the southeast of Locality 15;   d   Burrow-fill structure consisting of thick saucer-shaped chambers stacked vertically and recording the vertical migration of the burrow. Unit H, Locality 6;   e   Spreite burrow in cross-section (cf. Seilacher 1967, fig. 4b). Largest dimension about 5 cm. Unit G or H, Locality 18;   f   Tubular burrow with enlarged chamber. Silty shale layer approximately 4 cm thick. Upper part of Unit F, Locality 11.

Ichnogenus SCALARITUBA Weller 1899

This monotypic genus was first described from Lower Mississippian occurrences in the midwestern United States. It is present in Sappington Units E, F and H, and also occurs in F-equivalent beds in the Leatham Formation of Utah. *Scalarituba missouriensis* Weller was studied in some detail by Conkin and Conkin (1968).They found that the ichnospecies has a geologic range of Ordovician to Permian, and interpret the fossil as the trace of a worm or wormlike animal inhabiting a tidal flat environment. Those authors also note that the sediment-feeding burrower usually had few faunal associates.

Scalarituba and *Cosmorhaphe?* are present in calcareous shales carrying marine fossils in beds contemporary with the oncolite bank community of Unit E. These beds are on the flanks of the oncolite bank. The ichnofossil continues this peripheral development into the shales and siltstones of Unit F as the bank is buried. A similar situation is present in the Lodgepole Limestone (Fig. 3) where a fossiliferous bank is developed in the lower part of the Sacagawea Peak Section. Equivalent rocks to the west at Logan contain abundant *Scalarituba* and *Cosmoraphe?* in the muddy bank margin sediments. These occurrences suggest that *Scalarituba* may have preferred the muddy margins of organic concentrations where there was abundant nutrient matter in the sediments.

Scalarituba is present in the siltstones of Unit H although there are no known organic build-ups in these sediments. Its presence can probably be explained by the recurrence of silty sediments or it may have invaded muds in marine bar silts. The ichnofossil is especially abundant in Unit H at Locality 5, and is present also in correlative rocks, again siltstones, in the Exshaw Formation at Jura Creek (type section), Moose and Sulphur Mountain sections in Alberta, Canada. The association of *Scalarituba* with *Zoophycos,* as in Unit H and in the Paine Member, has been reported previously (Henbest 1960; Seilacher 1964; Seilacher and Meischner 1965), but the ichnogenus is clearly present in sediments reflecting shallower depths, as is the case in Unit F of the Sappington and its Leatham correlatives.

Ichnogenus ZOOPHYCOS Massalongo 1855

This ichnofossil or group of ichnofossils has a lengthy history of discussion and speculation with respect to its origin. Many workers now agree that *Zoophycos* and related forms represent the foraging burrow activity of sedentary polychaetes (see Webby 1969); however, Simpson (this volume) has offered an attractive alternative hypothesis.

Sappington specimens of *Zoophycos* from the top of Unit H are few in number, restricted to the southeast edge of its areal extent, simple in form, and developed along the bedding (Pl. 7a). The specimen illustrated resembles a feeding burrow, but lacks a marginal tube. The specimens from the Cottonwood Canyon Member are more complex, spirally coiled, and penetrate the entire thickness of the beds (Pl. 8 a-d). Paine specimens are numerous, but of the simple type developed along the bedding (Pl. 10d) in shaly partings. From a regional viewpoint, *Zoophycos* occurs lower in the Lodgepole Limestone in sections west of Logan as one approaches the axis of the miogeosyncline.

5. Carbonate and ichnofacies models

An area of study which seems to have potential is the development of relationships between the Ichnofacies Model, as developed by Seilacher (1964; 1967), and the modern Carbonate Model which has evolved through the efforts of numerous workers (see Bathurst 1967; Laporte 1969a for key references). The model is shown in a preliminary graphic synthesis, along with the Ichnofacies Model, as Figure 6. It is suggested here that parallel use of the Carbonate and Ichnofacies Models may reduce the uncertainties (Bathurst 1967 p. 467) inherent in seeking bathymetric evidence in carbonate sediments. As applied to the rocks in the present study, the position of the stromatolites (oncolites) of the Sappington-Leatham is clearly intertidal to shallow subtidal, embracing the bathymetric range of the *Cruziana-Glossifungites* ichnofacies. The evidence provided by shelter-seeking borers (although these may be found in deeper water) and a prolific sessile filter-feeding epibenthic community is in agreement with this conclusion. The presence of Waulsortian-type carbonate banks (Cotter 1965) in the lower Lodgepole carbonates of the southern Bridger Range near Bozeman, Montana, and the general absence of oolitic beds in the carbonate sequence, is suggestive of somewhat greater distance from shore. The extensive burrowing activity recorded in these lower beds indicates that the depth was not great, however. Somewhat higher in the carbonates, the appearance of characteristic fodinichnia-dominated ichnocoenoses (*Zoophycos* ichnofacies) suggests continued moderate deepening, but still in the upper (shallower) limits of this ichnofacies type. Crawling tracks identified as *Cruziana?* suggest fluctuations with somewhat shallower conditions.

6. Palaeoecological resumé

The palaeoecological interpretation of late Devonian Sappington-Leatham strata and early Mississippian Lodgepole Limestone in western Montana and northern Utah will begin with the Sappington-Leatham lower black shale, Unit C (Fig. 1). This conchostracan shale facies is known to occur along the length of the Cordilleran miogeosyncline in western United States and Alberta, Canada (Gutschick and Sandberg, in preparation); thus it provides a good datum. The restricted brackish water organic dark shale environment was followed by development of the oncolite bank, Unit E.

The oncolite bank was a large community of invertebrate animals, dominated by suspension feeders, shell-borers, and algae. The latter developed as spherical or nodular forms through encrustment of shelled organisms followed by rolling about on the shallow sea floor. The oncolites are apparently shallow subtidal or intertidal structures. There is evidence of boring activity, which may be attributed to polychaete worms, barnacles, and probably other unknown types. Many shelled animals were attacked while living and before burial; others were bored after envelopment by algal circumcrust and deposition of silty sediments.

Organisms responsible for *Scalarituba* and meander trails encroached along the southeastern margin of the bank where they are associated with marine invertebrates in calcareous shales of Unit E. Muds and silts choked off continued development of the oncolite bank and inundated it with sediments. This change to fine clastic sediments in Unit F accelerated burrowing activity. *Scalarituba* flourished in silts along the southeastern, as far as northern Utah, and the northwestern margins of the former bank during Unit F time. *Bifungites* got its start in an area where the former bank had its maximum development. Extensive influx of mud (Unit G) over much of southwestern Montana resulted in maximum burrowing activity ("burrow facies"). *Bifungites* became abundant, and is found in thin, platy, lenticular siltstones which alternate with muddier sediments in the upper part of the unit. Burrowing activity is shallow (1-2 inches) with tubular-shaped structures and U-shaped burrows. Similarity with the bar-margin facies of Cretaceous rocks in Nebraska (Exum and Harms 1968) is noted.

Bifungites and *Scalarituba* occur throughout Unit H but within beds and from place to place are mutually exclusive. *Bifungites* appears on bedding surfaces in flaggy siltstones, and *Scalarituba* in argillaceous matrix within siltstone beds. These ichnofaunas precede influx of simple *Zoophycos* during late H time, followed by more complex feeding burrows during deposition of the Cottonwood Canyon Member. This may imply somewhat deeper water conditions during the deposition of the latter unit as is also suggested by regional physical relations (Sandberg and Klapper 1967).

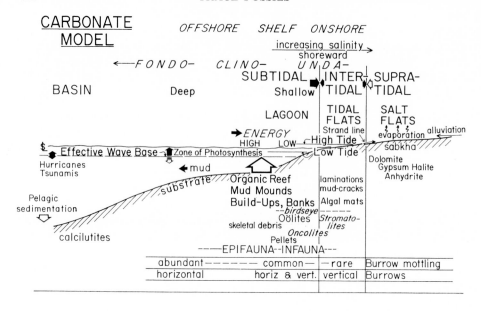

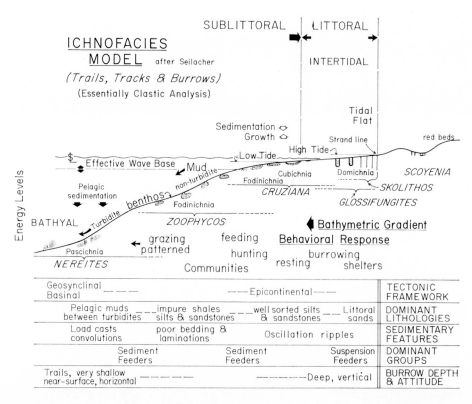

Fig. 6. Combination Carbonate and Ichnofacies Models to summarize characteristics of modern and ancient analog of bathymetry, energy levels, sediments and sedimentation, organisms and their behavioural preference, patterns, niches, structures, and substrate to aid in any environmental analysis of trace fossils in carbonate and clastic sediments. There is no intended significance to the difference in width of the intertidal area shown in both diagrams.

The sedimentation regime changed from extra-basinal clastics to intrabasinal carbonates. Waulsortian-type carbonate banks, like those reported in the Big Snowy Mountains to the east (Cotter 1965), developed in the southern part of the Bridger Range. *Scalarituba* and *Cosmorhaphe?* dominated the life marginal to the bank. Basin subsidence produced the ichnofacies progression to the *Zoophycos* Ichnofacies which persisted with some oscillations (*Cruziana?*) during Paine deposition. The seas shoaled late in Lodgepole time, and the area became intertidal, lagoonal, and supratidal during Mission Canyon shallow-water sedimentation.

Acknowledgments. Financial support for the field studies came from National Science Foundation research grants GE-363 (JR), GP-1197 (RG), and GP-4513 (RG). The field work was based at Indiana University Geological Field Station and we are grateful to the staff and personnel who gave their help. We also acknowledge National Science Foundation Undergraduate Research Participation grants G-16222 (RG) and GE-2612 (RG). Dr. L. J. Suttner and M. J. McLane are thanked for their perceptive and careful observations and notes and Thomas Hanley and James Sprinkle for their help. Appreciation is expressed to Dr. Charles Sandberg, U.S. Geological Survey, Denver, for sharing his information and experience in the field. The authors also wish to acknowledge the assistance of their wives.

Locality List

1 Almart Mtn. Lodge: SE¼ SW¼ sec. 22, T. 8 S., R. 4 E., Crown Butte Quadrangle, Gallatin County, Montana.

2 Antelope Valley: NW¼ NE¼ sec. 2, T. 1 S., R. 2 W., Jefferson Island Quadrangle, Madison, County, Montana.

3 Bacon Rind Creek: SE¼ SE¼ sec. 22, T. 10 S., R. 5 E., Tepee Creek Quadrangle, Gallatin County, Montana.

4 Baldy Mountain, Bridger Range: SW¼ NE¼ sec. 11, T. 1 S., R. 6 E., Sedan Quadrangle, Gallatin County, Montana.

5 Beaver Creek: NW¼ SE¼ sec. 32, T. 13 N., R. 1 W., Nelson Quadrangle, Lewis and Clark County, Montana.

6 Brownback Gulch: SE¼ sec. 20, T. 1 S., R. 3 W., Waterloo Quadrangle, Madison County, Montana.

7 Cave Mtn.: NE¼ SE¼ sec. 6, T. 11 S., R. 5 E., Monument Ridge Quadrangle, Madison, County, Montana.

8 Cottonwood Creek North: NE¼ NW¼ sec. 16, T. 2 N., R. 6 E., Sedan Quadrangle, Gallatin County, Montana.

9 Frazier Lake North: NW¼ SE¼ sec. 9, T. 2 N., R. 6 E., Sedan Quadrangle, Gallatin County, Montana.

10 Lewis and Clark Caverns: SW¼ NW¼ sec. 16, T. 1 N., R. 2 W., Jefferson Island Quadrangle, Jefferson County, Montana.

11 Logan: S½ SW¼ sec. 25, T. 2 N., R. 2 E., Manhattan Quadrangle, Gallatin County, Montana.

12 Milligan Canyon: NE¼ SW¼ sec. 36, T. 2. N., R. 1 W., Three Forks Quadrangle, Jefferson County, Montana.

13 Milligan Canyon East: NE¼ SW¼ sec. 31, T. 2 N., R. 1 W., Three Forks Quadrangle, Broadwater County, Montana.

14 Nixon Gulch: N½ SW¼ sec. 14, T. 2 N., R. 3 E., Manhattan Quadrangle, Gallatin County, Montana.

15 Peak 9559: SW¼ SW¼ sec. 22, T. 2 N., R. 6 E., Sedan Quadrangle, Gallatin County, Montana.

16 Sacagawea Peak: NW¼ sec. 27, T. 2 N., R. 6E., Sedan Quadrangle, Gallatin County, Montana.

17 Sand Creek: SW¼ NE¼ sec. 4, T. 1 S., R. 1 W., Three Forks Quadrangle, Gallatin County, Montana.

18 Sheep Mountain: NW¼ SW¼ sec. 28, T. 14 S., R. 1 W., Upper Red Rock Lake Quadrangle, Beaverhead County, Montana.

19 Sixteen Mile Creek: SE¼ SW¼ sec. 4, T. 4 N., R. 3 E., Toston Quadrangle, Broadwater County, Montana.

20 Targhee Peak: SW¼ SW¼ sec. 9, T. 13 S., R. 43 E., Targhee Peak Quadrangle, Fremont County, Idaho.

21 Leatham Hollow: NW Corner sec. 34, T. 11 N., R. 2 E., Logan Quadrangle, Cache County, Utah.

PLATES

Plate 1

UND number refers to University of Notre Dame repository.

a, b Cylindrical boring on umbonal region of brachial valve (**a**) and pedicle valve (**b**) of *Rhipidomella*, Leatham Formation, oncolite biostrome, Locality 21. **a.** × 0.8, UND 501, **b.** × 1.7, UND 502.

c Oblique cylindrical borings on interior of a *Rhipidomella* valve, Sappington Member, Unit E, Three Forks Formation, Locality 2, × 1.7, UND 503.

d-e Oblique cylindrical boring, exterior and interior views, on pedicle valve of *Rhipidomella*, Sappington Member, Unit E. Three Forks Formation, Locality 2, × 4, UND 504.

f Tangential or incomplete polychaete (?) boring, posterior of both valves of *Rhipidomella*. Leatham Formation, oncolite biostrome, Locality 21, × 1.7, UND 505.

g Burrow-fill passing between valves of *Rhipidomella*. Note small cylindrical hole near shell centre and incomplete hole in left posterior. Sappington Member, Unit E, Three Forks Formation, Locality 13. × 3.3, UND 506.

h Burrow-fills penetrating a partially dissolved oncolite. Note three cylindrical burrows at upper left; a fourth burrow pierces a small strophalosiid brachiopod (lower right) and continues in a curving path. Same specimen as Fig. **g**, × 3.

i Burrow-fill penetrating *Rhipidomella* shell. The brachiopod forms the oncolite nucleus. Thin section photograph of oncolite cross-section demonstrating post-algal penetration by the burrow. Thin section MG 2, Sappington Member, Unit E, Three Forks Formation, Locality 12, × 2.7, UND 508.

Plate 2

a, b Linear (**a**) and curvilinear (**b**) *Vermiforichnus* boring of unknown polychaete in *Rhipidomella*. Fine *Conchotrema* borings and tolypamminid foraminifera epizoans are also present in (**a**). Sappington Member, Unit E. Three Forks Formation. **a.** × 4.2, UND 509; **b.** × 2.5, UND 510.

c-d *Conchotrema* borings in *Rhipidomella*, pedicle and brachial valves, respectively. Pyrite crystals, epizoans and some matrix are present on former and tolypamminid foraminifera on the latter. Leatham Formation, Locality 21. × 2·5, UND 511.

e Interior of a *Rhipidomella* shell with *Conchotrema* and tolypamminid foraminifera. Leatham Formation, Locality 21, × 2. 3. UND 512.

f Pedicle valve of *Syringothyris* bored by *Conchotrema*. Leatham Formation, Locality 21. × 1.6, UND 513.

Plate 3

a Posterior portion of *Syringothyris* shell bored by *Conchotrema,* enlargement of specimen in Pl. 2**f**, × 4.2.

b Platycerid gastropod extensively bored by *Conchotrema.* Note circular perforations as well as branching tunnels. Leatham Formation, Locality 21, × 3.3, UND 514.

c Portion of specimen in Fig. **b**, × 5.

d Incomplete spiriferid pedicle valve exhibiting curvilinear polychaete boring, slit-like barnacle borings, and *Conchotrema.* Sappington Member, Unit E, Three Forks Formation, × 1.2, UND 515.

e Enlargement of left posterior of shell in Fig. **d**. Note elongate elliptical barnacle borings and *Conchotrema,* × 5.

f Barnacle borings and *Conchotrema* in a small tetracoral. Sappington Member, Unit E Three Forks Formation, × 4.2, UND 516.

Plate 4

"Burrow facies" in Sappington Member, Unit G, Middle Shale, western Montana.

a Bioturbate structure in alternating light siltstone and dark shale layers. Black arrow shows upward orientation of bedding. Photomicrograph of thin section DMsg5 (40 × 55 mm), Locality 10, UND 517.

b-d Portion of top surface of rock slab with circular, vertical, compacted horizontal burrows, and U-shaped tubes. Saw cut across slab in Fig. **b** is through the U-shaped burrow shown in cross-section in Figs. **c** and **d**. Burrow gives orientation of bedding. Locality 10, UND 518a, b.

e Tubular burrow-fill structures, orientation ranging from vertical to horizontal, in thin discontinuous siltstone layers and alternating shales. Locality 19.

Plate 5

Bifungites facies in Sappington Member, Units F-G-H, Western Montana.

a Siltstone double arrow found loose on bedding surface. Locality 19, UND 519.

b Thin (1-12 mm) siltstone layer with smooth burrows of *Planolites* sp. on sole face, positive hyporelief. This specimen is similar to the ledgy resistant layers in Pl. 4e. Top of Unit G or base of Unit H, Locality 9, UND 520.

c Slab showing distribution of *Bifungites* on a bedding surface of sharp crested oscillation ripple marks with interference pattern. Silt casts of *Bifungites* stand above bedding surface, positive epirelief. Locality 19 UND 521.

d Portion of large *Bifungites* showing well-formed arrow-shaped termination. Unit G, Locality 6 UND 522.

e *Bifungites* in bold relief on the undersurface, positive hyporelief, of siltstone layer. There are three subcircular broken surfaces where the tubular portion was separated along the bedding surface between the siltstone and underlying shale. Locality 19 UND 523.

f *Bifungites* superposed specimens on sole face, positive hyporelief. Locality 19, UND 524.

Plate 6

Scalarituba facies of Sappington Member, Unit H, Upper Siltstone.

a Association of *Scalarituba missouriensis* Weller and fine meandering traces resembling *Cosmorhaphe.* Slab shows density of trace fossils. UND 525.

b *Scalarituba missourinesis* Weller showing segmented winding burrows in which the dark clay has been washed out and burrows stand out in relief. Locality 5, UND 526.

c *Scalarituba missouriensis* Weller, UND 527.

d Close-up view of slab similar to that in Fig. **c**, UND 528.

a, b Locality 5; **c, d** Locality 3.

Plate 7

Trace fossils in Sappington Member, Unit H, Upper Siltstone, Western Montana.

a *Zoophycos* burrowing along bedding surface in cardboard siltstone layers. Photo shows undersurface of bed, positive hyporelief, marked by X. Associated with small amplitude ripple marks in adjacent beds. Locality 20, UND 529.

b *Planolites* burrows on underside, positive hyporelief, of siltstone layer. Locality 2, UND 530.

c Conchostracan cyziciid trail with smooth bilobate furrows separated by lower median ridge. Float from Sappington Member, Upper Siltstone, upper 15 feet, Locality 2, UND 531. Positive epirelief.

d *Crossopodia?* bilobate burrow with transverse ridges and median furrow. Note several other groups of parallel ridges. Locality 19, UND 532.

e Trail of unknown affinity. Note suggestion of uniserial pattern and V-shaped termination on the anchor-like extension. Locality 9, UND 533.

Plate 8

Zoophycos facies of Cottonwood Canyon Member of Lodgepole Limestone, Western Montana.

a *Zoophycos* (spiral form) with top of bedding surface upward towards the reader. Siltstone beds at top of Cottonwood Canyon Member, Locality 4, UND 534.

b, d *Zoophycos* (non-planar) within siltstone bed, medium and large-sized varieties. Photograph was taken of these fossils *in situ* looking upwards into underside of beds as outcrop is marked in Fig. **b**. Locality 14 (see Text, Fig. 2).

c *Zoophycos*, large variety, in siltstone. Loose slab, unoriented, Locality 2, UND 535.

Plate 9

"Burrow facies" Lodgepole Limestone, Paine Member, Western Montana.

a Burrowed surface in thin-bedded limestone. Arrow directed towards top of bedding as verified by burrows. Lodgepole Limestone, 533 feet above base, Locality 16.

b Tubular burrow fill of coarse detrital limestone penetrating light-coloured micritic limestone. Lodgepole Limestone, sample L540A, 620-621 feet above the base, Locality 11, UND 536.

c Cross-section of elongate vertical burrow in crinoidal limestone. Photo is made from acetate peel taken along planar sawed surface normal to bedding. Note light-coloured granular walls and dark central limonitic tube. Dark grains in light matrix are echinodermal skeletal elements, possibly faecal ejecta. Acetate peel BBR7, Lodgepole Limestone, 2-2.5 feet above base. Locality 6, UND 537.

d *Cruziana?* positive hyporelief. Upper part of Lodgepole Limestone, Locality 6, UND 538.

e Photomicrograph of burrowed limestone. Thin-section 1963-L227B, Lodgepole Limestone, 242-243 feet above base, Locality 11, UND 539.

Plate 10

Trace fossils in the Lodgepole Limestone, Western Montana.

a Rhizocorallid spreite burrows along interference ripples on top surface of limestone slab. Note two opposing burrows are parallel to and disrupting ripple crests. Burrows have prominent tubular flanks with numerous intervening spreite traces. Float slab, Lodgepole Limestone. Figure from field Kodachrome transparency, image illusory (negative rather than positive relief). Large slab not collected. North Cottonwood Creek, NE¼ NW¼ sec. 16, T. 2 N., R. 6 E. Sedan Quadrangle, Bridger Range, Montana.

b *Cruziana?* positive hyporelief. Light-coloured material is rusty weathered fine argillaceous dolomite and dark surface is crinoidal limestone. Crest of trace is weathered. Lower Lodgepole Limestone along ridge, SE¼ sec. 9, T. 2 N., R. 6 E., Sedan Quadrangle, Bridger Range, Montana, UND 540.

c Trail of unknown affinity, possibly *Phycodes* on sole face, positive hyporelief, marked by X. Note chatter marks in the centre of track-way which may represent shell drag. Finer winding feather-like trail is very similar to one interpreted as drag mark made by telson of swimming young limulid, Bandel 1967. Lodgepole Limestone near top, north side of Brownback Gulch, Tobacco Root Mts., Montana, UND 541.

d *Zoophycos* along plane of bedding surface *in situ*. Lodgepole Limestone, 307 feet above base, Locality 16.

e Petaloid ichnofossil resembling *Stellascolites?* and *Asterophycus?* (feeding burrow). Light-coloured lobes of yellow-orange fine argillaceous dolomite, in a darker crystalline limestone. Lodgepole (Paine) Limestone float, 295-300 feet above base of section, Locality 16, UND 542.

PLATE 1

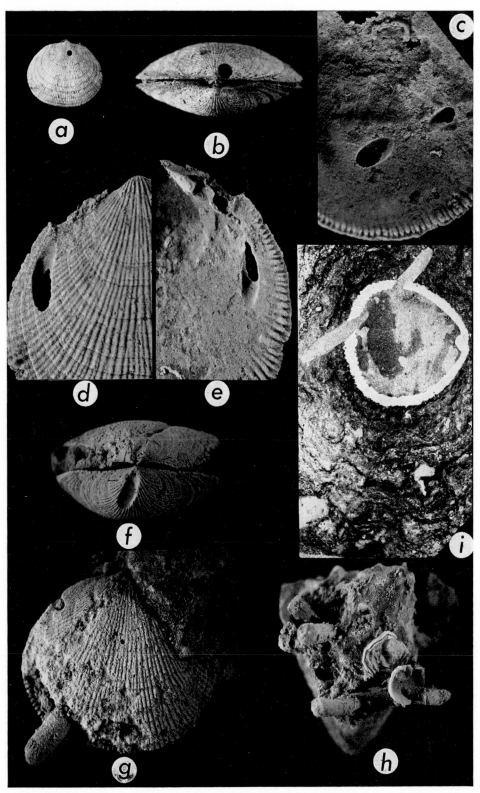

PLATE 2

PLATE 3

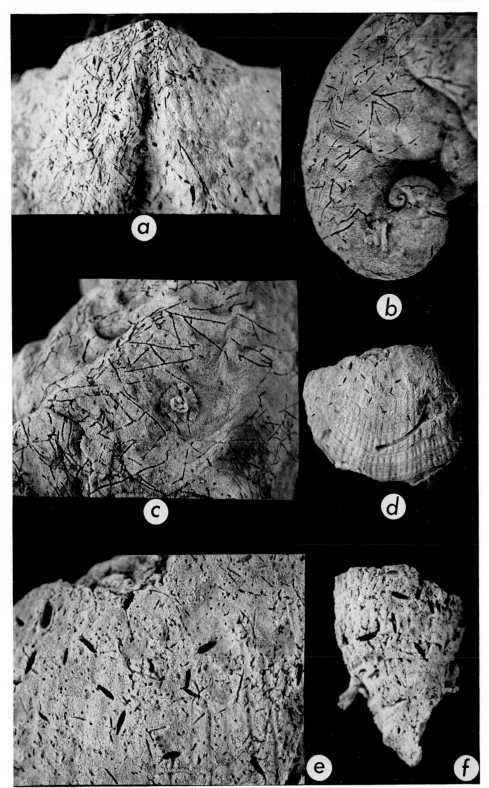

PLATE 4

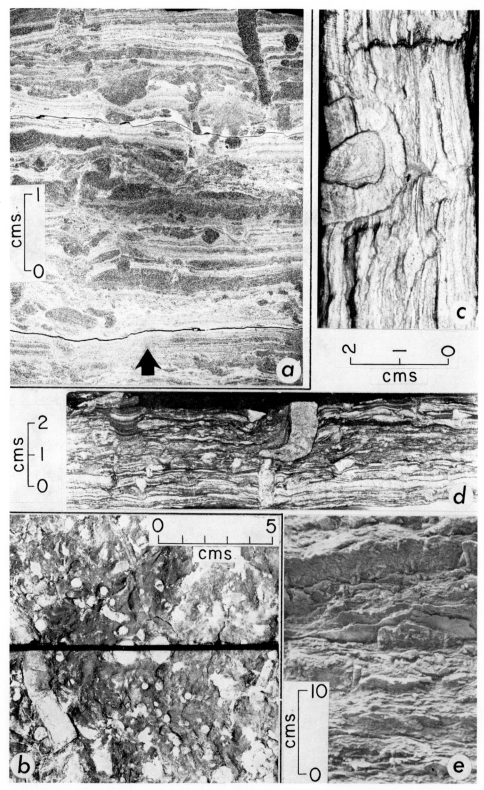

PLATE 5

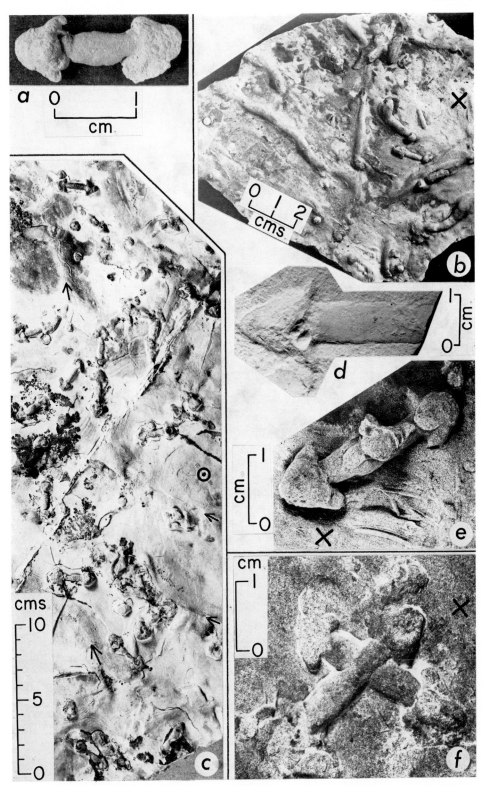

PLATE 6

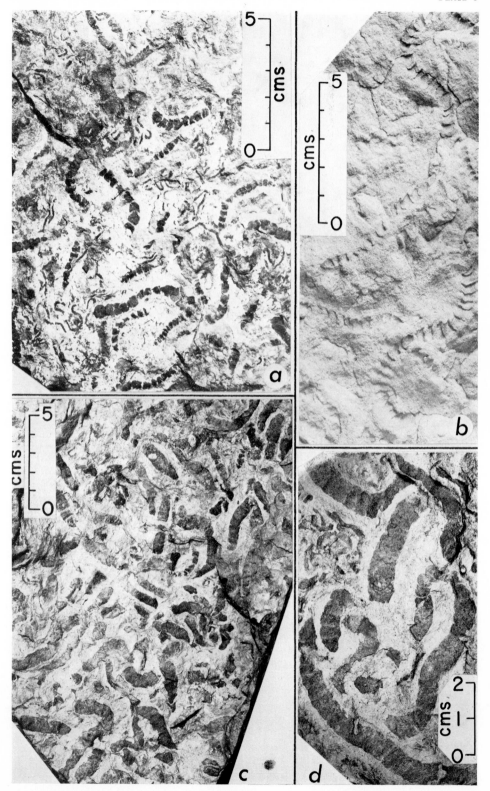

PLATE 7

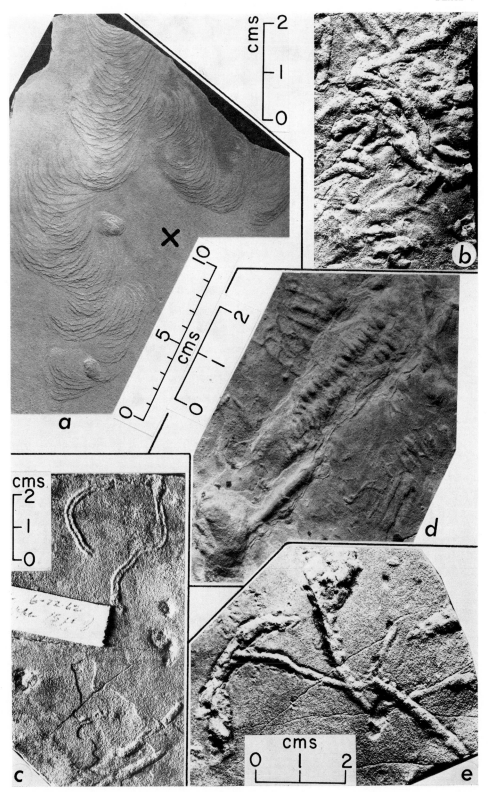

PLATE 8

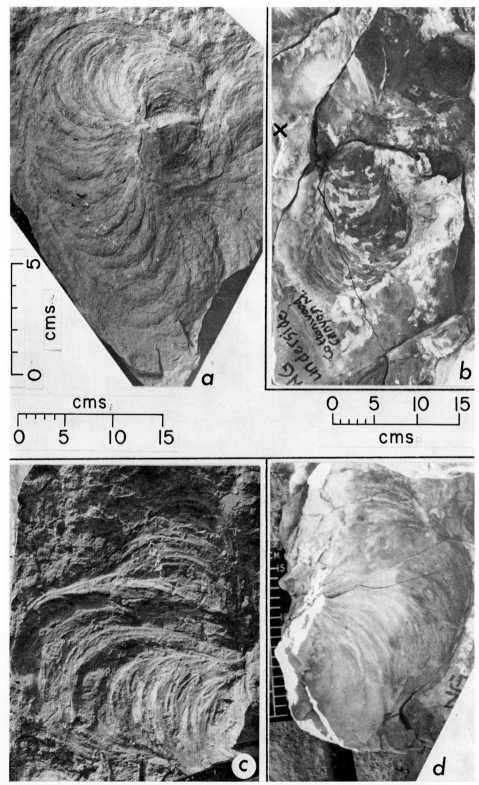

PLATE 9

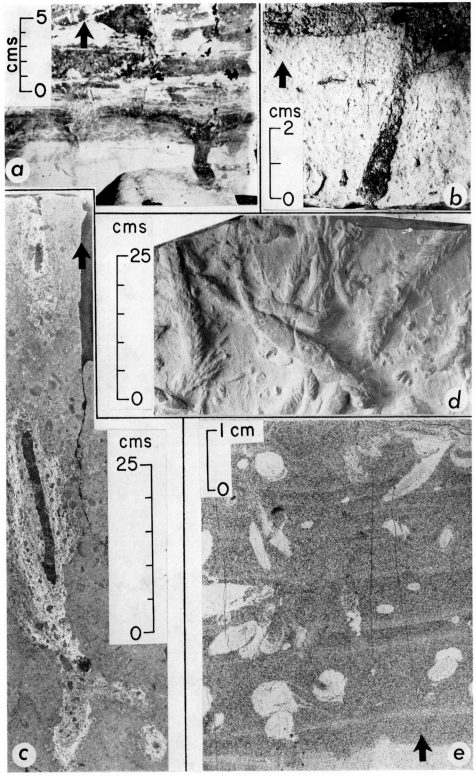

PLATE 10

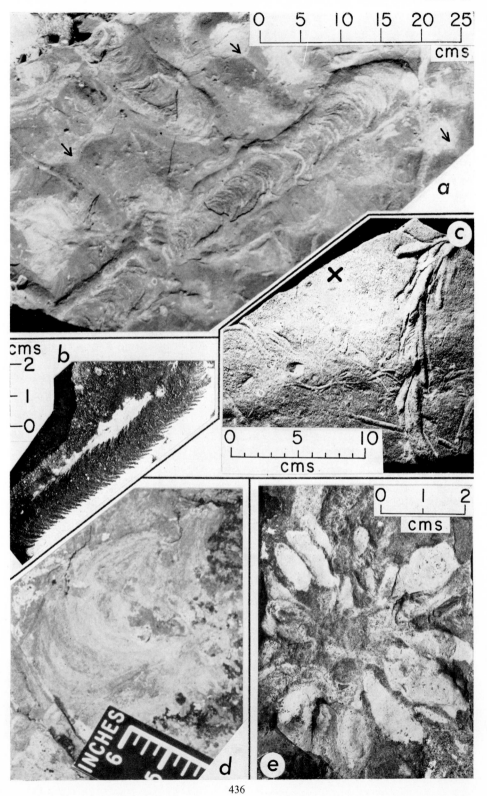

References

BANDEL, K. 1967. Isopod and limulid marks and trails in the Tonganoxie Sandstone (Upper Pennsylvanian) of Kansas. *Paleont. Contr. Univ. Kansas* Paper 19.

BATHURST, R. G. C. 1967. Depth indicators in sedimentary carbonates. *Mar. Geol.* **5**, 447.

BOEKSCHOTEN, G. J. 1966. Shell borings of sessile epibiontic organisms as palaeoecological guides (with examples from the Dutch Coast). *Palaeogeogr. Palaeoeclimatol. Palaeoecol.* **2**, 333.

—— 1967. Palaeoecology of some Mollusca from the Tielrode sands (Pliocene, Belgium). *Ibid.* **3**, 311.

BRUNTON, H. 1966. Predation and shell damage in a Viséan brachiopod fauna. *Palaeontology* **9**, 355.

BUEHLER, E. J. 1969. Cylindrical borings in Devonian shells. *J. Paleont.* **43**, 1291.

CAMERON, B. 1967a. Oldest carnivorous gastropod borings, found in Trentonian (Middle Ordovician) brachiopods. *J. Paleont.* **41**, 147.

—— 1967b. Fossilization of an ancient (Devonian) soft-bodied worm. *Science, N.Y.* **155**, 1246.

—— 1969. Paleozoic shell-boring annelids and their trace fossils. *Am. Zoologist* **9**, 689.

CARRIKER, M. R. and YOCHELSON, E. L. 1968. Recent gastropod boreholes and Ordovician cylindrical borings. *Prof. Pap. U.S. geol. Surv.* **593-B**, B1.

CLARKE, J. M. 1908. The beginnings of dependent life. *Bull. N. Y. St. Mus.* **121**, 146.

—— 1921. Organic dependence and disease, their origin and significance. *Ibid.* **221-222**, 113.

CONKIN, J. E. and CONKIN, B. M. 1968. *Scalarituba missouriensis* and its stratigraphic distribution. *Paleont. Contr. Univ. Kansas* Paper 31.

COTTER, E. 1965. Waulsortian-type carbonate banks in the Mississippian Lodgepole Formation of central Montana. *J. Geol.* **73**, 88.

DESIO, A. 1940. Vestigia problematiche Paleozoiche della Libia. *Annali Mus libico Stor. nat.* **2**, 47.

DUBOIS, P. and LESSERTISSEUR, J. 1964. Note sur *Bifungites*, trace problematique du Devonien du Sahara. *Bull. Soc. géol. Fr.* **6**, 626.

FISCHER, P. H. 1962. Perforations des fossiles pre-Tertiares attribuées à des gastéropodes predateurs. *J. Conch, Paris* **102**, 68.

GOLDRING, R. 1964. Trace fossils and the sedimentary surface in shallow-water marine sediments. *Developments in Sedimentol, Deltaic and Shallow Marine Deposits* (Ed. L. M. J. U. Van Straaten). Elsevier, Amsterdam **1**, 136.

GUTSCHICK, R. C. 1964. Transitional Devonian to Mississippian environmental changes in western Montana. *Bull. Kansas geol. Surv.* **169**, 171.

—— SUTTNER, L. J. and SWITEK, M. J. 1962. Biostratigraphy of transitional Devonian-Mississippian Sappington Formation of southwest Montana. *13th Ann. Field Conf. Billings Geol. Soc.* p. 79.

HECKER, R. F. 1965. *Introduction to paleoecology.* Elsevier, New York.

HENBEST, L. 1960. Fossil spoor and their environmental significance in Morrow and Atoka Series, Pennsylvanian, Washington County, Arkansas. *Prof. Pap. U.S. geol. Surv.* **400**, 383.

HOLLAND, F. D., Jun. 1952. Stratigraphic details of Lower Mississippian rocks of northeastern Utah and southwestern Montana. *Bull. Am. Ass. Petrol. Geol.* **36**, 1697.

LAMONT, A. In REED, F. R. C. 1954. Lower Carboniferous brachiopods from Scotland. *Proc. Leeds phil. lit. Soc., Sci. Sect.* **6**, 180.

LAPORTE, L. F. 1969a. Recognition of a transgressive carbonate sequence within an epeiric sea: Helderberg Group (Lower Devonian) of New York State. *Spec. Publs. Soc. econ. Paleont. Miner.* **14**, 98.

—— 1969b. Paleozoic carbonate facies of the Central Appalachian shelf. *Bull. Am. Ass. Petrol. Geol.* **53**, 728 (Abstr.).

McKINNEY R. A. 1966. A bored ectoproct from the Middle Mississippian of Tennessee. *S East Geol.* **9**, 165.

REYMENT, R. A. 1966. Preliminary observations on gastropod predation in the western Niger Delta. *Palaeogeogr. Palaeoclimatol. Palaeoecol.* **2**, 81.

RICHARDS, R. P. and SHABICA, C. W. 1969. Cylindrical living burrows in Ordovician dalmanellid brachiopod beds. *J. Paleont.* **43**, 838.

RODDA, P. U. and FISHER, W. L. 1962. Upper Paleozoic acrothoracic barnacles from Texas. *Tex. J. Sci.* **14**, 460.

RODRIGUEZ, J. and GUTSCHICK, R. C. 1968. *Productina, Cyrtina,* and *Dielasma* (Brachiopoda), from the Lodgepole Limestone (Mississippian) of southwestern Montana. *J. Paleont.* **42**, 1027.

—— and —— 1969. Silicified brachiopods from the lower Lodgepole Limestone (Kinderhookian), southwestern Montana. *Ibid.* **43**, 952.

SAINT-SEINE, R. DE 1955. Les cirripedes acrothoraciques echinicoles. *Bull. Soc. géol. Fr.* **5**, 299.

SANDBERG, C. A. and KLAPPER, G. 1967. Stratigraphy, age, and paleotectonic significance of the Cottonwood Canyon Member of the Madison Limestone in Wyoming and Montana. *Bull. U.S. geol. Surv.* **1251-B**.

—— and MAPEL, W. J. 1967. Devonian of the northern Rocky Mountains and Great Plains. *Int. Symp. Dev. Syst. Alta. Soc. Petr. Geol.* **1**, 843.

SCHLAUDT, C. M. and YOUNG, K. 1960. Acrothoracic barnacles from the Texas Permian and Cretaceous. *J. Paleont.* **34**, 903.

SEILACHER, A. 1964. Biogenic sedimentary structures. In *Approaches to paleoecology* (Ed. J. Imbrie and N. D. Newell) Wiley, New York. p. 296.
—— 1967. Bathymetry of trace fossils. *Mar. Geol.* **5**, 413.
—— 1968. Swimming habits of belemnites recorded by boring barnacles. *Palaeogeogr. Palaeoclimatol. Palaeoecol.* **4**, 279.
—— 1969. Paleoecology of boring barnacles. *Am. Zoologist* **9**, 705.
—— and MEISCHNER, D. 1965. Fazies-analyse in Palaozoikum des Oslo-Gebietes. *Geol. Rdsch.* **54**, 596.
SILER, W. L. 1965. Feeding habits of some Eocene carnivorous gastropods. *Tex. J. Sci.* **17**, 213.
SIMPSON, S. 1957. On the trace fossil *Chondrites*. *Q. J. geol. Soc. Lond.* **112**, 475.
TASCH, P. 1964. Conchostracan trails in bottom clay muds and on turbid water surfaces. *Trans. Kans. Acad. Sci.* **67**, 126.
TEICHERT, C. 1945. Parasitic worms in Permian brachiopod and pelecypod shells in Western Australia. *Am. J. Sci.* **243**, 197.
TOMLINSON, J. T. 1963. Acrothoracican barnacles in Paleozoic myalinids. *J. Paleont.* **37**, 164.
VOIGT, E. 1965. Über parasitische Polychaeten in Kriede-Austern sowie einige andere in Muschelschalen bohrende Würmer. *Pälaont. Z.* **39**, 193.
WEBBY, B. D. 1969. Trace fossils *Zoophycos* and *Chondrites* from the Tertiary of New Zealand. *N. Z. J. Geol. Geophys.* **12**, 208.
WELLER, S. 1899. Kinderhook faunal studies 1: the fauna of the vermicular sandstone at Northview, Webster County, Missouri. *Trans. Acad. Sci. St. Louis* **9**, 9.

J. Rodriguez, Department of Geology, Hunter College, City University of New York, Box 615, New York, NY 10021, U.S.A.

R. C. Gutschick, Department of Geology, University of Notre Dame, Notre Dame, Indiana, U.S.A.

Borings and burrows in the Eocene littoral deposits of the Tatra Mountains, Poland

P. Roniewicz

Large numbers of sponge borings and less frequent borings of polychaetes and bivalves have been found in dolomite pebbles of Eocene conglomeratic organodetrital limestones of the Tatra Mountains, Poland. Outlets of borings are usually damaged, and some pebbles have algal coatings showing that they were redeposited. Borings have not been observed in the Eocene substratum nor in the massive basal conglomerates; consequently it is thought that the substratum was probably covered with waste during the transgression. Intensive wave action and reworking of waste, resulted in an environment unfavourable for lithophages. Their development was only possible when the supply of shore-derived material decreased, i.e. when the deposition of conglomeratic organodetrital limestones took place. Tube-like burrows orientated perpendicular to the bedding and formed of flat foraminiferal tests (predominantly of *Discocyclina*) have also been found in the organodetrital limestones and detrital dolomites. The regular outline of these structures and the shape selection of foraminifer tests suggest that the tube-like burrows resulted from intentional activity of animals, probably decapods.

1. Introduction

The nummulitic Eocene of the Tatra Mountains (Fig. 1) comprises four nummulite subhorizons namely: I *Nummulites brongniarti*, II *Nummulites perforatus*, III *Nummulites millecaput*, IV *Nummulites fabiani*. The first three belong to the Upper Lutetian, and the fourth to the Lower Bartonian (Bieda 1963). Various deposits, mostly of littoral origin, constitute this nummulitic Eocene series. They start with polymict conglomerates, and grade into detrital carbonates and then organodetrital and organogenic rocks.

The rock-boring assemblage occurs within the detrital carbonates (Roniewicz 1966). This unit does not occur in all sections of the nummulitic Eocene. It is often lacking in places where the detrital dolomites and conglomerates are thick. It is well developed in sections of reduced thickness, where it appears just above the basal conglomerates and continues to the top of the nummulitic Eocene and into a facies which is transitional to the flysch deposits (Fig. 2). This unit is represented in various sections by different nummulite subhorizons (from II to IV) but is most frequently represented by the nummulites of the third and fourth subhorizons.

The burrows to be described occur in the top part of the detrital limestone and dolomites and the overlying organodetrital limestones.

2. Characteristics of the lithophages

The lithophage borings are normally only to be found in pebbles and rock fragments which are sparsely spaced in organodetrital limestones. One pebble with bivalve borings has, however, been found at the top of the cliff conglomerate at Wysoki

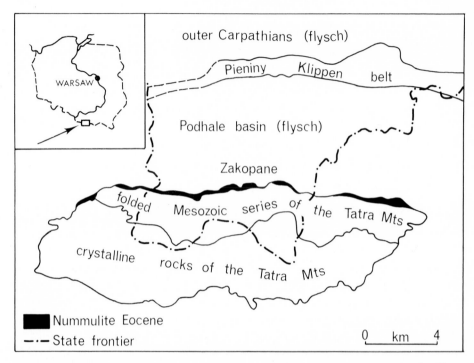

Fig. 1. Schematic map showing the occurrence of the nummulitic Eocene in the Tatra Mountains.

Regiel (Fig. 2a and Roniewicz 1969). The lithophages normally inhabited yellow-weathering dolomites of the sub-tatric Middle Triassic (Pl. 1).

The sponges are most abundant: *Cliona celata* Grant, *Cliona vastifica* Hancock, *?Cliona albicans* Volz, and also *Cliothosa* sp.. Polychaetes such as *Polydora ciliata* (Johnston) and *Potamilla reniformis* (O. F. Müller) are less common. Borings of bivalves, *Lithophaga* sp. and *Gastrochaena* sp. are relatively rare. The amount of destruction of the rock fragments differs and is best illustrated by sponge borings. Some specimens show only single holes while others are intensely bored.

Rock fragments were destroyed uniformly on all sides, suggesting that they were moved along the bottom. In many cases the outlets of borings are damaged, clearly showing that such pebbles were scoured after inhabitation by the lithophages. Concentric coatings of calcareous algae are also common. In many cases the thickness of such a coat greatly exceeds the diameter of the rock fragment. Structures of this type are known to have been formed during the transport of rock fragments (Roniewicz 1966). Bivalve shells are not often preserved and were probably removed during transport of the pebbles. All these observations demonstrate that the lithophages lived in a relative shallow zone with frequent bottom currents.

3. Origin of the lithophocoenoses

The occurrence of the lithophocoenoses in the pebbles of the relatively thin organo-trital limestones, together with their absence in the thicker conglomerates and detrital carbonates suggest that they favoured areas with slow sedimentation. The occurrence of bored and non-bored rock fragments together and the record of a single pebble with *Lithophaga* sp. in the basal conglomerate suggests that some of the bored material was transported from a distant littoral zone where the boring organisms were common and material was available for boring from the destruction of nearby cliffs.

Scouring of rocks with lithophages and the development of algal coatings might, however, occur by the action of waves and weak currents without transport over

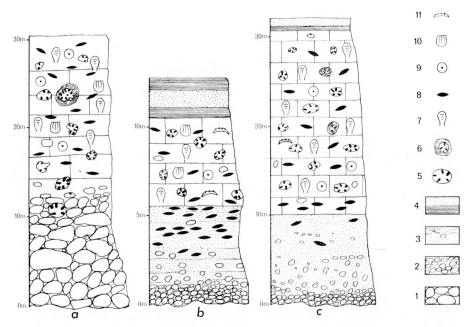

Fig. 2. Schematic profiles of the nummulitic Eocene with lithophage assemblages.   a   Wysoki Regiel Hill;   b   Spadowiec Valley;   c   Molkówka locality. *1.* the basal cliff conglomerate; *2.* the basal waste conglomerate; *3.* detrital dolomites and limestones; *4.* calcareous and clayey mudstones and sandstones (flysch sequence); *5.* pebble with lithophage borings; *6.* pebble with calcareous algal coatings; *7.* calcareous algae; *8.* tests of large foraminifera; *9.* crinoid ossicles; *10.* bivalve shells (*Pecten* sp.); *11.* oyster shells.

long distances. In this case almost all the rock fragments would be inhabited by lithophages as occurs in some of the material investigated. Thus two distinct environments appear to have been present.

A comparison of the Tatra Eocene lithophocoenoses with others occurring in the Palaeogene of Fergana (Hecker *et al.* 1962), the Tortonian of the Holy Cross Mountains (Radwański 1969) or in Recent environments (Volz 1939) shows that the basement rocks of the Tatra Eocene could have been a good environment for lithophages. Nevertheless there are no lithophages there or in the densely packed bottom conglomerates.

PLATE 1

442

This lack of lithophages in the basement rocks suggests that during the transgression the basement was covered with a regolith consisting of relatively small fragments of basement rocks. This cover was washed out by the encroaching sea and formed the basal conglomerates. During the washing process the small fragments were probably in constant motion with much attrition. Such conditions would be unfavourable for the settling of lithophages; this would only be possible after the shoreline encroached upon the land and the rock fragments were then more sparsely distributed. It might also have occurred in that part of the seashore in which either there was smaller quantity of debris, or its rate of supply was lower. Such were the environmental conditions when the conglomeratic organodetrital limestones were formed, and the lithophages found favourable habitats. Lithophage development ceased when the basin deepened and deposition of carbonate siltstones and pure argillites began and initiated the flysch deposition of the Inner Carpathians.

4. Occurrence of tubes lined with foraminifera

In the nummulitic Eocene tests of large foraminifera occur in plenty in the top part of detrital limestones and dolomites and in the overlying organogenic limestones.

These large tests do not normally show any orientation. Some concentrations caused by currents and wave action are met, however, and in such cases the tests are oriented and the concentrations are layer-like or lens-like in shape, but of variable size (Roniewicz 1969). Apart from these mechanical concentrations there are also some disturbances in test arrangement which are known to have been caused by mud-eaters. These animals penetrated loose sediment, in which there were abundant tests of large foraminifera, and caused concentrations of the latter at the rims of canals (see Roniewicz 1969 fig. 19, pl. 11 fig. 2). Tube-like structures lined with foraminifera found recently by J. Kraszewski and E. Olempska (Pl. 2) are, however, enigmatic. These structures occur within organodetrital limestones rich in tests of large foraminifera such as *Discocyclina* and *Nummulites*, and also in detrital dolomites in layers in which these tests are not rock forming components.

5. Description of the tube-like structures

The tube-like structures are built of flat tests, mainly of *Discocyclina*, but the interior is filled with sediment that bears few or no tests (Pl. 2a, b, d).

Three main types can be distinguished by shape and details of structures:

Plate 1

Dolomite pebble of Middle Triassic age with assemblage of Eocene lithophages:

A *Cliothosa* sp.

B *Cliona celata* Grant.

C *Lithophaga* sp.

D *Polydora ciliata* (Johnston) ×1.

PLATE 2

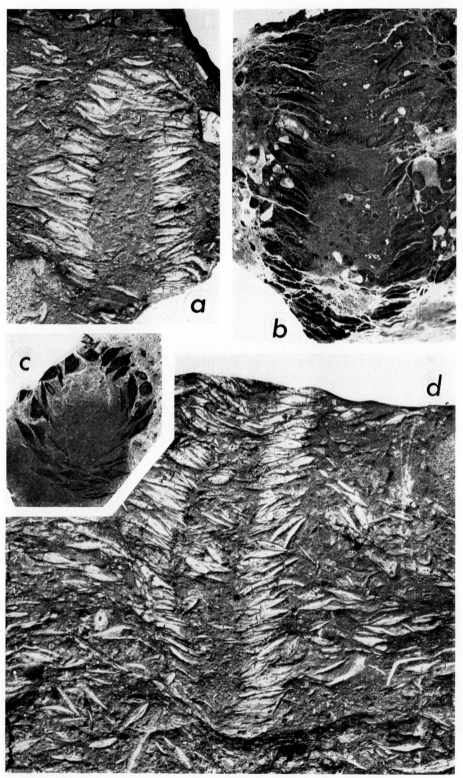

(i) Tubes with walls of width 1 to 1·5 times the diameter of the tests that form them. Here the tests are densely spaced one over another forming a narrow U-shape in vertical section (Pl. 2b, d; Fig. 3). The tests may lie flat or more frequently are slightly tilted toward the centre of structure, and less frequently outwards. The structures are usually perpendicular to the bedding. In some cases they are slightly oblique, and project as oval in section (Pl. 2a; Fig. 3). The length of these structures is from 5 to 25 cm and the width from 2 to 5 cm, with a direct relationship between them. They occur in groups of up to ten or more in a single layer, usually at the top. In detrital dolomites they are less frequent but sometimes occur in small groups.

(ii) The second type is similar in shape to the first. It differs in the arrangement of the tests, the maximal sections of which are almost parallel to the axis of the structure (Pl. 2c; Fig. 3). This type is less frequent and is found in detrital dolomites.

(iii) The third type consists of test concentrations of nest type in the centre of which is situated a space devoid of tests. The shape is that of tube opening upwards. The thickness of the wall in such a structure built of tests is from several to over ten test diameters. They are tilted towards the axis of the structure. These forms are rare and occur only in detrital dolomites.

6. Interpretation of the tube-like structures

Their regular structure, particularly in the first type, and their occurrence in deposits that do not show selection of detrital material or orientation of foraminifera tests, demonstrates convincingly that they could not have been formed mechanically by current or wave action. The layers with *Discocyclina,* in which these structures occur, consist of organic material and fine carbonate silt suggesting rather calm conditions of deposition. It may therefore be assumed that these structures (burrows) have been formed as a result of animal activity on the sea bottom: they were probably dwelling structures. The size of the whole structure, particularly its diameter, depended on the size of the animal. It may be calculated from the average size of these structures that the animals were from one to several centimetres in diameter. The differentiation of sizes is then a function of the sizes of the animals, and reflects the age of the individuals. It is very characteristic that the animals carefully selected the material for the construction of their dwellings avoiding the convex nummulite tests and rock pebbles and choosing only the flat tests of *Discocyclina.* In the case of the structures in detrital dolomites the tests were clearly transported from a distance because they are absent in the surrounding sediment. In a loose sediment transported by currents, as shown by cross-bedding (Roniewicz 1969), the tube-like burrows served as a shelter against the currents and covering by dolomite sand.

The origin of the third type is more complicated. Most probably the animals used these natural, mechanical, concentrations of tests, digging down into the lens-

Plate 2

The tube-like burrows built of tests of large foraminifera:

a, b, d Structures of the first type (explanation in the text) section perpendicular to bedding × 1.

c Structures of the second type (explanation in the text) on a bedding plane × 1.

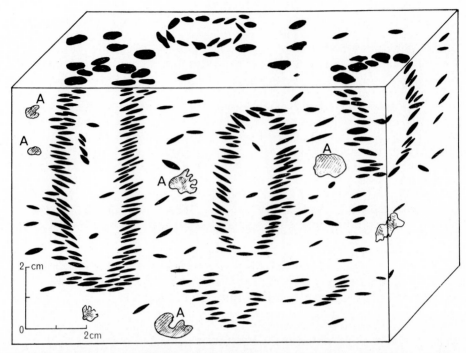

Fig. 3. Block-diagram illustrating the tube-like structures built of the tests of large foraminifera.
    A   dolomite pebbles with lithophage borings.

like agglomeration of tests. As a result of this the tests are orientated obliquely to
the channel axis. In this way such a burrow would be an intermediate one between
the nest-type test concentration, the mud-eater channels and structures built from
purposefully collected and arranged tests.

It is highly probable that arthropods could have been the inhabitants of such
tube-like burrows; decapods, particularly crabs, seem to be the most likely.

References

BIEDA, F. 1963. Larger foraminifers of the Tatra Eocene. *Trav. Inst. geol. Pol.* **37**, 1.
HECKER, R. Th., OSSIPOVA, A. I. and BELSKAYA, T. N. 1962. *Ferganski zaliv paleogenovovo mora.*
    Akad. Nauk U.S.S.R. **2**, 1.
RADWAŃSKI, A. 1969. Lower Tortonian transgression on to the southern slopes of Holy Cross
    Mts. *Acta geol. pol.* **19**, 137.
RONIEWICZ, P. 1966. New data on sedimentation of Eocene organodetrital limestones in the
    Tatra Mts. *Bull. Acad. pol. Sci.* **14**, 165.
—— 1969. Sedimentation of Nummulite Eocene of the Tatra Mts. *Acta geol. pol.* **19**, 591.
VOLZ, P. 1939. Die Bohrschwämme/Clioniden der Adria. *Thalassia* **3**, 2.

P. Roniewicz, Institute of Geology, Warsaw University, Warsaw 22, Poland, Al. Zwirki-i-
    Wigury 93.

Cruziana stratigraphy of "non-fossiliferous" Palaeozoic sandstones

A. Seilacher

Marine sandstones that contain practically no other remains may preserve abundant trace fossils. Among these, trilobite burrows (*Cruziana*) are shown to be valuable index fossils, provided preservational and behavioural variability is also taken into account. Some of the 30 species recognized in this paper have world wide distribution.

1. Introduction

Trace fossils are, as a rule, poor time markers (Seilacher 1960). Not only are they strongly facies-restricted but they also have notoriously long time ranges. This is even true for highly specialized and distinctive types such as the worm track *Gyrochorte* which ranges from the Carboniferous to the Tertiary, without sufficient changes to distinguish different species. Vertebrate footprints, on the other hand, express the taxonomic personalities of their producers much more clearly and can be used as index fossils in place of skeletal remains.

Tracks of larger arthropods are similar to vertebrate tracks, in that they often show distinctive "fingerprints". The "fingerprints" are not restricted to surface trackways, but may also be preserved in burrows, which, by their deeper penetration into the sediment, had a higher fossilisation potential. Trilobite burrows, found in shallow marine sandstones of the early Palaeozoic all over the world, show these "fingerprints" particularly well. Their scientific name, *Cruziana,* was given by d'Orbigny (1842) in honour of Andrés de Santa Cruz who from 1836 to 1839 united Bolivia and Peru under his rule. The more descriptive name *Bilobites* is invalid under the rules of zoological nomenclature (Sinclair 1951), but continues to be used as an open, non-Latin term in scientific literature. Being sizeable and conspicuous, trilobite burrows are easily recognized in the field, and it is not too difficult to distinguish different species by shape and surface ornamentation. These ichnospecies correspond to certain, though unknown, trilobite taxa, and there is no reason why they should not be similarly reliable as stratigraphic guides. Limitations, at present, are due rather to the small number of biostratigraphically defined occurrences but it is to be hoped that this number will increase with the growth of interest in trace fossils.

So far, the results of *Cruziana* stratigraphy are quite encouraging: the new tool allows one to correlate whole series of shallow water marine sandstones which, for preservational reasons, contain no other index fossils. This situation most commonly arises in cratonic areas with purely clastic sedimentation, but the guiding *Cruziana* species have first to be standardized in non-cratonic sections, where sandstones are interbedded with fossiliferous shales and limestones.

Compared to body fossils, *Cruziana* species are remarkably widespread and

447

little diversified. At present about 30 species can be distinguished. Of these, more than two-thirds are as yet stratigraphically defined, and more than a dozen have already been found in widely separated areas, many in different continents. During a recent visit to the Tassili (Central Sahara) seven *Cruziana* species were found, ranging in age from Lower Ordovician to Lower Devonian. Four of them were new to Africa, but only one was so far unknown. This trend indicates that the number of *Cruziana* species, while being sufficient for gross correlation, will never grow into a taxonomic jungle which only the specialist dares to penetrate.

Difficulties may rather come from the high intraspecific variation of trilobite burrows. This variation is due not only to anatomical differences (as in body fossils) but also to varying ecological intentions, behavioural responses, and, last but not least, to preservational differences. Therefore it will be necessary in this paper to discuss some general questions, before proceeding to the descriptive presentation of the material.

2. General considerations

Intra-sedimentary origin. There is no doubt that *Cruziana* burrows were dug at the water/sediment interface. But there are also strong indications that what we usually find as casts on sandstone sole faces are not the true surface structure, but its under-track duplicate formed under a thin layer of sand. This becomes most obvious in situations like the one shown in the block diagram of Figure 1; but it is also indicated by the fact that claw marks and burrow contours are hardly ever blurred by subsequent water action. As a consequence, we have to allow not only for a higher fossilisation potential, but also for a higher variability in outline (Fig. 1), of the undertrack bilobites as compared to the corresponding surface impressions.

Attribution to trilobites. Today it is hardly necessary to repeat Nathorst's (1886) emphatic plea for the trace fossil origin as opposed to the old seaweed interpretation of *Cruziana* (Saporta and Marion 1883; Delgado 1885–87). Nevertheless, the question whether these trace fossils were made by trilobites is still the subject of discussion.

The usual objection is that some sandstones have their bedding planes covered with *Cruziana* without yielding a single trilobite fragment. For the ichnologist this fact only illustrates the familiar antagonism in the occurrence of trace fossils versus body fossils (Fuchs 1895 p. 67): the sands that favour the preservation of trace fossils are usually too permeable to retain their shelly fossils during diagenesis. Moreover, burrowing arthropods are usually less calcified, and therefore less easily preserved to begin with, than the epibenthonic ones.

Under these conditions it is not surprising that there are only one or two cases in which the trilobite carapace was found preserved within its burrow (Osgood 1970). In most species we have to rely on indirect evidence:

(i) *Cruziana* species correspond in time range and size to the evolution of the trilobites. They are most diversified in sandstones of Cambrian age, reach maximum size in the Ordovician, and diminish in size, frequency and diversity in the Silurian and Devonian.

(ii) The number and uniformity of the claw marks, as well as the tapering outline of the resting tracks (*Rusophycus*), does not fit any other arthropod group of comparable body size.

(iii) Some burrows show impressions of the cephalon, pygidium, or pleural spines

PRESERVATIONAL   VARIATION

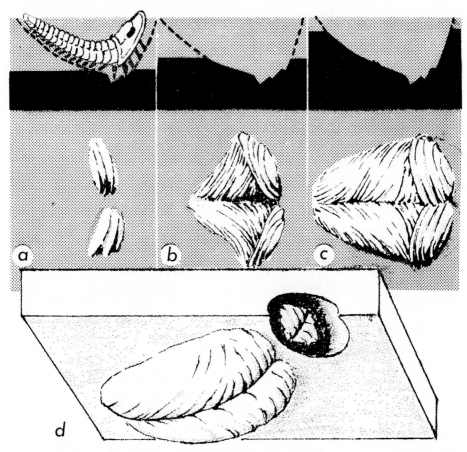

Fig. 1.   a-b   *C. barbata* (M. Cambrian, near Boñar, N. Spain).   c   *C. dispar* (L. Cambrian, Lugnås, Sweden). If these occurred together, they could be considered as preservational aspects of one species;   d   An intra-sedimentary origin is indicated by *Cruziana* specimens continuing into mud pebbles of the overlying sand layer thus explaining major variations between shallow and deeper undertracks.

on their lateral surfaces (Fig. 2). These specimens also clarify the problem of head- and tail-ends in trilobite burrows.

It should be noted that the second criterion does not apply to all species described in this paper. Some of them (*almadenensis* group) indicate a differentiation of the cephalic versus abdominal legs which is unknown in trilobites and might rather suggest a merostome origin. It was mainly for practical reasons that they were here included in the same ichnogenus together with undoubted trilobite burrows.

Digging action of the endopodites.   Trilobite digging was mainly done by the endopodites. Their claws left the scratches which cover the basal surface of most bilobites.

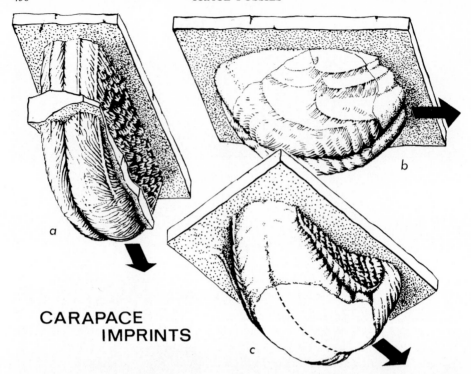

CARAPACE
IMPRINTS

Fig. 2. Occasional carapace impressions link the burrows with more familiar aspects of trilobite morphology and indicate the animal's orientation (arrow = anterior end).   a   *C. rugosa* with pygidial (?) grooves in addition to the marginal pleural grooves. Khabour Quartzite (Arenig), Sinat, N. Iraq. Tüb. cat. 1392/1, × 0·5.   b   Obliquely dug specimen of same species with impressions of a rounded cephalic edge reminiscent of *Illaenus*. Khabour Quartzite (Arenig), Ora, N. Iraq. Tüb. cat. 1392/2, ×0·6.   c   Oblique specimen of *C. dispar* with impressions of pointed pleural ends. Mickwitzia Sandstone (L. Cambrian), Lugnås, Sweden. Tüb. cat. 1392/3, ×0·7

Leg movement was towards the median line and mostly with a backward component, as can be concluded from the profile of the scratches and from the lack of marginal heaps. Only in a few species did the front legs work with a forward component, producing a more or less pronounced divide against the posterior set of scratches (see *C. barbata* Fig. 1a, b).

The scratches are not simple, but consist of two or more parallel or slightly diverging grooves produced by multiple or serrate claws (Seilacher 1962 fig. 2). Sometimes it may be difficult to single out multiple scratches from a multitude of sub-parallel markings. Still it is worth trying to distinguish them as they represent the most specific clues left by the burrowing trilobites. Since the scratches have been produced by a part of the body which is known only in very few trilobite species, they are of little help in linking trace and body fossil taxa. Nevertheless, they are useful for telling apart different *Cruziana* species (Seilacher 1962).

The functional co-ordination between the burrowing endopodites could hardly be derived from the morphology of the burrows alone. But we can assume that it was the same as in the walking trilobite, i.e. with the wave of motion passing from rear to front along the body (Seilacher 1955 p. 345).

INSTRUMENTAL
VARIATION

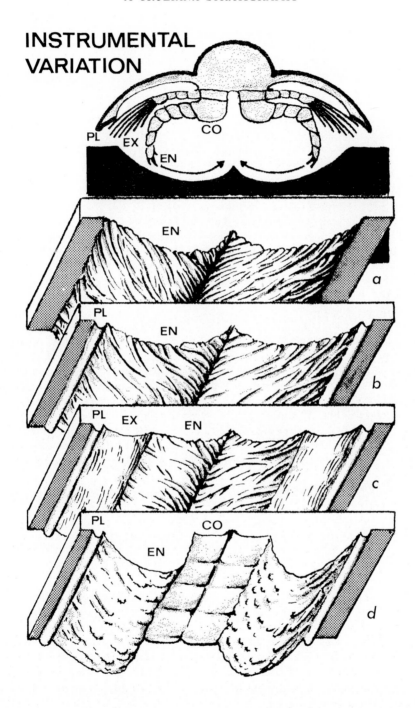

Fig. 3. The endopodites (EN) did most of the digging but pleurae (PL), expodites (EX) and coxae (CO) may have assisted in many cases. Their appearance in the trace record may be controlled by specific structure, behavioural variation, or preservational situation (see Fig. 4).

Additional tools used by the burrowing trilobite (Fig. 3). Some *Cruziana* species, as for instance *C. semiplicata,* have four, rather than the usual two lobes. The additional outer lobes are either completely smooth or bear multiple scratch marks that are finer and more longitudinal than those of the inner lobes. They are probably the work of the exopodites (pre-epipodites) which in addition to their respiratory, swimming, and food gathering functions (Bergström 1969) may well have assisted in burrowing with a kind of backward sweep.

More commonly one finds impressions of genal and pleural spines, dragged out into a narrow marginal groove on either side of the burrow.

Along the median line, the inner lobes usually meet, or if the animal did not burrow deep enough into the track-bearing interface they leave a band of the bedding surface undisturbed. In some of the shorter resting tracks, however, the inner lobes gape apart and between them, at a higher level, additional impressions become visible (Radwański and Roniewicz 1963 pl. 2; Fig. 7-11 and 7-16). These are more regular and less numerous than the endopodal scratches and suggest a longitudinal action, if any. They can be reasonably referred to the trilobite *coxae.*

The broad tail lobes of the *almadenensis* group superficially resemble coxal impressions. But their size and the fact that true coxal impressions occur between them (at least in *Cruziana almadenensis*), indicates a different origin. Whether they are dug out by specialized swimmer-like endopodites of the abdominal region, remains an open question.

Influence of body attitude (Fig. 4). Even in trilobites with essentially uniform appendages, gradational differences did exist in size, shape, and activity of the different claws along the body. This can be shown in short *Cruziana,* or resting tracks. The longer furrows, since they often receive their final touch only from one body end, look very different if ploughed by a head-down (*procline*) or a tail-down (*opisthocline*) trilobite. This effect may also modify the claw markings. In *Cruziana semiplicata,* for instance, the heavy trifid scratches made by the front legs look very different from the finer and nondescript scratches of the rear legs. They would easily pass as characteristics of different species, were they not found together in the same burrow (Pl. 1f).

Different burrowing techniques (Fig. 5). In deeper resting tracks and "nests" the excavated material from the anterior slope of the burrow tends to be pushed out towards the front instead of being passed all along under the body. This could be done either by shovelling with the head shield or simply by a forward component in the front leg digging, each method resulting in very different burrows.

Biological motivation (Fig. 6). While the forementioned effects modify the sculpture of the burrows, their different outlines and patterns are largely related to different biological motivations, and may thus express different ecological conditions. General types as distinguished in non-arthropod trace fossils can thus be matched by trilobite burrows, of which Figure 6 shows only some representative examples.

What features are taxonomical? Most of the variations discussed in the previous chapters are controlled primarily by function, behaviour, and preservation. They could potentially represent a single species, or even one individual and should rightly be disregarded as biostratigraphic indications. In the whole array of variables, however, every species has specific preferences, which cannot be predicted but have to be discovered by field experience.

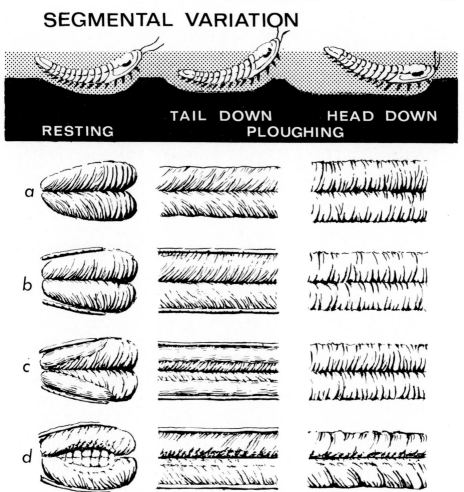

Fig. 4. Gradients in digging direction (smaller angles towards tail end) and additional structures (see Fig. 3) along the trilobite body are evident in complete resting tracks; in elongate furrows they cause different structures if the animal maintains a tail-down (opisthocline) or head-down (procline) position.

Some *Cruziana* species, for instance, occur only as resting tracks, while others are restricted to deep "nests" or elongate ploughing patterns. The choice of burrowing technique and attitude may be similarly specific, and in one case the undertrack level has proven to be stratigraphically significant: The Lower Cambrian species *C. dispar* is dug deep into the underlying mud (Fig. 1c; Fig. 2c), while *C. barbata* of Middle Cambrian age, otherwise very similar, stopped soon after reaching the interface (Fig. 1a, b). Even the population density on a track-bearing bed helps to distinguish different species. *C. almadenensis,* for instance, is fairly common wherever it has been observed, while it takes hours to find one or two specimens of *C. pedroana* in spite of its close similarity.

Thus it is clear that few of the features observed in *Cruziana* are directly related to anatomical structures of their producers. These features should form the basis of

VARIATION OF BURROWING TECHNIQUE

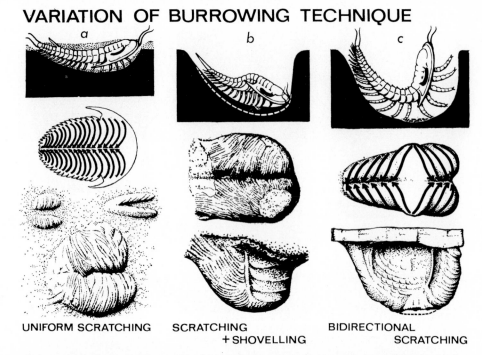

UNIFORM SCRATCHING   SCRATCHING   BIDIRECTIONAL
                       +SHOVELLING   SCRATCHING

Fig. 5. While shallow resting tracks can be dug out with fairly uniform endopodite action, deeper "nests" require modification of the digging process at the steep front and of the burrow. a *C. fasciculata*, L. Cambrian, Pakistan; b *C. jenningsi*, L. Cambrian, Alberta, with impressions of shovelling head shield; c *C. dispar*, L. Cambrian, Sweden; with proverse front leg markings (after Seilacher 1959 fig. 4).

a stratigraphically oriented classification. The functional, behavioural, and preservational differences of the burrows are in part also genetically controlled, but their value as additional characteristics can only be based on empirical evidence.

3. Taxonomy

Original description of taxon indicated with asterisk

Ichnogenus CRUZIANA d'Orbigny 1842

Synonyms:
    1839 *Bilobites* d'Orbigny (*non* Dekay 1824, *nec* Rafinesque 1831; see Sinclair 1951 and Häntzschel 1965 p. 16).
    *1842 *Cruziana* d'Orbigny.
    1852 *Rusophycus* Hall.

Diagnosis. Burrows of trilobites and trilobite-like arthropods, comprising two lobes of endopodal scratches, with or without additional impressions of coxae, exopodites, and carapace edges.

Type species. C. rugosa d'Orbigny (see Häntzschel 1965 p. 27).

Remarks. The nomenclatural history of this genus has been, and still is, largely influenced by varying interpretations. Exponents of body fossil interpretations (bivavles, d'Orb.; sponges, Lebesconte; sea weeds, Delgado *et al.*) tend to rely on

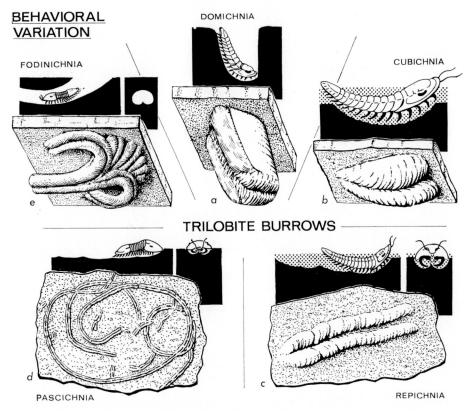

BEHAVIORAL VARIATION

DOMICHNIA

FODINICHNIA

CUBICHNIA

e   a   b

TRILOBITE BURROWS

d   c

PASCICHNIA   REPICHNIA

Fig. 6. Behavioural response to different biological situations is reflected in the geometry of the burrow.   a   Deep "nest" (cf. *C. jenningsi*) dug in head-down position. U. Cambrian, Bell Island, Newfoundland. Tüb. cat. 1392/4. 0·3;   b   Shallow resting track for temporary hiding in the sand;   c   Ploughed furrow. L. Cambrian, Salt Range;   d   Scribbling pattern made by foraging trilobite. L. Ordovician, Iraq (compare Pl. 1a);   e   Palmate feeding burrow (*C. ancora*). Silurian, Tschad.

features that would pass as functional and preservational "noise" in trace fossil morphology. This explains the large number of species distinguished in early descriptions.

The ichnologist, on the other hand, normally emphasises the behavioural and ecological framework used for the classification of taxonomically undefined trace fossils such as the various "worm"-tracks. Therefore, different generic names were initially used (Seilacher 1955) to distinguish trilobite resting tracks from elongate furrows. As it has become possible, however, to attribute burrows of very different outline to the same animals by means of "fingerprints", this procedure is no longer justified.

It is now suggested, as a matter of convenience, that all presumable trilobite burrows be comprised as different ichnospecies under the one ichnogenus *Cruziana*. Tentative subgroups that might technically range as subgenera are labelled "*semiplicata* group", "*almadenensis* group", etc. Just as "resting track" or 'deep undertrack" stand for a particular ecological or preservational situation, these open terms serve their purpose without nomenclatural complication and commitment.

This paper deals almost exclusively with *larger* burrows, more than one or two centimetres wide. In the field, one finds them often associated with the smaller burrows produced by the young, or by smaller species, of trilobites. Only in rare cases, or after careful preparation (Pl. 1h) however, do the small ones show the claw marks on which an adequate determination should be based. Not only specific distinction, but also the reference to trilobites, and hence even the gross indication of Palaeozoic age and marine environment, becomes doubtful in the smaller size class. Other small arthropods, particularly of the phyllopod group, and even worms and gastropods, seem to be responsible for very similar bilobed burrows. One type (*Isopodichnus* Bornem.) has even become a facies indicator in Palaeozoic, as well as Mesozoic, non-marine sandstones (Seilacher, 1963a), but so far we have no sound morphological criteria, except size, by which to distinguish *Isopodichnus* from true trilobite burrows.

I. FASCICULATA GROUP

This group is characterized by bundles of 4–6 subequal scratches. The scratches are usually finer than in the *rugosa* group and do not diverge. They also form a more obtuse angle with the median line, without running transversely as in the *pudica* group. Known members are of Lower Cambrian age.

Cruziana cantabrica ichnosp. nov.

Figure 7–1, 2

Diagnosis. Large front leg markings, rarely fusing to form true bilobites. Each marking has on its front face up to 6 shallow but acute scratches running parallel to each other in sigmoidal, antero-medial direction.

Remarks. It took some time before this trace fossil was recognized as a trilobite burrow, because the markings, although being sizeable and common enough, often occur isolated and have unusually steep posterior edges. They rarely link to moustache-like resting tracks or to elongate bilobites, which also contain nothing but front leg markings due to a strongly procline mode of burrowing. The species is provisionally attributed to the *fasciculata* group which otherwise has finer striae.

Width. 8–12 cm.

Occurrence. (i) Lower part of Porma Sequence 3b (L. Cambrian, Lotze 1961 p. 349), below zones of *C. fasciculata* and *C. carinata*, Cerezedo near Boñar, León Province, Spain = type locality. Common, 8 specimens in Tübingen coll. (ii) Jalón River near Calatayud (Zaragoza Province, Spain). Specimen No. 69/es 9, collected and kindly lent for inspection by U. Schmitz, Univ. of Münster collection.

Cruziana fasciculata ichnosp. nov.

Figure 7–3, 4

Diagnosis. Typical species of the group, with endopodal marks forming bundles of 5 or more fine scratches. These run almost transverse in the front part, gradually turning to about 30° postero-medial direction in the rear part of the resting burrow.

Remarks. Although it has been found so far only in one locality, this species is well defined. It occurs mainly in the form of resting burrows, which may be aligned to form longer, but irregular, furrows.

Much smaller but deeper forms from the Lalun Sandstone of Iran, irregular burrows from the Salt Range, and poorly preserved specimens from Sweden, are provisionally assigned to this species because they have similar claw marks.

Width. 5–7 cm (Boñar); 1·5–3 cm (Iran); 5·5–8 cm (Salt Range); 3 cm (Hardeberga).

Occurrence. (i) Middle part of Porma Sequence 3b (L. Cambrian between zones of *C. cantabrica* and *C. carinata;* Lotze 1961 p. 350), Rio Porma near Cerezedo, north of Boñar, León Province, Spain = type locality), Very common, 16 specimens in Tüb. coll. (ii) Lalun Sandstone (L. Cambrian, Stocklin, Ruttner and Nabavi 1964; Allenbach 1966); Sirgesht, Eastern Iran (see Pl. 1h). 6 specimens in Tüb. coll. (courtesy of Dr. Ruttner, Teheran/Vienna). (iii) Neobolus Beds (Seilacher 1955 fig. 5, nos. 3 and 8) and Magnesian Sandstone (*ibid.* pl. 21), both L. Cambrian with *Redlichia*, Salt Range, Pakistan. 6 specimens in Tüb. coll. (iv) Hardeberga Sandstone (L. Cambrian), Hardeberga, Sweden. One specimen in Tüb. coll. similar to the one described by Bergström (1969).

II. DISPAR GROUP

This group comprises forms with several, but unequal, sharp scratches within each endopodal marking. They indicate a claw formula similar to *Dimorphichnus obliquus* (Seilacher 1955) with two main and two small anterior claws, the scratches of which appear on the large and proverse front leg markings. The divide between proverse and obverse markings is obvious, particularly in resting burrows which form the most common type in this group.

Cruziana dispar Linnarsson

Figure 1c, 2c, 5c

1869 Linnarsson pp. 403-405 (without plate)

Diagnosis. Deep resting tracks or nests. The proverse front leg markings with impressions of at least two small side claws on exposed front sides. Rear leg markings retroverse and finer, but always preserved except in rare procline furrows.

Remarks. Distinction from the M. Cambrian *C. barbata* may be difficult for individual specimens, but becomes clear in larger populations.

Width. 3·0–8·5 cm.

Occurrence. (i) Mickwitzia Sandstone (Lower Cambrian on the basis of inarticulate brachiopods and *Volborthella*), Lugnås. Sweden = type locality. Common, many specimens particularly in Stockholm and Tüb. colls. (ii) Lower Cambrian, Holy Cross Mountains, Poland. See Orłowski, Radwański and Roniewicz in this volume.

Cruziana barbata ichnosp. nov.

Figure 7—6, 7

Diagnosis. Resting tracks similar to *C. dispar,* but difference between rear and front leg markings more pronounced. Since the animals did not dig deeply into the undertrack interface, rear leg impressions are either invisible or preserved only as short "lips" under the prominent "beard" of the front leg markings. Furrows rare, procline.

Remarks. Differences from *C. dispar* are so small that they might have passed unrecognized if only a few specimens had been found, but they are consistent in all occurrences.

Width. 3–8 cm.

Occurrence. (i) M. Cambrian (defined by trilobites in underlying carbonates; Lotze 1961), Cerezedo near Boñar, León Province, Spain = type locality. Very common; track-covered slabs in Tüb. coll. (ii) M. Cambrian (Embider Schichten; Lotze 1961) Najerilla Dam near Rioja Baja, Sierra de la Demanda, Spain. 6 poorly preserved specimens in Tüb. coll. (iii) Churin Beds (Färber and Jaritz 1964, M. Cambrian age endorsed by this species), Concha de Artedo Asturias, Spain. Several poorly preserved specimens, 3 of them in Tüb. coll. (iv) Unnamed sandstones, M. Cambrian (age based only on this trace fossil), Hassa, Amanos mountains, S. Turkey. 8 small specimens in Tüb. coll. (v) Flathead Sandstone (M. Cambrian), Lewis and Clarke Reserve, Montana. Together with *C. arizonensis*. Several good specimens in U.S. Nat. Museum.

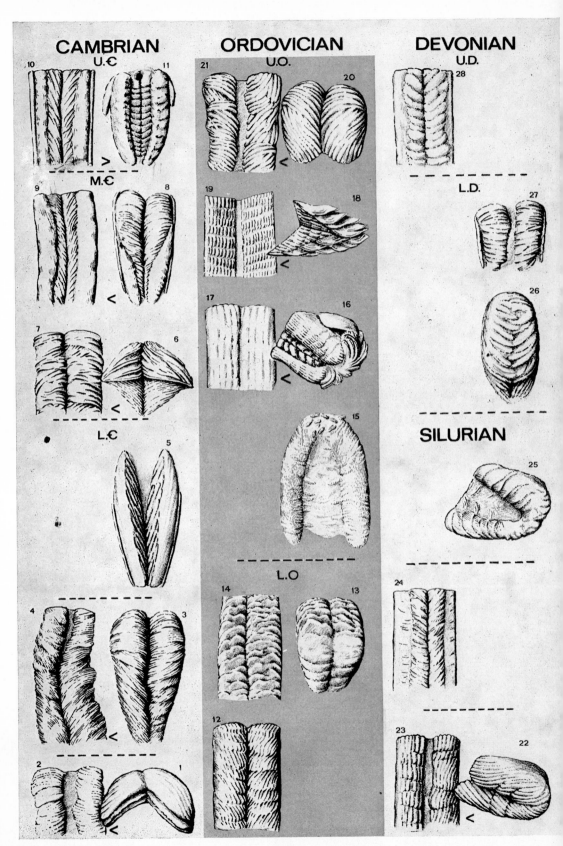

CAMBRIAN

U.Є

M.Є

L.Є

ORDOVICIAN

U.O.

L.O

DEVONIAN

U.D.

L.D.

SILURIAN

Fig. 7

458

Cruziana grenvillensis Dawson

Figure 8

*1864 *Rusichnites grenvillensis* Dawson fig. 1.

Diagnosis. Deep resting tracks similar in outline to *C. dispar*. Endopodal markings insufficiently preserved, but probably different from *C. dispar*.

Remarks. Several specimens, kindly supplied by Dr. H. Hofmann (Montreal) show clear impressions of the pleural edges and a division of leg markings at the deepest point of the burrow. The sandstone is too coarse to show clearly the claw arrangement, but they seem to be multiple and subequal in contrast to the Cambrian species.

Width. 7·5–9 cm.

Occurrence. Chazy (M. Ordovician), Grenville, Canada = type locality. Apparently common, 4 specimens (courtesy of Dr. H. Hofmann, Montreal) in Tüb. coll.

In addition to the species mentioned, several other known occurrences should probably be included in this group. Among these are specimens from the Dead Sea (Picard 1942 fig. 4–5)

Fig. 7. Combined sequence of *Cruziana* species from Palaeozoic sandstones of Europe, N. Africa, and S.W. Asia. > and < signs indicate whether the furrow (left) or the resting track expression (right) is more common. Forms not separated by a broken line may occur in the same unit.
1–2 *C. cantabrica* ichnosp. nov. Porma Sequence 3b, lower part (L. Cambrian, Lotze 1961), Cerezedo. N. Boñar, Spain. 1 Tüb. cat. 1392/5. 2 from field photograph.
3–4 *C. fasciculata* ichnosp. nov. Porma Sequence 3b, middle part (L. Cambrian, Lotze 1961), Cerezedo. 3 Tüb. cat. 1392/6. 4 Tüb. cat. 1392/7.
5 *C. carinata* ichnosp. nov. Porma Sequence 3b, upper part (L. Cambrian, Lotze 1961), Cerezedo. From field photographs.
6–7 *C. barbata* ichnosp. nov. Lower Boñar Beds (M. Cambrian, Lotze 1961), Cerezedo. 6 Tüb. cat. 1392/7. 7 Tüb. cat. 1392/8.
8–9 *C. arizonensis* ichnosp. nov. 8 Flathead Sandstone (M. Cambrian), Lewis and Clark Reserve, Montana. U.S. Nat. Museum. 9 U. Tapeats Sandstone (M. Cambrian): Kaibab Trail, Grand Canyon, Arizona. Tüb. cat. 1392/9.
10 *C. semiplicata* Salter, Ffestiniog Stage (U. Cambrian); Cwm Graianog, N. Wales. Tüb. cat. 1392/10.
11 *C. polonica* ichnosp. nov. U. Cambrian, Holy Cross Mts, Poland (after Radwański and Roniewicz 1963 pl. 2).
12 *C. rugosa* d'Orb. Khabour Quartzite (Arenig), N. Iraq. Drawing from photographs.
13–14 *C. imbricata* n.n. 13 Vire du Muflon, Unité II (Arenig), Tassili n'Ajer, Algeria. Tüb. cat. 1392/11. 14 Arenig, Serra de S. Miguel, Portugal. Schematized after Delgado 1885 pl. 34 fig. 1 and Original in Serv. Geol., Lisboa.
15 *C. lineata* ichnosp. nov. *Sabellarifex* Sandstone (Caradoc), Sahl el Karim. S. Jordan. Schematized from Tüb. cat. 1392/12.
16–17 *C. almadenensis* ichnosp. nov. Quarcitas de Canteras (Caradoc), Almadén, Spain. 16 Tüb cat. 1392/13. 17 Tüb. cat. 1392/14.
18–19 *C. flammosa* ichnosp. nov. *Sabellarifex* Sandstone (Caradoc), Sahl el Karim, S. Jordan 18 Tüb. cat. 1392/15. 19 Tüb. cat. 1392/16.
20–21 *C. petraea* ichnosp. nov. *Sabellarifex* Sandstone (Caradoc), Sahl el Karim, S. Jordan 20 Tüb. cat. 1392/17. 21 Tüb. cat. 1392/18.
22–23 *C. acacensis* ichnosp. nov. Lower Acacus Sandstone (U. Silurian), Wadi Tacharchuri near Ghat, S. Libya. 22 Tüb. cat. 1392/19. 23 Tüb. cat. 1392/20.
24 *C. quadrata* ichnosp. nov. Upper Acacus Sandstone (U. Silurian), Wadi Tanezzuft near Ghat, S. Libya. Tüb. cat. 1392/21.
25 *C. pedroana* ichnosp. nov. San Pedro Sandstone (U. Silurian), Felechas near Boñar, Spain. Tüb. cat. 1392/22.
26 *C. uniloba* ichnosp. nov. L. Devonian, Plateau du Fadnoun, Tassili Externe, Algeria. Tüb. cat. 1392/23.
27 *C. rhenana* ichnosp. nov. Nellenköpfchen-Beds (Emsian), Nellenköpfchen near Koblenz, Germany. Tüb. cat. 1392/24.
28 *C. lobosa* ichnosp. nov. Aouinet Ouenine Formation, Unit III. (Frasnian), Pagoda Hill, Aouinet Ouenine, Libya. Tüb. cat. 1392/25.

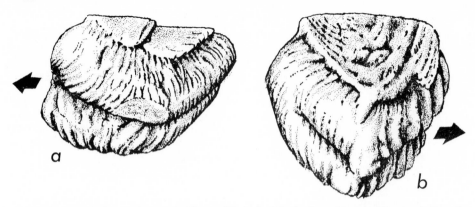

Fig. 8 *C. grenvillensis* (Dawson). Chazy (M. Ordovician), Grenville near Montreal, Canada. Tüb. cat. 1392/26(a) and 27(b) ×0·5 Note change from proverse to obverse scratches and carapace impressions. Arrow = anterior end.

and Sardinia (*C. sardoa* Meneghini 1885). They all need to be re-studied with adequate material. Specimens of the Jordanian (Geol. Survey, Amman) and Sardinian form (Univ. of Pisa collection) present only series of front leg impressions and contain no clear resting track. In the descriptions of *C. sardoa* (Meneghini 1883, 1885; Ciarpi 1901) and in later field studies (Schwarzbach 1952), bilobed but full relief gastropod burrows (*Scolicia*) were evidently combined with the true trilobite burrows.

III. SEMIPLICATA GROUP

Lateral lobes of finer exopodal "brushings" are the diagnostic features of this group. Since they may be missing in procline burrows, a larger sample should always be studied.

Cruziana arizonensis ichnosp. nov.

Figure 7–8, 9

1918 Walcott pl. 39 fig. 1, 3, 4 pl. 41.
1956 Seilacher pl. 8 fig. 5.

Diagnosis. Mainly resting tracks. Towards the rear end the sharp endopodal scratches are bordered, and eventually covered, by "brushed" exopodal lobes.

Remarks. This species, which is mainly found in North America, differs from *C. semiplicata* in the prevalence of short resting tracks and in the rarity of pleural impressions.

Width. 2·5–5·5 cm.

Occurrence. (i) Upper Tapeats Sandstone (M. Cambrian), Kaibab Trail, Grand Canyon, Arizona = type locality. Several good specimens in U.S. Nat. Mus., about 5 in Tüb. coll. (Walcott 1918). (ii) Flathead Sandstone (M. Cambrian), Dearborne River, Lewis and Clark Reserve, Montana. Together with *C. barbata*. Several good specimens in U.S. Nat. Museum (Walcott 1918). (iii) Cambrian Antelope Butte (T 54 N, R 88 W; Wyoming). Several specimens (Acquis. No. 180535) in U.S. Nat. Museum. (iv) L. Boñar Beds (Lotze 1961), (M. Cambrian age based on trilobites in underlying carbonates), Cerezedo near Boñar, León Province, Spain. Two specimens together with many *C. barbata*, Tüb. coll. (v) Deadwood Formation (U. Cambrian), Granite Creek, Bighorn Mts, Wyoming. 6 specimens in Univ. of Wyoming, Laramie; plaster casts in Tüb. coll. (courtesy of Dr. D. W. Boyd). (vi) Lower Cochise Formation? (U. Cambrian, lower part), Middle Canyon, Whetstone Mts, Arizona. 4 specimens in Tüb. coll. (courtesy of Dr. Chr. Lochmann).

Cruziana semiplicata Salter

Figure 7–10,   Pl. 1a–g

*1854 *Cruziana semiplicata* Salter.
1950 *Cruziana ortigosae* H. Sampelayo pl. 1 fig. 1–4, pl. 2 fig. 1, 2.

Diagnosis. Long and even furrows that indicate extensive ploughing. In typical cases, endopodal lobes are bordered by exopodal lobes and pleural grooves. Procline ploughing produces stronger, tricuspidate endopodal markings and coarser exopodal brushings.

Remarks. The tendency of this species to occur in large numbers makes it possible to study the whole range of variation. Procline ploughing, for instance, may completely suppress the exopodal lobes. Special food-conditions, on the other hand, may provoke systematic foraging patterns such as shown in the slab from the Sierra de la Demanda (Pl. 1a and Seilacher 1967 p. 73) and similar occurrences in Asturias. Resting tracks similar to those of *C. arizonensis* are unknown. A rare but distinctive type of resting track sometimes associated with *C. semplicata,* is considered as a different species (*C. polonica*).

Width. 2–7 cm.

Occurrence. (i) Ffestiniog Stage (U. Cambrian, age defined by succession, Crimes 1968), Cwm Graianog, N. Wales = type locality. Very common, extensive material in the collection of Dr. T. P. Crimes and also Tüb. coll. (ii) U. Cambrian, Wielka Wisniowka, Holy Cross Mountains, Poland (Radwański and Roniewicz 1963 pl. 4–7). (iii) "L. Silurian" (U. Cambrian age defined by this trace fossil), Hainichen near Leipzig (Germany; Pietzsch 1910). (iv) Demanda Beds (Lotze 1961 p. 340, U. Cambrian age confirmed by trilobite remains, Colchen, personal communication), Najerilla valley, Sierra de la Demanda, Burgos Province, Spain. Described as *C. ortigosae* Sampelayo 1950. Large slab and additional specimens in Tüb. coll. Other specimens collected during field work were kindly sent to the author for inspection by Colchen (1964). (v) U. Cambrian to Tremadocian (personal communication of V. Josopait and U. Schmitz, who collected specimens now in Univ. of Münster collections), Jalón valley near Calatayud, Zaragoza Province, Spain. (vi) Molinos Beds (Färber and Jaritz 1964, U. Cambrian age defined here by this trace fossil), Cabo Vidio near Soto de Luina, Asturias, Spain. Common; several well preserved specimens in Tüb. coll. (Seilacher and Crimes 1969). (vii) Wabana Group (Considered as L. Ordovician by Walcott 1918 pl. 40 fig. 2 and Nautiyal, personal communication; U. Cambrian age suggested on the basis of this trace fossil), East coast of Bell Island Conception Bay, Newfoundland. Common in association with *C. jenningsi*; several specimens in U.S. Nat. Museum (Walcott material) and Tüb. coll. (Seilacher and Crimes 1969). (viii) Kistedal Formation (U. Cambrian), Digermul Peninsula, Northern Norway (Strand 1935). Material collected by Reading (see 1965 p. 175) at present being studied by Dr. T. P. Crimes.

Cruziana jenningsi Fenton and Fenton

Figure 5b, 6a

*1937 *Cruziana jenningsi* Fenton and Fenton fig. 1, 2.
1937 *Cruziana irregularis* Fenton and Fenton fig. 4.
1937 *Cruziana navicella* Fenton and Fenton fig. 5, 6.

Diagnosis. Strongly procline nests with transverse endopodal markings in the deepest part, while exopodal lobes with longitudinal brushings prevail on the rear slope. Front side almost vertical and smoothened by edge of cephalic shield.

Remarks. This species may be too comprehensive, as it now includes occurrences of quite different age. But specimens collected by P. E. Cloud (University of California, Santa Barbara) in the Lower Cambrian of the Canadian Rocky Mountains are very similar to the Upper Cambrian ones from Bell island. Comparison with the Fenton material should clarify their relationship to *C. jenningsi* and the question as to whether the associated shallower burrows (*C. irregularis* and *C. navicella*) should not be considered as behavioural variations of the same species.

Width. 2·5–5·5 cm.

Occurrence. (i) Lake Louise Shale (L. Cambrian), Mt Assiniboine, Alberta, Canada = type locality (Fenton and Fenton 1937). (ii) Wabana Group (?) (Considered as Upper Cambrian on the basis of *C. semiplicata*), Ferry landing at East coast of Bell Island (type locality). Common in association with *C. semiplicata, Diplocraterion* and *Spiroscolex*. Many specimens in Tüb. coll. (collected with the kind help of the late Dr. Lilly).

Cruziana carinata ichnosp. nov.

Figure 7–5

Diagnosis. Large elongate resting tracks with exopodal lobes bordering the endopodal lobes along prominent crests that converge towards the rear end. Endopodal markings coarse, at acute angles to median line.

Remarks. Known only from a few specimens, which are impossible to salvage without blasting, but are distinctive enough to be considered as a new species. Affiliation with the *semiplicata* group is tentative, but endorsed by a specimen of *C. arizonensis* from the Grand Canyon (Tüb. coll.) in which the exopodal lobes culminate in a similar crest.

Width. 6–10 cm.

Occurrence. Upper part of Porma sequence 3b (a few metres above *C. fasciculata.* Lower-Cambrian defined by superposition with trilobite-bearing Middle Cambrian), Rio Porma north of Cerezedo near Boñar, León Province, Spain = type locality. About 6 specimens on the path along the river.

A single specimen described by (Weissbrod 1969 pl. 4, fig. 2) and kindly sent to the author for inspection is a procline furrow with tricuspidate front leg markings, but lacks exopodal and pleural markings. Without additional material it is impossible to decide whether it is related to *C. semiplicata* or to *C. omanica.*

IV. RUGOSA GROUP

This group occurs in great abundance and world-wide distribution. Its most distinctive features are multiple and sharp scratches indicating up to 12 subequal claws in one endopodite (Seilacher 1962 fig. 2, pl. 25 fig. 4). In contrast to the *fasciculata* group, these sets of scratches tend to diverge towards the median-posterior side. There is also a strong prevalence of long ploughings, or deeper cuts

---

Plate 1

a–g Variations of *Cruziana semiplicata* Salter, Upper Cambrian.

a Clockwise "scribbles", made by one individual, probably express a primitive type of foraging behaviour. Inked field photograph of tectonically deformed slab. Tüb. cat. 1392/33 (Seilacher 1967 p. 73). Najerilla valley, Sierra de la Demanda, Spain. ×0·08.

b–f Varieties due to different attitudes of the animal while ploughing through the sand (see Fig. 4). Cwm Graianog, N. Wales .Tüb cat. 1392/34–38. ×0·75—Strongly procline burrowing (b) has left only strong markings of the front endopodia. Less procline burrows (c) show coarse exopodal markings and pleural grooves in addition. In opisthocline position the endopodal scratches become more retroverse and finer (d) or disappear completely (e), while the exopodal lobes become smooth and more prominent. Lateral inclination (f) may cause predominance of front leg markings on the one, and of finer rear leg markings on the other endopodal lobe.

g Coarse scratches of front exopodites. They indicate a comb-like structure, the elements of which were tricuspidate as the endopodal claws in f. Jalon valley near Calatayud (Spain). Specimen collected by V. Josopait, now in Univ. of Münster collection. ×1·5.

h Well preserved and sand-blasted specimens of *C. fasciculata* ichnosp. nov. show fine claw markings rarely preserved in such small burrows. Lalun Sandstone (L. Cambrian); Sirgesht area, Iran. Tüb. cat. 1392/39. ×1·6.

PLATE 1

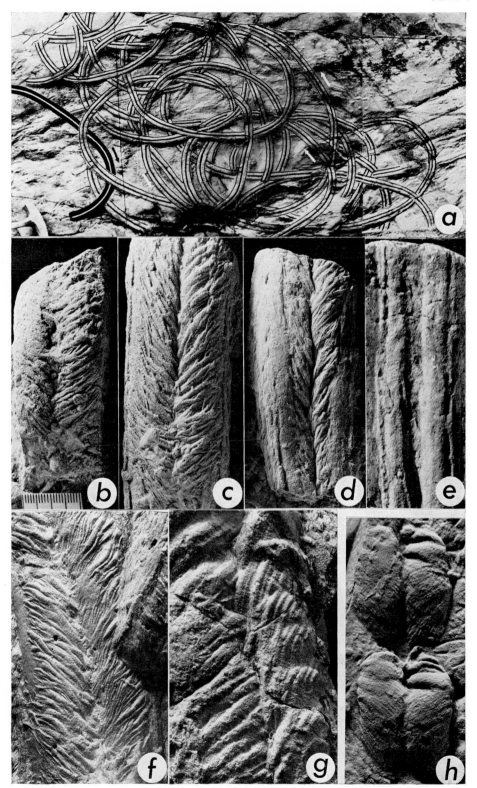

(Seilacher 1959 fig. 5E), over resting tracks which are virtually unknown in this group.

Earlier authors (Delgado 1885–87) have distinguished a large number of species, most of them being behavioural and preservational variations which may be found in different parts of a single burrow. Nevertheless, some of the occurrences seem to lack one or the other of these variants. Since this lack may be stratigraphically significant, the main variants are here listed separately.

Cruziana rugosa d'Orbigny

Figure. 7–12

1842 *Cruziana rugosa* d'Orbigny p. 30 pl. 1 fig. 1.
1946 Bibliography in Peneau.

Diagnosis. Deep bilobites of limited length. Endopodal markings, rather clearly separated, each with a marked discontinuity, producing strong corrugations across the lobes. Without pleural furrows.

Remarks. This variant should be considered the type of the genus (Häntzschel 1965). It is produced by the front legs and occurs on the front slope of deeper burrows, for instance on the other side of the specimen (Fig. 2a) as well as in procline ploughing. Among the abundant material of the "Vire du mouflon" (Unité II, Tassili) not even a single specimen of this variant was found.

Cruziana furcifera d'Orbigny

1842 *Cruziana furcifera* d'Orbigny p. 21 pl. 1 fig. 2–3.

Diagnosis. Long furrows with endopodal markings criss-crossing at acute angles and not clearly separated. Without pleural furrows.

Remarks. The most general type of the group and therefore found in all occurrences, but less distinctive than the other variants.

Cruziana goldfussi (Rouault)

1850 *Fraena goldfussi* Rouault p. 10.
1883 *Cruziana goldfussi* (Rou.) Lebesconte pl. 21 fig. 5; pl. 22 fig. 12.

Diagnosis. Long furrows with fine and fairly parallel retroverse scratches which make it difficult to separate individual leg markings. Pleural groove on either side.

Remarks. This variant is probably produced by the rear part of the body and thus occurs on the rear slope of deeper burrows (Fig. 2a) or on opisthocline ploughings. In smaller specimens the lobes are often smooth, probably due to preservation.

Width. For all three variants: 0·8–14 cm.

Occurrence. All three variants: Since this species tends to occur in abundance and has been found in many parts of the world no complete list of formations and localities, but only of areas can here be given: Bolivia (d'Orbigny 1842; Haug 1908 pl. 78); Argentina (Borrello 1966 pl. 17); Newfoundland (Seilacher and Crimes 1969); Portugal (Delgado 1885; Thadeu 1956); Spain (Barrois 1882; Hernandez-Pacheco 1908; own observations in Asturias, Meseta, Keltiberian Mts, Cantabrian Mts); France (Lebesconte 1886; Peneau 1946; Thoral 1946; own observations in Brittany and Montagne Noir); Wales (Crimes 1968; Seilacher and Crimes 1969); Turkey (Frech 1916; own observation in Amanos Mts); Jordan (Bender 1963 pl. 13 fig. 4); Central Sahara (Desio 1940; Gubler *et al.* 1966; own observations in Tassili Mts); Iraq (Seilacher 1963b); Afghanistan (Lapparent, personal communication); China (Yin 1932).

Age. Tremadoc to Llandeilo.

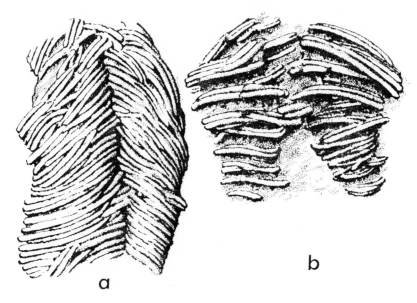

Fig. 9. *C. omanica* ichnosp. nov.   a   Procline furrow, ? Ordovician, Oman. Holotype; Tüb. cat. 1392/28. ×0·5.   b   Resting track. Tomahawk beds (? Lower Ordovician), Georgina Basin, Australia. Tüb. cat. 1392/29.×0·6. For claw shape compare Seilacher (1962).

V. IMBRICATA GROUP

This group contains only one species that cannot be grouped with others.

Cruziana imbricata n.n.

Figure 7–13, 14

1883 *Rysophycus rouaulti* Lebesconte (non *Cruziana rouaulti* Lebesc.) p. 67 pl. 21 fig. 9.
1885 *Rhysophycus rouaulti* Lebesc.—Delgado p. 72 pl. 34.

Diagnosis. Mainly resting burrows without scratches. Front leg markings scale-like, often with a lobate front edge.

Remarks. While the general shape and the mode of preservation leaves no doubt that we are dealing with a true *Cruziana,* the markings are difficult to interpret in terms of the digging action. Nevertheless, they cannot be a preservational feature, since the form occurs in different countries at the same level and may be associated with burrows of the *rugosa* group on the same slab.

Width. 4–5 cm.

Occurrence. (i) Grès Armoricain (Arenig), Bouexière, Ille-et-Villaine, France = type locality (Holotype as well as specimens from Chateaubriant and Pontréan in Nantes Museum.) (ii) Armorican Quartzite (Arenig), Serra de San Miguel, Portugal, 3 specimens figured by Delgado, now in the collection of the Serv. Geol. Portug., Lisbon. (iii) Vire du Mouflon, Unité II (Lower Ordovician, age based on trace fossil *Cruziana goldfussi*); Tassili n'Ajer (Stops B_2 and E_4 of Inst Alger. Petrole Guidebook), 30 specimens in Tüb coll.

VI. PETRAEA GROUP

While the *rugosa* group is characterized by multiple, but sharp claw marks, the scratches in this group are rounded, indicating broad, shovel-shaped claws. The number of claws recorded varies from three to about five.

Cruziana omanica ichnosp. nov.

Figure 9

1962 Seilacher pl. 25 fig. 2–3.

Diagnosis. Resting burrows or procline furrows with long, blunt tricuspidate endopedal markings, in which the median scratch is stronger than the lateral ones. Front leg markings proverse.

Remarks. Although only one complete specimen and a few isolated scratches are as yet known from the type locality, there is no question that we are dealing with a new species. But without additional specimens it is difficult to define the typical outline and to confirm the identity with the Australian specimens which are similar in size, claw formula and digging technique.

Width. 8–9 cm.

Occurrence. (i) ?Ordovician (no body fossil control), Oman = type locality. Two specimens in Tüb. coll. (courtesy of Iraq Petroleum Company, London, through Dr. R. Jefferies). (ii) Tomahawk beds (Upper Cambrian or Lower Ordovician age indicated by associated olenid pygidia), Georgina Basin, Australia. 3 specimens in Tüb. coll. (courtesy of Société Nationale des Petroles d'Aquitaine).

Cruziana petraea ichnosp. nov.

Figure 7–20, 21

1963 Bender pl. 12 fig. 3.

Derivation of name. From the ancient name, Arabia petraea, for the region around the Nabotaean city of Petra.

Diagnosis. Steep-sided resting burrows having 3 heavy, rounded and *subequal* scratches in the leg markings. These are proverse near the steep front end, with a directional divide in the deepest part of the burrow.

Remarks. This well represented species is distinguished from *C. omanica* by the claw formula and from *C. acacensis* by more transverse diggings and broad outline. Longer furrows are rare and discontinuous (horizontal repetition) and occur mainly in upstream orientation.

Width. 4–8 cm.

Occurrence. Sabellarifex Sandstone (Caradocian age defined by body fossils Bender, personal communication) and *Cruziana almadenensis*; Sahl el Karim, Southern Jordan = type locality. Common; representative material in Tüb. coll.

Cruziana acacensis ichnosp. nov.

Figure 7–23, 24

1940 Desio pl. 4 fig. 3; pl. 5 fig. 3.

Derivation of name. From Acacus Mountains that also gave name to the sandstone containing the tracks.

Diagnosis. Deep resting burrows, or nests, dug in head-down position. Front of burrow often undercut. Leg markings strongly retroverse or longitudinal, comprising up to five rounded and subequal scratches.

Remarks. This species is well represented and easy to recognize. The deepest part of the burrows tends to narrow, giving them a tongue-like outline. Impressions of the cephalon edge are sometimes preserved at the steep or undercut front slope.

Longer furrows are less frequent. They usually form by extension of the rear end of a resting track. Series of short isolated leg marks do also occur.

Width. 2·6–5·5 cm.

Occurrence. (i) Acacus Sandstone (Upper Silurian age defined by Llandovery graptolites in underlying shales, see Klitzsch 1964), Wadi Tacharchuri near Ghat, S. Libya. Common, 13 representative specimens in Tüb. coll. (ii) Lower part of "zone de passage" between Llandovery graptolite shales and Lower Devonian sandstones, stop F4 of Inst Alger. Petrole guidebook, Tassili Externe, S. Algeria. Not very common, 7 specimens in Tüb. coll.

Cruziana ancora Lessertisseur

Figure 6e

1956 Lessertisseur pl. 3 fig. 2–6.

Diagnosis. Small species characterized by regular anchor- or palm tree-shaped feeding burrows. Claw markings rounded and almost longitudinal.

Remarks. These unique burrows, whose shape is reminiscent of *Arthrophycus,* bear indistinct scratches similar to *C. acacensis.* Since only the anchor forms have been collected, we do not know about other, less obvious variants that may be associated.

Width. 1·5 cm.

Occurrence. Silurian, together with *Arthrophycus* and *Spirophyton,* Fada Oasis, Ennedi, Tschad. Common at this locality, 17 specimens in Jardin des Plantes Museum, Paris.

VII. ALMADENENSIS GROUP

Mainly procline resting tracks with deeply impressed markings of strong front legs contrasting with smoother lobes probably produced by rear legs and coxae. Possibly made by arthropods other than trilobites.

Cruziana almadenensis ichnosp. nov.

Figure 7–16, 17

Diagnosis. Deep and strongly procline resting tracks or nests. 3–4 pairs of multiple front leg markings form a radiating, palm tree-like pattern in the deepes tpart. Rear slope formed by two broad lobes with about 10 regular longitudinal grooves. Between the two lobes and less deeply dug out are smooth, but clearly segmented impressions suggesting coxal digging. The semicircular edge of the head shield may be impressed on the steep front slope.

Remarks. This species is well represented and easy to recognize, even if only the strong, radiating front leg markings are preserved in lower undertracks. Associated long furrows, with longitudinal canelure reminiscent of the rear lobes of the resting tracks, are tentatively assigned to the same species.

Width. 5–15 cm.

Occurrence. (i) Quarcitas de Canteras (Caradocian age according to Almela *et al.* 1962, defined by fossiliferous succession) Sierra del Carcel, Almadén, Spain. Common, 14 specimens in Tüb. coll. (ii) *Sabellarifex* Sandstone (Bender 1963; Upper Caradocian age supported by a few trilobite and brachiopod remains according to personal communication of Dr. Wolfart, Hanover). Sahl el Karim, Southern Jordan. 3 specimens in Tüb. coll. (iii) Unnamed sandstones and shales (Caradocian age based on this species), Kizlac, Amanos Mountains, Turkey. 3 specimens in Tüb. coll. (iv) Upper part of Unité III (IAP Guidebook, Stops D_1 and D_2; Caradocian age defined by this trace fossil, consistent with the occurrence of Arenig *Cruziana* in the underlying, and by Caradocian trilobite remains in the overlying, unit). Tassili n'Ajer, Algeria. 6 very large and well preserved specimens in Tüb. coll.

Cruziana flammosa ichnosp. nov.

Figure 7–18, 19

Derivation of name. From flame-like front leg markings.

Diagnosis. Procline, but shallow and often elongate resting tracks with flame like front leg marks near pointed anterior end. Posterior part with deeply impressed lateral margin from which the two lobes slope evenly before meeting in the median line. They bear up to 11 broad and distinct longitudinal grooves, each with a median keel. Rear end swallow-tailed.

Remarks. Although found only in one place close to occurrences of *C. almadenensis*, the species is clearly distinct and easy to recognize.

Width. 4–8 cm.

Occurrence. Lower *Sabellarifex* Sandstone (Caradocian age suggested by *C. almadenensis* occurring a few metres above), Sahl el Karim, Southern Jordan. 6 specimens in Tüb. coll.

Cruziana perucca ichnosp. nov.

Figure 10

Derivation of name. Name refers to wig-like appearance.

Diagnosis. Small procline resting burrows in which front leg action has produced a deep, wig-like structure. Posterior slope bilobed, smooth.

Remarks. At the bottom of a major channel fill, large surfaces are covered with these tracks, the arthropod origin of which may at first appear dubious. But their general plan is so similar to other species in the *almadenensis* group that they must have had a similar origin. The smoothness of the posterior part may be only a matter of scale. Sculptures comparable to *C. lineata* would probably be too minute in such small forms to be recorded in the sandy matrix.

Rheotactic orientation with the front end pointing upcurrent is particularly obvious in this species, because a large number of specimens can be observed on each slab.

Associated bilobed furrows are much shallower and seem to consist of oblique and multiple claw impressions. Similar tracks in the Cincinnatian are tentatively assigned to trinucleid trilobites by Osgood (1970). Trinucleids were perhaps also responsible for *Cruziana perucca* which would size-wise fit this interpretation. In this case the perforated brim of the head shield could have acted as a sieve for finer food particles set against the drifting sand, while the front legs kept digging free a hollow trap (the "wig") underneath the brim.

Width. 1·2–1·9 cm.

Occurrence. Sabellarifex Sandstone (Caradocian), at the bottom of a larger channel fill, Sahl el Karim, Southern Jordan. Very common in this particular place; two slabs with about 20 resting tracks and 2 furrows in Tüb. coll.

Cruziana lineata ichnosp. nov.

Figure 7–15

Diagnosis. Shallow and elongate resting tracks with flat, rounded lobes that are completely covered with fine oblique lines, up to about 17 in one lobe.

Remarks. Fig. 7-15, is a restoration combined from several specimens. In the field it is difficult to recognize the complete outline, because specimens are intercrossed, and because a slight lateral inclination is sufficient to exclude one of the two flat

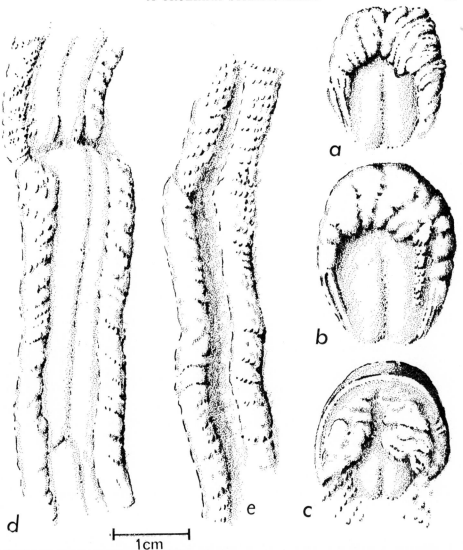

Fig. 10. *C. perucca* ichnosp. nov. *Sabellarifex* Sandstone (Caradoc); Sahl el Karim, S. Jordan; Tüb. cat. 1392/30 (Holotype).   a–c   Procline resting tracks with impressions of genal spines and cephalic rim.   d–e   Associated furrows.

lobes from undertrack preservation. The lineation, however, is distinctive enough to separate the species from the related forms *C. almadenensis* and *C. flammosa,* which have much coarser grooves. Associated deep scratches may be produced by the front legs, but they are much smaller than in these two species and do not form a distinct pattern.

Width. about 14 cm.

Occurrence. Sabellarifex Sandstone, together with *C. almadenensis,* indicating Caradocian age, Sahl el Karim (Bender 1963 pl. 11 fig. 4), Wadi Ram area, Southern Jordan. 2 fragmentary specimens in Tüb. coll. all from one large slab.

Cruziana pedroana ichnosp. nov.

Figure 7–25

1965 Rupke fig. 6.

Derivation of name. From San Pedro Sandstone.

Diagnosis. Strongly procline resting burrows. Shape of front leg markings unknown. Sloping rear lobes segmented, with very fine and regular oblique striation which is visible only on best preserved segments. Indications of similar segments sometimes visible in the depression between the lobes.

Remarks. This form is very distinctive in spite of the fact that no complete specimens have as yet been discovered. It resembles *C. almadenensis* in outline but has stronger transverse corrugations and finer and more oblique striation on the posterior lobes.

Width. 13 cm.

Occurrence. (i) San Pedro Sandstone (Upper Silurian age based on succession and body fossils; Rupke 1965), Corniero near Crémenes, Felechas, = type locality, and Barrios de Luna Northern Spain. 5 specimens in Tüb. coll. (ii) Uppermost beds of Zone de Passage (U. Silurian), about 3 m below erosional contact with Devonian sandstones; Tassili Externe (Stop No F6 of IAP Guidebook). 1 specimen in Tüb. coll. (iii) Upper part of Acacus Sandstone (U. Silurian age derived from graptolites in underlying shales), Wadi Tacharchuri, Libya, personal observation.

VIII. QUADRATA GROUP

Broad and smooth cuttings probably made by a to and fro motion of the carapace, bearing two narrower lobes of high-angle scratch marks. Group based on a few specimens and possibly quite artificial. I provisionally include shallow ploughings, in which the pleural grooves run at some distance from the endopodal lobes.

Cruziana quadrata ichnosp. nov.

Figure 7–22

1969 *"Cruziana I"* Seilacher pl. 1.

Diagnosis. Deep furrow with rectangular cross section. Narrow endopodal lobe of oblique multiple scratches on either side of the median line. Pleural lobe smooth with few transverse scratches.

Remarks. Only two well preserved burrows known. They are clearly distinct from *C. acacensis* found at a lower level within the Acacus Sandstone. *Cruziana* (*Rusophycus*) *clavata* (Hall 1850) from the Clinton of Hartford, N.Y. is much smaller (width 1–1·5 cm) and poorly preserved, but similar in sculpture and cross section.

Width. 4–6·5 cm.

Occurrence. (i) Acacus Sandstone (U. Silurian), E. side of Wadi Tanezzuft, north of Ghat, Southern Libya. One specimen, now Tüb. cat. no. 1361/3 (Holotype). (ii) Middle Part of "Zone de Passage" (U. Silurian age defined by stratigraphic position between Lower Silurian and Devonian), Tassili Externe (stop F5 a of Inst. Alger. Petrole Guidebook). One specimen showing well preserved endopodal markings, each with up to 6 subequal scratches, now in Tüb. coll.
   Since this specimen was found at an intermediate level between *C. acacensis* (below) and *C. pedroana* (above) in the same section, the isolated occurrence near Ghat has probably the same position (instead of below *C. acacensis* as suggested by Seilacher 1969)

Cruziana lobosa ichnosp. nov.

Figure 7–28

Diagnosis. Deep furrow with almost transverse leg markings that are rounded with blunt ends instead of bearing distinct claw marks.

Remarks. One might suspect preservational reasons to be responsible for this unusual sculpture. But the multiple occurrence suggests taxonomic significance.

Width. 4·5–5 cm.

Occurrence. Aouinet Ouenine Formation, Unit III (M. Devonian age based on abundant body fossils; Petroleum Exploration Society of Libya Guidebook 1963), Aouinet Ouenine, Fezzan, Libya.

Cruziana cf. *quadrata*

Remarks. Shallow furrows, in which the pleural grooves (smooth or segmented) run at some distance along the herringbone-sculptured endopodal lobes are provisionally assigned to the *quadrata* group, because one specimen was found associated with *C. quadrata* in Southern Libya. But similar forms, probably representing a similar mode of preservation rather than a taxonomic group, occur in various formations.

Occurrence. (i) Acacus Sandstone (U. Silurian), E side of Wadi Tanezzuft, north of Ghat, Southern Libya. One shallow epichnial furrow with segmented pleural grooves, found together with *C. quadrata* and now in Tüb. coll. (ii) Lower part of Nautiloid Sandstone (Bender 1963), Caradocian age based on trilobite and brachiopod remains determined by Dr. Wolfart (personal communication). 30 km SE of Mudawwara, Southern Jordan, 1 specimen in Tüb. coll. (courtesy of Dr. F. Bender), 2 cm wide, with segmented pleural grooves. (iii) Cincinnatian (U. Ordovician), Cincinnati, Ohio. Small form (about 1 cm wide), specimens in U.S. Nat. Museum, Washington. (iv) Tuscarora Sandstone (L. Silurian), Delaware Water Gap. 5 specimens (3·5 cm wide with bifid endopodal markings and smooth pleural grooves) in Tüb. coll.

IX. PUDICA GROUP

Mainly resting tracks with sharp and multiple endopodal scratches that run mainly transverse. Probably made by calymenid trilobites. This group needs to be revised before it can possibly be used stratigraphically.

Cruziana pudica (Hall)

Figure 11a

1852 *Rusophycus pudicus* Hall, pl. 8 fig. 6a.

Diagnosis. Fairly deep resting burrows with irregular transverse scratches and often with impressions of pleural spines and genal angles.

Remarks. The holotype is very poorly preserved, but better specimens from the same horizon are indistinguishable from the Cincinnatian form. At this locality specimens have been found which preserve the carapace of *Flexicalymene* within its burrow (Osgood 1970). A larger, but shallower form from Jordan is also included.

Width. 1·8–4 cm.

Occurrence. (i) Clinton Group (M. Silurian), Clinton, N.Y. Holotype in U.S. Nat. Museum, Washington. Better specimens in N.Y. State Museum, Albany. (ii) Cincinnatian (U. Ordovician), Cincinnati, Ohio. Many excellent specimens in University of Cincinnati and Harvard collections. (iii) *Conularia* Sandstone (Bender 1963; probably Caradocian), Southern Jordan. 1 specimen in Tüb. coll. (fig. 11a).

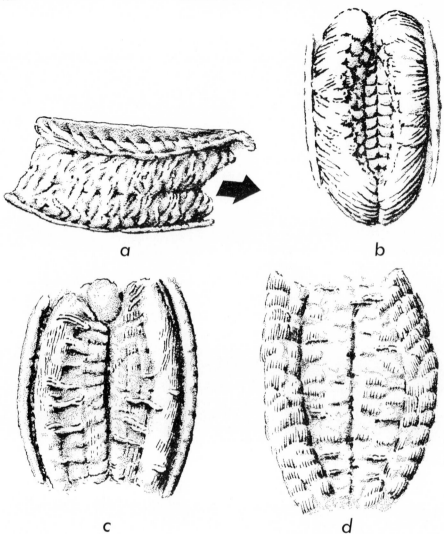

Fig. 11 a *C. pudica* Hall. *Conularia* Sandstone (Caradoc), S. Jordan, Tüb. cat. 1392/31. Shallow isocline resting track with impressions of pleural spines. Since the endopodal markings are transverse, the head end (arrow) has to be determined from outline and pleural impressions; b *C. carleyi* James. Cincinnatian (U. Ordvocian), Cincinnati, Ohio. Dyer collection, Harvard. Note coxal impressions between endopodal lobes. c *C. dilatata* ichnosp. nov. San Pedro Sandstone (U. Silurian), Felechas near Boñar, Spain. Holotype; Tüb. cat. 1392/32, nat. size. d *C. dilatata* ichnosp. nov. ? Ordovician; Toko Range, W. Queensland, Australia. After photograph of specimen in Brisbane Museum.

Cruziana rhenana ichnosp. nov.

Figure 7–27

Derivation of name. From typical occurrence in the Lower Devonian of the Rhine valley.

Diagnosis. Short and shallow resting tracks with transverse endopodal scratches and a marginal pleural groove.

Remarks. Poor preservation and the shortness of most tracks make it difficult to tell apart front and rear ends. Trilobites of the genus *Homalonotus,* with the smoothened carapace well adapted to a burrowing mode of life and fitting the size of the burrows occur in the same bed at Nellenköpfchen. They are probably responsible for many of the burrows in this as well as in other horizons of the Lower and Middle Devonian.

Much larger forms the Lower Devonian of North Africa are tentatively assigned to the same species.

Width. 3·3–4·3 cm (Nellenköpfchen),
12·13 cm (Libya).

Occurrence. (i) Nellenköpfchen Beds (Emsian, L. Devonian), Nellenköpfchen near Koblenz, Germany = type locality. Holotype and 4 cotypes in Tüb. coll. (ii) Upper Tadrart Formation (U. Devonian), Wadi Ahar, S. Libya. 2 specimens without pleural lobes in Tüb. coll.

Cruziana uniloba ichnosp. nov.

Figure 7–26

Diagnosis. Small but deep resting tracks in which coarse endopodal scratches of the two sides interfinger, thus almost eliminating the median groove typical for most other species.

Remarks. At the type locality these burrows cover whole bedding surfaces. They are mostly deeper than wide and somewhat broader and steeper at their front ends. Pleural lobes have not been observed.

Width. 2—2·5 cm.

Occurrence. L. Devonian, Tassili Externe (Algeria). Very common in places; about 20 specimens in Tüb. coll.

X. CARLEYI GROUP

Isocline resting tracks with oval outline that show coxal markings between the deep endopodal lobes. They may be the expression of a similar mode of burrowing rather than taxonomic relationship. Impressions of the cephalic spines are often seen near the front end which can be recognized from the direction of the endopodal scratches or slight divergence of the endopodal lobes.

Cruziana polonica ichnosp. nov.

Figure 7–11

1963 *Rusophycus* sp. Radwański and Roniewicz pl. 2 fig. 1–8.

Diagnosis. Oval resting tracks with about 12 pairs of coxal impressions between deeply impressed endopodal lobes on which the transverse or slightly retroverse markings are often indistinct. Pleural and genal impressions may occur.

Remarks. This form occurs in association with *C. semiplicata,* to which it is similar in size. Still it is probably produced by a different trilobite species because it has no exopodal markings in spite of being deeply impressed, and because it does not occur in all *semiplicata* occurrences.

Width. 1·1—4·5 cm.

Occurrence. (i) Upper Cambrian, Wielka Wisniowka, Holy Cross Mountains, Poland (Radwański and Roniewicz 1963). (ii) Ffestiniog Stage (U. Cambrian), Cwm Grainiog, N. Wales. Rare, several specimens in collection of Dr. T. P. Crimes.

Cruziana carleyi James

Figure 11b

1885 James p. 155 pl. 8 fig. 1.

Diagnosis. Deep resting tracks with oval outline and about 10 pairs of smooth coxal impressions between endopodal lobes. Endopodal markings multiple, running in transverse to slightly retroverse direction and forming an irregular and steep escarpment towards the coxal impressions. Pleural groove often preserved on either side.

Remarks. This type of burrow is discussed in detail by Osgood (1970) who relates it to isotelid trilobites occurring in the same formation.

Similar forms, but with endopodal markings less clearly preserved, occur in Arenig Quartzites.

Width. 4–6 cm.

Occurrence. (i) Cincinnatian (U. Ordovician), Cincinnati, Ohio. Many good specimens, particularly in collections of Cincinnati and Harvard Universities. (ii) Uppermost part of Armorican Quartzite (? Arenig), Camaret, Finistère (France), photograph of two similar specimens (4–6 cm wide) supplied by I. D. Bradshaw. (iii) Arenig Quartzites, Serra de Bussaco, Portugal. Specimen figured by Delgado 1885 pl. 33 fig. 1 in Serv. Geol. Portugal collection, Lisbon. (iv) Khabour Quartzite (Arenig) Ora, N. Iraq. Small specimen (3 cm wide) photographed in the field.

Cruziana dilatata ichnosp. nov.

Figure 11c, d

Diagnosis. Very flat resting tracks with longitudinal brushings on narrow and widely gaping lobes as well as on the broad central area which is divided by straight median line. A few trifid endopodal markings crossing brushed areas. Pleural lobes may be present.

Remarks. Although poorly represented, this form is clearly distinct from other recognized species. For practical reasons, a small specimen from the San Pedro Sandstone has been selected as holotype. Similar, but much larger forms seem to occur in the Ordovocian of Australia and Canada.

Width. 4·5 cm (S. Pedro), 15 cm (Australian form).

Occurrence. (i) San Pedro Sandstone (U. Silurian, Rupke 1965). Felechas near Boñar (N. Spain) together with *Cruziana pedroana* = type locality. 1 specimen in Tüb coll. (Fig. 11c). (ii) ? Ordovician, Toko Range, Western Queensland, Australia, Photograph of large specimen in Brisbane Museum, kindly supplied by Dr. R. Goldring (Fig. 11d). (iii) ? Laval Formation (Chazy Gr., M. Ordovician), St. Martin, Quebec, Canada. Photograph of imperfect, but fairly large specimen, kindly supplied by Dr. H. J. Hofmann.

Acknowledgements. Many colleagues, beyond those mentioned in the text, have contributed specimens and information for this study. Grants from the Deutsche Forschungsgemeinschaft (Se 48/2, Se 48/3 and Se 48/14) enabled the author to make field observations and collect reference material overseas. But the expeditions in desert areas would have been impossible without the guidance of experts such as Dr. F. Bender in Jordan and of Dr. E. Klitzsch in Libya. Special thanks are due the Algerian and French organizers of the sedimentological field symposium in the Tassili (January 1970), which provided a unique platform for interdisciplinary research and discussion, and to Dr. T. P. Crimes who not only offered his guidance in Wales but also organised the first and very impressive trace fossil conference, which has eventually triggered the completion of this paper.

References

ALLENBACH, P. 1966. Geologie und Petrographie des Damavand und seiner Umgebung (Zentral-Elburz), Iran. *Mitt. geol. Inst. Zurich* **63**.

ALMELA A. *et al.* 1962. Estudio geológico de la region de Almadén. *Boln. Inst. geol. min. Esp.* **73**, 193.

BARROIS, C. 1882. Recherches sur les terrains anciens des Asturies et de la Galice. *Mém. Soc. géol. N.* **2**, 630.

BENDER, F. 1963. Stratigraphie der "Nubischen Sandsteine" in Süd-Jordanien. *Geol. Jb.* **81**, 237.

BERGSTRÖM, J. 1969. Remarks on the appendages of trilobites. *Lethaia.* **2**, 395.

BORRELLO, A. V. 1966. Trazas, restos tubiformes etc. *Paleontografia Bonaerense* **5**.

CIARPI, B. 1901. La Cruziana (bilobites) Sardoa MGH. *P.-v. Soc. tosc. Sci. nat.* p. 3.

COLCHEN, M. 1964. Sur une coupe a travers les formations Paléozoiques de la Sierra de la Demanda (Burgos-Logrone, Espagne). *C. Som. Séanc. Soc. géol. Fr.* **10**, 442.

CRIMES, T. P. 1968. Cruziana: A stratigraphically useful trace fossil. *Geol. Mag.* **105**, 360.

DAWSON, J. W. 1864. On the fossils of the Genus Rusophycus. *Can. Naturalist* **1**, 363.

DELGADO, J. F. N. 1885. Estudo sobre os bilobites etc. (*Terrenos Paleozoicos de Portugal*). Lisboa.

——1887 *Ibid.* Supplement.

DESIO, A. 1940. Vestigia problematiche paleozoiche della Libya. *Annali Mus. libico Stor. nat.* **2**, 47.

FÄRBER, A. and JARITZ, W. 1964. Die Geologie des westasturischen Küstengebietes zwischen San Esteban de Pravia und Ribadeo (NW-Spanien). *Geol. Jb.* **81**, 679.

FENTON, C. R. and FENTON, M. A. 1937. Trilobite "nests" and feeding burrows. *Am. Midl. Nat.* **18**, 446.

FRECH, F. 1916. Geologie Kleinasiens im Bereich der Bagdadbahn. *Z. dt. geol. Ges.* **68**, 1.

FUCHS, T. 1895. Studien über Fucoiden und Hieroglyphen. *Denkschr. Akad. Wiss. Wien Math.-nat. Kl.* **62**, 369.

GUBLER, T. *et al.* 1966. Essai de nomenclature et caractérisation des principales structures sédimentaires. Edition Technip, Paris.

HALL, J. 1850. On the trails and tracks in the sandstones of the Clinton group of New York etc. *Proc. Am. Ass. Advmt Sci.* **2**, 256.

—— 1852. *Paleontology of New York.* Albany. **2**.

HÄNTZSCHEL, W. 1965. Vestigia invertebratorum et problematica. (*Fossilium Catalogus I Animalia,* pars 108) Junk,'s-Gravenhage.

HAUG, E. 1908. *Traité de géologie.* Colin, Paris. **2**.

INSTITUT ALGER. PETROLE, 1970. Voyage d'étude sédimentologique. Paleozoique inférieur du Sahara. *Inst. Alger. Petrole* **175**.

JAMES, J. F. 1885. The fossils of the Cincinnati Group. *J. Cincinn. Soc. nat. Hist.* **7**, 151.

KLITZSCH, E. 1964. Zur Geologie am Ostrand des Murzuk-Beckens (Prov. Fezzan, Libyen). *Oberrhein. geol. Abh.* **13**, 51.

LEBESCONTE, P. 1883. *Oeuvres posthumes de Marie Rouault. Suivie de: Les Cruziana et Rysophycus connus sous le nom général de bilobites sont-ils des végétaux ou des traces d'animaux.* Rennes.

—— 1886. Constitution générale du Massif Breton comparé à celle du Finisterre. *Bull. Soc. géol. Fr.* (3), **14**, 776.

LESSERTISSEUR, J. 1956. Sur un bilobite nouveau du Gothlandien de L'Ennedi (Tchad, A.E.F.), Cruziana ancora. *Bull. Soc. géol. Fr.* (6), **6**, 43.

LINNARSSON, J. G. O. 1869. On some fossils found in the Eophyton sandstone at Lugnas in Sweden. *Geol. Mag.* **6**, 393.

LOTZE, F. 1961. Das Kambrium Spaniens. I. Stratigraphie. *Abh. mat. naturw. Kl. Akad. Wiss. Mainz* no. 6.

MENEGHINI, G. 1883. Le Cruziane o bilobiti dei terreni Cambriani in Sardegna. *P.-v. Soc. tosc. Sci. nat.* **3**, 256.

——1885. Bilobiti Cambriane di Sardegna. *P-v. Soc. tosc. Sci. nat.* **5**, 184.

NATHORST, A. G. 1886. Nouvelles observations sur des traces d'animaux et autres phénomènes d'origine purement mécanique décrits comme "Algues fossiles". *K. svenska Vetensk. Akad. Handl.* **21**, no. 14.

d'ORBIGNY, A. 1839. Atlas to *Voyage dans l'Amérique méridionale.* Levrault, Paris and Strasbourg.

—— 1842. *Voyages dans l'Amérique méridionale.* Bertrand, Paris and Levrault, Strasbourg. 3 (4) partie (Paleontol.).

OSGOOD, R. G. 1970. *Trace fossils of the Cincinnati area. Palaeontographica Americana.* **6**, 41.

PACHECO, E. H. 1908. Consideraciones respecto a la organizazion, genero de vida y manera de fossilizarse algunos organismos de la epoca silurica y estudio de las especies de algas y huellas de gusanos arenicolas del silurico inferior de Alcuescar (Caceres). *Boln. R. Soc. esp. Hist. nat.* **75**.

PENEAU, J. 1946. Étude sur l'Ordovicien Inferieur (Arenigien = Gres Armoricain) et sa faune (specialement en Anjou). *Bull. Soc. Etude scient. Angers* n.s. **74–76**, 37.

PETROLEUM EXPLORATION SOCIETY OF LIBYA, 1963. Field trip guidebook of the excursion to Aouinet Ouenine. *Petrol. Explor. Soc. Libya. Saharan Symposium.* Tripoli.

PICARD, L. 1942. New Cambrian fossils and Paleozoic problematica from the Dead Sea and Arabia. *Bull. geol. Dep. Hebrew Univ.* **4**, no. 1.

PIETZSCH, K. 1910. Cruzianen aus dem Untersilur des Leipziger Kreises. *Z. dt. geol. Ges.* **62**, 571.

RADWAŃSKI, A. and RONIEWICZ, P. 1963. Upper Cambrian trilobite ichnocoenosis from Wielka Wisniowka (Holy Cross Mountains, Poland). *Acta palaeont. pol.* **8**, 259.

READING, H. G. 1965. Eocambrian and Lower Paleozoic geology of the Digermul Peninsula, Tanafjord, Finnmark. *Norg. geol. Unders.* **234**, 167.

ROUAULT, M. 1850. Note preliminaire sur une nouvelle formation decouverte dans le terrain silurien inferieur de la Bretagne. *Bull. Soc. géol. Fr.* (2), **7**, 724.

RUPKE, J. 1965. The Esla Nappe, Cantabrian Mountains (Spain). *Leid. geol. Meded.* **32**, 1.

SALTER, J. W. 1854. On the tracks of a crustacean in the "Lingula Flags". *Q. J. geol. Soc. Lond.* **10**, 208.

SAMPELAYO, P. H. 1950. Nuevas especies silurianas en la Sierra de la Demanda. *Inst. Geol. Miner. Espana, Libro jubil.* **1**, 145.

SAPORTA, G. and MARION, A. F. 1883. *Die paläontologische Entwickelung des Pflanzenreiches.* Leipzig.

SCHWARZBACH, M. 1952. Zur Stratigraphie des sardinischen Kambriums. *Neues Jb. Geol. Paläont. Mh.* p. 65.

SEILACHER, A. 1955. Spuren und Lebensweise der Trilobiten. In *Beiträge zur Kenntnis des Kambriums in der Salt Range (Pakistan)* by O. H. Schindewolf and A. Seilacher, *Abh. mat. naturw. Kl. Akad. Wiss. Mainz* no. 10, 86.

—— 1956. Der Beginn des Kambriums als biologische Wende. *Neues Jb. Geol. Paläont. Abh.* **103**, 155.

—— 1959. Vom Leben der Trilobiten. *Naturwissenschaften* **46**, 389.

—— 1960. Lebensspuren als Leitfossilien. *Geol. Rdsch.* **49**, 41.

—— 1962. Form und Funktion des Trilobiten-Daktylus. *Paläont. Z.* (H. Schmidt-Festband), 218.

—— 1963a. Lebensspuren und Salinitäts-Fazies. *Fortschr. Geol. Rhein.d Westf.* **10**, 81.

—— 1963b. Kaledonischer Unterbau der Irakiden. *Neues Jb. Geol. Palänt. Mh.* **10**, 527.

—— 1967. Fossil behavior. *Scient. Am.* **217**, 72.

—— 1969. Sedimentary rhythms and trace fossils in Paleozoic sandstones of Lybia. *Petrol. Explor. Soc. Libya, guidebook,* 117.

—— and CRIMES, P. 1969. "European" species of trilobite burrows in Eastern Newfoundland. *Mem. Am. Ass. Petrol. Geol.,* **12**, 145.

SINCLAIR, G. W. 1951. The generic name bilobites. *J. Paleont.* **25**, 228.

STÖCKLIN, J., RUTTNER, A. and NABAVI M. 1964. New data on the Paleozoic and Pre-Cambrian of North Iran. *Rep. geol. Surv. Iran* no. 1.

STRAND, T. 1935. A Cambrian fauna from Finnmark, Northern Norway. *Norsk geol. Tidsskr.* **15**, 19.

THADEU, D. 1956. Note sur le Silurien beiro-durien. *Bolm Soc. geol. Port.* **12**, 1.

THORAL, M. 1946. Cycles géologiques et formation noduliferes de la Montagne Noire. *Nouv. Archs Mus. Hist. nat. Lyon* **1**.

WALCOTT, C. D. 1918. Appendages of trilobites. *Smithson. miscn. Collns* **67**, 115.

WEISSBROD, T. 1969. The Paleozoic of Israel and adjacent countries. II. The Paleozoic outcrops in Southwestern Sinai and their correlation with those of southern Israel. *Bull. geol. Surv. Israel* **48**.

YIN, T. H. 1932. On the occurrence of *Cruziana* (bilobites) in Yunnan and Szechuan. *Bull. geol. Soc. China* **12**, 75.

A. Seilacher, Institut für Geologie und Paläontologie der Universität, 74 Tübingen, Sigwartstrasse 10, West Germany.

Ichnology of Palaeozoic sandstones in the Southern Desert of Jordan: a study of trace fossils in their sedimentologic context

R. C. Selley

This paper describes trace fossils in Lower Palaeozic sandstones and shales in the Southern Desert of Jordan. Emphasis is placed on the mode of occurrence of the fossils rather than their taxonomy.

A vertical sequence of three facies crops out in this region. Overlying the Precambrian basement are 700 m of coarse pebbly cross-bedded fluvial sandstones. Near the top trails attributed to *Cruziana furcifera* occur in silt-filled abandoned channels.

This succession is overlain by 250 m of medium-fine grained, well sorted sandstones with thin silt sheets. These contain *Harlania*, *Cruziana* and *Sabellarifex*. This is believed to be a marine shelf facies.

The third facies consists of coarsening upward cycles of clay to fine sand. In the lowest cycle shales with *Didymograptus bifidus* pass up through turbidite sandstones into a channel sand at the top. Succeeding cycles pass up from shale through interlaminated shale and silt with *Sabellarifex* into channel sands. The tops of the channels are cut by *Sabellarifex* and covered by *Rusophycus* and tracks and trails attributed to *Rouaultia*, *Diplichnites* and *Merostomichnites*. The last facies is believed to be deltaic.

1. Introduction

The stratigraphy of Palaeozoic sandstones in the Southern Desert of Jordan has been studied by Bender (1963; 1968). Trace fossils found during this work were described and figured by Huckriede (in Bender 1963) and mentioned by Seilacher (1968). Recently the author has carried out a detailed sedimentological study of these rocks, the results of which will be published elsewhere. During this project new trace fossils were found, and abundant and diverse collections made from formations previously thought barren.

The purpose of this paper is to describe these trace fossils with particular emphasis on their sedimentological context. A discussion of their taxonomy has been avoided and, to prevent confusion, the nomenclature of Huckriede (in Bender 1963) is used as far as possible.

The area studied is shown in Figure 1. Palaeozoic sandstones cover this region except in the south where Precambrian igneous rocks crop out beneath a subplanar unconformity.

The stratigraphy, sedimentology, fauna and environmental interpretation of the Palaeozoic section of the Southern Desert reveals that there is a vertical sequence of three facies. This is summarized in Figure 2. The sedimentology of each facies will now be briefly summarized, its environment deduced, and its fauna described and discussed.

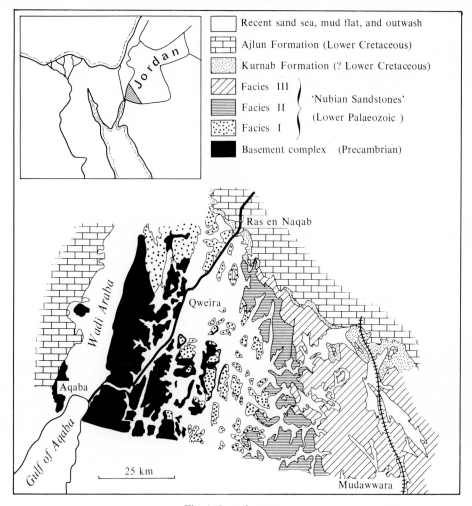

Fig. 1. Location map.

2. Pebbly channel sand facies

2a. Sedimentological summary

Stratigraphically this facies includes the Saleb, Ishrin and Disi Formations of Lloyd's classification (1968), i.e. the Bedded Arkose Sandstone, Massive Brownish Weathered Sandstone and Massive Whitish Weathered Sandstone of Bender's terminology (1963; 1968).

These formations all have sheet geometries which can be traced over the whole of the Southern Desert with little regional variation.

Grain size in this facies ranges from conglomerate to silt, but is largely in the medium to coarse grade (Wentworth Scale). Extra-formational conglomerates are mainly restricted to the Saleb Formation, though pebble-bearing sandstones and pebbly bands are common throughout the sequence. Intra-formational siltstone conglomerates and thin siltstone units are a rare but persistent feature of the whole section. Sorting is variable and appears to be controlled by bed form rather than

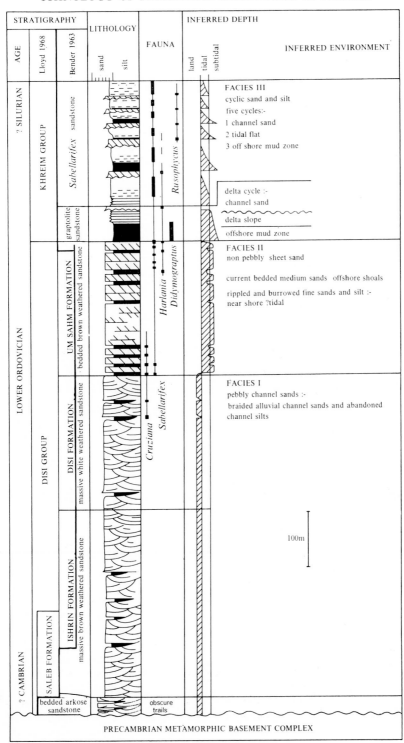

Fig. 2. Stratigraphic summary of the sedimentary rocks of the Southern Desert, Jordan. For key see Figure 3b.

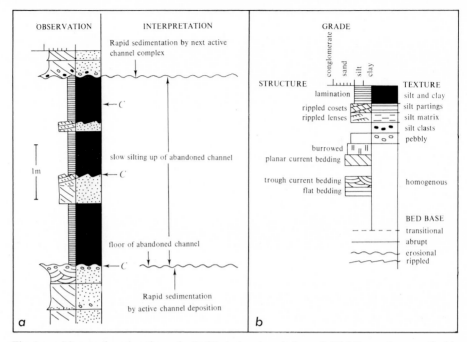

Fig. 3. a   Measured section through silt-filled abandoned channel. Disi Formation, north side of Qa Disi. Palestine Grid Reference 204895. Note location of *Cruziana,* indicated by letter c, to right of log;   b   Key to Figures 2, 3, 4 and 5.

stratigraphy. There is no obvious sign of cyclicity except at the base of the Ishrin Formation where fining up sequences are present.

Cross-stratification is the most prominent sedimentary structure. Both tabular planar and trough cross-bedding occur. Flat bedding is also present in all grades of sediment but is quantitatively subordinate to cross-bedding. Cross-lamination is restricted to the very rare fine sand and silts. Primary bedforms often show secondary deformation attributable to quicksand movement. Both recumbent foresets and streamer structure (Selley *et al.* 1963) are common.

The bedforms just described occur in channels up to 5 m deep and 300 m wide. These are only conspicuous when east-west trending cliffs are viewed from a considerable distance (i.e. those faces which are perpendicular to the palaeoslope). Channels are most obvious where adjacent shoestrings show marked contrast in grain size, as for example where granulestone units are present in the Saleb Formation and siltstones higher up the sequence. The latter are of particular significance since they always lie between two erosion surfaces. The upper one is generally planar, though locally load-casted and grooved into the underlying siltstone. The contact is marked by a thin conglomeration of quartz and silt pebbles. The lower erosion surface, underneath the siltstone, is concave upwards and is marked by a thin pebble conglomerate. Within these silt units thin sheets and lenses of micro-cross-laminated fine sands occur (Fig. 3). Owing to the excellent exposure it is possible to produce isopach maps of such channels and to demonstrate their trend and scale. They can sometimes be traced for up to 300 m downstream.

Palaeocurrents determined from cross-bedding and channel trends indicate deposition by unimodal northerly flowing currents, though there is some regional and stratigraphic variation in mean direction.

Geometry, sedimentary structures, grain size and palaeocurrents show that this facies was deposited in channels by unidirectional aqueous traction currents. These flowed mainly in the upper part of the lower flow regime (see Simons *et al.* 1965), though the rarer horizontally bedded sands indicate that transition flow regime deposition sometimes occurred. Silt partings between major bedding surfaces indicate pauses in current flow. Channel fill siltstones lying between erosion surfaces represent abandoned channel deposits due to avulsion. The hydraulic conditions deduced above are exclusive to braided rivers. Harms and Fahnestock's (1965) description of alluvial channel deposits of the present day Rio Grande can be applied almost *verbatim* to this facies of the 'Nubian Sandstones'.

2b. Trace fossils

Mr. J. Lloyd has shown the author obscure trails in the upper part of the Saleb Formation, and has observed similar trails in the Ishrin Formation.

Bender (1963; 1968) found trails attributable to *Cruziana furcifera* d'Orbigny *C. goldfussi* (Rouault) in two shale bands near the top of the Disi Formation. The authors' studies indicate that these shales are channel infillings of the type previously described (p. 480, and Fig. 3). *Cruziana* occurs on the pebble strewn channel floor (Pl. 1a), within the silt layers infilling the channel and on the upper rippled surfaces of fine sand layers. Two distinct types of *Cruziana* occur, a smaller variety (width about 1 cm), and a larger variety (about 8 cm wide) (Pl. 1 b, c). Apart from the size differences the two types appear to be morphologically similar.

More rarely two other types of track occur. The first of these consists of two parallel rows of laterally oriented short grooves or pits whose outside widths may attain 5 cm. Morphologically these are comparable to illustrations in Häntszchel (1962) figured under the names *Diplichnites, Ichnyspica, Incisifex* and *Tasmanadia.*

The second type consists of two parallel rows of laterally oriented kidney-shaped depressions. The outside width of this type of track is 7 cm. Individual footprints are about 1 cm wide, deep on their convex side, shallowing to the concave side (Pl. 1d). This type of track is comparable to *Merostomichnites* as figured by Häntzschel (1962 p. W 203).

On the assumption that *Cruziana* were made by trilobites, and that trilobites were exclusively marine organisms, Bender assigned the whole of the Disi Formation to a marine environment. (Bender 1963; 1968). However the author's studies show that this formation is sedimentologically comparable with those beneath, and that the facies is of fluvial type. One is faced therefore with the problem of trilobite tracks in ancient braided alluvium.

Braided river systems are often characterized by seasonal floods with long intervening dry spells when the channel systems dry out. Where braided alluvial plains impinge on marine shorelines sea water will infill the distal ends of channel systems during the dry spell. On such occasions marine organisms can perhaps temporarily inhabit fluvial channel systems. Such a situation could perhaps explain the presence of *Cruziana* in the fluvial sandstones. It is unlikely that the *Cruziana*-bearing channels can be regarded as estuarine in the normal sense of the word. There is no sign of bipolar palaeocurrents within the channels. They were unimodal and coincide with the palaeocurrent trend determined from sandstones above and below the channel complexes. It is perhaps significant that, though silt-filled abandoned channels occur throughout the whole fluvial sequence, *Cruziana* is restricted to two regionally widespread channel complexes only 50 m below the junction of the fluvial facies with overlying marine strata. This perhaps indicates therefore the first sign of the subsequent marine transgression.

PLATE 1

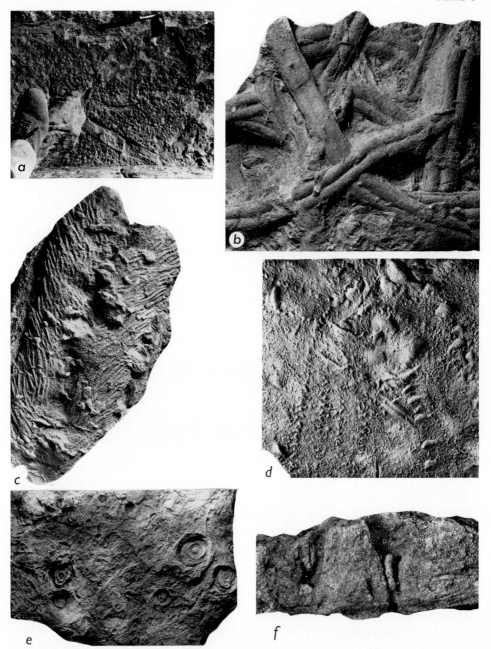

Plate 1

a Pebble covered channel floor with *Cruziana* trails. Disi Formation. Palestine Grid Reference 208888. Boot gives scale (one foot long).

b Small variety of *Cruziana* width 1·1 cm, Um Sahm Formation. Location shown in Figure 4.

c Large variety of *Cruziana*, width 8 cm, Disi Formation. Southeast side of Qa Disi. P.G.R. 207889.

d Base of fine sand layer in silt-filled abandoned channel complex. Disi Formation. P.G.R. 207889. Track attributable to *Merostomichnites* (Packard) trends from bottom right to top left. Various other tracks and organic markings also present.

e Bedding surface with *Sabellarifex* 'trumpets'. Location shown in Figure 4.

f Vertical section through *Sabellarifex* showing 'trumpet' and median 'spine'.

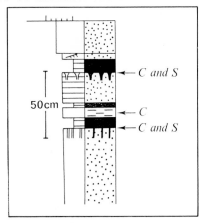

Fig. 4. Measured section of silt unit within the Um Sahm Formation. Southeastern side of Qa Disi. Palestine Grid Reference 207889. C location of *Cruziana*; S location of *Sabellarifex*. For key see Figure 3b.

3. Non-pebbly sheet sand facies

3a. Sedimentological summary

The pebbly channel sand facies just described is overlain by about 250 m of non-pebbly sands with sheet geometries. This is the 'bedded brown weathering sand-stone' of Bender (1963; 1968), the Um Sahm Formation of Lloyd (1968).

This facies is composed largely of fine to medium grained, well sorted, sand-stones which are massive or show tabular planar cross-bedding, set heights 5–15 cm.

At several levels there are layers, only a metre or so thick, of laminated grey silt and micro-cross-laminated fine sand. The ripples occur in lenses separated from one another by thin silt laminae. In contrast to the silt units of the preceeding facies these have sheet geometries and can be traced for kilometres along both the palaeodip and palaeostrike. They seldom show signs of erosion at their upper surfaces, and never at their bases.

Palaeocurrents determined for this facies were unimodal, directed slightly east of north. The cross-bedding and sheet geometry of the sands of this facies indicate deposition by unidirectional open-flow (i.e. not channel confined) currents in the upper part of the lower flow regime. The rippled fine sands are due to deposition in the lower part of the lower flow regime. The fact that the ripples occur in isolated lenticular sets bounded by silt laminae suggest pulsing current conditions. Rippled cosets indicative of steady flow, such as may be found in river channels, are absent. Considered overall therefore, a marine shelf environment is highly probable for this facies. The cross-bedded well sorted sands being deposited by downslope migrating shoals and bars in the offshore zone, while the silts and rippled fine sands suggest lower energy conditions, perhaps shallow and nearshore.

3b. Trace fossils

The author has found a diverse and abundant trace fossil suite distributed throughout the succession. Traces occur, almost exclusively, in the thin silt and fine rippled sand sequences, a typical example of which is shown in Figure 4. This shows that trace fossils are preserved on the upper surfaces of fine rippled sand-stone units where they are overlain by siltstone. The top of the sands are commonly cut by burrows similar to those recorded from the overlying facies and described by Huckriede (in Bender 1963) under the name *Sabellarifex dufrenoyi* (Rouault). Häntzschel (1962 p. W215) considers this form to be 'like *Skolithos* but individual tubes less straight and not as crowded'. These burrows also sometimes fall within the ichnogenus *Tigillites*, described in Häntzschel (1962 p. W218) as 'simple vertical burrows without special lining, smooth or regularly annulated, openings may be funnel shaped, not crowded like *Skolithos*' and regarded as a synonym of *Monocraterion* (Torell).

The burrows are vertical, generally less than 10 cm deep but may penetrate to 30 cm. Width varies from 1-5 mm. They are sometimes trumpet shaped at the top, the maximum observed width of the single trumpet being 1·8 cm. Internally the tube may be simple, infilled by sand, or silt. In some specimens a central sand column 1 mm wide is surrounded by horizontally laminated silt (Pl. 1e, f).

It is possible that the various types of burrow just described were made by different organisms. However, since forms transitional with the end members are common it is considered more likely that the burrows were all made by the same creature. The different burrows may be due to variations in sediment type and hence the style of preservation. Alternatively the creatures may have produced different burrows according to environmental factors. Thus Hallam and Swett (1966) attribute *Skolithos* to a suspension feeding worm-like organism during periods of negligible sedimentation, while they believe that *Monocraterion* was produced by the same organisms during more rapid sedimentation.

In addition to the vertical burrows just described the sandstone bedding surfaces often have *Cruziana*. These are morphologically similar to those found in the previous facies, and again two sub-types may be defined according to size. *Cruziana* also occurs within the rippled sands and on their bases where they overlie siltstone. A particular feature of this mode of occurrence is that *Cruziana* sometimes occurs in steep sided grooves deeper than they are wide (Pl. 2a).

The third type of trace fossil found in this facies occurs in a prominent silt sheet about 60 m from the top of the formation. Here, where a fine sand bed overlies a siltstone, are abundant trace fossils similar to those found by Bender in the overlying facies and described by Huckriede (in Bender 1963) as *Harlania alleghaniensis* (Harlan) (Pl. 2b). *Harlania* is known by the synonyms *Arthrophycus* Hall and *Phycodes* Richter (See Häntzschel 1962 p. W184).

4. Cyclic sand and silt facies

4a. Sedimentological summary

Stratigraphically this facies includes the Khreim Group of Lloyd (1968), the Graptolite Sandstone and *Sabellarifex* Sandstone of Bender (1963; 1968). Over 200 m thick the facies consists of six upward coarsening cycles of clay to fine sand (Fig. 2). The lowest cycle, the Graptolite Sandstone of Bender (*ibid.*) consists of laminated green shales with *Didymograptus bifidus* (Hall) which pass up through the fine grained sandstone turbidites into a cross-bedded channel sand complex at the top. In the overlying cycles (*Sabellarifex* Sandstone) the turbidite sequence between the shale and channel sand is replaced by rippled inter-laminated very fine sand, silt and clay (Fig. 5).

Sequences showing coarsening upward grain-size are produced today by prograding deltas, or prograding linear shorelines. Deposition by prograding deltas rather than beaches is the more likely explanation for this facies since the base of the upper sand unit is erosional and channelled, not transitional. Furthermore, this unit is cross-bedded, whereas flat bedding is more characteristic of Recent beaches.

PLATE 2

a Vertical section through *Cruziana* grooves. Note steep sides. Width at base 1 cm. Um Sahm Formation. Location shown in Figure 4.

b Lower surface of fine sandstone unit overlying silt with *Harlania*. Prominent silt sequence 60 m from the top of the Um Sahm Formation. P.G.R. 209890.

c Linearly arranged *Rusophycus* from the base of a sand bed at the top of the channel sand in the third cycle of the Khreim Group. P.G.R. 222879.

485

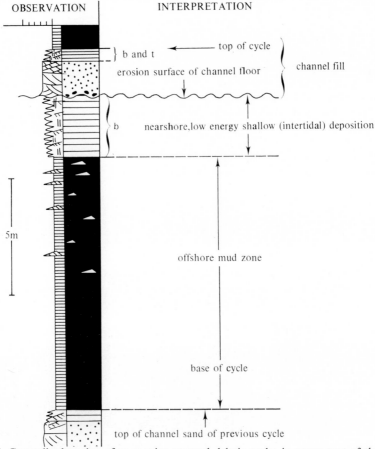

Fig. 5. Generalized section of coarsening upward deltaic cycles in upper part of the Khreim Group. (*Sabellarifex* Sandstone.)   b   burrows;   t   trails. For key see Figure 3b.

The lowest cycle (the Graptolite Sandstone) would seem to have been produced by deltaic distributary channels which built out lobes of mud which were buried under delta slope turbidite sands.

The succeeding five cycles (*Sabellarifex* Sandstone) indicate a slightly different environment, since the central turbidite unit is absent, being replaced by rippled and interlaminated very fine sand, silt and clay with abundant *Sabellarifex*. This lithological and faunal association suggests a gently sloping, shallower low energy environment, perhaps intertidal.

4b. Trace fossils

The cyclic sand and silt facies contains an abundant and diverse trace fossil suite whose distribution is closely controlled by sedimentology. The laminated shales, and the turbidite sandstones are barren, except for the graptolites already mentioned, but the interlaminated very fine sand, silt and clay units in the centre of the cycles show abundant burrows attributed to *Sabellarifex dufrenoyi* (Rouault) by Huckriede (in Bender 1963). Morphologically these are comparable to those described from the previous facies. Again there are both trumpet and vertical tubes, which may or may not show a central pipe within the burrow. The burrows are often very closely spaced, which together with the rippling and lamination, gives the rock an aspect typical of recent tidal flat sediments.

The cross-bedded channel sands are internally devoid of fossils. However, the upper, generally rippled, surface of each channel is covered by a variety of tracks in addition to being pierced by *Sabellarifex*.

Three main types of trace are present. The first two are similar to those previously described (p. 481) from the pebbly channel sand facies and are attributable to *Diplichnites* and *Merostomichnites*.

The third type of trace is about 0·5 cm wide, straight or gently curved and bilobate. The surfaces of the two lobes are generally smooth, but in some cases bear numerous striae running parallel to the trace. This type of trace is comparable to *Rouaultia*.

In addition to these three trails, sand filled casts occur which were illustrated by Huckriede (in Bender 1963) as *Rusophycus*. These occur both singly, and sometimes in linearly arranged columns of three or four casts (Pl. 2c.). Individual specimens have lengths from 5–7 cm and widths 5–8·5 cm. The average length: width ratio is 1:0·8.

Rusophycus and the three types of trace just described have all been attributed to trilobites (references in Häntzschel 1962).

Considering the cyclic deltaic facies as a whole it is apparent that there was a very close control of the fauna by sedimentation. During the deposition of the shales and turbidites when sedimentation was probably too rapid to permit benthonic activity, only the pelagic graptolites could survive. The apparent absence of trace fossils in the turbidites is unusual since the facies is often highly fossiliferous. This is the *Nereites*-facies of Seilacher (1964; 1967). The absence of trace fossils in the cross-bedded channel sands is to be expected, both because the current velocity may have been too strong for benthonic organisms, and because the homogenous nature of the sediment would be unfavourable for trace preservation.

Only in the tidal flat facies and in the last phase of channel infilling are signs of benthonic activity abundant. In both cases the sedimentology indicates deposition by pulsating currents. These allowed the deposition of mud from suspension to alternate with periods of lower flow regime traction currents which laid down the rippled sand layers. It may only be a quirk of preservation potential but whereas burrowing occurred both in the tidal flat deposits, and during the waning phases of channel infilling, trilobite traces are preserved only in the last environment.

5. Conclusions

The Lower Palaeozoic sediments of the Southern Desert of Jordan contain a vertical succession of three facies with a total thickness of more than 1000 m.

At the base are about 700 m of coarse pebbly cross-bedded fluvial channel sandstones with rare silt-filled abandoned channels. Two such silt shoestring complexes about 50 m from the top of the sequence contain *Cruziana*. This facies is overlain by some 250 m of finer well sorted sands, hitherto thought to have been unfossiliferous. Thin sheets of silt and fine rippled sand contain *Cruziana, Sabellarifex* and *Harlania*. This second facies is believed to have been deposited on a marine shelf. The third facies consists of coarsening upward shale: sand cycles attributed to a deltaic environment. *Didymograptus bifidus* at the base of this facies indicates a Llanvirn age. Tidal flat sediments half way up the deltaic cycles contain many *Sabellarifex*. The tops of the channel sands at the end of each cycle also contain *Sabellarifex* and various kinds of traces which have been attributed to trilobites.

This study may prove of more than local interest since this sequence of facies and trace fossil faunas can be traced from Jordan and Saudi Arabia (Helal 1968) across the Sahara at least as far as the Murzuk basin in southwestern Libya (Klitzsch 1966).

Throughout the Jordan sequence there is a close correlation between sedimentology and trace fossils. As previous studies have pointed out, this is probably due not only to common environment factors, but also to the preservation potential of sub-environments.

Seilacher's classification (1964) of trace fossil faunas holds good in this area. It is apparent that the whole sequence belongs to his *Cruziana*-facies. However, his refined (1967) facies classification does not fit. It is quite clear that *Cruziana* in the lowest facies is much less marine than *Skolithos*—(i.e. *Sabellarifex*) facies. In the two upper marine facies *Cruziana* and *Sabellarifex* are so commonly found together that it is impossible to use them as indicators of distinct trace fossil facies.

Acknowledgements. Financial support for this project has been provided by the National Environmental Research Council. Logistic support in the desert was kindly provided by the Natural Resources Authority of the Hashemite Kingdom of Jordan. Personal thanks are due to Mr. Omar Abdullah, Director of the N.R.A. and to his staff, also to Messrs. M. Barber and J. Lloyd of the United Nations Development Project: "Sandstone Aquifers of Jordan". It is a pleasure to acknowledge assistance in the field from Mr. Ahmed Tell and driver Fuad Sheik, whose skill in finding trace fossils in the most improbable places generated this paper. The author has also had the benefit of discussions with Dr. F. Bender, Dr. R. Goldring and Dr. T. P. Crimes.

References

BENDER, F. 1963. Stratigraphie der 'Nubischen Sandsteine' in Sud-Jordanien. *Geol. Jb.* **81**, 237.
—— 1968. *Geologie von Jordanien. Beiträge zur regionalen Geologie der Erde* **7**. Borntraeger, Berlin.
HALLAM, A. and SWETT, K. 1966. Trace fossils from the Lower Cambrian pipe rock of the north-west Highlands. *Scott. J. Geol.* **2**, 101.
HÄNTZSCHEL W. 1962. Trace fossils and problematica. In *Treatise on invertebrate paleontology* (Ed. R. C. Moore). Part W p. W 177.
HARMS, J. C. and FAHNESTOCK, R. K. 1965. Stratification, bed forms, and flow phenomena (with an example for the Rio Grande). In *Primary sedimentary structures and their hydrodynamic interpretation* (Ed. G. V. Middleton). *Spec. Publs econ. Palaeont. Miner., Tulsa* **12**, 84.
HELAL, A. H. 1965. Stratigraphy of outcropping Paleozoic rocks around the northern edge of the Arabian Shield (within Saudi Arabia). *Z. dt. geol. Ges.* **117**, 506.
KLITZSCH, E. 1966. Comments on the geology of the central parts of Southern Libya and Northern Chad. In *South Central Libya and Northern Chad* (Ed. J. J. Williams). Petrol. Explor. Soc. Libya. p. 1.
LLOYD, J. 1968. *The hydrogeology of the Southern Desert of Jordan.* Unpublished report. United Nations Development Project: Sandstone Aquifers of Jordan.
SEILACHER, A. 1964. Biogenic sedimentary structures. In *Approaches to paleoecology* (Ed. J. Imbrie and N. D. Newell). Wiley, New York. p. 296.
—— 1967. Bathymetry of trace fossils. *Mar. Geol.* **5**, 413.
—— 1968. Trilobitenspuren als Zeitmarken im jordanischen Paläozoikum. *Z. dt. geol. Ges.* **117**, 502.
SELLEY, R. C., SHEARMAN, D. J., SUTTON, J. and WATSON, J. 1963. Some underwater disturbances in the Torridonian of Skye and Raasay. *Geol. Mag.* **100**, 224.
SIMONS, D. B., RICHARDSON, E. V. and NORDIN, C. F. 1965. Sedimentary structures generated by flow in alluvial channels. In *Primary sedimentary structures and their hydrodynamic interpretation* (Ed. G. V. Middleton). *Spec. Publs Soc. econ. Palaeont. Miner., Tulsa.* **12**, p. 34.

R. C. Selley, Department of Geology, Imperial College, London, S.W.7, U.K., and Geology Research Laboratory, Oasis Oil Company of Libya Inc., P.O. Box 395, Tripoli, Libya.

The relation of trace fossils to small scale sedimentary cycles in the British Lias

B. W. Sellwood

Several types of small scale sedimentary cycle occur in the Raricostatum and Jamesoni Zones of the British Lias. Three of these consist of coarsening upward sequences in which the sediments, trace and body fossils indicate increasing environmental energy toward the cycle tops.
    Cycle Type I has clays at the base with a pectinid-nuculid faunal assemblage, and small pyritic burrows. The clays pass up into silts and fine sand with abundant suspension-feeding bivalves (e.g. myids), and a trace fossil assemblage dominated by *Rhizocorallium* and *Diplocraterion*.
    Cycle Type II occurs in the more calcareous facies. These cycles are the "limestone-shale" rhythms of previous authors. "Limestone" units represent the coarser portion of each cycle. Similar trace fossil changes are seen as in Cycle Type I.
    Cycle Type III consists of silty clays becoming more silty upward. The common occurrence of *Pinna*, a more argillaceous nature, and the presence of fewer trace fossils distinguish this Cycle Type from Type I. From the base, the fauna changes from a pectinid-nuculid assemblage to a *Pinna*-myid assemblage near the cycle tops where *Chondrites* occur. The remainder of the cycle contains tubular pyritic burrows.
    The cycles are probably related to variations in water depth. These variations are tentatively related to eustatic instability combined with tectonic subsidence, the two processes acting upon the North European epeiric seas of the Mesozoic.

1. Introduction

Part of the Lower Jurassic of Britain is characterised by rhythmic units, the rhythms being defined by variations in either the carbonate to clay content, or sand and silt to clay content. The present paper is mainly concerned with the ammonite zones which fall below and above the Sinemurian-Pliensbachian boundary, namely the Raricostatum and Jamesoni Zones. The beds of these zones crop out in excellent coast sections (Fig. 1) at Charmouth in Dorset (Lang *et al.* 1928), Robin Hood's Bay in Yorkshire (Tate and Blake 1876; Fox-Strangways 1892), the Inner Hebrides (Peach *et al.* 1910; Lee *et al.* 1925), and on the east coast of Scotland at Golspie (Lee in Read *et al.* 1925; Hallam 1965). Inland exposures exist, but are poor.

In this paper, the term "small-scale" refers to cyclic sedimentary units from a variety of facies, in which the individual cycles range up to about 4m in thickness, and may, with favourable exposures, be traced laterally over a distance of about 5 km.

Cycles of a similar type have been described before from the British Jurassic by Brinkmann (1929) and Hallam (1960; 1964). Hallam (1960) revived the old controversy about the origin of "limestone-shale rhythms" in the Blue Lias of southern England (Hettangian-Lower Sinemurian), and from the evidence of the trace fossils, sedimentary structures, and other features, he concluded that their origin was, composite, being partly primary and partly secondary.

A similar facies to the Blue Lias occurs in the lowermost Pliensbachian (Jamesoni

Table 1.

	Stages	Zones
LOWER JURASSIC (LIAS)	TOARCIAN	
	PLIENSBACHIAN	*Pleuroceras spinatum* *Amaltheus margaritatus* *Prodactylioceras davoei* *Tragophylloceras ibex* *Uptonia jamesoni*
	SINEMURIAN	*Echioceras raricostatum* *Oxynoticeras oxynotum* *Asteroceras obtusum* *Caenisites turneri* *Arnioceras semicostatum* *Arietites bucklandi*
	HETTANGIAN	

Modified from Dean, Donovan and Howarth (1961).

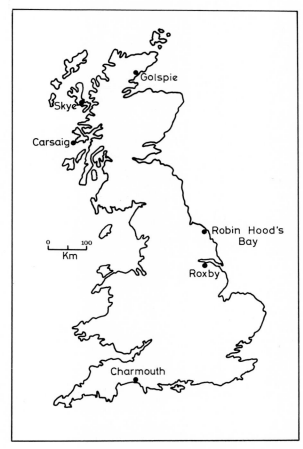

Fig. 1. Locality map.

and Ibex Zones) at Charmouth Dorset. These beds are termed the Belemnite Marls, and except for the fact that they have experienced less diagenesis than the Blue Lias, they are similar to the latter in many respects.

The "limestone-shale" cycle is the most obvious type. Other cycles in more clastic facies also occur, significantly in beds equivalent in age to the Belemnite Marls in the north of Britain. Here also, obvious cycles exist in rocks of the pre-ceeding (Raricostatum) Zone. Unfortunately, exposures are not good enough to enable facies changes to be laterally traced.

In this paper, an attempt is made to present as much as possible of the available biological, sedimentological and geochemical evidence as a facies analysis for each type of cycle and then to suggest a way in which the cycles may be inter-related. Ecological considerations of the possible modes of life of trace fossil producers in most part follows Seilacher (1967), while other interpretations are based on work carried out by Reineck et al. (1967), and McGinitie (1934). Where trace fossils and body fossils occur together, as for example myids and *Diplocraterion*, a suspension feeding mode of life for the animal which produced the latter would seem reasonable and a shallow water environment suggested. Clear cut associations such as these are seldom seen; the more common and rather diverse assemblages must be interpreted on their own merits. Distributions of suspension feeding animals are believed to be related primarily to depth and environmental energy, thus following Seilacher (1967), Jørgensen (1966) and Bordovisky (1965).

2. Types of cycle

2a. Type I (thickness 1·4–3·6 m)

This cycle type is common in beds of Raricostatum zone age at Robin Hood's Bay (Yorkshire) and part of the Jamesoni zone at Carsaig Bay (Mull). A generalized cycle is given in Figure 2, and is seen to consist of a coarsening upward sequence, commencing at the base in poorly micaceous clays, often rich in pyritic ammonites. The clay becomes more micaceous upwards, and discrete, but often bioturbated, laminations of silt a few millimetres thick, appear. Upward these laminae generally become more common and thicker, often forming discrete lenticular laminations of silt. Trace fossils in the more argillaceous portions are limited to irregular pyritic tubes with diameters ranging up to 5 mm.

Scour-structures which are circular in plan, with diameters up to 1 m and depths of 100 mm may occur anywhere within the cycle. Crinoid debris often forms lag deposits at the bases of these scours. Generally the scours are filled with well sorted fine sand, and sedimentary structures within the filling sediment consist of sandy and silty streak (de Raaf et al. 1965), and often there are numerous levels marked by oscillation ripples, each level giving a different orientation of ripple axes. Occasional grazing trails traverse the rippled surfaces, while animal escape structures sometimes penetrate the thinner scour-fills.

Simple (as opposed to vertically retrusive) *Rhizocorallium* often penetrate the topmost laminae of the scour fills; these burrows are here filled by the overlying silty clay. Rare and rather small *Chondrites* (1 mm diameter) may also penetrate the top few laminae of the scour fills; these burrows, like the *Rhizocorallium*, are filled with silty clay. The *Rhizocorallium* found at this level within the cycles are also simple spreiten "U" tubes, as opposed to the vertically retrusive forms which occur in the upper levels (Pl. 1b).

Toward the top of the cycle, and where the silt laminations are more persistent, *Rhizocorallium* structures are commonly found. The benthonic fauna of the more

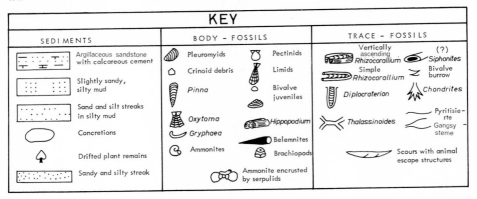

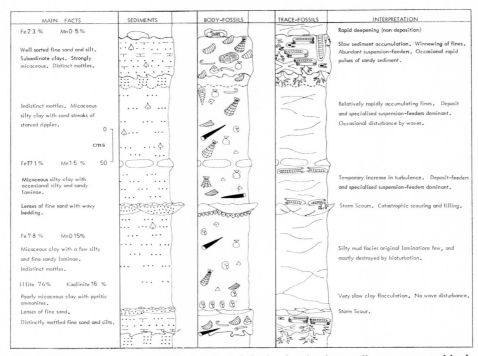

Fig. 2. Diagrammatic section through a Type I Cycle, showing how sediments trace and body fossils change through it. Fe and Mn percentages are of the total oxides (Fe_2O_3 and MnO respectively).

Plate 1

a Slightly sandy silty mud toward the top of a Type I Cycle. Arrow indicates burrow of *Pholadomya* at the lithological change to more sandy sediments nearer to the Cycle top. *Chondrites* may be seen piping light-coloured sandy sediment down into the underlying silty clay. Length of hammer handle 270 mm.

b Vertically retrusive *Rhizocorallium* from a sandy unit near a Cycle top, Robin Hood's Bay. Match Box 53 mm long.

PLATE 1

argillaceous portions of the cycles is typified by *Camptonectes, Plagiostoma, Ento-lium,* and *Nucula.* The topmost 300 mm of the cycles show a marked increase in the proportion of coarser material, and here, a distinct change in the trace and body fossil assemblage occurs. The junction has been emphasised by the burrowers, but was probably gradational originally. *Chondrites* pipe the white silt and sand 100 mm down into the darker silty clay (Pl. 1a, Fig. 2), and *Thalassinoides* become apparent at the silt to clay/silt contact. Vertically retrusive *Rhizocorallium* (Pl. 1b) become very abundant, but lack a specific orientation. The body fossils also change as myid bivalves, *Hippopodium* and *Gryphaea* become dominant. The myids are particularly common, and are mostly preserved in life position, many being vertically retrusive like the *Rhizocorallium,* suggesting for both a response to sediment influx. *Rhizocorallium* remains dominant, with *Thalassinoides, Chondrites* and *Siphonites*(*?*) along with *Diplocraterion.* The latter seem to penetrate down from the cycle tops. *Teichichnus*-like burrows also may be seen, but on close inspection usually turn out to be retrusive *Rhizocorallium* with only one arm of the burrow system exposed. Trough-like bedding structures also occur, and these result from the interference of retrusive burrow systems. An attempt to show how these burrow systems may appear in outcrop is given in Figure 3.

The tops of the cycles are marked by hummocky surfaces produced by the burrowers. These surfaces are draped by the basal clay unit of the succeeding cycle. Variations from this idealised cycle are often seen. Where scours directly overlie the cycle tops, the surfaces tend to be planar. Calcareous nodules crowded with amonites, and shell filled "runnels" similar to those described by Häntzschel *et al.* (1968) may also be found at the cycle tops. Ammonites within the nodules are frequently encrusted with serpulids on their upper surfaces.

Interpretation of the cycle. The basal clay unit of the cycle constitutes a slowly accumulating deposit below the influence of wave action. Trace fossils like the tubular burrows (*pyritisierte Gangsysteme*) of Schlotz (1968) represent the tunnels of infaunal deposit feeders. The nuculids were similarly infaunal (Yonge 1939; Stanley 1968). The pectinids were probably byssally attached, and following Yonge (1953a) were able to keep their mantles free of mud because of their valve-clapping habit; they could thus survive in a muddy environment.

The association between sandier sediment and *Rhizocorallium* could mean that during the long phases when argillaceous material predominated, the *Rhizocorallium* animal was not present, or that if it was, it remained undetectable, or that it was present and adopted a different feeding mode which did not involve the construction of the typical burrow form. In the tops of the cycles however, in addition to the intermittently rapid sedimentation which induced the retrusive structures, there were also phases of slower sedimentation. Wave and current action was probably quite strong as is suggested by the well sorted (even though burrowed) nature of the sandy beds. The bivalves and *Diplocraterion* are all essentially suspension feeding types, and following the work of Seilacher (1967) and many others, this suggests water that the final phase in the cycle represents very shallow and turbulent conditions.

The mode of life of the *Rhizocorallium* animal is more difficult to interpret; Seilacher (1967) has suggested a deposit feeding habit. By applying a simple calculation the volume of sediment removed and reworked from such a system can be estimated. For a *Rhizocorallium* system 0·4 m long showing no retrusive component, an average of 275 cc of sediment will have been worked. Such a volume of sediment would probably not have been enough to sustain an animal which employed only a sediment eating mode of life unless it constantly redug new burrows elsewhere. Also, the vertically retrusive nature of many burrow systems, as shown

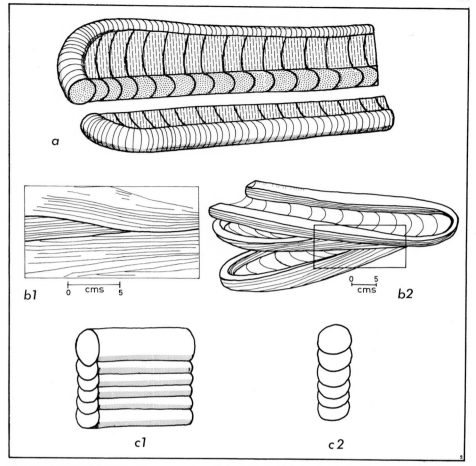

Fig. 3a. Exploded block diagram of a non-retrusive *Rhizocorallium* which could give the appearance of certain other "meniscus filled" burrows in some exposures (cf. Kennedy 1967a fig. 6). × 0·5.

    b. 1. Enlargement of area boxed in b2, showing an oblique section through three super-imposed, vertically retrusive *Rhizocorallium* burrows. The enlargement shows how such a situation might be mistaken for small-scale trough-cross bedding.

    c. 1. Lateral view of one "arm" of a vertically retrusive *Rhizocorallium,* showing how in outcrop such a system could be mistaken for *Teichichnus.* 2. shows same situation viewed from the front. Both × 0·5.

in Plate 1b is not altogether compatible with a sediment feeding habit, especially if the upward building in both myids and *Rhizocorallium* was in response to the same stimulus, namely influx of sediment. Sedimentation would probably not adversely affect an animal living solely as a detritus feeder, except that the burrow entrances would need to be re-opened.

    It seems likely therefore, that the *Rhizocorallium* animal was similar in its mode of life to some recent callianassid crustaceans, which exhibit deposit- and suspension-feeding at different stages in their life history to suit the particular requirements of the time. These callianassids deposit-feed whilst they excavate the systems and then suspension-feed once the systems have been completed (McGinitie 1934). It is probable that the crustaceans which constructed *Rhizocorallium* burrows also adopted this form of dual existence.

Thalassinoides, although it occurs mainly towards the bases of the more sandy units in these cycles, may have occurred throughout the sandy portion, only to be re-worked and obliterated by the later burrowers.

From Figure 2, Fe/Mn concentrations are seen to be high in the concretions within the clays, but extremely low at the cycle tops where the Fe is replaced by Ca. Such a situation has often been interpreted as reflecting a change from terrigenous to more marine influence (Curtis and Spears 1968; Hallam 1967). A probable still-stand in sedimentation and transgressive phase is marked by the calcareous nodules rich in ammonites at the cycle tops.

The entire cycle probably represents a shallowing upward sequence, with possibly quite rapid deepening occurring whilst the very topmost portions of the cycles were being burrowed. The rapidity of the deepening is inferred from the abrupt change from sand to clay at the cycle tops which gives an extreme asymmetry to the cycles. The presence of burrowers probably caused the removal of some fine grained components in the upper portions of the cycles, by their throwing of fines into suspension and the subsequent winnowing action of currents.

The scour structures were cut and filled very rapidly. They generally lack burrowing except in their uppermost laminae and occasional vertical tubes which are attributed to escape structures. Sole markings occur on the bases of some of the sand lenses. These sole marks consist of scoured burrows and are therefore pre-scour structures reminiscent of those described by Seilacher (1962). The sandy-streak and oscillation ripples suggest that the scours resulted from strong wave action possibly induced by storms. The scours being produced by eddies which acted around inhomogeneities on the sea bed such as small communities of crinoids or occasional ammonites.

2b. Type II (thickness 0·15–0·9 m)

This type of cycle is seen in the beds of Jamesoni-Ibex Zone age in the Belemnite Marls of Charmouth (Dorset), where lithologies similar to those in the Blue Lias of Dorset can be seen. The Blue Lias has received much attention from Lang (1924) and Hallam (1960; 1964). The stratigraphy of the Belemnite Marls was described by Lang *et al.* (1928), and were mentioned by Hallam (1964), but apart from a few comments made by Simpson (1957) they had not received a detailed sedimento-logical study. They do, however, exhibit largely unaltered examples of what have often been termed "limestone-shale rhythms". The quite obvious, and rather profound diagenetic redistributions of carbonate which affected the Blue Lias, seem for the most part not to have affected the Belemnite Marls which thus show the best evidence for the origin of this type of sequence.

The evidence, and an interpretation from three cycles, is summarised in Figure 4. From this figure it may be seen that burrows are most evident at lithological junctions, whilst within the beds (apart from *Chondrites*) only general biogenic mottling is seen.

The terms "limestone" and "marl" have so far been used in a rather loose way. The "marls" in the context of this paper are predominantly argillaceous sediments with carbonate contents ranging from 30% to 60%. The "limestones" also contain considerable amounts of clay, but have a carbonate content usually in excess of 50% but less than 75%. Thus the terms "limestone" and "marl" are merely relative, but "limestones" have higher carbonate contents than the adjacent "marls". Significantly, the three beds which exceed 80% in their carbonate content have undergone considerable diagenesis, and exhibit a similar nodularity to limestone units in the Blue Lias with comparatively high carbonate values.

The carbonate component within these cycles has long been a cause of controversy. When etched specimens of "limestone" from the Belemnite Marls are viewed under a binocular microscope, the coarser grained constituents may be seen to consist of small echinoid spines, faecal pellets and small bivalve (ostracod) shells. These components are often collected together as micro-lag deposits at the bases of burrow fills. The fine-grained matrix which makes up some 60% or more of the "limestone" units is more difficult to examine. From studies made with the electron microscope, a contribution to the carbonate component in the cyclic units is seen to be made by numerous sub-microscopic elliptical calcareous rings which superficially resemble Chalk nanno-fossils. The remainder is microcrystalline calcite growing on the clay flakes, and the origin of this, although diagenetic, remains unknown. Within the "marl" units, the bioclastic debris is less common. Clay mineral compositions of the insoluble fraction of both "marl" and "limestone" units are identical at about 95% illite, 5% kaolinite.

As illustrated in Figure 4, there are several sharp junctions within these rhythmic units, and it may be argued that cycle tops and bases could be placed at any of these. By comparison with the Type 1 cycle, certain similarities are seen to exist, especially in the occurrence of trace fossils. Trace fossil distributions are seen to be markedly asymmetric, with *Diplocraterion* usually only present at the tops of "limestone" units, piping the overlying darker "marl" down into the "limestone" below.

Scour structures similar in some respects to those seen in the Type 1 cycles also occur, but in these cases are filled only with biogenic material, especially crinoid and belemnite remains. These scours, where present are generally limited to the tops of "limestone" units.

The "limestones" themselves are conspicuously mottled by *Rhizocorallium, Thalassinoides* and a very small form of *Chondrites* (tube diameter 0·1-1·0 mm) *Thalassinoides* and *Rhizocorallium* are especially obvious at the lower junctions of "limestones" with "marls" whilst the *Rhizocorallium* also occur at the tops of the "limestone" units. A large form of *Chondrites* (or perhaps it is *Pygospioides* (Häntzschel *et al.* 1968)) with tube diameters ranging from 2-5 mm, as well as smaller forms, ubiquitously pipe white "limestone" into the darker "marls". Careful study has shown only a very few occasions where the larger *Chondrites* penetrate a limestone unit from above. Where "marl" units are thin enough for burrow impingement from the overlying "limestone", instead of penetrating the more calcareous bed, the large *Chondrites* follow down the marly fills of *Rhizocorallium*, or *Diplocraterion* burrows (Simpson 1957). *Chondrites* within the "limestone" units tend to be the very small forms mentioned above.

Occasionally, a few centimetres of calcareous shales with bituminous laminae occur within the "marl" units; in these cases, the "marls" below become gradually more bituminous and finally pass up into the shales. The top surfaces of such shales are sharply defined, and penetrated by a few small *Chondrites* burrows filled with overlying "marl". Other trace fossils are not seen at these junctions. The sharp junction that we now see from "marl" up to "limestone" was probably originally gradational, the junction having been exaggerated by the burrowers.

Apart from belemnites, the fauna of the Belemnite Marls is really quite poor in terms of its diversity. This is partly because of removal of the originally aragonitic elements during diagenesis. The lack of casts and moulds suggests that there may never have been a diverse fauna anyway. *Plagiostoma, Inoceramus* and *Chlamys* are the most important bivalves, whilst cidarid, diadematid and crinoid fragments dominate the finer grained fraction.

Interpretation of the cycle. This is again summarised in Figure 4. Basically, each cycle, like that of Type 1, represents a regressive sequence reflecting an increase in

INTERPRETATION	MAIN FEATURES	CARBONATE % 40 60 80	LITHOLOGY
REGRESSION			
TOP OF CYCLE. SHALLOWEST. Shallow water, winnowing of clays. Occasional scouring by storms. Suspension-feeders reflect shallow agitated water conditions.	Strongly mottled argillaceous calcilutite ("limestone") scoured at the top of the bed. Scours filled with crinoid, echinoid and other bioclastic debris. *Diplocraterion* (or *Corophioides*) descend from the top of the unit. "Marly" fill of these, and *Rhizocorallium* is re-worked by large *Chondrites* which penetrate from the top of the "limestone" bed above. Brachiopods commoner in "limestone" than in underlying "Marl". *Inoceramus* and *Plagiostoma* occur, while echinoderm debris is abundant, and submicroscopic calcareous (?) nannoplankton is common.		
	SHARP CONTACT, VERY REWORKED by *Thalassinoides, Chondrites, Rhizocorallium*		
Clay flocculation dilutes carbonate component. No winnowing of clays, but anaerobic conditions. Prevented by sluggish water movements.	Calcareous mudstone ("Marl") with occasional echinoderm debris, foraminifera, *Plagiostoma*, and *Inoceramus*. Belemnites and ammonites occur throughout. *Chondrites* filled by overlying "limestone" (much higher carbonate content) than surrounding "Marl". Small pyritic tubular burrows common.		
	----- LIMIT of PENETRATION by LARGE *CHONDRITES* -----		
Slow clastic sedimentation, no winnowing. Anaerobic. RAPID DEEPENING NON DEPOSITION	SHARP CONTACT WITH SOME *CHONDRITES*, no burrowing. TRANSITION. Laminated bituminous shale. Calcareous mudstone with some features as that above the shale.		
REGRESSION			
TOP OF CYCLE. SHALLOWEST. Winnowing of clays. Complete reworking by burrowers. Slow deposition.	Strongly mottled argillaceous calcilutite ("limestone"). Abundant very small *Chondrites*. No large *Chondrites* except those reworking marly fills of *Rhizocorallium* burrows. Fauna and (?) flora as in argillaceous calcilutite at top of succeeding cycle.		
	SHARP CONTACT, VERY REWORKED by *Thalassinoides, Chondrites, Rhizocorallium*		
Original transition exaggerated by burrowing. Accumulation of fines with little winnowing. No stagnation because of sluggish water movements. RAPID DEEPENING NON DEPOSITION	Calcareous mudstone ("Marl"). Small *Chondrites* penetrate less far into the bed than the large *Chondrites*. Pyritised tubular burrows (2 mm in diameter), often containing faecal pellets, are abundant.		
	----- LIMIT of PENETRATION by LARGE *Chondrites* -----		
REGRESSION			
TOP OF CYCLE. SHALLOWEST. Scouring, turbulence. Suspension-feeders.	SHARP CONTACT, VERY REWORKED by *Thalassinoides, Chondrites, Rhizocorallium*		
Original transition exaggerated by burrowers.	Strongly mottled argillaceous calcilutite. Scours at the top of the bed filled with bioclastic debris. *Diplocraterion* or *Corophioides* descend from the top of the bed.		

Fig. 4. Diagrammatic section through three Type III Cycles showing lithologies and burrow relationships.

turbulence toward the cycle top. This is demonstrated by the dominance of suspension feeding forms (Seilacher 1967) in the "limestones" related to the "limestone" tops. The sequences may be broadly termed "coarsening upward" in view of
the abundant bioclastic material which is present in the "limestone" units relative
to that in the "marls" and bituminous shales. Although the biogenic material is
fine, it represents a much coarser fraction than the clay portion. Thus, the "limestones" may represent "winnowed" horizons (as did the sands in Type 1 cycles).

These cycles, like those of Type 1, are markedly asymmetric, and if the differences
outlined above are due to depth and turbulence, the asymmetry at the tops of the
"limestones" suggests quite a rapid raising of wave base (deepening?); and where
bituminous shales occur, the transgressive episode was probably prolonged, so that
even argillaceous sedimentation was minimised. The lack of turbulence, and slow
organic rich sedimentation resulted in stagnation of the bottom sediment.

Inoceramus is by far the best preserved and most abundant bivalve; *Plagiostoma*
and *Chlamys* occur less commonly. The latter genera were byssally attached, and
adapted to a life in mud as explained earlier. *Inoceramus* occurs commonly in
facies of this type, often to the exclusion of most other biota, and was probably
specialised to withstand the ensuing muddy conditions.

The larger forms of *Chondrites* are confined to the "marls", whilst very small
forms remain in the "limestones". There are a number of reasons why this distinction should occur. Firstly, the more calcareous beds may represent some chemically
unfavourable substrate which repelled the larger forms. Secondly, the food content
of the limestones may not have been amenable to them; or thirdly, some physically
inhibitory phenomenon may have ensued, such as inter-stratal hardening of the
more calcareous units. Preservational and observational reasons are not thought to
be likely, because these burrows are very obvious where they are present in the few
exceptional cases.

Chondrites has been considered the burrow of a deposit feeding animal since the
classic work of Simpson (1957). As with *Rhizocorallium*, the burrowing "efficiency"
of the animal can be assessed by comparing the potential workable volume of
sediment against actual worked volume. From observations on the large *Chondrites*
(*?granulatus*) in the Belemnite Marls it may be seen that the potential volume of
sediment that could be worked by the animal approximates to that of a teardrop.
The volume worked can be measured by point counting "burrow" against
"matrix" for individual systems and deducting this volume from that of the
calculated "potential volume". The large *Chondrites* (*?granulatus*) seems to have
been about 30–40% efficient in its mining programmes. Systems with a mean

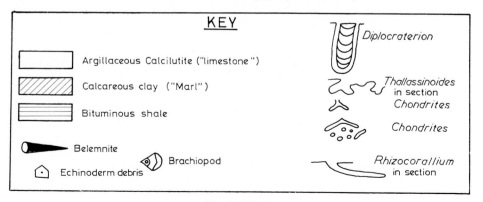

Key to Fig. 4.

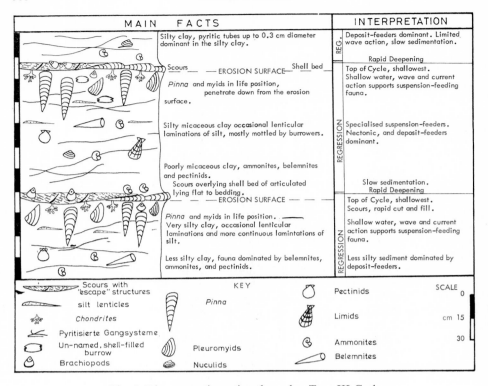

MAIN FACTS	INTERPRETATION
Silty clay, pyritic tubes up to 0.3 cm diameter dominant in the silty clay.	REG. Deposit-feeders dominant. Limited wave action, slow sedimentation.
	Rapid Deepening
Scours —— EROSION SURFACE —— Shell bed	Top of Cycle, shallowest. Shallow water, wave and current action supports suspension-feeding fauna.
Pinna and myids in life position, penetrate down from the erosion surface.	
Silty micaceous clay occasional lenticular laminations of silt, mostly mottled by burrowers.	REGRESSION Specialised suspension-feeders. Nectonic, and deposit-feeders dominant.
Poorly micaceous clay, ammonites, belemnites and pectinids. Scours overlying shell bed of articulated lying flat to bedding. —— EROSION SURFACE ——	Slow sedimentation. Rapid Deepening Top of Cycle, shallowest. Scours, rapid cut and fill.
Pinna and myids in life position. Very silty clay, occasional lenticular laminations and more continuous laminations of silt.	REGRESSION Shallow water, wave and current action supports suspension-feeding fauna.
Less silty clay, fauna dominated by belemnites, ammonites, and pectinids.	Less silty sediment dominated by deposit-feeders.

KEY

Scours with "escape" structures

silt lenticles

Chondrites

Pyritisierte Gangsysteme

Un-named, shell-filled burrow

Brachiopods

Pinna

Pleuromyids

Nuculids

Pectinids

Limids

Ammonites

Belemnites

SCALE 0

cm 15

30

Fig. 5. Diagrammatic section through a Type III Cycle.

burrow diameter of 6 mm have excavated *c.* 250–450 cc of sediment, and would therefore seem to have been quite efficient deposit feeders, as was suggested by Simpson (1957).

Thus it is quite evident that with the Belemnite Marls, the cyclicity is due to some primary sedimentary difference between "marls" and "limestones". Many hypotheses have been advanced in the past to explain similar types of cyclicity. From the evidence of the burrows, an entirely diagenetic origin for the cyclicity can be ruled out. It seems more probable that it resulted from variations in clay and other insolubles. The variations are influenced by the degree of winnowing of the insoluble fraction. From the presence of scour-structures at the cycle tops and the *Diplocraterion,* a shallowing upward sequence is believed to be represented, with the overall shallowing resulting from wave-base lowering.

2c. Type III (thickness 0·3–1·5 m +)

This type of cycle contains only limited trace fossils, but is included in this paper for completeness. This type is common in part of the Jamesoni Zone at Robin Hood's Bay and Carsaig Bay (Fig. 1). A generalised cycle is given in Figure 5, from which it may be seen that the facies is clastic and the bulk of the cycle consists of silty clay which sometimes exhibits lenticular laminations and more continuous laminations of silt. The silty clay contains a fauna similar in many respects to that of the clay units in Type I cycles, namely *Plagiostoma, Chlamys, Camptonectes,* belemnites and ammonites. The bivalves are mostly disarticulated in the lower portions but toward the top *Pinna* and myids (mostly *Pleuromya* and *Pholadomya*) occur in life position. The first *Pinna* are present some 0·3–0·4 m below the top of the cycle, and seem, like the myids, to be anticipating the occurrence of the erosion surface which cuts the top of the cycle. The erosion surface is marked by the presence of exhumed, but articulated, *Pinna* lying flat to the bedding. These shells often show a preferred orientation. Mostly, the *Pinna* are encrusted by what were, in life, commensal serpulids which colonised the posterior (projecting) shell margins. A few laminae rich in exhumed *Pinna* have been found encrusted by serpulids. This encrustation occurred after the erosional event, when the shells lay exposed.

Overlying the shells, there are usually found scour structures similar in respect of their scale and sedimentary structures, to those described from Cycle Type I. They are dissimilar in the fact that the shell beds which underlie them although only one or two shells thick, may be traced several metres away from the scours. In many cycles, it was possible to predict the position of a shell bed and scour surface after finding the first *Pinna* in life position.

Trace fossils in this cycle are limited to the *"pyritisierte Gangsysteme"* of Schlotz (1968); some peculiar shell filled burrows which have yet to be described; escape structures in the scour-fills, and a few small *Chondrites* penetrating down from the erosion surface at the cycle top.

Interpretation of the cycle. The silty clay unit is analogous to the silty clay in Type 1 cycles, probably having been deposited in water which was subject to intermittent and very slight wave and/or current action. The bivalve and trace fossil association support this interpretation. The incoming of an abundant suspension feeding bivalve fauna which in every case anticipates the succeeding erosion surface, suggests an increase in environmental energy (lowering of wave base?) towards the tops of the cycles. This increase in environmental energy culminated in a phase of scouring and exhumation of the infauna, and particularly the *Pinna*. Yonge (1953b), in his study of *Pinna*, has shown that once tipped over, the animals are unable to re-bury themselves.

After the phase of scouring, quite a rapid reversion to silty mud sedimentation occurred, which suggests a much lower environmental energy. The sedimentary reflection of this change gives the asymmetry of the cycles. In only one or two cases do *Pinna* in life position continue immediately above the erosion surfaces, and here, the change in energy regime probably occurred at a slower rate.

When one considers the scale of all three types of cycle, it becomes apparent that the biotic and lithologic changes which occur within them cannot be easily explained in terms of conventional models. If the conventional interpretation concerning shallowing, and its reflection by the faunal and sedimentological changes are accepted; then the question of the mechanism which induced the shallowing is of extreme importance. It is not likely that an accretion of sediment only a metre or so thick should have caused the changes which have been described from all three cycle types. This leaves the somewhat larger scale variables like sea level fluctuations and tectonism, and in order to explore this possibility the cycles that have been described should be compared with those from other formations.

3. Small scale cycles from other formations

Blue Lias Cycles from Dorset, Britain. Lithologically, these are similar in most respects to the Belemnite Marl cycles (Type II). They differ in respect of the diagenesis which has affected them. Diagenesis in the Blue Lias has tended to exaggerate the "limestone" units, and has apparently occurred as a result of both

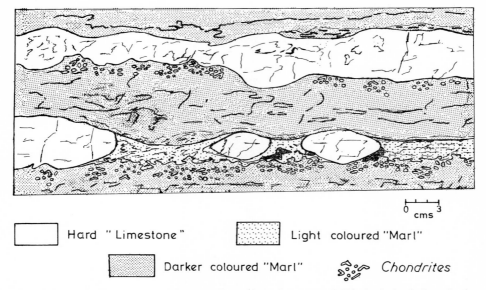

Hard "Limestone"   Light coloured "Marl"

Darker coloured "Marl"   *Chondrites*

Fig. 6. Drawing made from a photograph, to show burrow and lithological relations in the Blue Lias. Hard "limestones" pinch and swell, but pass laterally into light-coloured "marl". Both the hard "limestones" and the light "marl" are piped down into the underlying darker "marls" by *Chondrites* and other burrows. Diagenetic migration of carbonate occurred both vertically and laterally.

vertical and lateral migrations of carbonate. This has produced the characteristic nodularity so typical of some of the "limestone" units. Often a relationship such as that shown in Figure 6 may be seen, which confirms the view that in some cases at least, the diagenesis involved the exaggeration of some primary sedimentary difference. The Glamorgan Lias does not show the differences in burrow structures from cycle to cycle (Hallam 1960), and diagenetic factors are probably paramount in this sequence.

Chalk cycles. Calcareous cycles in the Lower Chalk (Cenomanian) were described by Kennedy (1967a, b). Similar cycles in the *Actinocamax plenus* Marls (Turonian) were noticed by Jefferies (1963).

The Chalk cycles closely resemble the Type II Lias cycles described here. Cycle tops are sometimes marked by scour surfaces, or abruptly overlain by argillaceous chalks rich in glauconite and phosphate, suggesting very slow sedimentation.

In other respects, the cycles differ. In the Chalk, the primary carbonate component is biogenic, consisting of coccoliths. Some of the Plenus Marls cycles are traceable over the whole of the Anglo-Paris Basin, suggesting that something more than local factors controlled the cyclicity.

4. Possible interpretations

There are a number of possible interpretations which could be applied to individual cycle types. Because of the similarities between the Lias cycles, and those from other formations, a more general interpretation may be necessary. As has been mentioned, individual units, especially those of the Plenus Marls, and several others reviewed in Hallam (1961), may be traced over considerable distances. This suggests that some broad causal mechanism may be required, and possibly on a large, rather than small or local scale.

The types of cyclicity which have been described have been common features of epeiric sea sedimentation. These seas were vast shallow epicontinental areas with probably reduced tidal and other circulations (Shaw 1964), and they would tend to be rather subtle indicators (in terms of facies shifts and sedimentation changes) of small scale volumetric changes affecting the oceans as a whole. There is also the evidence from the northern European Mesozoic basins for there having been considerable subsidence throughout the era. An interaction between sea level fluctuations (eustasy), and tectonic subsidence (epeirogenesis) was quite possibly responsible for the small scale cyclicity. From the cycles themselves and the record of changing environmental conditions within them, a number of interpretations can be made concerning the various possible controls. Features that they all show are firstly the asymmetry suggesting rapid deepening; and secondly a gradual coarsening upward with a concomitant faunal change which suggests a rather gradual shallowing, as also suggested by Duff *et al.* (1967).

It has been shown that the well known "limestone-shale" rhythms have their probable equivalents in clastic facies. To control the facies on a regional scale requires some overriding tectonic, eustatic (Hallam 1969) or local tectonic, combined with eustatic changes.

Tectonic subsidence has not occurred regularly over wide areas, as evidenced by the numerous local basins which have been recognised in the British Lias by previous workers. On the other hand, eustasy would affect all areas, but the results such eustatic change would cause would depend upon the tectonic stability of particular areas. Basically, a broad tectonic control is not considered likely, but as a local factor would have been of considerable importance.

Fluctuations at inconstant rates both of eustatic changes and tectonic subsidence could produce the cyclicity demonstrated. Gradual shallowing phases and rapid deepening phases have been suggested, and a tectonic/compactional subsidence, combined with a eustatic rise would lead to a relatively rapid deepening. If subsidence were intermittent, and eustatic rises and falls of 10 m or so were superimposed on this pattern, then small scale cycles would result like those described here.

The epeiric seas, characterised by their vast scale and overall shallowness would be subtle indicators of small scale changes, which in other strongly tidal, non-epeiric seas, would probably go unnoticed in the geological record.

Acknowledgements. I gratefully acknowledge the aid given by Drs. W. J. Kennedy, A. Hallam, W. S. McKerrow and H. G. Reading, and Mr. N. L. Banks at Oxford; Miss J. D. Newman and all those colleagues at Oxford with whom many of the problems were discussed. The work was carried out during the tenure of an N.E.R.C. grant which is acknowledged with gratitude.

References

BORDOVISKY, O. K. 1965. Sources of organic matter in marine basins. *Mar. Geol.* **3**, 5.

BRINKMANN, R. 1929. Statistich-biostratigraphische Untersuchungen an mitteljurassischen Ammoniten über Artbegriff und Stammesentwicklung. *Abh. Ges. Wiss. Gottingen. Math-Phys. Kl.* n.f. **13** (3).

CURTIS, C. D. and SPEARS, D. A. 1968. The formation of sedimentary iron minerals. *Econ. Geol.* **63**, 257.

DEAN, W. T., DONOVAN, D. T. and HOWARTH, M. K. 1961. The Liassic ammonite zones and subzones of the north-west European province. *Bull. Br. Mus. nat. Hist., Geology* **4**, 435.

DUFF, P. McL., HALLAM, A. and WALTON, E. K. 1967. *Cyclic sedimentation*. Elsevier, Amsterdam.

FOX-STRANGWAYS, C. 1892. The Jurassic rocks of Britain (Yorkshire). *Mem. geol. Surv. U.K.* **1**.

HALLAM, A. 1960. A sedimentary and faunal study of the Blue Lias of Dorset and Glamorgan. *Phil. Trans. R. Soc.* **243 B**, 1.

—— 1961. Cyclothems, transgressions and faunal changes in the Lias of North-West Europe. *Trans. Edinb. geol. Soc.* **18**, 124.

—— 1964. Origin of the Limestone shale rhythm in the Blue Lias of England. A composite theory. *J. Geol.* **72**, 157.

—— 1965. Jurassic, Cretaceous and Tertiary sediments. In *Geology of Scotland* (Ed. G. Y. Craig). Oliver and Boyd, Edinb.

—— 1967. Siderite- and calcite-bearing concretionary nodules in the Lias of Yorkshire. *Geol. Mag.* **104**, 222.

—— 1969. Tectonism and eustasy in the Jurassic. *Earth-Sci. Rev.* **5**, 45.

HÄNTZSCHEL, W., REINECK, H. E. and GADOW, S. 1968. Fazies-Untersuchungen im Hettangium von Helmstedt (Niedersachsen). *Mitt. geol. StInst. Hamb.* **37**, 5.

JEFFERIES, R. P. S. 1963. Stratigraphy of the *Actinocamax plenus* Subzone (Turonian) in the Anglo-Paris Basin. *Proc. Geol. Ass.* **74**. 1.

JØRGENSEN, C. B. 1966. *Biology of suspension feeding*. Pergamon, Oxford.

KENNEDY, W. J. 1967a. Burrows and surface traces from the Lower Chalk of Southern England. *Bull. Br. Mus. nat. Hist., Geology* **15**, 128.

—— 1967b. Field meeting at Eastbourne, Sussex, Lower Chalk sedimentation. *Proc. Geol. Ass.* **77**, 365.

LANG, W. D. 1924. The Blue Lias of the Devon and Dorset coasts. *Proc. Geol. Ass.* **35**, 169.

——, SPATH, L. F., COX, L. R. and MUIR-WOOD, H. M. 1928. The Belemnite Marls of Charmouth, a series in the Lias of the Dorset coast. *Q. J. geol. Soc. Lond.* **84**, 179.

LEE, G. W., BAILEY, E. B., BUCKMAN, S. S. and THOMAS, H. H. 1925. The pre-Tertiary geology of Mull, Loch Aline, and Oban. *Mem. geol. Surv. U.K.* (*Scotland*).

McGINITIE, G. E. 1934. The natural history of *Callianassa californiensis* (Dana). *Am. Midl. Nat.* **15**, 166.

PEACH, B. N., HORNE, J., WOODWARD, H. B., CLOUGH, C. T., HARKER, A. and WEDD, C. B. 1910. The geology of Glenelg, Lochalsh, and south-east part of Skye. *Mem. geol. Surv. U.K.* (*Scotland*).

RAAF, DE, J. F. M., READING, H. G. and WALKER, R. G. 1965. Cyclic sedimentation in the Lower Westphalian of North Devon. *Sedimentology* **4**, 1.

READ, H. H., ROSS, G. and PHEMISTER, J. 1925. The geology of the country around Golspie, Sutherlandshire (Strathfleet, Strath Brora, and Glen Loth). *Mem. geol. Surv. U.K. (Scotland)*.

REINECK, H. E., GUTMANN, W. F. and HERTWECK, G. 1967. Das Schlickgebiet südlich Helgoland als Beispiel rezenter Schelfablagerungen. *Senckenberg. leth.* **48**, 219.

SCHLOTZ, W. 1968. Über Beobachtungen zur Ichnofacies und Uber umbelagerte Rhizocorallien im Lias α Schwabens. *Neues Jb. Geol. Paläont. Mh.* **11**, 691.

SEILACHER, A. 1962. Paleontological studies on turbidite sedimentation and erosion. *J. Geol.* **70**, 227.

—— 1967. The bathymetry of trace fossils. *Mar. Geol.* **5**, 413.

SHAW, A. B. 1964. *Time in Stratigraphy*. McGraw-Hill, New York.

SIMPSON, S. 1957. On the trace fossil *Chondrites Q. J. geol. Soc. Lond.* **112**, 475.

STANLEY, S. M. 1968. Post-Paleozoic radiation of infaunal bivalve mollusca—a consequence of mantle fusion and siphon formation. *J. Paleont.* **42**, 214.

TATE, R. S. and BLAKE, J. F. 1876. *The Yorkshire Lias*. Van Voorst, London.

YONGE, C. M. 1939. The Protobranchiate mollusca: a functional interpretation of their structure and evolution. *Phil. Trans. R. Soc.* **230 B**, 79.

—— 1953a. The monomyarian condition in the Lamellibranchia. *Trans. R. Soc. Edinb.* **62**, 443.

—— 1953b. Form and habit in *Pinna carnea* (Gmelin) *Phil. Trans. R. Soc.* **237 B**, 335.

B. W. Sellwood, Department of Geology, The University, Parks Road, Oxford OX1 3PR, U.K.

Notes on *Zoophycos* and *Spirophyton*

S. Simpson

The ichnogenus *Zoophycos* as it has been understood by Häntzschel (*Treatise on Invertebrate Paleontology*) consists of two disparate elements. The genus is redefined so as to exclude the helical spiral forms for which the name *Spirophyton* is revived. New material yielding additional morphological detail allows the formulation of a hypothesis as to the ethological process involved in its formation. It is shown that an essential feature of the fossil is its constitution, in part, of selectively concentrated clastic grains when present in an arenite or calcarenite. The lateral growth of the fossil does not take place by the lateral displacement of a tunnel as in such spreitenbauten as *Diplocraterion*, but by successive branching probings along nearly parallel lines. The probing process suggests a relationship to *Chondrites* and the existence of an intermediate form in *Lophoctenium* is commented on. A possible connection with *Chomatichnus* is discussed. The mode of occurrence in British examples suggests a vagile rather than a sedentary form and the normal facies it occurs in is that of a typical shelf-sea environment.

1. Introduction

Although the spirally wound and spirally striated fossils with which this paper is concerned are widespread, and have been familiar for a long time, progress in understanding them has been slow. In spite of a number of recent papers on them it is clear that much remains to be discovered. This is in part because the fossil is so large that commonly only fragments are collected. Moreover collectors in the past have usually not understood the general form of the fossil and have so failed to observe it properly in the field before collecting. Further advance will only come from much more study of specimens *in situ*.

The purpose of this paper, then, is not to attempt prematurely a comprehensive monograph of the known material. Nor will any account of the extensive literature on *Zoophycos* and related fossils be attempted; a good lead into the literature can be found in Taylor (1967). Instead notes will be made on a number of particular aspects of *Zoophycos* and a hypothesis to explain the origin of the fossil, taking into account particularly the detailed structure of major and minor lamellae discovered by Taylor, will be proposed. It is to be hoped that by directing attention to these particular matters some useful progress may be stimulated.

I wish to express my gratitude to Dr. B. J. Taylor for letting me see his interesting *Zoophycos* material from the Antarctic. It is the remarkable mode of preservation of this material that has revealed details not previously observed.

2. Nomenclature

The name *Zoophycos* Massalongo 1855 was the first of a number of names to be published for what we now recognise to be one of a distinctive group of trace fossils consisting of a spreite which is in some degree spirally organised.

While it is clear that there are a number of junior synonyms of *Zoophycos*, yet it is also true that some of the fossils that have been called *Zoophycos* can be distinguished as separate ichnogenera. At one extreme Häntzschel (1962) in the *Treatise on Invertebrate Paleontology* lumps all these forms together under *Zoophycos*, on the other Bischoff (1968) would restrict the name to forms close to *Z. brianteus* (Villa).

One of the names that has been included in the synonymy of *Zoophycos* is *Spirophyton* (Hall 1863). This name was proposed by Hall, in ignorance of the European Cretaceous *Zoophycos*, for a variety of forms (including some which had long been familiar as *Fucoides cauda galli*) that occur at a number of horizons in the Devonian of the eastern United States. Kayser (1872) recognised forms in the German Devonian resembling one of Hall's species, *Spirophyton typus*, and provided a reconstruction (inverted) of the Eifel material under the name *Spirophyton eifelense*. This fossil is widespread in the Lower Devonian of Europe where the Rhenish facies is developed. It is also common in the Devonian of the Sahara. In all probability it is confined to the Devonian. Because it is quite distinctive and separable from *Zoophycos* it is proposed that the name *Spirophyton* should be retained in a restricted sense for forms like *S. eifelense*. The typical *cauda galli* fossils of the Devonian and Carboniferous, which have often been called *Spirophyton* following Hall, cannot be distinguished from *Zoophycos* of the Mesozoic or Tertiary.

3. Preservation

While the structure of most kinds of trace fossils is revealed by the deformation of pre-existing surfaces bounding sediments of different composition, in the case of *Zoophycos* the structure is revealed by the contrast between the composition of the sediment of the enclosing stratum and the composition of a material derived from that sediment by a special sorting activity of the organism. This has been demonstrated (Donaldson and Simpson 1962) in material from a bioclastic limestone from the Lower Carboniferous of Lancashire, and is familiar to the author in other Lower Carboniferous limestones.

In other cases the fossil is developed, in the sense in which a photographic film is developed, by subsequent chemical alteration during diagenesis or early metamorphism. A striking example of this latter effect is provided by the low grade alteration of the sediments yielding *Zoophycos* in the Aptian of Alexander Island described by Taylor (1967). In these rocks which are affected by the quartz-prehenite stage of the prehenite-pumpellyite metagreywacke facies and the laumontite stage of the zeolite facies, the sorted sediment consists of a white material which is totally absent from the dark rock of the containing strata.

Diagenetic development is exhibited by differential dolomitization in specimens from the Carboniferous limestone of South Wales in which the sorted material, being of coarser grain than the surrounding sediment, has been less dolomitized and has therefore been more readily dissolved away during weathering.

Another example is provided by the replacement of chalk by flint nodules which results in showing up parts of *Zoophycos* specimens replaced by flint while the part remaining in the Chalk is invisible. This has been described by Voigt and Häntzschel (1956).

4. Morphology

In the following account an attempt is made to generalise the morphology of the forms which are near to *Z. brianteus* from the Cretaceous and Eocene as well as those from the Devonian, Carboniferous and Permian. The fossil is constituted of three parts as first noted by Sarle (1906): (i) the lamina ("plate" of Sarle), which has the structure of a spreite. (ii) the lamellae, which are contained within the lamina and which may be differentiated into major and minor; and (iii) the tunnel, which consists of an axial and a marginal part ("marginal cylinder" of Sarle).

An additional, fourth part may well be a mound of faecal castings at the top of which is the opening of the axial tunnel. This was suggested by the author and D. Donaldson (Donaldson and Simpson 1962).

4a. The lamina

This has the form of a sheet wound in a helicoid spiral, like a spiral staircase, round an axis which is normal to the bedding. At the same time the lamina slopes outwards from the axis so that a single volution has the form of a cone. The amount of this slope varies greatly within a single specimen, increasing steadily either from the top or from the bottom. Very little is known about the form of complete specimens because normally only that part of the whole which has a low transverse slope, generally about one whorl, is observed or collected.

Most specimens seen tend to be almost flat, for not only do they lack transverse slope, but the spiral is of very low pitch and often difficult to detect. The outline of the lamina in such specimens is often roughly circular, but there is much variation. Figure 1 illustrates some common variants. Arcuate outlines such as Figure 1b are familiar as *cauda galli*. They are obviously incomplete and resemble isolated lobes of a form such as Figure 1c. There is much variation in the relative size and number of the lobes from specimens such as Figure 1c, with highly isolated tongue-like lobes, to such as Figure 1d with more numerous, less isolate lobes, or Figure 1e with rather few broadly based lobes.

To a considerable extent the various types of outline seem to characterise certain horizons, but this is probably a result of different modes of preservation. Both Seilacher (1967) and Bischoff (1968) have described the way in which some specimens have the early whorls highly lobate, but the later whorls more nearly circular in outline.

4b. The lamellae

General. The relation of the lamellae to the lamina is like that of the slats of a Venetian blind to the blind as a whole. The lamellae are, however, lunate in cross-section, as shown in Figure 2. It will be convenient to refer to the concave side of a lamella as its *front* surface and to the convex side as its *back* surface.

Further the lamellae are not parallel, but radiating from the axis of the lamina; and not straight, but swept into a curve. This curve, seen in tangential sections of the lamina, is convex forwards (i.e. to the front side). The general pattern of the lamellae in the plane of the lamina is thus spiral, like the hair on the crown of the head. If the lamina as a whole is wound right-handedly the lamellae will constitute a left-hand spiral and *vice versa*.

Major and minor lamellae. The lamellae never cross one another. But they may branch, and Lessertisseur (1955 p. 73) has referred to "une fine reticulation plus ou moins regulière" which he illustrates (*idem* pl. 10 fig. 5, 6) and which is in fact due to branching. This branching is very clearly displayed in the material described by Taylor (1967) and is also evident in specimens from the Carboniferous limestone

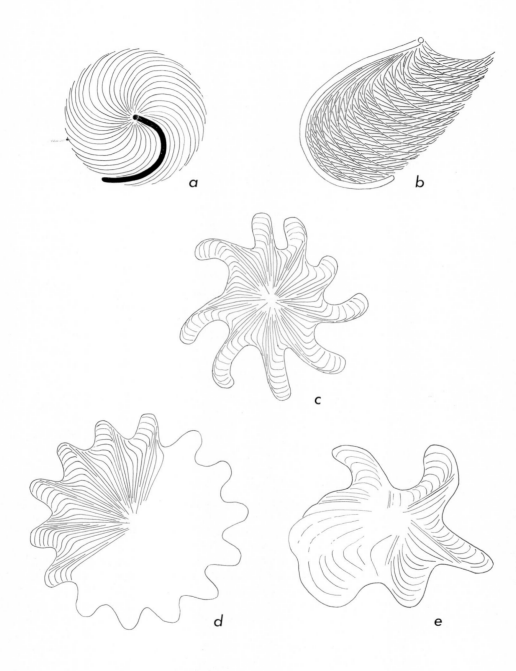

Fig. 1. Various shapes taken by the outline of the lamina.   a   Circular as in *Spirophyton*;
b   Arcuate. *Cauda-galli*;   c Lobed. Based on figure in Seilacher (1967);   d   Numerous
lobes. Based on figure in Seilacher (1967);   e   Few lobes. Based on Venzo (1951 fig. 8).

Fig. 2. Cross-section of the lamina. Black, undisturbed sediment; white, sorted grains constituting lamellae.

(Exeter University collection specimens 100 and 101.) The branches arise from the front surface of the main (major) lamellae and constitute minor lamellae. These minor lamellae are also lunate in section. They branch off at rather an acute angle in an inward direction (i.e. towards the axis) and persist until they make contact with the next major lamella. They do not fuse with this but stop up short on making contact (see Fig. 3).

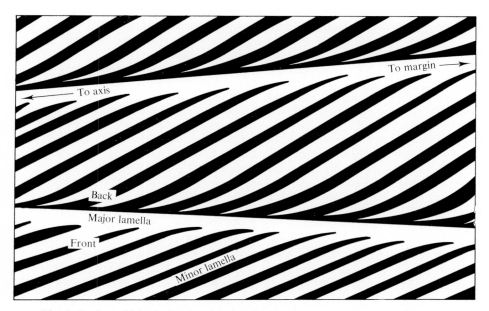

Fig. 3. Section within the lamina showing the course of major and minor lamellae.

The specimen illustrated by Taylor (1967 fig. 3, 7f) clearly shows (as noted by Taylor) how the space between the two major lamellae is filled in with a set of minor lamellae which are separated from one another by narrow screens of normal, unworked sediment. In this specimen the total number of minor lamellae between two major ones is greater than 20, and at any one point eight or nine may be present.

The degree of differentiation of the lamellae into major and minor is a feature of variable development as between specimens from the same horizon or locality. The thickness of the minor lamellae in comparison with that of the major lamellae is inversely proportional to their number per major lamella. This is because the major lamellae are in fact built up by the fusion of minor lamellae. It would appear that in some cases only a few minor lamellae are associated with each major lamella. In such cases the size difference is not very marked, the branching angle is more acute and the presence of minor lamellae is easily overlooked. When the number of minor lamellae is very great they are very thin, and if preservation is not very good they are in this case also easily overlooked.

The lamellae and lobes. In unlobed forms the backward curvature of the lamellae when traced outwards from the axis may constitute a more or less circular arc (see Fig. 1a). Where lobes are present the successive lamellae radiate in fairly straight lines from the axis before swinging backwards in a rather tight curve. In successive lamellae the straight portion increases in length while the curved portion remains of fairly constant size. Thus a tongue-shaped lobe originates (see Fig. 1c). A rather sudden change affects the front portion of the lobe. The lamellae become straight throughout their length and at the same time they become shorter. Thus each lobe is composed of two parts, a rearward part in which the lamellae are curved and a forward part in which they are straight. In some specimens, e.g. that figured by Venzo (1951 fig. 8) a thick rib-like lamella separates the two parts. The next lobe is commenced by the initiation of a forward curve or bulge of the lamellae which grows progressively more marked.

4c. The axial and marginal tunnel

This is a cylindrical structure with diameter equal to the thickness of the lamina, which, descending perpendicular to the bedding, constitutes the axis of the spiral lamina. At the base it bends through a large angle and continues roughly in the bedding, running parallel with the lamellae and bounding the lamina on its forward and part of its lateral edge. This relationship is illustrated in Figure 1b. In some material, e.g. that described by Bischoff (1968), the tunnel continues further along the periphery of the lamina for its whole length, winding round the lobes of the initial, lobate, part of the whole structure. So, too, Seilacher (1967) considers that the tunnel opens to the sediment surface at both ends. It must be said, however, that this does not appear to be a necessary feature and is not observed in most specimens. On the other hand a tunnel extending around the periphery for about half a volution of the lamina is normally present.

4d. *Chomatichnus*

This trace fossil was described and named (Donaldson and Simpson 1962) from material occurring on the upper surface of two limestone beds of Lower Carboniferous age at Wegber Quarry in Lancashire. It consists of a mound of faecal castings thrown up from a vertical burrow and having a close superficial resemblance to the piles of castings thrown up by the contemporary *Arenicola marina*. It was suggested that the fossil might be associated with the *Zoophycos* (referred to as "*cauda galli*") occurring within both of the limestone beds concerned. Although no further evidence has been obtained it seems certain now that *Chomatichnus* is the product of the *Zoophycos* animal and that the axial tunnel of *Zoophycos* is the continuation of the *Chomatichnus* burrow in depth. The lining of the *Chomatichnus* burrow may well be the continuation of the packing of "special" sediment which constitutes the lamellae of *Zoophycos*.

5. Morphology of *Spirophyton*

The structure of *Spirophyton* has been well described by Antun (1950). It has in common with *Zoophycos* a spirally wound lamina which is composed of lamellae in a similar way. It differs from *Zoophycos* in having a strictly circular outline to the lamina with no tendency to lobation, and a considerably smaller size. Its characteristic feature, however, is that the lamina does not slope outwards from the axis to the periphery. It does start to slope outwards from the axis but soon flattens and is then flexed upwards to the margin. The resulting cross-section is a smooth, nearly semi-circular curve, concave upwards.

6. Ethological interpretation

There are probably a number of quite distinct kinds of spreite. Certainly that of *Diplocraterion* (Goldring 1962) is entirely distinct from that of *Zoophycos*. The spreite of *Diplocraterion* is produced during the continuous migration of the transverse portion of the U-burrow. Presumably the sediment is entirely disaggregated on the leading side of the burrow and transferred to the trailing side where it is redeposited.

The spreite of *Zoophycos* on the other hand is the product of a discontinuous process. If it were a continuous process the result would not be a series of separate lamellae of worked sediment but a continuous sheet. The reason for the difference is that the *Zoophycos* organism was concerned not merely with the lateral displacement of the burrow but was engaged in feeding on the sediment. The lamella of sorted large grains constitutes only a small part of the volume of sediment moved in the driving of a tunnel: the bulk of the material was presumably ingested and voided at the surface. The branching pattern of the lamellae makes it quite evident that what is involved is not the lateral displacement of a single burrow, but the successive driving of a series of tunnels, one after the other. The screens of unworked sediment separating the lamellae of worked-over material are a necessary consequence of the organism's mode of working. It does not feed from one side of a pre-existing tunnel but feeds at the end of a tunnel as it is driven forward within the sediment.

The physical pattern of the lamellae described in section 5 is explicable in terms of a pattern (program) of behaviour as follows. A tunnel is driven radially outwards from the axis to the periphery. The organism withdraws to the axis and then commences to tunnel outwards again, but this time in a direction making an angle with the last. The tunnel is extended, but with a backward curvature so that contact is soon made with the first tunnel. The organism withdraws again, but only partially, remaining in occupation of the proximal portion of the second tunnel. It then extends again in the straight line of this proximal portion but soon diverges to parallel the foregoing lateral excursion. Contact is made with the first tunnel and the process is repeated: withdrawal, extension of the radial proximal portion, backward divergence to make contact with the first tunnel. The extension in the direction of the initial radial portions of the second tunnel continues until it reaches the length of the first tunnel. This completes an element of the pattern and the full cycle is then repeated by the initiation of a new radial tunnel making an angle with the last.

This interpretation is based on the relation between the major and minor lamellae. The major lamellae correspond with the radial tunnels and the minor lamellae with the backwardly diverging serial tunnels which lie between them. A major lamella results from the infilling of the last formed radial tunnel by the confluence of successive minor lamellae in it. This implies that the organism depositing a minor lamella on reaching the radial tunnel advances into it for a short distance before withdrawing to commence the next serial tunnel (see Fig. 4).

In order that successive tunnellings should be kept in touch, and so as to avoid omission of areas from exploitation, it would appear that the organism advanced

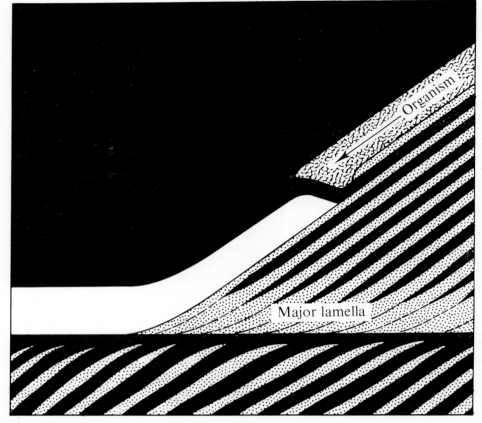

Fig. 4. Diagram to explain hypothetical mode of working. White, open tunnel; black, sediment (unworked); dotted, lamellae.

partly within the last-formed tunnel and partly outside it. As the head advanced it would displace, into the tunnel it was following, a screen of sediment which its more posterior part would pack against the tunnel wall. Subsequently selected grains rejected in the feeding proccesses would also be packed against the back side of the tunnel to form a minor lamella.

The essence of the *Zoophycos* tunnelling programme is that it solves the problem of the complete exploitation of a volume of sediment within a definite radius by working successive sectors limited by radial lines to which the major lamellae correspond. The space between the diverging radii is worked by successive probings (to which the minor lamellae correspond) unilaterally branching off the leading radial tunnel and terminating against the rearward radial tunnel. This is, however, very much the pattern of formation of the lobes of lobate examples described on page 510. Thus, for instance, the broad ribs which separate the lobes in the specimen figured by Venzo (1951) may be considered to be major lamellae, and all the curving traces between them, minor lamellae.

Looked at in this way the difference between lobate and non-lobate laminae is determined by the magnitude of the angle between successive major lamellae. If this angle is large, say of the order of 60°, as in the specimen figured by Venzo, there will be about six lobes in a volution. If the angle is about 30° then about 12 lobes will be present (e.g. a form figured by Seilacher 1967), and the outline of the lamina will not be very obviously lobate. With smaller angles still the margin of the lamina will be entire.

7. Diagnoses

It is now possible to summarise the account of the ethology deduced in section 6 to provide diagnoses of the ichnogenera *Zoophycos* and *Spirophyton*.

Zoophycos: trace fossils resulting from the driving of a series of tunnels of constant diameter from the bottom of a vertical shaft which descends from the sediment-water interface. These tunnels are of two kinds: (i) radial composite tunnels, and (ii) simple oblique tunnels. The radial tunnels descend at an angle to the horizontal, each successive one making a definite lateral angle with the last. The space between one radial tunnel and the next is worked by successive oblique tunnels, the radial proximal portions of which come to constitute the later radial tunnel while the distal oblique portions diverge backwards to make contact with the earlier radial tunnel. At the same time the vertical shaft is progressively deepened so that the whole system acquires the form of a conical spire of diameter up to 60 cm.

Spirophyton: like *Zoophycos* but radial tunnels not descending outwards for their full length. Instead they are curved upwards towards their ends. Much smaller than *Zoophycos*: diameter up to 8 cm.

8. Discussion

Its possession of a spreite has tended in the past to obscure the fact that *Zoophycos* has much in common with a form such as *Chondrites*. Both consist of radiating and descending tunnel systems with lateral branching which achieve complete coverage of the potential area of exploitation by working systematically backwards to the limit of the area already covered at any given stage. In both too the tunnel system may change its attitude to become almost parallel with the bedding, presumably in order to work a stratum particularly rich in nutriment. In both forms the tunnels maintain a quite constant diameter throughout their length and branches diverge at a constant angle.

It was argued in the case of *Chondrites* (Simpson 1957) that the regularity of the tunnel pattern and the integration of the whole implied that the organism was not an errant animal, of small size relative to the dimensions of the whole tunnel system, but a large sedentary animal which drove the tunnels by means of an extensible proboscis. If, however, the *Zoophycos* organism operated in a similar way to the *Chondrites* animal, then it too must have been large and sedentary. On the other hand, if the *Chomatichnus* mound is the termination of the *Zoophycos* axial tunnel there is no room for a large body.

It must be admitted that the very uniform tunnel diameter is a character more easily understood, if produced by an organism resembling *Arenicola,* than by a sipunculoid. What still remains a difficulty however is that an errant form with relative dimensions like *Arenicola* should (*a*) be restricted in the length of its lateral tunnelling, and (*b*) be able to execute a pattern of tunnelling of such geometrical regularity.

The discovery by Häntzschel (1960) and Bischoff (1968) of small ovoid impressions on the tunnel walls of *Zoophycos* is of great interest in connection with the comparison with *Chondrites*. The appearance of these impressions as illustrated by Bischoff (1968 pl. 180 fig. 1) is virtually identical with the well-known impressions on the tunnel walls of *Chondrites granulatus* that the writer has discussed (Simpson 1957).

A feature which contradicts an affinity between *Chondrites* and *Zoophycos* is the alleged existence of a continuation of the marginal tunnel around the entire periphery of the lamina of *Zoophycos*. This would seem to imply an opening at the surface at both ends of the tunnel (Seilacher 1967) and would suggest an affinity with forms such as *Diplocraterion*. It would rule out any significant relationship with *Chondrites* which existed successfully without any second connection with the surface, and whose branches are blind. A solution of this contradiction must await further research.

References

ANTUN, P. 1950. Sur les *Spirophyton* de l'Emsien de L'Oesling. *Annls Soc. geol. Belg.* **73**, 241.

BISCHOFF, B. 1968. *Zoophycos*, a polychete annelid, Eocene of Greece. *J. Paleont.* **42**, 1439.

DONALDSON, D. and SIMPSON, S. 1962. *Chomatichnus*, a new ichnogenus, and other trace fossils of Wegber Quarry. *Lpool Manchr geol. J.* **3**, 73.

GOLDRING, R. 1962. The trace fossils of the Baggy Beds (Upper Devonian) of North Devon, England. *Paläont. Z.* **36**, 232.

HALL, J. 1863. Contributions to palaeontology. *Ann. Rep. New York St. Cab.,* **16**, App. D.

HÄNTZSCHEL, W. 1960. Spreitenbauten (*Zoophycos* Massal.) im Septarienton Nordwest-Deutschlands. *Mitt. geol. StInst. Hamb.* **29**, 95.

—— 1962. Trace fossils and problematica. In *Treatise on invertebrate paleontology* (Ed. R. C. Moore). Geol. Soc. Am., New York and Univ. of Kansas Press, Lawrence. Part W, p. W177.

KAYSER, E. 1872. Neue Fossilien aus dem Rheinischen Devon. *Z. dt. geol. Ges.* **24**, 691.

LESSERTISSEUR, J. 1955. Traces fossiles d'activité animale et leur signification paléobiologique. *Mem. Soc. géol. Fr.* n.s. **74**.

MASSALONGO, A. B. 1855. *Zoophycos:* novum genus plantarum fossilium. *Studii Palaeontologici* **5** (2), 43.

SARLE, C. J. 1906. Preliminary note on the nature of *Taonurus*. *Proc. Rochester Acad. Sci.* **4**, 211.

SEILACHER, A. 1967. Fossil behaviour. *Scientific American* **217** (2), 72.

SIMPSON, S. 1957. On the trace fossil *Chondrites*. *Q. J. geol. Soc. Lond.* **112**, 475.

TAYLOR, B. J. 1967. Trace fossils from the Fossil Bluff Series of Alexander Island. *Br. Antarct. Surv. Bull.* **13**, 1.

VENZO, S. 1951. Ammoniti e vegetale Albiano Cenomaniani nel flysch del Bergamasco occidentali. *Atti Soc. ital. Sci. nat.* **40**, 175.

VOIGT, E. and HÄNTZSCHEL, W. 1956. Die grauen Bänder in der Schreibkreide Nordwest-Deutschlands und ihre Deutung als Lebensspuren. *Mitt. geol. StInst. Hamb.* **25**, 104.

S. Simpson, Department of Geology, The University, Exeter, U.K.

Traces and significance of marine rock borers

J. E. Warme

Marine rock borers are under investigation on the seafloor and on the walls of submarine canyons off southern California. All submarine exposures of sedimentary rocks that have been studied are bored to some degree, but generally the most intensely attacked rocks are soft, fine-grained, and calcareous.

A sequence of excavation results in destruction of the rocks. Initial borers are pholadid bivalves and *Lithophaga*, which produce auger-like borings at all angles to exposed rock surfaces, and polychaete annelids and sipunculids, which excavate sinuous passageways concentrated along bedding planes. Abandoned borings are modified and deepened by nestling bivalves, gastropods, polychaetes, arthropods, and several other taxonomic groups. In advanced stages the borings become interconnected to form a network of passageways extending one to several decimetres into the rock. Tunnels thus formed exhibit a variety of geometries, diameters (1–30 mm), and wall sculptures, and contain a diverse fauna. At least 20 species are clearly borers, and it is probable that many other species also participate.

The activity of these borers not only leaves evidence of their life habits, but also results in significant submarine erosion and provides detritus for the local sedimentary regime.

1. Introduction

Taxa belonging to several different animal phyla attack rock outcrops in the marine environment. Clapp and Kenk (1963) summarize the literature on marine rock borers, and the symposium volume edited by Carriker *et al.* (1969) treats marine borers that penetrate calcareous substrates such as shell and limestone. Little information is available on marine animals which bore or otherwise excavate terrigenous sedimentary rocks, or igneous and metamorphic rocks.

Submarine outcrops of sedimentary rocks were studied near San Diego in southern California. Intertidal outcrops of Cretaceous sandstones and mudstones were collected at Bird Rock, a landmark in La Jolla, adjoining the north end of San Diego. A variety of Eocene sedimentary rocks were collected at the north end of Del Mar beach, 15 km north of La Jolla. Subtidal outcrops were sampled near Scripps Institution of Oceanography in La Jolla: Cretaceous sandstones and mudstones were from an area offshore between Point La Jolla and La Jolla Submarine Canyon, at depths of 10 to 30 m; Eocene sandstones and mudstones were collected in Scripps Submarine Canyon at depths from 15 to 40 m (for locations, see Warme and Marshall 1969 fig. 1).

The purpose of this paper is to document the more common borers present, to describe their borings, and to report the kinds of rocks and water depths in which these borings occur. This is part of a larger study of the borers and faunal communities associated with submarine outcrops of clastic terrigenous rocks of the Pacific Coast.

A great variety of borings are present in the study area. Pholadid and mytilid bivalves, annelids, and sipunculids are the most prominent borers, and attack

rocks exposed at all depths thus far investigated. The borings are of palaeontological interest because many resemble those that mark unconformities and
"hardgrounds" in the fossil record. Some systems of borings also possess the
basic geometry and detailed morphology of trace fossils commonly regarded as
originating in soft, unconsolidated sediments.

Many borers require a substrate of calcium carbonate in order to penetrate.
The amount of carbonate necessary for an animal to bore, however, appears to
differ among taxa. In order to investigate the range of lithologies that are
inhabited by different taxa, both the properties of the rocks and the boring fauna
are being studied.

2. Methods

Intertidal samples were collected at low tide, using hammer and chisel to acquire
rock specimens. Subtidal samples were collected *in situ* with the aid of SCUBA.
Plastic or canvas bags were used to carry the smaller samples to the surface,
and "bubble bags" to lift heavier rocks. The latter resemble parachutes, which
are filled with air underwater and used to raise objects by flotation. Rocks weighing
up to 50 kg were recovered with this method.

Some rock samples were kept in aquaria for observation and recovery of live
borers. Other samples were frozen at about $-20°$ C in an attempt to fix the borers
in their proper positions in the rocks. Samples were then thawed in a 5 per cent
solution of formaldehyde to preserve the fauna, and were shipped from La Jolla
to Houston for laboratory study.

The rocks were investigated in thin sections, and carbonate and carbon from
"organic matter" determined by the induction furnace method (carbon oxidized,
carbon dioxide collected and measured in a gas-operated burette).

Most samples were radiographed prior to dismantling in order to determine
where the excavations lie and to avoid indiscriminate destruction of the borings
(see Figures). Stereo X-ray radiography is useful to see the three-dimensional
relationships between borings inside the rocks.

3. Rock borers and their borings

Collections of bored rocks contain many species belonging to several different
invertebrate phyla. Commonly it is difficult to determine which animals are responsible for the borings (primary borers), and which ones modify abandoned
boring by their subsequent occupation or merely reside in ready-made borings
(nestlers). Although the taxa boring into these rocks are well described, the
geometry, scale, and extent of their excavations are only poorly known.

Three basic kinds of primary borings have been identified; however, a formal
classification of borings is not proposed herein:

(i) Auger-like and piercement borings, with straight or slightly curved axes e.g.
bivalves, some sipunculids.

(ii) Slot-shaped borings, U-shaped tubes, or extended U-tubes; may become
sinuous and/or deviate from the original plane of boring with development,
resembling more-or-less parallel double tracks with filled loose material between
e.g. some polychaetes and (?) crustaceans.

(iii) Sinuous borings; may be entirely or largely confined to a single plane
e.g. sipunculids, polychaetes, and (?) crustaceans.

3a. Bivalves

At least 7 species of bivalves are primary borers in the rocks studied. These include 5 species in the Family Pholadidae, which bore mainly by mechanical means (see Turner 1954; 1955), and two species in the Mytilidae which bore mainly by chemical means and generally require a calcareous substrate (Yonge 1955). At least 7 additional bivalve genera nestle in borings vacated by mortality of the original occupants (Keen 1963 p. 104) and modify these to varying degrees.

Pholadids recovered thus far are dominated by *Penitella penita* Conrad and *Nettastomella rostrata* Valenciennes (genus *Netastoma* Carpenter of Keen 1963 p. 93), both of which occur from the intertidal zone to depths of at least 40 m. The shells of both species have a wide anterior gape, through which a strong foot extends to make contact with the substrate. Although the exact method of boring certainly differs between species of pholadids, they bore chiefly by pushing their shells against the substrate with the foot and rocking or rotating, thus scraping the substrate.

P. penita (Pl. 1a) secretes a callum that wholly or partially seals the pedal gape upon reaching adulthood (Turner 1955). It bores faster and deeper into softer mudstones than into sandstones (Evans 1968a). The shells reach a length of 9 to 10 cm and can bore at least twice this distance into the rock. The borings rarely intersect, even under crowded conditions, and can curve and turn to avoid another boring, an obstacle, or to keep from boring completely through small pieces of substrate or narrow ledges into which they penetrate. Evans (1967; 1968a, b) has discussed aspects of the ecology and geological significance of *P. penita*.

Nettastomella rostrata is a diminutive pholadid (Pl. 1c, 3a). The shells grow to a length of about 12 mm in addition to a calcareous siphonoplax extending 8 to 10 mm from the posterior margin of the shell towards the opening of the boring (Turner 1955 p. 144). This species can be very abundant, and penetrate 2 to 3 cm into the rock. *N. rostrata* borings are club-shaped, and usually curve gently into the substrate. If the substrate is a fragment or thin slab of rock the borings may curve sharply, and the siphonoplax may then be strongly inflected towards the surface opening. The siphonoplax is calcareous, inflexible, and firmly attached to the shell, and when curved prohibits rotation of the animal. It is probably secreted only after the bulk of the boring is completed.

Because some pholadid borings of large diameter (2 to 3 cm) are heart-shaped in cross-section, it is likely that they do not always rotate when boring. Penetration can also be accomplished by up- and down-movements in combination with a scissors-like motion from alternate expansion of the anterior and posterior margins of the shell, using the maximum diameter (from umbos to ventral margin) as a fulcrum (Turner 1954 p. 6).

The mytilids *Lithophaga plumula* Hanley and *Adula californiensis* Philippi are primarily chemical borers, removing loosened substrate with a ciliary mucus and mantle cavity currents (Yonge 1955). These species commonly bore into limestone, and require some measure of carbonate in order to penetrate (Hodgkin 1962). *A. californiensis* was collected in only one sample, a mudstone from 20 m depth in Scripps Submarine Canyon (Pl. 3). Although the animals were abundant, the rock contained only 4·2 per cent calcium carbonate, and both *Adula* and *Lithophaga* were present. *Adula* does not rotate in its boring, thus leaving a heart-shaped cross-section, and those in this sample were oriented with the longest axis of the shell and boring in a vertical position (Pl. 3a). *Lithophaga* borings with heart-shaped cross-section have not been observed, although impressions of the anterior end of the valves may be separated by a median ridge at the head of their borings (Yonge 1955).

PLATE 1

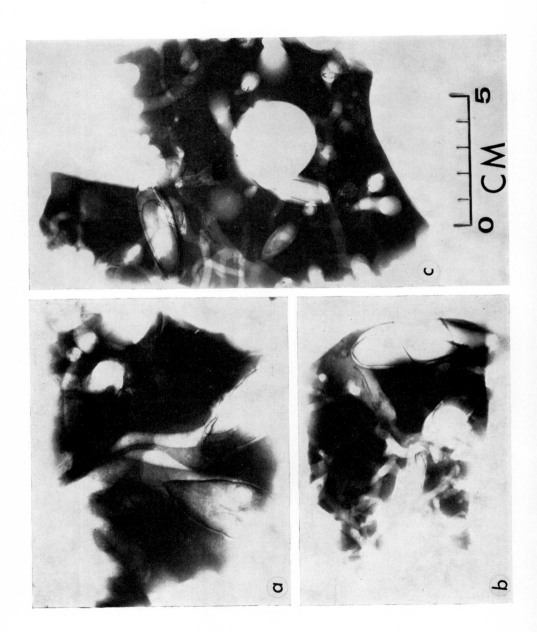

Lithophaga plumula constructs a loose fitting boring (Pl. 1b, c, 3a). It has a measure of anterior-posterior movement by pulling on byssal threads fixed to the side of the boring. When excavating it moves to the anterior end of the boring and appresses an extended part of the mantle that chemically dissolves or loosens the calcareous components of the substrate (Yonge 1955). *L. plumula* also moves anteriorly when feeding. In this position it can open its valves and extend the siphons to the posterior and out of the opening. If disturbed, the animal first moves slightly more to the anterior, retracts the siphons completely within the shell, and then moves to the posterior until the blade-like "posterior prolongations" (Turner and Boss 1962 p. 4) of the valves protrude slightly from the boring and tightly seal it from predators or other disturbance.

L. plumula borings are lined with a laminated calcareous sheath (Pl. 1b, c, 2, 3). It is first secreted just inside the opening of the boring, but eventually lines the whole interior and may protrude outward from the aperture where the extended siphons are situated during feeding. The sheath is usually absent or only partially developed in small specimens, and completed after individuals reach full size. In many specimens collected off California, the sheath is secreted along one side of the boring only. This occurs if the boring is intersected by another borer, either *Lithophaga* or other species, commonly polychaetes, and represents a change in position of the axis of boring. The animal secretes the sheath near the disturbance and excavates on the opposite side of the boring, resulting in a lateral shift of the axis of boring (Pl. 3a).

3b. Polychaete annelids

At least 20 species of polychaetes are significant borers on the Pacific Coast, and the actual number may be two or three times that many (T. Scanland 1969, personal communication). The excavating activities of spionids such as *Polydora* and *Boccardia* are well known. *Polydora* constructs a U-shaped boring, filling the space between the limbs of the "U" with material excavated from the sides and base, as described by Boekschoten (1966) and many others.

The borings of *Boccardia uncata* Berkeley are common along bedding planes, which provide a zone of weakness that is more easily penetrated than across the bedding. *B. uncata* makes a U-shaped boring, but with development it becomes sinuous, more-or-less parallel tracks that wander along bedding planes (Pl. 3b). *Boccardia* also constructs burrows in abandoned bivalve borings by filling the void with sediment, in which it builds an irregularly coiled tube (Pl. 1c, 3a).

Plate 1

a Contact print of radiograph of Eocene sandstone from lower intertidal zone at the north end of Del Mar beach, southern California. The holes are borings of *Penitella penita*. Two shells of this species are visible within slightly curved borings at the bottom; they tightly fit their borings. Specimen on the left has a well developed chitinous siphonplax flaring from the posterior end of the shell. Rock fragment is 9 × 12 cm; maximum thickness 6 cm (JW-69-12).

b Radiograph print of mudstone from Scripps Submarine Canyon, depth 35 m. Sample is 8 × 10 × 2 cm (JW-69-22). Sinuous borings on left yielded 15 sipunculids, one nereid, and countless other small annelids. Two *Lithophaga plumula* shells and sheaths are visible at right and bottom centre.

c Radiograph of sample shown in Plate 2.

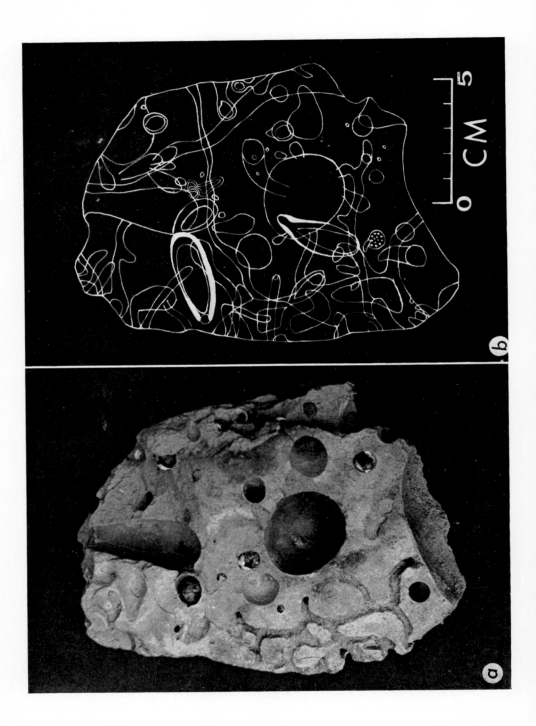

PLATE 2

Another boring polychaete that makes a modified U-shaped boring is the capitellid *Dasybranchus glabrus*. This is a large species, constructing a boring of wandering parallel tracks that may extend 20 cm or more into the rock. *D. glabrus* excavates at the sides and base of its boring similar to *Polydora*, moving the material to the central filling between the limbs (Pl. 4), but on a much larger scale. *D. glabrus* borings may exhibit knobbly indentations on the walls, resembling sites where the animal repeatedly placed parapodia when moving. The commensal polinoid *Lepidasthenia gigas* was living with almost every *D. glabrus* collected. *D. glabrus* borings are similar to some examples of the trace fossil *Rhizocorallium*, considered to be formed in unconsolidated sediments (Häntzschel 1962 p. W207). The central filling between the limbs of the boring is comprised of material derived from the host rocks, and if collected as a fossil it would be difficult, based on morphology alone, to determine if the excavation was made in soft sediment or consolidated rock.

Preliminary investigation shows that several other species of polychaetes are present in rather irregular, sinuous borings that may extend several decimetres into the rock. Some of these are shown in Plate 1c.

3c. Sipunculids

Two kinds of sipunculid borings have been identified (Pl. 1b). One is a club-shaped boring, with only one opening and occupied by a single individual. These are difficult to separate from pholadid borings in which the shell has been removed, and are similar to sipunculid borings figured by Rice (1969 p. 806). The other is a sinuous, irregular boring with multiple branches, more than one opening to the surface, and commonly occupied by two or more individuals, which are probably vagrant in the system of excavations. These are similar to the excavations of some polychaetes, with which they are commonly associated.

3d. Crustaceans

Samples of excavated rocks commonly contain pistol shrimp (*Crangon* sp.) and several other species of brachyurans and anomurans. Although the excavating activities of these taxa are not known, it is likely that at least some of them are responsible for the systems of passageways and galleries shown in the Figures. These exhibit a variety of wall sculpture that suggest scrape marks of chelae (Warme and Marshall 1969 p. 770) and likely represent enlargement of natural cavities or other borings in the rocks.

Larger systems of passages with smooth walls are more puzzling. Plate 3b illustrates the extensive excavations in the walls of Scripps Submarine Canyon.

Plate 2

a Photograph of bedding plane in fragment of Eocene mudstone from 20 m depth, Scripps Submarine Canyon. Rock is $11 \times 15 \times 3$ cm (JW-69-32).

b Plot of some of the borings in the specimen as seen on radiograph of Plate 1c. Club-shaped boring at top and hemispherical borings in centre are by pholadid bivalves. The exposed anterior edge (pedal gape) of several *Nettastomella rostrata* are visible. Two *Lithophaga plumula* have secreted sheaths; one is not exposed in Pl. 2a, and the anterior end of the other can be seen at the upper left. Sinuous borings concentrated along bedding planes are largely made by sipunculids, with some polychaete borings also present. Circle with dots near bottom is small pholadid boring filled with sediment and penetrated by the irregularly coiled tube of *Boccardia uncata* (see Pl. 1c).

JJ

PLATE 3

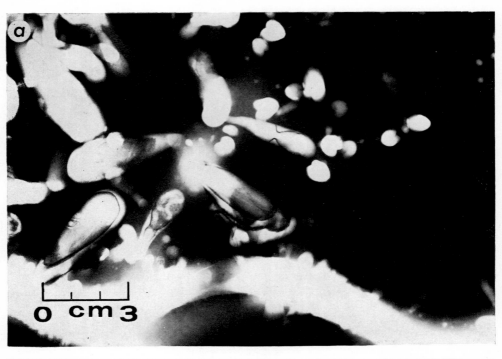

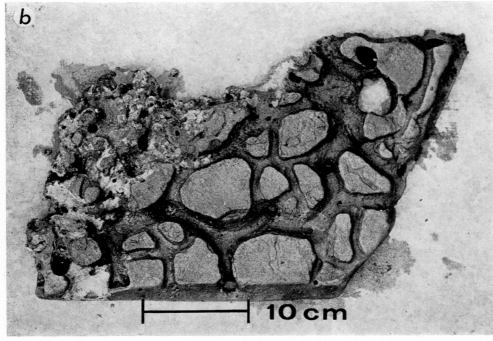

The size and geometry of these borings are identical with examples of *Thalassinoides* often described in the literature (Häntzschel 1962 p. W218) and commonly attributed to decapod crustaceans such as *Callianassa* (Bromley 1967). Underwater excavations made by hand in Scripps Submarine Canyon at a depth of 30 m penetrated up to 0·4 m into the rock walls and failed to reach the end of the borings. It is not yet known what animals are responsible for this bioerosion.

4. Conclusions

(i) Marine borers attacking rocks off southern California can be categorized as those that pierce or rotate into the rocks in a straight line or axis, those which make U-shaped or modified U-shaped borings, and those which excavate in no clear pattern. Diameters of borings in all three categories range from 1–2 mm to 2–3 cm or more.

(ii) There appears to be an evolution of excavation activities in these rocks, beginning with the first category of borings and ending in a complex tunnel and gallery system.

(iii) Rocks that are soft, fine-grained and calcareous are most intensely attacked. Calcareous substrates are penetrated by chemical borers regardless of grain size or induration. Some chemical borers penetrate rocks with less than 5 per cent carbonate content, and with grain size from claystones to medium-grained sandstones.

(iv) Marine rock borers live in water depths of at least 40 m and are abundant when rocks are favourably located away from shifting sediment or other hazards. Some species are apparently depth limited, but others extend from the intertidal zone to the deepest samples collected in this study (40 m).

(v) Penetration of marine rocks by borers provides a protected habitat for other borers, nestlers, and many other taxa, significantly increasing species diversity in the habitat.

(vi) Borings in these rocks commonly resemble those described as trace fossils in ancient rocks. The Plates show sinuous excavations made in hard rocks that are similar to trace fossils commonly regarded as originating in soft sediments.

Plate 3

Flat bedded Eocene mudstone from 20 m depth, Scripps Submarine Canyon. Slab is $51 \times 30 \times 2 \cdot 6$ cm (JW-69-37), with 4·2 per cent $CaCO_3$.

a Contact print of radiograph of portion of rock (12×17 cm). Seaward edge is towards left, where larger proportion of rock is excavated. Large spindle- or club-shaped voids with dark rims are *Lithophaga plumula* borings with sheaths. Shells of *Lithophaga* can be seen in two borings. Specimen near centre has shifted the axis of boring, as evidenced by a compound sheath. Small club-shaped borings, none of which are lined, were made mostly by *Nettastomella rostrata;* one shell is prominent in boring just above centre. Some *Nettastomella* borings are filled with tubes of *Boccardia uncata,* and others are empty. Heart shaped borings are by *Adula californiensis;* most are empty, but some still have the shells intact. Small sinuous lines at top centre are polychaete or sipunculid borings. Sinuous white line on bottom is part of a system of large (1·5-2·0 cm diam.) borings by unknown animals.

b Bottom surface of slab. Encrusted and intensely bored surface at upper left was exposed to the sea. Large sinuous borings along bedding plane provided access to the interior of the rock for larval settlement of abundant *Nettastomella rostrata*. Small sinuous borings along bedding are made by *Boccardia uncata*.

PLATE 4

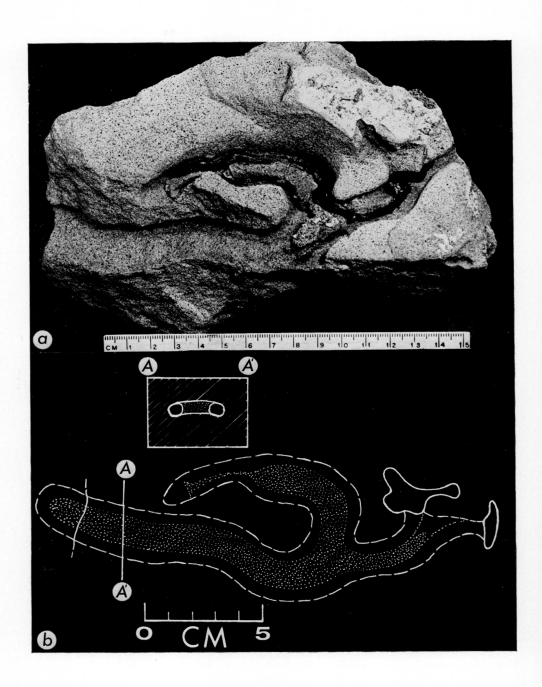

524

Acknowledgements. I gratefully acknowledge all those at Scripps Institution of Oceanography who have given advice and helped collect samples, particularly N. Marshall, T. Scanland, and A. Flechsig. T. Scanland identified the polychaete annelids. This work has been supported by National Science Foundation Grant GB 14321, by the Department of Geology at Rice University, and by numerous courtesies of E. W. Fager of Scripps Institution of Oceanography.

References

BOEKSCHOTEN, G. J. 1966. Shell borings of sessile epibiontic organisms as palaeoecological guides (with examples from the Dutch Coast). *Palaeogeogr. Palaeoclimat. Palaeoecol.* **2**, 333.

BROMLEY, R. G. 1967. Some observations on burrows of thalassinidean Crustacea in chalk hardgrounds. *Q. J. geol. Soc. Lond.* **123**, 157.

CARRIKER, M. R. SMITH, E. H. and WILCE, R. T. 1969. Penetration of calcium carbonate substrates by lower plants and invertebrates. *Am. Zoologist* **9**, no. 3, ed. 2.

CLAPP, W. F. and KENK, R. 1963. *Marine borers, an annotated bibliography.* Office Naval Research (ACR-74), Washington.

EVANS, J. W. 1967. Relationship between *Penitella penita* (Conrad, 1837) and other organisms of the rocky shore. *Veliger* **10** (2), 148.

—— 1968a. The effect of rock hardness and other factors on the shape of the burrow of the rock-boring clam, *Penitella penita. Palaeogeogr. Palaeoclimatol. Palaeoecol.* **4**, 271.

—— 1968b. The role of *Penitella penita* (Conrad 1837) (Family Pholadidae) as eroders along the Pacific Coast of North America. *Ecology* **49**, 156.

HÄNTZSCHEL, W. 1962. Trace fossils and problematica. In *Treatise on invertebrate paleontology* (Ed. R. C. Moore). Geol. Soc. Am., New York and Univ. of Kansas Press, Lawrence. Part W, p. W177.

HODGKIN, N. M. 1962. Limestone boring by the mytilid *Lithophaga. Veliger* **4**, 123.

KEEN, A. M. 1963. *Marine molluscan genera of western North America.* Stanford Univ. Press, Stanford.

RICE, M. E. 1969. Possible boring structures of sipunculids. *Am. Zoologist* **9**, 803.

TURNER, R. D. 1954. The family Pholadidae in the western Atlantic and the eastern Pacific, Part I—Pholadinae. *Johnsonia* **3**, no. 33, 1.

—— 1955. The family pholadidae in the western Atlantic and Eastern Pacific, Part II—Martesiinae, Jouannetiinae and Xylophaginae. *Johnsonia* **3**, no. 34, 65.

Plate 4

a Polychaete boring in lower intertidal Cretaceous sandstone from Bird Rock, La Jolla. Preserved worm is a nereid. The boring was probably made by the capitellid *Dasybranchus glabrus,* and was also occupied by the commensal polynoid *Lepidasthenia gigas.*

b Plan view diagram of boring. Solid lines on left represent openings of boring; solid line on right is where rock is broken in photograph above. Dots represent sand filling in centre of boring, most of which is removed in photograph. Inset represents cross section of boring along A-A'.

TURNER, R. D. 1954 and Boss, K. J. 1962. The genus *Lithophaga* in the western Atlantic. *Johnsonia* **4**, no. 41, 81.

WARME, J. E. and MARSHALL, N. F. 1969. Marine borers in calcareous terrigenous rocks of the Pacific Coast. *Am. Zoologist* **9**, 765.

YONGE, C. M. 1955. Adaptations to rock boring in *Botula* and *Lithophaga* (Lamellibranchia, Mytilidae) with a discussion on the evolution of this habit. *Q. J. micros. Sci.* **96**, 383.

J. E. Warme, Department of Geology, Rice University, Houston, Texas, 77001, USA.

Brookvalichnus, a new trace fossil from the Triassic of the Sydney Basin, Australia

B. D. Webby

A new trace fossil, *Brookvalichnus obliquus* ichnogen. et sp. nov., is described from a fossiliferous shale lens of possible lacustrine origin in the Hawkesbury Sandstone (Middle Triassic) of the Sydney Basin. It is characterised by inclined, ribbon-like structures, which seem to have originated by the collapse of tube-like dwelling burrows. These may have been formed by a freshwater, worm-like organism or an insect larva.

1. Introduction

Apart from the records of 'vertical cylindrical and almost cylindrical sand-casts up to five inches in length' and of 'worm tracks' in the Gosford Formation (Lower Triassic) of the Narrabeen Group (Osborne 1948), there are virtually no references to trace fossils in the literature on the Triassic of the Sydney Basin. A silty shale lens in the Hawkesbury Sandstone (Middle Triassic) contains the new trace fossil, *Brookvalichnus obliquus* ichnogen. et sp. nov.

The Hawkesbury Sandstone typically consists of cross-bedded and massive quartz sandstones, from medium to coarse grade (Standard 1969). Large scale cross-bedding occurs (Conolly 1964; 1965) and, locally, there are thin quartz pebble bands, large-scale slump structures, sometimes involving cross-bedded units, and lenses of siltstone and silty shale. The unit is up to 900 feet (274 m) thick, and has a broad distribution in the Sydney metropolitan area and the Blue Mountains.

Thick lenses of silty shale are prominent in only a few areas of outcrop, and tend to be developed in the upper part of the unit (Standard 1961). They may be traced for about one mile (1·8 km), and reach a maximum thickness of 30 feet (9·1 m). From one such lens, at the Beacon Hill Quarry, Brookvale, a fauna consisting of a labyrinthodont, *Paratosaurus brookvalensis* (Watson 1958), some 29 species of fish, including the lungfish *Ceratodus,* several insects, two crustaceans and a freshwater bivalve of *Unio* type has been reported (Wade 1931; 1935; McKeown 1937; Watson 1958; Welles and Cosgriff 1965), together with plant remains. Most of the Beacon Hill fossils have come from the lower part of the silty shale lens, now no longer exposed.

The trace fossil, *Brookvalichnus obliquus,* was found to occur in abundance in the higher part of the silty shale at Beacon Hill Quarry. It obliquely cuts and disrupts the prominent lamination in the silty shales.

2. Systematic Description

Ichnogenus BROOKVALICHNUS nov.

Type species. B. obliquus ichnosp. nov.

Diagnosis. As for the species.

Brookvalichnus obliquus ichnosp. nov.

Plate 1 a-g

Holotype SUP 21872 in the Palaeontological Collection of the Department of Geology and Geophysics, University of Sydney.
Paratypes SUP 13017, 13043, 21871, 21873–75.
Locality and horizon. Silty shale lens in upper part of Hawkesbury Sandstone at Beacon Hill Quarry, Brookvale, New South Wales. Preserved as full and semirelief in laminated grey silty shales.

Diagnosis. Inclined, straight to gently sinuous, ribbon-like trails, having an overall width of 3·5–4·0 mm, and representing collapsed, lined, originally tube-like burrows. The wall of the burrow is composed of an inner, thin, transversely annulated layer, and an outer, thicker, structureless dark shale layer.

Description. Ribbon-like trails varying from straight to sinuous, sometimes in groups approximately parallel to one another and cutting lamination obliquely (Pl. 1b). Trails are normally inclined about 10–15° to the horizontal. They show no branching, and are up to 93 mm long; they maintain a uniform width. The trails are highly compressed and have outer width of 3·5–4·0 mm. The outer dimensions include the width of the dark structureless shale band on either side of the inner, lighter-coloured, ribbon-like trail. Inner dimensions, measured just across the ribbon-like trail, are from 2·5–3·0 mm. The trails represent two-layered, collapsed burrows; the inner, ribbon-like part has a paper thin wall, and exhibits a transversely annulated form, including aligned, scattered fragments of carbonaceous material (Pl. 1d). They are up to 1 mm long and 0·3 mm wide. A few trails show arching of the annulations (Pl. 1e). The outer wall is thicker (0·4–0·75 mm wide), and composed of structureless dark grey shale (Pl. 1c).

Plate 1

a-g *Brookvalichnus obliquus* ichnogen. et sp. nov. Shale lens in Hawkesbury Sandstone, Brookvale, N.S.W.

a Vertical view of holotype SUP 21872, × 1, showing straight to gently curving ribbon-like trails.

b Side view of holotype SUP 21872, XO.75, showing the flat, ribbon-like trails cutting lamination obliquely.

c Detail of portion of holotype SUP 21872, × 3, to show inner (lighter coloured) ribbon flanked by outer band of dark grey structureless shale.

d Detail of another part of holotype SUP 21872, × 4, exhibiting transversely annulated inner ribbon. Note the relatively large, transversely aligned fragments of carbonaceous material. Outer dark band not exposed.

e Vertical view of paratype SUP 21873, × 2.5, showing specimens with curved annulations (top) and longitudinal crease (bottom), the latter probably due to compressional effects.

f Vertical view of paratype SUP 21874, × 1.5, exhibiting a moderately sharply bent ribbon.

g Oblique view of paratype SUP 21871, × 1.25, to show relationship between lamination and obliquely-cutting, ribbon-like trails. Note dark, narrow, outer bands and transverse annulations (with carbonaceous flecks) in inner, lighter ribbons.

PLATE 1

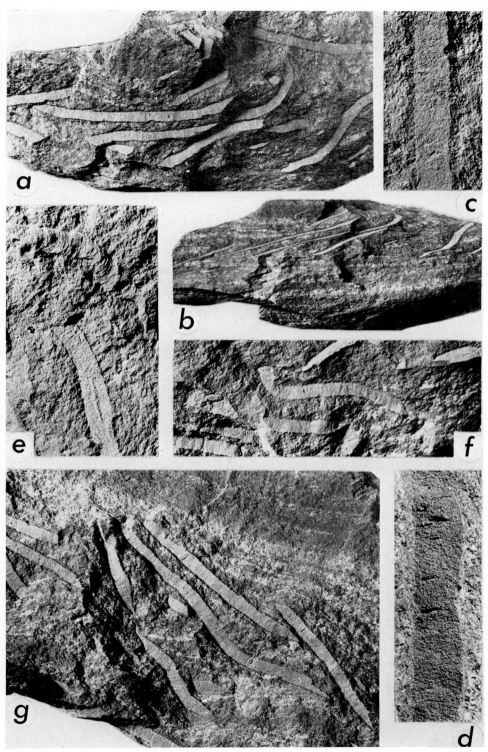

Remarks. B. obliquus seems to represent collapsed, two-layered dwelling burrows, mucus-lined on the inside, and formed by a freshwater(?) worm-like organism or insect larva. It is interpreted as a trace fossil rather than a body fossil because its construction below the sedimentary interface has involved the disruption of lamination. A form like the oligochaete *Tubifex* could have been responsible. *Tubifex* dwells in tubes which are part burrows and part chimneys above the bottom.

Aquatic earthworms are active in the mud of ponds, but there is little information as to whether the burrows exhibited a distinctive pattern or not. However they seem rather unlikely originators because of their deposit-feeding habit. From the construction of the *Brookvalichnus* trace, it seems more likely to have been a dwelling burrow, possibly permanently occupied by a suspension feeder.

Again, it may have been built for temporary occupation of an early growth stage such as an insect larva, or used by a free-living vagile organism for protection. Insect larvae, like midges, produce inclined, randomly arranged tubes held together by secretion of their own silk glands on the pond bottom. However, the rather considerable length of the burrows tends to weigh against this suggestion. The shape, form of layering and the close spacing of some of the burrows preclude any possibility of *Brookvalichnus* originating from the activity of gastropods or other molluscs.

No other trace fossils are known to be strictly comparable with *B. obliquus*.

References

CONOLLY, J. R. 1964. Trough cross-stratification in the Hawkesbury Sandstone. *Aust. J. Sci.* **27**, 113.
—— 1965. Large-scale cross-stratification in Triassic sandstones, Sydney, Australia. *J. sedim. Petrol.* **35**, 765.
MCKEOWN, K. C. 1937. New fossil insect wings (Protohemiptera, Family Mesotitanidae). *Rec. Aust. Mus.* **20**, 31.
OSBORNE, G. D. 1948. A review of some aspects of the stratigraphy, structure and physiography of the Sydney Basin. *Proc. Linn. Soc. N.S.W.* **73**, iv.
STANDARD, J. C. 1961. A new study of the Hawkesbury Sandstone; preliminary findings. *J. Proc. R. Soc. N.S.W.* **95**, 145.
—— 1969. Hawkesbury Sandstone, Triassic system. In *The geology of New South Wales* (Ed. G. H. Packham). *J. geol. Soc. Aust.* **16**, 407.
WADE, R. T. 1931. The fossil fishes of the Australian Mesozoic rocks. *J. Proc. R. Soc. N.S.W.* **64**, 115.
—— 1935. *The Triassic fishes of Brookvale, New South Wales.* British Museum (Nat. Hist.), London.
WATSON, D. M. S. 1958. A new labyrinthodont (*Paracyclotosaurus*) from the Upper Trias of New South Wales. *Bull. Br. Mus. nat. Hist. Geology* **3** (7), 235.
WELLES, S. P. and COSGRIFF, J. 1965. A revision of the labyrinthodont family Capitosauridae. *Univ. Calif. Publs geol. Sci.* **54**, 1.

B. D. Webby, Department of Geology, The University, Sydney, N.S.W. 2006, Australia.

Trace fossil index

Figures in **bold type** indicate pages on which the trace fossil is figured.
An asterisk * indicates a new trace fossil genus, species, or form.

Zapfellidae Code and Saint-Seine 1957, 69.

Zoophycos Massalongo 1855, 6, 12, 15, 17, 102, 141, 145, **147,** 148, 155, 156, 159, 161, 206, 221, 223, 263, **268, 271,** 272, 273, 279, 281, 283, 314, 316, 317, 318, 319, 320, 321, 361, **363, 367,** 368, 369, 407, 408, 409, 415, 416, 417, 418, 420, 421, 422, 423, **433, 434, 436,** 438, 505, 506, **508,** 510, 511, 512, 513, 514; *briantius* (Villa 1844), 273, 506, 507; *caput-medusae* Massalongo 1855, 273; *circinnatus* (Brongniart 1828), 363, 364, **365;** *massalongi* Plička 1968, 363, 364.

Subject index